BEYOND AESTHETICS

Beyond Aesthetics brings together philosophical essays addressing art and related issues by one of the foremost philosophers of art at work today. Countering conventional aesthetic theories – those maintaining that authorial intention, art history, morality, and emotional responses are irrelevant to the experience of art – Noël Carroll argues for a more pluralistic and commonsensical view in which all of these factors can play a legitimate role in our encounter with artworks. Throughout, the book combines philosophical theorizing with illustrative examples including works of high culture and the avant-garde, as well as works of popular culture, jokes, horror novels, and suspense films.

Noël Carroll is the Monroe C. Beardsley Professor of the Philosophy of Art at the University of Wisconsin-Madison. Former president of the American Society for Aesthetics, he is the author of seven books including *The Philosophy of Mass Art, The Philosophy of Art,* and *Theorizing the Moving Image.*

BEYOND AESTHETICS

Philosophical Essays

NOËL CARROLL

University of Wisconsin–Madison

CAMBRIDGE
UNIVERSITY PRESS

PUBLISHED BY THE PRESS SYNDICATE OF THE UNIVERSITY OF CAMBRIDGE
The Pitt Building, Trumpington Street, Cambridge, United Kingdom

CAMBRIDGE UNIVERSITY PRESS
The Edinburgh Building, Cambridge CB2 2RU, UK
40 West 20th Street, New York, NY 10011-4211, USA
10 Stamford Road, Oakleigh, VIC 3166, Australia
Ruiz de Alarcón 13, 28014, Madrid, Spain
Dock House, The Waterfront, Cape Town 8001, South Africa

http://www.cambridge.org

First published 2001

Printed in the United States of America

Typeface Bembo 10.5/12.5 pts. and Centaur   *System* Quark XPress™   [HT]

A catalog record for this book is available from the British Library.

Library of Congress Cataloging in Publication Data

Carroll, Noël (Noël E.)
Beyond aesthetics: philosophical essays/Noel Carroll.
p. cm.
ISBN 0-521-78134-5 (hb) – ISBN 0-521-78656-8 (pbk.)
1. Art–Philosophy. 2. Arts–Philosophy. 3. Aesthetics. I. Title.
BH39. C3752 2001
111′.85–dc21   00-059887

ISBN 0 521 78134 5 hardback
ISBN 0 521 78656 8 paperback

Dedicated to my teacher
George Dickie

CONTENTS

FOREWORD

The second half of our century has witnessed a remarkable revival of interest in philosophical speculation centering on the fine arts. Not since the flowering of German Romanticism have so many philosophers of the first rank taken aesthetics and the philosophy of art as an area of special interest.

The publication of Arthur Danto's *The Transfiguration of the Commonplace,* in 1981, ushered in a period in the aesthetic revival of which I speak that, at least in Anglo-American circles, has been largely dominated by Danto's philosophical presence.

The Transfiguration of the Commonplace is philosophy of art in the "grand manner": in the universe of the arts, a "theory of everything." I myself think it will be the last such grand speculative venture in the field for a very long time: how long a time I cannot possibly guess. But we are, in any case, entering a new period in the ongoing philosophical exploration of the fine arts. If the age of Danto was the age of the hedgehog, who knows one big thing, we are entering, now, the age of the fox, who knows a lot of little things. And the big fox on the block, at least from where I sit, looks to be Noël Carroll. If the age to come in philosophy of art and aesthetics is the age of the fox, it may very well be the age of Carroll.

I should say a word, though, about foxes. The philosophy of art has had, over the past half-century, its *little foxes.* These have been people who have found one area of the discipline particularly amenable to their efforts and talents: one has worked only on literary interpretation, another only on music, a third specializes on problems of pictorial representation, and so on. The hedgehog knows one big thing, the little foxes one little thing. The little foxes are by no means to be despised. They also serve, and have, together, made an enormous contribution.

What makes the big fox *big* is that he knows not just one little thing but a lot of little things. And if they are important, central things, then, like the hedgehog, he is a master of the whole discipline. Noël Carroll is, by any standard, a very big fox.

The essays in your hands cover a wide range of topics in the philosophy of art and aesthetics; and their range, of course, is one of the collection's most impressive features. But one can, after all, range over trivial and peripheral topics, as well as over deep and central ones. It is the depth and centrality of the issues Carroll is willing to confront that makes these essays such a substantial contribution to the field, and their author one of its dominant figures. Issues that the faint of heart shy away from for fear of their difficulty Carroll takes on with a kind of confident common sense that makes us all wonder what there was to be afraid of, and why *we* didn't think of the answer ourselves.

A look at the organization of this volume, the topics covered, and some of the theses advanced will give the reader some small idea of what Carroll's contribution to the main issues in aesthetics and the philosophy of art has been, and why it has earned him, in my eyes and the eyes of many others, such distinction in the field.

In Part I of this collection, Beyond Aesthetics, Carroll broaches what I take to be one of the two most central questions in the philosophy of art since its founding in the first half of the eighteenth century. The other of these central questions is the definition of art, which Carroll takes up in Part II.

Although Kant did not use the word "aesthetic" in the ways we do, he nevertheless laid the groundwork for *one* of our two basic usages – namely, as a word to describe certain formal and sensual properties of works of art, as well as of Nature. The *other* way we tend to use it is simply as synonymous with "artistic," "pertains to art *qua* art." When the two are conflated, it has the result that the *only* properties of art *qua* art that there are – the only properties of art that are relevant to art *qua* art – are its "aesthetic," which is to say formal and sensual properties. This view of art, sometimes called "formalism," has had a profound and baleful influence on our thinking about art and the aesthetic. Carroll argues, convincingly, I think, that this conflation should *not* be allowed to take place: that "(1) the philosophy of art and aesthetics should be spoken of as two areas of inquiry since (2) failure to do so has been and continues to be a source of philosophical confusion" ("Beauty and the Genealogy of Art Theory"); and, further, he disputes "both the thesis that aesthetic responses are definitive of our responses to artworks and the thesis that art is to be characterized exclusively in terms of the promotion of aesthetic responses" ("Art and Interaction").

In his claims about art and the aesthetic, Carroll exhibits a healthy philosophical pluralism that runs through all his work. I shall return to this theme in my conclusion to these brief remarks.

Part II, Art, History and Narrative, as the title suggests, contains essays having to do with the nature both of artistic and historical narrative structure. But the three major essays have, rather, to do with the second of the two central issues of modern philosophy of the arts, which is to say, the nature of art itself, with narrative as the essential, defining idea.

The three dominant theories of art in our time have been George Dickie's "institutional" theory, Arthur Danto's "aboutness" theory, and Morris Weitz's Wittgensteinian "no theory" theory. The options have been, then, the theory that something is a work of art if and only if it has been enfranchised by the "artworld"; the theory that something is a work of art if and only if it at least makes sense to ask what it is about (and that it fulfills certain other conditions on its "aboutness" too elaborate to go into here); and the theory (if you want to call it that) that "art" is an "open concept" and therefore cannot be defined at all.

To these three approaches to defining art we must now add Carroll's "narrative" definition, the first new approach since Danto became the dominant figure in the field. As Carroll sees the novelty of his suggestion, "the question 'What is art' changes its thrust. 'Art' in our query no longer refers primarily to the art object; rather what we wish to know about when we ask 'What is art?' predominantly concerns the nature and structures of the practices of art – things, I shall argue, that are generally best approached by means of historical narration" ("Art, Practice, and Narrative").

Carroll's idea, then, is that something is a work of art if and only if it can be connected with other, bona fide cases of art by a convincing historical narrative. As he puts the view, "I propose that ... we identify works as artworks – where the question of whether or not they are art arises – by means of historical narratives which connect contested candidates to art history in a way that discloses that the mutations in question are part of the evolving species of art. I call these stories 'identifying narratives'" ("Historical Narratives and the Philosophy of Art").

On Carroll's view, attempts to define art are driven, particularly in our century, by the avant-garde, which continually challenges the reigning definitions with "problem objects," bizarre entities that it seems impossible to see as possessing anything in common with art "properly so-called." With regard to such objects of the avant-garde, it is a virtue of Carroll's account that we are looking not for some common property in the object, even in Danto's liberating sense of "something the eye cannot descry," but for something not belonging to the artwork at all – rather, an art-historical narrative in which the problem object can, as it were, play a believable role. It may also prove more effective than Danto's approach with "problem objects" not of the avant-garde but ones that have been around to plague us since the very beginning of the art-defining project, which is to say, works of *absolute music*.

Absolute music in the eighteenth century, as now, was a plague and a nuisance to would-be art definers. Its at least apparent lack of representational or semantic content, and the absence of consensus over whether its "expressive" features can make up for that lack, are themselves "content," have made it recalcitrant to any theory of art that posits "content" of any kind as a necessary condition, even Danto's, with its subtle "aboutness" criterion, requiring merely that the "aboutness" question can relevantly be asked. Carroll's theory sidesteps this problem, requiring but that absolute music be worked into an "identifying narrative," connecting it with other, standard cases of "art" properly so-called. What its "inner" nature may be is not material for this narrative maneuver.

All prospective "definitions" of "art" must, in the event, steer between the Scylla of *exclusion* and the Charybdis of *inclusion:* they must, that is, be so framed as to not exclude from the precincts of art those problematic objects of the avant-garde driving the enterprise, and, on the other hand, they must not, in so doing, *include* objects no one recognizes intuitively as "art." It is my suspicion that Charybdis is the danger to Carroll's project. But the ultimate fate of that project is yet to be played out.

The publication of a little essay by William K. Wimsatt and Monroe Beardsley, called "Intention," in 1942, the theme of which was later developed more fully in their "The Intentional Fallacy," in 1954, had two important results: it made the topic of literary interpretation a central one for the philosophy of art, and made the relevance of authorial intention the crucial question. Wimsatt and Beardsley argued with great persuasiveness, and, indeed, succeeded in persuading many, that the author's intentions are irrelevant to literary interpretation; that, in fact, to treat them as relevant is a "fallacy": the "intentional fallacy," as they called it.

Carroll takes on this long-debated issue in Part III, Interpretation and Intention. Characteristically, his position is commonsensical, and appeals to "everyday" experience. "In the normal course of affairs," Carroll writes, "when confronted with an utterance, our standard cognitive goal is to figure out what the speaker intends to say" ("Art, Intention, and Conversation"). If this is true in ordinary conversation, he asks, why should it be any less true in our encounters with literary (and other) works of art that, Carroll suggests, can usefully be thought of as, so to speak, "conversations" with their creators? As he puts the point: "When we read a literary text or contemplate a painting, we enter a relationship with its creator that is roughly analogous to a conversation. Obviously, it is not as interactive as an ordinary conversation, for we are not receiving spontaneous feedback concerning our own responses. But just as an ordinary conversation gives us a stake in understanding our interlocutor, so does our interaction with an artwork" ("Art, Intention, and Conversation").

To many, this answer to the much debated question as to the relevance of authorial intention to artistic interpretation will seem too simple to be true. Simplicity of theory is much admired in the mathematical sciences, but not in philosophy, where bogus profundity thrives on unintelligible complexity. My own feeling is that Carroll's answer to the question of authorial intention is too simple *not* to be true.

The section of Carroll's collection called Art, Emotions, and Morality takes on two question about art that have only recently regained an importance they once had. They are the questions of whether moral value is relevant to artistic value, and how ordinary, garden-variety emotions like anger, hope, fear, sorrow, and so forth, can be aroused in audiences to fictional works of art. The reason for their eclipse has been, I believe, the general acceptance, in recent philosophy, of what is sometimes called the "autonomy of art," or, more colloquially, "art for art's sake." Fueled, certainly, by formalism, the belief has gained currency among "sophisticated" lovers of art that its values, even where it seems to have reference to the world beyond its boundaries, must be found within *its* world alone. Both the ideas that we should evaluate fictional works even partly for their moral content, or that it can be part of their function to arouse in us the ordinary emotions of our everyday lives, ideas once accepted as a matter of course by experts and the laity alike, were, until recently, considered discredited vestiges of Romanticism, not worthy of philosophical notice.

Carroll is not alone in reconsidering these issues and, as a matter of fact, his account of how fiction arouses the garden-variety emotions is a developed version of a theory that others have propounded. The problem is that emotions are standardly aroused by beliefs about what are taken to be actual states of affairs. Thus, I am angry at my landlord for raising the rent. But why, so the skeptical argument goes, should I get angry at a fictional landlord who raises the fictional rent of a fictional lady in distress, since there is no landlord, no lady in distress, no rent to be raised?

The answer that Carroll and others have come up with is that mere "thoughts" of things happening can arouse the garden-variety emotions. The mere thought of my landlord's raising the rent, even though I do not presently believe the landlord is going to raise my rent, can make me angry, so this account has it. As Carroll puts his point, "it seems indisputable that emotions can be engendered in the process of holding propositions before the mind unasserted. While cutting vegetables, imagine putting the very sharp knife in your hand into your eye. One suddenly feels a shudder" ("Art, Narrative, and Emotion"). And applying this conclusion to fictional works of art, "Fictions, construed as propositions to be imagined, supply us with the relevant, unasserted propositional content, and in entertaining that content, we can be emotionally moved by fictions" ("Art, Narrative, and Emotion").

Armed with this account of how fictional works of art can move us to the garden-variety emotions, Carroll goes on, in Part IV, to investigate, among other things, the role of these emotions in narrative in general, in horror, and in suspense. He argues against both the ancient Platonic theory that emotions in fiction are aroused in us by "identifying" with fictional personages, and its present-day reincarnation, called "simulation theory," which has it that "By simulating the mental states of fictional characters, we come to experience what it would be like – that is, for example, what it would feel like – to be in situations such as those in which the characters find themselves" ("Simulation, Emotions, and Morality").

With regard to the issue of moral value in art, Carroll advocates, characteristically, a view he calls "moderate moralism." I say "characteristically" because here, as elsewhere, Carroll exhibits his innate common sense and commonsensical pluralism. *Of course,* the layperson, untainted with theory, wants to say that moral value is neither *all* there is to artistic value; but nor is it *nothing:* it is part of artistic value, in some kinds of artworks, some of the time. This, essentially, is the moderate claim.

Carroll's argument is that narrative, at least as we know it, works, in part, by engaging our moral concepts, attitudes, feelings, sympathies. "Part of what is involved, then, in the process of filling in a narrative is the activation of the moral powers – the moral judgments and the moral emotions of audiences" ("Moderate Moralism"). And that being the case, "the moderate moralist also contends that moral evaluation may figure in our evaluations of some art. For inasmuch as narrative artworks engage our powers of moral understanding, they can be assessed in terms of whether they deepen or pervert the moral understanding" ("Moderate Moralism"). That sounds like common sense to me. I am not saying that common sense always makes philosophical sense – but it is an encouraging start.

I said that what characterizes these essays of Carroll's, and makes them such a substantial contribution to aesthetics and the philosophy of art, is their wide-ranging coverage of the central, most difficult, and most contested issues. The final section, however, Alternative Topics, shows that there is yet another side to Carroll's impressive range of philosophical interests: a lighter side, shall we say, as evidenced by such essays as "On Jokes," "The Paradox of Junk Fiction," and "On Being Moved By Nature." That Carroll can interest himself not only in the core issues of his field but in the peripheral ones as well makes him truly the "complete" philosopher of art. There is no one I know who can come even close to him in either breadth or depth.

The theme of Carroll's work in aesthetics and the philosophy of art, I have maintained, is a healthy kind of commonsensical pluralism: the tendency to avoid those overarching theories that tell us art is *all* one thing, or *never* another, and to say, rather, perhaps it is more things than one. In its favoring of practice over theory it is Aristotelian rather than Spinozistic (to appropriate a distinction Stuart Hampshire once applied to moral philosophy). For those who think philosophy must be high and mighty, this philosophy is not for you. For those who think the truths of art and the aesthetic could be right in front of your nose, where you suspected all along that they were, Noël Carroll will give you the best arguments you are ever likely to get for your intuitions. In the postmodern age of outrageous paradoxes, you will find here an oasis of sanity.

Peter Kivy

INTRODUCTION

This volume is a selection of my essays on the philosophy of art and aesthetics written between 1985 and 1999. The earliest essays in the volume coincide with the beginning of my career as a professional philosopher while working at Wesleyan University; the more recent articles, composed at Cornell University and the University of Wisconsin-Madison, seem as though they were written yesterday – undoubtedly a flaw of memory attributable to advancing age. When I look back at these essays, however diverse they may appear to the reader, they strike me as being united by several recurring threads.

The most pronounced thread is a reactive one: an opposition to aesthetic theories of art broadly and to its more distinctive variant, formalism, most particularly. Tutored in its discipline as an undergraduate, I have spent much of my career as a philosopher attempting to combat the limitations that aesthetic theories and formalism impose on the philosophy of art. It is from this reaction formation that the present volume derives its title – *Beyond Aesthetics: Philosophical Essays.* For, in a nutshell, the dominant recurring theme in this book is that we much reach beyond aesthetic theories of art and their various prohibitions.

That is, we must not identify the essence of art with the intended capacity of artworks to afford aesthetic experiences. Nor must we agree with aesthetic theorists of art and formalists that art history, authorial intentions, garden-variety emotions, and morality are alien to proper commerce with artworks. My campaign against aesthetic theories of art, in a manner of speaking, organizes the first four parts of this book.

The first section — Beyond Aesthetics — initiates the argument against aesthetic theories of art, while also propounding a genealogy of the ways in which this theoretical disposition has shaped and distorted the evolution of the philosophy of art. The next section, Art, History, and Narrative, argues (against aesthetic theorists of art, like Clive Bell) for the the importance of art history to the philosophy of art, while also advancing an alternative to aesthetic definitions of art for identifying artworks.

Whereas aesthetic theorists of art typically question the relevance of authorial intentions to interpretation, in the next section, Interpretation and Intention, I defend the appeal to authorial intentions in the analysis of artworks. Likewise, where aesthetic theorists of art tend to regard only aesthetic experience as constituting the essential, appropriate kind of response to art, I maintain in the section

Art, Emotion, and Morality that garden-variety emotional responses and moral responses are not only art-appropriate responses to art, but also that they are relevant to the evaluation and analysis of artworks. Indeed, in this section I also attempt to provide analyses of selected emotional responses of this sort, including suspense, horror, and amusement.

Undoubtedly, part of my animus against aesthetic theories of art derives from my having studied with George Dickie, to whom this volume is dedicated. From him, I inherited my abiding philosophical interests in the concepts of "the aesthetic" and "art." Like Dickie, or perhaps because of Dickie, I have always resisted the idea that art can be defined in terms of the intended capacity of certain objects to support aesthetic experiences as well as the idea that the aesthetic is best conceptualized in terms of disinterestedness.

I have also always thought that Dickie's classic article "The Myth of the Aesthetic Attitude"[1] can best be read as a demolition of the notion of "the aesthetic" for the purpose, ultimately, of undermining aesthetic theories of art – thereby paving the way for his own Institutional Theory of Art. That interpretation, moreover, is borne out in his book *Art and the Aesthetic,* in which the best known candidates for "the aesthetic" this-or-that are successively derailed in the explicit process of defending the Institutional Theory.[2] And something like Dickie's strategy – challenging aesthetic theories of art as a first step in generating new theories – has become my own.

Part I: Beyond Aesthetics can be regarded as a continuation of Dickie's project. The first essay, "Art and Interaction," criticizes the limitations of aesthetic theories of art outright, specifically by emphasizing the way in which interpretation (in contrast to aesthetic experience) is an art-appropriate response at least as significant as aesthetic experience. Here, as elsewhere, the implicit dependence on Arthur Danto is evident, while my use of Monroe Beardsley, in this essay and others, as my leading foil also shows the influence of George Dickie, since it was Dickie who taught me always to consult Beardsley's work for the most worked-out and authoritative position on any subject in aesthetics, even if, in the end, I wound up criticizing it. There are more ways than one to stand on the shoulders of giants.

"Beauty and the Genealogy of Art Theory" does not confront the aesthetic theory of art directly, but instead attempts to disclose its subterranean influence on the contours of the philosophy of art. If one accepts the arguments that I have made concerning aesthetic theories of art, then, this essay functions as a debunking genealogy, one that traces various tendencies in the philosophy of art – such as the prohibitions against art history, authorial intention, garden-variety (as opposed to aesthetic) emotional responses, and moral responses – as flowing from historical misinterpretations and prejudices that have remained unexamined for too long.

In "Four Concepts of Aesthetic Experience," I take a closer look at the concept of aesthetic experience that serves as the fulcrum of aesthetic theories of art. I argue against three well-known views of aesthetic experience: the pragmatic (Dewey's), the allegorical (Marcuse and Adorno's), and the traditional account (almost everyone else's).[3] But this essay is not merely critical. It concludes with a positive characterization of aesthetic experience that I label the deflationary account. In the vocabulary of my first essay in this volume, "Art and Interaction," it is what I call a content-oriented account. Unlike George Dickie, I do not contend that aesthetic experience is a myth, but rather that something is an aesthetic response if it involves design appreciation or the detection of aesthetic or expressive properties or the contemplation of the emergence of formal, aesthetic, or expressive properties from their base properties, or a combination of any or all of these responses.

Dickie, I have argued, parlayed his attack of aesthetic experience (and intimately connected aesthetic theories of art) into the case on behalf of his Institutional Theory. I have not traveled all the way with Dickie to embracing the Institutional Theory. However, I agree with him that the putative failure of aesthetic theories of art puts pressure on us to find some other way to account for how we go about identifying objects and performances as artworks.

In Part II: Art, History, and Narrative, my solution to this problem is the suggestion that we achieve this result by means of historical narratives.[4] Just as the biological concept of a species is a historical one, so I maintain, is the concept of art. That is, we determine membership in the category of art by providing narratives or genealogies of the descent or lineage of present candidates from their established forebears.

The essay "Art, Practice, and Narrative" represents my first attempt to craft a historical account for classifying artworks as artworks. As the result of criticism of it, I produced two more overlapping essays – "Identifying Art" and "Historical Narratives and the Philosophy of Art" – in order to refine and defend the historical approach. Since the notion of narrative figures so importantly in this section, and others, I have also included the essay "On the Narrative Connection" to provide a clarifying account of what I mean by "narrative" in the most abstract sense. And finally, since I uphold a realist account of historical narratives, including art-relevant identifying narratives, I conclude this section with a defense against the relativist view of narrative propounded in the influential writings of Hayden White.

As already noted, an opposition to the relevance of authorial intention to the interpretation and evaluation of artworks is a recurring theme of aesthetic theorists of art, such as Clive Bell and Monroe Beardsley. For them, it diverts attention away from the artwork itself to something outside the work, namely, the author's intention. In Part III: Interpretation and Intention, I try to reinstate the acceptability of the relevance of authorial intention.

The opening essay, "Art, Intention, and Conversation," attempts to refute the major arguments of anti-intentionalists like Monroe Beardsley and Roland Barthes, while also invoking what I call our conversational interests with respect to artworks (which involve, among other things, certain moral considerations) in order to say why authorial intentions are relevant constraints on our interpretive practices. Since one of my complaints against the way in which debates over the relevance of authorial intention usually proceed is that they are overly focused on questions of linguistic meaning, I use examples from outside literature where the lack of conventional semantic and syntactic structures clearly require hypothesizing authorial intentions as the royal road to interpretation, due to absence of anything like conventions (rather than, say, merely rules of thumb).[5]

In "Anglo-American Aesthetics and Contemporary Criticism," I attempt to defend intentionalism against recent critics who indulge in what is called the "hermeneutics of suspicion." In this essay, I show that rather than being antithetical to the aims of politicized criticism, intentionalism is not only compatible with them, but even generally presupposed by them.

"Art, Intention, and Conversation" was attacked from two directions. First, predictably enough, by anti-intentionalists; but also from a position within intentionalism itself, called hypothetical intentionalism (the view that the correct interpretation of an artwork corresponds to our best hypothesis of authorial intention, even where the author's actual intentions are known to deviate therefrom). I address the anti-intentionalist challenge in "The Intentional Fallacy: Defending Myself" and the second attack in "Interpretation and Intention: The Debate Between Hypothetical and Actual Intentionalism."[6]

Garden-variety emotional responses (as opposed to the alleged aesthetic emotions) and moral responses to artworks have been traditionally regarded as not part of (and even at variance with) aesthetic experience and, therefore, have fallen outside the purview of the philosophy of art, notably as that is construed by the aesthetic theory of art. As a result, they have not received the philosophical attention they deserve. Part IV: Art, Emotion, and Morality seeks to repair this lacuna. The opening essay "Art, Narrative, and Emotion" sets out a framework for philosophically examining the relations that obtain between these terms, while the subsequent essays – "Horror and Humor" and "The Paradox of Suspense" – extend this framework by considering several case studies.

Similarly, "Art, Narrative, and Moral Understanding" introduces a general framework for discussing questions of art and morality, while "Moderate Moralism" defends the moral evaluation of artworks as a legitimate form of artistic evaluation against the aesthetic viewpoint that I call autonomism.[7] Part IV concludes with an essay entitled "Simulation, Emotions, and Morality" that critically considers a framework, simulation theory, that is a rival to the one developed in this section.

If the range of topics belonging to the catch area of philosophical aesthetics (or the philosophy of art) has been narrowly circumscribed under the influence of an aesthetic conception of art, my own view of our field of research is much wider. Thus, in the last section of this book – Part V: Alternative Topics – I include a handful of essays that examine a group of disparate topics I believe are worth pursuing once we divest ourselves of our obsession with Aesthetics and Art (both with capital As). My alternative topics include: jokes, junk fiction, visual metaphors, and the appreciation of landscape. Of course, further topics are readily imaginable. But my essays about them, of course, remain to be written, let alone anthologized.

PART I: BEYOND AESTHETICS

ART AND INTERACTION

Ideas of the aesthetic figure largely in two crucial areas of debate in the philosophy of art. On the one hand, *the aesthetic* often plays a definitive role in characterizations of our responses to or interactions with artworks. That is, what is thought to be distinctive about our commerce with artworks is that these encounters are marked by aesthetic experiences, aesthetic judgments, aesthetic perceptions, and so forth. Furthermore, the use of aesthetic terminology in such accounts of our interactions with artworks is, most essentially, "experiential" or "perceptual" where those terms are generally understood by contrast to responses mediated by the application of concepts or reasoning.

Second, notions of the aesthetic are also mobilized in theories of the nature of art objects; the artwork, it is claimed, is an artifact designed to bring about aesthetic experiences and aesthetic perceptions, or to engender aesthetic attitudes, or to engage aesthetic faculties, et cetera. Thus, these two claims – that aesthetic responses distinguish our responses to art, and that art objects can be defined in terms of the aesthetic – though ostensibly independent, can, nevertheless, be connected by means of a neat, commonsensical approach that holds that what an object is can be captured through an account of its function. The art object is something designed to provoke a certain form of response, a certain type of interaction. The canonical interaction with art involves the aesthetic (however that is to be characterized). So the artwork is an object designed with the function of engendering aesthetic experiences, perceptions, attitudes, and so forth.

The purpose of this essay is to dispute both the thesis that aesthetic responses are definitive of our responses to artworks and the thesis that art is to be characterized exclusively in terms of the promotion of aesthetic responses. It will be argued against the first thesis that many of our entrenched forms of interaction with artworks – what may be neutrally designated as our art responses or art experiences – are not aesthetic in nature nor are they reducible to aesthetic responses or experiences. The argument here proceeds by enumerating and describing several of our nonaesthetic though eminently characteristic responses to art objects. That is, along with doing things like attending to the *brittleness* of a piece of choreography – a paradigmatic

From: *The Journal of Aesthetics and Art Criticism,* XLV, No. 1 (Fall 1986), 57–68.

aesthetic response – we also contemplate artworks with an eye to discerning latent meanings and structures, and to determining the significance of an artwork in its art historical context. These art responses, often interpretive in nature, are, it will be claimed, as central as, and certainly no less privileged than, aesthetic responses in regard to our interactions with artworks.[1] Moreover, if an expanded view of the art response is defensible, then our concept of art, especially when construed function-ally, must be broadened to countenance as art objects that are designed to promote characteristically appropriate art responses or art experiences distinct from aesthetic responses. And this, in turn, has consequences for attempts by theorists, armed with aesthetic definitions of art, who wish to exclude such objects as Duchamp's *Fountain* from the order of art.

This essay is motivated by a recent development in the philosophy of art, namely the popularity of aesthetic definitions of art. As is well known, the antide-finitional stance of post-World War II philosophers of art provoked a reaction for-mation called the Institutional Theory of Art.[2] Dissatisfaction with the Institutional Theory has, in turn, elicited several countermoves of which the aes-thetic definition of art is one species. For though the Institutional Theory has been judged wanting in numerous respects, it has reestablished the respectability of attempts to define art.

Examples of this development include articles such as "An Aesthetic Definition of Art" by Monroe Beardsley and "Toward an Aesthetic Account of the Nature of Art" by William Tolhurst.[3] These writers attempt to construct theories that dis-criminate between art and nonart by reference to aesthetic experience, which is taken as the canonical mode of our interaction with artworks. In this, I think that these authors are symptomatic of the tendency within much contemporary philos-ophy of art to equate the art experience with the aesthetic experience. Given this propensity, both articles define an artwork as an object produced with the intended function of fostering aesthetic experiences. Beardsley's statement of the theory is "An artwork is something produced with the intention of giving it the capacity to satisfy the aesthetic interest."[4] To have an aesthetic interest in an object, for Beards-ley, is to have an interest in the aesthetic character of experience that a given object affords. Simply put, our aesthetic interest in an object is predicated on the possibil-ity of our deriving aesthetic experiences from the object.

Tolhurst's statement of the aesthetic theory of art is more complex. As a rough indication of the way in which an aesthetic definition might go, Tolhurst writes

> A thing, x, is a work of art if and only if, there is a person, y, such that 1) y believed that x could serve as an object of (positive) aesthetic experiences, 2) y wanted x to serve as an object of (positive) aesthetic experiences, and 3) y's belief and desire caused y (in a certain characteristic way) to produce x, to create x, or to place x where x is, etc.[5]

Both Beardsley and Tolhurst are involved in the attempt to limit the range of things we shall count as art. Broadly speaking, this attempt is carried out by two maneuvers: invoking the condition that the producer of a putative artwork had an appropriate intention, which, in turn, is specified in terms of a plan to afford aesthetic experience. Given this twofold requirement, Beardsley believes that he can deny the status of art to such things as Edward T. Cone's "Poéme symphonique" – a composition that involves one hundred metronomes running down – and to Duchamp's *Fountain*. In a similar gesture, Tolhurst thinks that Duchamp's *L.H.O.O.Q.* and *L.H.O.O.Q. Shaved* are not art. With such cases, Beardsley and Tolhurst believe that the artists could not possibly have been motivated by the intention of promoting aesthetic experience.

For the purposes of this essay I shall put the issue of the intentional component of the aesthetic theory of art somewhat to one side. I am more interested in the job that the concept of aesthetic experience is supposed to perform in the theories. It must be said that the commonsense approach of the aesthetic theory of art is very attractive. It conceives of the artwork as an object designed with a function, a function, moreover, that is connected with what a spectator can get out of an artwork in virtue of its facilitating or promoting certain types of responses or interactions. As a theory of art, it has the strength of acknowledging the mutual importance of the artist, the object, and the audience; it does not emphasize one element of the matrix of art over others in the manner of a Croce or a Collingwood with their preoccupations with the artist and his expression of intuitions.

Also, this type of theory puts its proponent in a strong position to systematically tackle further questions in the philosophy of art, such as what is the value of art and why are we interested in seeking out artworks? Clearly, the aesthetic theorist of art can answer that the value of art and the interest we have in pursuing artworks reside in whatever positive benefit there is in having the types of experiences and responses that art objects are designed to promote.

On the other hand, the delimitation of the relevant art experience to the aesthetic experience – the maneuver that gives the aesthetic theory of art much of its exclusionary thrust – appears to me to be a liability. The aesthetic definition of art privileges aesthetic experience to the exclusion of other nonaesthetic forms of interaction that the art object can be designed to promote. I shall argue that there is no reason for the aesthetic experience to be privileged in this way insofar as it seems to me that we cannot rule out other, nonaesthetic forms of response to art as illegitimate on the grounds that they are not aesthetic responses. Indeed, when discussing these other responses to works of art. I think I will be able to show that denying the status of art to such works as *L.H.O.O.Q.* and "Poème symphonique" is a mistake.

Before charting several forms of nonaesthetic responses to art, it will be helpful to clarify the notion of an aesthetic response to art. One problem here is that there are a number of different, ostensibly nonequivalent characterizations available. Let a sample suffice to initiate the discussion. Tolhurst intentionally refrains from characterizing aesthetic experience, though Beardsley, of course, has offered a number of accounts. Writing on aesthetic enjoyment, which as I take it is nothing but positive aesthetic experience, Beardsley has claimed that

> Aesthetic enjoyment is (by definition) the kind of enjoyment we obtain from the apprehension of a qualitatively diverse segment of the phenomenal field insofar as the discriminable parts are unified into something of a whole that has a character (that is, regional qualities) of its own.[6]

This account offers what might be thought of as a content-oriented characterization of positive aesthetic experience. It is "content-oriented" because it stresses the properties of the object, here "regional qualities," to which attention is directed. This approach corresponds to J. O. Urmson's notion that what marks an aesthetic reaction is its attention to how things look and feel especially in terms of qualities such as appearing spacious, swift, strong, mournful, cheerful, and so on.[7] I will take it that one major variation of the aesthetic response approach – the content-oriented approach – designates a response as aesthetic when it takes as its focus the aesthetic or expressive or "qualitative" appearances of the object. I will argue that this leaves us with a particularly impoverished view of our customary reaction to art that has extremely problematic consequences for any theorist who would want to use aesthetic experience as definitive of the function, vis-à-vis the spectators' reaction, which artworks are designed to produce.

Beardsley has not always characterized aesthetic experience primarily by reference to content. Often he attempts to characterize aesthetic experience through the analysis of its internal-feeling-structure, which we might call an affect-oriented account of aesthetic experience. In recent essays, Beardsley has placed more weight than the previous quotation did on the affective features of aesthetic experience. In a formal statement of his criteria for aesthetic experience, one mirrored informally in *What Is Art?*, Beardsley says that an experience has an aesthetic character if it has the first of the following features and at least three of the others. For Beardsley, the five relevant features of aesthetic experience are: object directedness, felt freedom, detached affect, active discovery, and wholeness, that is, a sense of integration as a person.[8] Apart from "active discovery," these criteria allude to affective attributes of experience. And even in the case of "active discovery" the criterion is a case of both content-oriented and affect-oriented considerations, for though said discoveries are achieved through seeing connections between percepts and meanings, such insights are to be accompanied by a sense of intelligibility.

There are many problems with this characterization of aesthetic experience. First, it is possible that either there is no experience that meets this account or, if this account can be read in a way that grants that some experiences meet it, then other-than-aesthetic experiences, for example, solving theorems in nonapplied mathematics, may also meet it. But, most important, it is clear that many of our typical responses to art will, under a rigorous reading of Beardsley's formula, not stand up as aesthetic, with the consequence that objects that support only certain typical but nonaesthetic interactions with art will not count as art. Of course, the desiderata canvassed in what I've called the content-approach and the predominantly affect-oriented approach do not reflect every belief about aesthetic experience found in the tradition; other beliefs will be mentioned in the ensuing discussion of nonaesthetic responses to art. However, frequent return to these two models of the aesthetic response will be useful in discussing typical nonaesthetic interactions with art.

A great many of our typical, nonaesthetic responses to art can be grouped under the label of interpretation. Artists often include, imply, or suggest meanings in their creations, meanings and themes that are oblique and that the audience works at discovering. Mallarmé wrote

> To actually name an object is to suppress three-quarters of the sense of enjoyment of a poem, which consists in the delight of guessing one stage at a time: to *suggest* the object, that is the poet's dream... There must always be a sense of the enigmatic in poetry, and that is the aim of literature.

And in a similar vein, John Updike says "I think books should have secrets as a bonus for the sensitive reader". These statements are by writers but there are artists in every artform who strive to incorporate oblique or hidden meanings or themes, and nonobvious adumbrations of the oblique themes in their work.[9] In Peter Hutchinson's interpretation of *Tonio Kroger,* we find an example of an oblique theme, that of the split personality, and of an adumbration thereof, the use of the character's name to convey, in a camouflaged way, extra inflection concerning the nature of the split personality, Hutchinson writes

> In *Tonio Kroger,* Mann's most famous early story, the eponymous hero bears features of two distinct qualities in his name: those of his artistic mother, and the more somber ones of his self-controlled father. It is his mother from whom Tonio has inherited his creative powers – she comes from "the South," a land lacking in self-discipline but rich in self-expression, and its qualities are symbolized in his Christian name (with its clear Italian ring). His father, on the other hand, the upright Northerner, the practical man of common sense and sound business acumen, bears a name suggestive of dullness and solidity (it derives from the Middle Low German 'Kroger,' a publican). The very sound of each component reinforces those ideas and explains the split in Tonio's character, the major theme of this Novelle.[10]

The presence of such obliquely presented themes and adumbrations occurs frequently enough, especially in certain genres, that audiences customarily search for hidden meanings that are likely to have been implanted in the artwork. Though Hutchinson's interpretation might be thought of as "professional," I think that it is reflective of one central way in which we, in general, have been trained to think, talk, and in short, respond to art. This training began when we were first initiated into the world of art in our earliest literature and art appreciation classes. Moreover, we have every reason to believe that our training in this matter supplies dependable guidelines for appropriate art responses since our early training is reinforced by the evident preoccupation with oblique meanings found in discussions of art by critics, scholars, and connoisseurs in newspapers, journals, and learned treatises. And clearly our training and behavior regarding the search for hidden meanings are not beside the point since artists, steeped in the same hermeneutical traditions that spectators practice, have often put oblique meanings in their works precisely so that we, excited by the challenge, exercise our skill and ingenuity, our powers of observation, association, and synthesis in order to discover oblique themes and to trace their complex adumbrations.

With certain forms of interpretation, the spectator's relation to the artwork is gamelike. The spectator has a goal, to find a hidden or oblique theme (or an oblique adumbration of one), which goal the spectator pursues by using a range of hermeneutical strategies, which, in turn, place certain epistemological constraints on his or her activity. This interpretive play is something we have been trained in since grammar school, and it is a practice that is amplified and publicly endorsed by the criticism we read. The obliqueness of the artist's presentation of a theme confronts the audience with an obstacle that the audience voluntarily elects to overcome. How the artist plants this theme and how the audience goes about discovering it – in terms of distinctive forms of reasoning and observation – are primarily determined by precedent and tradition, though, of course, the tradition allows for innovation both in the area of artmaking and of interpretation. Within this gamelike practice, when we discover a hidden theme we have achieved a success, and we are prone, all things being equal, to regard our activity as rewarding insofar as the artwork has enabled us to apply our skills to a worthy, that is, challenging, object. But this type of interpretive play, though characteristic of our interaction with artworks, and rewarding, exemplifies neither the content-oriented form, nor the affect-oriented form of aesthetic response.

Though so far I have only spoken of the interpretation of obliquely presented meanings, it should be noted that our interpretive, nonaesthetic responses also include the discernment of latent structures. That is, when we contemplate art, we often have as a goal, upon which we may expend great effort, figuring out the way in which a given painting or musical composition works. In the presence of an artwork, we characteristically set ourselves to finding out what its structure is as well as often asking the reason for its being structured that way. Or, if we sense that an artwork has a certain effect, for example, the impression of the recession of the central figure in Malevich's *Black Quadrilateral,* we examine the formal arrangement and principles that bring this effect about.[11] Again, this is something we have been trained to do and something that pervades the discussion of art in both informal and professional conversation. Indeed, some radical formalists might hold that understanding how a work works is the only legitimate interest we should have in art and the only criterion of whether our response to art is appropriate. This seems an unduly narrow recommendation given art as we know it. My claim is only that identifying the structure or structures of a work – seeing how it works – is, like the identification of a hidden meaning, one criterion of a successful interaction with art. Moreover, this form of interaction is not "aesthetic," as that is normally construed, but it should not, for that reason, be disregarded as a characteristic and appropriate mode of participating with artworks.

So far two types of interpretive play have been cited as examples of characteristic responses to art that tend to be overlooked when philosophers of art accord a privileged position to aesthetic responses as the canonical model of our interaction with art. And if interpretation is ignored as an appropriate art response while only aesthetic experience is so countenanced, and if art is identified in relation to the promotion of appropriate responses, then objects devoted exclusively to engendering interpretive play will be artistically disenfranchised. But, of course, one may wonder whether it is correct to claim, as I have, that the philosophers of art tend to ignore the importance of interpretation. For much of the literature in the field concerns issues of intepretation. This, admittedly, is true in one sense. However, it must be added that the attention lavished on interpretation in the literature is not focused on interpretive play as a characteristic form of the experience of interacting with artworks but rather revolves around epistemological problems, for example, are artist's intentions admissible evidence; can interpretations be true or are they merely plausible; and so forth. This epistemological focus, moreover, tends to take critical argument as its subject matter. Thus, the fact that philosophers have such epistemological interests in interpretation does not vitiate the point that interpretive play is an ingredient in our characteristic experience of artworks which philosophers, by privileging the aesthetic, have effectively bracketed from the art experience proper. Indeed, within the philosophical tradition, the kind of intellective responses I have cited under the rubric of interpretation are not part of the experience, proper, of art. Hume, for example, tells us that though good sense is necessary for the correct functioning of taste, it is not part of taste.[12] Rather, the picture he suggests is that the prior operation of the understanding, engaged in doing things like identifying the purpose and related structure of the artwork, puts us in a position to undergo, subsequently, the central experience of the work, namely, for Hume, a feeling of pleasure.

This citation of Hume provides us with one reason why philosophers are tempted to exclude interpretive play from the art experience proper. The essential experience of art, for them, is a matter of feeling pleasure either of the undifferentiated Humean sort or of the disinterested Kantian variety. Interpretive activity, on the other hand, it might be said, has no obvious connection with pleasure. But I'm not so sure of this.

I have asserted that art spectatorship is a practice, a practice linked with other practices, such as artmaking, within the institution of the artworld. I follow MacIntyre when he writes that

By a "practice" I am going to mean any coherent and complex form of socially established cooperative human activity through which goods internal to that form of activity are realized in trying to achieve those standards of excellence which are appropriate to, and partially definitive of, that form of activity, with the result that human powers to achieve excellence, and human conceptions of the ends and goods involved, are systematically extended.[13]

Within the practice of art spectatorship, among the goals of the enterprise, we find the making of interpretations of various sorts. Finding hidden meanings and latent structures are goods internal to the activity of art spectatorship. Pursuit of these goals in our encounters with artworks occupies large parts of our experience of artworks. Our interpretations can succeed or fail. They can be mundane or excellent. When our interpretations succeed, we derive the satisfaction that comes from the achievement of a goal against an established standard of excellence. That is, satisfaction is connected with success, within the practice of art spectatorship, when we are able to detect a latent theme or form in an artwork. Moreover, I see no reason to deny that this type of satisfaction is a type of pleasure even though it differs from the type of pleasurable sensation, or thrill, or beauteous rapture that theorists often appear to have in mind when speaking of aesthetic experience. The exercise of the skills of art spectatorship is its own reward within our practice. This is not to say that interpretive play is the only source of pleasure, but only that it is a source of pleasure. Thus, the worry that interpretive play is remote from pleasure should supply no grounds for excluding interpretive play from our characterization of the art experience proper.

Apart from the argument that interpretive play is not connected with pleasure, there may be other motives behind the tendency not to include interpretive play in the account of the art experience proper. One concern might be that interpretive play is not essential or fundamental to the art experience because it fails to differentiate the interaction with art from other experiences. In this context, the putative virtue of the notion of the aesthetic experience of art is that it can say how our experiences of art differ from other types of experience. The proponent of the aesthetic experience approach might argue that the interpretive play I refer to regarding the art response is not different in kind from that activity in which a cryptographer indulges.

Of course, it is not clear that aesthetic-experience accounts can do the differentiating work they are supposed to do. First, those versions of aesthetic experience that rely on notions of detachment and disinterest may just be implausible. Second, even an account as detailed as Beardsley's affect-oriented one doesn't differentiate the aesthetic experience of art from all other activities. For example, assuming that there are acts of disinterested attention, Beardsley's affect-oriented account might not differentiate aesthetic experience from the mathematician's experience of solving a problem that is divorced from practical application. So if the argument against including interpretive play in our account of the art experience is that interpretive play does not differentiate that experience from other kinds whereas the notion of aesthetic experience does, then we can say that neither of the putatively competing accounts succeeds at the task of essentially differentiating the art experience. Thus, essentially differentiating the art experience from others might not be a desideratum in our characterizations of it.

I suspect that since art evolved over a long period of time and through the interactions of many different cultures, it may support a plurality of interests such that the art experience is comprised of a plurality of activities of which having aesthetic experiences of some sort is one, while engaging in interpretive play is another. There are undoubtedly more activities than only these two. Furthermore, it may be the case that none of the multiple types of interactions that comprise the art experience is unique to encounters with art. Of course, this might be granted at the same time that the proponent of the aesthetic theory urges that nevertheless aesthetic experience is a necessary component of any experience of art whereas other responses, like interpretive play, are not. At that point, the aesthetic theorist will have to show that aesthetic experience is such a necessary component. And, at least for those who hold an aesthetic definition of art, that will not be easy to do without begging the question. Suppose my counterexample to the notion that aesthetic experience is a necessary component of every art experience is Duchamp's *Fountain*. I note that it is an object placed in a situation such that it has an oblique significance that supports a great deal of interpretive play. But it does not appear to promote the kinds of response that theorists call aesthetic. So it affords an art experience that is not an aesthetic one. Moreover, the interpretive play available in contemplating *Fountain* involves an art experience of a very high degree of intensity for its kind. The aesthetic theorist can attempt to block this counterexample by saying that *Fountain* is not an artwork and that an interpretive response to it, therefore, is not even an experience of art. But one can only do this by asserting that aesthetic experience is definitive of art and of what can be experienced as art. Yet that begs the question insofar as it presupposes that a work designed to provoke and promote interpretive play cannot be art because interpretive play is not a criterion of the kind of experience appropriate to art.

One might argue that interpretive play is not fundamental to the art experience in the sense that it is not the original purpose for which the works we call art were created. But this faces problems from two directions. First, hermeneutics has been around for a long time and may even predate our notion of taste. Second, if one makes this argument with aesthetic experience in mind, can we be so certain that promoting aesthetic experience was the original purpose for which many of the more historically remote objects we call art were made? Moreover, if it is claimed that many of the ancient or medieval artifacts we call art at least had a potentially aesthetic dimension, it must be acknowledged that most of the self-same objects also possessed a symbolizing dimension that invited interpretive play.

Perhaps it will be argued that interpretive play is inappropriate to the art response proper. This tack seems to me an implausible one since all the evidence – our training in art appreciation and the behavior of the majority of our leading connoisseurs – points in the direction of suggesting that interpretative play is one of the central and esteemed modes of the practice of art spectatorship. Indeed, how would one go about showing that a behavior as deeply entrenched and as widely indulged in a practice as interpretive play in art spectatorship is inappropriate to the practice? Practices are human activities constituted by traditionally evolved purposes and ways of satisfying those purposes. The active traditions of such practices determine what is appropriate to a practice both in terms of the ends and means of the practice. Thus, in art, the continuing tradition of interpretation establishes the appropriateness of the kinds of hermeneutical responses that we have been discussing.

One might try to show the inappropriateness of interpretive play as an art response by arguing that it interferes with some deeper goal of the practice of art. But what could that be? Perceiving aesthetic properties might be one candidate. However, in some cases interpretive play may, in fact, enhance the perception of aesthetic qualities. Nor does this suggest that interpretive play is subservient to the goal of perceiving qualities. For in some further instances, perceiving qualities may be valuable for the way in which it enables the discovery of a richer interpretation, while in other cases the interpretive play and the aesthetic response may remain independent of one another, supplying spectators with separate focii of interest in the work. Of course, proponents of the aesthetic approach may assert that theirs is the only proper response to art, but that, as I have, I hope, shown, is only an assertion.

I think that it is obvious that the types of activities I have used, so far, to exemplify interpretive play diverge from what was earlier called the content-oriented version of the aesthetic approach. There the notion was that an aesthetic response to art was one that was directed at the qualitative features of the object, such as its perceptible or expressive features. And though interpretation may, in different ways, sometimes be involved with aesthetic responses, it should be clear that interpretive play is not equivalent to aesthetic or expressive apprehension both because it is not evident that interpretation is an element in all instances of aesthetic perception, and because the objects of interpretive play extend beyond aesthetic and expressive qualities to themes and their adumbrations, and to structures and their complications.

But what about the affect-oriented variant of the aesthetic approach? First, it should be noted that many of the candidates in this area rely centrally on a characterization of aesthetic experience that rests on notions such as disinterested pleasure or detachment from practical interest. But one may successfully engage in interpretive play without being devoid of practical interest – one may be a critic whose reputation has been built on clever interpretations. So interpretive play differs from aesthetic experience as the latter is typically explicated.

But the Beardsleyan affect-oriented account of aesthetic experience is more detailed than many of its predecessors and it seems to have room for interpretive play. That is, in later versions of his account of aesthetic experience, Beardsley includes a new feature to the characterization of aesthetic experience – namely, active discovery – which is not included in previous accounts, either his own or, to my knowledge, those of others. By the inclusion of active discovery, it may be felt that interpretive play has been successfully wedded to aesthetic experience.

I disagree. For even in Beardsley's new variant, a response still requires much more than active discovery to amount to an aesthetic experience. It would also have to be at least object-directed as well as meeting two of the following three criteria: afford a sense of felt freedom, detached affect, or a sense of wholeness. But surely we could, via interpretive play, engage in active discovery without felt freedom – that is, the absence of antecedent concerns – and without detached affect – that is, emotional distance. Imagine a Marxist literary critic, pressed by a deadline to finish her paper on the hidden reactionary meaning of a Balzac novel. Nor does it seem likely that interpretive play often correlates with Beardsley's criterion of wholeness, that is, a sense of integration as a person. Indeed, I suspect that this is a rather unusual concomitant to expect of many interactions with art. And, furthermore, many instances of interpretive play may not meet the requirement of object directedness. A work like Duchamp's *Fountain* surely supports a great amount of interpretive play although most, if not all, of this can be derived from attention to the art historical context in which it was placed rather than to the object itself.

Even Beardsley's account of the element of active discovery, as it is involved in the art response, has an affective component. For under the rubric of active discovery, he not only has in mind that we actively make connections but that this be accompanied by a feeling of intelligibility. One is uncertain here whether this feeling of intelligibility is simply seeing a connection or whether it is something more. If the former, then it is true of every interpretive insight. But if it is the latter, which is a more likely reading given Beardsley's overall program, I am not sure that a sense of intelligibility accompanies every interpretive insight. I may come to realize that *The Turn of the Screw* is structured to support at least two opposed interpretations but that doesn't result in a sense of intelligibility.

What these considerations are meant to show is that even with the inclusion of active discovery in Beardsley's formula, interpretive play remains a mode of response to art that is independent of and not subsumable under aesthetic experience. Often, instances of interpretive play will not amount to full-blown, Beardsleyan-type aesthetic experiences because they will not score appreciably in terms of the criteria he requires over and above active discovery. And it may also be the case that instances of interpretive play may not even count as examples of Beardsleyan active discovery because they will not result in the appropriate sense of intelligibility.

But interpretive play nevertheless still remains a characteristic form of interaction with artworks. And, *pace* aesthetic theorists of art, I think that if we encounter an object designed to support interpretive play, even though it affords no aesthetic experience or aesthetic perception, then we have *a* reason to believe it is an artwork. Of course, an aesthetic theorist might try to solve this problem by saying that interpretive play, sans any particular affect or perceptual focus, is a sufficient condition for calling a response "aesthetic." However, this move involves abandoning not only the letter but also the spirit of the aesthetic approach, for the tradition has always used the idea of the "aesthetic" to single out a dimension of interaction with objects that is bound up with perceptual experience, affective experience, or a combination thereof. In short, to assimilate interpretive play as a mode of aesthetic experience misses the point of what people were trying to get at by use of the notion of the "aesthetic."

One key feature of the notion of the aesthetic, mentioned by Beardsley and others,[14] is object directedness. In this light, having aesthetic experiences or aesthetic perceptions is, in large measure, a matter of focusing our attention on the artwork that stands before us. The implicit picture of spectatorship that this approach suggests is of an audience consuming artworks atomistically, one at a time, going from one monadic art response to the next. But this hardly squares with the way in which those who attend to art with any regularity or dedication either respond to or have been trained to respond to art. Art – both in the aspect of its creation and its appreciation – is a combination of internally linked practices, which, to simplify, we may refer to as a single practice. Like any practice,[15] art involves not only a relationship between present practitioners but a relationship with the past. Artmaking and artgoing are connected with traditions. As artgoers we are not only interested in the artwork as a discrete object before us – the possible occasion for an aesthetic experience – but also as an object that has a place in the tradition. Entering the practice of art, even as an artgoer, is to enter a tradition, to become apprised of it, to be concerned about it, and to become interested in its history and its ongoing development. Thus, a characteristic response to art, predictably enough, is, given an artwork or a series of artworks, to strive to figure out and to situate their place within the tradition, or within the historical development and/or tradition of a specific art form or genre. This implies that important aspects of our interaction with artworks are not, strictly speaking, object directed, but are devoted to concerns with issues outside the object. We don't concentrate on the object in splendid isolation: our attention fans out to enable us to see the place of the art object within a larger, historical constellation of objects. Nor is this attending to the historical context of the object undertaken to enhance what would be traditionally construed as our aesthetic experience. Rather, our wider ambit of attention is motivated by the art appreciator's interest in the tradition at large. Yet this deflection of attention from the object is not an aesthetic aberration. It is part of what is involved with entering a practice with a living tradition.

To be interested in the tradition at large is to be interested in its development and in the various moves and countermoves that comprise that development. For example, encountering one of Morris Louis's *Unfurleds,* we may remark upon the way in which it works out a problematic of the practice of painting initiated by the concern of Fauvists and Cubists with flatness. The painting interests us not only for whatever aesthetic perceptions it might promote, but also for the way in which it intervenes in an ongoing painterly dialectic about flatness. To be concerned with the significance of the painting within the tradition of modern art is not inappropriate, but rather is a characteristic response of an appreciator who has entered the practice of art. From one artwork to the next, we consider the way in which a new work may expand upon the dialectic or problematic present in earlier works. Or, a later work may, for example, amplify the technical means at the disposal of a given artform for the pursuit of its already established goals. So we may view a film such as Griffith's *The Birth of a Nation* as the perfection of primitive film's commitment to narration. Such an interest in *The Birth of a Nation* is neither the viewpoint of an antiquarian, a filmmaker, or a film specialist. It is rather the response of any film appreciator who has entered the practice of film spectatorship.

Confronted with a new artwork, we may scrutinize it with an eye to isolating the ways in which it expands upon an existing artworld dialectic, solves a problem that vexed previous artists, seizes upon a hitherto unexpected possibility of the tradition, or amplifies the formal means of an artform in terms of the artform's already established pursuits. But a new artwork may also stand to the tradition by way of making a revolutionary break with the past. A new artwork may emphasize possibilities not only present in, but actually repressed by, preceding styles; it may introduce a new problematic; it may repudiate the forms or values of previous art. When Tristan Tzara composed poems by randomly drawing snippets of words from a hat, he was repudiating the Romantic poet's valorization of expression, just as the Romantic poet had repudiated earlier poets' valorization of the representation of the external world in favor of a new emphasis on the internal, subjective world. Tzara's act wasn't random; it made perfect sense in the ongoing dialogue of art history. Concerned with the tradition at large, we as spectators review artworks in order to detect the tensions or conflicts between artistic generations, styles, and programs. We interpret stylistic choices and gambits as repudiations and gestures of rejection by later artworks of earlier ones. This is often much like the interpretation of a hidden meaning; however, it requires attention outside the work to its art historical context. The significance we identify is not so much one hidden in the work as one that emerges when we consider the work against the backdrop of contesting styles and movements. Call it the dramatic meaning of the artwork. But as participants in a tradition, we are legitimately interested in its historical development and especially in its dramatic unfolding. Recognizing the dramatic significance of an artwork as it plays the role of antagonist or protagonist on the stage of art history is not incidental to our interest in art but is an essential element of immersing ourselves in the tradition. Following the conflicts and tensions within the development of art history is as central a component of the practice of art spectatorship as is having aesthetic experiences.

The "other directed," as opposed to the "object directed," interpretive play we characteristically mobilize when interacting with art takes other appropriate forms than those of detecting stylistic amplifications and repudiations. For example, we may wish to contemplate lines of influence or consider changes of direction in the careers of major artists. These concerns as well are grounded in our interests, as participants, in an evolving tradition. However, rather than dwell on these, I would rather turn to a proposal of the way in which the detection of a repudiation – insofar as it is an important and characteristic interpretive response to art – can enable us to short-circuit the dismissal, by aesthetic theorists of art, of such works as Duchamp's *Fountain*.

Let us grant that Duchamp's *Fountain* does not afford an occasion for aesthetic experiences or aesthetic perceptions as those are typically and narrowly construed. Nevertheless, it does propose a rich forum for interpretive play. Its placement in a certain artworld context was designed to be infuriating, on the one hand, and enigmatic and puzzling on the other. Confronted by *Fountain,* or by reports about its placement in a gallery, one asks what it means to put such an object on display at an art exhibition. What is the significance of the object in its particular social setting? And, of course, if we contemplate *Fountain* against the backdrop of art history, we come to realize that it is being used to symbolize a wealth of concerns. We see it to be a contemptuous repudiation of that aspect of fine art that emphasizes craftsmanship in favor of a reemphasis of the importance of ideas to fine art. One might also gloss it as a gesture that reveals the importance of the nominating process, which George Dickie analyzed, of the institution of the artworld. And so on.

Now my point against aesthetic theorists of art is that even if *Fountain* does not promote an aesthetic interaction, it does promote an interpretive interaction. Moreover, an interpretive interaction, including one of identifying the dialectical significance of a work in the evolution of art history, is as appropriate and as characteristic a response to art as an aesthetic response. Thus, since *Fountain* encourages an appropriate and characteristic art response, we have an important reason to consider it to be a work of art even if it promotes no aesthetic experience.

Aesthetic theorists hold that something is art if it has been designed to function in such a way as to bring about certain appropriate responses to art. This seems to be a reasonable strategy. However, such theorists countenance only aesthetic responses as appropriate. Yet there are other characteristic and appropriate responses to art. And if an object supports such responses to an appreciable degree, then I think that gives us reason to call the object art.

One objection to my reclamation of *Fountain* might be that my model of the standard artgoer is unacceptable. It might be said that someone involved in trying to decipher the moves and countermoves of artists within the historically constituted arena of the artworld is not the standard spectator but a specialist or an art historian. My response to this is to deny that I am speaking of specialists and to urge that I take as my model someone who attends to art on some regular basis, and who is an informed viewer, one who "keeps up" with art without being a professional critic or a professor of art. It is the responses of such spectators that should provide the data for philosophers of art concerned to discuss the experience of art.

On the other hand, I am disquieted by the implicit picture that aesthetic theories project of the standard artgoer. For them, it would appear, the spectator is one who goes from one encounter with art to the next without attempting to connect them. Such a person, for example, might read a novel every year or so, hear a concert occasionally, and go to an art exhibition whenever he or she visits New York. But why should the casual viewer of art be our source for characterizing the art experience? If we want to characterize what it is to respond to baseball appropriately, would we look to the spectator who watches one game every five years? Of course, this is an *ad hominem* attack. Aesthetic theorists don't say that we should use such casual artgoers as our model of the standard spectator. Nevertheless, there is something strange about their standard viewer, namely, that he or she responds to each work of art monadically, savoring each aesthetic experience as a unitary event and not linking that event to a history of previous interactions with artworks. As a matter of fact, I think this picture is inaccurate. Such an artgoer would be as curious as the dedicated baseball spectator who attends games for whatever excitement he can derive from the contest before him and who does not contemplate the significance of this game in terms of the past and future of the practice of baseball.

The aesthetic theorist may, of course, admit that interpretive responses to the hidden meanings, dramatic significance, and latent structures are appropriate within the practice of spectatorship. But he might add that they are not basic because the practice of art spectatorship would never have gotten off the ground nor would it continue to keep going if artworks did not give rise to aesthetic experiences. Our desire for aesthetic pleasure is the motor that drives the art institution. These are, of course, empirical claims. Possibly aesthetic pleasure is what started it all, although it is equally plausible to think that the pleasure of interpretation could have motivated and does motivate spectatorship. But, in any case, this debate is probably beside the point. For it is likely that both the possibility of aesthetic pleasure and the pleasure of interpretation motivate artgoing, and that interacting with artworks by way of having aesthetic perceptions and making interpretations are both appropriate and equally basic responses to art.

My dominant thesis has been that there are more responses, appropriate to artworks, than aesthetic responses. I have not given an exhaustive catalogue of these but have focused upon various types of interpretive responses. This raises the question of whether or not something like the aesthetic definition of art, amplified to incorporate a more catholic view of the appropriate experiences art avails us, couldn't be reworked in such a way that the result would be an adequate theory of art. The theory might look like this: "A work of art is an object designed to promote, in some appreciable magnitude, the having of aesthetic perceptions, or the making of various types of interpretations, or the undertaking of whatever other appropriate responses are available to spectators."

Attractive as this maneuver is, I doubt it will work. It does not seem to me that any given type of response is necessary to having an appropriate interaction with the artwork. With some artworks, we may only be able to respond in terms of aesthetic perceptions while with others only interpretive responses are possible. Nor, by the way, does any particular response supply us with sufficient grounds for saying something is a work of art. Cars are designed to impart aesthetic perceptions but they are not typically artworks, while we might interpret one artist throwing soup in another artist's face as the repudiation of a tradition without counting the insult as art. Likewise an encoded military document with a hidden message is not art despite the interpretive play it might engender.

At the same time, if we are trying to convince someone that something is an artwork, showing that it is designed to promote one or more characteristic art interactions – whether aesthetic or interpretive – supplies *a* reason to regard the object as art. Suppose we are arguing about whether comic book serials like *The Incredible Hulk, Spiderman,* and the *Fantastic Four* are art. And suppose we agree that such exercises do not afford aesthetic experiences of any appreciable magnitude.

But, nevertheless, suppose I argue that these comic books contain hidden allegories of the anxieties of adolescence, such that those allegories are of a complexity worthy of decipherment. At that point, we have *a* reason to regard the comics
as art, and the burden of proof is on the skeptic who must show that the alleged
allegories are either merely fanciful concoctions of mine or are so transparent that
it is outlandish to suppose that they warrant a response sophisticated enough to be
counted as an interpretation.

℮〜

BEAUTY AND THE GENEALOGY
OF ART THEORY

Within the analytic tradition, those of us who take art as our field of study call
ourselves either philosophers of art or aestheticians. From one perspective,
these alternative labels could be seen as a harmless sort of shorthand. For two
major concerns of the field, however it is named, are the theory of art, which
traditionally pertains to questions about the nature of the art object, and
aesthetic theory, which pertains primarily to certain dimensions of the experience of art (and also to the experience of certain features of nature). Thus,
rather than identifying ourselves longishly as philosophers of art *and* philosophers of aesthetics, for economy's sake, we may simply refer to ourselves as one
or the other, leaving the remaining label unstated, but understood. And where
this is the motive behind the alternations of title, the ambiguous labeling seems
quite harmless.

However, the ambiguity can also be understood to rest on a substantive and
controversial claim – namely, that the theory of art and the theory of aesthetics are
conceptually linked in such a way that the former can be reduced to the latter;
that, in other words, there are not two, generally independent areas of philosophical inquiry here, but one unified field. Thus, we are called either philosophers of
art or philosophers of aesthetics because, in most contexts of any significance,
those titles signal a concern with the selfsame issues.

The view that the philosophy of art and the philosophy of aesthetics are conceptually linked is explicitly stated in what have been called aesthetic theories of art. On
this approach, which is enjoying quite a resurgence nowadays,[1] the artwork is functional; such works are designed to create a certain experience in spectators, namely, an
aesthetic experience. Thus, with aesthetic theories of art, our conception of aesthetic
experience is the most crucial feature in the identification of artworks. In effect, the
theory of art is virtually reduced to aesthetics, insofar as aesthetic experience is the

From: *The Philosophical Forum*, XXII, no.4 (Summer 1991), 307–34.

"first among equals" of the conditions the theory proposes to be necessary for discriminating artworks from other things. (That such works be *intentionally designed* to bring about said experiences is another, frequently invoked, condition.)

On the aesthetic theory of art, then, the philosophy of art and the philosophy of aesthetics become roughly the same enterprise, thereby apparently making the ambiguity of the name of the field a matter of indifference. And the reason for indifference here is that the philosophy of art just is a branch of aesthetics. But since the aesthetic theory of art is quite controversial, the ambiguity in the name of our field may be problematic insofar as it masks an implicit allegiance to one, highly disputed theory of the way our philosophical inquiries should proceed. That is, the ambiguity facilitates confusing one rival philosophical position about the field with the structure of the field itself.

Now I think that something like this confusion – which involves a conflation of art and the aesthetic in decisive ways – occurs often. It appears overtly in aesthetic theories of art, but it also has covert ramifications that surface in supposed intuitions about what is irrelevant to a proper philosophical consideration of art. That is, the convictions that artistic intention, art history, morality, politics, and so on are not germane to the theory of art are, in fact, subsidiary tenets of the reduction of the philosophy of art to aesthetics.

Moreover, if the aesthetic theory of art and the "intuitions" that accompany it are false, then the easy slippage from talk of the philosophy of art to talk of aesthetics is not so innocent, since it at least helps to obscure and possibly encourages confusions about some of the deepest controversies in the field: the status of artistic intention, of art history, of the role of morality and politics in art, and so on. That is, the question of "What's in a name?," in this case, could have substantial repercussions for philosophical progress.

My own view is that we should be sticklers in talking about the philosophy of art, on the one hand, and about aesthetics, on the other. Nor, I shall argue, is this simply a matter of standing on ceremony. For since I believe that aesthetic theories of art and the "intuitions" that issue from them are misguided, I would like to discourage usage that may, in part, be motivated by a tacit or unrecognized acceptance of them. So, central among the points that I would like to make in this essay are that: (1) the philosophy of art and aesthetics should be spoken of as two areas of inquiry *since,* (2) failure to do so has been and continues to be a source of philosophical confusion.

Furthermore the ambiguity between the philosophy of art and the philosophy of aesthetics – where that is facilitated by the explication of the concept of art by means of the category of the aesthetic – penetrates the discourse of the field quite profoundly. For when the philosophy of art becomes aesthetics, the *agenda* of what philosophers in this area will and will not talk about is subtly set. Art history and the relation of art to morality, politics, and, indeed, to the world at large – topics of deep concern to theorists of art in nonanalytic traditions – for example, are primarily ignored or even actively denied to be issues of philosophical interest. At the very least, I think that anyone familiar with the analytic tradition will acknowledge that questions about art history, and of the moral and political status of art, have not received a great deal of attention. Where these topics do receive attention is often in the context of showing that they are irrelevant to the proper concerns of the field. Part of the purpose of this essay is to diagnose how and why this blindspot, whether maintained complacently or through explicit argumentation, afflicts the analytic tradition.

My hypothesis is that there is a major tendency in the tradition – implicit on the part of many, explicit in aesthetic theories of art – to systematically subsume the concept of art under the category of the aesthetic. Moreover, I think that one strategy for curing these afflictions is to show how this tendency originates in an error that is only further compounded by the passage of time.

I do not claim to be the first philosopher to have noticed the danger of linking the theory of art with aesthetic theory. Some such recognition provides an underlying principle for much of George Dickie's work in the field. One reading of George Dickie's overarching project might note that his classic dismissal of aesthetic attitudes and experiences as myths and phantoms[2] functions as the key move in a dialectical argument in favor of his Institutional Theory of Art and its successor, the theory of the Art Circle.[3] That is, one way to read Dickie is to construe him as operating in opposition to skepticism about the possibility of art theory (Weitz et al.[4]), on the one hand, and opposition to aesthetic theories of art – conceived of as the most persuasive candidates for art theory – on the other. He defeats the skeptical, open-concept view of art after the fashion of Maurice Mandelbaum[5]; and he attempts to dismiss aesthetic theories of art by challenging a representative sample of the ways in which its central defining term, the aesthetic, has been construed. Thus, with respect to the latter strategy, if there is no viable concept of the aesthetic, then there can be no aesthetic theory of art. And if, *pace* skeptical proponents of the open-concept approach, art theory is possible, and the aesthetic theory of art has been removed as a serious contender, then the logical space has been secured to at least advance something like an Institutional Theory of Art, modified as a theory of the Art Circle.

If this interpretation of Dickie is correct, then his famous attacks on the aesthetic are an integral and coherent part of the project of defending institutional-type theories. That Dickie's rejection of the various notions of aesthetic faculties/attitudes/experiences comes prior to his proposals concerning the theory of art can be seen as part of an argumentative, ground-clearing operation, one devoted to dismissing aesthetic theories of art as viable contenders in the realm of art theory by calling into question the acceptability of any characterization of the correlative state in spectators that artworks putatively engender. This, of course, severs the bond between the philosophy of art and the philosophy of the aesthetic, though it remains somewhat unclear, given the skeptical nature of Dickie's arguments about anything aesthetic, what Dickie thinks remains for aestheticians to study.

I believe that Dickie's objections to aesthetic theories of art and to the various formulations of the idea of the aesthetic attitude or experience are sound. What I want to do in this essay is to develop an alternative line of argument against the reduction of art to aesthetics that, while rejecting that reduction, also shows how this tendency emerged, why it seemed and, for some, continues to be seen to be plausible, and what some of its consequences are in terms of the supposed intuitions that it reinforces.

In order to do this, I will tell a narrative or genealogy about the evolution of the field that discloses how it happened that aesthetic theory came to be confused with art theory. This will be a highly selective narrative but not, I think, a distortion. For the figures it singles out as seminal — Francis Hutcheson, Kant, Clive Bell, and Monroe Beardsley — are already central characters in the field's narratives of itself, and, therefore, one surmises, are major influences on the shape philosophical conversation has taken.

The story that I want to tell has a point and to make the story flow smoothly, it is useful to state that point from the outset. The most important concern of early aesthetic theorizing (and here I have Hutcheson and, with certain qualifications, Kant in mind) is the analysis of the beautiful — the beautiful in the narrow sense of the term, such as it figures in locutions like "a beautiful sunset." Indeed, the best candidates for the subjects of early aesthetic theorists, it seems to me, were natural beauties. Thus, when later theorists attempt to exploit the findings of earlier aesthetic theorists in their characterizations of the nature of art, they are, in effect, transposing the theory of beauty onto the theory of art. Stated more tendentiously, later theorists are treating art as if it was a subspecies of beauty. Of course, stated this way proponents of the aesthetic theory of art would undoubtedly claim that they are being unduly caricatured. So the burden of my little story will be to show that this is not a caricature.

I am presuming here that if it is the case that it can be shown that aesthetic theories are reducing art to beauty, narrowly construed, then those theories are clearly false. Much art may correlate with beauty, but much may not, and, therefore, much need not. The issue of caricature here is especially important, for if it can be shown that aesthetic theories of art essentially reduce art to a matter of beauty, then they are certainly wrong.

Moreover, hypothesizing that there is a strong tendency in the tradition to reduce art to beauty, at the theoretical level, has the advantage of explaining certain of the "intuitions" one finds in the tradition, such as: the irrelevance of artistic intention, the irrelevance of art history, the irrelevance of the moral and political dimension of art, and so on. For a plausible case might at least be made that these things are irrelevant to an experience of beauty — for example, the experience of a beautiful landscape — in the narrow sense of beauty. And if art is conceptualized as an instrument for bringing about the experience of beauty, then it may seem to be plausible to regard such things as intention, history, morality, and politics as irrelevant to our intercourse with it. Or, at least, it will seem plausible to those who accept, either implicitly or explicitly, the reduction of art to the aesthetic. The rest of us, however, are unlikely to see anything wrong or conceptually confused about responding to the political or moral commitments of a novel, thinking about a painting as a product of a historical context or evolution, or speculating about an author's intentions. With respect to the relevant sorts of artworks, we will take these to be appropriate responses. That is, by attributing a powerful tendency to reduce art theory to beauty, and, correspondingly, to reduce art to a subspecies of beauty, we can explain why certain deep philosophical "intuitions" seem so counterintuitive.

The charge that art theory has been reduced to beauty theory requires some clarification, since the term *beauty* is notoriously ambiguous and, in addition, there are a wide variety of beauty theories. The sense of beauty that I have in mind is very narrow. It appears to have been introduced by the Sophists, who defined beauty as "that which is pleasant to sight or hearing,"[6] a notion that I think that later theorists, in the dominant tradition that concerns us, attempted to further refine by means of ideas like disinterested pleasure. This concept of beauty should be distinguished from an even narrower one that is said to originate with the Stoics and that specifies the relevant source of pleasure in proportion.[7] That is, for our purposes, beauty is a concept that applies to such things as pleasing shapes, sounds, and colors, and, most important, to their combinations in pleasing forms: however, these forms need not be associated with classically identifiable proportions such as, for example, the Golden Section. The sense of beauty at issue here should also be separated from broader, expressionist or romantic usages in which one might speak of the manifestation of a *beautiful* spirit in a given poem or painting. And, likewise, the notion of beauty I will discuss, because it is the one that I think has had the most material impact on the analytic tradition, does not see the good as a direct constituent of the beautiful.

We may profitably begin our story about the reduction of art theory to beauty theory by considering Francis Hutcheson's *Inquiry Concerning Beauty, Order, Harmony, Design*. This treatise is not concerned with defining art, but it does popularize a conception of beauty that will supply central ingredients to those theorists of art who attempt to define art in aesthetic terminology. Indeed, it is pretty clear, I think, that Hutcheson himself would not have concocted what we are calling an aesthetic theory of art, for he notes quite explicitly that beauty is not the only relevant property in this neighborhood. Objects, presumably including artworks, might please because they project grandeur, novelty, and sanctity, among other things.[8] That is, for Hutcheson, artworks can engender important experiences other than that of beauty, and there is no reason to suppose that he believes that beauty is an essential correlative of artworks.

Hutcheson's project is twofold: to define what beauty is, on the one hand, and to ascertain what causes it, on the other hand. Expanding upon the empiricist psychology of Locke, he regards beauty as a sensation, one for which we have a faculty of reception, namely, the faculty of taste. What kind of a sensation is it? Most important, it is an immediate and disinterested sensation of pleasure. What causes this sensation? Objects that possess the compound property of uniformity amid variety.

In order to follow Hutcheson's treatise, it is important to realize how very narrow its focus really is. He is attempting to characterize one very particular dimension of experience, the experience of beauty that paradigmatically accompanies our positive response to things such as "the moonlight reflecting like gems off the bay on an otherwise dark night." It is a characterization, in the spirit of Lockean empiricism, of that sort of feeling that his theory is primarily designed to analyze. And of that feeling, he says that it is pleasurable, immediate, and disinterested.

That such experiences, all things being equal, can be sources of pleasure is, I think, uncontroversial. But Hutcheson also says they are immediate. He writes:

> Many of our sensitive perceptions are pleasant, and many painful, immediately, and that without any knowledge of the cause of this pleasure or pain or how the objects excite it, or are the occasions of it, or without seeing to what farther advantage or deteriment use of such objects might tend. Nor would the most accurate knowledge of these things vary either the pleasure or pain of the perception, however it might give a rational pleasure distinct from the sensible; or might raise a distinct joy from a prospect of farther advantage in the object, or aversion from an apprehension of evil.[9]

and

> This superior power of perception is justly called a *sense* because of its affinity to other senses in this, that the pleasure does not arise from any *knowledge* of principles, proportions, causes or of the usefulness of the object, but strikes us first with the idea of beauty. Nor does the most accurate knowledge increase this pleasure of beauty, however it may superadd a distinct rational pleasure from prospects of advantage, or from the increase of knowledge.[10]

The leading notion in these quotations is that beauty is a feeling in the subject, like a perception, that is felt as pleasurable and that is immediate in the sense that it is not mediated by knowledge – neither the knowledge of what in the object causes the sensation of pleasure, nor knowledge of the potential uses to which the object might be put, nor knowledge of the nature of the thing. That is, a response to the beauty of a forest vista in foliage season is not a function of knowledge of an ecological structure of the forest, of the economic uses to which it might be put, or even explicit knowledge of the variables that cause the sensation of beauty in us. We look at the forest and we experience beauty just as we taste sugar and experience sweetness.

Sugar does not taste sweeter to us if we know its subatomic structure or if we know that the sugar we are tasting is very expensive or if some special variety has a beneficial medicinal effect. These may be reasons to be interested in the sugar or to desire to possess more of it. But they do not make the sugar literally taste sweeter. Similarly, Hutcheson wants to say that with respect to the beautiful, we are consumed by a feeling of pleasure immediately, that is, independently of the knowledge we have of the object. We see or feel that x is beautiful without any inference based on knowledge of the nature or use of the object and, furthermore, knowledge of these things does not make the object feel any more beautiful.

For example, we may be struck by the beauty of the ornamentation of a tribal costume without knowing that it is an article of clothing, without knowing how it is made or what it symbolizes, and without knowing that it is a very valuable artifact. Nor will learning any of these things make it more beautiful. Of course, this knowledge may make the artifact more interesting or it may prompt a wish to acquire it. But it doesn't make it more beautiful. Beauty it might be said, though Hutcheson doesn't state it this way, is closer to the surface of the experience.

Clearly, Hutcheson wants to contrast the feeling of beauty with knowledge, a contrast that portends subsequent contrasts, within the tradition, between the aesthetic and the cognitive. Hutcheson contrasts the feeling of beauty with knowledge in two ways, maintaining that it is both a feeling and that it is immediate, that is, not involving further inferences. It is a sensation of pleasure unmediated by inferential reasoning. We don't look at an object, for example, note that it has a compound ratio of uniformity amid variety and surmise that it is beautiful. We look at a sunset and, all things being equal, we undergo a sensation of beauty. That there are such experiences seems fair to suppose. It also seems correct to suppose that they are very special and need not exclusively constitute our only appreciative response to objects, including art objects. As Hutcheson admits, objects, including art objects, may also have other sources of pleasure, such as independent rational pleasures, that will reward our attention to them.

In discussing the response to beauty, Hutcheson not only contrasts the sensation of beauty to that of knowledge but also contrasts it to pleasure instilled through the prospect of advantage.[11] He writes:

> And farther, the ideas of beauty and harmony, like other sensible ideas, are
> *necessarily* pleasant to us, as well as immediately so. Neither can any resolu-
> tion of our own, nor any prospect of advantage or disadvantage, vary the
> beauty or deformity of an object. For as in the external sensations, no view
> of interest will make an object grateful, nor view of detriment distinct
> from immediate pain in perception, make it disagreeable to the sense. So
> propose the whole world as a reward, or threaten the greatest evil, to make
> us approve a deformed object, or disapprove a beautiful one; dissimulation
> may be procured by rewards or threatenings, or we may in external con-
> duct abstain from any pursuit of the beautiful, and pursue the deformed,
> but our *sentiments* of the forms, and our *perceptions,* would continue invari-
> ably the same.
>
> Hence, it plainly appears that some objects are *immediately* the occa-
> sions of this pleasure of beauty, and that we have senses fitted for perceiv-
> ing it, and that it is distinct from the *joy* which arises upon prospect of
> advantage.[12]

The point Hutcheson is after here is often summarized by saying that the pleasure involved in the sensation of beauty is disinterested. If I see the cornfield as beautiful, I do so independently of my knowledge of its use to the community for nourishment or its value to me as its owner. The look of it enraptures me: it would be no more enrapturing in terms of its look, if I were suddenly to learn that it is mine. Personal advantage is irrelevant to the perception of beauty. I can be taken

with the beautiful pattern on the skin of a deadly snake, and knowing the disutil-
ity of such snakes will not diminish its beauty. The beauty of such things is a matter of the pleasure derived from the look of them apart from their advantages and
disadvantages for humans in general or me in particular. Emphasizing the disinterested nature of this pleasure is a way of signaling that the pleasure is derived from
the look or sound or pattern of the thing apart from other concerns. Indeed,
whether the pleasure involved in an experience is disinterested could in fact be
regarded as the *test* of whether or not one's feeling was one of beauty. If something
seems more attractive to me because I own it than it does when it is contemplated
independently of considerations of ownership by anyone, including myself, then
my pleasure is *not* rooted in a sensation of beauty.

Hutcheson wants to separate our sense of beauty from our desire for beautiful
objects. If we know a beautiful object is also valuable or advantageous, that may
enhance our desire for it, but not our sensation of beauty. Knowing the diamond
is valuable, or that it is mine, doesn't make it look more beautiful to me, though
knowing it has these attributes may make it more desirable to me. This is not to
say that beautiful things *qua* beautiful things are not desirable, and that we do not
seek after them, perhaps aided by formulas like Hutcheson's idea of uniformity
amid variety. However, the sensation of beauty is independent from the desire for
it, and we cannot will something either to be beautiful or to be more beautiful
than it is. Our desires in all cases leave the status and degree of beauty untouched.
Genuine experiences of beauty are independent of our desires and interests; they
are disinterested.

Whether or not we can agree that there are experiences of beauty may be controversial, but, if we agree that within the range of human experience, there is a
certain feeling of pleasure that is a function solely of the appearance and forms of
things, then some such notion of disinterest, as specified nominally by Hutcheson,
at least initially seems like a plausible, if rough and ready, way to ascertain whether
the pleasure we derive from a flower is, on a specific occasion, exclusively derived
from the look and the configuration of the object. This is not said in order to
endorse the notion of disinterest, but only to admit that it is not implausible to
hypothesize that it may be the marker of a very narrow band of human experience
– call it the experience of beauty and agree that it can occur in nature as well as art.

However, though Hutcheson's suggestion that considerations of knowledge
and interest are somehow bracketed from the experience of pleasure associated
with beauty may have some plausibility as a mark of that type of experience, it
should be evident that if his conception of beauty is taken as a model for a definition of art and a measure of what can be appropriately contemplated with respect
to artworks, then it is quite clear that many characteristic features of artworks and
their standard modes of appreciation and evaluation are likely to go by the board.
If the origin of an object is irrelevant to its identification as a beautiful thing, and
knowledge of the origin in no way enhances its appreciability *qua* beauty, then, by
extension, knowledge of art history will be irrelevant to the identification and
appreciation of artworks. If the moral and political disadvantages of an atomic

mushroom cloud are irrelevant to an assessment of its degree of beauty, then, by analogy, considerations of the moral and political consequences of a novel are irrelevant in its evaluation.

Again, I hasten to add that Hutcheson, himself, does not make these moves. For he is analyzing beauty rather than art in general, and he does not appear to think that these are coextensive, not only because the class of beautiful things also includes natural objects and geometrical theorems, but, furthermore, because he does not appear committed to maintaining that beauty is the only or even the essential feature of art. However, in introducing a characterization of beauty as divorced from interest and cognition, he, perhaps inadvertently, laid the seeds for the aesthetic theory of art.[13]

Before leaving the discussion of Hutcheson, it is important to underscore that his theory of beauty is not only empiricist but also functionalist and formalist. Beauty is an experience that is a function of the form – the compound ratio of uniformity and variety – in the object of our attention. Furthermore, that the experience is brought about in the percipient, without any knowledge of the precise mechanism that causes it, fits nicely with Hutcheson's opinion that the experience is universally available. That is, despite the strain that this would appear to put on some of his examples, banishing knowledge from the experience of beauty appears to support the view that the experience of beauty is available cross-culturally (insofar as the variability of knowledge between cultures is discounted as relevant to the experience).

Kant is the next stage in our survey of the evolution of art theory. His is an immensely complicated theory. I will not attempt to characterize its richness, but only to make some points about his view of what is called free, as distinct from dependent, beauty. I will talk about free beauty, even though it seems that art as we know it is generally more a matter of dependent beauty, first, because I think that his account of free beauty has had more influence on the tradition than his account of dependent beauty, and, second, because his account of dependent beauty is in some ways inconclusive and ambiguous (which is, perhaps, why it has been less influential on the tradition).

Before delving into the substance of Kant's position, it pays to note one significant divergence in vocabulary between Kant and Hutcheson. Whereas Hutcheson speaks of taste and beauty, Kant adds to this terminology the notion of aesthetics, a terrain of judgment concerned to a large extent with beauty (along with the sublime). This term, of course, was introduced by Baumgarten to demarcate the realm of perception in general, and, in Kant's third critique, it is used as a label for judgments of taste in general. This change in terminology I think may be significant to our story because in referring to beauty by means of the concept of the aesthetic, one may come to think that the two are distinguishable when one is really only talking about beauty, narrowly construed, rather than something more encompassing. Thus, when J. O. Urmson tells us what makes a situation aesthetic, his criteria primarily targets forms and appearance that favorably address the senses – in other words, beauty as Hutcheson conceives it (although to be fair,

Urmson's use of *aesthetic* is also a bit broader, since it also includes negative appreciative judgments in terms of ugliness).[14]

With respect to beauty, Kant's focus in the *Critique of Judgment* is on aesthetic judgments such as "*x* is beautiful." In terms of such judgments of free beauty, Kant wants to explain how these judgments can be universal and necessary – commanding the assent of all – despite the fact that they are based on no more than the particular sensation of pleasure that we, responding as a single individual to a subjective state, feel in response to an object. Summarizing drastically, Kant's view, with regard to free beauty, is roughly that "*x* is beautiful" is an authentic judgment of taste (or an aesthetic judgment) if and only if it is a judgment that is: (1) subjective,[15] (2) disinterested, (3) universal,[16] (4) necessary,[17] and (5) singular,[18] concerning (6) the *contemplative pleasure* that everyone ought to derive from (7) cognitive and imaginative free play in relation to (8) forms of finality.[19]

In terms of our narrative, the important elements in this account are that aesthetic judgments are disinterested and contemplative, that they are rooted in cognitive and imaginative *free* play, and that they are directed at forms of finality.

Kant unpacks the notion of disinterestedness by means of the apparently radical idea of indifference to the existence of the object. He writes:

> Now, where the question is whether something is beautiful, we do not want to know whether we, or anyone else, are, or even could be concerned in the real existence of the thing, but rather what estimate we form of it on mere contemplation (intuition or reflection). ... All one wants to know is whether the mere representation of the object is to my liking, no matter how indifferent I may be to the real existence of the object of this representation. It is quite plain that in order to say that the object is *beautiful*, and to show that I have taste, everything turns on the meaning which I can give the representation, and not on any factor which makes me dependent on the real existence of the object. Every one must allow that a judgment on the beautiful which is tinged with the slightest interest, is very partial and not a pure judgment of taste. One must not be in the least prepossessed in favour of the real existence of the thing, but must preserve complete indifference in this respect, in order to play the part of judge in matters of taste.[20]

Here, as in Hutcheson (and possibly in response to Hume's failure to distinguish pleasure in the moral from pleasure in the beautiful), we find disinterestedness being used as a test of whether the response concerns the beauty of something. The idea seems to be that such a response, if authentically aesthetic, is a matter of pleasure in reaction to the appearance of a thing. Whether the thing exists, then, is irrelevant to its beauty. Our feeling of the magnificence of a divinely appointed palace would be no less one of beauty were the palace an hallucination. The notion of indifference to the existence of the object seems to be a way to get at the idea that beauty, narrowly construed, is pleasure taken in the appearance or configuration of the object.

Kant also makes the point that our judgments of beauty will be tainted if guided by our practical interests in the object – interests we can only plausibly sustain if we take the object to exist. But, at the same time, the notion of existence-indifference is an attempt to locate the aesthetic response, the response to beauty, as taking as its object the perceptual appearance and form of things. Thus, the aesthetic response, on this account, is targeted at what might be thought of as, first and foremost, the phenomenal properties of objects. Though perhaps not correct, this is at least a reasonable hypothesis to conjecture, if what one is interested in is a conception of the phenomenon of beauty very narrowly construed.[21] Whether it can be extrapolated, across the board, to the far more complicated phenomenon of artworks in general, rather than to simply artworks marked by beauty, is another question, one that will be forced upon us when we recall theorists like Monroe Beardsley who attempt to classify all artworks within the broad category of phenomenal fields.[22]

Kant's view of free beauty is formal in a number of obvious and important respects. The objects of aesthetic judgments are *forms* of finality. That is, the sense of beauty is raised by a *sense* of the purposiveness or design of a configuration, rather than through a comprehension of the purpose that the object might serve. If one is genuinely struck by the beauty of the crenelations of the turrets of a medieval castle, this will be a function of perceiving the orderliness, design, and, in this sense, the purposiveness of the pattern, and not by a recognition of the practical purposes of fortification that the architectural structure serves. One, of course, might appreciate the ingenuity and utility of the structure from a military point of view; but such a judgment is not an aesthetic one. The aesthetic judgment focuses on the configuration – and the feeling of purposiveness and pattern it affords – without regard to the actual purpose or utility of the object. Here, the notion of a form of finality does much of the work that the interaction of uniformity and variety does in Hutcheson's theory, and that significant form will do in Bell's argument.

In respect to our response to form, the application of our cognitive and imaginative capacities in the contemplative act is one of *free play* since tracking unfolding designs and their interrelations is not governed by comprehending how the design serves some practical purpose or utility. The play of our faculties of imagination and the understanding is harmonious because it is directed at forms of finality that impart purposiveness, and that play is free because it is not subservient to a consideration of practical concerns. The play of cognition and imagination might also be thought of as free in the sense that the object of its attention is singular – that is, not subsumable under a rule or concept – as would be the case with the object of a rational judgment. And the free and harmonious play of cognition and imagination, independent of the claims of purpose, practicality, and knowledge, gives rise to a special form of pleasure, aesthetic pleasure, pleasure in the purpos*ive* rather than the purpose*ful* configuration of the object of attention. Again, even if it is not ultimately compelling, this type of formalism may appear at least initially appealing if one wishes to analyze the type of pleasure encountered in tracing out the exfoliating design of a Persian rug, something which, though it may be art, is hardly paradigmatic of art as we know it.

Though Kant and Hutcheson say a great deal about art, their theories are not theories of art. They are theories of beauty – and, in Kant's case, of the sublime as well. Their observations can be extended to beautiful art, to sublime art, and to the role of what Kant calls aesthetic ideas in art. But they do not propose anything remotely like definitions of art. Nevertheless – and here the plot thickens – many of their claims, especially about beauty, become the basis of attempted definitions of art, and this importation of the vocabulary and conceptual framework of beauty theory, as developed by Hutcheson and Kant, into art theory has vast repercussions, virtually initiating art theory as a branch of aesthetics (conceived of as the philosophy of taste).

A crucial figure here is Clive Bell. Bell's project is explicitly concerned with the proposal of an *essential* definition of art. He regards the central problem of the philosophy of art – specifically of painting, but with ramifications for other media as well – to be to identify the common feature or set of features of the field's objects of study. He approaches this task with a predisposition to empiricism and functionalism. That is, he searches for the answer to his problem by looking for a certain invariant experiential or feeling state that always accompanies art (the empiricist component[23]) as a way to isolate the invariant feature of artworks that causes or functions to bring about the invariant responses that all and only art-works educe (the functionalist component). As is well known, Bell calls our characteristic experience of art *aesthetic emotion* and he regards *significant form* to be its causal trigger.

In striking respects, Bell's theory of art resembles Hutcheson's theory of beauty, with Kantian elements thrown in for added effect. Roughly, significant form plays the role that uniformity amid variety plays for Hutcheson, while in place of the feeling of beauty, Bell has the notion of having an aesthetic emotion. The latter is an experience that Bell does little to specify, but, whenever he does, it is in language that is unmistakably derivative from the kind of beauty theory we have been discussing. For example:

> ...to appreciate a work of art we need bring with us nothing from life, no knowledge of its ideas and affairs, no familiarity with its emotions. Art transports us from the world of man's activity to a world of aesthetic exaltation. For a moment we are shut off from human interests; our anticipations and memories are arrested; we are lifted above the stream of life.[24]

Bell repeatedly asserts that this rapturous emotion is independent of concerns of practical utility,[25] and cognitive import (see particularly his caustic remarks on the Futurists).[26] The aesthetic emotion is a state brought about in percipients as a function of attention to significant form. Significant form pertains to the combination of lines, colors, shapes, and spaces. It is a matter of pure design that elicits a response, that, like its object, significant form, contains no residue of ordinary experience. In all likelihood, like Kant, Bell believes that one cannot antecedently supply rules for what forms will be the significant ones. Rather, the only test for whether an object is an instance of significant form is that it engenders an aesthetic experience, a sense of rapture divorced from practical life and its interests, or, in the language with which we are already familiar, a sense of rapture that is disinterested.

Bell, himself, rejects labeling this emotion in terms of the feeling of beauty. He maintains that the term "beauty" has too many misleading connotations in ordinary language. However, it is quite clear that his conception of aesthetic emotion is a derivative from the technical conception of beauty that we have seen developing in Hutcheson and Kant. Caused by the appearance of things and their forms, the aesthetic emotion is nothing but the feeling of beauty in the technical sense. And using the mark of beauty to isolate art is to commit oneself to the view that art is a subspecies of beauty, technically construed.

Of course, Bell's view is not exactly that of Hutcheson's. Not only does Bell attempt to reject beauty talk, he also refuses the idea that the experience in question is quintessentially one of pleasure. Bell, again unlike Hutcheson, regards it to be a function exclusively of art, and not of nature. Bell also parts company with Hutcheson insofar as Hutcheson, in his account of relative beauty, believes, perhaps inconsistently,[27] that representation *qua* representation can sustain this disinterested sensation, whereas Bell is famous for claiming that representation is altogether irrelevant to the aesthetic emotion.

However, what is more important is the way in which Bell appears to appropriate some of the leading concepts of aesthetic theory, or, as I prefer to call it, beauty theory, to conceptualize art. Clearly, he is exploiting the tradition of beauty theory that emphasizes the appearance of things, as well as exploiting the notion of disinterestedness to flesh out this conception. This leads him to assert the irrelevance of a great many things in the appreciation of art. Artworks are not to be appreciated for their practical utility, nor as sources of knowledge, whether moral, political, social, or otherwise. For these things are irrelevant to having aesthetic emotions, which are emotions, that, by definition, do not take such things as their objects. The ideal spectator stays riveted to the surface of the art object; that is the appropriate object of the emotion in question. Among other things, this is thought to entail that considerations of art history and authorial intent are out of bounds when one talks about genuine responses to art, since they are not part of the appropriate object of the aesthetic emotion, which, in turn, is thought to isolate the art object.

In effect, Bell endorses what has come to be known as the genetic fallacy, of which the intentional fallacy is the best known example. He writes: "To appreciate a man's art I need know nothing whatever about the artist; I can say whether this picture is better than that without the help of history."[28] Furthermore, he continues: "I care very little when things were made, or why they were made; I care about their emotional significance to us,"[29] where by "emotional significance" he is, of course, speaking of aesthetic emotion, or what I would call disinterested rapture, that is, the sense of beauty.

For Bell, the only relevant dimension of interaction with art *qua* art is sensibility, the conduit of aesthetic emotion. Art is that which engages this emotion by means of significant form. Knowledge of art history, concern with authorial intent, the practical consequences of the object, its contributions to knowledge – moral, social, or otherwise – are all bracketed from the operation of sensibility. As noted earlier, perhaps a case could at least be made for all these exclusions when one is explicitly talking about the experience of beauty, narrowly construed. However, under Bell's dispensation, by assimilating beauty theory to art theory, art, despite its multiplicity of functions, traditions, and levels of discourse, is effectively reduced to nothing more than the contemplation of beauty.

One way in which Bell appears to me to differ in his invocation of disinterestedness from Hutcheson and Kant is that they seem to regard disinterestedness as a test of whether the sensation in question is aesthetic, that is, a feeling of beauty, whereas, for Bell, disinterestedness is the very result sought after in interacting with artworks. With Hutcheson and Kant we feel pleasure that is disinterested. But with Bell we seek out aesthetic emotions because when we are in their thrall we are released from or detached from the stream of everyday life. Where for Kant and Hutcheson disinterest is the mark of the state in question, for Bell, disinterested or detached experience would appear to be the whole point of having the aesthetic experience. Where in Kant the play of our faculties is free because it is unconstrained by concepts and purposes, in Bell the very value of art seems to be liberation from purpose; that is what is good about having the aesthetic emotion.[30] In this respect, Bell's theory of art recalls Schopenhauer's insofar as the very point of art seems to be identified with bringing about a divorce from everything else, rather than this sort of detachment being a concomitant of a certain form of contemplation.

(Of course, if art is identified with separating ourselves from everything else by restricting the art object *qua* art to its form, itself conceived to be divorced from everything else, then Bell's essentialist view of art is guaranteed, since art and our responses to art have been isolated, by definition, from everything else. In other words, an essentialist conclusion almost falls out, so to speak, from Bell's theorization of aesthetic emotion.)

Insofar as Bell regards disinterestedness or detachment to be the point of art appreciation, things like concern with art history, morality, authorial intent, knowledge, and utility are distractions. They stand in the way of securing aesthetic emotions. On Bell's functionalist model of the aesthetic stimulus, attending to these sorts of things draws attention away from its appropriate focus, upsetting the causal conditions that guarantee the production of aesthetic emotions. Centering attention on anything but significant form destroys or dilutes aesthetic emotion. This, moreover, would appear to be predictable because if one takes things like morality as the content (or part of the content) of one's appreciative response, then one is unlikely to become entirely detached from the stream of life.

In order to ensure that detachment or disinterestedness is the output of our interaction with art, the input has to be gerrymandered. In Bell's case this is done by reducing the artwork *qua* art to significant form, while in Beardsley the artwork becomes a phenomenal or perceptual field, separated from its conditions of production and isolated from all its potential consequences, save the provocation of aesthetic experience. In both cases, it is hard to avoid the conclusion that these theorists are extrapolating from the view that the locus of beauty is the appearance or form of the object, independent of its nature, its genesis, and its consequences.

It is this very "phenomenalist" or "perceptualist" bias in art theory – developed perhaps from the notion of existence-indifference, found in Kant, and rooted in one traditional theorization of beauty – that Arthur Danto, in effect, rejects when he argues that art is not something that the eye could descry, and that art theory is to be built on the method of indiscernibles. If art were significant form, it could be "eyeballed," and art history would be irrelevant to the identity of the work of art. That the method of indiscernibles points to the importance of art history to answering the question, "What is art?," is of a piece with Danto's rejection of aesthetic phenomenalism. Similarly, Danto's tendency to regard the response to art as cognitive, rather than aesthetic (in the traditional sense) – a matter primarily of thought rather than simply feeling – also distinguishes him from aesthetic theorists of art.[31]

Bell's theory of art confronts many frequently rehearsed problems of detail, such as its inability to specify significant form independently of aesthetic emotion, and its difficulty in making sense of the notion of bad art.[32] This is not the place to recount all of the theory's failings. However, one critical point is worth dwelling upon with respect to the aesthetic emotion. Namely, it is not clear that there is any reason to believe that a state, like the one Bell discusses, appropriately characterizes our responses to art.

When we look at a painting or read a book, we may be intently preoccupied by it. We may, for the time being, leave off worrying about our own troubles, and put thoughts of making money on the back burner along with anxieties about current events and moral outrages. That is, we may be intently absorbed and closely attentive to an artwork. But this need not be described in terms of some total, principled detachment from ordinary concerns. Rather, it is a matter of focusing our attention, or of the artwork's holding our attention, and nothing more.

There is no special, disinterested state here, just rapt absorption. In fact, our absorption and interest in a novel or a picture can be enhanced by noting that it reflects upon pressing political and social issues, makes a novel observation about life, strikes a courageous moral stance, and so on. That is, in order to hold our attention in the way described above, there is no need for facilitating disinterest in the sense we have used that term in this essay. There is no need to be lifted out of the concerns of our common life. Indeed, attentiveness can be quickened in artworks by means of reference to the world, by imparting knowledge about it, and by encouraging us to think of moral, practical, and political consequences. Disinterest is not a fruitful notion with which to attempt to characterize the preoccupied attention we lavish on artworks.

Though it *may* be true (or at least not implausible) to think that considerations of knowledge and utility do not enhance our sense of *beauty* in an object, there is no reason to suppose that those things will not accentuate our interest and attention in other contexts, contexts not restricted to assessments of *the beautiful,* including the context of the art gallery. Thus, if disinterestedness and detachment are proffered as concepts that capture our focused attentiveness to art, they are off the mark. For this indiscriminately transposes frameworks of thought that are (at best) *possibly* relevant to the perception of the beautiful, but not to the reception of art as we comprehensively know it.[33]

Given the role that significant form plays in Bell's theory, he is often referred to as a formalist. Aesthetic emotion is triggered by form, which, since it is bereft of reference to life, detaches us from quotidian concerns. Just as Bell's essentialism is tied to his characterization of aesthetic emotion – that is, since it is separate from everything else, art or the only relevant aspect of it is essentially distinct from every other enterprise – so Bell's formalism is tied to the account of aesthetic emotion. The object needs to originate in appearance or form disconnected from knowledge, utility, and so on, lest the emotion have content of a "nondetached" variety.

If Bell's theory can be seen as an updated version of Hutcheson's, Beardsley's work is an extremely sophisticated development of Bell's. Where Bell is weak on specifying the nature of significant form, Beardsley, in his book *Aesthetics,* spends over one hundred and fifty pages reviewing the formal structures of literature, fine art, and music for the purpose of showing how these practices can be spoken of in terms of a uniform language of unity, intensity, and complexity, the formal features of artworks that, on Beardsley's view, give rise to aesthetic experience.[34] That is, where Bell is criticized for lacking an independent account of significant form, Beardsley gives a painstaking enumeration of the constituent elements of artistic form.

These formal arrangements, in turn, cause an aesthetic experience, a state that Beardsley has variously characterized in the course of his career. At first Beardsley thought of it as composed of (1) attention firmly fixed upon a phenomenal field (2) that yields an intense, (3) coherent, (4) complete, (5) complex experience that (6), as a result of the preceding conditions, is detached or insulated from practical action.[35] Because of this aura of detachment, Beardsley calls aesthetic objects, objects *manqués,*[36] though one wonders whether the language here is not misleading. Is it not the case that the objects in question do not spur us to immediate practical action because they are generally fictions or representations that call for no pressing practical response, rather than that they cause some special state of contemplation that is insulated from practical concern?

Unlike Bell, Beardsley tells us what the relevant features of the art object are – they are unity, complexity, and intensity, which cause unity, intensity, and complexity in our experience. But, like Bell's, Beardley's theory is functionalist, regarding the aesthetic object as a causal instrument, and empiricist, regarding experience as the key to an object that itself is explicitly called *phenomenal.* Furthermore, again like Bell, the detached affect is an effect of the aesthetic interaction, one that is a constituent of the value of the experience, and not merely a mark or test of the aesthetic, as it is in Hutcheson and Kant.

Toward the end of his career, Beardsley proposed another characterization of aesthetic experience that does not explicitly deploy the language of unity, complexity, and intensity, but which from our perspective is even more telling for its outright use of the elements of beauty theory. In "Aesthetic Experience," he writes: "an experience has aesthetic character if and only if it has the first of the following features and at least three of the others." The features are: object directedness; felt freedom (a sense of release from antecedent concerns); detached affect (emotional distance); active discovery (a sense of intelligibility);[37] and wholeness (contentment, and a freedom from distracting and disruptive impulses).[38]

The conditions of felt freedom, detached affect, and wholeness seem somewhat repetitive and, as well, rehearse the test for beauty in the theories of Hutcheson and Kant. In each case, they appear motivated by the attempt to capture the degree to which we can be caught up in an artwork, and, to that extent, might simply be read as elaborations of the first condition, the requirement for object-directedness, which, to my way of thinking, indicates that they are simply garden-variety elements of any act of absorbed attention, whether to aesthetic objects, artworks, newspaper articles, philosophical treatises, and so on.

Furthermore, within the totality of Beardsley's interlocking system, these features of experience are advanced as a means of identifying artworks. For in Beardsley's view an artwork is something produced with the intention of giving it the capacity to satisfy the aesthetic interest, that is, the interest in having aesthetic experiences.[39] Thus, logically, in order to be art, an object must be produced with the intention of satisfying at least two experiential features of the sort that we have identified with beauty theory, though as noted previously, the language of beauty theory here may have been misapplied in the attempt to phenomenologically characterize a level of preoccupation that has nothing particular to do with art – that is, that would equally characterize our attentiveness to an interesting lecture.[40]

That Beardsley identifies artworks with causing aesthetic experiences, where these experiences are portrayed in the language of beauty theory, has several, by now, predictable repercussions for his theory of art as a whole. Since having an aesthetic experience is a function of the artwork, the artistic stimulus needs to be gerrymandered so that it raises a disinterested affect. Beardsley's formidable energies in gerrymandering the artwork are evident throughout his career. Artworks are said to be *phenomenal* objects that give pleasure in virtue of their form (recalling what we earlier earmarked as a Sophist conception of beauty). Beardsley also consolidated and consistently defended the notion of the genetic fallacy, and, most particularly, the intentional fallacy.[41] In effect, these can be read as arguments that tell us what is not part of the art object and, therefore, what is not appropriate to consider when attending to artworks – for to attend to such things, as the New Critics would put it, is to go *outside* the text, inviting attention to elements that will interfere with aesthetic experience proper.[42] That is, on the functionalist model of the artwork, genetic considerations, such as authorial intent, are the wrong input where aesthetic experience is the expected output.

Beardsley's arguments about the limits of art history's relevance to art criticism – which he inevitably links with assessments of the potential for causing aesthetic experience – though thoughtful and not to be rejected out of hand, are also of a piece with his desire to restrict the artwork proper to a formal stimulus (thereby focusing the appreciative response so as to assure its "disinterestedness").[43] Likewise, Beardsley's continual arguments with Goodman about the centrality of reference to art and about the cognitive status of art, though again, not to be discounted because they are part of a systematic project, nevertheless, must be understood as connected to Beardsley's conviction that the artwork, like the object of beauty, is detached from the world, on the one hand, and a source of unique value (aesthetic not cognitive), on the other.[44]

Like Bell, Beardsley attempts to distance his own theory from beauty theory. It seems to me that his strongest argument to this effect is that a canonical beauty theory takes beauty to be intrinsically valuable,[45] whereas his view is that having aesthetic experience is a value in human life in general.[46] This, however, is not fully persuasive, since figures like Hutcheson certainly thought that aesthetic experience was a constituent of the good life. Bell, under the influence of Moore, might have said that aesthetic experience was an intrinsic good and that this was connected to its detached nature. But it seems to me that the commitment to intrinsic goodness is an optional feature of beauty theory; detachment, which itself may or may not be of intrinsic value, is the essential, recurring feature of the dominant characterization of beauty in the tradition. And, on that basis, Beardsley remains grounded in beauty theory. Indeed, he admits as much when he writes that we can dispense with the term "beautiful" in favor of terms like "aesthetically valuable,"[47] that is, promoting a high degree of aesthetic experience.

With Beardsley, we find the most systematic reduction of art theory to aesthetic theory, which I have tried to show means essentially a reduction to beauty theory. Given the notion of beauty dominant in the tradition, the concept of disinterestedness or detachment comes to play a large role in the characterization of the nature of artworks, since what is appropriate to our concern with artworks must be adjusted and delimited in such a way that our intercourse with them will result in detachment. This systematically requires that questions of art history, authorial intent, utility, cognitive content, and so on be bracketed, as they are in testing for beauty in the treatises of Hutcheson and Kant.

That Beardsley chose to call his landmark treatise *Aesthetics* is telling in this regard. For aesthetic theory or, as I prefer to call it, beauty theory is the fulcrum upon which his entire theory of art was organized. Through the notion of aesthetic experience, he is able to answer such fundamental questions as: What is art, What is good art, What are the relevant reasons in assessing art critically, and What value does art have for human life? This is quite an awesome accomplishment, though, of course, it relies on reducing art theory to beauty theory.

Like Bell's theory, Beardsley's is essentialist in identifying a common feature or set of features that differentiates artworks from everything else. Since the feature is the capacity to cause an aesthetic experience, which itself is detached from everything else, artworks are divorced, in their essential nature from other realms of human commerce, most notably cognition and morality. Artworks are functional, since they are viewed as instrumentalities for causing aesthetic experiences, and the theory is formalist since satisfying the requisite causal conditions for having an aesthetic experience demands focus on the forms of art objects. The theory is empiricist not only in its reliance on experience as its central term, but also in its construal of the art object proper as a phenomenal field, one constituted, for purposes of appreciation, of perceptible form and appearance. Moreover, in terms of all these features, save essentialism, Beardsley's theory corresponds to Hutcheson's initial theory of beauty.

One index of Beardsley's transformation of a Hutchesonian-type theory of beauty into a theory of art is that avant-garde art often tends to be excluded from the order of art. For works in which the contemplation of the object for its formal qualities is not relevant and/or the response sought after is not detached or disinterested will not turn out to be art on this approach. Such works need not be avant-garde, but often are. For Beardsley, then, a piece like Duchamp's *Fountain* will not be art because Duchamp could not (and, in fact, did not) produce it with the intention of satisfying an aesthetic interest; he had a point to make and contemplation of the design of the urinal was irrelevant to a proper appreciation of the point. Beardsley creates a special category for such works; he calls them comments on art.[48] My own diagnosis of this move is that it is virtually an inevitable consequence of building a theory of art on a theory of beauty. Obviously, much avant-garde art is explicitly designed to defy traditional senses of beauty. Saying that the problem with such art is that it fails to afford an aesthetic experience or that it could not have been made with the intention to afford said experience is just a roundabout way of repeating the evident – namely, that the works in question have purposes or express purposes, other than facilitating the experience of beauty, such as subverting, displacing, replacing, ignoring, or criticizing it.

Beardsley, of course, is not alone in this response to avant-garde art. It is a tendency of aesthetic theorists of art in general to treat the avant-garde in a dismissive fashion. Invoking traditional notions of the aesthetic, Harold Osborne says: "in its purest form Conceptual art abolishes the art object altogether ... as something to be contemplated and appreciated for itself, reducing it to a mere instrument for communicating an idea," while the shapelessness of Joseph Beuys' *Fettecke* and the spectator involvement in Herman Nitsch's butcher-block performances interfere with such aesthetic desiderata, respectively, as form and detachment.[49] Indeed, the "intuitions" of the aesthetic approach to art run so deep that even Wittgensteinians, like Benjamin Tilghman, who are skeptical, in principle, of the prospects of art theory, invoke the notion of an "aesthetic character" in order to challenge the artistic status of Warhol's *Brillo Boxes* and Oldenburg's *Placid City Monument*. This character is said to involve qualities such as those of organization, design, composition, balance, plot structure, thematic and harmonic structure, expressive and emotional qualities, qualities of style, and so on – in short, for the most part, the elements focused on in traditional beauty theory.[50]

The problem that aesthetic theorists have with much avant-garde art is not one unique to the avant-garde. For many of the concerns of the avant-garde, with knowledge, morality, politics, and so on, are not anomalous given the range of pre-occupations found in traditional art. Thus, the avant-garde crystallizes general issues concerning aesthetic theory rather than being a special case. That much avant-garde work eschews the role of promoting aesthetic experience, narrowly construed, is of a piece with Romantic pretensions to epistemology, and realist commitments to social description and even explanation. The rejection of much avant-garde art by aesthetic theory, then, exemplifies its perennial discomfort with a great deal of what one pretheoretically identifies as the traditional concerns of art.

Our position, of course, is that the discomfort rests on an error – the dubious way in which beauty theory metamorphosed into art theory. Of particular importance in that process is the transformation of a test for beauty – disinterestedness – into the very point or purpose of artworks. For even if one accepts the controversial but at least plausible view that disinterestedness is a litmus test for whether the pleasure I take in a moonlit bay is aesthetic – that is, originating in the form or appearance of the visual array – it is clearly wrong, as an unprejudiced view of the historical record indicates, to suppose that engendering this experience is the sole or defining or even characteristic purpose that all art has served.[51]

When one is thinking about a variety of beauty that pertains to natural objects as well as artworks, questions of intention do seem misplaced since natural objects have no authors. And a similar point might be made with respect to considering the purposes – cognitive and moral – of natural beauty. But these observations, far from supporting the aesthetic approach to art, should lead us to conclude that the aesthetic approach, modeled on a theory of beauty that gains its greatest plausibility from its concern with nature, is just the wrong framework for thinking about art.

I have repeatedly asserted that it is obvious that beauty, narrowly construed, cannot be a useful starting point for art theory. But if this is so obvious, one wonders why theorists are drawn into this error so often. I think that there are two major reasons that make this putative error so attractive and that they are most evident in Beardsley's extremely sophisticated version of the approach.

First, if one takes aesthetic experience as the central concept of one's theory of art, one can use it, as Beardsley did, to systematically answer a great many other questions about art. One cannot only define art functionally, but can go on to develop evaluative criteria for works of art in terms of the amounts of aesthetic satisfaction an artwork delivers, a critical vocabulary keyed to pinpointing the features of artworks that cause aesthetic experience, and an explanation of the value of art in light of the instrumental value of having aesthetic experiences in human life. That is, one may be attracted to the aesthetic approach because of its systematicity – because of its capacity to answer a great many theoretical questions with a highly interconnected and interdefinable set of theoretical terms. Indeed, one suspects that Beardsley persisted in defending an aesthetic approach – in the face of Dickie's indefatigable refutation of every characterization of aesthetic experience – because he was swayed by the elegance and economy that an aesthetic theory of art would have – if only its central concept, aesthetic experience, could be adequately defined.

The second, ostensible advantage of the aesthetic approach to art theory is that, if one's aim is to produce an *essential* definition of art, then aesthetic theories at least appear to do this quite expeditiously. The reason for this, of course, has to do with the supposed nature of aesthetic experience. That is, if aesthetic experience is, by definition, divorced or detached from cognition, morality, utility, and every other realm of human life, and the art object *qua* art is reduced to whatever will bring about the relevant detached experience, then, as the source of the detached experience, the gerrymandered artwork will predictably be separate from everything else. It will not be a cognitive or a moral instrument, for that would interfere with its function as that which engenders aesthetic experience. The artwork, in other words, will be essentially differentiated from other realms of human experience just because its purpose has been defined in terms of detaching us from everything else. An essentialist account of art – of art as distinct from everything else – then issues almost effortlessly, so to speak, from attributing detachment as its function.[52] And insofar as theorists are obsessed with the importance of identifying the essence of art, they will be drawn to aesthetic theories, despite their awkward mismatch with the facts of artistic practice.

But however attractive the aesthetic approach is, these benefits cannot overweigh its evident shortcomings. On the one hand, it must confront what can be called the Dickie problem – that is, we need an account of aesthetic experience that persuasively shows that our intense attention to artworks can be described in virtue of a conception of disinterest or detachment that is different in kind from the focused way in which we follow anything, including baseball games, magazine articles, and scholarly treatises, in which we take an interest. And, on the other hand, the elegance and economy of a system like Beardsley's must be weighed against its evident failures in comprehensiveness, not only with respect to what it excludes from the corpus of art but also in terms of what it strictly isolates as the sources of artistic value.

Many philosophers, of course, do not explicitly espouse an aesthetic theory of art. However, they do often advance as intuitions such notions as that authorial intent, art history, and cognitive, moral, and political content are irrelevant to considerations of art proper. These intuitions are not generally shared once one leaves the precincts of analytic philosophy. On our account, these intuitions are not intuitions at all but really lingering fragments of a theory of the sort that Bell popularized and Beardsley perfected. Within the context of such theories, these exclusions make some systematic sense. But divorced from the system as a whole, the notions that one might not appreciate a painting *qua* artwork because of the way it solves an art-historical problem, or that literature *qua* literature might not be valued for moral or cognitive insight rubs against deeply ingrained practices with respect to art.

Something like aesthetic theories of art operate, in a manner of speaking, as the subconscious of the field, a subconscious shaped by the historical emergence of art theory from beauty theory. In this light, this essay is meant to be analogous to a kind of conceptual psychoanalysis; it is a retelling of the story of the field in a way that reveals how a series of confused associations have kept art theorists in the grip of a misplaced obsession with disinterest and detachment.

Moreover, this obsession runs even deeper than the tendency of art theorists to advance "intuitions" that are little more than fragments of aesthetic theories. The very contour of the field of art theory shows the underlying influence of the formative prejudices of the aesthetic approach. Scanning the analytic literature, for example, one is struck by how little writing one finds on topics excluded from the consideration of art proper by the aesthetic approach. The exception here is the issue of authorial intention, the exclusion of which is still debated because of the implications of influential views, such as those of Grice, in the philosophy of language. However, while the cognitive and moral significance of art is rarely discussed in analytic theory, it occupies a position at center stage among nonanalytic theorists of art; and the relevance of art history has always figured as an important element in Hegelian and Marxist thinking. That these are not topics of concern in the analytic tradition is a function of the tendency, perhaps subconscious, within that tradition to conflate art theory with beauty theory.[53]

In conclusion, it seems eminently clear that the theory of beauty is distinct from the theory of art. There may be points of tangency between the two, such as in the case of discussing beautiful art. However, an at least plausible test for beauty, such as disinterestedness, can hardly be advanced as the intended causal output or defining purpose for every kind of artwork. Nor can it be used to circumscribe the boundaries of legitimate inquiry in art theory. But, if my story is persuasive, this is what has happened in the analytic philosophy of art. That beauty theory can be referred to as aesthetic theory may obscure this. Nevertheless, beauty theory, and the aesthetic theory that is preoccupied with its problems, deal with quite a different set of questions than does art theory. Models derived to accommodate, first and foremost, our response to natural beauty do not promise to be fruitful in discussing art. Progress in art theory depends on realizing that the frameworks developed to answer questions in the aesthetic domain, narrowly construed as beauty theory, deal with distinct, though sometimes tangential, problems. Speaking very roughly, the problems of art theory fall *more* on the side of culture, while those of aesthetics fall *more* on the side of nature.[54] Mixing these problems together – confusing art theory and aesthetics – will guarantee that we will solve none of them.

FOUR CONCEPTS OF AESTHETIC EXPERIENCE

INTRODUCTION

A salient feature of critical practice over the last three decades has been an almost exclusive emphasis on interpretation as the primary mode of the analysis of artworks.[1] Roughly put, the output of such analyses is a message – a set of propositions that the artwork is said to imply or to entertain, or a conceptual schema (e.g., an interpretation may disclose that in the world of a fiction women are all sorted into the categories of madonnas versus whores). These messages, then, are often further evaluated in terms of whether they are progressive or reactionary politically. This approach to criticism, moreover, contrasts with alternative views, such as the notion that what a critic does is to point to features of an artwork in order to elicit a certain kind of experience from the audience.

For instance, the critic points to one part of a painting and then to another, foregrounding similarities, in order to enable the viewer to experience the unity of the painting; or the critic describes the dancer's movement in such a way that on subsequent evenings viewers are able to perceive its qualities of lightness or airiness. Whereas the output of interpretive criticism is a message, the output of what we might call demonstrative criticism is, ideally, the promotion of a certain kind of experience – what is generally called an aesthetic experience – in the audience.

The point of demonstrative criticism is to call attention to the variables that make aesthetic experiences possible. The idea is that by encouraging audiences to dwell on certain features of the work in a certain way, audiences will undergo the relevant experiences. In literary studies, certain exercises of New Criticism are examples of demonstrative criticism, predicated on enabling readers to experience the ambiguity of the pertinent poems. In film criticism, André Bazin's emphasis on deep focus photography guided viewers to apperceive the experience of multiplanar complexity in the cinema of Welles and Renoir.

If recent critical practice has gravitated more toward interpretation than to demonstrative criticism – to deciphering messages rather than encouraging aesthetic experiences – then it seems worth noting that a similar emphasis on the message is also in evidence in much contemporary art, especially gallery art. Installation artworks, for instance, typically function as rebuses, gnomically suggesting messages through the juxtaposition of disparate components. Recent performance art, as well, has come to be dominated by identity politics, rhetorically advancing, for the sake of emancipatory empowerment, claims for equal treatment toward women, gays, the disabled, and ethnic and racial minorities. Disgruntled opponents of such artworld tendencies bewail the contemporary artworld emphasis on what they perceive to be political propaganda, and they call for artists to return to the vocation of producing beauty, where "the production of beauty" is shorthand for the "promotion of aesthetic experiences."

If it is true that *the message* has been in the limelight in contemporary critical and artistic practice, then perhaps that provides a clue to the current renewed interest in aesthetic experience. I have said that overt preoccupation with the message is a recent development. It has most often been championed as an antidote to aestheticism, the view said (undoubtedly hyperbolically) to have been dominant in years gone by, that art is for its own sake and not about sending messages into the world. Engaged in an almost oedipal struggle with aestheticism, contemporary critics and artists have focused obsessively on the semiotic dimension of art. As a result, aesthetic experience, the very fulcrum of aestheticism, has been put on the back burner, if not taken off the stove altogether.

But even if aestheticism represents a false view of the comprehensive nature of art, as I believe it does, it does not follow that there is no such thing as aesthetic experience. The promotion of aesthetic experience may not be the sine qua non of art, yet artworks, even artworks of a primarily semiotic cast, may often possess an aesthetic dimension. And it is my hypothesis that the realization of this fact is an important motivating factor in the current interest in aesthetics, evinced by recent lecture series at Wesleyan, Brown, Rutgers, and the University of Wisconsin at Milwaukee. If more semiotically oriented art and criticism can be understood as a corrective to an earlier aestheticism, the still ongoing interlude of preoccupation with the message is calling forth its own corrective in the form of a renewed interest in aesthetic experience.

In the artworld, minimalism, with its premium on the perceptual experience of the work, was superseded by postmodernist pastiche with its penchant for allusion and discourse on real-world commodification. But as postmodernism appears to have become the established norm, artists and critics are on the lookout for alternative projects, of which the return to aesthetic experience is predictably one. I say this not to endorse the sentiments of conservative critics who urge artists to abandon politics in favor of aesthetics, because I do not think that the choice here is mutually exclusive. However, such critics are an index that something has been neglected in recent advanced artistic practice – something whose exile may be about to be ended.

Similarly, criticism itself, after a sustained period of refining sophisticated batteries of interpretive frameworks, may be coming to an awareness that it has left something out of its purview. Exegesis has flourished as many new strategies for interpreting art have been developed, but little effort has been spent in evolving vocabularies for discussing and conceptualizing aesthetic experience. At the very least, this places the academic critical estate at some distance from audiences, since probably what audiences – including our students – often care about most is aesthetic experience. But also, no comprehensive approach to the arts can ignore aesthetic experience. Thus, the renewed interest in aesthetics can only be regarded as a salutary corrective. Nor do I regard research on aesthetic experience as a replacement for interpretation, including political interpretation, but I do regard it as at least a supplement. There is no reason to suppose that interpretive criticism and aesthetic criticism cannot coexist; indeed, they are generally mutually informative and often complementary.

So far, the phrase "aesthetic experience" has been bandied about rather freely. But what is aesthetic experience? Before any new vocabularies are invented to analyze it, we need some idea of what we are analyzing. This question, of course, is a troubled one in the history of philosophy, notably since the eighteenth century. In what follows, I will review four theories of aesthetic experience in the hope of arriving finally at an account that I think will be useful for contemporary criticism. I call the accounts, respectively: the traditional account, the pragmatic account, the allegorical account, and the deflationary account. Maybe, needless to say, the last account, the deflationary account, is my own – which, if I've rigged this essay correctly, should appear to be the most persuasive.

THE TRADITIONAL ACCOUNT

A bland statement of the traditional account of aesthetic experience goes something like this: an aesthetic experience of an artwork involves contemplation, valued for its own sake, of the artwork. That is, aesthetic experiences are self-rewarding. Some variations of the traditional account, such as those of Kant and Hutcheson, are framed in terms of pleasure: for them, an aesthetic experience of an artwork is one in which pleasure is taken from contemplating an artwork for its own sake, or, in other words, the pleasure taken from contemplating the artwork is disinterested. These latter formulations, however, are too narrow, since it is generally agreed that aesthetic experience may not be pleasurable. It may, for instance, involve horror. So the blander formulation is to be preferred initially; if we are horrified by contemplating the artwork, and we value that experience of disturbance for its own sake, then, according to the traditional view, it is an aesthetic experience.

The key element in traditional accounts of aesthetic experience is the notion that such experience is valued for its own sake and not for the sake of something else. This is what, along with a few more qualifications, allegedly hives aesthetic experience off from other sorts of experience. *Ex hypothesi,* we value the experience of flying because it gets us to our destination. Likewise, we study physics in order to accumulate knowledge. But aesthetic experience, putatively, is sought out for its own sake, because it is held to be intrinsically, rather than instrumentally, valuable.

When attending to objects aesthetically, our attention is said to be disinterested – a perhaps misleading term – that really means our attention is engaged without instrumental or ulterior purposes. When I attend to the landscape aesthetically, I have no practical purposes in mind, unlike the geologist who surveys the landscape looking for signs of profitable mineral deposits.

If questioned after reading a poem as to why you did it, and you answer because you found the experience worthwhile in and of itself – or even pleasurable in and of itself – then you are adverting to the standard idiom of the traditional account of aesthetic experience. Your attention to the poem was disinterested, not in the sense that you were not interested in the poem, but in the sense that your keen interest was not predicated on any instrumental considerations, like impressing your lover. You simply find reading the poem its own reward – end of story.

The traditional account of aesthetic experience comes in for a lot of bad press most often because of the doctrines with which it has been associated historically. These include the aesthetic theory of art, of which formalism is the most notorious variation. Such theories use the notion of aesthetic experience as the central term in comprehensively defining the nature of art. The general form of such theories is: something is an artwork if and only if it is designed with the intention to afford aesthetic experience. Such theories include the qualification that there must be the relevant intention with respect to artworks in order to distinguish between artworks and things like sunsets, which, though they may afford aesthetic experience, do not do so intentionally.

Formalism is the best known example of an aesthetic theory of art. For the formalist, such as Clive Bell, the focus of aesthetic experience is, as the name suggests, artistic form. With respect to paintings, artistic form comprises relations between lines, colors, vectors, spaces, and the like. These are said to be the appropriate objects of attention for painting *qua* painting and focusing upon them – comprehending their studied articulation – yields a self-rewarding experience, one that banishes practical concerns from the mind in favor of absorption in the abstract structure of the work.

Undoubtedly, formalists place emphasis on abstract structures just because those are less likely to invite contemplation of the artwork in terms of ulterior interests, like political content. This is also why formalists like Bell maintain that the representational content of a work is at best irrelevant to its status as art, since at worst representational elements are apt to entice the viewers into thinking about the practical world of affairs, instead of contemplating the object for its own sake. And, perhaps needless to say, it is this attempt to bracket considerations of the practical world of affairs, including social relations, that has gained formalists the reflex opprobrium of contemporary politically minded scholars.

Though formalism did provide a serviceable foundation for certain types of art appreciation, it is an unpersuasive theory of art for the obvious reason that much art has not been produced with the intention to afford appreciable experiences of structure. Historically, most art has been designed with the intention to serve practical or instrumental purposes, including political and religious purposes. Much art has been produced to reinforce national and cultural identities, to bolster the ethos of the group, to encourage pride and commitment, to celebrate or memorialize important occasions, to enlist support, to mourn, to commemorate, and the like. Statistically, formalism fails dismally to reconstruct the concept of art as we typically employ it. Thus, those dissatisfied with formalism because it is apolitical can add to their budget of complaints that it also fails to be a comprehensive theory of art empirically.

Nor does it make much sense for the formalist to allege that patriotic responses to artworks designed to elicit nationalism are somehow inappropriate, if that is the aim of the genre to which the work in question belongs. Rather, patriotism seems to be precisely the appropriate response to such artworks. And, in any case, formalism proposes a questionable account of artistic attention – insofar as formalism suggests that representional content is strictly irrevelant for appreciating artworks *qua* artworks – for the simple reason that tracking representational content is frequently an ineliminable precondition for discovering formal relations. You won't grasp the formal organization of Brueghal's *The Fall of Icarus* unless you also contemplate the story.

Likewise the structure of many novels (including the Harry Potter series) is practically impossible to discern if one does not access one's cognitive and emotive stock about the real world. Though literary comprehension, including the discovery of structure, involves many other things, it typically requires the mobilization of cognitive and emotive scripts and schemas drawn from everyday life and applied in a comparable manner to characters and situations. It is hard to imagine, for instance, how ordinary readers would detect structures of dramatic conflict otherwise.

Of course, formalism is not the only aesthetic theory of art. And a more generic statement of the theory can remedy some of formalism's shortcomings. For example, if we say that something is an artwork if and only if it is intended to afford aesthetic experience *and* we do not stipulate that the object of aesthetic experience is artistic form, many of the previous objections to formalism fall by the wayside, since contemplating the representational content of artworks, including its political content, can count, on the generic aesthetic theory, as aesthetic experience, so long as the experience is valued for its own sake. Whereas dwelling on the moral observations in a novel by Henry James does not count as aesthetic experience for the formalist, a proponent of what I'm calling the generic aesthetic theory will accept it as such, so long as the reader finds the experience intrinsically valuable. Nor on the generic view is there any problem with finding the representational content of the artwork relevant in any way, so long as it subserves the cultivation of an experience that is valued for its own sake.

Though the generic aesthetic theory escapes some of the troubles of formalism, as a comprehensive theory of art, it is nevertheless inadequate. It is too exclusive. There are works of art that are not intended to afford the relevant kinds of aesthetic experiences. Many cultures, for example, produce demon figures that are intended to drive off intruders by means of their terrifying visages. It is implausible to imagine that these figures were designed to be contemplated for their own sake. Such responses would contradict the very purpose these artifacts subserve. But nevertheless we count figures and masks such as these as artworks.

So far I haven't said much about aesthetic experience. I've concentrated on theories of art that mobilize aesthetic experience as the central element in their definitions of art. I've done this because of my suspicion that much of the prevailing skepticism about aesthetic experience is connected to people's dismissal of the theories of art, like formalism, in which the notion of aesthetic experience plays a crucial role. However, it is of the utmost importance to emphasize that the notion of aesthetic experience can be detached or decoupled from formalism and aesthetic theories of art. That those theories fail as comprehensive theories of art does not entail that there is something wrong with the notion of aesthetic experience in its own right – that is, apart from its putative role in defining art. Aesthetic experience may not – indeed, I claim that it does not – define art; nevertheless, there is still something that we refer to by means of the concept of aesthetic experience.

The traditional characterization of aesthetic experience identifies it as an experience necessarily valued for its own sake. With respect to artworks, my experience is aesthetic when, guided and directed by the artwork, said experience is intrinsically valued by me. If you ask the rich man why he attended the concert and he indicates he did it in order to show the world he is a philanthropist, his experience of the music is not aesthetic. If you ask his impoverished aunt why she attended and she says that she went in order to have an intrinsically valuable experience of the music, hers is an aesthetic experience. For her, the having the experience is its own reward; she did not seek it out for some ulterior purpose.

But what is it to have an intrinsically valuable experience of the music? Is it that certain experiences just are intrinsically valuable, irrespective of the agent's beliefs about them, or is what makes an experience intrinsically valuable a person's beliefs about it, namely, that she believes it valuable for its own sake, and not for the sake of something else? Let us call the first of these options the objective conception of intrinsic value, and the second the subjective conception.

The objective conception of intrinsic value hardly seems promising. How can we tell which experiences are valuable for their own sake? Aesthetic experiences are said to be valuable for their own sake. They involve things like recognizing patterns and structures, on the one hand, and detecting expressive properties, on the other hand. But it is plausible to hypothesize that these activities have, unbeknownst to us, some subtle, adaptive value and are, therefore, instrumentally valuable from an evolutionary point of view.

Aesthetic experiences of form may exercise and enhance our capacities for recognizing regularities in the environment, while the detection of expressive properties in artworks may nurture and contribute to our ability to scope out the emotional states of our conspecifics – a clearly advantageous capability for social beings like us.

Of course, I don't know for sure whether aesthetic experiences are instrumentally valuable in these ways, though the idea that the seemingly nearly universal capacity for having them provides no benefit whatsoever to the organism is hard to square with a scientific worldview. But, in any event, the bottom line is that no one really knows enough psychology to be sure whether aesthetic experiences are instrumentally or instrinsically valuable irrespective of what the agents undergoing the experience believe about them. For all we know, aesthetic experiences might be instrumentally valuable, especially adaptively, without the agents' being aware of that value.[2]

At this point in the debate, it is open to the friend of the traditional account of aesthetic experience to opt for the subjective interpretation of valuation for its own sake. On this construal, when we say that an experience is valued for its own sake, we have in mind that what explains the agent's participation in the experience is that he or she believes that it is valuable intrinsically. That is, the belief that the experience is valuable for its own sake is the internal mechanism that motivates the agent to engage in certain behaviors, like attending the theater.

Ask the theatergoer why she is spending her time that way. Is it to make money or impress her friends? No. Is it to show solidarity with the oppressed? No. It is, she says, because having the experience itself – perhaps she calls it a pleasurable experience – is valuable in and of its own right. She goes to the theater in order to undergo such an experience – in anticipation that it would be pleasur-

able, or moving, or interesting just to have that kind of evening. We buy a choco-
late bar because we believe the taste of it, irrespective of its practical, nutritional
value (if any), is a satisfying experience on its own terms. Similarly, we seek out
certain artworks given our belief or expectation that they will afford experiences
that will be satisfying on their own terms. This belief is what in large part causes
or motivates our commerce with many artworks, and when it is borne out, under
the guidance of the artwork, our experience is said to be an aesthetic experience.

One thing to notice about the subjective version of the traditional account of
aesthetic experience is that it identifies aesthetic experiences not in terms of
internal features of the state, but in terms of the causal conditions that abet the
state, namely, the agent's belief that the experience is intrinsically valuable. That is,
this characterization of aesthetic experience says little about the content of the
experience, but instead isolates aesthetic experiences in terms of whether they are
caused and sustained by the right sort of beliefs. Yet this seems to me to guarantee
that the traditional account of aesthetic experience is mistaken.

The traditional account presumes that a necessary condition for aesthetic
experience is the belief that the experience is valuable for its own sake. But this is
false. Let us agree with the formalist at least this far: that appreciation of the form
of an artwork is one kind of aesthetic experience. Now let's also imagine two reasonably informed artgoers: Oscar, who believes experiencing artworks is valuable
for their own sake, and Charles, an evolutionary psychologist, who believes experiencing artworks is valuable for honing one's cognitive and perceptual abilities.

Oscar and Charles listen to the same piece of music, attending to the same
musical structures – both track the same repeating motifs and note how cleverly
they are interwoven. Both find the work unified, in the same way, and both are
moved by its expressive qualities. Both run the exactly same computations relevant to processing the formal features of the work. Pretheoretically, I think that we
are disposed to say both of them had aesthetic experiences. After all, the content
of their experience is exactly the same; their computational states are type-identi-
cal. If we had a science-fiction device, call it a cerebroscope, that enabled us to get
inside their experiences, we would detect no differences in kind between their
mental activities.

Nevertheless, the traditional account seems driven to the counterintuitive
conclusion that, despite the sameness in content of their mental states, Oscar is
having an aesthetic experience, but Charles is not, since Charles believes his state
is instrumentally valuable – that it improves his cognitive and perceptual abilities –
whereas Oscar thinks the experience is valuable for its own sake. But this scarcely
seems to mark a categorical difference, if we grant that both Oscar and Charles are
attending to the same things, in the same ways – ways, moreover, that are appropriate, given the nature of the music in question.

Furthermore, imagine that Charles' theories, whether or not they are true,
become so popular among educators worldwide that at some date in the distant
future, everyone is taught and comes to believe that attending to artworks in the
way that Oscar and Charles do is instrumentally valuable for the reasons Charles

says they are. That is, everyone avidly consumes artworks because they believe that the activity improves their cognitive and perceptual abilities. In such a world, the traditional account would be forced to conclude that there is no longer any aesthetic experience, despite the fact that it might be the case that more people could be consuming more art with more acuity and perceptiveness than ever before.

Of course, the friend of the traditional account may claim that though people like Charles *say* explicitly that they believe that experiencing artworks improves them and that this is why they do it, deep down what they really believe is that such experiences are valuable for their own sake. The proof of this might be that if their beliefs in the self-improvement value of art were proven to be false, they would continue to seek out artworks. Why? Because, *ex hypothesi,* they subconsciously find the experiences intrinsically valuable. But insofar as this prediction assumes, overconfidently in my opinion, that were these people truly to believe that art affords no opportunities for improvement, they would continue to consume it, the traditional account of aesthetic experience still seems to me to rest on a highly shaky conjecture. For people like Charles might go Gragrind were their beliefs in the improving value of art undermined – after all, others have – and, furthermore, this behavior would not in any way alter the fact that in their pre-Gragrind days, they were still having aesthetic experiences despite the fact that they believed them to be instrumentally valuable.

In short, the traditional account requires for an experience to be aesthetic that the agent believe or find the experience to be valuable for its own sake. But surely an agent can appreciate the form or expressiveness of an artwork while regarding these experiences as instrumentally valuable in some manner. That is, from the viewpoint of artistic appreciation, the mental processing activities and attendant qualities of Oscar's experience and Charles' experience can be the same in every way. It seems arbitrary to say that one is having an aesthetic experience and the other not. But if valuation for its own sake is not a necessary condition of aesthetic experience, then that scotches the traditional account.

THE PRAGMATIC ACCOUNT

I've called the next account "the pragmatic account" because its leading advocate was John Dewey. It might just as easily be called the structural account, since it characterizes aesthetic experience in terms of its putative internal structure or rhythm. The pragmatic account contrasts nicely with the traditional account. Whereas the traditional account attempts to define aesthetic experience in terms of the agent's beliefs about that experience, the pragmatic account focuses squarely on the content of the relevant experience and tries to generalize about its recurring internal features.

Unlike many theories of aesthetic experience, Dewey's does not propose a distinction between aesthetic experience and other kinds of experience. For Dewey, aesthetic experience exemplifies the fundamental structure of anything that we would be willing to call "*an* experience" as that phrase is used in expressions like "now that was *an* experience." Dewey does not think that aesthetic experiences are uniquely correlated to artworks, but rather that aesthetic experiences of artworks can be used by us as instructive guides for fashioning everyday experiences and our lives. Aesthetic experiences can function in this way because, according to Dewey, they represent in a more realized manner the structure toward which all potentially vivid experiences naturally gravitate. Or, putting the point in a different way, for Dewey anything we are disposed to call *an* experience in ordinary language always already has a latent aesthetic character that we can learn to bring into the foreground through cultivating the aesthetic experiences available to us via artworks.

Commenting on the aesthetic nature of experience, Dewey says:

> we have *an* experience when the material experienced runs its course to fulfillment. Then and only then is it integrated within and demarcated in the general stream of experience from other experiences. A piece of work is finished in a way that is satisfactory; a problem receives its solution; a game is played through; a situation, whether that of eating a meal, playing a game of chess, carrying on a conversation, writing a book, or taking part in a political campaign, is so rounded out that its close is a consummation and not a cessation. Such an experience is a whole and carries with it its own individualizing quality and self-sufficiency. It is *an* experience.[3]

Dewey says of such an experience that "it is a thing of histories, each with its own plot, its own inception and movement toward its close";[4] and that "in such experiences, every successive part flows freely without seams and without unfilled blanks, into what ensues. At the same time there is no sacrifice of the self-identity of the parts."[5] For "in an experience, flow is from something to something. As one part leads to another and as one part carries on what went before, each gains distinctness in itself. The enduring whole is diversified by successive phases that are emphases of its varied colors."[6] And lastly, such an experience has a unity that is "constituted by a single quality that pervades the entire experience in spite of the variation of its constituent parts."[7]

Dewey's phenomenological description of aesthetic experience here and elsewhere sounds like an abstract scenario. Moments flow into moments under the selective guidance of a single quality until they reach closure or, as he says, are consummated. Moments are integrated, like a plot, and the congruence of the interphasing moments make the experience stand out against backgrounds of either nondescript monotony or bustling confusion. Some experiences are like this, especially some aesthetic experiences of artworks. The issue is whether this structural account of some aesthetic experiences can be generalized across the board.

Dewey is a slippery writer. One cannot always be sure what he is saying or whether he is always saying the same thing. However, he does seem committed to the idea that an aesthetic experience must have a temporal dimension; it evolves over time; it has duration. Moreover, structurally, it has closure; it doesn't just end. This gives the experience unity, as does the fact that it possesses some distinctive quality in contrast to the often bland experiences of ordinary life. Since this does not differentiate the aesthetic experience of art from many other sorts of experience, these criteria – duration, qualitative unity, and temporal integration and closure – don't, as Dewey would probably be the first to admit, supply sufficient conditions for identifying the relevant experiences, but they do appear to be necessary conditions for him.

And yet obviously they are too restrictive. Not all aesthetic experiences of artworks extend over any appreciable duration. Some paintings just overwhelm you in one shot. Pow! Some Rothkos are like this. Their sublimity envelops you all at once. Of course, many paintings are designed so that their parts will be taken in and imaginatively reconstructed over time. But that is not enough to support Dewey's generalizations, because many other paintings – say minimalist paintings bereft of parts – are composed to elicit immediate rather than durative experiences. Nevertheless, we still regard experiences of those kinds of paintings as aesthetic, though they do not abet experiences of temporal integration or evolution, nor does it make much sense to speak of experiential closure with respect to them.

Likewise, the requirement that aesthetic experiences be qualitatively unified seems too narrow. Dewey thinks that with regard to encounters with artworks something like a qualitative feeling tone emerges that selectively governs our sense of what belongs and what doesn't in our experience, thereby setting up an internal boundary between aesthetic experiences and surrounding circumstances. But, of course, many modern artworks, like John Cage's *4′33″*, are designed to subvert the kinds of aesthetic experiences Dewey regards as the norm. By mobilizing chance techniques, Cage renders unlikely the operation of any principle of selection of the sort that would impart a feeling of qualitative unity to an experience of a performance of *4′33″*. Moreover, *4′33″* does just end; it does not consummate. Instead of erecting a boundary between that experience and the experiential surround, Cage blurs it. He fosters an experience of dispersion, arbitrary juxtaposition, and openness rather than that of a bounded unity, thereby defamiliarizing the quotidian so that it can be heard afresh.

Similarly, many of Robert Morris's installations make the experience of disarray their subject, while Antonioni's films of the early sixties portray scarcely storied events in order to place the loose-endedness of lives lived under the cinematic microscope. But if experiences of quotidian dispersion, openness, disarray, arbitrariness, loose-endedness, of endings without consummation, and so on can all be aesthetic experiences, designed to blur the distinction between Dewey's capital letter E Experiences and the more desultory and disconnected sorts of daily experience, then the pragmatic account of aesthetic experience, no matter how influential on twentieth-century educational theory, must be abandoned.

THE ALLEGORICAL ACCOUNT

Though perhaps never stated with the utmost clarity and explicitness in the writings of Critical Theorists, the allegorical account of aesthetic experience of art is strongly suggested by the later works of Herbert Marcuse and T. W. Adorno. In order to get the gist of this position on aesthetic experience, let me begin with some quotations from Marcuse. He writes:

> Art breaks open a dimension inaccessible to other experience, a dimension in which human beings, nature, and other things no longer stand under the law of the established reality principle. Subjects and objects encounter the appearance of that autonomy which is denied them in their society. The encounter with the truth of art happens in the estranging language and images which make perceptible, visible, and audible that which is no longer, or not yet, perceived, said and heard in everyday life.[8]

Because genuine artworks are autonomous in the sense that they afford disinterested experiences, they provide us with a sense that society could be different, that it could be ruled by different principles. Of Mallarmé's poety, Marcuse writes: "his poems conjure up modes of perception, imagination, gestures — a feast of sensuousness which shatters everyday experience and anticipates a different reality principle."[9] In this regard, the aesthetic experience of genuine artworks is utopian — it provides a taste of qualities of experience typically not available in capitalist and totalitarian societies, dominated as they are by exchange value and instrumental reason, the profit motive and the performance principle.

That is why Marcuse claims of fiction that "the encounter with the fictitious world restructures consciousness and gives sensual representation to a countersocial experience."[10] By being unreal, in other words, fiction awakens experience to the possibility that things could be otherwise — experience in general could be more like what is now often only found in aesthetic experience, an opportunity to allow imagination and sensibility free rein. In this way, aesthetic experience looks forward to a time when "imagination, sensibility and reason will be emancipated from the rule of exploitation."[11] Aesthetic experience, in short, functions as a beacon, encouraging us to realize a new social order where our species-being, in terms of our powers of imagination and sensibility, can flourish.

Genuine art has a utopian side, inasmuch as the aesthetic experience that it affords sustains faith in the possibility of a different social order, one where imagination and sensibility rather than instrumental reason and the performance principle preside.[12] At the same time, by being different from the social order that exists, art, through the agency of aesthetic experience, implicitly criticizes what is. It negates the existing social order by drawing a revealing contrast between everyday experience under the present dispensation and the creativity and imaginativeness available through aesthetic experiences of genuine works of art. Art, in virtue of aesthetic experience, is revolutionary — it negates the modalities of existing social reality: at once holding out the promise of the possibility of a utopian alternative, while also accusing, indicting, and criticizing what we have instead.

In order to understand what Marcuse is trying to do here, it is helpful to recall that he is attempting to find a political significance for art and aesthetic experience that does not tie them to the propaganda function of art. That is, he wishes to argue that art can be politically emancipatory, irrespective of its overt political content, rhetoric, and purpose. He wants to argue, for example, that Mallarmé can be regarded as revolutionary from a Marxist point of view. In this respect, Marcuse's project is not so different from the one that Kant undertook in his *Critique of Judgment* where he was at pains to show the moral significance of art apart from and even despite its lack of moralizing content. To a comparable end, Marcuse focuses on aesthetic experience, taking it to symbolize experientially the possibility of a more humanly fulfilled way of life, while, at the same time, it also implicitly functions to criticize our present form of social existence.

Though Adorno's theory, which Marcuse acknowledges as an immense influence, is far more complicated, and less sanguine, than Marcuse's, it also emphasizes the potential of the aesthetic experience of art to be a demystifying agency. Adorno says:

> What is social about art is not its political stance, but its immanent dynamic in opposition to society. Its historical posture repulses empirical reality, the fact that works of art *qua* things are part of that reality notwithstanding. If any social function can be ascribed to art at all, it is the function to have no function. By being different from ungodly reality, art negatively embodies an order of things in which empirical reality would have its rightful place. The mystery of art is its demystifying power.[13]

That is, because the work of art is autonomous or lacking any other function than that of producing aesthetic experience (which itself is free of any instrumental, practical, and, therefore, social interest), art may serve as an occasion for a demystifying, negating experience of existing social reality – an experience embracing both social promise and social criticism. Adorno, of course, as well as being far less conventional than Marcuse with respect to his aesthetic taste, is also dramatically less hopeful than Marcuse about the prospects for art to transcend altogether the social circumstances from which it emerges, though nevertheless he would still appear to grant aesthetic experience the same kinds of powers of negation Marcuse does, even if he is far more emphatic about the limitations of their efficacy.

Because their language is so different, it may not be obvious that there is an important correspondence between the traditional account of aesthetic experience and the allegorical account. Nevertheless, both accounts share a central premise in regarding aesthetic experience as disinterested – that is, not a matter of the pursuit of any practical, instrumental, moral, or, broadly social value.[14] It is because artworks are said to promote this sort of disinterested experience that Marcuse and Adorno regard genuine artworks to be autonomous or, at least, in Adorno's case, headed in the direction of autonomy. That is, the autonomy of art is constituted by its capacity to promote aesthetic experience. Or, to say it differently, the key to understanding the notion that art is autonomous is the presupposition that it specializes in the promotion of disinterested experiences, since such experiences are said, by definition, to be aimed at something valuable for its own sake, rather than in the service of social and instrumental interests.

Of course, the reason that both the traditional account and the allegorical account of aesthetic experience converge on this commitment to disinterestedness is primarily a shared heritage, notably the writings of Kant. However, the allegorical account relies far more heavily on Kantian aesthetics than does the traditional account.

For Kant, an aesthetic experience of the relevant sort – an experience of free beauty – is, in part, a subjective, disinterested feeling of pleasure that results from the free play of the imagination and understanding in response to forms of purposiveness. Unpacking this formula, we can say: such experiences are subjective, because they obtain inside the percipient. They are disinterested because they are valued for their own sake. And, the pleasure they provoke is a function of the imagination and the understanding in free play.

That is, the imagination and the understanding are active in aesthetic experience, but not in the way they are standardly deployed in theoretical and practical reason. Instead of being involved in subsuming particulars under determinate concepts and purposes, as in the manner of instrumental reason, during aesthetic experience, the imagination and understanding are exploratory; they are free to examine particulars without the pressure to classify them under a general concept or purpose. In a typical aesthetic experience, of which contemplating a metaphor may be one, the imagination probes the particular for its possible meanings, constructing alternatives, and is open to diverse and vagrant sensations rather than attempting to corral the experience under a single determinate concept, including the sort that would be useful or serve a purpose.

The object of aesthetic experience presents us with the form of purposiveness – that is, it looks to be the product of intentional activity – but we don't examine it in terms of the purpose it does or might serve. Instead, we absorb it imaginatively and openendedly. We savor the colors in the painting of a tree for their richness and variety rather than using them to tell ourselves what kind of tree it is. We imaginatively explore the multiple, metaphorical, shifting meanings that a heraldic emblem might have, rather than simply, practically regarding it as the insignia of a certain family or clan.

There are two different, discriminable, though relatable, kinds of freedom here folded into the Kantian aesthetic experience. There is the freedom the experience sustains insofar as it is disinterested – valuable intrinsically and, therefore, divorced, that is to say "free from," any other sort of interest: practical, moral, financial, political, and so on. But the experience is also free in the sense that during it the imagination and understanding are free from the governance of concepts. The imagination and understanding explore particulars in their richness without the compulsion to subsume them under concepts. Moreover, this concept-freedom of the imagination may relate back to the disinterested freedom of the experience both positively and negatively. Positively because this imaginative exploration is self-rewarding and negatively because the subsumption of particulars under concepts generally serves practical purposes. Thus, where the imagination eludes conceptualization, in the same stroke, it functions outside a network of purposes.

These two freedoms are especially crucial for the allegorical account of aesthetic experience. On the one hand, it is the notion of disinterestedness that encourages proponents to identify the experiences afforded by genuine art with an indictment of market value and the utopian promise of more humane value, since aesthetic experience itself is putatively, in principle, independent from any sort of exchange value. So to engage aesthetic experience through artworks then is to find oneself necessarily outside the reach of exchange value.

On the other hand, the freedom of the imagination from concepts when immersed in aesthetic experience is also implicitly utopian and accusatory, since subsuming particulars under concepts is the hallmark of instrumental reason. Thus, insofar as the operation of the imagination in aesthetic experience amounts to a form of cognition free from the subsumption of particulars under concepts, aesthetic experience represents a cognitive free zone outside the processes of instrumental reason. For Adorno, it represents a kind of cognition or rationality outside the perimeter of the sort of the instrumental rationality that dominates capitalist and totalitarian societies, thereby holding forth an alternative kind of reason, whose possibility also indicts instrumental rationality. Moreover, to the degree that imaginative cognition without concepts emphasizes the experience of particularity, it resists the totalizing demands of existing forms of existing social reality.

The allegorical account of aesthetic experience also reflects certain tendencies in the self-conception of modernist art. Accosted somewhere in the nineteenth century by rude commercial ambitions bent on reducing all value to utilitarian or economic value, some modernist artists began to represent themselves as trying to set up a firebreak — called art for art's sake — in order to sustain an autonomous realm of value independent of the dollar sign. That is, in the context of earlier culture wars, the putative autonomy of art was mobilized by many modernist artists historically as a sign of resistance to the perceived threat of the reduction of all value to market or instrumental value through bourgeois contagion.

The allegorical account of aesthetic experience provides a philosophical grounding for this modernist tendency, explaining ostensibly how art can secure autonomy because of its capacity to engender aesthetic experiences that are disinterested and impractically valuable as well as, in principle, free from the protocols of instrumental reason. That is, the allegorical account provides a theoretical rationale for the modernist's conviction that art can defend the possibility of value beyond instrumental value, of which market value is a particularly pronounced and threatening example.

I have called this account allegorical. Perhaps now we have reached a point where I can explain my choice of nomenclature. In order to limn the significance of aesthetic experience, proponents of this approach embed aesthetic experience in a larger dramatic conflict in which aesthetic experience figures as the protagonist and instrumental reason and market rationality as the antagonists. The putative mental state of disinterested valuing and the capacity to imagine and reflect sans the guidance of concepts are opposed to instrumental reasoning and market rationality not only in the sense of being different, but also in the sense of some-how being rivals or competitors.

In the Kantian system, aesthetic experience or aesthetic judgment occupies a niche in a static architectonic schema. What the allegorical account does is to dynamize that schema, thematizing the parts and turning it into a story. In addi-tion, the allegorical account, then, also appears to historicize the story, associating certain aspects of reason with the marketplace and totalitarianism, on the one hand, and drafting aesthetic experience and the imagination as a significant, if ulti-mately doomed, antidote to the encroachment of the sort of rationalization Max Weber identified with modernity. The allegorical account treats aesthetic experi-ence as a counter against instrumental reason, narrativizing mental processes in an agonistic struggle, one made more poignant by being superimposed onto disturb-ing social tendencies, especially ones relevant to modern capitalism.

In some of the most obscure passages of Kant's *Critique of Judgment,* Kant conjec-tures that the aesthetic experience of nature is the symbol of morality – by which he means that it is a metaphor for morality that enables humans to grasp the idea intu-itively or experientially. My suspicion is that the allegorical account of aesthetic expe-rience is in the same ballpark. It is an attempt to locate the significance or symbolic import of aesthetic experience, notably for the age of instrumental reason. Thus, the account is allegorical because it takes a certain conception of aesthetic experience, derived from Kant, and attempts to make it a metaphor or symbol for something else – the affirmation of autonomy, criticism of the status quo, and so on.

However, for the metaphor to work, aesthetic experience needs to have just the features attributed to it. It would have to be necessarily disinterested and it also would have to deploy the imagination without dependence on determinate con-cepts. If not, the allegory would not work on its own terms. Moreover, despite the authority of Kant, we have already seen in our discussion of the traditional account of aesthetic experience that the supposition that aesthetic experience is necessarily disinterested is dubious. Is the conjecture that in aesthetic experience the imagination functions without the direction of determinate concepts any bet-ter off? For if it is not, the putative rivalry between aesthetic experience and instrumental reason is undermined.

If what we are talking about is the aesthetic experience of artworks, as opposed to natural vistas, it is difficult to credit the idea that concepts play no role in aesthetic contemplation. With respect to artworks, very frequently, if not most frequently, a decisive portion of our cognitive activity is spent placing the artwork in its correct category or genre, which, in turn, gives us a sense of its likely pur-poses, which, then, enables us to appreciate the suitability of its formal articula-tion. Part of what it is to experience *Oedipus Rex* aesthetically involves identifying it as an example of the category of tragedy and using what one knows about the purposes of that genre in order to isolate and size up its structural modifications.

This is not to say that every artwork falls neatly into one category. Some straddle or synthesize categories; some amplify already existing categories in inno-vative directions; some may even repudiate familiar categories, erecting, in effect, countercategories. But in responding to even these examples, categorical thinking plays a major role in much, perhaps even most, aesthetic experiences of artworks. Yet if categorical thinking is not an alien part of aesthetic experience, then how can aesthetic experience be allegorized as the antithesis of instrumental reasoning, where categorical thinking is taken as an index of instrumental reasoning?

Kant, of course, thought of aesthetic judgment as falling into two kinds: judgments of free beauty and judgments of accessory or dependent beauty. Only the former are issued without determinate concepts; the latter – judgments of accessory beauty – require concepts. To judge something a beautiful car in Kant's dependent sense, we need the concept of the kind of car in question and the purposes it serves. And similarly, a vast number of the judgments we make concerning artworks involve situating them in the relevant categories. That is, even within the Kantian scheme of things, the aesthetic experience of artworks is hardly devoid of the cognitive deployment of the imagination and reflection in order to categorize. And outside the Kantian orthodoxy, opinion strongly favors the view that the aesthetic experience of art is an affair involving categorical thinking as standardly an ineliminable, generally constitutive element.

Taking something like the Kantian portrait of the aesthetic experience of free beauty as the model for the aesthetic experience of art – even of great art or what might be called genuine art – results in an extraordinarily narrow, revisionist, and almost stipulative construal of the aesthetic experience of artworks, including modernist artworks. Nevertheless, some such maneuver appears required by proponents of the allegorical account if their homology contrasting aesthetic experience versus instrumental reason is to click. But if the aesthetic experience of artworks requires as much categorical thinking as I have indicated – and not exclusively imaginative free play, as is assumed – then aesthetic experience is not an apt figure for the allegorical role assigned to it.

One set of problems for the allegorical approach, then, is that it presupposes that aesthetic experience is a matter of the disinterested free play of the imagination, untethered by determinate concepts. These features of aesthetic experience must obtain if aesthetic experience is to be allegorized as a site of resistance against exchange value and instrumental reason. However, arguably neither disinterestedness nor cognitive free play are necessary ingredients of the aesthetic experience of artworks, thereby compromising the allegory internally.

In addition to being skeptical about the premises of the allegorical account, one must also voice reservations about its form. It appears to treat aesthetic experience as a symbolic figure. But how theoretically informative is this? Clearly it is not being claimed that aesthetic experiences induce people who undergo them to imagine utopia or to criticize the status quo on any regularly recurring basis. But what exactly is being asserted?

I suspect it is that the aesthetic experience of autonomous art can be made to symbolize freedom in an unfree world. This involves selectively hypostasizing complementary mental processes like the free imagination and subsumptive reasoning and then mapping them, in a manner that involves drastic simplification, onto conflicting social tendencies, exploiting associative ambiguities in the relevant senses of "freedom" all the way. That is, to get the relevant binary symbolic oppositions in place, both the mental processes and the social forces they are correlated to will need to be radically gerrymandered theoretically beyond empirical recognition.

Now I have no doubt that this can be done with great elan. However, I wonder whether it wouldn't be just as easy to tell alternative allegories about aesthetic experience by selecting some of its other putative features and weaving them into different social dramas, in which the aesthetic experience of art takes on a less ennobling role. Imagine radical environmentalists who, noting the absorptive quality of aesthetic experiences of art, castigate it as an opiate that stands for the repression and degradation of our capacities for communing with nature. Aesthetic experiences of art, for them, will symbolize the epitome of the anthropocentric narcissism that increases exponentially with the march of history.

Of course, as liberally educated folk, we will reject this allegory, preferring ones that assign the aesthetic experience of art a more heroic role. But aside from being uplifting for people like us, does the allegory of aesthetic experience that we encountered in Marcuse stand on any firmer ground than that of the environmentalists?

The problem with allegories, especially highly selective ones, of aesthetic experience is that alternative, different, and even incompatible allegories are easily available. There seems to be no principled reason to accept one such allegory over another. The allegory Critical Theorists offer us does not force us on pain of philosophical necessity to accept it, since it rests on ideas of disinterestedness and on the concept of free deployment of the imagination that themselves lack philosophical necessity.

Nor can the allegory be recuperated as an empirical reconstruction of the rationale behind all genuine modern art, except by courting circularity, since much modern art, such as Soviet Constructivism, rejects any commitment to disinterestedness. At best, the allegorical account provides useful insight into the ambitions of *some* modern art, but it does not afford a comprehensive way of conceptualizing the aesthetic experience of art, even in the twentieth century. It may be an interesting story, but inasmuch as other interesting stories, including incompatible ones, are readily imaginable through other homologies, the allegorical account is not finally compelling.

In summary, if the allegorical account is supposed to figure aesthetic experience as a metaphor for the possibility of noninstrumental, nonmarket rationality, then, since the features of aesthetic experience (distinterestedness and the concept of free imaginative play) it valorizes seem questionable, the metaphor is inapt. But even if the metaphor were more persuasive, the question of its genuine theoretical informativeness would linger, since alternative, nonconverging metaphors – alternative allegories – appear equally conceivable.

THE DEFLATIONARY ACCOUNT

So far we have not had much success attempting to characterize the aesthetic experience of art. But the problems with the preceding accounts provide us with clues about how to proceed, if only by flagging some of the pitfalls in our path. Attempts to portray aesthetic experience in terms of disinterestedness fail because, rather than focusing on what goes on during aesthetic experiences, they emphasize the beliefs in intrinsic value that putatively attend such experiences, in terms of causing them and sustaining them. So one way to repair this shortcoming may be to take note of what goes on during the aesthetic experience of art – to attend, that is, to the content of such experiences.

The pragmatic account does do this, of course, as does the emphasis on the concept-free play of the imagination. However, in both cases, there is a tendency to overgeneralize – to treat certain kinds of aesthetic experience or certain aspects of some aesthetic experiences as the essence of all aesthetic experience. Thus, given this background of difficulties, a promising line suggests itself, namely, to characterize the aesthetic experience of artworks by focusing on the content of said experiences without overgeneralizing.

But what goes on – what do we do – during what, with respect to artworks, are typically called aesthetic experiences? Two things spring to mind immediately. One is that we attend to the structure or form of the artwork, taking note of how it hangs, or does not hang, together. The formalists were wrong to think that this is the only sort of thing that counts as aesthetic experience. But surely it is one of the possible ways of attending to artworks that we standardly refer to as aesthetic experience. We can call it design appreciation. Where our experience of an artwork involves an attempt to discern its structure or form, that is a case of design appreciation. And if our experience of the artwork or part of our experience is dedicated to design appreciation – if our experience is in whole or in part preoccupied with discovering the structure of the work – then that is an aesthetic experience.

By calling this activity design appreciation, I do not intend to imply that it must involve liking the work or admiring it, though a frequent consequence of design appreciation may be a feeling of satisfaction. All I mean by design appreciation is that we are involved in sizing up the work, in attending to how the work works – that is, we are trying to isolate the ways in which the relevant choices the artist made realize or fail to realize the point or purpose of the artwork. Someone, the content of whose attention to a work concerns its design or form, is, during the pertinent time span, having an aesthetic experience of it.

But design appreciation is not the only type of experience we typically call aesthetic. Also paradigmatic is the detection of the aesthetic and expressive qualities of an artwork – noticing, for instance, the lightness and grace of a steeple, or the anguish of a verse. This sense of aesthetic experience is very close to the notion that Baumgarten had in mind when he introduced the neologism *aisthisis* in the eighteenth century as the label for a species of sensuous cognition. Attending to a vase, not only observing its weight, shape, and size, but its appearance of elegance is an aesthetic experience.

That is, an experience whose content is the response-dependent, qualitative dimension of the object is an aesthetic experience. Explaining the ontological and psychological conditions of such experiences is, of course, still an enormous project. Nevertheless, that such experiences obtain is a fact of human existence, and where responses to artworks involve them, they are uncontroversially called aesthetic experiences.

So if an experience of an artwork is a matter of design appreciation or of the detection of its aesthetic and/or expressive qualities, then it is an aesthetic experience. Design appreciation and quality detection are each disjunctively sufficient conditions for aesthetic experience. Moreover, neither of these experiences requires the other. One could apprehend the aesthetic qualities of a work without scrutinizing its form, or examine the structure of the work without detecting its aesthetic qualities (perhaps because it has none). Yet, design appreciation and quality detection often come in tandem: frequently, the search for structure involves isolating the artistic choices on which salient aesthetic qualities supervene, while attention to the aesthetic qualities of an artwork is generally relevant to discovering its design. Thus, we may at least hypothesize that design appreciation and/or quality detection are aesthetic experiences – that, independently or together, they provide sufficient conditions for classifying an experience as aesthetic.

This way of characterizing aesthetic experience avoids overgeneralization, since it does not take one kind of aesthetic experience for the whole phenomena. At least two discriminable kinds of experience belong to the concept: design appreciation and quality detection. The formulation also allows that there may be other kinds of experience that also deserve the label "aesthetic experience," though these two, disjunctively or in concert, command our immediate attention, since it seems perfectly uncontroversial to call the activities of design appreciation and quality detection aesthetic experiences.

A ruckus might be raised were we to say that only design appreciation is aesthetic experience; but calling design appreciation a major mode of aesthetic experience should raise no hackles. Moreover, other candidates can be added to this list, where they track the ordinary and traditional application of the concept of aesthetic experience as unproblematically as do design appreciation and quality detection – that is, with the same intuitive fitness and convergence on precedent.

This account of aesthetic experience is deflationary. It identifies aesthetic experience in terms of the content of certain experiences whose objects it enumerates as, first and foremost, the design of artworks and their aesthetic and expressive qualities. It does not propose some common feature between these two kinds of experience, like disinterestedness, that constitutes the essence of aesthetic experience. On its behalf, one can say of the deflationary, content-oriented, enumerative account of the concept aesthetic experience that calling an experience an aesthetic experience because it involves either design appreciation, quality detection or both (1) accords with a tradition of usage that has recurrently selected form and/or qualitative appearance as its primary conditions of application and (2) that such usage is unobjectionably recognizable as correct by those who talk about aesthetic experience. Moreover, the deflationary account is more informative than the traditional account, whose guiding concept – disinterestedness – tells us almost nothing, since it is virtually exclusively negative (an account of what the experience is not).

Perhaps one reason that the deflationary account may sound inadequate is that sometimes people take the notion of an aesthetic experience of an artwork to be an umbrella concept for any appropriate experience of art. On this construal, a response of political indignation to the situation depicted in a novel about racism appears unjustifiably disenfranchised as an appropriate response to the work, since it is not an aesthetic response according to the obviously narrower deflationary account.

But from my perspective, there are many different kinds of appropriate responses to artworks, of which aesthetic experience is only one. Though moral indignation, inasmuch as it need not involve design appreciation or quality detection, may not be an occasion for aesthetic experience, that does not preclude its status as an appropriate response to a work that, given its purposes, lays political matters before its readers for their consideration. It is simply an art-appropriate response that is different from aesthetic experience.

According to the deflationary account, aesthetic experience is neither the only, the central, nor the best kind of appropriate response to an artwork. The notion of aesthetic experience is not being used honorifically, but only descriptively, of one set of transactions audiences may have of artworks.[15] Once it is acknowledged that no special virtue attaches to the aesthetic experience of artworks – that it is one sort of art-appropriate response among others – then anxiety over the apparent narrowness of the deflationary account should subside. Different artworks ask for or mandate or prescribe many different kinds of responses, whose appropriateness is best assessed on a case-by-case basis. To attempt to call them all aesthetic experiences or to reserve that label for only the best of them simply courts confusion and even, unfortunately, rancor.

Some may be surprised that I have not included interpretation, along with design appreciation and quality detection, as an instance of aesthetic experience. I have refrained from this in order to respect an influential tradition that, though not unchallenged, regards the deciphering of the thematic messages of artworks to be a different, and by some accounts opposed, activity to aesthetic experience. Nevertheless, I have not caved into that viewpoint altogether, since the deflationary account can still acknowledge and explain a close relation between interpretation and aesthetic experience.

For insofar as design appreciation involves discerning the structure of an artwork relative to its points or purposes, design appreciation will generally require interpretation in order to isolate those points and purposes. Likewise, quality detection will usually be ineliminable in interpreting the thematic viewpoints of artworks. So even if interpretation does not represent an uncontroversial paradigm of aesthetic experience, it can still be shown to be intimately related to activities that are.

Recently, the notion of aesthetic experience has fallen under a pall because, given the residual reputation of ideas of disinterestedness, it is perceived as claiming insulation from political concerns. However, on the deflationary account of aesthetic experience, there is no necessary disjunction between attending to aesthetic experience and political analysis. On the one hand, design appreciation includes the sizing up of the rhetorical structures of the work that will be relevant to most imaginable political analyses; while, on the other hand, political analyses can hardly encourage confidence, unless they are responsive to expressive qualities. However, the moratorium on discussing aesthetic experience in the humanities needs to end not only because aesthetic experience is relevant to political analysis, but because as audiences and educators the whole gamut of art appropriate responses, including aesthetic experience, is our province.

PART II: ART, HISTORY, AND NARRATIVE

❧

ART, PRACTICE, AND NARRATIVE

I

The purpose of this essay is to attempt to reorient one of the central questions of philosophical aesthetics, namely, "What is art?" The direction that this reorientation proposes relies upon taking advantage of the practice, or, more aptly, the practices of art as the primary means of identifying those objects (and performances) that are to count as art. Roughly put, the question of whether or not an object (or a performance) is to be regarded as a work of art depends on whether or not it can be placed in the evolving tradition of art in the right way. That is, whether an object (or performance) is identified as art is a question internal to the practice or practices of art. In this respect, the question "What is art?" changes its thrust. "Art" in our query no longer refers primarily to the art object; rather what we wish to know about when we ask "What is art?" predominantly concerns the nature and structures of the practices of art − things, I shall argue, that are generally best approached by means of historical narration.

This essay is written within the context of the philosophy of art as that has evolved in the Anglo-American tradition. The positive proposals I advance, as a result, need to be seen against that background of debate; indeed, part of the confidence that I have in the view developed in ensuing sections rests on my belief that my view manages to avoid the most decisive objections made against earlier, rival positions in the ongoing debate concerning the nature of art.

Space does not permit a detailed review of the evolution of that debate. However, brief mention of three of the major moments in that dialectic will be useful. For the positive position advanced in this essay is supposed to have the advantage of overcoming the liabilities of these earlier interludes in the discussion.

Within the Anglo-American tradition, one initially compelling picture of what is at stake in answering the question "What is art?" involves envisioning a cosmic warehouse full of objects (henceforth, "objects" is often shorthand for "objects and performances") to be sorted into piles of art and nonart.[1] Many proposals about the way in which this sorting is to proceed have been

From: *The Monist,* vol. 71, no. 2 (April 1988), 140–56.

proffered, each with its own shortcomings. Three that have been particularly influential are:

A. *Stage-one essentialism.*   Figures such as Bell, Croce, Collingwood, Tolstoy, and Langer have been associated with this approach. Their theories of art are at least said to be attempts to specify, by means of real definitions, the identifying features of art objects, which definitions, in turn, would then be used to carry through the sorting described above. These real definitions, that is, would be used as rules assigning objects to the realm of art or nonart. Candidates for the identifying marks of art include significant form, clarified intuition or emotion, the capacity to elicit aesthetic experience, forms of feeling, and so on. Ostensibly, whether an object possesses the relevant, manifest properties can be determined from a point of view external to the artworld – as if artworks were natural kinds. And, furthermore, possession of such properties is taken to satisfy necessary and sufficient conditions for regarding an object to be art.

B. *The open concept approach.*   This view, as popularized by Morris Weitz,[2] depends upon the anti-essentialism of Wittgenstein's later writings, explicitly applying those criticisms to that which has just been called stage-one essentialism. Against any variant of stage-one essentialism, Weitz denies that art can be defined by necessary and sufficient conditions. Weitz's leading notion is that art is an open concept – one that is applied without reference to necessary and sufficient conditions. The ground for suspecting that art is such a concept is not that past theoretical attempts to define said conditions have all failed – though that seems to be the case – but rather that the arena demarcated by the concept of art is one in which we legitimately expect novelty, innovation, and originality. In a manner of speaking, previous art theory, of the stage-one essentialism variety, was doomed to fail just because in codifying the necessary and sufficient conditions of the class of artworks up to the present no accommodation could be guaranteed for the innovations of art of the future. Such definitions of art, one worried, function as rules in a forum of activity valued for not being strictly rule governed.

On the positive side, Weitz also suggested a way in which to sort the art from the nonart. Following Wittgenstein's analysis of the concept of games, Weitz maintained that membership in the class of artworks was to be determined on the basis of family resemblances. Shakespeare's *Pericles* resembles Homer's *Odyssey* by virtue of certain manifest plot motifs and, whereas neither obviously resembles Goya's *The Sleep of Reason,* both resemble *Hamlet,* which shares darkly brooding, manifest expressive qualities with *The Sleep of Reason.* The family of art, so to speak, is bound together by strands of discontinuous though interlacing resemblances.

But this invocation of family resemblances was quickly challenged. It rests on an analogy between family resemblances and relations of similarity between artworks. However, the analogy is incongruous. The relationships of resemblance among members of a family are significant, that is, are *family* relations, because they are the result of an underlying generative mechanism. They are not merely surface resemblances. Mere resemblance between people, and, by extension between artworks, does not portend inclusion in a family unless that resemblance can be shown significant by reference to a specifiable generative process. Moreover, by overlooking the importance of underlying, nonmanifest generative processes, proponents of the open concept approach missed the possibility that one might develop a theory of what is common to the members of the order of art in terms of their origination through a shared generative process or procedure.[3]

   C. *The Institutional Theory of Art.*   This approach, in its classic statement by George Dickie,[4] identifies an artifact as art only if it is generated by the right process, an institutional process, which Dickie initially thought of as the conferral of status of candidate for appreciation by some person or persons acting on behalf of the artworld. In certain respects, the Institutional Theory of Art reminds one of a positivist theory of law. X is a law if and only if it is generated by the right procedure, for example, passage by Congress. Likewise, an artifact is a work of art if it is introduced by the right persons for the right purposes – for example, as a candidate for appreciation. Dickie's theory is what can be thought of as stage-two essentialism for it is stated as a real definition. However, it is not threatened by the anxiety of foreclosing artistic innovation that perplexes the Wittgensteinian proponents of the open concept approach for insofar as one reads the Institutional Theory of Art as a pure procedural theory for generating art, no expressive, thematic, aesthetic or formal breakthrough is blocked, so long as it is presented by the right person for the right purpose. Furthermore, the theory exploits what was overlooked in the open concept approach by focusing on the nonmanifest, relational properties of putative artworks, that is, on their common relation to the generating procedure of the artworld.

   However, despite the ingenuity of Dickie's theory in evading the drawbacks of its predecessors, it too has been subjected to much criticism. One notable line of rebuttal zeroes in on the notion that the artworld is an institution analogous to a legal system or a religion. Specifically, it is argued that it is implausible to regard the artworld on a par with such social formations. Within any given legal system or established religion, the roles, powers and objects of concern – the players and the pieces, if you will – are strictly regulated. In fact, the regulations here are what make institutions out of these practices. But where are the regulations in Dickie's artworld? What specified conditions does one have to meet in order to act on behalf of the artworld and are there really any minimal conditions for being a candidate for appreciation? One might attempt to say that the rules of the artworld are informal, but in response it can be stressed that it is exactly the formality and explicitness of specific legal systems and religions that makes *institutions* of them. *Pace* Dickie's classic formulation of his theory, art is not an *institution* if that concept is to be rigorously applied.

   Our view – of art as a cultural practice – attempts to negotiate through the pitfalls in previous theorizing. It does not foreclose artistic innovation while it does attend to the generative process*es* through which objects enter the realm of art. In some ways, it resembles the institutional approach; however, it does not claim that art is an institution but only makes the less ambitious observation that it is a cultural practice. Also, it regards the question of whether an object is art as one internal to the cultural practices of the artworld and goes on to discuss the coherence of that practice.

II

Calling art a cultural practice, it is to be hoped, is noncontroversial. To refer to something as a practice in its simplest sense is to regard it as an activity that is customarily or habitually undertaken; a cultural practice, in this sense, applies to the customary activities of a culture. Shaking hands is a customary activity of greeting in our culture. But though custom and habit have a large part to play in what I am calling a cultural practice, they are by no means the whole of it.

The sense of cultural practice I have in mind here is that of a complex body of interrelated human activities governed by reasons internal to those forms of activity and to their coordination. Practices are aimed at achieving goods that are appropriate to the forms of activity that comprise them, and these reasons and goods, in part, situate the place of the practice in the life of the culture. Such practices supply the frameworks in which human powers are developed and expanded.

Custom, tradition, and precedent are integral components of a cultural practice. Nevertheless, cultural practices need not be static. They require flexibility over time in order to persist through changing circumstances. They tolerate and indeed afford rational means to facilitate modification, development into new areas of interest, abandonment of previous interests, innovation, and discovery. Practices sustain and abet change while remaining the same practice. Practices do this by a creative use of tradition, or, to put the matter another way, practices contain the means, such as modes of reasoning and explanation, that provide for the rational transformation of the practice.

In one sense, callng art a practice in the singular is misleading. For art is a cluster of interrelated practices. The plurality of practices here involves not only the diversity of artforms, whose interrelations are often evinced by their imitation of each other, but also by the different, though related, roles that different agents play in the artworld.

Of special note here are the roles of makers and receivers. In many respects, the activities or practices of these two groups diverge. And yet, at the same time, they must be linked. For art is a public practice and in order for it to succeed publicly – that is, in order for the viewer to understand a given artwork – the artist and the audience must share a basic framework of communication: a knowledge of shared conventions, strategies, and of ways of legitimately expanding upon existing modes of making and responding. This point is often partially made by saying that the artist is her own first audience; artistic practices must be constrained by the practices of response available to audiences in order to realize public communication. A similar constraint operates with the audience not only to assure communication in the basic sense, but, in the long run, to keep the activities of the artworld coherently related.

Two points in the preceding, rather general, discussion of a cultural practice need to be connected. Art is a cultural practice. A cultural practice is an arena of activity that governs itself such that it reproduces itself over time. A cultural practice, to speak anthropomorphically, needs to provide for its continuance over time. In one sense, it must replicate itself. However, this replication cannot be absolutely rote. For the practice must also readjust itself and evolve, in order to adapt to new circumstances. Thus, a cultural practice requires rational means to facilitate transition while remaining recognizably the same practice. That is, a cultural practice must reproduce itself while also being able to change, without becoming an alien practice; it must have not only a tradition, but ways of modifying that tradition so that past and present are integrated.

Furthermore, the essential publicity of art requires that these modes of reproducing and transforming the practice be available to both the makers and receivers of putative artworks, not only so that they have the possibility of understanding each other but also so that the practice evolves coherently. To put the matter more concretely, an artist needs to know the constraints on diverging from the tradition in such a way that her activity changes it rather than ends it, and the audience, or at least certain members of it, needs to share the knowledge of the modes of expanding the tradition in order not only to understand the artist's work, but, even more fundamentally, to recognize it as a development within the tradition.

One mark of a practice is that participants be able to self-consciously identify themselves as participating within the practice. But if practices change, this requires that the participants have the means to self-consciously identify themselves as partaking of the same practice through change and transition.

This, of course, through a roundabout route, returns us to the initial question of how we identify works of art. That is, as the cultural practice of art reproduces and transforms itself, makers and receivers need ways in which to identify newly produced objects as members of the same tradition as antecedently existing artworks. In our own time, this question is made especially urgent by the avant-garde. But it has been an issue for art throughout its history, given its proclivity for self-transformation.

As I have already intimated, I think that the means for identifying a new object as part of the corpus of art are internal to the practice of art, and, furthermore, are related to the reproduction of the practice as a self-transforming tradition. The means of identification, here, are rational strategies rather than the types of rules that are, for example, identified with stage-one essentialism. That is, given a new work of art, we do not have a rule or set of rules to determine whether it deserves inclusion in the order of art; rather we have several strategies for thinking about the object and for justifying its acceptance in the tradition. Moreover, these strategies need not converge on a single theory of the nature of the artwork.

Perhaps an analogy with morality is useful here. Even if the practice of morality is not founded upon a single moral doctrine of the good act, from which all moral precepts flow (in the way championed by Kantians and utilitarians), we still have rational strategies with which to reasonably conduct moral debate. Con-

fronted by an action we adjudge immoral, we may press its perpetrator by pursuing certain well-known lines of argument: for instance, pointing out that she
would not like the same act visited upon her, or that he would abhor the consequences of everyone behaving in the manner he does. These argumentative strategies do not in themselves amount to a unitary moral theory; however, they do
provide immensely serviceable means with which moral practitioners can adjudicate disputes. Similarly, I hold that with respect to the artworld there are strategies
of reasoning, as opposed to rules, definitions, first principles or unitary theories,
which enable practitioners to identify new objects as art.

The best way to convince you that there are such strategies is to call your
attention to some of them. Three spring immediately to mind. Confronted with a
new object, we might argue that it is an artwork on the grounds that it is a repetition, amplification, or repudiation of the works that are already acknowledged to
belong to the tradition.[5] In each case, given the need of the cultural practice to
reproduce itself, we connect the new object to past artworks, but the nature of
that connection differs with each strategy of argumentation.

The simplest form of argumentation is to note that the object in question is a
repetition of the forms, figures, and themes of previous art. For example, the ballet *Giselle* (choreographed by Coralli and Perrot) could have been identified as art
by its original audience in virtue of the way in which it repeated the vocabulary,
themes, and genre conventions of *La Sylphide* (choreographed by F. Taglioni). Similarly, the works of contemporary portrait painters and of authors of *bildungsromans*
are counted as art because of the way in which they repeat the structures, techniques, données, and themes of previous art. Where narrative arts are concerned, a
repetition involves a modification or variation in the particularities of content of
a genre or form; character, events, and places change while basic narrative techniques and genre conventions remain intact. Identification as an artwork in such
cases involves demonstrating the way in which the later work repeats the form,
conventions, and effects of past work.

This can fail in various ways: the forms of the past or present works can be
misdescribed, for example, or the repetition noted in the present work may only
be of vaguely peripheral significance to the traditional forms or genres cited as
precedents. As well, repetition, in the relevant sense, is not exact duplication.
Baldly copying a previous artwork so that it cannot be distinguished from its
model cannot count as art under the rubric of repetition. It is either plagiarism,
or, if it is art, it's so classified generally because it can be interpreted as some form
of complex repudiation.

An amplification is a formal modification that expands the presiding means for
achieving the prevailing goals of a given genre or artform. In identifying new
works as art, amplification figures importantly in the problem/solution model of
discussing art history. A form or genre is presented as dealing with a problem, and
later works, which diverge in evident respects from the earlier work in the tradition, are said to solve the problems that beset previous practitioners. The history of
Western painting essayed in Gombrich's *Art and Illusion* is perhaps the stellar

example of this approach. Stylistic divergences of later stages are shown to be continuously integrated with the work of earlier pictorial traditions, in Gombrich's account, insofar as the later work introduces new techniques for the purpose of realizing the antecedent goal of "capturing reality."

Likewise, at a given point in film history – one often associated with the name of Griffith – devices such as parallel editing and the close-up were introduced, producing movies of a new sort. These could nevertheless be identified as continuous with previous filmmaking, since they were amplifications of the preestablished aim of making film narratives. The earlier films in this tradition, as well, could have been identified as art by showing the ways in which they repeated the données of existing forms such as narrative painting, theater, and the novel. Traveling forward in film history, the work of the Soviet montage school could be identified as art by virtue of the way in which it amplified the goals of the Griffith-type editing to which we have already alluded.

Through the use of the notion of amplification, we see *one* way that the cultural practice of art has for expanding itself by enabling practitioners – both artists and audiences – to identify new work as developments of the tradition. In this manner, the view of art as a cultural practice assimilates the point of the open concept approach that the originality of art must be respected. However, there also is *another* way in which the artworld supplies its practitioners with the means both to produce and to track legitimate expansions of the tradition. An artwork need not only stand in relation to the tradition as an amplification; it may also function as a repudiation of an antecedent style and its associated values.[6] For an object to count as a repudiation, it must not only be different from what has preceded it, it must also be interpretable as in some sense opposed to or against an antecedent artistic project.

When an artwork is regarded as a repudiation of a preexisting style or form of art, it appears, in the culture from which it emerges, to stand to what it repudiates somewhat like a logical contrary. We think this way, for example, of the tension between Classicism and Romanticism, on the one hand, and between Soviet montage and deep-focus realism in cinema, on the other. A repudiation is not simply different from the art that precedes it, but is opposed to it in a way that gives the repudiation's relation to the past a distinctive structure. To identify a new object as art by virtue of its being a repudiation, one must show exactly along what dimensions the object rejects the tradition as well as showing that just that sort of rejection was conceivable in the context in which the work appeared (i.e., Duchamp's readymades, as Danto teaches us, could not have been intelligible as a repudiation in the artworld of Cimabue). History and tradition, in other words, supply information that constrains what at any given time can function as a plausible repudiation and, thereby, a radical expansion of the frontier of art.

The cultural practice of art transforms itself through amplification and repudiation. Amplification might be thought of as an evolutionary mode of change; in contrast, repudiation is revolutionary. We think of artistic development not only in terms of the smooth process of solving self-generated problems, but also in terms of the eruption of conflict between opposing movements and artistic generations. Repudiation is the category meant to capture this latter process. But it needs to be emphasized that an artistic repudiation is not a total break with the past. Rather, repudiation typically proceeds by maintaining contact with the tradition in several ways that enable us to view it as a continuity within the cultural practice of art.

First, and most obviously, the artistic repudiation stays in a structured relation with the tradition insofar as it proposes itself as contrary to prevailing practices. The object that counts as a repudiation is not an ineffably alien creation but, in the Hegelian sense, is a determinate negation of certain tendencies of its predecessors. It remains, so to speak, in an essential conversation, no matter how acrimonious, with its generally immediate forebears. Second, it is interesting to note another characteristic relation that works of repudiation maintain with the past. Usually, though repudiating art rejects the styles and values of its *immediate* predecessors, it often at the same time claims affinity with *more temporally distant* exemplars in the tradition. The German Expressionists, for example, while decrying the limitations of the realist project, cited the expressivity of medieval painters, such as Grünewald, to warrant their figural distortions. The predecessor program of realism, that is, was rejected by the Expressionists in the name of the exclusion or repression of qualities, such as expressive distortion, that could be found in the work of more remote practitioners of the tradition, which possibilities, by the way, had earlier been repudiated by realists.

It is easy to multiply cases of this sort. In the sixties, ambitious American novelists rejected the psychological realism of much dominant postwar fiction in favor of gargantuan comic escapades in which characters were types. But this rejection of psychological realism was accompanied by the reminder that such forms were in the older tradition of the picaresque. The newer works, by people like Pynchon, were not repetitions of the picaresque, but developments in the light of the experience of the psychological novel. Likewise, postmodern architects, such as Venturi, advance their position not only by rejecting the modern tradition of figures like Le Corbusier, but *also* by citing the influence of Renaissance Venetian cityscapes. The point illustrated by these examples is that even in cases of artistic revolution, the break with tradition is anything but complete. Not only does a work that repudiates a tradition remain conceptually tied to the predecessor program that it rejects, but also the qualities that the predecessor program is said to preclude or repress are argued to have precedent in more temporally remote tendencies in the tradition.[7]

Through contrast and precedent, then, the repudiation remains continuous with the tradition of the cultural practice. In order for an artist to have a new work accepted as an example of art through the rubric of repudiation, as well as for a critic or spectator to argue concordantly, it must be maintained that the work in question determinately negates one part of the tradition while rediscovering or reinventing another part. Obviously, if no connections could be found between a new work and the practice, we would have no reason to call it art.

Art is a cultural practice that supplies its practitioners with strategies for identifying new objects as art. Since cultural practices tend to reproduce themselves and to negotiate their self-transformations in ways that sustain continuity between the existing tradition and expansions thereof, the modes of identifying new objects as art make essential reference, though in different ways, to the history of the practice. New objects are identified as artworks through histories of art, rather than theories of art. Artists and audiences share strategies for identifying new objects as art. The artist is concerned with these strategies in order to present new artworks, while the audience is concerned with them in order to recognize new artworks. Primary, though not necessarily exhaustive, examples of these strategies involve regarding whether the objects in question can stand as repetitions, amplifications, or repudiations of acknowledged artistic tendencies in the tradition.[8] Moreover, these strategies are not necessarily mutually preclusive. A given avant-garde work may be a repetition of a stylistic gambit of a contemporary art tendency – for example, the displacement of popular iconography *à la* postmodernism – while also being a repudiation of preceding art movements – for example, of minimalism.

Confronted by a new object, a practitioner of the artworld considers whether it can be shown that the new work is a repetition, amplification, or repudiation of the tradition. These strategies are key means of identifying artworks. They are not definitions of art but rely on identifying new artworks by a consideration of the history of the artworld. Their essential historical reference is grounded in art's being a self-transforming historical practice with a flexible tradition that facilitates innovation. If this sounds somewhat like the family resemblance approach, insofar as it underscores correspondences (albeit not necessarily manifest ones) between new art and past art, it nevertheless evades the crushing objection to that conception since it also relies on genetic links between such works. Nor does it claim that art is an institution, but rather makes the weaker point that art is a cultural practice, though, of course, cultural practices are the sorts of things from which institutions may emerge.

III

So far an attempt has been made to maintain that the way in which we identify objects as art is to rely upon strategies internal to the practice of art, which enable us to situate objects that repeat, amplify, or repudiate already accepted artworks as contributions to the expanding tradition of art. The question of "What is art?" – where it is construed as a question of identifying artworks – is deferred as an issue internal to the artworld, which provides procedures, rather than real definitions, in order to ascertain which objects are artworks. But this may be thought to be a dodge.

To say that objects are identified as artworks in virtue of strategies internal to the practice of art invites reframing the issue as a request for a statement of the identifying conditions of the practice of art. That is, if we deflect the demand to supply an account of the essential nature of the artwork by an invocation of the practice of art, we will soon be asked to specify the conditions that differentiate the cultural practice of art from other cultural practices.

But I would like to suggest that the practice of art need not be characterized by means of setting forth the necessary and sufficient conditions of this realm of activity. The cultural practice of art may be elucidated by means of narration rather than by means of an essential definition. That is, pressed to portray the unity and coherence of the practice of art, we propose rational reconstructions of the way in which it historically evolved. The identity of art, in other words, is conceived to be historical. One would not attempt to characterize a nation's identity by means of sets of necessary and sufficient conditions. For a nation is an historical entity whose constituent elements came together as a result of certain patterns of development, whose guiding purposes emerged in certain circumstances, and whose interests can be transformed in response to subsequent pressures. The unity of this sort of entity is best captured by an historical narrative, one that shows the ways in which its past and present are integrated. Similarly, though differences between art and a nation are readily to be admitted, the cultural practice of art is essentially historical, and accounting for its coherence primarily involves narrating the process of its development, highlighting the rhyme and reason therein.[9]

The historical or narrative approach to the cultural practice of art has already been foreshadowed in our discussion of some of the key strategies for identifying new objects as artworks. For repetition, amplification, and repudiation are obviously, though implicitly, narrative frameworks. They are story forms or genres, if you will, to be filled in with details of the artistic tendencies, movements, and presuppositions of one stage of development that give rise to a later stage in virtue of, for example, one of the processes discussed. At any point in the history of the practice (or practices) of art, the unity of a later stage of development is rendered intelligible or explained within the practice by filling in the narrative of its emergence from an earlier stage by means of such processes as repetition, amplification, and/or repudiation.

What is called Early Modern Dance, for example, is intelligible within the practice of art as a repudiation of European ballet, while Impressionism in painting can be viewed as an amplification of the realist project in fine arts. Perhaps MTV, or at least some of it, could be shown to be art by pointing to the ways in which it repeats the techniques of avant-garde film. Such narratives are open to criticism. Their reports must be based on evidence. They must be accurate as well as plausible historically, and their descriptions of the objects under scrutiny must be appropriate.

Such narratives reveal the unities within the practice of art, its coherence, so to say. Moreover, these narratives are rational in that they aim to make optimal sense out of their materials by integrating past and present. The significance of later works is rendered intelligible in light of relations with past works. At the same time, in examining such processes as repudiation, the significance of past, perhaps forgotten art is brought to our attention. New works can inform our understanding of past art, while past art informs our understanding of new art. This under-standing proceeds by historical narration, which is both forwards- and backwards-looking, and which discloses lines of development through such recurring patterns as repetition, amplification, and repudiation.

Moreover, the contents of these patterns of development are neither preor-dained nor closed but depend, at any given point, upon the antecedent evolu-tion of the artworld. Narrative provides us with a means for tracing the unity of the practice of art without prejudging what art of the future will be. For the art of the future may branch out from the present not only through various processes of change, but also with respect to a multiplicity of various dimen-sions. That is, what aspect of an artform might be repudiated or amplified next is not strictly predictable.

Thus far, our approach to questions about the unity or identity of the practice of art has been to suggest that we can cut into the history of the putative practice at any point and present narrative explanations of the way in which a given stage developed from an earlier one and portended a later one, by, for example, intro-ducing or extending a problematic, or promoting studied reactions. Such histori-cal narratives reveal the coherence of the practice of art; they disclose its identity as an *integrated* historical process.

This narrative procedure, of course, presupposes that we need to begin by pre-suming that we have knowledge that some objects are art, as well as knowledge of the salient features of those objects. However, once that rather reasonable assump-tion is granted, we can move forwards or backwards from a given point in the his-tory of the practice to show its unity and coherence with past and future stages.

Nevertheless, here it may be objected that what can be shown is at best the unity of certain portions of the practice rather than the unity of the practice as a whole. But I see *no reason in principle* why a narrative approach is fated to fail in this matter. Undoubtedly, a narrative of every stage in the history of the practice would be a herculean project and probably a tedious one, given the long swaths of repetition we are likely to encounter. But, for example, granted that certain ten-dencies of the present are art, I see no reason why we cannot move backwards through history applying the strategies of repetition, amplification, and repudia-tion, along with whatever other narrative-developmental frameworks we discover, to reconstitute the trajectory of the tradition in reverse, so to speak.[10]

Admittedly, when present tendencies change, we may have to readjust our characterizations of art history, just as the significance of the historical past in gen-eral alters with the unfolding of contemporary events. However, each in-princi-ple-possible revision would give us a characterization of the practice of art as we know it. As it is, of course, we do not demand accounts of the historical unity of the entire cultural tradition of art, but only more localized accounts of apparent breaks with and striking departures from the normal, that is to say, repetitive development. For, given the massive amount of obvious repetition within the tra-dition, a full sketch of its unity is effectively besides the point. But, again, there is no reason to think that such a sketch is impossible in principle.

Talk of tracing the unity of the practice backwards raises questions about the origin of the practice and, thereby, focuses questions about its purity. For as we trace the development of the practice it becomes clear that it is not entirely disjunct from other cultural practices. Specifically, it is widely held that the practices we regard as art emerged from religious concerns. Objects were made for the purposes of representing (in some sense of the term) gods and myths, and such objects were replete with potently expressive qualities, were inscribed with hermetic messages, and reflected cultural self-conceptions. Spectators responded to these objects by, among other things, recognizing their referents, by being moved affectively, and by interpreting their significance. The possibilities of these sorts of broadly described interactions were probably put in place by religion, but they were gradually developed independently and, ultimately, secularly through processes such as repetition, amplification, and repudiation in ways that have generated the history of the practice of art.[11]

This line of historical conjecture, however, would appear to pose a problem for purists. For it freely acknowledges that the practice of art did not spring into existence by way of Apollo's neatly and decorously distributing clearly defined roles to a covey of muses. But this type of purity does not seem likely as a description of the emergence of many human practices. Practices begin in a mess of activities, often borrowed or derived from preexisting cultural realms, and some of these begin to coalesce. Interrelations between these activities become refined as practitioners become self-conscious and enter a self-interpretive conversation in what starts to dawn as a tradition.

Of course, to admit that a practice starts ill-defined does not mean that its cluster of originating activities are arbitrarily united. For a certain sense can be discerned in the way in which they coalesce. In the case of art, supposing that representation, expression, decoration, and communication, broadly characterized, were, from the production side, the initial core activities of the practice of art, a certain functional logic appears to ground their cohesion. For what an object represents constrains, and, in that sense, partially determines what it expresses, while the expressive and aesthetic qualities of the object significantly inflect what the object communicates. Or, to state the matter from the spectator's vantage point, what an object is recognized as representing modifies what expressive and aesthetic qualities we can derive from it, and these in turn contribute importantly in structuring our interpretations of the work. This is not said in order to demand that artworks be representative, expressive, and/or communicative, but only to note that when these activities are combined, their logical interconnections would indicate that their coalescence as deep-rooted activities of the practice is not sheerly arbitrary.

As the preceding speculation concerning the origins of our cultural practice of art indicates, when we begin to reach the boundaries of the tradition, our characterization of its intelligibility tends toward considerations of function.[12] However, once the core activities and accompanying objects within the tradition are so located, the process of identifying the new objects to be included in the series is pursued by means of narratives whose elaboration, in turn, explains the historical unity of the practice to us.

Basically, by way of considering art as a cultural practice, I have advanced narrative as a primary means of identifying artworks and of characterizing the coherence of the artworld, in contrast to the inclination to deal with these matters by proposing defining sets of necessary and sufficient conditions. Roughly stated, I have advocated what might be called narrativism over essentialism. This reorientation, moreover, correlates with a growing tendency in many schools and areas of inquiry on the contemporary intellectual landscapes.[13]

IDENTIFYING ART

As a student of George Dickie's, I have been profoundly influenced by his contributions to the philosophy of art. I believe that his criticisms of the notions of aesthetic perception, aesthetic attitudes, aesthetic experience, and so on remain fundamentally sound. And, as well, they place important constraints on theories of art. Notably, they preclude the possibility of sustaining what are currently called aesthetic theories of art: that is, theories of art that propose to define art in terms of the engendering of aesthetic experience. George Dickie's rejection of aesthetic experience, of course, set the stage for the proposal of his own variations on the institutional theory of art by effectively removing one sort of rival − aesthetic theories of art − from the playing field. And I am convinced that this move is still decisive.

George Dickie also successfully undermined the open concept/family resemblance approach to identifying art as a way of dialectically arguing in favor of institutional-type theories of art. In this matter, too, I believe Dickie's arguments are still powerful.

In challenging the viability of aesthetic theories of art and the open concept/family resemblance approach, George Dickie showed the importance of social context for the prospects of identifying art. His own variations on the institutional theory of art are contested, but his emphasis upon the relevance of social context represents a major contribution to the philosophy of art. In my own work, I have become suspicious of the plausibility of institutional theories of art, including its most recent reincarnation. I have argued that art is not identified by definitions, institutional or otherwise, but by narratives. The essay that follows is an attempt to provide further clarification of the narrative approach, which I advocate, to the problem of identifying art.[1]

From: *Institutions of Art,* ed. by Robert Yanal (University Park: Penn State University Press, 1993), 3–38.

Nevertheless, though I have departed from the letter of George Dickie's approach, I am still touched by its spirit, especially by its emphasis on the central-ity of context. And, as well, my conception of the structure of the dialectical field on which debates about identifying art are staged is deeply indebted to Dickie's always careful and clear way of setting up the problem.

IDENTIFICATION, ESSENCE, AND DEFINITION

One of the central questions of analytic philosophy in the twentieth century – notably in the second half of the twentieth century – has been "What is art?" Whether it was an issue of much urgency earlier is a matter of genuine historical dispute. And even in the second half of the twentieth century, there have been dis-tinguished theorists – like Nelson Goodman[2] and Kendall Walton[3] – who have wondered whether there is much profit to be found in this issue. Indeed, in his landmark treatise *Aesthetics,* Monroe Beardsley did not bother to address the ques-tion in its canonical form.[4] Nevertheless, the sheer statistical evidence seems enough to warrant the claim that it has been *a* central question of analytic philos-ophy even if, at the same time, it is true that our energies might have been spent more fruitfully elsewhere.

However, even if it is granted that this has been *a* central question for philoso-phers, it has been noted less often that this question may be taken in a number of different ways – ways that diverge from the interpretation that contemporary philosophers are often predisposed to give it, and ways that do not connect in a neat package of interrelated answers. That is, the question "What is art?" may, at different times, signal a request for different kinds of information, and that infor-mation, furthermore, may not be linked logically in the manner most contempo-rary philosophers anticipate.[5]

Some of the primary issues that the question "What is art?" may serve to introduce include the following. First of all, how do we identify or recognize or establish something to be a work of art? That is, how do we establish that a given object or performance is an artwork? This request for information has, of course, become increasingly pressing for nearly a century, a period that we might label the "age of the avant-garde." For in its urge to subvert expectations, the art of the avant-garde, which would appear to have the most legitimate historical claim to be the high art of our times, has consistently and intentionally produced objects and performances that challenge settled conceptions about what one is likely to encounter on a visit to a gallery, a theater, or a concert hall. It can be no accident that the art theorists of the last century have become so obsessed with the ques-tion "What is art?" during the age of the avant-garde. For theory here would appear to be driven by practical concerns: that is, given the consistently anomalous productions of the avant-garde, how does one establish that these works are art-works? Indeed, recalling what Stanley Cavell has identified as the modern audi-ence's fear that it might be the butt of a continuously floating confidence game, we surmise that the issue is one of how we are to go about establishing that the works in question *are* works of art in the face of worries, if not downright skeptical objections, to the contrary.[6] Again, it can be no accident that one of the most tempting theories of art to emerge in this period was George Dickie's Institutional Theory of Art, which, if nothing else, was perfectly suited to perform such a service for the works of Dada and its heritage.

This, of course, is not said in order to claim that in previous times there never arose the question of how to identify something as a work of art. The explosion of romanticism certainly anticipates some of the quandaries of the age of the avant-garde. And there are other precedents. My point is simply that in the age of the avant-garde, the question of how one recognizes and establishes something to be a work of art is irresistible in a way that is reflected by the concerns of contemporary philosophy of art. Moreover, the question of how one establishes that something is a work of art gives rise to a deeper philosophical vexation: Are there indeed reliable methods for establishing or identifying something to be a work of art?

Another issue that might be introduced by asking "What is art?" may be the question of whether art has an essence. Here, following T. J. Diffey,[7] by essence I mean some general, shared feature or features of artworks that are useful to mark but that are not shared by artworks alone. When Plato and Aristotle agree that poetry and paintings are imitations, they point to what they take to be such an essence, though this feature, despite its significance for art as they knew it, was also shared, even in their own times, by childhood games of emulation. In this sense, an essence may be a necessary condition, and it is my suspicion that art theory before the age of the avant-garde was concerned primarily to isolate only such conditions, especially where identifying these shed illumination on artistic practices. To say that art is essentially communication or that it is essentially historical is to claim that art has an essence in this sense, which is a matter of pointing to an informative general feature of art without maintaining that it is a feature that uniquely pertains to art. When, for example, George Dickie says that an artwork is of a kind designed for public presentation,[8] he marks an essential feature of art, though neither essential public presentability, nor historicity, nor communicativeness is a property of art alone. In asking "What is art?" we may be introducing the question of whether art has a noteworthy essence or necessary condition – a question that, if answered affirmatively, will be followed by a specification of what that general feature might be. Moreover, citation of that feature need not be proposed for the sake of saying something unique about art, but only as something that helps us understand art – that points us in the direction of something we have missed or helps us get out of some problem into which we have backed ourselves. Again, much previous art theory might be read profitably as presenting answers of this general sort.

Third, "What is art?" may also be taken as a request for a *real* definition in terms of necessary conditions that are jointly sufficient. This is the interpretation of the question that Morris Weitz attributed to the conversation of art theory that preceded his neo-Wittgensteinian de-Platonization of it. Whether Weitz's diagnosis of the tradition was an historically accurate conjecture is open to debate. However, the particular spin that Weitz put on the question – construing it as a request for a real definition – is the one that subsequent theorists, like George Dickie, have taken to be the most "natural" interpretation (though it pays to remark here that it may only seem natural in the context of a debate where Weitz and the other neo-Wittgensteinians had laid down the dialectical challenge that it cannot be done).

These three issues – Is there a reliable method for identifying art? Does art have an essence? and Does art have a real definition? – are the primary questions that may be introduced by asking "What is art?" However, there are two other questions worth mentioning, even though I will have little to say about them. They involve requests for information about the importance of art as a human activity, which some theorists, though not I, regard as inextricably linked with what I have identified as our three primary questions.[9] These questions – which I think of as secondary – are as follows. First: Why is art valuable as a human activity? Here we might be told that art is a cognitive instrument or a means of moral education. Moreover, this request can be made in an even more demanding manner. Specifically, we may be asked what makes art *uniquely* valuable – that is, What is the peculiar value of art in contradistinction to the values available in every other arena of human activity?

Now it seems to me that the reason all these questions – ranging from "How do we tell something is art?" to "What is the peculiar value of art?" – have been lumped together is that there is an underlying philosophical dream such that, ideally, all the relevant answers in this neighborhood should fit into a tidy theoretical package.

Consider the primary variants of our question: Is there a reliable method for identifying artworks? Does art have (some) essential feature(s)? Can art be defined? The philosophical dream to which I have alluded wants to answer each of these questions affirmatively, in such a way that each affirmation supplies the grounds for subsequent affirmations. That is, an affirmative answer to the question of whether art has any essential features may be registered in the expectation that these can be worked into a real definition such that the relevant necessary conditions are jointly sufficient for identifying something as an artwork. Thus, the definition functions as the reliable standard for assessing whether or not something is a work of art.

Of course, there is an even more ambitious dream in these precincts, one that hopes not only to link up the answers to our primary questions but to link up our secondary answers as well. That is, there is the expectation that we shall be able to say why art is important, even uniquely important, in the course of defining art. Here there is the conviction that, among the necessary conditions listed in our definition, there will be some feature or features whose citation makes it evident that art has value or even a unique value. An example of this variation of the dream is Monroe Beardsley's aesthetic definition of art, in which affording aesthetic interest is related to the value of art as a human activity. That Beardsley supposes that some such account of the value of art should be part of the definition of art, moreover, is indicated by Beardsley's criticism of the Institutional Theory of Art in terms of George Dickie's failure to say anything about the "pervasive human needs that it is the peculiar role of art to serve."[10]

Stated in its most ambitious form – that an identifying, real definition of art will yield an account of what is uniquely valuable about art – the dream seems exactly that. For, save embattled defenders of aesthetic theories of art, the remaining consensus is that art may serve a motley of purposes and, in consequence, that it possesses a motley assortment of values. But even the less ambitious dream – that artworks might be identified by means of a real definition that comprises sets of necessary conditions that are jointly sufficient – is dubious. For as the neo-Wittgensteinian's – Weitz, Kennick, perhaps Ziff, and others – maintain, it is at least possible to answer what I have called our three primary questions in ways that are independent of each other. That is, there may be no reason to suppose that the relevant answers dovetail – indeed, they may come apart.[11]

For example, it is possible to deny that a real definition of art is possible, as Weitz did,[12] and to deny that artworks share any general features or essences, as Kennick did,[13] and still argue that we do possess reliable methods for identifying or establishing that a given object or production is a work of art. That is, we may be able to identify candidates as art even if art lacks an essence. After all, we manage to identify a great many other things for which we lack a real definition. Of course, the leading candidate for a reliable method of art identification – the one that the neo-Wittgensteinians championed – was the notion of family resemblance. In fact, it may be the only well-known alternative to definition to be found in the literature so far, though, by way of preview, I should say that I plan to introduce narration as another alternative.

On one variation of the family resemblance approach, we begin with a set of cases of acknowledged or paradigmatic artworks. Given a new candidate for membership in the set, one identifies it or establishes it to be a work of art by determining whether it is sufficiently similar to our starting cases in a number of respects. This resemblance to our paradigm is called a family resemblance. Establishing that something bears a family resemblance to our paradigms, or to works whose resemblance to our paradigms has been previously recognized, is enough to establish a new candidate to be an artwork. However, whether the family resemblance approach is a reliable method is subject to a number of challenges.

The first objection takes note of the logic of resemblance. Starting with a handful of paradigms, we can identify a second generation of what Arthur Danto has called "affines" – things that share discernible similarities with our paradigms.[14] Yet these affines also have a great many properties that are not shared with our initial group insofar as things that are similar to each other in some respects also differ from each other in further respects. Consequently, a third generation of affines can be constructed that bears a large number of resemblances to the second generation but few to the first. Clearly, in the fourth and fifth generations of affines, we can get very far away from the package of properties possessed by the first generation. In fact, in short order, since it is also a feature of the logic of resemblance that everything resembles everything else in some respect, enough generations of affines of the sort that I have in mind can be arrayed so that anything can be said to bear a family resemblance to either an artistic paradigm or an affine thereof.

Now this may not seem to be a particularly bothersome consequence in a world that has been shaken by Dada. However, the family resemblance method seems liable to identify anything as art for the wrong reason. A given snow shovel might be recognized to be art as it is in the case of Duchamp's *In Advance of a Broken Arm;* but I cannot claim that my snow shovel, which resembles Duchamp's in a hundred ways, is art on that basis. Perhaps my snow shovel could be made into a work of art – maybe as a deadpan counterexample to the family resemblance method. But it would require more than resemblance for that. In such a case, it would require what Danto calls a "background of theory."[15]

One may worry whether the preceding demolition of the family resemblance approach has not proceeded too hastily. For the family resemblance approach depends upon our starting with some paradigmatic exemplars, and one might suspect that the use of paradigms here could provide some constraints that would halt the headlong rush to the conclusion that everything is art. For example, the relevant resemblances, which this approach invokes, are said to be family resemblances. So perhaps that places suitable restraints upon what resemblances can count in the process of establishing that a candidate in question is art. That is, the collection of paradigms is a family, and any candidate that is to resemble them in a family way must share whatever property (or properties) makes the collection a family. But, of course, it has long been a criticism of the family resemblance approach that the notion of "family" that figures so prominently in its name really performs no work in the theory.[16] Nor is this an accidental oversight, given the other commitments of the most radical neo-Wittgensteinians. For if there were criteria of family resemblance or criteria for what sort of resemblances count as family resemblances, then the neo-Wittgensteinians would appear to be committed to the concession that there are at least necessary conditions for art. And that is *not* a concession they will make.

At this point, one attempted rejoinder might be to say that the neo-Wittgensteinians need not rely upon the notion of necessary conditions in order to cash in the idea of family resemblance, but instead need only claim that a family resemblance to our paradigmatic artworks is a resemblance by virtue of correspondence to one or more members of a disjunctive set of the paradigmatic artmaking properties of our paradigmatic artworks – that is, those properties by virtue of which the artworks in question belong to our collection of paradigms. In other words, our collection of paradigmatic artworks yields a disjunctive set of paradigmatic artmaking properties; and, so, a family resemblance is a similarity to the paradigms in terms of one or more paradigmatic artmaking properties. Thus, not just anything could become art, because in order to be art a candidate would have to possess one or more of a disjunctive set of paradigmatic artmaking properties.

However, this maneuver is not open to the neo-Wittgensteinian because such a theorist is committed to the view that one cannot fix a paradigmatic set of artmaking properties. And if such a set cannot be fixed, then we are back to sorting candidates in terms of resemblance rather than family resemblance. And that, combined with the principle that everything resembles everything else in some respect, will leave intact the *reductio ad absurdum* initiated four paragraphs earlier.

The preceding dilemma demonstrates the inadequacy of the family resemblance approach as a reliable method for identifying artworks. And this, along with the recognition that, *pace* Weitz, a definition of art, properly framed, need be no impediment to artistic creativity, encouraged a return to the dream of finding an identifying definition of art in terms of sets of necessary conditions that are jointly sufficient. This drama has been played out most explicitly with reference to Dickie's institutional theory of art.[17] Yet, to date, despite the voluminous exchanges on the topic, the prospects for securing a real definition of art along institutional lines seem slim.

George Dickie's most recent version of an institutional theory is advanced in his monograph *The Art Circle*. The core of the theory is a definition that proposes that "a work of art is of a kind created to be presented to an artworld public."[18] This definition, in turn, is elucidated by the following four definitions: "A public is a set of persons the members of which are prepared in some degree to understand an object which is presented to them"; "An artworld system is a framework for the presentation of a work of art by an artist to an artworld public"; "An artist is a person who participates with understanding in the making of an artwork"; and "The artworld is the totality of all artworld systems."[19] The first thing to note about this set of definitions is that it is circular insofar as the concept of a work of art is material to the definition of the artist, which, of course, is presupposed by the definition of an artworld system that, in turn, supplies the basis for identifying an artworld public upon which the very notion of a work of art depends. Of course, noting this circularity is no news. Dickie himself calls attention to it, arguing that the definition is circular because the concept of art, like other cultural concepts, is inflected. Perhaps, however, rather than saying that the concept of art requires a special sort of inflected definition, it might be more to the point to admit that this reformulation of the institutional theory of art has just given up the aim of producing a real definition of art where that is understood in terms of the challenge that the neo-Wittgensteinians advanced.

Moreover, it seems to me, there is a real question as to whether the new institutional theory is really a theory of *art*. For the inflected set of definitions, though mentioning "art" at crucial points, could be filled in just as easily with the names of other coordinated, communicative practices like philosophy or wisecracking. For example, we might say that "a work of philosophy is a discourse of a kind created to be presented to a philosophyworld public" or that "a wisecrack is a discourse of a kind created to be presented to a jokeworld public" while also adjusting the related, elucidating, inflected propositions so that the structure they picture is analogous in terms of functional positions to the artworld and its systems.

But then the question arises as to whether George Dickie has really said anything specific about art, as opposed to merely producing something like the necessary framework of coordinated, communicative practices of a certain level of complexity, where such practices cannot be identified in terms of their content.

Art is an example of such a practice. But in illuminating certain necessary structural features of such practices, Dickie has not really told us anything about art *qua* art. Rather, he has implied that art belongs to the genus of complex, coordinated, communicative practices, and he has shown us by example some of the features that such practices presuppose by way of interrelated structural functions. Undoubtedly, such an analysis is not without interest. But it is not what disputants in the conversation of analytic philosophy expected in the name of a definition.

Another way of making this point might be to agree that Dickie's new version of the institutional theory does tell us something about the necessary conditions of art insofar as art is the product of a coordinated social practice. But the necessary conditions in question are features shared also by social practices other than art. This is not to say that the reformulation is uninformative. It points in the direction of a social framework for artmaking that many philosophers may have heretofore ignored. However, if at best George Dickie can claim only to have elucidated some necessary conditions for artmaking of the sort shared by comparable coordinated social practices, then he should give up talking about defining art. For he is no longer playing that game according to its original rules, and it only confuses matters to pretend that a real definition is still in the offing.[20]

Dickie's response to the failure of family resemblance as a reliable means for identifying artworks was to return – undoubtedly egged on by Weitz's challenge – to the project of framing a real, identifying definition of art. However, there may be another lesson to be derived from the neo-Wittgensteinian episode and another response to the failure of the family resemblance method. We may provisionally accept the neo-Wittgensteinian suggestion in one of its weaker forms – to wit: that a real definition of art is at least unnecessary – and agree that we nevertheless have reliable means at our disposal for establishing whether or not a given candidate is an artwork. Such a method will not be the family resemblance approach, of course, since the objections of George Dickie and others do seem pretty compelling. However, the refutation of that particular approach does not preclude that there may be other methods for establishing that something is art and that these other methods are not susceptible to the objections leveled at the family resemblance approach. The particular method I have in mind is historical narration of the sort that I will characterize in the next section of the present essay.[21]

But before turning to that analysis, let me summarize my argumentative strategy in light of the framework set forth in the preceding pages. I intend to answer the question "What is art?" (where that question is taken to pertain to answering affirmatively whether we have a reliable method for identifying art) by specifying the nature of that method. My proposal is that we do have a reliable method for identifying a candidate to be an artwork and that that method is historical narration.[22]

Concerning the question of whether art may be characterized by means of a real definition, I remain agnostic: not only have George Dickie's attempts to provide one failed, but, as I shall try to show in a later section of this essay, recent attempts by Jerrold Levinson and Arthur Danto appear deeply problematic as well. Needless to say, such failures do not prove that there is no essential definition of art. But since I maintain that we do not really need such a definition, our agnosticism is not of the anxious variety. For the question of whether art can be defined is "academic" in the strong sense of the term, since artworks can be identified by other means.

NARRATION AND IDENTIFICATION

As previously suggested, a major impulse for a great deal of what we call art theory derives from the practical pressure of adjudicating momentous shifts within the practice of art. This is an historical conjecture. Perhaps some evidence for this conjecture is that the greatest variation in art theories corresponds to the period in Western art history that is marked by the fastest rates of innovation and change. That is, the most seismic shifts in art theory have occurred during what I referred to previously as the age of the avant-garde. Again, this is not said with the intention of denying that in previous epochs major changes called for theoretical accommodation; I claim only that the seminal role of theory in negotiating spiraling historical transitions becomes particularly salient in the age of the avant-garde.

The dialectical conversation of the analytic philosophy of art has unfolded against the backdrop of avant-garde practice. Whether or not this has always been explicitly acknowledged by the major participants in that conversation, it should be clear that developments in the avant-garde have motivated what are identified as the crucial turning points in the dialogue. Implicit in the theories of Clive Bell[23] and R. G. Collingwood[24] are defenses of emerging avant-garde practices – neoimpressionism, on the one hand, and the modernist poetics of Joyce, Stein, and Eliot on the other. Indeed, these theories might be read as an attempt to realign the compass of art in general according to a grid extrapolated from the previously mentioned avant-garde movements. Susanne K. Langer's theory of dance, in turn, might be read as a gloss on the aesthetics of modern dance;[25] while, given the premium they place on innovation and originality, neo-Wittgensteinians would appear to have virtually incorporated the ideals of avant-gardism into their concept of art.

Likewise, George Dickie's initial version of the institutional theory of art requires something like the presupposition that Dada is a central form of artistic practice in order for its intuition pumps (like Walter de Maria's *High Energy Bar*) to work; while Arthur Danto wondered at the end of his "The Last Work of Art: Artworks and Real Things" whether his essay was not just another avant-garde artwork.[26] In any case, Danto has freely admitted that the historical conditions for initiating a philosophy of art, as he construes it, were secured by the avant-garde production of what he calls "indiscernibles," such as Warhol's famous Brillo boxes.[27]

Moreover, the linkage between art theory and avant-garde practice is evident outside the canonical progression of analytic philosophers of art. Russian formalism was intimately connected with Russian futurist poetry,[28] while the recent influential essays of Barthes and Foucault concerning the death of the author promote the explicit modernist ideals of cited authors, such as Mallarmé and Beckett, as the conditions of all writing.[29]

The recurring correspondence between developments in art theory and developments in the avant-garde supplies a clue to the aims of art theory. Though art theory may appear to be a purely abstract activity, it, like other forms of theory, has a point and a purpose within the tradition and practice from which it has emerged.[30] Stated bluntly, the task of art theory in the age of the avant-garde has been, in fact, to provide the means for explaining how the myriad modern subversions of traditional expectations about art – or at least some subset thereof – could count as art. The question "What is art?" as it is posed by the art theorist in the age of the avant-garde has generally, though perhaps in many cases only tacitly, been a question of fitting innovations into the continuum of our artistic practices. That is, on my interpretation of the history of art theory, the task of modern analytic aesthetics has really been one of providing the means for identifying the revolutionary productions of the avant-garde as artworks. Theory does not blossom in a vacuum; it is formulated in a context that shapes its agenda. And the context that motivates theoretical activity in the branch of art theory concerned with the question "What is Art?" is one in which change, transition, or revolution is a central problem.

As noted above, in many cases in the analytic tradition it is said that the answer to the problem is sought in terms of real definitions; however, the family resemblance method has also attracted a vocal minority. So far, neither of these strategies has proven to be entirely satisfactory. So perhaps another approach – the narrative approach – is worth considering.

On my view, the paradigmatic problem that is, in effect, addressed by contemporary art theory is one in which the public is confronted with an object or performance that is presented by an artist but is at odds with the public's expectations about what counts as art. Some, often outraged, members of the public and their critic-representatives charge that the new work is not art; others claim that it is art. The question of whether or not the work is art is then joined, with the burden of proof placed on those who maintain that the new work is art.

How does one go about meeting this challenge? I think that the most common way in which this is accomplished is to tell a story that connects the disputed work x with preceding artmaking contexts in such a way that the production of x can be seen as an intelligible outcome of recognizable processes of thinking and making within the practice.

Typically the question of whether or not x is art arises in a context in which a skeptic fails to see how the object in dispute could have been produced in the network of practices with which she is already familiar – that is, if those practices are to remain the same practices with which she is already familiar. There is a perceived gap, so to speak, between the anomalous avant-garde production x and an already existing body of work with an antecedently acknowledged tradition of making and thinking. In order to defend the status of x as art, the proponent of x must fill in that gap. And the standard way of filling in that gap is to produce a certain type of historical narrative, one that supplies the sequence of activities of thinking and making required to, in a manner of speaking, fill in the distance between a Rembrandt and a readymade.

In order to counter the suspicion that x is not a work of art, the defender of x has to show how x emerged intelligibly from acknowledged practices via the same sort of thinking, acting, decisionmaking, and so on that is already familiar in the practice. This involves telling a certain kind of story about the work in question: namely, a historical narrative of how x came to be produced as an intelligible response to an antecedent art-historical situation about which a consensus with respect to its art status already exists. With a contested work of art what we try to do is place it within a tradition where it becomes more and more intelligible.[31] And the standard way of doing this is to produce an historical narrative.

The paradigmatic situation I have asked you to recall in order to motivate my hypothesis is one in which a work is presented and challenged and in which the challenge is met by means of a narrative. However, equally typical is the situation in which the narrative is told proleptically – that is, told ahead of time in order to forestall an anticipated challenge. This proleptic story may be told or published by an artist, perhaps in the form of a manifesto or an interview, or, more likely, by a critic. Indeed, much of the task of the critic who champions the work in question is to place it in a framework that will render its connections with acknowledged portions of the tradition intelligible.[32]

For example, in order to allay misgivings about a painting by Morris Lewis, Clement Greenberg provides a narrative that connects it to the program of analytical cubism. To a certain extent, the choice of the starting point of the narrative may be strategic. That is, the defender of the disputed work x begins the story with a body of artmaking techniques and purposes that she supposes the target audience acknowledges to be within the artistic tradition. However, in principle, such narratives are always open to being, so to say, pushed back further in time under the pressure of skeptical questioning. Thus, if analytical cubism is not a pragmatically effective starting point for defending the painting by Lewis, one may have to tell the narrative that gets us from impressionism or even realism to analytical cubism before one tells the narrative from analytical cubism to Lewis.

Nevertheless, though these narratives may be "strategic" in the sense in which I have just conceded, this does not entail that they are arbitrary or imposed in the way that historical constructivists maintain. For there is no reason to suspect that the historical connections that figure in our narratives are not literally truth-tracking.

Obviously, this method for identifying or establishing a proffered work x as an artwork presupposes some body of work and associated practices that are agreed to be artistic by the various parties involved in a given debate. That is true, but it is not a problem for the narrative approach to identifying artworks. For example, it makes no sense to charge the narrative approach with circularity on the basis of these assumptions. For circularity is a defect in real definitions, and the narrative approach to identifying art does not entail definitions. Narratives are not definitions.

Furthermore, presupposing that we approach our problem knowing some examples of artworks and their associated practices is an assumption made not only by the narrative approach but by its competitors as well. Clearly, the family resemblance approach makes such assumptions in presuming that we can designate a set of paradigmatic artworks. Likewise, George Dickie admits that knowledge of art as we know it is requisite for mobilizing his conception of the art circle; at the same time, definitionists in general must allow that we have some core knowledge of art and its practices in order to frame their theories and to weigh the force of counterexamples. Consequently, the presupposition that the narrative approach assumes – that there is already some knowledge about art and its practices – should be no obstacle to its potential as a means for identifying art.

Previously I claimed that the question "What is art?" serves as an umbrella under which a series of questions might be advanced, including these: Is there a reliable method for identifying artworks? Does art have any essential or general features? and Can art be defined? The narrative approach answers the question about whether there is a reliable method for identifying art affirmatively. That is, the narrative method is one reliable method. On the question of whether art can be defined, we are, as noted, agnostic; like many agnostics in the realm of religion, though, we are not tortured by our suspense in this matter. For if our earlier historical conjecture is correct, if what drives art theory is the quest for a reliable means of identifying artworks, then the narrative method satisfies our needs in a way that makes answering the question of art's definition academic. Whether art has a definition may remain a question of some marginal philosophical interest; but art theory can discharge its duties without answering it.

I have supplied answers to two of the three primary questions sketched earlier, but the issue remains as to where the narrative approach stands on the matter of whether art has any essential or general features. Here the version of the narrative approach that I wish to defend delivers an affirmative answer. Though I am convinced that art has more than one essential or general feature, for the purpose of advancing my narrative approach it is necessary only to argue that art has at least one necessary feature: historicity.

Art, as R. A. Sharpe nicely puts it, is an affair of ancestors, descendants, and postulants.[33] Each artist is trained in a tradition of techniques and purposes to which her own work, in one way or another, aims to be an addition.[34] The artist learns the tradition, or at least crucial parts of it, in the course of learning certain procedures of production, along with their attending folkways, self-understandings, rules of thumb, associated values, and even theories. In producing artworks, the artist remains in conversation with her teachers – sometimes repeating, sometimes improving upon, and sometimes disputing their achievements. But in every instance, the artist is always involved in extending the tradition; typically, even the artist who repudiates large portions of it does so in order to *return* it to what she perceives to be its proper direction.

Alongside the artist's traditions of production, there are also traditions of reception – that is, traditions of appreciating and understanding works of art on the part of audiences – that include paradigms for looking at, listening to, and interpreting works of art. However, such traditions are not entirely disjunct from those of production, if only because artists are audiences as well. That is, they attend to their own works and to those of others in the ways provided by our traditions of reception and, in consequence, these artists then produce works governed by the internalized norms and purposes that they, the artists, have derived from our practices of appreciation and understanding. Of course, to a lesser extent, especially in modern society, audiences are also introduced to the artist's side of the exchange, typically receiving some rudimentary training in some art-making practice *along with* training in various practices of appreciation (e.g., interpreting stories for their morals).

The coordinated traditions of production and reception provide artists, audiences, audience/artists, and artist/audiences with the means for orienting their activities. Understanding a work of art, in large measure, is a matter of situating it, of placing it in a tradition. This may not be immediately apparent to some because the degree to which historical sensitivities, categories, and concepts are enmeshed in our art education blinds us to the influential, sometimes constitutive, role that they play in our appreciative responses. People deploy far more art-historical knowledge than they are often self-consciously aware of deploying. But even the simple identification of a drama as Shakespearean or a film as a silent comedy mobilizes historical knowledge that, in turn, shapes appreciation in terms of appropriate modes of response, including the postulation of relevant comparisons, expectations, and norms. Producing art, on the other hand, also, often unavoidably, involves awareness of the tradition – awareness of precedents and predecessors, of available techniques and purposes, of influences and the anxieties thereof,[35] of audience expectations, and of the historically rooted reactions that are apt to be engendered by subverting such expectations at a given moment.

Art has an inexpugnable historical dimension because it is a practice with a tradition. Moreover, this tradition is taught historically. Artists study their predecessors, their aims, and their breakthroughs in order to prepare themselves for their own contribution to the tradition. And the audience learns to appreciate and to interpret the productions of artists in terms of period concepts, in terms of generational strife and competition between artists, in terms of evolutionary solutions to preexisting problems as well as through historically grounded standards such as innovative/conservative, original/unoriginal, revolutionary/retrograde, not to mention the very idea of the avant-garde. Without art history, there is no practice of artmaking as we know it, nor is there the possibility of understanding that practice to any appreciable extent. In this sense, history is a necessary condition for art; and, thus, art has at least one essential feature.

Moreover, the assertion that art has this essential feature is connected to the strategy – historical narration – that I advocate as a reliable method for identifying art. If understanding a work of art involves placing it within a tradition, then challenging a particular claimant amounts to the charge that it cannot be placed in any intelligible way within the tradition. Meeting that challenge, then, is a matter of placing the claimant within the tradition. The challenge, if unwarranted, is a failure of historical understanding. Deflecting the challenge involves delivering historical understanding. And the most straightforward way of supplying historical understanding is historical narration.

Of course, I have said that a historical narrative will do the job if the challenge is unwarranted. This allows that a challenge may be warranted, which, at the very least, effectively implies that there is no adequate historical narrative available to connect the work in question to the tradition.

The perplexity that the work of the avant-garde provokes in the skeptic is a function of the skeptic's inability to discern a plausible connection between the work in dispute and the rest of the tradition. The task of historical narration in this context is to make such a connection visible to the skeptic. Historical narration is an appropriate means for establishing whether or not the work under fire is art because it is a way of showing whether or not the work is part of a developing tradition.

So far, a great deal of weight has been placed on the role of historical narratives in identifying art. However, little has been said about the nature of these narratives. At this juncture, then, it will be useful to characterize the relevant features of the species of historical narrative that we deploy in order to identify and establish a claimant to be a work of art.

The first and perhaps most obvious thing to say about such narratives is that insofar as they are *historical* narratives, rather than fictional narratives, they are *committed* to reporting sequences of events and states of affairs accurately or truthfully. That is, in order to succeed fully in establishing the claim that a given work is a work of art by means of a historical narrative requires at the very least that the narrative be true. This means that the reports of events and states of affairs that constitute the narrative must be true and that the asserted connections between those events and states of affairs must obtain. If it is an ingredient in the narrative that x influenced y, then it must be true that x influenced y. If the narrative in question is at best plausible, given our state of knowledge, then it must be plausible that x influenced y.

The historical narratives that identify art are, among other things, *ideally* accurate reports of sequences of events and states of affairs. That they are accurate reports of sequences indicates that they respect a certain temporal order. A narrative is a time-ordered series of events and states of affairs. This does not mean that the order of exposition in the narrative must mirror the order of the chronology to which it refers, but only that the actual chronology of events be available from the narrative. This is consonant with the requirement that the narratives be truthful, since in order to be truthful the narrative should not rearrange the chronology of events. But this requirement does not follow from the demand for truthfulness, since the requirement for time-ordering would be violated where it is impossible to discern the actual sequence of events and not only where the proposed time-ordering is false.

Thus far we have said that the relevant type of narrative aspires to be an accurate report of a time-ordered sequence of events. In other words, it must be at least what is often called a chronicle.[36] But more is required for the sort of narrative we need. The kind of narrative we are looking for has an explanatory role to play: it has to explain how an anomalous work in the present is part of the previously acknowledged practices of artmaking. Before undertaking a narrative of this sort, we already know where it must end in order to be successful. Specifically, it needs to end with a presentation of the work or works, or the performance or performances, whose status is contested. The task of the narrative is to show that this event is the result or outcome of a series of intelligible decisions, choices, and actions that originate in and emerge from earlier, already acknowledged practices of artmaking. That is, the narrative must represent the presentation of the contested work as part of a whole process that can be recognized to be artistic.[37] Moreover, though it may be controversial to claim that all historical narratives have unified subjects, the historical narratives discussed here will have such a subject insofar as they are organized around the dominant purpose of explaining why some contested work is art.[38]

The endpoint of such a narrative – its moment of closure, if you will – is the presentation or production of the contested work. On the other hand, the *beginning* of the story sets the stage by establishing the art-historical context of the work – generally by describing a set of prevailing artmaking practices about which there is consensus that the works produced in that context are bona fide art. Pragmatic considerations may determine how far back into history the story must go in order to be convincing for given audiences. However, wherever the story begins, it must be connected to the subsequent events recounted in terms of real historical relations such as, for example, causation and influence. Pragmatically, the choice of where to begin such a narrative may be relative to an audience's consensus about what is indisputably art, but whether the states of affairs are part of the series of events recounted is not arbitrary. And, perhaps needless to say, I am presuming that there will always be some earlier point in time about which there is consensus about acknowledged artmaking practices.

By now, we have some sense of where the kinds of historical narratives in question begin and end. But what constitutes the middle of the story or, as I would prefer to call it, the complication?

The narrative begins by describing an acknowledged artmaking context. For simplicity's sake, let us imagine that there is consensus about the art status of the artistic practices that exist just prior to the appearance of the disputed work. In this case, the story begins with a sketch of the relevant artworld at the time the artist, whose work is contested, enters it. Thus, if our subject is the work of Isadora Duncan – of which Vaslav Nijinsky charged, "[H]er performance is spontaneous and cannot be taught. … [I]t is not art"[39] – then we are likely to begin our story with an account of the turn-of-the-century theatrical dance scene in the West that was dominated by academic ballet.

The complication in the story then emerges as we outline the artist's assessment of the artworld as she finds it. Of course, an artist may assess a given artworld to be unproblematic and simply go on to produce works in the same manner to which she has become accustomed.[40] But then the story is a very short one. However, in the case of innovative work of the sort that is likely to cause dispute, the artist is apt to assess the existing artworld as requiring change or alteration either in the direction of solving some problem internal to existing artworld practices or in the direction of radically reorienting the project of the relevant artworld.[41]

Duncan, for example, assessed the ballet-dominated dance scene in late-nineteenth-century America to be tired, rigid, and stifling – features she associated with the Old World. In contrast, she searched for forms that were spontaneous and natural (by her lights) and would serve to emblematize the Whitmanesque strains of her vision of the American spirit.[42]

The complication in our narratives commences as we introduce the artist's conception of the context in which she finds herself. The story gets rolling when we establish that the artist is resolved to change that context in one way or another. In noting the artist's conception of the situation and her resolve to change it, we elucidate the impetus of her assessment of the need or opportunity for change. Here the impetus may come from pressure within the artworld or from concerns derived from broader cultural contexts, or from a mixture of the two. In Duncan's case, for example, the aim of rejuvenating dance as well as the impulse to align it with romantic aesthetics might be thought of as imperatives internal to the artworld, while the desire to forge a style of dance with a distinctly American identity implemented a broader cultural politics, one heralded, for example, in Emerson's essay "The American Scholar."

Once we have established the artist's resolve to change artworld practices, and once we have shown how it is intelligible that someone in that context might come to have the resolve in question, then we go on to demonstrate how the artist's choice of the means to her end makes sense in the historical context under discussion. That is, we show how the means adopted would be deemed appropriate for securing the artist's purposes given the alternatives the situation afforded. Or, in other words, we must show that what the artist did in the existing context was a way of achieving her purposes. This involves sketching the situation in such a way that it becomes evident why certain artistic choices make sense given the values, associations, and consequences that are likely to attach to them in the pertinent historical context.[43]

Thus, to return to the case of Isadora Duncan, we continue her story by noting the way in which her choice of the bare foot as her medium contravened the constrained pointwork of ballet in a way that within the presiding cultural framework would be associated with freedom, spontaneity, and naturalness. Similar observations might be made about her choice of loose-fitting tunics in opposition to tight ballet corsets.

In order to show that the disputed work of an artist is art, we must show in the course of our narrative that the artist's assessment of the initiating situation and the resolve she formulated in response to that assessment were intelligible. To do this we need to show that the artist had a reasonable interpretation of certain general understandings of the purposes of art that were abroad and alive in her culture. These general understandings include such purposes as the following: that art is expressive, or that it challenges complacent moral views, or that it is about itself. It is the artist's reasonable interpretation of these general purposes that ground her assessment and her resolve. In the case of Duncan, her claim to return to the natural expressivity of Greek art situated her revolution in recognizable artistic purposes.

Once it is established, by narrating the conditions that give rise to her assessments, that the artist's resolve is intelligible, we go on to show that the techniques, procedures, and strategies she enlists are effective ones for realizing her purposes, given the lay of the artworld – that is, given the alternative, available strategies and their associated values.[44] Finally, this elaboration of choices and rationales – including, possibly, a citation of the artist's experimentation with different alternatives – eventuates in the production of the contested work. My claim is that if through historical narration the disputed work can be shown to be the result of reasonable or appropriate choices and actions that are motivated by intelligible assessments that support a resolution to change the relevant artworld context for the sake of some recognizable aim of art, then, all things being equal, the disputed work is an artwork.[45]

In theory, these stories sound immensely complicated; in practice they are not. For example, gathering together the fragments, recited so far, of the Isadora Duncan story, when someone denies that her barefoot prancing and posing in *Chopin Waltzes* is art, we could tell the following narrative:

> Turn-of-the-century theatrical dance in the West, excluding Russia, was dominated by forms of academic ballet that contemporary commentators, like Bernard Shaw, felt had become tired and cliched. From Isadora Duncan's point of view, the problem was that ballet was an ossified discipline, mechanical and uninspired. As a child of the New World, she saw in it all the vices Americans attributed to Europe. It was artificial, lifeless, and formal. It was the epitome of the Old World. Duncan aspired to new dance forms that were spontaneous and natural. She found her sources in disparate places, including social dancing, physical culture, gymnastics, and the Delstarte deportment movement. From 1904 to 1914, Duncan was at the peak of her career. She replaced the toeshoe and the corset of ballet with the bare foot and the loose tunic. And her ebb-and-flow movement in pieces like *Chopin Waltzes* was designed to recall the natural rhythms of waves. At the same time, the use of running and walking in her choreography exchanged the measured and predetermined cadence of academic ballet for the more personally inflected gesture. Undoubtedly her conception of art as a means to individual expression derived as much from romantic poetry as it did from the tradition of American individualism. But Duncan did not see herself as creating something completely new. She conceived of herself as returning the dance to the founding values of naturalness which she identified with Greek art. Thus, with *Chopin Waltzes,* Duncan was able to solve the problem of the stagnation of theatrical dance by repudiating the central features of the dominant ballet and by reimagining an earlier ideal of dance.

Narratives like this can be expanded in many directions. Further details may be included about the initial art-historical context: more background on the artist's influences, assessments, and decisions can be added, along with further descriptions of central and/or exemplary events, experiences, and experiments that contributed to the artist's resolutions and actions. Such narratives may appear seamless in the hands of an accomplished art critic, but they have a great deal of structure. So, to return from simple practice to abstract theory, let me try to capture that structure with a formula:

> x is an identifying narrative only if x is (1) an accurate and (2) time-ordered report of a sequence of events and states of affairs concerning (3) a unified subject (generally the production of a disputed work)[46] that (4) has a beginning, a complication, and an end, where (5) the end is explained as the outcome of the beginning and the complication, where (6) the beginning involves the description of an initiating, acknowledged art-historical context, and where (7) the complication involves tracing the adoption of a series of actions and alternatives as appropriate means to an end on the part of a person who has arrived at an intelligible assessment of the art-historical context in such a way that she is resolved to change (or reenact)[47] it in accordance with recognizable and live purposes of the practice.

Undoubtedly some clarificatory remarks about this formula are in order. My point has been that art theory has been driven by the question of how we identify innovative works as art, especially in contexts where such works are subject to dispute. I claim that the way in which this is done is by historical narratives of the sort we call "identifying narratives." An adequate identifying narrative establishes that a work in question emerged in recognizable ways from an acknowledged artworld context through an intelligible process of assessment, resolution, and action.

If we review the conditions I have advanced for an identifying narrative, it is probably pretty apparent that the explanatory force of this sort of narrative relies on the fact – most evident in my characterization of the complication – that underlying this narrative is the structure of practical reasoning.[48] The artist's assessment leads to a resolution, which leads to the choice from alternatives of means to that end, which choices then ensue in the action we want explained – the production of the disputed work. If in our reconstruction of this process we are able to show that the assessments, resolutions, and choices were intelligible in context, we are well on our way to showing that the work in question is an artwork.

It is not my contention that the explanatory power of *all* historical narratives rests on an underlying structure of practical reasoning, but only that the explanatory power of many historical narratives, including identifying narratives, does so. That many narratives are similarly based in the structure of practical reasoning should be noncontroversial. Think of the degree to which most popular narrative films, like *Terminator 2,* are founded almost exclusively on the problem/solution structure. That it should turn out that identifying narratives are also of this sort would seem to follow from a natural interpretation of the question that motivates them. That is, when confronted with an anomalous production that forces the question of whether it is art, a natural path to the answer is to hypothesize why someone would, in a given context, produce such an object for presentation to an artworld audience. And answering that question is a matter of reconstructing a process of intelligible assessment, resolution, choice, and action.

Though the example I have developed of the identifying narrative is relatively simple, it is easy to envisage more complex, expanded identifying narratives. Identifying narratives may include "embedded" narratives – for example, identifying narratives within identifying narratives dealing with cases where certain avant-garde experiments prove unsatisfactory (from the artist's point of view) until the final production of the disputed work. And identifying narratives can be "enchained" – that is, several identifying narratives may be arrayed "back to back," as in our example concerning the Morris Lewis painting.[49]

Furthermore, though the reliance on practical reasoning seems to restrict identifying narratives exclusively to the productions of individuals, there really is no reason why identifying narratives cannot be extended to movements. That is, not only may we mobilize identifying narratives to say why Richard Long's huddle of rocks called *Cornwall Circle* is art, but we may also employ such narratives to say why movements like Dada, given the Dadaists' assessments and resolutions, confronted the artworld with certain objects and antics. Ultimately, such narratives may have to be cashed in with reference to the activities of specific artists. But if that constraint is understood, there is no problem in depicting a movement in terms of its corporate assessments, resolutions, and choices when we explain why the movement in question produces the kind of objects it does.

One objection to the narrative approach might be that there are intelligible processes of assessment, resolution, and choice in artworld contexts that do not issue in artworks. Thus, identifying narratives of certain objects and performances might be told of productions that are not art. In the lore of film history, for example, the story is told that as a result of their heated and long-standing debate about the nature of film montage, Sergei Eisenstein named his dog "Pudovkin" in dishonor of his rival V. I. Pudovkin. In this, Eisenstein was not some sort of precursor of William Wegman. Eisenstein was not turning his dog into an artwork. He meant to insult his competitor Pudovkin. But surely a true story could be told about the way in which Eisenstein, in the context of an artistic debate, came to an assessment that resulted in the naming of his dog Pudovkin as a means of expressing his resolution that the "linkage" version of montage (Pudovkin's version) be discarded. Does this show that Eisenstein's dog was a work of art? How can the narrative approach keep dogs out of the artworld?

But, of course, we do not really want to keep dogs out of the artworld *simpliciter*. We only want to keep Eisenstein's dog out of the Soviet filmworld in particular and out of the pre-World War II Soviet artworld in general. In order to do so, it seems that we need to add to our account the constraint that the thinking and making that our identifying narratives reconstruct be localized to activities occurring within recognizable artworld systems of presentation: that is, artforms, media, and genres that are available to the artist in question. Thus, Eisenstein's naming of the dog Pudovkin, though a creative act by an artist, is not counted among the accomplishments of the golden age of Soviet art because the relevant thinking and

acting was not transacted in the context of a recognizable artworld system of presentation. Surely the dog was not a film or a poem. Soviet Russia before World War
II simply lacked a structure or convention of presentation in which Eisenstein's dog
could – through an act of christening – become an artwork.

To say that the solution to this problem is that identifying narratives be
restricted to thinking and making within recognizable artworld systems of presentation may appear simply to move the problem up a notch. But I would prefer to
say that what it does is move the *solution* up a notch. The putative problem with
relying on recognizable systems of artworld presentation is this: How are we to
identify those systems? Here I feel we can say that, for the most part, there is an
acknowledged consensus about a large body of available artworld systems of presentation in our culture, just as there is a large body of objects that we agree are
art. In most cases, the question of whether the relevant thinking and making transpired in such a system can be settled straightforwardly. Of course, we can also
point to cases in which there are disputes about whether or not a putative system
of presentation is an artworld system. The issue then becomes a matter of how one
identifies a system of presentation as a recognizable artworld system that is available to the artist in question.

Not surprisingly, perhaps, my answer to the question of how we go about
establishing that certain presentational systems are artworld systems is "by means
of historical narration."

Novel artworld systems of presentation do not simply appear on the landscape
by magic or by acts of nature. They are evolved from preexisting artistic practices
by their proponents through self-conscious processes of thinking and making.
Early filmmakers succeeded in turning a new technology into a recognizable artworld system of presentation by initially adapting it as an effective means for discharging the preexisting purposes of already acknowledged arts such as theater,
painting, the short story, and the novel. Establishing that film was an artworld presentation system is a matter of explaining how the choices of early filmmakers
flowed in a recognizable manner from the intelligible assessments and resolutions
they made with respect to the artistic potential of the new technology.

Of course, there are other ways of introducing novel presentational systems. Film
was introduced initially by mimicking existing, acknowledged forms of artmaking
and their purposes. But novel presentational systems have been introduced in living
memory by other strategies. For example, "happenings" seem to have developed as a
reaction to existing artworld practices, notably practices in the precincts of painting
and sculpture. Artists like Allan Kaprow, feeling the constraints of a high modernist
aesthetic that bracketed the exploration of space and content from the canvas and
prized what was called "objecthood" (by the likes of Michael Fried) over participation, invented the happening as the arena in which those preexisting artistic concerns that had been repressed under the Greenbergian dispensation could return.
Similar and indeed related stories can be told about the emergence of conceptual art
and performance art. But in all these cases, the point remains the same. Contested
presentation systems are established to be artworld systems when we can account for

their emergence through narratives of thinking and making that connect them in recognizable ways with preexisting artworld systems and their purposes. Eisenstein's dog Pudovkin was not art because there was no artworld system available to Eisenstein through which he might have implemented an intention to make his dog art. That Eisenstein might have introduced such a system is irrelevant. For that is quite literally *another* story.[50]

LEVINSON AND DANTO

The narrative approach I have developed for identifying art emphasizes the importance of art history. However, it is not the only contemporary approach to look to art history for ways of answering the question "What is art?" Powerful, alternative, historicist theories have been advanced by Jerrold Levinson and Arthur Danto. In this section, I would like to examine the viability of these rival theories.

One difference, of course, between the narrative approach and the theories of Levinson and Danto is that their approaches remain definitional. That is, they attempt to provide the means for identifying and establishing that something is art by means of real definitions.

Levinson's method, which he explicitly calls *defining* art historically,[51] contends that

> X is an artwork at t = df. X is an object of which it is true at t that some person or persons, having the appropriate proprietary right over X, non-passingly intends (or intended) X for regard-as-a-work-of-art – i.e., regard in any way (or ways) in which objects in the extension of 'artwork' prior to t are or were correctly (or standardly) regarded.[52]

This is a definition of art at a given time (t) in terms of what art has been in past times. To be art at t is to be intentionally related in the required way to something that is art prior to t. Furthermore, the intention has to be stable or, as Levinson puts it, "nonpassing." That is, in order to turn something into a work of art it is not enough just to have it flash momentarily through your mind that a certain object might be regarded as an artwork; Duchamp would not have turned a urinal into an artwork if he just momentarily thought that a urinal might become an artwork. The intention required has to be long-lived, firm, and stable; as Levinson puts it, nonpassing. And lastly, the artist in question has to have a proprietary right over the object. This stipulation appears to be intended by Levinson to block the possibility of artists scurrying willy-nilly through the world, christening as art everything in sight.

Levinson's theory contains two necessary conditions – the proprietary condition and the intention condition – that are jointly sufficient. Let us look at these proposals in turn.

The proprietary right condition seems irrelevant to the question of art status. Suppose a well-known artist stole her painting materials – stole the canvas, stole the paints – and painted the work during hours when she was contracted to be doing some other project. Nevertheless, she paints the work with the nonpassing intention that it be regarded in an art-historically, well-precedented mode of appreciation. Such a work might involve illegality, but surely, all things being equal, it would be a work of art.

Questions of legality are independent of art status. There may indeed be certain art forms, like urban graffiti, that require as a condition of class membership that they be illegal – that the graffiti be drawn on objects, like subway cars or tenement walls, over which the artist possesses no proprietary rights.

The motivation behind this condition is Levinson's desire to block certain types of appropriationist or conceptual art. Levinson wants to deny that simply by pointing at something – or by writing out a specification of what an audience is supposed to look at (à la conceptual art) – the artist can turn Marilyn Monroe, the Empire State Building, or a slice of life of a family in Queens into a work of art.

But even if these things cannot be turned into works of art, the reason cannot be that the artist does not own them. For, presumably, if the artist did have a proprietary right – if Marilyn Monroe and the Queens family consented to being artistically transfigured, or if the artist bought the Empire State Building – then anyone who was inclined to be skeptical about the art status of the result would still be skeptical.

Levinson appears to presuppose that where an object is used to realize two conflicting intentions – where one of the intentions attaches to the owner and the other to an appropriator – the intention that determines its use is the owner's. So the appropriationist artist's intention that the object be used to support some art-historical regard will be trumped by the owner's intention wherever it conflicts with the artist's. But I do not see why the owner's intentions have so much ontological weight. Someone can certainly use my shotgun to shoot me despite my intentions that my shotgun not be so used. I might wish that my shotgun not have the status of a murder weapon. It might not be very nice to shoot me with my shotgun; but you can do it nonetheless. Similarly, I do not see how my ownership of the Empire State Building would be enough to stop someone else from turning it into a readymade.

My recommendations about identifying art come closest to Levinson's with respect to his second condition.[53] However, even though he speaks of his method as a matter of defining art historically, Levinson's theory is really very ahistorical. For Levinson supposes that something might be art now just in case it supports *any* type of regard, treatment, or mode of appreciation that was appropriate to at least some works of art in the past. The problem here is that not *every* mode of appreciation that was lavished on artworks in the past is eternally available. Some modes may have become historically obsolete. Making artworks in the present to support such obsolete, historically outmoded, and historically unavailable modes of appreciation should not, on the face of it, result in things that we now count as artworks. Levinson's theory is ahistorical at least in the respect that it does not allow for the historical obsolescence of art regards. He treats his art regards as ahistorically eternal – as always available modes of appreciation. But modes of appre-

ciation may pass away. This is something that any theory claiming to be historically sensitive should acknowledge. But Levinson's does not.

This may sound like a somewhat abstract objection. Let me introduce a counterexample in order to give it some purchase.

It seems fair to suppose that sometime in the past artworks were thought to
perform such services as propitiating the gods. That is, artworks – such as those
performed at religious festivals – were offerings to the gods (offerings predicated
on either exciting their favor or, at least, mitigating their disfavor). Since this was
once a function of what we call artworks, presumably one way of appreciating
such artworks was in terms of how suitable or how effective such works were in
propitiating the gods. Perusing some works in this light, we might think that they
were very powerful examples of propitiation; other works might be assessed as less
powerful. We might appreciate such works with respect to propitiation in the way
that we appreciate thoroughbreds with respect to their racing potential.

Now if what I have said so far is plausible, then assessing, appreciating, or
regarding some historically acknowledged artworks as vehicles of propitiating the
gods was an appropriate way of regarding artworks. On Levinson's view, it must
count as an integral form of artistic regard. It is, in other words, a form of regard
that a contemporary artist might seek to facilitate with respect to a contemporary
candidate for the status of artwork.

But consider this case. Jones is a person who knows something of the history
of art. He knows that artworks were sometimes used to propitiate certain gods.
Let us even suppose that Jones believes in these gods and thinks that they ought to
be propitiated. Jones also owns a chicken farm and an automatic assault rifle. He
has a proprietary right over both the relevant chickens and the rifle. By dint of
these property rights and a certain intention, Jones sets out to make an artwork.
Specifically, he shoots a mass of chickens in record time in order to propitiate the
gods. Moreover, he presents the massacre as an artwork: onlookers are invited to
appreciate it, assess it, or regard it in terms of its effectiveness as a means of propitiating the gods. This was a correct way of regarding some artworks in the past;
and Jones intends to facilitate this way of regarding his massacre of the chickens as
a means of producing a contemporary artwork.

Here it is important not to confuse Jones's activity with the activities of other
proponents of the art of slaughtering chickens. Jones is not a conceptual artist
who seeks to make some kind of statement about art or life by means of slaughtering chickens; nor does Jones hope to turn chicken-slaughtering into art by creating something that is full of dramatic excitement and color. His intention is
simply to make something that is to be regarded and assessed as an effective vehicle for propitiating the gods, where propitiating the gods *was once* an acknowledged purpose of art and where regarding the work's viability in discharging this
function is one correct way to treat artworks.

So Jones makes a work at *t* – September 25, 1992 – with the nonpassing intention that it, the chicken massacre, be an object for regard as an artwork. In particular, it is to be regarded in terms of its efficacy for propitiating the gods – which,

of course, was a way of correctly regarding artworks in the past (prior to September 25, 1992).

It is hard to see how Levinson's theory can avoid admitting Jones's chicken massacre to the roster of art. But surely Jones's chicken massacre is *not* a work of art, even if an indiscernible chicken massacre by the modern artist Herman Nietze is. There must be something wrong with Levinson's theory if it entails that Jones's chicken massacre is art.

Moreover, I do not think that this counterexample is idiosyncratic. Rather, it points to a systematic flaw in Levinson's theory – namely, that it is ahistorical (despite its claims to being historical) in the sense that it fails to take account of the fact that some regards-as-a-work-of-art may pass away. Indeed, it is very easy to multiply counterexamples of this sort when one recalls that a great deal of art in the past was produced for religious purposes and was properly regarded as the focus of devotion. But when I was a first-grade student in Catholic school and I put two Popsicle sticks together in the shape of a cross with the intention that it be a devotional object, the result was not a work of art, even though it was correct to regard some artworks in the past as devotional objects. Obviously, the religious functions of art and their attending regards can produce, in fairly predictable ways, a substantial number of problem cases for Levinson's theory.

Arthur Danto's theory of art is another rival to my narrative approach, for in it, too, art history performs an important role in identifying works of art. But Danto's theory, like Levinson's, differs from the narrative approach insofar as it proposes a definition as the reliable means for identifying art.

Danto never states his definition of art outright. But he does seem to believe that something is a work of art just in case it (1) is about something (2) about which it projects some attitude or point of view (this is what Danto means by the work's possession of a style) (3) by means of metaphorical ellipses that (4) depend on some enthymematic material from the historico–theoretical artworld context (this material is generally what Danto thinks of as art theories), and that (5) engage the audience in interpreting the metaphors elliptically posed by the work in question.[54]

This is an immensely complicated theory of art, and full justice cannot be given to it in a page or two. But, *prima facie,* it does seem to be far too exclusive to serve as an adequate definition of art. Surely some tap dancing, such as the work of Honey Coles, counts as art. But that work need not be about anything; it need not propose a metaphor about anything; it does not engage or require an interpretation about its (probably nonexistent) metaphorical import by audiences; and its reception does not depend upon art history, where that is construed narrowly in terms of art theory.

Admittedly, it will require some art-historical background to establish that such dancing is art, if it is challenged; but it need not be background of the order of art theories. Rather, that background can be woven into suitable art-identifying narratives without recourse to theories of dance. For there is probably nothing that we would count as a theory of dance in the actual historical background of

Honey Coles's tap dancing. That is, where Danto proposes to identify artworks in terms of their connection to historically existing art theories, I think it is enough to tell stories about their connection to preexisting art contexts which may or may not possess anything like art theories.

Of course, Danto might modify his view, as he sometimes seems to do, by dropping the emphasis on the background of art theory. But even with this modification, his definition seems too strict. Surely some artworks are not about anything. Do not certain works of pure pattern count as art? And even of those remaining works that are about something – those that have a semantic component – many need neither be construed as metaphors nor interpreted that way. There are plain-speaking works of art. Hogarth's "Cruelty in Perfection," from his *The Four Stages of Cruelty,* is not a metaphor (not even a visual metaphor), and it does not elicit or require metaphorical interpretations from viewers. Indeed, it is not clear that the work requires any sort of interpretation, metaphorical or otherwise, if one agrees with Annette Barnes's argument that interpretation is an activity we engage in only when the point of what we are attending to is not obvious.[55]

Perhaps Danto thinks that all works of art are about something because they "comment" on their tradition. But surely this is a figurative use of the notion of commenting. Many works of art bear relations to their tradition upon which we comment. It is strained, however, to relocate what are *our* comments in the work of art. Moreover, there is no reason to suppose that those works of art that do comment on other works of art always do so in a metaphorical mode. Daumier's 1856 lithograph *Photographie: Nouveau Procede* comments disparagingly on the art of photography, but without metaphor.

Danto's emphasis on the importance of the art-historical context, especially where the latter is not associated strictly with existing art theories, is a valuable insight. In fact, it is an insight that led me to my own thoughts about the role of historical narration in identifying art. However, many of the other conditions that Danto adds to the condition of historical relevance seem to render his theory far too exclusive.

The theories of Danto and Levinson seem the closest competitors to the sort of historical approach I advocate. Their accounts, of course, are both definitional. The problems I have sketched in regard to their theories reveal that there are continued difficulties with definitional approaches, even when putatively informed by historical considerations. In a dialectical sense, the failure of these theories at least recommends attention to the narrative approach.

In the present essay I have maintained that in asking the question "What is art?" we may be requesting different types of information. We may be asking whether there are reliable methods for identifying and establishing that something is art; whether art has any general or essential features; whether there is a real or essential definition of art. Moreover, as a historical conjecture or diagnosis, I have claimed that the actual project of philosophical art theory in the age of the avant-garde is, in fact, the issue of how to identify and establish whether the often unex-pected productions of the avant-garde are art. In this context, I have proposed that identifying narratives provide us with a reliable method for establishing the artis-tic status of the works in question. Such narratives ideally explain the way in which a disputed production is an artwork by showing how it emerged through intelligible processes of assessment, resolution, choice, and action from acknowl-edged artworld practices within a context of recognizable presentational systems. Securing such narratives for contested artworks represents a sufficient condition for establishing that such candidates are art. Moreover, my invocation of acknowl-edged artworld practices and systems should raise no worries about circularity, since we are talking about identifying art, not defining it.

One criticism of my emphasis on identifying narratives rather than on art def-initions might be that this is not really philosophy. But isolating the reliable meth-ods of reasoning and argument that we use in our practices certainly has a *prima facie* claim to the status of philosophy. Another worry about the narrative approach might be that it makes it seem easy to establish that something is art. This does not strike me as a problem. Establishing that something is art is generally not a very daunting task.

The narrative approach offers a way of answering the question "What is art?" that is different from the one George Dickie proposed. It employs narration rather than definition, and it makes much more explicit reference to art history than Dickie's more explicitly sociological approach does. However, the move to art history that I advocate might be thought of as a matter of seizing an opportunity opened by Dickie's seminal emphasis on the indispensability of context for art theory.

HISTORICAL NARRATIVES
AND THE PHILOSOPHY OF ART

I. SETTING THE STAGE

If one surveys the canonical history of the philosophy of art in the English-speaking world – as it is enshrined in numerous textbooks and anthologies[1] – it is difficult to resist the conjecture that it has been driven by the development of the avant-garde. This may appear to be a controversial hypothesis because it does not seem to square with the field's explicit understanding of itself. For on that understanding, the dom-inant view is that the philosophy of art has been concerned with successive attempts to characterize the nature of art from an ahistorical point of view. However, a close

From: *The Journal of Aesthetics and Art Criticism,* 51, 3 (Summer 1993), 313–26.

look at the way in which later philosophers have dialectically constructed their views against the backdrop of earlier, rival philosophies of art reveals an unmistakable trend – namely, later philosophers in the historical series are attempting to come to terms with certain recent mutations in the practice of art that were not accommodated by the proposals of earlier philosophers of art.

For example, as is well known, Clive Bell's dismissal of imitation theories of art and his defense of formalism were motivated by his perception of the conceptual failure of earlier approaches to art to accommodate neo-impressionism. R. G. Collingwood's philosophy of art attempts to create a space for the modernist poetics of Eliot, Joyce, Pound, and Stein; while the theories of George Dickie and Arthur Danto emerge in the process of taking Dada seriously.

In his recent book, *Definitions of Art,* Stephen Davies draws a distinction between functional and procedural definitions of art.[2] Functional definitions attempt to define art in terms of some function or point that art has – such as the production of aesthetic experience – whereas procedural theories identify objects as artworks in virtue of their introduction by means of certain procedures – such as the conferral of art status.

Monroe Beardsley's aesthetic theory of art – which might be thought of as a summation of views that flourished in the nineteenth and early twentieth centuries – is the most sophisticated functional theory of art, while George Dickie's institutional theory is a major example of the procedural approach to art. Davies himself notes that procedural theories of art have an edge over functional theories of art because the practices of art have departed from the initiating functions or point of art.[3] Obviously, anti-aesthetic art cannot be theorized in terms of the production of aesthetic experience. Other approaches, such as, Davies surmises, those advanced by proceduralists, need to be found in order to secure the wherewithal to identify art in the age of the avant-garde.

Of course, Davies' account of the functional/procedural distinction confirms my historical conjecture. Whereas functional theories – such as the imitation theory or the aesthetic theory – tracked earlier art (art created to acquit certain specifiable functions) somewhat adequately, as art began to depart from those initiating functions – as art became for example, anti-mimetic and anti-aesthetic – procedural theories came to the fore. Procedural theories are more comprehensively sensitive to the range of modern art. That is, procedural theories are more attractive because they are better suited to accommodate the developments of avant-garde art.

My point in alluding to Davies' distinction is not, however, to argue in favor of procedural definitions of art. Rather, I mention Davies' account in order to bolster my historical conjecture that what has been the driving, though perhaps not fully acknowledged, force behind the philosophy of art for at least a century – a century that not coincidentally could be called the age of the avant-garde – has been the startling innovations of modern art. It is no accident, in other words, that the philosophy of art, as we currently conceive it, is primarily a creature of the twentieth century. For it is in the twentieth century that the theoretical task of coming to terms with virtually continuous revolutions in artistic practice has become urgent. That is, it is in the twentieth century that the problem of identifying art has become persistently unavoidable.

Undoubtedly, this is not the way that most practitioners of the philosophy of art would articulate their project. Many would be prone to say that they have concocted ahistorical theories of art that in the process of capturing the essence of art, of course, apply both to the art of the present as well as the art of the past. But this account is insensitive to the flagrant historical fact that what we call the philosophy of art has consistently reawakened from its dogmatic slumbers at the prodding of momentous mutations in artistic practice. Thus, a better diagnosis of the project of the philosophy of art as we know it is that its underlying, though not generally explicitly avowed, task has been to provide the theoretical means for establishing that the mutations issued from avant-garde practice belong to the family of art. That is, the recurrent task of the philosophy of art, as a matter of fact, has been to provide means to identify new and emerging work, particularly work of a revolutionary sort, as art.

Resistance to this hypothesis may derive from the view that philosophical positions address problems from the standpoint of eternity, situated somewhere near erehwon. But theory in general is beholden to practice and it finds its problems in specific historical contexts. And this is true of art theory as well.[4] Moreover, if we attend to what philosophers of art have done, as opposed to what they say, it appears undeniable that most of the activity of theory construction on the part of modern philosophers of art has been devoted to establishing theoretical connections between the innovations of the avant-garde and the body of work antecedently regarded as art.[5] In a manner of speaking, one might say that a great deal of modern philosophy of art is an attempt to come to a philosophical understanding of the productions of the avant-garde.

If it is plausible to hypothesize that the underlying task of the philosophy of art historically has been to supply the means by which innovative mutations – especially avant-garde mutation – in artistic practices are to be counted as art, it is even less historically adventurous to note that the most popular approach to discharging this task has been to propose definitions of art. That is, the dominant presumption has been that what are called real definitions of art – definitions in terms of necessary conditions that are jointly sufficient – provide us with the means to identify objects and performances (whether they be strikingly innovative or traditional) as artworks.

Typically, the philosopher of art propounds a definition of art that foregrounds some feature putatively made salient by innovative art – such as significant form or institutional status – and then attempts to show that this is also a necessary feature of antecedently acknowledged art. Thus, the means for identifying avant-garde art is the same as the means for identifying previous art, namely, the application of a formula that sorts artworks from everything else. A commonly accepted way to introduce the philosophy of art is to recite the succession of these formulas, where, as I would emphasize, later definitions in the sequence are continuously adjusted in order to, among other things, secure the identification of emerging mutations as artworks.

However, once we agree that the central task of the philosophy of art has been to isolate a method for identifying artworks, then it should be clear that we have no prima facie reason to expect that that task must be fulfilled by means of a theory in the form of a definition. For we are able to identify a great many things without resort to definitions. That is, we often have reliable methods for identifying objects and actions as members of a class where we lack real definitions. Thus, it is possible that the solution of the task of the philosophy of art – the task made pressing by the historical avant-garde – need not involve the production of a real definition of art. The task of the philosophy of art – the identification of objects and performances (most pertinently avant-garde objects and performances) as art – may be satisfied by some instrument other than a real definition, which alternative instrument nevertheless presents a reliable method for determining that the candidates in question are artworks.

The solution that I propose to the central problem of the philosophy of art is an alternative to the definitional approach. Whereas the definitional approach presumes that we identify art – including, most particularly, avant-garde art – by means of real definitions, I propose that a compelling alternative view is that we identify works as artworks – where the question of whether or not they are art arises – by means of historical narratives that connect contested candidates to art history in a way that discloses that the mutations in question are part of the evolving species of art.[6] I call these stories "identifying narratives," and it is the purpose of this essay to analyze these narratives. It is also the contention of this essay that identifying narratives provide the philosopher of art – in search of a reliable method for identifying art – with an attractive alternative to real definitions.[7]

One way in which to situate the strategy that underpins my advocacy of identifying narratives is to recall the neo-Wittgensteinian approach to art theory popularized by people like Morris Weitz.[8] According to this view, a real definition of art is impossible, but we may nevertheless still possess reliable methods for identifying candidates as artworks. The reliable method that Weitz had in mind was what was called the family resemblance method. That method, of course, was subjected to a number of decisive criticisms.[9] And, historically, the defeat of the family resemblance approach heralded a return to the project of defining art essentially (most notably in terms of George Dickie's institutional theory of art).

However, the rebuttal of the family resemblance approach should not obscure one of its founding insights, namely, that there may be reliable means for identifying something as an artwork apart from real definitions. That criticism has shown that the family resemblance approach is not such a method does not preclude the possibility that there may be some other method that reliably identifies artworks sans real definitions. It is my view that identifying narration provides such a method.

Weitz believed that he possessed an argument that foreclosed the prospects for real definitions of art on logical grounds. For he contended that the very concept of art implied commitments to originality, creativity, and innovation that are conceptually inimicable to the treatment of art as a closed concept, susceptible to real definition. Weitz's so-called argument was undermined by counterexamples –

such as Dickie's Institutional Theory of Art that, despite being a real definition, placed no constraints on what kind of thing[10] could be art and, therefore, no limitations on artistic originality and creativity. Moreover, Weitz's view that somehow real definitions contradict the concept of art and its implied commitments to innovation has always seemed to me doubly murky insofar as it is difficult to understand exactly what he means by the concept of art, and, therefore, rather unfathomable to ascertain whatever it implies and contradicts. Consequently, I, unlike Weitz, do not think that we have any principled reason to believe that a real definition of art will never be constructed. Rather, all we have before us is the continued failure of attempts to construct such definitions.

However, it is possible to make an end run around this apparent impasse. For though Weitz was mistaken in his conviction that he had demonstrated the logical impossibility of a real definition of art, his contention, along with that of other neo-Wittgensteinians, that artworks can be identified reliably without recourse to real definitions, remains quite sound. Though we may not be able to prove that a real definition of art is impossible, it may nevertheless turn out that a real definition of art is unnecessary. For if identifying narratives realize the task of the philosophy of art by providing a reliable method for determining whether or not a candidate – especially an avant-garde candidate – is art, then, if my historical conjecture is correct, the issue of whether or not art is accessible to real definition becomes somewhat marginal and academic. That is, if the following account of identifying narratives is persuasive, then the central problem – as I have characterized it – of the philosophy of art can be addressed while bypassing the question of the real definition of art.

II. THE ROLE OF IDENTIFYING NARRATIVES

I have claimed that, in fact, the central problem of the philosophy of art has been that of identifying – or of finding *ways* to identify – objects and performances as art. This is a problem because art mutates and evolves historically.[11] Art today may look and even communicate very differently than art of yesteryear. Indeed, art often mutates radically. The task of the philosophy of art, first and foremost, is that of handling such radical mutation, a task that dominates the foreground in the age of the avant-garde.

The characteristic situation in which this problem arises is one in which a public is presented with an object that defies its expectations about what counts as art and, thereby, leaves the public bewildered. One might hear it said: "That's not art; a child could do it." Frequently, when confronted with such art, the public, or its representatives in the critical estate, charge that the work in question is tantamount to a practical joke or a confidence trick. For example, Jules Renard wrote in response to the first performance of Alfred Jarry's *Ubu roi:* "If tomorrow Jarry does not write that it was all a hoax, he's finished."[12] Such outrage signals disbelief that the work in question is art. And the burden of proof weighs upon those who contend that the new work is art.

How is this challenge met? Generally, the proponent of the work in question responds by telling a story that links the contested work to preceding art making practices and contexts in such a way that the work under fire can be seen as the intelligible outcome of recognizable modes of thinking and making of a sort already commonly adjudged to be artistic.

When the public and/or some of its designated critics react incredulously to a mutation like *Ubu roi*, it is a function of their inability to locate the work in question within the context of the artistic practices with which they are already familiar. Their problem is one of how to "place" the work. And this is a problem of historical under-standing. The more that we know of the history of a work – of the tradition from which it emerges – the "more rapidly we 'place' a work we are hearing, reading, or seeing for the first time; once we 'place' it we know what to look for, and so the work becomes intelligible more quickly."[13] For example, we begin to understand Yambo Ouologuem's *Le Devoir de violence* when it is historically situated as a reaction against Chinua Achebe's *Things Fall Apart* and Camara Laye's *L'Enfant noir.*[14]

Avant-garde mutations often strike the public and some critics as unintelligi-ble, and, therefore, as not art, because such audiences are unable to place the work in question in the tradition of what they already regard as art. They fail to be able to respond to the work correctly because they lack a recognizable context. The way to assuage their apprehension is to supply the context by telling a story about the way in which the work in question derives – through recognizable processes of thinking and making – from a background of practices that they already acknowledge to be artistic.

Confronted by a postmodernist pastiche like Ronnie Cutrone's 1984 *Idolatry* – a painting of an outsized Smurf figure stretching before posterlike cultural icons of John Wayne and Elvis Presley – one may be tempted to reject the work as romper-room or adolescent wall decoration. However, the piece can be profitably situated in an intelligible artworld tradition, one centered around the notion of critique.

Paintings by Cubists are said to be critiques of the conditions of painting, which critiques proceed by acknowledging the flatness of the picture plane; while subsequent large canvasses by Pollack are explained in terms of a similar reflexive gesture whereby line and color are saliently advanced as the basic constituents of painting. In turn, the minimalists who succeeded Pollack's generation expanded their field of critique, making works that were structured in a way intended to transform the spectator into an amateur phenomenologist, reflecting self-con-sciously upon the ways in which the painting or sculpture shaped and modified the spectator's attention. The name of the game was still critique but whereas the object of critique for Pollack was the painting itself, the object of critique for the minimalists was the conditions of pictorial and sculptural perception.

The advent of what is called postmodernism on the gallery scene marks a shift from the idiom of phenomenology to that of semiotics and poststructuralism. The basic constituents of painting are no longer identified as lines and colors, but signs. The object of critique, in turn, becomes signs, and the task of the postmodernist artist becomes the critique of signs, particularly the signs and symbols of contem-porary culture. The thought that motivates *Idolatry,* then, is that by thrusting Smurfs, John Wayne, and Elvis Presley on our attention, Cutrone promotes the spectator's reflection upon the status of signs and their circulation in our culture. Cutrone, by displaying Smurfs with the salience Pollack displayed line and color, invites the spectator to enter into a process of critique of the kind the artist engaged in originally structuring the work.

By showing – through a historical narrative of the sort exemplified above – that *Idolatry* belongs to a continuous artistic tradition (call it that of "artworld critique"), we produce evidence that it is a work of art and not romper-room wallpaper. The preceding narrative does not establish that it is *good* art, but it provides a prima facie reason to accept the work's claim to art status. That is, if the historical account that we have offered of the emergence of *Idolatry* from the series of historical events and motivations is accurate, then we have established that *Idolatry* is an artwork (or, at least, we have shifted the burden of proof to the skeptics).

Of course, pragmatically speaking, our particular narrative will only work for listeners who are prepared to accept what I have dubbed "artworld critique" as an acknowledged practice of art. However, if the starting point of my story here is controversial, that is of little moment, since I can always begin the story at an earlier historical juncture – say impressionism or the work of Cézanne – that is uncontested and from which the notion of "artworld critique" itself can be sensibly derived by means of a plausible, art-historical narrative.

Another example of the role of historical narration in accommodating artistic mutation can be found in the notion of the shifting dominant that was introduced by the Russian Formalists and exploited by the Prague Structuralists. To audiences mystified by the *arrythmia* of then-contemporary Czech poetry, Roman Jakobson pointed out that Czech poetry was always comprised of several components – including rhyme, a syllabic scheme and intonational unity – but that in different periods these components stood in different orders of hierarchy.[15] In the fourteenth century, rhyme dominated, but was displaced in importance in the realist Czech poetry of the second half of the nineteenth century in favor of emphasis on syllabic pattern. Then, under the pressure of innovation in the twentieth century, the role of the dominant feature in verse shifted again, giving intonational unity pride of first place. The emphasis on intonational unity evolved from a recognizable tradition of Czech poetry by means of an intelligible artistic concern, the pressure for innovation and differentiation. Skeptical challenges to the artistic status of the new poetry are met by telling the story of its evolution by means of straightforwardly artistic processes from acknowledged poetic practices.

Of course, not just any story can be told in order to secure the art status of an embattled work or practice. Insofar as the stories told are historical narratives, they are committed to historical accuracy. The stories must aspire to truth. Historical narratives may be challenged epistemically. They may be rejected where they are factually flawed or where the modes of thinking and making to which they advert are anachronistic. However, if such a narrative connects a disputed work to antecedently acknowledged art by way of narrating a satisfactory historical account of the way in which the work in question emerged intelligibly from previous artistic practices, then its defender has established its art status.

So far, I have characterized the paradigmatic situation in which identifying narratives are mobilized to identify and establish the art status of contested works as one in which a candidate is put forward and then challenged by skeptics. However, nowadays, especially, it is often customary for the identifying narrative to be advanced prior to skeptical challenges. That is, the identifying narrative takes, so to speak, the form of a preemptive strike. Through artistic manifestos, interviews, critical reviews, and lectures, the story of the place of a new work in an evolving tradition is told and publicly circulated – via art journals, gallery handouts, symposia, catalogues, lecture-demonstrations, and so on – prior to or in tandem with the new work. These stories articulate the art-historical considerations that led to the production of the work – the constraints the producer was working with or against as well as the recognizably artistic motives that prompted her to negotiate those constraints in the way she did – and, thereby, these stories attempt to make the new work accessible to audiences. At the same time, they function to explain why the work in question is art.

It is an expectation of artists that they be concerned to make original contributions to the tradition in which they work. These contributions can range along the creative scale from slight variations in established genres to revolutions. In this respect, Jeffrey Wieand has pointed out that art history is analogous to a conversation in which each artist-conversationalist makes or, at least, is expected to make an original contribution to the discussion.[16]

However, as in a conversation, the contribution must also have some relevance to what has gone before. Otherwise, there simply is no conversation. Wieand writes: the artist must be "asking or answering a question, elaborating on what someone else has done or disagreeing with it, demonstrating that something is possible, and so on. The artist's contribution should in this way be relevant to the existing practice, concerns, and interests of the kind of art he makes."[17]

Of course, the problem presented frequently by avant-garde art is that the artist's interlocutors – the public – often fail to catch the relevance of the artist's "remark" to the ongoing conversation in its artistic context. The audience may discern, so to say, the "originality" of the work, but not its relevance. There is, in a manner of speaking, a gap or a glitch in the conversation. But if this is the problem, then it is easy to see how to repair it: reconstruct the conversation in such a way that the relevance of the artist's contribution is evident – bring perhaps unremarked presuppositions into the open, point to overlooked features of the context, make the intentions the artist intends to convey explicit, show that said intentions are intelligible in terms of the conversation and its context, and so on. Moreover, reconstructing the conversation in this way amounts to a historical narrative. Where something is missing from the conversation – some connection – it is supplied by a retelling of the conversation that historically reconstructs it.

An identifying narrative establishes the art status of a work by connecting the production of the work in question to previously acknowledged artistic practices by means of a historical account. In this respect, this procedure requires that there be a consensus about certain objects and practices in the past. That is, we must agree that we know that certain objects and practices already count as art. Historical narratives then connect contested works to works already identified as art.

For those who confuse the narrative approach with the definitional approach, this may seem problematic; they might worry that this method is circular. However, whereas circularity is a problem for definitions, there is no problem of circularity with narratives. It is not circular, for example, to identify rapping as a recognizable variation of traditional forms of African-American performance by arguing that it has emerged from a continuous process of evolution from such practices as, among others, The Dozens and The Toast.

Moreover, it needs to be noted that no procedure for identifying art can proceed without the antecedent conviction that some objects and performances are art. Definitions require agreement about some clear-cut cases in order to be motivated, while some knowledge about what is and is not art is necessary to adjudicate counterexamples. Likewise, the family-resemblance approach to identifying art requires that we begin with paradigm cases that afford us the basis for charting correspondences between new works and acknowledged works. Thus, insofar as the narrative approach presumes that we know that some past objects, performances, and practices count as art, it makes no assumption not made by competing approaches to identifying art.

As noted earlier, the narrative approach to identifying art has more in common with the family-resemblance approach than it has to the definitional approach. However, it is not susceptible to the line of criticism customarily leveled at the family-resemblance approach. For when the narrativist draws correspondences between contested candidates for art status and past artworks, those correspondences are not merely grounded in manifest or exhibited similarities between the old and the new. For the narrativist, the antecedent artworks and practices in question play a generative role in the production of the new work – a role that the narrative makes explicit in its reconstruction of the causes and effects, and the influences and intentions that give rise to the work in question.

Identifying narratives are genetic accounts of the provenance of artworks; they do not simply track manifest resemblances.[18] Whereas a proponent of the family-resemblance approach might defend the art status of Manet's *Olympia* or *Le Dejeuner sur l'herbe* by noting that his use of nudes resembles previous uses, the narrativist explains that Manet is explicitly working in the historically established genre of nude, making a modern, revolutionary statement by populating that genre with contemporary figures, such as the *grande horizontale,* in strident, intentionally outrageous opposition to the more typical mythological or exotic damsels who standardly inhabited the genre.

III. THE STRUCTURE OF
IDENTIFYING NARRATIVES

An identifying narrative is a historical narrative. This entails that it has the features that we expect from any genuine historical narrative, namely, that it portray a sequence of past events and states of affairs whose time-ordering is perspicuous;

that the events and states of affairs it portrays be connected; and that the account be committed to rendering the past accurately – that is, the events, states of affairs, and the connections between them that the narrative depicts should all obtain.

The point of an identifying narrative is to situate a candidate for art status in the history of art in such a way that the work can be placed as an intelligible contribution to the tradition. This aim implies where the stories in question will end; they end with the production of the work whose art status is contested. Challenged by Renard's charge that *Ubu roi* is a hoax, the defender of Jarry proposes a historical narrative that shows how the play emerged through intelligible processes of thinking and making from recognizable artistic practices. The culmination or resolution of the story is the production and presentation of *Ubu roi*.[19]

The narrative plays the role of an argument in which the conclusion is the production of *Ubu roi*. The narrative elucidates the way in which *Ubu roi,* as a set of choices, issues from acknowledged modes of thinking and making, pursued within a known artistic framework. The argument concludes when the production of *Ubu roi* is shown to follow from the logic of the situation as it is or was reasonably construed by someone like Jarry. Thus, the story ends with an account of the presentation and production of a contested work such as *Ubu roi*.

If the identifying narrative ends with the production of *Ubu roi,* where does it begin? Identifying narratives establish the art status of contested works by connecting the works in question to artworks and practices already acknowledged to be art. Thus, an identifying narrative will begin with some art historical juncture that is recognized by all concerned to be uncontested. That is, since the aim of the identifying narrative is to demonstrate the art status of the contested work by explaining how it emerged through recognizable processes of making and thinking from acknowledged practices, the narrative must begin in a context where acknowledged practices preside. Consequently, an identifying narrative sets the stage or establishes the context of the action by starting with a set of circumstances already known to be artistic.

Moreover, the beginning of an identifying narrative, like the beginnings of narratives in general, is, as Aristotle observed, such that it "does not necessarily come after something else, although something else exists or comes about after it."[20] In other words, the beginning of the narrative establishes a background or context sufficient for what follows to be narratively comprehensible – that is, the beginning introduces a context that is adequate for understanding what follows and as such does not necessarily require reference to earlier points in time. Thus, the identifying narrative begins by establishing a state of affairs that is rich enough to support and to motivate the ensuing story and is also such that all the disputants grant its status as an ensemble of artistic practices.

Often with avant-garde productions the relevant context – the beginning of the story – involves the state of the artworld immediately prior to the innovations under dispute. For, it is most frequently the case that avant-garde art is a reaction to or repudiation of prevailing artistic practices.[21] The task of the identifying narrative, then, is to show how such reactions to prevailing (acknowledged) art represent intelligible responses to existing, acknowledged artworld practices.

To return to the case of *Ubu roi,* for example, one may profitably begin an identifying narrative by sketching the state of the theatrical milieu in which Jarry operated, a milieu dominated, on the one hand, by the escapist, bourgeois entertainments of Alexandre Dumas *fils,* Victorien Sardou, Emile Augier, Jacques Offenbach and Edmond Rostand, and, on the other hand, by the realist project of figures like André Antoine, which project itself was, in part, a reaction formation to the aforesaid bourgeois escapism.

An identifying narrative formally ends with its recounting of the final completion of the work in question and/or its presentation to the public. The narrative begins by establishing the relevant artistic background from which the work in question emerges. The middle or complication of the narrative functions to connect the beginning of the narrative to the end; the middle is what gets us from the beginning to the end of the story.

In recounting the context in which an artist like Jarry finds himself, the narrator includes a sketch of the artist's assessment of that context, highlighting the ways in which the artist perceives the initial state of affairs as one that invites change – either because the initial state of affairs confronts internal problems that call for solutions, or because it contains heretofore unexploited opportunities, or because it has come to hamper expression, or because it is stagnant, or because it is corrupt.

Jarry, for example, assessed the dominant bourgeois theater of his day as corrupt, as bereft of serious content, as escapist. At the same time, he, like contemporary Symbolists, was also opposed to the realist reaction to the dominant bourgeois theater because he feared that the literal, naturalist approach limited "the intelligent spectator's imaginative freedom to construct in his mind his own, pure and perfect set in response to the poet's words."[22] Jarry's assessments of the limitations within prevailing theatrical practice led him to resolve to change that practice. Moreover, the kind of reasons that led Jarry to this resolve – his low estimate of the vapid escapism of the so-called "well-made play" and his suspicion that realism thwarted imagination – are ones that are perfectly intelligible to anyone familiar with art history; they represent well-known art-historical motives for reform and for revolution.

The identifying narrative begins in an acknowledged artworld context. Complications start when we take note of the artist's assessments of such a context, which assessments motivate the artist's resolution to change said context. The changes the artist introduces – such as the avant-garde innovations that often initially mystify the public – are woven into narrative accounts in terms of the ways in which these changes implement the artist's conception of what must be done in order to rectify, reform, or revolutionize preexisting practices. That is, the artist's innovations are explained as decisions predicated upon improving or correcting prevailing practices in light of the artist's assessments of those practices and their shortcomings, and in light of his or her resolution to change those practices.

In the case of *Ubu roi,* an identifying narrative explains that Jarry assaulted bourgeois theater not only through fusillades of obscenity, but through the comic-infantile portrayal of the topic of political assassination (thereby, all-but-explicitly travesty-ing the high seriousness of *Macbeth*). Indeed, many of the stylistic, structural and the-matic choices of *Ubu roi* can be readily understood as part and parcel of a concerted effort to outrage the bourgeoisie. Moreover, this assault was not simply rooted in a desire to shock, but rather also to confront the consumer of escapist theater with a view of human nature that such theater suppressed – namely, that of the ignoble, instinctual, darker side of humankind that Freud would later explore.

However, at the same time that many of Jarry's decisions were aimed at chal-lenging bourgeois theater, a narrative of the production of *Ubu roi* would also note that many other choices were directed against the practices of realist theater. These stylistic and structural choices were often predicated upon deploying abstract (as opposed to literal or realist) devices for the purpose of encouraging the spectator's use of her imagination.

For example, Jarry advocates "A single set or, better still, a plain backdrop, eliminating the raising and lowering of the curtain during the single act. A for-mally dressed character would enter, as in puppet shows, to put up signs indicating the location of the scene. (Note that I am convinced that such signs have far greater 'suggestive' power than any set. No set or extras could convey the sense of 'the Polish army on the march in the Ukraine'.)"[23] Likewise Jarry favored the use of masks and of a single soldier to depict an army because he believed that such abstract devices prompted the spectator to employ her imagination whereas real-ism in its putative attempt to counterfeit the literal appearance of things engenders passive perception.

An identifying narrative comprises a beginning, a middle or complication, and an end. The complication segues into the end as the distinctive, problematic choices of the work in question are motivated in light of the artist's assessments of the way in which acknowledged artistic practices need to be changed. The identifying narrative begins by sketching or establishing an initial context about which there is consensus concerning its positive art status. Where that set of circumstances provides the context for the avant-garde work in question, the narrative proceeds by elucidating the artist's assessment of the situation, indicating not only how that assessment leads the artist to resolve to transform the art in question, but also showing how it is intelligible that someone in such a context might come to have that resolution.

Once the artist's assessment of the situation is explained and her resolution to change the artworld motivated, the narrator goes on to show how the choices that compose the artwork in question are sensible or appropriate means to the artist's end – that is, her resolution to change the artworld in a certain direction in light of her assessments of its shortcomings. The complication of the identifying narra-tive shows how the artist comes upon her innovations as means for securing her purposes; it illuminates the way in which what the artist did in the existing con-text was a way of achieving her resolution. This involves describing the situation in such a way that it becomes evident why certain artistic choices make sense given the values, associations, and consequences that are likely to accrue to such choices in the pertinent historical context.

In the case of *Ubu roi,* for instance, an identifying narrative attempts to show that given a background correlation between realism and passive perception, the choice of abstract theatrical devices was an intelligible move to make in the name of the imagination. Moreover, it is important to emphasize that in explicating an artist's assessment of the situation and her choices of the means for transforming artworld practice in an intended direction, we only require that her thinking be intelligible, not that it be veridical.

Jarry's assessment of the bourgeois and realist theater of his day might not coincide with the assessments of present-day theater historians. However, the identifying narrative need only show that Jarry's assessment was an intelligible assessment, an assessment of the situation that would be reasonable for someone in that context to make applying certain general acknowledged understandings of the aims of art – like encouraging the imaginative activity of the spectator – that were abroad and alive in the pertinent context.

Once we establish, by narrating the conditions that give rise to the artist's assessments, that the artist's resolution is intelligible, the story continues, explaining how the techniques, procedures, themes, and strategies that the artist mobilizes involved intelligible choices for realizing the artist's goals, given the structure of the relevant artworld – that is, given the alternative, available strategies and their associated values in the art-historical context under examination.

Again, we do not demand that the artist's practical reasoning in this matter be veridical; Jarry's psychological presuppositions about realism and the imagination could be mistaken. Rather, we only require that Jarry's thinking and his choices be intelligible in context. The question of truth only arises with respect to the identifying narrative when we come to evaluate the narrator's hypotheses. That is, our conjectures about the beliefs that went into the thinking and making of Jarry's *Ubu roi* should be accurate, if our identifying narrative is to be successful.

The identifying narrative begins with some state of affairs whose art status is acknowledged. Change enters our story when we introduce the way in which an artist assesses that state of affairs such that she resolves to transform it. The artist's assessment of the situation, however, is still connected to acknowledged artistic practices insofar as she is guided by accepted construals of the aims of art. The bulk of the middle or complication of an identifying narrative comprises the narrative elaboration of the choices and rationales – including, possibly, the description of the artist's experimentation with different alternatives – that eventuate in the production and presentation of the contested work to the public.

My central claim throughout has been that if through a historical narrative of this sort a disputed work – generally an avant-garde work – can be shown to be the result of reasonable or appropriate choices and actions that are motivated by intelligible assessments that support a resolution to change the relevant artworld context for the sake of some live, recognizable aim of art, then, all things being equal, the disputed work is an artwork. That is, we establish that a disputed work is an artwork in the face of skeptical opposition by explaining via narration how it emerged from an acknowledged artistic context though a process of thinking and making in virtue of recognizable motives, conceptions and construals of the kind already precedented in artistic practice.

So, when confronted by the charge that *Ubu roi* is a hoax, we defend the play by telling the story of how it and its outrageous stylistic strategies emerged from an acknowledged artistic state of affairs as a consequence of assessments and choices of the sort that people with an acquaintance with art history recognize to be familiar. We say, for example, that given the practices of bourgeois theater, on the one hand, and realist theater, on the other, Jarry criticized the former for its saccharine escapism and the latter for its disavowal of the imagination; in order to redress these limitations, Jarry opted for the grotesque, for the obscene and for travesty as an antidote to bourgeois sentimentalism and for abstract, antirealist devices to jump-start the spectator's imagination. Of course, the preceding is just a skeleton of the identifying narrative that could be told to establish that *Ubu roi* is art. Such a narrative becomes more and more compelling as detail is added in a way that makes Jarry's ensemble of choices more intelligible.

Assembling the various elements of our characterization of identifying narratives so far, then, we contend that: *x* is an identifying narrative only if it is (1) an accurate (2) time-ordered report of a sequence of events and states of affairs (3) that has a beginning, a complication and an end, where (4) the end is explained as the outcome of the beginning and the complication, where (5) the beginning involves the description of an initiating, acknowledged art historical context and where (6) the complication involves tracking the adoption of a series of actions and alternatives as appropriate means to an end on the part of a person who arrived at an intelligible assessment of the art historical context in such a way that she is resolved to change it in accordance with recognizable and live purposes of the practice.

The preceding qualification – that the artist's resolution be made in terms of purposes that are live in the practice – is meant to avoid one of the problems of attempts to define art historically. Jerrold Levinson[24] and Stephen Davies[25] maintain that, for a work to be art, it necessarily must be produced with the intention that it be viewed in one of the ways that art has been correctly viewed in the past.[26] But this condition is not fine-grained enough, for it makes no provision for the fact that past ways of viewing art may become obsolete. If I wield my camcorder at the family picnic with the intention that what results be appreciated for its perceptual verisimilitude, that hardly supports any claims for the art status of my videotape because perceptual verisimilitude in and of itself is no longer a living mode of artistic commerce, though it once was. Consequently, when proposing a narrative of the artist's assessments of prevailing, acknowledged artistic practices, the artist's assessments should be based on extant understandings of the aims of art, if the narrative is to be successful.

The point of an identifying narrative is to establish that a candidate is an artwork by explaining how the work emerged from an artworld context through assessments whose presuppositions about the aims of art are already precedented and through choices that are intelligible. The explanatory power of such narratives

— as scrutiny of the sixth condition above quickly reveals — resides in the fact that such narratives are underwritten by the structure of practical reasoning.[27] The artist's assessment leads to a resolution that leads to the choice from alternative means to that end, which choices, then, result in the action that we want explained — the production of a contested and/or befuddling work such as *Ubu roi*. If we can explain the production of such a work in terms of intelligible processes of making and thinking in an acknowledged art context, then if our narrative is true, the art status of the work is secured.

Identifying narratives rest on the presumption that the artist is a rational agent. If our narrative genuinely illuminates the way in which the production of the artwork historically flows from an established artworld starting point by way of assessments that are recognizable as of a precedented kind and which assessments are subsequently implemented by intelligible decisions, given the logic of the situation, then the grounds for conceding the art status of the work seem irresistible. Of course, one might still question the merit of the work in question. However, the question of merit is independent of the question of its art status.

IV. SOME OBJECTIONS

1. In his *Definitions of Art*, Stephen Davies objects to Levinson's historical definition of art on the grounds that it places too much authority in the artist's intention. For Levinson, if x is an artwork, then necessarily the work has been created with the intention that it be regarded in one of the ways some preexisting artworks were correctly regarded. My own approach, though not definitional, like Levinson's, places decisive weight on the artist's intentions for the purpose of identifying artworks. Thus, if Davies' objection to Levinson is persuasive, it threatens the narrative approach as well.

According to Davies, the way in which we regard an artwork is not restricted to the way in which the artist intended us to regard the work — even in those cases where the artist intended an art historically correct regard. Rather, we may regard the work in any way that is consistent with our conventions for regarding and interpreting artworks and which accord with the facts of the work in question. That is, an interpretation of an artwork is legitimate if it is consistent with a true description of the artwork and if it abides by our conventions for regarding or interpreting artworks — even if said interpretation is at variance with or diverges from an interpretation based on an artist's intention.

Why? Because according to Davies art has a point — namely, the maximization of aesthetic interest (understood as the having of the richest possible experience of artworks) — and this point or interest is best served by conventional interpretations rather than intentional interpretations. Indeed, where a conventional interpretation and an intentional interpretation are rivals and the former promises a richer aesthetic experience, it always trumps the intentional interpretation.

Two points need to be made concerning Davies' case against the role of establishing authorial intentions in the matter of identifying art — whether by definitionalists or narrativists. First, it is certainly logically possible for someone to argue that though identifying the artist's intention is relevant for establishing art status, it may not be relevant for interpretation. Monroe Beardsley's aesthetic theory of art explicitly endorsed such a view, and, if I am not mistaken, Davies himself does as well, since Davies, like Levinson, tends to believe that it is a necessary condition for art status that "the art maker intends her product to be viewed in one or another of the ways that art has been correctly viewed in the past."[28]

It is only a historical fact about Levinson that he is intentionalist in both the interpretation and the definition of art. One could be intentionalist in the matter of identifying art and nonintentionalist in one's approach to interpretation, as Davies is. Thus, what we might call Davies' conventionalism with respect to interpretation has no implications for intentionalism in the matter of identification.

Second, I wonder whether Davies is correct in claiming that there is a point to art – the maximization of our aesthetic interests – such that conventional interpretations always trump intentionalist interpretations. There are currently interpretations of B-movies, such as Ed Wood's *Plan 9 from Outer Space,* that interpret its sloppy editing and narrative lapses as if they were avantgarde gestures of subversion, aimed at deconstructing the techniques of the classically edited, Hollywood cinema. In fact, the film looks the way it does because it is a slapdash exploitation quickie, made in a hurry and on a shoestring budget.

Given the protocols of contemporary film criticism, the avant-garde-primitive modernism-account of the film is available, and mobilizing it in such a way that each gaff in the film's style is a transgressive gesture certainly makes a more exciting item out of the movie. But this interpretation does not square with anything that we would be willing to say about the film on the basis of Wood's intentions. And, I submit everyone – save the most committed lovers of the world's worst films – will agree that, though the primitive-modernist interpretation is available within the conventions of film criticism, it should not be endorsed because it is implausible to believe that Wood could have intended *Plan 9 from Outer Space* as an exercise in modernist transgression.

There were, of course, filmmakers, like Luis Buñuel and other surrealists, who could have made a transgressive film in the nineteen fifties of the sort that some have said that Wood attempted. But given what we know of Wood, it is outlandish to attribute such intentions to him. Thus, in this case, I maintain that on balance we prefer the intentionalist interpretation over an available conventional one which would make our encounter with *Plan 9* more exciting.[29] Therefore, it seems dubious that conventional interpretations always trump intentional ones. Nor does it seem that there is some point of art – such as the maximization of aesthetic experience – that always overwhelms intentionalist considerations. That is, we do not have to foreswear intentionalism when it comes to interpretation. Consequently, even if there was some way in which emphasis on intention in the matter of identifying art was tied logically to our interpretive practices, it is not clear that our interpretive practices are as decisively conventional as Davies maintains.

2. One might worry that identifying narratives are too powerful – that they can be deployed in such a way as to defend the art status of objects and performances that are not art. For example, it is well known that van Gogh cut off his ear lobe after an argument with Gauguin. Suppose that their conversation concerned artistic matters. Further suppose that van Gogh mutilated himself as an expression of frustration with that debate. Indeed, let us go so far as to imagine that van Gogh mutilated himself in order to symbolize the plight of his artistic convictions in the face of Gauguin's criticisms. If we imagine all this to be fact, then couldn't an identifying narrative of the sort discussed previously be mounted to support the claim that van Gogh's mutilated ear is art. But even if what we have supposed were factual, I predict most of us would still hesitate to count the ear as art, despite an accompanying narrative.

This hesitation seems to me correct. And yet the reason that most of us have for withholding art status from van Gogh's ear can be turned to the advantage of the narrativist. Van Gogh's ear is not precluded art status because it is the product of self-mutilation. In the second half of the twentieth century in that subgenre of performance Art often called Body Art, there are examples of artworks – of which the most notorious was Rudolf Schwarkolger's fatal, self-castration – which, however gruesome, self-destructive, disgusting, and immoral have a discernible, if lamentable, place on the contemporary landscape of the arts.

What Schwarkolger had at his disposal – which van Gogh lacked – was a recognized framework in which self-mutilation could be presented as art. Van Gogh's act occurred outside any artworld system of presentation – outside any of the artforms, media, and genres known to him and his public – whereas Schwarkolger's self-mutilation was a nearly predictable move in a recently entrenched genre.

Now if this analysis is correct, it indicates that in order to establish the art status of a contested work, one needs not only to tell an identifying narrative that connects the work in question with acknowledged art practices, but, as well, one needs to establish that the thinking and making that the identifying narrative reconstructs be localized to activities that occur within recognizable artworld systems of presentation – that is, artforms, media, and genres that are available to the artist and the artworld public under discussion. That is, identifying narratives must be constrained to track only processes of thinking and making conducted inside the framework of artworld systems of presentation or recognizable expansions thereof. Moreover, where this constraint is honored, identifying narratives will not commit the error of overinclusiveness.

In most cases, we will have little difficulty determining whether a work is produced in a recognizable artworld system of presentation. No one disagrees about whether poetry, the opera, the novel, and so on are artworld presentational systems. However, there may be cases when disputes arise about the status of a presentational practice. So the question that faces us finally is how we are to establish that disputed presentational practices are artworld systems of presentation. Here I think that once again narrative is our most reliable method.

New artworld systems of presentation – like photography, cinema, performance art, and so on – appear frequently. But such systems do not spring from nowhere. They are evolved by their practitioners through self-conscious processes of thinking and making from earlier artistic systems and practices. Establishing that a candidate practice is an artworld system of presentation becomes a matter of reconstructing that process of thinking and making in such a way that a narrative of its development out of existing, acknowledged practices can be perspicuously charted.

For example, photographers, like Edward Steichen, strove to have their medium accepted as an art by making photos that achieved the same ends as state-of-the-art painting. Of his *The Frost-Covered Pool,* he wrote: "The picture, if picture you can call it, consisted of a mass of light gray ground, with four or five vertical streaks of gray upon it … Among artists in oil and water colors the impressionist leaves out of his picture much, if not all, of the finer detail, because he assumes … that the public can supply this detail much better than he can portray it … What is true of the oil or water color is equally true of the photograph."[30] By telling the story of the way in which photographers like Steichen adapted their medium to acquit existing aims of art, we explain how a new artworld system of presentation is introduced.

Of course, new artworld systems of presentation may arise in many different ways. Art photography emerges from the aesthetics of painting, in part, by mimicking prevailing artistic styles and their purposes. But new artworld systems of presentation can follow alternative pathways of evolution. What is called Conceptual Art, for instance, emerged by repudiating the art object as a commodity fetish – by effectively leaving the gallery-market system with nothing to sell. This antipathy to the commodification of art, needless to say, was already a well-known stance by the late nineteenth century. Thus, the new arena of artmaking, Conceptual Art, though it produced works of an unprecedented variety, can be connected to previous artworld endeavors as a means to an already well-entrenched conception of art's purpose.[31]

In many cases, there is a great deal of consensus about which practices constitute recognizable artworld systems. Where questions arise about a candidate, like Conceptual Art, a narrative of its emergence from acknowledged artworld practices can establish its status as an artworld system of presentation. The kinds of narratives that are applied to such conclusions are various. In some cases, new systems of presentation may be plotted as emerging from established systems by processes of repetition, amplification and/or repudiation, though sometimes we will have to map even more complex routes.[32]

Identifying narratives of contested artworks, then, are constrained to tracking processes of thinking and making within the framework of established artworld systems of presentation. Explaining – by way of a narrative – that a contested candidate is the intelligible outcome of processes of thinking and making in response to acknowledged artistic practices in the context of a recognizable artworld system of presentation is sufficient for establishing the art status of the work in question.[33]

3. Lastly, it may be argued that the narrative approach to identifying art is not really philosophical. It reduces the philosophy of art into the history of art – a charge that some have leveled at Hegel.[34] However, it should be recalled that philosophical research is traditionally concerned with epistemological questions. And the theory of identifying narration presented in this essay is an attempt to analyze and motivate what I claim is a reliable method for establishing that a candidate is art. It may be true that – in contrast to definitionalists – metaphysics is not my concern. But epistemology – or a species of naturalized epistemology – is, and that is certainly philosophical.

Moreover, if the diagnosis that I offered of the philosophy of art in the opening stages of this essay is correct, what has animated the philosophy of art as we know it is the problem of the avant-garde – the problem of coming to terms with stylistic upheaval in the practice of art. This problem is that of how to comprehend and incorporate radical innovation. The solution that I recommend is identifying narration.

℮৲

ON THE NARRATIVE CONNECTION

Narrative is a topic of increasing interest across the humanities and the social sciences today. Even philosophers like Richard Rorty and Alastair MacIntyre invoke it, often against something they call theory. However, although the notion of narrative frequently figures in many discussions in the university, it is not often defined. The purpose of this essay is to advance a characterization of our ordinary concept of narrative in terms of one of its crucial ingredients, and to explore some of the ramifications of that definition in light of how we might begin, in part, to understand narrative comprehension.

Of course, narratives come in many different sizes and shapes. What is called a narrative history, for example, may mix different expositional forms, including not only narration, but argument and explanation. Likewise, a novel may contain elements of commentary, description, and decoration in addition to strictly narrative elements. It is not the purpose of this paper to define such large-scale units of discourse. My aim is much more modest. I would like to attempt to define something more discrete – what I call "the narrative connection."

I suspect that when we call more large-scale discourses, such as histories or novels, narratives, we do so because they possess a large number of narrative connections or because the narrative connections they contain have special salience or a combination of both. I will not speculate on what proportion of narrative connections a discourse must possess or on what degree of salience said connections must

From: *New Perspectives on Narrative,* ed. by Will van Peer and Seymour Chatman (Albany: SUNY Press, 2000).

exhibit in order for a large-scale discourse to be called a narrative. At present, I am only concerned to characterize the nature of the narrative connection.

If this is all I intend to do, does this justify my previous claim about characterizing narrative? I think that it does. For fundamental to our identification of a given novel or history as a narrative is its possession of narrative connections. Histories and novels may contain more than narrative connections. But it is their possession of narrative connections that leads us to call them narratives. Thus, even if we are not prepared to say what proportion and what degree of salience of narrative connections provide grounds for calling a history or a novel a narrative, the possession of narrative connections is an essential feature of anything that we would want to call a narrative. Therefore, we need a characterization of the narrative connection before we attempt to explore the grounds on which we call large-scale mixed discourses narratives.

I. DEFINING THE NARRATIVE CONNECTION

The first step in defining the narrative connection is to consider its proper domain. I hope that it is uncontroversial to say that the domain of narrative discourse is at least comprised of events and states of affairs. I will assume this much. However, the statement "There was an old lady who lived in a shoe" is not a narrative, although it describes a state of affairs. Why not? Because narratives contain more than one event and/or state of affairs. Narratives represent a series of events and/or states of affairs. Thus, the first necessary condition for what constitutes a narrative representation is that it refer to at least two, though possibly many more, events and/or states of affairs. "There was an old lady who lived in a shoe" is not a narrative, but "There was an old lady who lived in a shoe that was very small, so she went looking for a boot" looks more like a narrative, since this involves two things, a state of affairs – living in a shoe – and an event – "searching for a boot."

A narrative connection represents a series of events and/or states of affairs. Mention of a *series* here implies that narratives contain the citation of at least two, but possibly more, events and/or states of affairs. But is any series of events and/or states of affairs a narrative? Here, following the lead of linguists, let us test our intuitions against an example. Is the following a narrative?

"The Tartar hordes swept over Russia; Socrates swallowed hemlock; Noël Carroll got his first computer; Jackie Chan made his most successful movie; and dinosaurs became extinct." Is this a narrative? I suspect that almost everyone will agree that this is not a narrative. Why not? One reason is that this particular discourse, though it contains more than enough events and states of affairs to qualify as a narrative, fails to be about a unified subject. It seems as though it is about four disconnected subjects. Thus, I hypothesize that to count as a narrative connection, a discourse representing a series of events must be about a unified subject (though, I admit, more will have to be said about what makes a subject unified).

Of course, saying even this much allows that a narrative may be about more than one unified subject. Large-scale narratives, such as a history of France, will often be about more than one subject; and narratives of all sizes may develop parallel stories concerning different subjects; moreover, in addition, narratives may contain nonnarrative material. But to qualify as a narrative connection, the discourse must manifest at least one unified subject. Perhaps so much is implied by calling the phenomenon under discussion the "narrative *connection*." That is, the events and/or states of affairs must be *connected;* they cannot simply be a list of *disconnected* events and/or states of affairs.

Now test another example against your intuitions: "The President talked to his adviser; the President ate a piece of cheese; the President jogged; the President waved to reporters." This discourse string takes note of apparently more than one event and it appears to have a unified subject – namely, the President's activities. But let me suggest that it is not a narrative. Why? Because it lacks a discernible temporal order. One cannot divine the order in which the preceding events occurred. Perhaps, the President jogged in the morning, then ate the cheese, and on the next day he talked to his adviser and, at the same time, waved to the reporters. From a logical point of view, assuming the President did do all these things, the discourse string as a whole would be true whether the President jogged first and then waved to the reporters or vice versa. But narrative structure makes demands over and above logical structure. Narrative requires that the events and/or states of affairs represented be perspicuously time-ordered. A narrative is not simply a series of events arranged helter-skelter; a narrative is at least a *sequence* of events, where "sequence" implies temporal ordering.

Perhaps my example is a little confusing. Some may feel that the previous recounting of the President's activities are, in fact, time-ordered. But I submit that if you think that, then it is because you are assuming that the order of the sentences represents the order of the events in question. But why assume that? If you look closely at the discourse string in terms of the information it carries, I suspect that you will quickly realize that all the activities notated could occur at the same time. The discourse string is underdetermined with respect to the time-ordering of the events, even if initially it seems natural to suppose that they are occurring sequentially.

"John jumps; Mary sings; Harold bleeds" is not self-evidently a narrative not only because a unified subject eludes us, but also because it yields no reliable insight into the order of these events. Likewise, "The Tartar hordes swept over Russia; Socrates ate hemlock; Noël Carroll got his first computer; Jackie Chan made his most successful movie; and dinosaurs became extinct" is not a narrative not only because it lacks a central subject, but because it does not even conversationally implicate a perspicuous, reliable time ordering of the events it recounts. The narrative connection requires both a unified subject and a perspicuous temporal order where by a perspicuous temporal order I mean a retrievable one. This, of course, does not mean that the temporal order must be stated outright in the discourse string. Context and the knowledge that the intended, informed audience brings to the discourse may be enough for the intended reader, viewer, or listener to derive a perspicuous temporal ordering from an example.

So far I have alleged that a narrative connection is comprised of a series of events that is both possessed of a unified subject and perspicuously time-ordered. Moreover, it is important to realize that the requirements of a perspicuous time-ordering and that of a unified subject do not amount to the same thing. This can be seen by comparing the following two strings of discourse: "The Eastern Roman Empire falls in 1453; the American Constitution is accepted in 1789; Russia is defeated in 1905;" and "Hume publishes 'Of the Standard of Taste;' Hume fails to secure a professorship." Neither is a narrative because the first lacks a unified subject, though it is temporally ordered, whereas the second, though apparently possessing a unified subject (viz., Hume), lacks a perspicuous time-order – which came first the failure to secure a professorship, or the publication?

For classificatory purposes, following Morton White, we might call our first example – "The Eastern Roman Empire falls … etc. – an *annal*.[1] An annal is not a full-blooded narrative. On the other hand, it is not altogether without temporal order. So perhaps we should call annals members of the class of *story forms,* where story forms are any sort of temporally ordered discourse. But with respect to the annal, its principle of organization is simply temporal ordering.

However, the annal is not the only kind of story form. The *chronicle* is another. Where temporal ordering is combined with a unified subject, we arrive at a somewhat more complex structure than the annal, which has been called the "chronicle."[2] For example: "The French Revolution occurred in 1789; Napoleon became Emperor in 1805; Napoleon was defeated at Waterloo in 1815, after which the Bourbons were restored." This possesses a perspicuous temporal structure, as well as a unified subject, namely, French history.

In this example of a chronicle, each event is explicitly dated. However, in order to qualify as a chronicle, it is not necessary that the temporal order be made absolutely explicit in the text, so long as the reader, viewer, or listener is able to derive a reliable temporal order from it. Had our earlier example stated "First the President talked to his adviser; then he ate a piece of cheese; then he jogged; and, finally, he waved to the reporters," then this would be a chronicle, rather than an annal, for even though the temporal structure is somewhat imprecise, it nevertheless affords a rough order of occurrence.

Or, in some cases, it may be appropriate to presume that the temporal order is implicit for a target audience. Thus, "Kennedy is assasinated; Johnson becomes President" qualifies as a chronicle for informed audiences who are able to fill in the temporal order. A discursive representation that (temporally, but noncausally) connects at least two events in the career of a unified subject such that a reliable temporal ordering is retrievable from it (and/or from the context of enunciation) is a chronicle. Chronicles are certainly more complex structurally than annals. But are chronicles full-fledged narratives?

I conjecture that they are not, although I realize that this is open to terminological dispute. The reason I think that a mere chronicle is not yet a narrative is that it does not display any connection other than that of temporal succession between the events it recounts. If I say "I woke up; later I dressed; still later I went to class," I suspect that most people would agree that this falls short of a full-fledged narrative, although the events cited might be turned into ingredients of a narrative. But why isn't it a narrative properly so called? To put it vaguely – because the connection among the events alluded to by it is not tight enough.

Of course, as noted, this might be a controversial conclusion. Some theorists, like Gerald Prince, might be willing to call this a narrative.[3] However, I think that it is more profitable theoretically to discriminate between different sorts of temporal discourses or, as I call them, story forms – between, for example, annals, chronicles, and narratives proper. Having more distinctions at least has the advantage of affording more fine-grained structural insights. And what we have been talking about are important structural differences no matter what labels we finally settle on.

On my view, narratives proper require more than simply temporal ordering as a principle for connecting events and/or states of affairs. But in order to motivate my taxonomy, it is necessary for me to specify the nature of the connection I have in mind rather than simply saying it is more than merely a matter of temporal ordering.

What is the connection that obtains between events and/or states of affairs in a narrative proper? One popular candidate is causation. This seems eminently plausible, since narratives typically represent *changes* in states of affairs, and change implies some subtending causal process.

"Creon had Antigone executed; consequently, his son committed suicide, which caused his wife to commit suicide, and, as a result, Creon felt anguish." This is a narrative. It has a unified subject, Creon, and it is perspicuously time-ordered. But in addition to being time-ordered, the events are also causally linked. Earlier events in the discursive string are the causes of the later events in the string in the sense that the earlier events supply sufficient grounds, all things being equal, for the occurrence of the later event. This is certainly a "tighter" connection than mere temporal ordering. Is it the secret of the narrative connection?

It is not, if what we are after is the generic or comprehensive connection between earlier events and/or states of affairs and what follows. Admittedly, in some narratives, causation of this sort is what supplies the connection between earlier and later events. But causation in this sense – the sufficiency sense – is too strong a relation to hypothesize as the relevant connection operative in *all* narratives linkages. Were the relation causal on this understanding, that would suggest that earlier events in narratives causally entail later events. And although this may obtain in some cases, it does not obtain in all cases, nor does it seem to me to obtain in even most of the typical cases.

Most narratives are not strings of causal entailments. In most narratives, the earlier events in a sequence of events underdetermine later events. We read that a thief enters a bank and robs it; in the next scene, as he exits the bank, he is apprehended by the police whom we subsequently learn have been watching him all along. The first event did not entail the second event. Indeed, we may even be surprised by the appearance of the police when the thief leaves the bank. Nevertheless, "the thief enters the bank to rob it, but subsequently, as he exits, he is apprehended by the police" is a narrative, though, strictly speaking, the first event is not the fully determining cause of the second event. That is, although robbing the bank is causally relevant to the arrest, it does not causally entail the second event. That is why we cannot think of all narratives on the model of a series of causal chains in which earlier events and/or states of affairs function as the efficient causes of succeeding events and/or states of affairs.

Looking at the preceding counterexample concerning the thief and the bank may suggest a way of modifying the causal account. The first event by itself does not causally entail the second event, but the second event brings with it the causal information – the presence of the police observers – that explains the second event – the arrest – when it is combined with the first event – the robbery. We can call this addition, following William Dray, a causal input.[4] On this model, the narrative connection is a matter of the first event and/or state of affairs + a causal input + the second event. Does the causal input model yield a general picture of the narrative connection?

I think not, and again the problem is that it is too strong. Consider this narrative:

> Because the town refused to surrender, the invading army laid siege to it; because a message reached them that their base of operations was under attack, the besiegers soon withdrew, but, in withdrawing, their campaign fell into confusion.[5]

This seems to be an acceptable narrative. However, not every successive event in it can be subsumed under either the causal model or the causal input model. The first connection in the story – the refusal to surrender/the siege – is arguably causal; the second connection – the message/the withdrawal – possibly involves a causal input; but the last connection – the withdrawal/the confusion – is causally underdetermined. Withdrawing from the siege might have integrally contributed to the campaign falling into confusion. But it does not necessitate it. Withdrawing troops does not causally entail falling into confusion. Nevertheless, this last connection seems like a legitimate narrative connection. Indeed, this sort of connection appears quite often in narratives. But it does not fit either the deterministic causal model or the causal input model. Thus, we need a characterization of the narrative connection that is not as strong as those provided by the causal model or the causal input model.

Since narratives represent change, it is natural to think that the narrative connection has something to do with causation. But it is too demanding to expect that, in all cases, the narrative connection involves an earlier event that causally necessitates the succeeding state. But though the earlier event need not be the cause, in this sense, of succeeding states, it is not causally irrelevant either. What might the narrative connection be if it need not be the sufficient cause of successive states, but is also somehow causally relevant to successive states? One obvious relation fitting these desiderata is that the earlier event and/or state of affairs in a narrative connection is a causally necessary condition for successive states (or a contribution to such a causally necessary condition).[6] That is, more precisely, the earlier event in a narrative connection is *at least* a necessary or indispensable contribution to a sufficient, though nonnecessary, condition for the occurrence of the relevant later event in the narrative complex (or, in other words, it is, at least, what J. L. Mackie calls an INUS condition).[7]

Referring to our robbery example, had not the earlier events cited obtained, the later events would not have obtained, though the earlier events in question do not guarantee the occurrence of the later events. In other words, had the robber not been pilfering the bank, *ceteris paribus,* the police would not have arrested him, but his robbing the bank, at that point in the story, did not guarantee his being arrested. (Here we are obviously talking about token causation, not type causation.)

Likewise, in the preceding story about the withdrawal of the army, the retreat from the town can be understood as a causally necessary condition for the army in question falling into confusion when it did. Other factors may also have conspired to cause the disarray of the army. But the preceding story tells us that a causally necessary condition for this particular instance of disarray was that the army was in the process of withdrawing. That is, if that army at that time had not been withdrawing, it would not have fallen into disarray.

Similarly, that the thief robbed the bank is a causally necessary condition for his arrest. Had he not robbed the bank, all things being equal, he would not have been arrested by the police observers when he was. The robbery was a necessary condition for his arrest.

On the strict, deterministic causal model of the narrative connection, the earlier events in the narrative necessitate the succeeding events and/or states of affairs. On the causal input model, the earlier event plus some causal input necessitate the succeeding event. But, as I have noted, the narrative relation is often weaker than that of necessitation or causal entailment. Rather, in a great many cases, earlier events merely function to make later events causally possible. Insofar as the earlier event is generally of the nature of a causally necessary condition (or a contribution to such a condition), the later event is often not predictable.

Many events share the same causally necessary conditions. The hero is rushing to save a child from an oncoming truck. This opens up the possibilities that either the child will be saved from the truck or not. That the oncoming truck is rushing at the child is a necessary condition for both the event of the child's destruction or its being saved by the hero. The earlier event does not necessitate the outcome, but it is, all things being equal, a necessary condition for either of the alternative outcomes.

The reason that we hesitated to identify strict deterministic causation as the relevant connective for all cases of narrative connection was that we noted that very often the earlier events and/or states of affairs in stories underdetermine the events that follow them. Hypothesizing that the earlier events and/or states of affairs are causally necessary conditions, however, cannot be defeated by this objection, since x's being a causally necessary condition for what follows is consistent with the appearance of a wide range of events and/or states of affairs. Moreover, hypothesizing that the earlier event is at least a *causally* necessary condition (in the sense of an INUS condition)[8] coincides with the intuition that many have that narrative has something to do with causation (if only because it is concerned with processes of change).

Of course, in saying that the earlier event in a narrative connection is *at least* a causally necessary condition in the sense stipulated, one leaves open the possibility that sometimes the relation may be stronger causally. Sometimes the earlier event may be the cause of a subsequent event and/or state of affairs in the sense of necessitation, or sometimes a series of earlier events and/or states of affairs may be jointly sufficient for the production of a later event. I do not preclude these possibilities in some cases. Rather, I deny that they supply an account across the board of the narrative connection. A better candidate for that account is that the earlier event and/or state of affairs in a narrative connection is at least a causally necessary condition or ingredient for bringing about later events (or a contribution to such a condition). This way of approaching the matter holds only that earlier events must figure in the causal network that gives rise to later events, but allows that it can figure in that network not only as a sufficient condition but as weakly as simply a causally necessary condition (or as a contribution thereto) that is indispensable to the sufficient but nonnecessary cause of the relevant later events.

Once it is proposed that the earlier events in a narrative are at least causally necessary conditions (in the sense of INUS conditions) of later events (or contributions thereto), it is natural to wonder whether this hypothesis isn't itself too strong. Perhaps it is too stringent to require that the earlier events be *causally* necessary conditions. Might they not be just necessary conditions?

Consider this putative narrative: "Aristarchus hypothesized the heliocentric theory thereby anticipating Copernicus' discovery by many centuries." This appears to have a unified subject – the heliocentric theory – and it is time-ordered – first Aristarchus hypothesized the heliocentric theory and then Copernicus had the same insight centuries later. Moreover, if this is what we might call a narrative of anticipation (or prefiguration), then the first event, Aristarchus' discovery, is a necessary condition for the anticipation (or prefiguration) of the second event, Copernicus' discovery. Thus, if this is a narrative, then it appears that a necessary condition, rather than a causally necessary condition is all that we need to require of a narrative connection.

Yet if there is no line of influence stretching from Aristarchus' discovery to Copernicus', I, at least, find it strained to think that this is narrative. It is an interesting series of events. Indeed, mention of the second event in this series retrospectively reveals something of the significance of the earlier event, and, as we shall see, retrospective significance is a frequently recurring feature of narrative. However, where the events bear no sort of causal relation to each other, they seem more of the order of coincidence than of narrative, at least if you agree that narrative involves changes in the career of a unified subject, where change is a function of causal processes.[9]

Assuming that the narrative connection involves the earlier event in the sequence playing the role of at least a causally necessary condition, the narrative connection is structurally more complex than the chronicle. However, the narrative connection bears an obvious relation to the chronicle, since a given narrative connection will imply a chronicle of events, that is, a time-ordered sequence of events. From any narrative connection proper, one can retrieve a time-ordering of the relevant events. A narrative connection, in other words, entails some chronicle, although a mere chronicle does not entail a narrative. Similarly, both a narrative proper and a related chronicle will imply some annal, though no annal strictly entails a chronicle or a narrative connection. In this way, our story forms are ordered hierarchically.

Of course, the order of presentation, as it is locally articulated, of a narrative connection – that is, the story as told (or what the Russian Formalists called the *syuzhet*) – may deviate from the chronological-causal structure of the narrative connection itself (from what the Russian Formalists called the *fabula*), since the exposition may involve all sorts of devices such as the flashback, the flashfoward, the hysteron proteron, and so on.[10] Nevertheless, in the narrative proper, the narrative connection (or *fabula*) should be retrievable from the exposition. If it is not, there is no narrative.

In the preceding paragraph, I introduced the idea of a *local articulation,* like a flashback. However, narratives as a matter of discursive practice are globally articulated in what might be called a forward-looking manner. Once we are in a flashback, for example, the events are told in a temporally progressive way. They are not told backwards, so to speak. This differentiates narratives from mere explanations of the form: x at $t3$ because of y at $t2$ because of z at $t1$.

"The battle was lost for want of a horse and the horse was wanting for lack of a horseshoe" is not a narrative, though "King Philip could find no shoe for his horse and could not ride into battle and as a result the battle was lost", is a narrative. The forward-looking aspect of narrative here is what might be called a discursive, rather than a logical requirement, of this particular story form.[11]

Summarizing my arguments, then, a narrative connection obtains when (1) the discourse represents at least two events and/or states of affairs (2) in a globally forward-looking manner (3) concerning the career of at least one unified subject (4) where the temporal relations between the events and/or states of affairs are perspicuously ordered, and (5) where the earlier events in the sequence are at least causally necessary conditions for the causation of later events and/or states of affairs (or are contributions thereto). I say that the earlier events must be *at least* causally necessary conditions in order to allow that they may also be sufficient or jointly sufficient conditions for the later events. Basically, what I am saying is required is that the earlier events fall into the causal network that gives rise to the later events where the weakest, but perhaps the most frequent, way of figuring in that causal network is as a causally necessary condition (or a contribution thereto) for the causation of later events. That is, the earlier event in the narrative connection must be causally relevant to the effect event.

Moreover, I have added parenthetically that the earlier events and states of affairs may merely be contributions to a causally necessary condition. This last qualification is meant to accommodate the fact that many of the descriptions and depictions of states of affairs in narratives may not themselves present causally necessary conditions for what is to come, but only elements of a causally necessary condition. For example, we may be told that a character was born in a humble neighborhood in Arkansas. Later we are told that he became President of the United States. Here the humble birthplace of the president is not itself a causally necessary condition to his presidency, but only a contribution to setting forth such a condition, since it is a requirement for the presidency that the candidate be an American citizen, which condition is satisfied by being born in Arkansas, however humbly. A great many of the details we encounter in narratives are of this sort; they do not constitute causally necessary conditions for later events, but are contributions to the characterization of such conditions.

In passing, I mentioned that a typical effect of a narrative is retrospective significance. That is, later events in a narrative disclose the significance of earlier events. For example, in the historical narrative "The Allies and the Central Powers had fought themselves to a standstill, but then the Americans entered the war and, as a result, Germany was defeated," the significance of America's entry into the war is made clear in terms of its contribution to the defeat of Germany. In this narrative, the significance of American's entry into World War I is foregrounded as a turning point in that conflict. The end of the story, so to speak, makes prior mention of America's entry into the war pertinent. It discloses the significance of that event; it makes the relevance of the inclusion of that event in the story clear. Likewise, a later event in the *fabula* of *Oedipus Rex,* the plague, makes an earlier event in the story, the murder of the stranger at the crossroads, retrospectively significant. Moreover, as this example perhaps suggests, it is the fact that narratives track causal networks that most frequently enables us to identify their subjects as unified, since we usually colligate or collect elements of a narrative under the overarching umbrella of some causal network. In narrative, causal relations are standardly the cement that unifies the subject of the story.

The account that I have offered of the narrative connection should help explain the phenomenon of retrospective significance. The earlier events in the narrative connection are at least causally necessary conditions of later events in the story. Thus, when later episodes are added to the story, they reveal the relevance and importance of earlier events in terms of the causally necessary roles they play – something that may not be evident when these events and/or states of affairs are first mentioned. Consequently, the characterization of the narrative connection I have offered can explain the phenomenon of retrospective significance that is typically observed to attend reading, viewing, or listening to narratives. On the other hand, retrospective significance, though a typically recurring and explicable feature of narrative, should not be mistaken as the mark of narrative.[12] For the temporally ordered discourse "Aristarchus hypothesized the heliocentric system and then centuries later Copernicus discovered it again" affords the apprehension of retrospective significance – it indicates the point of mentioning Aristarchus' discovery in light of Copernicus' – but it is not, as I have argued, a narrative proper inasmuch as it lacks a narrative connection.

Earlier I justified the taxonomy involving annals, chronicles, and narrative connections proper, rather than accepting any time-ordered series of events as constituting a narrative, on the grounds that it provides us with more theoretical precision. Now that I have developed my account of the narrative connection, I can perhaps offer a more powerful consideration in behalf of this taxonomy. It is this: when confronted by specimens of annals, chronicles, and narrative connections proper, and asked which most accords with what one expects of a full-blooded narrative, I predict that most respondents will choose the narrative connections proper. Narrative connections proper correspond best to our intuitions about what a narrative is. Moreover, this is because our intuitions are rooted in a vague sense that narratives have something centrally to do with changes of state and, thus, with causation. Other theorists may suggest that we deal with the preference for narrative connections proper by saying that they possess greater degrees of narrativity. But reverting to my earlier argument, I think that it is more enabling theoretically to talk about different structural variations, notably the structural variations between annals, chronicles, and narrative connections proper.

Perhaps a related consideration in favor of my view of narrative is that narrative is a common form of explanation. In ordinary speech, we use narratives to explain how things happened and why certain standing conditions were important. Narrative is capable of performing this role because it tracks causal networks. The rationale for citing earlier events in the course of an explanatory narrative is that they play some role in the etiology of the events we wish to explain. To perform that role they must minimally belong to the causal network, a requirement that can be satisfied by their being a causally necessary ingredient (or a contribution thereto). Thus, insofar as what we call narratives are explanatory, it seems advisable to regard narrative properly so called as connected to causation and not merely temporal succession.

II. SOME OBJECTIONS

This account of the narrative connection is likely to draw forth a number of criticisms. Though I cannot anticipate them all, let me mention a few. In literary studies, it is often customary to talk about narratives not only in terms of temporal and causal relations, but also spatial relations. However, I have not included spatial relations in my characterization of the narrative connection. Is this a problem?

Most narratives do involve spatial relations. However, since I am attempting to get at the essential features of our concept of narration, I do not invoke spatial relations, because it seems to me that there can be narratives bereft of spatial relations, though, on the other hand, narratives bereft of temporal and causal relations seem unfathomable to me. Consider this example: "This morning I was upset because I thought that I had forgotten how to add, but then I remembered that 2 + 2 = 4 and now I am so very happy." This seems to be a narrative to me, or, rather, to possess a narrative connection, but it doesn't involve spatial relations, since, of course, "I" might be a disembodied spirit. Nor is this simply an invented example. In various religious narratives we are frequently told of spirits and spiritual forces who undergo changes of state.

Another objection to my view involves a counterexample. Suppose we hear a story of the sort we are all likely to categorize as a full-blooded narrative – at least up to the last line of the story. But, then, the last line of the story says that everything has transpired in a logically possible world where there are no causes, just coincidences. In the world of the story, there are no causally necessary conditions. So, according to my view, there are no narrative connections in the story, and, hence, it is not a narrative, properly so called.[13]

This is an ingenious example. However, my temptation is to bite the bullet and to say that it is not a narrative. It looked like a narrative up until the very end, but then it turned out not to be. Is this simply arbitrary or questioning begging? I think not.

If one is attracted to this counterexample, it may be because one thinks that the tale being told is some kind of story, and that my claiming that it is not is simply dogmatic. However, I too can agree that it is a story – it is a chronicle on my accounting. It is not a narrative properly so called, but it still a representative of a story form. We thought at first that it was a narrative, but by its conclusion we realized it is a chronicle. Thus, denying it the status of narrative is not as drastic or counterintuitive as it may sound at first, since I am not claiming that the example fails to be any kind of story; it just fails to be a full-fledged narrative. Indeed, slotting it under the category of the chronicle may even be attractive, since it says precisely what story form it belongs to.

A related counterexample might be to imagine a race of alien peoples who have no concept of causation. They string together event-ordered series untethered by causal connections. On my account, these people would not have narratives even though they might spend most of their time recounting past events to each other. But once again, this sort of counterexample does not seem problematic to me. On the one hand, it seems to me clear that these people would not have our concept of narrative, and that is the concept I am trying to unravel. And, on the other hand, if we knew more about the kind of stories they tell, we might be able to identify them in terms of story forms other than narrative.

Literary and cinema scholars are apt to be distrustful of my characterizations because they are often concerned with modernist or avant-garde narratives. These are often antinarratives, like Kathy Acker's *Pussy King of the Pirates,* that are designed to disrupt or subvert ordinary narrative connections. These sorts of practices do not accord with my characterizations, since they are expressly intended to violate the standard conception of narrative. But, in that sense, these practices themselves must presuppose something like the ordinary concept of narrative in order to negate it. Such practices are parasitic on the ordinary concept of narrative. But so much concedes that there must be an ordinary concept that functions as their, so to speak, foil. I would argue that that is what my conception of the narrative connection models. Thus, practitioners and critics of the avant-garde antinarrative, oddly enough, need something like my concept of the narrative connection as a condition of possibility for their own practices and, in that way, they will confirm my theory, or something very much like it, if only backhandedly.

The picaresque is another genre that literary critics advance as a counterexample to theories like mine. However, this is to enter the debate over the identification of what I earlier called large-scale discourses. Picaresques, like *Tom Jones,* may recount the diverse adventures of a character over a long period of time and many of these events may not cohere in a connected causal network. That is certainly true. However, none of the best known picaresques are totally bereft of narrative connections. Actions and events within given episodes standardly evince what I have called narrative connections, not to mention the fact that there are often, even if not always, narrative connections between episodes. Thus, at least the best known picaresques will not be discounted as narratives proper on my characterization of the narrative connection. They will have some narrative connections, even if they contain fewer narrative connections than other genres like the classical detective mystery or the thriller.

III. NARRATIVE COMPREHENSION

Having outlined a theory of the narrative connection proper and having considered some objections to it, the question arises about whether this theory can contribute anything to our understanding of narrative comprehension. I think that it can. Comprehending a narrative involves following it. But following a narrative involves anticipation. It involves having a sense of where the narrative is headed. But what is the nature of this anticipation? In what sense does the reader, viewer, or listener intuit the direction in which the narrative is headed?

Where ideas about outcomes are at issue, it is natural to think in terms of prediction. And sometimes when reading, viewing, or listening to a narrative, we do predict what will come next. But this is not our typical posture toward future episodes in a narrative. For, as I have already noted, generally the earlier events in a narrative underdetermine the later events. Prediction would be a feasible mental state for readers, listeners, and viewers typically to be in if deterministic causal models of narration were persuasive. That is, presented with causes, we would predict the effects. But I have suggested that very frequently the connection between earlier events and later events in narratives is not that of a strict causal chain. Indeed, typically, earlier events in a narrative underdetermine later events. So prediction, in any strong sense of the term, seems an unlikely characterization of the sort of anticipation that characteristically accompanies narrative.

But if prediction is not the core of narrative anticipation, what is? On my account of the narrative connection, earlier events raise certain possibilities, rather than others. They, so to speak, open a range of possibilities about what might happen next. From the point of view of the reader, viewer, or listener, this is a matter of encouraging a range of expectations. Following the story involves having a broad sense of where it is headed – a broad sense of what might happen next – rather than having a definite sense of what will happen next (as would be the case with prediction). Thus, narrative anticipation is structured in terms of the reader's, listener's, or viewer's possession of a range of possibilities. When later events are then entered into the narrative, the audience finds them intelligible just because they accord with or fall into the range of possibilities suggested by the earlier events in the story.

This is not to say that the reader, listener, or viewer has an array of concrete possibilities before her mind as she processes the narrative. Rather, earlier events open a range of possibilities and when later events arrive, we recognize that they fall into that range. If ensuing events fail to fall into that range and are not recuperated by the addition of causal inputs, the narrative will appear incoherent and unintelligible. Following a narrative with understanding is a matter of seeing how the states of affairs that obtain in the narrative are possible, given the earlier events in the narrative. This involves, in short, recognizing that the earlier events presented conditions for the realization of the later events. Specifically, it involves recognizing that the earlier events were causally relevant conditions (or contributions thereto) for the occurrence of the pertinent later events in the story at hand.

These conditions make later events possible. Our sense of the direction of the narrative – of its intelligible unfolding – is rooted in our sense of what kinds of events are possible, given other events. Of course, causally necessary conditions can branch in many different directions. Many subsequent itineraries are possible. One causally necessary condition will support an indeterminate range of consequences. But, of course, this is consistent with the fact that our sense of the direction of a narrative may also be very indeterminate. Remember that following a narrative is not typically a matter of prediction.

On the other hand, that the direction of the narrative is indeterminate does not mean that it is wide open – that just anything can follow anything else. For the causally necessary conditions that access some lines of development will exclude other lines of development. So while earlier events open a range of possibilities, they also preclude (save the addition of extenuating causal inputs) other possibilities. Our sense of the direction of the narrative is not typically precise – we do not typically predict future narrative events with exactitude. But our sense of the direction of the narrative is not altogether without shape, even in the initial stages of narration. Presented with a boy and a girl, we entertain the possibility that they may or may not subsequently become lovers, but we do not, without the addition of more information, anticipate that Mars will explode. The presentation of a boy and a girl is not a causally necessary condition for a planetary eruption.

That our sense of the direction of a narrative is typically indeterminate fits nicely with our hypothesis about causally necessary conditions. That is, an indefinite though not wide-open sense of direction is what one would expect if the basis of the narrative connection is generally only a matter of causally necessary conditions (in the sense of INUS conditions), or contributions thereto. Or, alternatively, that the narrative connection depends primarily on such causally necessary conditions explains why our sense of the direction of a narrative is generally indeterminate (though not unbounded). Of course, as narratives proceed, piling up more and more causally necessary conditions, the range of possible subsequent events shrinks. We expect subsequent events to fall in the intersection of those events made possible by the combination of the antecedent causally necessary conditions. Indeed, the compilation of causally necessary conditions may even get so exhaustive that we treat them as jointly sufficient and predict subsequent events. But even when prediction becomes feasible, it is the special case and not the norm of narrative anticipation. That is, it is not what we are generally involved in doing when we follow a narrative, even if it is what we do at certain points in a narrative, especially with respect to penultimate episodes.

Rather, narrative anticipation is a matter of forming expectations on the basis of what events are possible, given earlier events in the story. Where do these expectations come from? Lots of places, including our knowledge of the world (our knowledge of what is causally possible in everyday life), our knowledge of what is possible within the conventions of a certain narrative genre, and our knowledge of what is thought possible given the beliefs of the culture in which the narrative is composed. These expectations are not always – indeed, possibly rarely – consciously articulated. Metaphorically speaking, they are like opening certain directories for access in our mental computer. I leave it to the psychologists to discover the actual mechanics of this process. Suffice it to say that the addition of such causally necessary conditions to the narrative prepares us mentally for certain kinds of possibilities rather than others, and when one of those possibilities is realized by subsequent events in a narrative, we find it intelligible if it accords with one of the kinds of lines of possibility we have been primed to expect.

Following a narrative involves understanding what is going on in the narrative. This is a matter of assimilating what is going on into a structure – of integrating earlier events and later events into a structure. That structure is comprised of possibilities opened by earlier events in the discourse that function at least as causally necessary conditions. The sense of intelligibility that attends the narrative connection is a matter of the later events falling into the range of possibilities opened by or proponed by earlier events.

Stated negatively, following a narrative is a matter of not being confused when later events arrive in a narrative. Stated positively, following a narrative involves a sense of the direction of the narrative as it unfolds, and a sense of intelligibility or fitness when earlier events are conjoined with later events in the narrative. These events can all be explained by the hypothesis that earlier events in narratives are at least (and perhaps typically) causally necessary conditions (or contributions thereto) for the later events in the story. We are not confused by later events in a narrative because they fall into the range of possibilities opened by earlier episodes that function at least as causally necessary conditions (or contributions thereto). Or, if we are confused, that can generally be explained by pointing out that the subsequent events do not appear to fall into the range of possibilities for which the earlier events have prepared us. When we follow a narrative successfully it is because we find subsequent events in the narrative rationally acceptable. The criterion of rational acceptability here is whether the subsequent events fall into the range of possibilities opened by earlier events and/or states of affairs in the narrative.

Likewise, when we say we have a sense of the direction a narrative is taking, we mean that its destination is roughly defined by the possibilities that the representation of earlier events and states of affairs have opened up. Figuratively, we might say that the narrative is "headed toward" those possibilities (and "away from" the ones precluded by earlier events and/or states of affairs).

Moreover, when the arrival of subsequent events in a narrative strike us as intelligible or fitting, that is because they accord with our sense of what is possible, given earlier events. This does not mean that we are not often surprised by subsequent events in a narrative. I was surprised when I learned who the culprit was in the movie *The Usual Suspects,* and in its spiritual forebear, the novel, *The Murder of Roger Ackroyd.* However, once the culprit was revealed, I recognized that he fell into the range of possibilities opened by earlier scenes, even though I had not explored that particular possibility in my own thinking about these cases. Moreover, being surprised is consistent with there being causally necessary conditions in the narration that are, so to speak, stylistically recessive. In the cases of *The Usual Suspects* and *The Murder of Roger Ackroyd,* we might say that they were downright "hidden."

In this essay, I have tried to develop a definition of the narrative connection, which connection I think is fundamental to our concept of narrative – to the way in which we go about categorizing large-scale discourses as narrative. The most controversial aspect of that theory, I predict, is my contention that the basis of the narrative connection is that earlier events and/or states of affairs are at least causally necessary conditions (in the sense of INUS conditions), or contributions thereto, for the occurrence of later events in the relevant stories. I have attempted to defend this hypothesis by contrasting the narrative connection with annals and chronicles, and by an appeal to our intuitions about narrative. I have also tried to use this notion to characterize and explain aspects of narrative comprehension, especially narrative anticipation and its role in following a narrative. If these explanations are attractive, it is my hope that they will make my hypotheses about the nature of the narrative connection even more compelling to you.[14]

INTERPRETATION, HISTORY, AND NARRATIVE

I. INTRODUCTION: HISTORICAL NARRATIVES AS FICTIONS AND AS METAPHORS

At present, one of the most recurrent views in the philosophy of history claims that historical writing is interpretive and that a primary form that this interpretation takes is narration. Furthermore, narration, according to this approach, is thought to possess an inevitably fictional element, namely, a plot, and, in this

From: *The Monist,* vol. 23, no. 2 (April 1990), 134–66.

regard, the work of the narrative historian is said to be more like that of the imaginative writer than has been admitted. The upshot of this philosophically, moreover, is the assertion that historical narrations, *qua* narrative interpretations, are to be assessed, in large measure, in terms of the kind of criterion of truth that is appropriate to literary works. And a subsidiary, though far less tendentious, consequence is that our understanding of historical interpretation can profit from literary or "discourse" analysis.

This position, which was perhaps anticipated by Nietzsche,[1] is suggested in varying degrees by Roland Barthes[2] and Louis Mink;[3] it has been developed most extensively by Hayden White;[4] and it commands a following among historians, literary critics, and philosophers of history.[5]

For White, historical writing is interpretive in several separable, though interrelated, registers. Historical argumentation in the dissertative mode involves a paradigm choice; second, in a broad sense, a historical tract requires the choice of an ideological perspective; and, also, a historical narrative itself enjoins a choice of a plot structure, which, in turn, is related to the discursive tropes that "figure" the writing of the text.[6] For the purposes of this essay, it is White's conclusions about the specific status that he assigns to narrative interpretation that preoccupy us.[7]

Stated roughly, White identifies historical discourse with interpretation and historical interpretation with narrativization. A historical narrative is not a *transparent* representation or copy of a sequence of past events. Narration irreducibly entails selecting the events to be included in its exposition as well as filling in links that are not available in the evidential record. The historian does not find or discover her narrative; she constructs it. This process of construction involves distortion[8] and the imposition of generic plot structures (such as Romance, Tragedy, Comedy, and Satire) on the sequence of past events. The plot structures that are culturally available to the narrative historian are inherently fictional; they are not merely neutral, formal armatures on which events are displayed; they have a content – hence, White's emphasis on the notion of the *content of form*. Moreover, that content is fictional.

This conclusion, however, does not lead White to argue that historical interpretations cannot be truthful. Rather they are truthful, but in the way that White takes fictions to be truthful. That is, historical narratives, like fictional narratives, are, by virtue of their plot structures, true in the ways that metaphors are true.

Marx's characterization of the Eighteenth Brumaire of Louis Bonaparte as a farce is assessable in the same way that the sentence "our last faculty meeting was a farce" is assessable. Here, the presiding idea is that there is a variety of metaphorical truth, in contradistinction to literal truth, and that fictions and that historical narratives (with plot structures derived ultimately from myths) are a subspecies thereof.

In according historical narrative this means, albeit fictional in nature, of characterizing reality, White stands at odds with various Continental theorists, such as Lévi-Strauss[9] and the *Annales* school,[10] who disparage narrative history as regressively unscientific, alternatively mythic and fantastic. White, in contrast, grants historical narration cognitive purchase, specifically in terms of metaphor (though sometimes he also uses the notion of allegory to make this point).

White summarizes his position succinctly by saying:

> To emplot real events as a story of a specific kind (or as a mixture of stories of a specific kind) is to trope these events. This is because stories are not lived; there is no such thing as a 'real' story. Stories are told or written, not found. And as for the notion of a 'true' *story,* this is virtually a contradiction in terms. *All* stories are fictions which means, of course, that they can be 'true' in a metaphorical sense and in the sense in which any figure of speech can be true. Is this true enough?[11]

Though as a slogan this is quite pointed, it does require some care in order to understand what White is asserting. Contra Paul Ricoeur's analysis of White,[12] White is not entirely erasing the distinction between fiction and historical writng. Historical writing does refer to past events and those references must be supportable on the basis of the evidential record. In virtue of this evidential requirement, historical writing can be assessed in terms of a literal criterion for truth in a way that fictional exercises should not be. However, in addition to this standard of truth, the historical narrative – that is, the selection, combination, and arrangement of events attested to by the record – is to be evaluated by another criterion, one shared with fictional narratives – to wit: metaphorical aptness.

In this regard, there is a superficial resemblance between the structure of White's account of historical interpretation and Joseph Margolis's notion of robust relativism. For Margolis, the descriptions that ground interpretations are susceptible to evaluation in terms of truth and falsity, whereas the overall interpretation requires some other sort of assessment, say in terms of plausibility.[13] For White, the notation of the events by the historian is responsible to literal canons of evidence, whereas the narrative constructions themselves are metaphorically true. The historian promotes understanding in her reader by casting a sequence of historical events in the form of a culturally shared and familiar narrative pattern (e.g., tragedy), and we assimilate the past under a common myth. This pattern of meaning – embodied in the plot structure, which itself has a kind of mythic content – illuminates insofar as it is a serviceable analog for the past.

So far, I have merely offered a sketch of historical constructivism *à la* White. In the next section, I will try to refine the various arguments that he uses to advance this position, and, in the concluding section, I will review the problems that confront White at almost every turn, along with offering a diagnosis of certain of the deep presuppositions that I believe lead White astray.

2. WHITE'S ARGUMENTS

White characterizes his approach as concerned with a *specifically* historical kind of writing[14] and he explicitly aligns himself with the narrativist, as opposed to a *scientific,* conception of historiography.[15] This seems extravagant to me, for clearly

science can be narrative in form – for example, the geological account of the disposition of the continents – without ceasing to be scientific, and, therefore, narrative cannot be the quiddity of history as differentiated from science.[16] However,
even if White's commitment to narrativism is sometimes overzealous, his position
is still a challenging one. For, obviously, history is often (most often?) presented in
narrative form – even if narration is not the essence of historical exposition – and,
thus, the finding (if it is that) that historical narrative is always in fundamental ways
fictional remains a significant epistemological thesis.[17]

White's leading idea is that historical interpretation is a construction or an
imposition on a sequence of past events insofar as it involves narration. The coherence that narration supplies to a sequence of events is an imaginative invention.
The historical series of events is not coherent – despite the claims of speculative
philosophers of history like Hegel; rather, historical events begin to take coherent
shape only through the historian's narrative efforts.

In this respect, White is not thoroughly antirealist; he does not deny that the
past existed. He is only opposed to the notion that there are "real stories," that is,
that narratives of the past reflect the structure of ongoing, successive, past events.
The past, in other words, is not storied, and representing sequences of events in
story form is, strictly speaking, adding something to them.

Furthermore, even if the references to past events in the historical account are
assessable in terms of truth or falsity, that added "something" – the narrative configuration or pattern (which is more than the conjunction of all the truth-func-
tional references in a historical account) – is not. It must be evaluated as metaphor
or allegory. That is, narrative histories must be thought of in terms of something
called *narrative truth,* which involves more than establishing the truth values of the
conjunction of the atomic sentences that comprise them and which is spoken of
as a different kind of truth.[18]

On White's account, typical historiographic practice proceeds under the
assumption that narrative historians are discovering the structure of past processes
– that is, "real stories." But for White stories are invented, not found, and their
invention by historians is structurally continuous with the efforts of authors of fiction. Thus, historical narratives are on a par with fictional narratives in this respect,
and their cognitive value, *qua* narration, is of a piece with things like novels –
namely, they are sources of metaphorical insight.

White attempts to support his view with a wide range of considerations, involving slogans, contrasts, and analyses of the nature of narrative. These different forms of
argumentation build on and segue with each other in various ways. Their effect, one
supposes, is meant to be cumulative, though one also suspects that White thinks that
each has force independently of the others. So for purposes of this presentation, I will
introduce them as separate considerations, while also taking note of the ways in
which later analyses and arguments build on and flesh out earlier ones.

White's often repeated[19] core slogan, which he shares with Louis Mink,[20] is
that lives are lived and stories are told. Our lives do not come packaged as stories;
we invent stories about them retrospectively through imaginative effort. Thus, the

historians' narrative cannot be taken as a reflection of the lives lived by historical agents. If historians think this way – as White believes they do, despite what they may say – then narrative historians are woefully mistaken.

Though the invocation of "lives" here, as we shall see, is too restrictive as well as infelicitous in other ways, what is intended can be put more rigorously and comprehensively: "Histories, then, are not only about events but also about the possible sets of relationships that those events can be demonstrated to figure. These sets of relationships are not, however, immanent in the events themselves; they exist only in the mind of the historian reflecting on them."[21]

This slogan is fleshed out in terms of various, further contrasts. Since the past is not storied, historical narratives are not *found* or *discovered;* rather they are *invented.*[22] In this sense, historical narratives are *constructions*[23] – constructions that give a sequence of events, such as one might find notated in a historical chronicle or annal, a *meaning.*[24] Historical narratives, in this regard, are also said to *constitute* meaning.[25]

But events, as lived, do not have meanings. They only get meanings by being invested with a function in a narrative. That the Battle of Stalingrad was the *turning point* of World War II, for example, acquires this significance by being a complication in a narrative plot about World War II. The Battle of Stalingrad, *qua* event, had no meaning; and, indeed, it could figure in other stories in which it would have a different meaning. (In an architectual history, for example, the significance of the battle might be that it occasioned the destruction of important buildings.)

Related to the meaning/real event contrast is a contrast between meaning and a copy of an event. Putatively, practicing historians have the naive view that their narratives could be *copies* of events past – by which I understand White to mean something like a perfect replica or mirror image.[26] But historical writing cannot afford a perfect simulacrum of the past. It involves selection and filling in; so it is actually a deviation from an exact copy or representation of the succession of events. In fact, White does not hesitate to call it a *distortion,*[27] presumably a distortion in contrast to whatever would count as a perfect replica or mirror image of a succession of past events.

Narration has its own conditions of intelligibility. Narrative coherence requires features like beginnings, middles, and ends – ends, particularly in the technical sense of closure. But, on what must be ontological grounds, White thinks it is obvious that events do not emerge from the flux of history closed. Closure is a product of narrative coherence. It is the aim of achieving narrative coherence that leads to the selection and hierarchical ordering that imbues the relevant events with meaning, while also *distorting* them in the sense at play in the preceding paragraph.

Narrative coherence, then, is an *imposition*[28] on the historical past. Moreover, the patterns of narrative coherence thus imposed upon (or constructed out of) a collection of historical events are *conventional* (rather than, say, realistically motivated).[29] This inventing, distorting, constructing, imposing, constituting, meaning-making (signifying), and convention-applying activity are all acts of the imagination (in contrast, one supposes, to some more literal information assimilating process). Moreover, this imaginative activity on the part of narrative historians is not different in kind from the activity of the literary fabulist and should be treated as telling us about the world in the same way.

White runs his various foils to actual sequences of events (and perfect replicas thereof) together rather indiscriminately. That is, imagining, constructing, distorting, signifying, constituting, and so on are never scrupulously and differentially defined, and they are all used to serve roughly the same purpose: to underpin the animating distinction between living (the succession of real events) and telling (narrating). One would think that signifying, imagining, distorting, conventionalizing, and so on – not to mention selecting – (though potentially interrelated in interesting ways) should not be lumped together so cavalierly. However, in White's brief they serve as "intuition pumps"[30] directed at consolidating the reigning slogan that distinguishes between living (history as process) and telling (history as narrative *artifact*). Each contrast, that is, is meant to convince us of a disjunction between a sequence of real events or a perfect replica thereof (whatever that might be) and a narrative structure that introduces fictional elements into the flow of events.

White expands upon and concretizes his slogans and intuition pumps by exploiting analyses of narrative by literary theorists – both those of the recent structuralist/poststructuralist dispensation, and that of Northrop Frye.

From continental literary theory, White derives the idea of what he calls "narrativizing discourse."[31] This is putatively discourse that gives the impression that there is no narrator. It is the discourse that in contemporary literary circles is often called "transparent," that is, writing that presents itself to the reader as unmediated and full – a transcription of reality without gaps: "the whole unvarnished truth and nothing but," so to speak. Such discourse, ostensibly appearing without a narrator, presents itself as if "the events seem to tell themselves."[32] The property of "events telling themselves" is called narrativity, and discourse that imbues the events it recounts with this property is narrativizing.

The transparency or narrativizing effect is the hallmark of what many literary theorists call the realist text, such as is supposedly found in the form of the nineteenth-century novel. In adopting the narrating strategies of the realist text, the historian, likewise, presents events as if they were "telling themselves." For White, this implies that naive, narrative historians really have a deep, though unacknowledged and even disavowed, affinity with substantive philosophers of history, like Marx and Hegel, who see the historical process as a single unfolding story – history speaking through the acts of humankind. Thus, if substantive philosophers of history are open to criticism, then less grandiose but nevertheless still narrativizing historians should be vulnerable to the same kind of criticisms.

So, both ordinary narrativizing historians and philosophers of history can be charged with distortion and with masking their highly selective procedures with an imaginary aura of coherence, integrity, and fullness that exploits our desires (for coherence, etc.), but misrepresents reality.[33] White writes, "Does the world really present itself to perception in the form of well-made stories, with central subjects, proper beginnings, middles and ends, and a coherence that permits us to see 'the end' in every beginning?"[34] Any form of narrativity – which is the presupposition that narrative structure literally corresponds to something in the historical past – amounts to the belief that "events tell themselves." But "real events should not speak, should not tell themselves. Real events should simply be."[35] Or, to return to White's earlier slogan: stories can't be found because *real stories* aren't out there in the world of the past to be found.

Though White uses the conceptual frameworks of continental literary theorists to augment his account of narrative history, the literary theorist on whom his argument most relies is Northrop Frye. As we have seen, White believes that narrative historians impose preexisting plot configurations on event series, thereby rendering them intelligible. But this raises the question of identifying some of the plot configurations that historians are supposedly employing. And it is in this context that White is able to use Frye in order to cash in his more philosophically motivated conceptions of historical narration.

According to Frye, there are certain master genres into which literary narratives fall.[36] These include Romance, Tragedy, Comedy, and Satire/Irony. On the basis of the analyses of nineteenth-century historical writing in *Metahistory* and of more recent figures, such as A.J.P. Taylor,[37] White advances the hypothesis that the kinds of narrative configurations identified by Frye in literary fictions are also operative in historical narratives. This empirical claim, if it is sustainable, gives White's more philosophical speculations real bite. For surely narrative configurations of the order of tragedy do have a content as well as generic conditions of coherence such that we would be prone to suspect a historian who selected events from the historical flow under their aegis of imposition in the epistemically dubious or distorting sense. Tragedies, comedies, romances, and satires do seem invented rather than found, at least for the most part. So, if historical narratives tend to have these structures with significant regularity, we might very well admit that the practice of historical writing is of a piece with fiction. For these patterns *are,* first and foremost, fictional genres.

One reason White advances in favor of the idea that historical narratives are impositions is that events can be emplotted in different stories. This, of course, becomes particularly convincing when we think of the stories in terms of generic forms like tragedy and comedy. For certainly the same events or cluster of events can figure in tragedies or comedies – for example, in *Hamlet* or *Rosencrantz and Guildenstern Are Dead.*

Moreover, if it is the case that historical narrative is as thoroughly dependent on generic structures at the level Frye describes them, then the idea that they illuminate metaphorically becomes more perspicuous. Actual series of events may not literally be satiric, but by emplotting them in a satiric structure the narrative historian may be seen to be exhibiting certain aspects of those events in a revelatory way. By likening a sequence of actual events to satire, an apparently desultory group of events takes on a familiar and understandable shape. Furthermore, the notion that these generic structures function as metaphors accommodates White's worries about the selectivity of narrative, for metaphors function cognitively by drawing selected, though ideally revealing, analogies.

Whether White is committed to the existence of only four generic plots is unclear. On the one hand, there are indications in his writings that there might be more, such as the epic;[38] on the other hand, Frye's recurring fourfold division is the most frequently invoked characterization of generic narrative configurations. However this issue is resolved, White does appear to believe that the number of narrative configurations culturally available to the historian is limited and the repertoire is at the level of generality found in Frye's typology. At the same time, White does not think that each historical narrative will be subsumable under one and only one of Frye's types, because some historical works will mix configurational options. Nevertheless, whether pure or mixed, all historical narratives will employ generic configurations and, therefore, possess an inexpungable fictional dimension.

Connected to White's theory of emplotment is his theory of tropology – the tropics of discourse. Not only are the events in historical narratives arranged or emplotted in accordance with a finite number of culturally available story forms (myths), but the events are described by means of tropes, notably metaphor, metonymy, synecdoche, and irony, *and* the tropes a historian favors influence or prefigure the choice of plot structure of the historian's narrative as a whole.

On White's view, since the historian, unlike the scientist, works, for the most part, in the medium of ordinary, rather than technical, language, his tendency will be toward the employment of tropes. A given historian will customarily gravitate toward the use of one trope over others. The use of a particular trope is likely to predispose her toward, or to correspond to, one form of culturally available emplotment over others. Thus, from the ground up, so to say, the work of the narrative historian begins to converge on that of the writer of literary fiction at the level of descriptive tropes that, in turn, portend the use of certain kinds of plots that are mythic in nature.

White writes:

> the four general types of tropes identified by neo-classical rhetorical theory appear to be basic: metaphor (based on the principle of similitude), metonymy (based on that of contiguity), synecdoche (based on the identification of parts of a thing belonging to a whole), and irony (based on opposition). Considered as the basic structures of figuration, these four tropes provide us with categories for identifying the modes of linking an order of words to an order of thoughts ... on the paradigmatic axis of an utterance and of one phase of a discourse with preceding and succeeding phrases ... on the syntagmatic axis. The dominance of one mode of associating words and thoughts with one another across an entire discourse allows us to characterize the structure of the discourse as a whole in tropological terms. The tropological structures of metaphor, metonymy, synecdoche, and irony (and what I take – following Northrop Frye – to be their corresponding plot types: Romance, Tragedy, Comedy and Satire) provide us with a much more refined classification of the kinds of historical discourses than that based on the conventional distinction between "linear"

and "cyclical" representations of historical processes. They also allow us to see more clearly the ways in which historical discourse resembles and indeed converges with fictional narrative, both in the strategies it uses to endow events with meanings and in the kinds of truth in which it deals.[39]

White, then, fills out and supports his claims about the invented or imposed nature of historical narration by means of three substantive, empirical claims: (1) historians structure their descriptions tropologically; (2) historians narrate through generic story forms; (3) the tropes a historian uses prefigure or, in some other way, correspond to her generic story forms. Crucial here is the assertion of the operation of generic story forms that can be supported either inductively through a sample of historical writing or (roughly) deductively as following from (1) and (3). Moreover, if (2) is defensible, then the claims that historical narratives are imposed and that they are fictional gain plausibility insofar as a series of past events would not (or, at least, would almost never) appear to be intrinsically comic or tragic. Consequently, if *narrative truth* is a matter of configurations at the level of such (fictional or mythic) plot structures, then it will not be assessable in terms of the truth of the conjunction of its constituent, atomic sentences. That is, if *narrative truth* is truthful, it must be evaluated on another model, which, logically speaking, opens the possibility that it is a subspecies of metaphorical truth.

3. RESISTING WHITE'S CONSTRUCTIVISM

Though the full force of White's position is best realized when his various intuition pumps are backed up by his empirical claims about the genre-derived nature of historical narratives and his tropology, it seems to me that his intuition pumps rely upon certain philosophical presuppositions that he believes will carry his assertion concerning the fictional nature of historical narrative independently of his general findings about generic emplotment and tropology. Thus, in dissecting his position, it is important to challenge those philosophical presuppositions before turning to his broad empirical claims about the kinds of generic structures found in historical narratives.

According to White, lives are lived and stories are told. The putative consequence of this is that insofar as historical narratives represent the lives of the past in story form, they do not correspond to what existed in the past and are, therefore, fictional. This is not compelling comprehensively. For it is often the case that we plan – if not our entire lives, at least important episodes therein – by means of telling or visualizing stories to ourselves, and, then, we go about enacting them. That is, lives can be storied; indeed there is a branch of psychology that uses this idea as a research hypothesis.[40] Consequently, with certain life episodes – and, in some cases, perhaps with some monomaniacal lives – there are stories, hatched by historical agents, that had causal efficacy in the past and could be discovered and written up by historians. Thus, to the extent that the contrast between lives and stories is not thoroughly exclusive, the conclusion that any historical narrative must be fictional is not without exception; there could be historical narratives of storied lives, or, at least, of storied episodes in the lives of historical agents.

Of course, this is not the real issue that the lives/stories dichotomy is meant to broach. For historians are not merely biographers in search of life stories. The contrast between lives and stories is meant to call to mind colorfully the idea that historical narratives are not found or discovered in the past, but are constructions or inventions. The notion of *invention* here is a bit tricky and open to equivocation. In one sense, historical narratives are inventions, namely, in the sense that they are made by historians; but it is not clear that it follows from this that they are *made-up* (and are, therefore, fictional).

Narratives are a form of representation, and it is true that historians do not go about finding their representations as one might find a lost picture, a lost photo, or a lost piece of film footage. Photos and filmstrips are made (invented) and they are not found. We could say that lives are lived, and home movies are invented. But this doesn't entail that a stretch of film footage cannot record the past or yield accurate information about it. Similarly, narratives are a form of representation, and, in that sense, they are invented, but that does not preclude their capacity to provide accurate information. Narratives can provide accurate knowledge about the past in terms of the kinds of features they track, namely, the ingredients of *courses of events,*[41] which include: background conditions, causes and effects, as well as social context, the logic of situations, practical deliberations, and ensuing actions.

For example, on July 3, 1989, the U.S. Supreme Court announced a decision that delegated responsibility for regulating the availability of abortions to the discretion of individual states. This decision was the result, in significant respects, of the success of the Reagan regime in appointing a series of like-minded, conservative judges to the Supreme Court. The appointment of those judges, including O'Connor and Scalia, in the context of a background project of contesting the perceived past liberalism of the Supreme Court, was part of a real historical process, a course of events, that culminated on July 3, 1989.

This is not to say that there will not be further consequences to the court's decision nor that this is the *final* culmination of Reagan's successful efforts to reorient the court. But the fact that there is more to come does not vitiate the fact that the Reagan administration's decisions and appointments were significant ingredients in a real historical process that had as one result – *one,* for there will be more – the decision on July 3, 1989. The historian who tracks these decisions and appointments, situating them in their social contexts, will make something – something that may take imagination to accomplish – namely, a historical representation. But there is no reason to suppose that such historical representations are necessarily *made-up* or invented unless, for some as yet undemonstrated reason, courses of events must be excluded from our ontology. Moreover, if courses of events are admissable ontologically, then they are there to be discovered and represented.

That my counterexamples so far often rely on the idea of deliberations and decisions implemented in ensuing actions may appear open to the objection that they presuppose a commitment on the part of historians to recreating the internal perspective of historical agents. This, in turn, would be criticized as problematic for two related reasons. First, that historians are not simply concerned with narrating events in terms of how the agents saw them *and* that, even if historians were so disposed, they should not be so exclusively preoccupied since it is often (most often?) the unintended consequences of people's deliberations and decisions about which we most care.

These objections, however, require two remarks. First, if there are courses of events that did issue as planned from the agent's perhaps storied deliberation, this would be enough to show that there is a sense in which the thesis that stories are never found fails to be fully comprehensive. But a second and more important point is that in speaking of courses of events, we are not committed to rendering them solely in terms of the original intentions of the agents involved in them. A course of events may involve failed attempts, like Reagan's nomination of Bork to the Supreme Court, which will result in more deliberative activity that may have further unintended consequences. Or, the agent's deliberative activity may involve miscalculations that call for the historian to illuminate the prevailing conditions that made the attempt misfire. That practical reasoning and its implementation in action provide some of the ingredients that make a course of events adhere in no way implies that the representation of a course of events will be a string of successful practical syllogisms. That practical, deliberative activity will supply some measure of cohesiveness to the narratives of human events does not restrict us to a form of historical intentionalism nor does it preclude discussion of corporate entities like states or classes.[42]

Of course, in speaking of courses of events, I do not mean to imply that any given event is only a member of one course of events. The appointment of Sandra Day O'Connor to the Supreme Court is part of the course of events that led to the decision alluded to above. But that event also undoubtedly figured in various other courses of events – some in the history of the O'Connor family and some concerning the social advancement of women in the United States. And, equally, the event of O'Connor's appointment will also figure in courses of events still in the making. The same event can be part of different courses of events, and, therefore, can be represented in different stories. But the fact that different events can figure in different stories in no way indicates that the stories are fictional. For this suspicion to counterfeit plausibility, we would have to assume that in order to be nonfictional, there would have to be only one relevant story, perhaps of the sort proposed by speculative philosophers of history, and that each event in it would be significant in one and only one way. That is, if there is more than one story, then stories are invented, and, therefore, fictional. But the presumed disjunction that either there is one real story or a multiplicity of fictional ones fails to accommodate the fact that courses of action intersect and branch off from shared events, which intersections and branches can be found or discovered.

In White's way of speaking, when a given event is situated in different narratives it can acquire a different meaning. That events have these differential meanings indicates that they are imposed and, therefore, fictional. But talk of meanings here may be a little misleading. Events have different significances in different courses of events.[43] Anthony Scalia's appointment to the Supreme Court has one significance in terms of the great abortion debate and another, though perhaps not completely unrelated, significance in the history of Italian Americans. In these examples, the idea of significance can be cashed in causally. If *meaning* here amounts to playing a role in a network of socially significant causation, then there should be no problems in admitting that Scalia's appointment may have a different meaning in different courses of events. This simply allows that a single event can play a different role in different causal chains. This does not indicate that a meaning has been imposed on the event. Again, the event may occur in different stories because the different stories track different courses of overlapping events.[44]

White's use of the notion of meaning in his arguments gives his thesis a semantic flavor, which perhaps suggests a level of arbitrariness that would warrant talk of imposition. However, it is important to stress that the kind of *meaning* that an event has in a narrative is a matter of its significance with respect to subsequent events, often in terms of causation and/or practical reasoning. And whether significance in this sense obtains is not arbitrary or imposed. That the historian wants to know what caused the American entry into World War II does not make her citation of the attack on Pearl Harbor an imposition on the historical train of events nor is her imputation of causal efficacy to the attack arbitrary in any way. This is not to deny that events in historical narratives will be events under a description; but within the context of a given research project, the description of a pertinent event is not arbitrary in the way that on some views of language the relation between a signifier and a signified is arbitrary. Similarly, it is not helpful to think of the historian's description of an action in terms of its significance in a course of events as constitutive of the event in any strong sense; whether Pearl Harbor, for example, was a cause of World War II is a fact even if it were not asserted in historical accounts.

White contrasts historical narratives replete with meanings to copies of the past. The historical narrative, involving selection and abduction, is not a copy of the past, and, therefore, is fictional. The contrast here seems forced; the visual references to copies and mirrors is particularly strained though revelatory of an empiricist residue in White's thinking. Obviously, historical narratives are not mirror images of the past; in general (save for things like cinematic documentaries) they are not even pictorial, let alone perfect pictorial replicas of anything. But why should the fact that they are not pictures imply they are fictions?

However, the preceding worry misses the point. The idea of a copy of the past should probably be understood metaphorically. A copy of the past would be a perfect reflection of everything that transpired in the relevant time span with nothing added or subtracted. It would bear an exact correspondence to all and only what came about, or, even more strictly, to what could have been perceived as past events unfolded. Anything that falls short of this is said to be fictional.

Of course, it is difficult to imagine that practicing historians pursue the production of such copies in their work, or that, informed as they are of the historical evidence, they construe their narratives as perfect replicas of the past. But White, it seems, wants to confront them with a dilemma. Either historical narratives are copies in the relevant sense or they are fictional. The way to deal with this dilemma is to reject it – to maintain that historical narratives are not and, in fact, should not be copies in the mirror sense while also maintaining that this does not make them fictional.

The notion that only copies in the mirror sense would not be fictional presupposes something like a narrowly empiricist, correspondence criterion of truth. White explicitly denies the viability of this approach in one sense – he denies that historical narratives could meet it. However, this does not seem to lead him to reject the criterion entirely. That is, he appears to continue to regard it as the ideal criterion for nonfictional historical exposition, even if it is an unrealizable ideal. And, to the extent that it is unrealizable, he consigns historical narration to the realm of fiction. But what is strange here is that White doesn't take the inapplicability of this ideal of truth as a grounds for advancing alternative criteria of nonfictional truth for historical narratives.

Confronted by the inapplicability of the copy ideal of an empiricist view of correspondence truth, it seems to me that the line one should take is to search for some other grounds for accommodating the truth of historical narratives construed as nonfictional. That is, we should hold onto the intuition that historical narratives can be truthful in the way that nonfictional discourse is true, drop the expectation that this is explicable in terms of a naive view of correspondence to the past as a whole, and explore alternative models. White, in effect, maintains the criteria of empiricist correspondence, which leads him to reassigning historical narration to the realm of fiction. In this respect, oddly enough, he turns out to be a closet empiricist – presupposing that anything that falls short of the correspondence standard is fictional.[45]

Undoubtedly, there is a parallel between White's strategy here and that of many deconstructionists. When they note the failure of certain theories of language on the grounds that no language is an absolute mirror of the world, they conclude that meaning is an arbitrary, infinitely fluctuating construct rather than surmising that the expectation that a language might absolutely mirror the world was a theoretical error to begin with, and that a better view of the way in which a language is objectively constrained should be sought. That is, they remain in the thrall of a bad theory of language, employing it to motivate their skepticism, at the same time that they agree that no language squares with the idealization. This is akin to reasoning that either existence has an absolute meaning ordained by God or it has no meaning; since there is no God, there is no meaning. This way of thinking shares the theistic assumption that only something like God could serve as a source of meaning. An alternative would be to search for other sources of meaning once the hypothesis that there is no God is endorsed. Similarly, in consigning historical narration to the realm of fiction on the grounds that it is not a perfect replica of the past, White remains implicitly in the very empiricist camp from which he explicitly wishes to part company.

Armed with the copy ideal of nonfictionality, White recycles the issue of selectivity, which must be the most perennial pretext for suspecting the objectivity of historical narration. Obviously, a narrative selects a subset of events and event relationships from the historical flow; thus, if candidacy for nonfictionality depends on correspondence to the whole past, or the whole past within certain stipulated time parameters, a historical narrative will be discounted. But, again, this should lead us to drop the copy ideal of nonfictionality and not to jettison the idea that historical narratives are nonfictional. This is not the place to review all the arguments that are designed to show that the selectivity of historical narratives need not be epistemologically problematic in any way that warrants special attention. Some historians may select the events they highlight in dubitable ways, but there are procedures for ascertaining whether the processes of selection a given historian employs are questionable. That is, historians may produce distortive representations of the past because of biased procedures, but this only goes to show that the selective attention of a given narrative may be distorting, and not that selectivity, in and of itself, is problematic. If it were, then scientific findings, which are also selective, would also, by parity of reasoning, be fictional.

White, himself, may remain unmoved by our last argument. For he is apparently convinced of the constructivist/conventionalist view of science. Thus, he seems to gain confidence by analogizing historical narratives with scientific theories, as construed by constructivists. Surmising that scientific theories are constructed on the basis of observational data that underdetermine theory choice, which data themselves are theory-laden, White thinks of narratives as similarly constructed, in contexts where the data would support alternative stories, and he thinks of narrative events as, so to speak, story-laden. Thus, if the adoption of a scientific theory is conventional, given the putative fact that it is one construction of the data within a range of equally acceptable ones, then historical narratives, assuming the analogy to scientific theories, are equally conventional. Their selective organization of the data does not correspond to reality, but is an invention developed within conventional choice procedures. Thus, one dispels the argument of the preceding paragraph by maintaining that scientific selectivity forces us to concede that scientific theories are imaginative constructions – and in that sense fictions – and, therefore, no incongruity is engendered by maintaining that comparable processes of selection with respect to historical narratives render them fictional as well.[46]

A major problem with this invocation of the philosophy of science is that it presumes that the facts of scientific theorizing pointed to by constructivists entail antirealism. But a solid case for the compatibility of scientific realism with the facts of the history of science, upon which constructivists rely, is available,[47] thereby blocking any facile attempt to derive historical antirealism with respect to narrative from scientific antirealism with respect to theories. That is, the selective procedures and inferred nature of theoretical entities does not commit us to antirealism; it does not force us to deny that scientific theories are approximately true. Therefore, even if suitable analogies could be drawn between constructivism in science and constructivism in historiography,[48] we would not have to regard historical narratives as fictional.

A course of events transpiring between $t1$ and $t5$ need not comprise every event or state of affairs in its temporal neighborhood. Therefore, a narrative representation that tracks that course of events need not refer to every occurrence in the stipulated time span. Narratives are selective, but this is appropriate given the nature of courses of events. Nor is it useful to call the reconstruction of a course of events distortive just because it involves selection. Indeed, from the perspective of attempting cognitively to assimilate a representation of the past, the portrayal of a course of events that chronicled all the events in the temporal neighborhood would distort insofar as it would muddy the links between the pertinent elements in the sequence.

Likewise, our narrative accounts may have to be revised in the light of subsequent events; this does not show that historical narratives are fictional, but only that there are always more stories to tell. Moreover, that some historical narratives may be superseded by ones that are more fine-grained no more shows that the earlier ones were fictional than the adjustment of one approximately true scientific theory with further details (atomic theory amplified by the characterization of subatomic particles) shows that the earlier viewpoint must now be evaluated according to a different standard of truth.

No historical narrative says everything there is to say, not even about all the events within the time frame that it discusses. The historian exercises choice in the sense that the linkage between some events and not others will be given salience in order to illuminate a given course of events. It is true, as White repeatedly emphasizes, that in charting these linkages and in making the relevant selections, the historian uses her imagination. But, *pace* White, it is quite a long throw from the historian's use of her imagination in discerning said linkages to the inference that the historian's narrative is on a par with that of the imaginative writer (i.e., the writer of fiction). White appears to presume that there is a correlation between the use of the imagination and fiction. But this is illicit. On many views of the imagination, such as Kant's, the imagination plays a role in perception, but my perception of my house is in no way fictional.

Many of White's arguments for the fictionality of historical narrative hinge on contrasting said narratives with copies of the past. Any addition (imaginative construction) or subtraction of detail (selection) from such a copy, conceived of on the model of a mirror, is evidence of fictionality. But the foil is inadmissable. Not only is the visual metaphor inapplicable – it is not the case that not being an exact copy of x entails being a fictional representation of x; but it indicates a residual commitment to a very radical version of an empiricist expectation of exact "perceptual" correspondence between a representation and its referent, which is not only philosophically bogus but is at odds with White's own suspicion of empiricism. Like the skeptic who arrives at her position by accepting a phenomenalist account of perception and who, therefore, remains effectively an empiricist, White regards historical narration as fictional, because he continues to employ something as implausible as perceptual correspondence as the standard of nonfictionality.

White's emphasis on the verbal dimension of historical narration sends him to contemporary discourse theory for insight. There he encounters the idea that narration in what is called the realist text gives the reader the impression that the text is transparent – that it is unmediated, for example, by a narrator exercising selectivity – indeed, that it is as if the text were reality narrating itself. This corresponds to White's own view that historians write as if they were discovering real stories, stories immanent in the historical process, whereas they are really fitting preexisting story templates onto past events. The ideas that "events narrate themselves" and that the historian, so to speak, records them as a dictaphone might, ostensibly shows acceptance of the disreputable assumption of speculative philosophers of history to the effect that the historical process is storied – that is, that historical events have a single significance in some overarching historical narrative.

This is a very perplexing argument. It begins by attributing transparency – or, narrativity, as White calls it – to realist texts. But to whom does the text appear transparent? Presumably, to naive readers and the naive historians who write under the supposedly misguided faith that they could track a historical course of events. These naive readers and writers are somehow possessed by the idea that reality is narrating itself. Stated this way, the belief attributed to them is at least obscure and, on a number of readings, absurd.

It is absurd to think of events as telling or narrating their own story in any literal sense, as White notes. But, in fact, it is so absurd on a literal reading that it is hard to believe that any readers or writers, no matter how naive, can be taken in by it. No one could believe that reality literally narrates itself, so it is an inadequate starting point from which to field a dialectically alternative account. It is, so to say, an argumentative red herring, rather than a genuine competing theory whose defeat gives way to White's alternative, fictional account of historical narration. That is, faced with a transparency account of historical narration and White's account, we are not moved to White's theory by the all-too-easy defeat of the attributed transparency view, but rather suspect that we have not started with a viable field of competing accounts.

Stated nonabsurdly, but still obscurely, the transparency effect might be thought of as the impression on the part of naive readers and naive historians that the text is unmediated, that it is without gaps, that it renders a full account of the past. However, this too seems to be such a bizarre conviction to attribute to anyone that it is a nonstarter. Historians obviously know that they are selecting a series of events from a larger sequence, and readers have only to look at the title page of the book to learn the identity of the narrator/mediator. No one, in short, believes that historical texts are unmediated; or, to put it positively, any informed reader or writer is aware that a text involves selection. In this, everyone agrees with White, and the view that some do not is a straw man. Where there is undoubtedly disagreement is in the assumption that selection implies fictionality. But the burden of proof is on White to show this, and, in my opinion, the only means at his disposal is the dubious, implicit assumption that nonfiction requires exact correspondence.[49]

Associated with White's implicit presumption of a standard of exact correspondence is his apparent view that if one assumes that there are "real stories," then said stories would have to be of the nature of what we can call absolute stories. For any series of events, an event emplotted in a narrative structure that is immanent in the historical process will have one and only one fixed significance. Something like this view is what leads him to believe that the narrative exploits of practicing historians correspond to those of substantive philosophers of history. I suppose that White is prompted to this intuition on the grounds that if one actually composed a nonfictional narrative in accordance with the exact correspondence standard, one would have a unitary picture of the past in which every event had a determinate place. Of course, White, and perhaps everyone else, thinks that this is impracticable. But White goes on to argue from the infeasibility of absolute stories to the fictionality of all historical narratives.

That is, given an event or a series of events, we can develop a number of stories. No event or event series has one final, that is, *single,* fixed significance for reasons rehearsed above. Events and event series can, through narration, be connected with alternative events and event series. A collection of events, in a manner of speaking, underdetermines the stories in which they can play a role. From this, White infers that there can be no "real stories"; if there were "real stories," immanent in the historical process, events would fall into one and only one train of events, said train inscribed in events like the evolution of Hegel's world spirit. Historical narrative presumes that the historical process is narrativized and if the historical process is narrativized and there are real stories, the significance of each event fits into one and only one story. So, since there is always more than one derivable story, there are no real stories.

But once again, the argument proceeds on the basis of a straw man. The requirement that "real stories" be absolute stories is exorbitant from the outset. Stories will be nonfictionally accurate insofar they track courses of events. But courses of events overlap and branch, and there is no need to presume – as perhaps Hegel did – that there is only one course of events. Thus, events and series of events may play different roles in different stories. But that events and series of events figure in different stories is no obstacle to those stories being nonfictional. There are different stories because there are discrete courses of events whose interest is relative to the questions the historian asks of the evidence. This relativity, which precludes the possibility of an absolute story, however, does not make the historical narrative fictional. Rather it makes the accuracy of the nonfictional account assessable in terms of what questions are being directed to the relevant courses of events.[50]

Like innumerable poststructuralist commentators, White appears to believe that agreement that there is no absolute interpretation, no final word, so to say, with respect to *x,* should impel us to avoid the imputation of truth to an interpretation of *x.* That is, if there are a multiplicity of interpretations available for *x,* then the question of literal truth goes by the boards. A true interpretation would have to be an absolute interpretation; an absolute interpretation would have to be the final word on its subject; but since there are no such absolute interpretations – here with respect to historical narratives – there is no question of literal truth.

Needless to say, this is a bad argument with respect to literary criticism. To say a literary interpretation is true if and only if it is the only acceptable account of a text is absurd; one does not deny the truth of a literary interpretation by showing that another interpretation is possible. For the other interpretation may be compatible with the interpretation under scrutiny. That a text supports a multiplicity of interpretations does not disallow the possibility that all of them are literally true; the epistemological issue with respect to a collection of interpretations of texts only becomes live when they are inconsistent.

But here it is important to keep two very different arguments separate: one says that truth is inapplicable to interpretations because there is always a multiplicity of acceptable interpretations of x available; the other says that truth is inapplicable to interpretations because there is always, at least in principle, a multiplicity of equally acceptable but inconsistent interpretations of x available. The former view is based on the truism that there may be no absolute interpretation of x, but from that truism it does not follow that several different interpretations of x cannot be conjointly true, for example, that *1984* is about totalitarianism *and* that it is about Stalinism. The pressure to abandon the question of truth with respect to interpretations only impinges when it can be argued that we are always confronted by a multiplicity of incompatible interpretations.

Turning from literary interpretation to historical narration, the pressing question is which of the preceding arguments can be sustained. Here, it seems to me that it is obvious that there are multiple stories that can be derived from a given set of events, but, without buying into White's confidence in generic emplotment, there is no reason to presume that these different stories must conflict, and, therefore, no reason to believe that they cannot be assessed in terms of literal truth.[51] Sandra Day O'Connor's appointment to the Supreme Court is part of the narrative of somewhat recent abortion decisions and part of the narrative of women's social empowerment. These stories need not conflict and both could be true. Insofar as White's arguments about historical narration, unlike Joseph Margolis's arguments about literary interpretation, do not show that different historical narratives can always in principle be nonconverging and inconsistent, historical narrations remain assessable in terms of literal standards of truth.

Again, the recognition that an event or an event series affords an ingredient for more than one story is a truism. It does not force us to concede that historical narratives cannot be assessed in terms of literal truth. Nor does it seem compelling to suppose that ordinary historians must buy into the presuppositions of substantive philosophers of history in order to regard their narratives in terms of truth. For there is no logical requirement that true narratives be absolutely true. Historians can trace alternative courses of events without presupposing that some one course of events is privileged because history is *the* story of human emancipation or class struggle.

So far we have been considering White's more abstract, philosophical arguments. Now we must evaluate his empirical theses. For it may be the case that White's abstract arguments, when filled in by his empirical claims, are more convincing. We have argued that the fact that an event may be incorporated in more than one story supplies no reason to believe that historical narratives cannot be literally true. But if we accept White's claim that all historical narratives are generically emplotted in terms of romance, tragedy, comedy, and satire, perhaps White's position can be given new life. For, on the one hand, most events do not seem to be intrinsically comic or tragic; and, on the other hand, if events are alternatively emplottable as comedies or tragedies, then alternative, equally acceptable, but incompatible interpretations seem available such that both cannot be literally true. That is, if one historian's narrative of an event sequence portrays it as comic and another portrays it as tragic, and both are acceptable, though incompatible, then what warrants these interpretations cannot be literal truth.

Of course, whether this argument is successful depends upon whether White is correct in claiming that all historical narratives are generically emplotted in terms of the sort of narrative forms that White suggests. Undoubtedly, some historians may deploy the kinds of mythic plots typified by Frye. But do all historical narratives do this? My own inclination is to think that they do not. For example, in a recent, randomly selected, narrative explanation of the perplexities confronting contemporary socialism, Michael Harrington writes:

> One might say from 1883 (when Marx died and the social democracy was about to enter its golden age) to 1945 the socialists attempted, with a notable lack of success, to figure out precisely what they meant by socialism. Then in the postwar age, it seemed that John Maynard Keynes had miraculously provided the answer that Marx had neglected: socialization was the socialist administration of an expanding capitalist economy whose surplus was then partly directed to the work of justice and freedom. When, sometime in the seventies, that Keynesian era came to an end, the socialists were once more thrown into confusion. Which is where we are now.[52]

This brief narrative does not seem to me to be identifiable as either a tragedy, a comedy, a romance, or a satire. And, furthermore, if most narrative writing of history is, as I suspect, as generically neutral as this example, then the importance of generic emplotment for the assessment of historical narration becomes extremely exiguous. Of course, whether, in fact, historical narration is typically plotted generically or is more like the preceding example is an empirical question. But even if my counterexample is not the norm, it still shows from the perspective of the philosophy of history that not all historical narratives are generically emplotted. Therefore, not all historical narratives can be matched with equally compelling alternatives in contradictory generic modes. Therefore, not all historical narratives raise the problem of the multiplicity of inconsistent interpretations in such a way that talk of literal truth is rendered problematic.

Moreover, assessing the empirical accuracy of White's theory of generic emplotment would be very difficult – not because there would be so many narratives to consider, but because White's characterization of his generic modes is so vague. Confronted by the preceding counterexample, White would probably attempt to show that it fits one of his genres. But his apparent success in this matter would be based on the fact that these genres are very loosely defined and there are no conditions of application for these modes in evidence. Consequently, some feature of Harrington's little narrative can probably be lined up with at least one feature of one of White's genres. However, White's freewheeling, associative manner of identifying genre membership not only makes his thesis suspicious, but unfalsifiable. Thus, the very *ad hoc* flavor of White's analysis undercuts its reliability as the basis for maintaining that for any historical narrative, there is an equally acceptable contradictory narrative – that is, a narrative in an incompatible genre – that forces us to concede that the criterion of truth is inapplicable to it.

On White's view, historical narratives will be emplotted in terms of romance, comedy, tragedy, satire, or a mode of comparable generality; those modes are said to be incompatible but alternatively available for a given series of events; so, no narrative can be literally true. I am not convinced that these genres are necessarily contradictory in the sense that the argument requires. However, even if they are, it seems to me that many (most?) historical narratives are not emplotted at this level of generality, but derive their plot structures by tracking causes, reasons and consequences in a way that allows for straightforward evaluation in terms of truth. This is not a matter of imposing cultural conventions (White's generic plots) on event series, so the putative undecidability between White's story-templates is of little moment in assessing typical historical narratives. Furthermore, if White wishes to dispute this claim, he will have to rigorously define his generic plots so that should he find them everywhere, we may rest assured that this is because they are everywhere and not because they are so carelessly characterized that they can be applied to anything.

Along with his theory of generic emplotment, White has his theory of tropes, which is meant to reinforce his theory of plots. Every historical narrative relies on tropes – specifically those of metaphor, metonymy, synecdoche, and irony – and the historian's choice of trope prefigures her choice of generic emplotment. Insofar as narratives are troped, they are emplotted in generic forms. Emplotment in generic forms, then, seems unavoidable, despite my protests to the contrary.

Unfortunately, many of the problems that afflict White's theory of emplotment also plague his tropology. On the face of it, it does not seem difficult randomly to peruse the work of narrative historians and to find long stretches of nonfigurative writing. White seems to think that because historians use ordinary language, they must use tropes. But since there is nonfigurative ordinary language, it is difficult to be persuaded by this argument.[53]

One would think that it would be easy to determine whether historical writing is dominated by the four tropes in the ways White argues. It should be a simple matter of statistically gauging their incidence (along with correlating that incidence with the frequency of the associated generic plots). However, the question is not so easily settled because White's idea of troping pertains not only literally to instances of figurative language but to modes of thought. Thus, to determine whether a given trope dominates a historian's writing may call for an interpretation of her style of thought and the correlation of that mode of thought with a trope. A historian, for example, who emphasizes the repetition of certain kinds of events in her narrative might be said to be thinking tropically in terms of metaphors. But as with White's plot categories, his trope categories are not tightly defined, and one worries that his attributions of this or that trope to a particular writer has an ad hoc ring to it. That White's discussion of tropes can shift between specific verbal structures and vaguely sketched styles of thought suggests a capacity for ambiguity that renders the claim that all historical writing is tropological disturbingly unfalsifiable.

Furthermore, construed as figures of thought, White's tropes bear a strong similarity to associationist principles for the connection of ideas. Thus, to the extent that such a theory represents a crude but still rather commodious cartography of mental operations, it will come as no surprise that examples of one or another connectives – for example, similarity, contiguity or contrast – will subsume virtually every example of human thinking. That is, whether thinking is articulated in ordinary language or scientific language, or whether it is narrative or analytic, it will exemplify fundamental associative principles. Thus, casting tropes at a level of generality such that they become indiscernible from associationist principles of thought undermines the attempt to separate historical narrative from other types of human thought, such as science. Indeed, tropes thought of as mental processes subvert the distinction between the literal and the figurative that White himself needs to particularize what he thinks is special about the way historical narratives inform us about the world.

Of course, if we think of tropes less expansively, then I think that we have no reason to think that historians must employ tropes at all, or that in actual practice a historian's writing will inevitably be figurative or dominated by the choice of a particular, dominating trope. And, as well, even if a historian's writing were figurative that would not force us to evaluate it according to some figurative or metaphorical standard of truth because even metaphors, conceived of as implied similes, can be straightforwardly said to be true or false.[54]

If it is not the case that all historical writing is tropological in some nonvacuous way, then it is not true that in virtue of their tropes all historical narratives correspond to a generic plot of the order of comedy, tragedy, romance, or satire. That is, the hypothesis of the pervasiveness of tropes cannot support the claim of the generality of generic emplotment nor the corresponding claim of the permanent possibility of conflicting interpretations.

However, even if it were plausible to maintain that all historical writing indulges in the use of the four tropes and that for any given piece of historical narration one of the four tropes is likely to dominate, the link between the choice of a trope and the choice of a generic mode of emplotment – the prefiguration thesis – remains persistently obscure. For example, White writes that "The *mythos* of Synecdoche is a dream of Comedy, the apprehension of a world in which all struggle, strife and conflict are dissolved in the realization of a perfect harmony."[55] Yet, granting the Frye-derived conception of comedy here, we still want to know what this has to do with any literal construction of the trope of synecdoche. Here we are likely to be told that the trope of synecdoche is integrative,[56] so the integrative trope goes with the integrative plot. But surely one can employ synecdoches, even a great many of them, without that resulting in a narrative of reconciliation. And, if we are told that what is at issue is not literal synecdochal structures but a style of thought that underlies the text, then we shall wonder whether we have two things here – synecdochal thinking and comic thinking – or just comedy, construed ever so broadly as integration, which has nothing to do with tropes except that White has implicitly stipulated that *synecdoche* can be an equivalent name for it. And, if this is the case, then we merely have a jerry-rigged definition masquerading as the discovery of the very causal-sounding relation of prefiguration.

Neither the generic emplotment hypothesis nor the tropological hypothesis seem to pertain to all historical narration. Nor does the idea – even if the tropological hypothesis were true – that choice of tropes prefigures choice of generic emplotment seem plausible. So accepting the hypothesis that all historical narratives are tropological would not entail that they were all generically emplotted. And if we have no reason to think that all historical narratives are generically emplotted in terms of romance, tragedy, comedy, and irony, then we are not threatened by the prospect that any given historical narrative will be in one of these genres but could be equally in another conflicting genre (events emplotted as comedy could always be emplotted in the incompatible genre of tragedy). Rather, historical narratives can be (and generally are) plotted at a lower level of structure, tracking courses of events in terms of such things as causes, reasons, and consequences. And there is no reason to think that there must be alternative, equally cogent, but incompatible narratives of given courses of events at this level of structure.

Underlying White's overall view, it seems to me, is a picture of the following sort: a narrative, specifically a nonfiction narrative, is a collection of sentences ordered in a certain way. Narratives, however, are not simply evaluated in terms of the truth or falsity of their constituent sentences. The way in which the sentences are ordered is also epistemically crucial. But this dimension of epistemic evaluation would not be assessed if the narrative were evaluated solely in terms of the conjunction of the truth values of its individual, fact-asserting sentences. Moreover, it seems to be presumed that saying a narrative's epistemic adequacy for White would have to be reducible to the assessment of the truth value of the conjunction of the constituent atomic sentences in the narrative. But since the adequacy of the narrative – with respect to its structure of ordering relations – involves something beyond the truth of the sum of the truth values of its atomic sentences, the narrative as a whole must, at least in part, be assessable in terms of some other standard.

Furthermore, White also appears to presuppose that the sole epistemic category relevant to the assessment of historical narratives is truth – either literal truth construed on the model of some picture theory in which each atomic sentence corresponds to some past fact (or facts), or to some kind of truth construed in other terms. White then worries that whatever governs the selective structure of a narrative may not correspond to anything in the past. Thus, the truth of that structure must be assessable in other terms, such as metaphorical accuracy.

Now if this diagnosis of White's presuppositions is correct, it is easy to avoid his conclusions. First of all, too much is being made of the idea of atomic sentences.[57] Narratives are typically written in sentences. But nothing of great importance should hinge on this. For where the relevant narrative linkages are of the nature of relations between background conditions, causes, effects, reasons, choices, actions, and the like, the text can be reconstructed perspicuously in terms of propositions that can, in turn, be straightforwardly evaluated with respect to truth. In some cases, these reconstructions will be a matter of paraphrasing the individual sentences in such a way as to make the relevant narrative relations obtaining between them evident. In other cases, the sentences found in the text will have to be expanded so as to make narrative linkages that are presupposed or conversationally implied explicit. But paraphrases and expansions of this sort in nowise mandate some special criteria of truth.

Undoubtedly, White might concede the preceding point, but still maintain that it does not get at the heart of his misgivings. For even allowing the paraphrases and expansions adverted to above, he will argue that narratives still add something and that this added something – the principles that guide the narrator's selections – is not to be literally found in the past. To the extent that that something is a matter of linkages like causes and reasons, White's argument is not compelling. However, he is right to point out that we will assess a given narrative as a good narrative in terms of criteria over and above the truthfulness of all its propositions even when suitably expanded and/or paraphrased. Should this drive us toward regarding narration as fictional and as assessable as metaphor?

I think not. To be an adequate narrative, indeed to be an adequate historical account of any sort, a candidate needs to do more than merely state the truth (indeed, an historical account could contain only true statements and yet be adjudged unacceptable[58]). It must also meet various standards of objectivity. For example, a historical narrative should be comprehensive; it should incorporate all those events that previous research has identified to be germane to the subject that the historian is seeking to illuminate.[59] A narrative of the outbreak of the American revolution that failed to recount the debates over taxation could include only true, chronologically intelligible statements and still be regarded as an inadequate standard. Like any other cognitive enterprise, historical narration will be assessed in terms of rational standards that, though they are endorsed because they appear to be reliable guides to the truth, are not reducible to the standard of truth.

Obviously, the selective procedures that historians respect in composing their narratives will be evaluated in terms of all sorts of rational standards, like comprehensiveness, that do not correspond to anything found in the past. However, this does not mean that the selections and deletions in a historical narrative are divorced from literal questions of truth or falsity. For the selections and deletions are assessed in terms of those sorts of standards that experience indicates reliably track the truth.

White's deepest problem seems to be that he believes that truth is the only relevant grounds for the epistemic assessment of historical narratives. And, since narrative selectivity cannot be epistemically assessed without remainder in terms of truth on his correspondence model, it must be assessed in terms of some other standard of truth, such as metaphorical truth. But we can dodge this dilemma by noting that the selections and deletions of a historical narrative are subject to objective standards, which though not unrelated to ascertaining truth, are not reducible to truth. Such standards may be considered our best means for discovering the truth. Desiderata – like comprehensiveness – are, so to speak, truth-tracking. Thus, in evaluating the selections and deletions the narrative historian makes, we need not feel that we must embrace some special standard of truth, like metaphorical truth. Rather, our concern with historical narratives is that they be true in the ordinary sense of truth and that our assessments of their adequacy in terms of standards like comprehensiveness are keyed to determining truth. That principles governing the inclusion of an event in a narrative, like comprehensiveness, are not reducible to the standard of truth in no way implies that the narrative is fictional, nor that it should be understood as some kind of metaphor. This alternative only presents itself if one mistakenly circumscribes the options for epistemically evaluating nonfiction narratives in the way White does.[60]

White believes that the selections and deletions in a historical narrative are to be explained in terms of literary exigencies. Events are included or excluded with respect to whether they can function as beginnings, middles, and ends in comedies, tragedies, romances, and satires. I doubt that every historical narrative falls or must fall into one of White's generic types, and I even doubt that historical narratives require middles, and ends, in the technical sense of closure. A historical course of affairs may have a turning point and it may have results, but these need not be taken to be mere literary artifacts. Similarly, White writes as though the coherence of a historical narrative is solely a function of a literary imposition. But events in human life very often appear coherent, unfolding in terms of causes, reasons, complications, and consequences, and elucidating these relations between actions and their background conditions need not be exercises in fiction.

White and his followers regard historical interpretation as fictional insofar as it relies on narrative. This follows from their conviction that narrative, as such, is fictional. However, neither the philosophical considerations nor the empirical theses advanced in behalf of these views seem persuasive. At the very least, the reduction of all narrative to the status of fiction seems a desperate and inevitably self-defeating way in which to grant the literary dimension of historiography its due.

PART III: INTERPRETATION AND INTENTION

ℰ⌁

ART, INTENTION, AND CONVERSATION

I

In the normal course of affairs, when confronted with an utterance, our standard cognitive goal is to figure out what the speaker intends to say. And, on one very plausible theory of language, the meaning of an utterance is explicated in terms of the speaker's intention to reveal to an auditor that the speaker intends the auditor to respond in a certain way.[1] That is, the meaning of a particular language token is explained by means of certain of a speaker's intentions.

Likewise, in interpreting or explaining nonverbal behavior, we typically advert to the agent's intentions. This is not to say that we may not be concerned with the unintended consequences of an action; but even in order to explain unintended consequences, one will need a conception of the agent's intentions. Nor is this reliance on intention something that is relevant only to living people; historians spend a great deal of their professional activity attempting to establish what historical agents intended by their words and their deeds, with the aim of rendering the past intelligible. Furthermore, we generally presume that they can succeed in their attempts even with respect to authors and agents who lived long ago and about whom the documentary record is scant.

Nevertheless, though it seems natural to interpret words and actions in terms of authorial intention, arguments of many sorts have been advanced for nearly fifty years to deny the relevance of authorial intention to the interpretation of works of art in general and to works of literature in particular. Call this anti-intentionalism. Whereas ordinarily we interpret for intentions, anti-intentionalism maintains that art and literature either cannot or should not be treated in this way, Likewise, where characteristically we may use what we know of a person – her biography, if you will – to supply clues to, or, at least, constraints on our hypotheses about her meanings,[2] many theorists of art and literature regard reference to an author's biography as either illegitimate or superfluous.

The realm of art and literature, on the anti-intentionalist view, is or should be sufficiently different from other domains of human intercourse so that the differ-

From: *Intention and Interpretation,* ed. by Gary Iseminger (Philadelphia: Temple University Press, 1992), 97–131.

ence mandates a different form of interpretation, one in which authorial intent is irrelevant. In this essay, I scrutinize some of the grounds for drawing distinctions between art and life that advance the thought that authorial intent is irrelevant; and, in contrast, I also try to suggest some hitherto neglected continuities between art and life that might motivate a concern for authorial intention in the interpretation of art and literature.

II

Historically speaking, anti-intentionalism, under the title of "the intentional fallacy,"[3] arose in a context in which biographical criticism flourished – that is, the interpretation of such things as novels as allegories of their authors' lives. Authors were geniuses whose remarkable personalities we came to know and appreciate all the more by treating their fictions as oblique biographies.[4] Undoubtedly, this sort of criticism promoted distorted interpretations – as any intentionalist would agree, insofar as it is not likely that Kafka intended to speak of his father in writing *The Metamorphosis*. But in banishing all reference to authorial intention, to authorial reports of intention, and to the author's biography,[5] anti-intentionalism was an exercise in overkill. That is, in performing the useful service of disposing of what might be better called "the biographer's fallacy," anti-intentionalists embraced a number of philosophical commitments that went far beyond their own purposes, as well as beyond plausibility.

Indeed, anti-intentionalism is often promoted as a means for rejecting critical practices that most of us would agree are misguided. It is generally unclear, however, whether one has to go all the way to anti-intentionalism in order to avoid the errors in question.

For example, anti-intentionalism was advocated as a principle that could dispense with taking outlandish authorial pronouncements seriously. Monroe Beardsley writes "if a sculptor tells us that his statue was intended to be smooth and blue, but our senses tell us it is rough and pink, we go by our senses."[6] This example is meant to serve as an "intuition-pump";[7] if we agree that a sculptor cannot make a pink statue blue by reporting that it was his intention to make a blue sculpture, then it must be the case that we regard such intentions – and such reports of intention – as irrelevant.

This solution to the case is too hasty, however, and the example need not force the intentionalist into anti-intentionalism. For with cases in which the authorial pronouncement is so arbitrary, we may discount it, not because we think that authorial intentions are irrelevant, but because we think that the report is insincere. That is, we do not believe that the sculptor in Beardsley's example really had the intention of making a blue statue by painting it pink.

Intentions are constituted, in part, of beliefs, on Beardsley's own view,[8] and we can resist attributing the belief to an artist that one makes something blue by painting it pink. We need not resort to the hypothesis of anti-intentionalism in such a case, but can instead suspect that the artist was putting us on, perhaps for the purpose of notoriety. That is, competent language users, especially trained artists, are presumed to know the difference between blue and pink. Flouting this distinction leads to the suspicion of irony.

For an actual literary example of the sort of problem that Beardsley has in mind, we could consider Andrew Greeley's sensational novel *Ascent into Hell*. Like many of Greeley's works, this story is a titillating tale of Catholic priests and sex, a kind of soft-core pornography, spiced with religious taboos. Greeley, however, has a note preceding the text of the novel entitled "Passover," in which he offers a symbolic reading of that ceremony, thereby perhaps insinuating that we should take the text of *Ascent into Hell* as an allegory of Passover.

Needless to say, it is difficult to regard the sexual escapades in the book as a serious Passover allegory. But the intentionalist is not forced to accept Greeley's implied intention at face value. One can simply, on the basis of the novel, note that Greeley could not genuinely have the belief that it could be read as that allegory, nor would he have written the text as he did if he had the desire – another component of intentions on Beardsley's view[9] – to render a modern-day Passover theme. In fact, one may hypothesize that Greeley included the red herring about Passover in order to reassure his Catholic readership that his book was not irreligious.

But, in any event, the intentionalist can reject the "Passover" interpretation of *Ascent to Hell* in the face of Greeley's implied intentions by denying that it is plausible to accept the authenticity of Greeley's ostensible intent. Thus, the problem of aberrant authorial pronouncements need not drive us toward anti-intentionalism.[10]

Another frequent intuition-pump, employed in early arguments against intentionalism, argues that commending poems insofar as they realize authorial intentions is usually circular. For in many (most?) instances, including those of Shakespeare and Homer, we have no evidence of authorial intention other than their poems. Consequently, if we commend such a poem on the basis of its realization of intentions, and our sole evidence for that intention is the poem itself, then our commendation is tantamount to the assertion that the poem succeeds because it is the way it is because it is the way it is.

We cannot, in these instances, have grounds for discerning failed authorial intentions because the way the artwork is provides our only access to the intention. If it appears muddled, then that is evidence that the artist intended it to be muddled and, therefore, that it succeeded in realizing his intention. That is, commending works of art for realizing authorial intentions when the way work is is our only evidence of intentions threatens to force us to the counterintuitive conclusion that all works of art are commendable.[11]

The unwarranted presupposition here, of course, is that the artwork cannot provide evidence of failed intentions. In the introduction to his *The Structure of Scientific Revolutions*, Thomas Kuhn writes at one point that "having been weaned on these distinctions [the "context of discovery" versus "context of justification"] and others like them, I could scarcely be more aware of their import and force."[12] Clearly, any alert reader will note that Kuhn has said the opposite of what he meant to say. He intended to communicate that he had been *nurtured* on these distinctions, and not that he had been *weaned* on them.[13]

The text itself, in terms of the entire direction of what is being said, makes evident what Kuhn has in mind. Also, we know that the confusion over the dictionary meaning of *weaned,* like the meanings of such words as *fulsome* and *sleek,* is quite common among contemporary English speakers; so it is easy to recognize that Kuhn should not have written what he, in fact, wrote, given his intentions. From the text itself and our knowledge of language usage, we can infer that the sentence failed to realize Kuhn's intentions and that, from his own viewpoint, it is not a great sentence. And, similarly, with artworks – given their genre, their style, their historical context, and their overall aesthetic direction – one can say by looking at a given work that the author's intention has misfired, whether or not we go on to commend or criticize it.

Undoubtedly, as the preceding discussion indicates, one of the deepest commitments of early anti-intentionalism was the notion that authorial intention is somehow *outside* the artwork and that attempts to invoke it on the basis of the artwork itself are epistemologically suspect. Underlying this view is a conception of authorial intentions as private, episodic mental events that are logically independent of the artworks they give rise to in the way that Humean causes are logically independent of effects. What we have access to, in general, for purposes of evaluation and interpretation is the work itself. The authorial intention is an external cause of the artwork of dubious availability.

However, this view of authorial intention gradually came to be challenged by another view – call it the neo-Wittgensteinian view[14] – according to which an intention is thought to be a purpose, manifest in the artwork, that regulates the way the artwork is. Authorial intention, then, is discoverable by the inspection and contemplation of the work itself.[15] Indeed, the artwork is criterial to attributions of intention.

Searching for authorial intention is, consequently, not a matter of going outside the artwork, looking for some independent, private, mental episode or cause that is logically remote from the meaning or value of the work. The intention is evident in the work itself, and, insofar as the intention is identified as the purposive structure of the work, the intention is the focus of our interest in and attention to the artwork. On the external-episode view, authorial intention is a dispensable, if not distracting, adjunct to the artwork, which adjunct is best ignored. But on the neo-Wittgensteinian approach, tracking the intention – the purposive structure of the work – is the very point of appreciation.

Given the conception of authorial intention as external to and independent of the artwork, the anti-intentionalist claim of its irrelevance to the meaning of the work is eminently comprehensible. But with developments in the philosophies of action, mind, and language, the neo-Wittgensteinian picture of authorial intention seems more attractive. The persuasiveness of anti-intentionalism comes to hinge on which view of intention in general theorists find more plausible. And to the extent that early anti-intentionalism was based upon a crude view of intention, its conclusions are questionable.[16] Moreover, the more attractive, neo-Wittgensteinian view of intention not only makes authorial intention relevant to the interpretation of artworks but implies that in interpreting an artwork, we are attempting to determine the author's intentions. Thus, at this point in the debate, if anti-intentionalism is to remain persuasive, it must do so not only without presupposing a crude view of intention but also must accommodate the neo-Wittgensteinian picture of intention.

With these dialectical constraints in mind, it seems that two anti-intentionalist strategies have become popular recently. The first relies on adducing ontological reasons based on the nature of artworks to deny the relevance of authorial intention to interpretation. The second argues for the irrelevance of intention by exploring the aesthetic interests that audiences have in art. That is, the first sort of argument – the ontological argument – advances anti-intentionalism on the grounds of the nature of the artwork, while the second sort of argument – the aesthetic argument – is grounded on what might be thought of as policy considerations about the best way to regard artworks for aesthetic purposes. Both kinds of arguments presuppose that artworks, for one reason or another, are to be or should be interpreted differently from ordinary words and actions.

III

As noted earlier, we ordinarily interpret words and deeds with the cognitive goal of ascertaining the intentions of authors and agents. As the investigations of historians reveals, there seems to be no principled difficulty in such practices even when the agents in question are long dead and the record fragmentary. Thus, the question arises, Why should matters stand differently when it comes to art? Should not artworks be interpreted in the way in which we customarily interpret other words and actions? At this point, the anti-intentionalist may attempt to argue that artworks are ontologically different from ordinary words and deeds, and therefore different interpretive practices are appropriate to them; specifically, given the nature of artworks in general and literature in particular, authorial intent is irrelevant to interpretation.

This conviction of ontological difference can be found in different and indeed widely disparate literary theorists. It is, for example, an article of faith of contemporary literary critics who endorse Roland Barthes's notion of "the death of the author."[17] And it is, at the same time, a view that underpins the more traditional approaches of the New Criticism, as that approach was defended by the late Monroe Beardsley.[18] Perhaps this convergence of theorists of different stripes on anti-intentionalism should be less surprising than it seems, for both Barthes and Beardsley arrived at their positions – albeit in different decades and in different countries – while in the process of reacting to what was earlier called biographical criticism.

Though Roland Barthes does not explicitly speak of the issue of intention, he clearly believes that, with a literary text, the reader's activity should not be constrained by the "myth" that the author is confiding in us. One reason advanced in support of this view is that writing is the destruction of every voice, of every point of origin. Writing is that neutral, composite, oblique space where our subject slips away, the negative where all identity is lost, starting with the very identity of the body of writing.

No doubt it has always been that way. As soon as a fact is *narrated* no longer with a view to acting directly on reality but intransitively, that is to say, finally outside of any function other than that of the very practice of the symbol itself, this disconnection occurs, the voice loses its origin, the author enters into his own death, writing begins.[19]

What Barthes seems to be getting at here is that once writing is divorced from ordinary usage – that is, when language does not serve the purpose of acting on reality – the relevance of an author's intention in writing drops out, and the word sequence is attended to in terms of its play of potential meaning ("the very practice of the symbol itself"). This is a feature of poetry explicitly recognized in modernist writing following Mallarmé, but it implicitly has been a feature of literature all along ("No doubt it has always been that way.")[20]

Ordinary language is tied to acting on reality, and that is the grounds for our preoccupation with authorial intent. But when language is detached from that purpose – when language is aesthetized? – the cognitive goal of fixing authorial intent becomes feckless. That literary language is not practical severs its conceptual connection to authorial intention. As soon as language is employed ("narrated...") in what theorists of a more traditional bent than Barthes would call an *aesthetic* way, the conceptual pressure to make sense of it in the light of authorial intent dissolves, and the reader can explore it for all its potential meanings and associations.

In his "Intentions and Interpretations: A Fallacy Revived," Monroe Beardsley, deploying the machinery of speech-act theory, independently evolves an argument that, though different from Barthes's, also parallels it in pertinent respects. The argument begins by drawing a distinction between performing an illocutionary action and representing one. When a pickpocket takes my wallet and I say, "You stole my wallet," I perform the illocutionary act of accusation. An illocutionary action is generated (according to Beardsley, following Alvin Goldman) by the production of a text under certain conditions, and according to certain language conventions.[21] In contrast, when a stage actor, playing a character, says, "You stole my wallet," to another actor, playing another character, she is not performing an illocutionary action; she is representing one.

The relation between performing illocutionary actions and representing them is to be understood on the model of pictorial representation. Just as Beardsley argues that the relation of a pictorial depiction to its referent is that of selective similarity, he maintains that the representation of an illocutionary action resembles the performance of illocutionary action in certain, selected respects (i.e., reproduces certain, but not all, of the conditions requisite for the performance of the illocutionary action). For example, when I accuse a culprit of filching my wallet, I believe that he has taken my wallet; an actor, though repeating much of the formula for accusation, does not believe her fellow actor has stolen anything. Thus, a representation of accusation resembles it in many respects, but not in every respect – for instance, it fails to fulfill the condition of conviction in the culprit's guilt.

Most ordinary discourse is preoccupied with the performance of a multitude of illocutionary actions. Literature, in contrast, specializes in the representation of illocutionary actions. In this respect, once the author's intent to represent illocutionary actions is recognized, thereby acknowledging the neo-Wittgensteinian claim of a conceptual relation between an act and its animating intention, the representation of the illocutionary action is regarded as a selective imitation of the performance of a fictional character – either the literal characters in the text or what has sometimes been called an implied narrator or an implied speaker or dramatis persona.

So when Wordsworth writes about England that "she is a fen," this is not Wordsworth directly performing an illocutionary act of accusation. Wordsworth, in writing poetry, signals his intent to represent the illocutionary act of accusation, which, in this case, is the imitation of an implied speaker's disparaging of England.

The language in the poem is not a performance of an illocutionary act of accusation by Wordsworth. It is a representation of such an action by an implied speaker. Thus, the meaning of the language token is not tied to Wordsworth's intention, nor need it be understood in the context of Wordsworth's biography. It is a representation that can be comprehended solely in terms of the conventions of language.

The author of the performance in the text, so to speak, is the implied speaker; since all we know of the implied speaker are the words in the text – since the implied speaker, a fictional entity, has no existence outside the text – there can be no question of his extratextual intentions. There is no extratextual author, so there are no governing, extratextual intentions. Just as the issue of the number of children Lady Macbeth has is underdetermined by the fiction, so there is no access to implied authorial intent beyond the page.

Beardsley agrees that in ordinary language the cognitive goal of interpretation is the discernment of the speaker's intentions. But the language in literature is not a matter of the author's performance of an illocutionary act. It is a representation of the illocutionary acts of characters and implied speakers. And such fictional speakers have no intentions beyond the words on the page, which must, in consequence, be understood solely in terms of the conventions of language (and without recourse to the intentions of actual authors). It is as if in creating fictional characters, through illocutionary-act representation, actual authors' intentions are ontologically detached from the language sequence in favor of the meanings of characters, both literal and implied, which in turn can, for metaphysical reasons,[22] only be a matter of grasping of linguistic conventions (the literal sense of the words, and the conventions or established strategies for comprehending the sense of verbal contexts and metaphors).

The language in a literary text in being represented language – perhaps, this is what Barthes intends by "narrated ... intransitively" – becomes the linguistic "performance" of the characters – implied and literal – and thereby is disconnected from the intentions of actual authors by means of a fictional frame (Barthes's notion that language is detached from acting on reality). Moreover, the "intentions" of characters have no existence beyond the page and are available solely in terms of linguistic conventions. Stated formally, Beardsley's argument seems to be as follows:

1. If x is a literary work, then x is only a representation of an illocutionary act.
2. Though actual authorial intentions are relevant to whether x is a representation of an illocutionary act, what x is a representation of (its meaning) is solely a matter of the relevant linguistic conventions (the literal sense of words and the conventions or established strategies for grasping the sense of a verbal context and metaphors) *and not* a matter of fixing authorial intent.
3. Therefore, if x is a literary work, then what x is a representation of is solely a matter of the relevant conventions.

Thus, in interpreting the language in a literary text, we will be concerned with the meanings of characters – literal ones, implied authors, or dramatis personae. And since these characters have no existence outside the words in the text, interpreting their meanings is exclusively a matter of convention. The actual author, metaphorically speaking, banishes himself from the text in the process of representing illocutionary actions. This argument grants some role to authorial intention as an ingredient in identifying the author's act as one of representing. But once the representational frame is in place, so to speak, the author's intentions are outside it. And given the ontological status of the representational frame, it is a category mistake to be preoccupied with authorial intent; it is metaphysically irrelevant.

(Moreover, though this argument is stated in terms of literature, one supposes that it can be extended to other art forms, given, for example, Beardsley's analogies between pictorial representation and illocutionary representation – perhaps landscapes are to be understood as vistas seen by implied observers.)

It is absolutely central in this argument that literary language and ordinary language be ontologically distinct. Literary language is a special zone, so, even if in ordinary language authorial intent is a guide to meaning, it is not relevant in literature because literature is not a performance but a representation. In ordinary language, we are prone to say that when a speaker disambiguates her earlier utterance, she has told us the meaning of the utterance. With literature, however, there is no comparable resort to the author's intent, for the relevant speaker is not the living author but various dramatis personae who are ontologically unavailable for comment. If their words are ambiguous, one suspects that Beardsley would be prone to say that the dramatic speaker is being represented as ambiguous.

The crux of Beardsley's argument is, given the distinction between performing and representing, the claim that literature is by definition a matter of representing illocutionary acts.[23] This effectively boils down to the assertion that all literature is essentially fictional. For even if a literary text does not deploy imaginary characters and places, it is involved in presenting its persons, places, and events through the fictional medium of an implied speaker or narrator. Such claims are not unfamiliar.[24] If anti-intentionalism depends on this generalization, however, it is surely in trouble.[25]

Pretheoretically, many works of what we classify as literature fall into the category of nonfiction. Lucretius's *Concerning the Nature of Things* is one example; *The Mahabharata* is another. Both appear to be illocutionary acts of assertion, even if what they assert turns out to be false. It does not seem correct to attribute to Lucretius the intention of representing the illocutionary acts of an Epicurean philosopher – he was an Epicurean philosopher philosophizing. Similarly, the authors of *The Mahabharata* were not imitating the telling of the history of their race; they were telling it. Nor do we need, I think, to travel to the distant past for our counterexamples. When in "Howl," Allen Ginsberg wrote "I saw the best minds of my generation destroyed by madness," there is every indication that, however hyperbolically, he is speaking in his own voice and not representing the illocutionary act of accusation of some "angel-headed hipster." The notion of implied narrators and dramatic speakers, no matter how useful in explicating a great deal of literature, does not afford a necessary condition for being a literary text.[26]

Thus, a literary text is not necessarily a representation of an illocutionary act; it may be a performance of an illocutionary act of assertion, accusation, and so forth. Therefore, the fact that many literary texts involve representations of illocutionary acts does not entail that every literary text must be interpreted without concern for authorial intent in contradistinction to ordinary language.

Of course, it would be a mistake to conflate the representations of illocutionary acts presented through fictional characters with the performance of illocutionary acts by actual authors. It would be an error to identify Emily Brontë with the narrator of *Wuthering Heights*. But that distinction can be readily marked without resorting to the extreme theoretical concession that the literary speaker is always fictional.

Not only are there entire literary works that it seems ill advised to regard as representations of illocutionary acts. There are also many parts of literary works that do not appear to be representations of illocutionary acts: the discourse on whales in Melville's *Moby Dick,* the history of symbols in Hugo's *Hunchback of Notre Dame,* and the philosophy of history in Tolstoy's *War and Peace.* Though housed in fiction, where they undeniably perform a literary function, they are also essays whose authors produced them in order to make assertions. In interpreting these interludes, one needs to approach them as one would any other form of cognitive discourse. Some may be tempted to prefer to read them as representations of illocutionary acts when one finds a particular author's ideas rather harebrained. But such considerations – however cosmetically well intended – are, in fact, irrelevant to the issue of whether the passages in question are performances of illocutionary acts rather than representations thereof. Furthermore, if, as I argue, these are performances of illocutionary acts of assertion, then in such instances, it will be appropriate, as Beardsley would appear compelled to admit, to interpret them with the cognitive goal of discerning what the authors intended.

So far, we have been whittling away at the first premise of Beardsley's arguments by finding poems and passages to which the generalization does not apply and by arguing that in these instances, given Beardsley's own views, interpreting with respect to authorial intention is as appropriate as it is in the case of ordinary illocutionary acts of assertion. But the million-dollar question is: How extensive a problem does this pose for the anti-intentionalist?

My own hunch is that the problem will be very extensive. For once we admit that there can be explicit nonfictional passages (which may range in scale from clauses and sentences to chapters and beyond) housed in fiction – and which are best construed as performances of illocutionary actions – the door is opened to the recognition that there are many implicit or implied propositions in literary works as well, which are also best conceived in terms of performances. *Brave New World* expresses a point of view about what Huxley sees as the prospect of utilitarian social control. I see no particular advantage in rephrasing this observation in terms of the point of view of a fictional dramatic speaker. And, of course, if it is suggested that we must advert to talk of implied speakers in order to deflect the worries of anti-intentionalism, that begs the question at issue.

Authors, in fact, often make political (Gorky's *Mother*), philosophical (Sartre's *Nausea*), and moral (James's *The Ambassadors*) points through their literary writings. This is a commonly known, openly recognized, and frequently discussed practice in our literary culture. These points are very often secured through oblique techniques – implication, allegory, presupposition, illustration (unaccompanied with explicative commentary), and so on. That is, such points need not be and often are not directly stated. For this very reason, they are one of the most common objects of literary interpretation. And there is no reason to believe that in every case the implicit points found in literary works are merely the notions of a fictional speaker or an implied author rather than the actual author.

This is not to deny that there may be literary works in which the moral, philosophical, religious, political, and other views are only constituents of dramatic speakers or implied authors. It is only to reject the position that all the implicit points made in literary works are the representations of the implied commitments of fictional speakers.

There may be no general epistemological principle that we can apply to tell whether, in a given instance, the implied point belongs to the actual author or to an implied author. We may have to proceed in this matter on a case-by-case basis, relying on the results of practical criticism (of a sort that at least countenances the applicability of intentionalist hypotheses). But given the practices of our literary culture, that seems a better procedure than negotiating our lack of an epistemological principle by jettisoning the idea that actual authors communicate their commitments to us through literary works[27] – or, to return the issue to Beardsley's idiom, that actual authors do not ever perform illocutionary acts, even in fiction, rather than merely, only, always representing them.

Often it seems that arguments about the relevance of authorial intent to interpretation become so preoccupied with the issue at the level of word sequences that sight is lost of the fact that much of our interpretive activity is spent in trying to ascertain the point, often the implicit or implied point, of large segments of discourse and entire works. For example, we may be concerned with what a whole novel is getting at – its thesis, as Beardsley once called it.[28] And it seems to me natural, in many instances, to regard the theses we encounter in literary works as that which the author intends, through the production of the text, that the reader recognizes as the intended point. If we can regard implicit thesis projection with nonfictional import as a form of illocutionary action, there is no reason to think that it cannot be performed by actual authors. Implicit thesis projection may be a device employed in the construction of an implied author. But I see no reason to agree that it is always so employed.

For example, in Donald Barthelme's story "Alice," there is a recurring strategy of surreal and disorienting lists. In interpreting this strategy, we are not primarily concerned with elucidating the meaning of words or word sequences, but, and this is more important, in ascertaining Barthelme's point in employing these lists – that is, we are concerned with why he made the story this way. A likely hypothesis is that he intended this mode of organization to suggest the currently fashionable, antihumanist notion that the subject is decentered.[29] Here the object of interpretation is what Barthelme has *done,* and even though what he has said in the narrow sense is material to what he has done, the intentionalist idiom of *action* seems central to the way in which we characterize thesis projection through artistic strategies.

Not all literature is fictional, and not even all the assertions in fictions are representations of illocutionary actions. Pretheoretically, literary works, including parts of some fiction, can involve performances of illocutionary acts. Thus, if it is an appropriate cognitive goal with respect to performances of illocutionary acts to read for intentions, then, in certain circumstances, reading literature for authorial intention is plausible. There indeed may be times when reading representations of illocutionary acts for authorial intent is misguided for the reasons Beardsley advances. Nevertheless, those reasons cannot provide the grounds for a comprehensive anti-intentionalism with respect to literature (not to mention art in general).

Moreover, if there is implicit thesis projection of nonfictional import – whereby actual authors express their views about life, society, morality, and so forth – and a great deal of literary (indeed, artistic) interpretation concerns the identification of such theses, then intentionalist criticism has a wide arena of legitimate activity.

So far, I have been concerned to undermine the first premise of my reconstruction of Beardsley's argument. Literary works need not only be representations of illocutionary actions. But Beardsley's second premise also bears scrutiny. Its purpose is to exclude intentionalist interpretive activity on the grounds that its meaning can only be a matter of conventions because its speakers (fictional characters and implied authors) do not exist and therefore have no intentions. And, in any event, even if in some sense "intentions" could be imputed to them, they are not the intentions of the actual author, since he or she is not the speaker.

This premise may have some plausibility if it is narrowly construed to pertain only to the meaning of word sequences. But literary meaning – that is, the object of literary interpretation – need not be concerned solely with the meaning of word sequences even when it comes to the representation of illocutionary acts. Literary interpretation may ask questions about the point of constructing a character in this or that way and thus may investigate the representation of illocutionary acts in a text in terms of the contribution it makes to the point of the character as an element in the overall design of the work.

That is, in representing a character or an implied author and his or her fictional illocutions in a certain way, a theme may be adumbrated. We may ask, why did so-and-so say that in that way at that point in the text – how does it fit into the larger argument of the story or poem? And such questions about the point of character construction and the representation of the illocutionary acts that constitute them seem to me referable to the intentions of the actual author, without risking the kind of ontological gaff Beardsley feels must arise when actual authors are introduced into the interpretation of the meaning of representations of illocutionary acts. Thus, even if it were true that all literary works are only representations of illocutionary acts, that would not preclude intentionalist interpretation of literary meaning in the broad sense.

Of course, we might also wonder whether the actual author is as remote from representations of illocutionary acts as Beardsley supposes. As a historian of philosophy, Beardsley himself, along with an entire profession, appears to find little problem in deriving Plato's doctrine from Socratic dialogues. Surely these are no less representations of illocutionary acts, in Beardsley's terminology, than is the experiential proof of God's existence offered at the end of *The Brothers Karamazov*. But if we can, at least sometimes, feel justified in treating Plato/Socrates intentionalistically, with respect to illocutionary representations, why should we hesitate treating Dostoyevsky/Alyosha similarly?

Problems arise, then, with both of Beardsley's premises. I have spent more time with Beardsley's formulation than with Barthes's, since I think that it is obviously more developed. Nevertheless, though Barthes does not mobilize speech-act theory, I think that his notion of the death of the author is susceptible to a number of the points made against Beardsley. Barthes apparently maintains that when language is divorced from the goal of acting on reality ("narrated … intransitively"), the relevance of the author disappears, and a space is opened for the reader to explore the text in terms of all its intertextual associations. The reader, in a manner of speaking, becomes a writer and the critic, a creator.

I am not sure that once language is used "intransitively," the author becomes irrelevant, since identifying such a use would appear to depend on fixing the author's intention to work in certain genres or forms, namely, those that function intransitively. That is, how will the interpreter know that the writing in question is of the right sort to be read in a writerly fashion without adverting to authorial intentions?

Barthes claims that when writing is divorced from the purpose of acting directly on reality, the author becomes irrelevant. Whether this is persuasive depends on what this divorce from reality amounts to. Does the notion of no longer operating directly on reality reduce to Beardsley-type claims about representations of illocutionary acts or to the notion that literature is essentially fictional? If so, Barthes must deal with the kinds of objections rehearsed already.[30] But if the notion does not dissolve into the view that all writing (literature?) is fiction, then one wonders how often writing is divorced from the purpose of acting on reality. That is, supposing Barthes is correct and once writing is detached from the purpose of acting on reality, the author becomes irrelevant, the crucial question concerns the frequency of this phenomenon.

Barthes clearly thinks it happens a great deal. But, generously construed, the idea of writing acting on reality seems to me to apply quite uncontroversially to much literature that is used to criticize society, to champion moral views, to afford insight into social behavior, to reinforce values, to encourage our sympathies, to elicit our hatred, to give voice to our experience, and so on. If this is said not to be a matter of *directly* acting on reality, we need an account of what Barthes means here. If he has the issue of fiction in mind, we have already provided the counterexamples. Moreover, if narrating intransitively means just any writing where the author is not in the presence of her or his audience – writing detached from the physical context of utterance – that, counterintuitively, implies that such things as book orders do not operate directly on reality.[31]

If Barthes has something else in mind, the burden of proof is on him (or his followers) to produce it. For insofar as it is common practice for authors to strive to affect reality by means of their writing and insofar as they appear in some sense to succeed, then it would seem, given Barthes's own argument, that in certain instances (many?), the author is not dead, and there is no conceptual pressure to treat him or her as such.

Undoubtedly, there may be poems – one thinks of the Exquisite Corpses of the Surrealists – in which the writer opens the text to the free play of the reader (though even here the author's intent to enable readers to see the world differently cannot be forgotten). Nevertheless, artistic attempts to secure the death of the author by, so to say, authorial suicide, no matter how interesting and legitimate experimentally, do not force us to concede that, in general the author is, in every respect, irrelevant to the interpretation of the text – even if we accept Barthes's criterion of acting or not acting on reality as the mark of authorial life and death.

Both Barthes and Beardsley frame their arguments in terms of literature, though I think that it is fair to say that both would advocate anti-intentionalism across the interpretation of the arts.[32] But their anti-intentionalism seems to me to be most persuasive when it is applied to such things as word sequences, whose meanings are extremely conventionalized. In other art forms, where there are not such highly articulated codes of meaning, our interpretations of artistic performances are more akin to discerning the sense of an action than to reading.

If a choreographer mounts a dance in a theater in the round rather than on a proscenium stage, we attempt to figure out the significance of this *choice* by thinking about what he or she is trying to do with respect to historical and contemporary theatrical practices relative to the work in question. The *meaning* of "theater in the round" is neither fixed nor semiotically bound to other theatrical "signs" in a way that can be read the way a text may be (either determinately, à la Beardsley, or intertextually, à la Barthes). Instead, its interpretation depends on locating the purpose that the strategy in question serves for what the author is attempting to do.[33] And it is hard to see how such artistic *doings* – which describe most activity outside literature[34] – can be explicated without reference to the *intentional* activity of authors.

IV

So far, we have explored anti-intentionalist arguments that preclude reference to authorial intent on the grounds of the putatively special ontological nature of art in general and literature in particular. Our own position has been that these considerations do not require us in general to treat literature differently from ordinary discourse, except perhaps in certain limited instances – for example, where the meaning of a character's or an implied narrator's literal utterance token, per se, is underdetermined due to the constraints of fiction. But even in the face of these limitations, there are many other cases and aspects of literary and fictional discourse where there is no ontological barrier to the cognitive goal of attempting to discern authorial intention as an object of interpretation. Thus, anti-intentionalism does not, on ontological grounds, afford grounds for believing that authorial intent is irrelevant in every instance of interpretation.

The ontological considerations of the anti-intentionalists, which were canvassed earlier, might be called "reasons of art" in that they declare reference to authorial intent out-of-bounds because of the special nature of art. With respect to discourse, such reasons of art presume that literary discourse is metaphysically different from ordinary discourse in a way that makes reading literature for authorial intent a kind of category error. We have challenged the generality and applicability of this position and concluded that there is no reason why, across the board, reading literary works with the cognitive goal of identifying authorial intentions is inadmissible; indeed, at times – for example, with respect to authorial *doings* – it seems the most plausible way to proceed.

There are other "reasons of art" that we have not yet considered. The idea behind the ontological arguments is that it is in some sense impossible to fix authorial intent and that the aim should be abandoned as any other impossible goal should be abandoned. Nevertheless, an anti-intentionalist might admit that the ontological arguments are not generally conclusive, yet adduce reasons of art that show that reading for authorial intent *should not* be pursued, even though it could be pursued. These reasons of art might be called aesthetic. That is, whereas ontological arguments advance reasons of art that maintain that intentionalism is, strictly speaking, impossible; aesthetic arguments admit that intentionalist criticism is possible, but *recommend* that it not be embraced for what might be called aesthetic policy reasons.

Isolating pure aesthetic arguments for anti-intentionalism is a bit difficult, since most anti-intentionalists believe in the ontological distinction between literary language and ordinary language, and as a result they weave their ontological and aesthetic arguments together in ways that are hard to disentangle. The supposed aesthetic advantages of anti-intentionalism are often introduced only to be ultimately backed up by ontological considerations. But it is possible to construct an aesthetic argument without reference to ontological claims about the nature of art in general or of literature in particular.

For example, Monroe Beardsley writes:

> What is the primary purpose of literary interpretation? It is, I would say, to help readers approach literary works from the aesthetic point of view, that is, with an interest in actualizing their (artistic) goodness. The work is an object, capable (presumably) of affording aesthetic satisfaction. The problem is to know what is there to be responded to; and the literary interpreter helps us to discern what is there so that we can enjoy it more fully.[35]

Here, the underlying idea is that an artistic object has a purpose: affording aesthetic satisfaction. This is why we attend to artworks. Our object is to derive as much aesthetic satisfaction as is possible from the object. The role of the interpreter is to show us what there is in the object that promotes aesthetic experience. Nevertheless, one can readily imagine that what an author intended to say by means of an artwork is less aesthetically provocative than alternative "readings" of the work. For Beardsley, these readings, with respect to literature, have to be constrained by what the words of the text mean conventionally. Even with this caveat, it is easy to imagine instances in which what the author intended is less aesthetically exciting than an alternate, conventionally admissible reading.

Moreover, since the point of consuming art, and of interpretation as an adjunct to artistic consumption, is to maximize aesthetic satisfaction, we should always favor those interpretations that afford the best aesthetic experience that is compatible with established textual meaning conventions. Furthermore, since aesthetic richness is our overriding concern, we need only interpret with an eye to that which is most aesthetically satisfying and linguistically plausible. Whether or not the meanings we attribute to the text were authorially intended is irrelevant. The proof of the pudding is in the tasting.

Of course, the best reading of the text – the one that is most aesthetically satisfying and also at least linguistically plausible – may coincide with the author's intended meaning, but that is of accidental importance. What is essential for the purposes of aesthetic consumption is that it be the best interpretation – the one that points to the maximum available aesthetic enjoyment – conceivable within the constraints of linguistic plausibility. Thus, for aesthetic purposes, we may always forgo concern for authorial intent in favor of the best aesthetic interpretation.

Where authorial intention and the best interpretation coincide, the reason we accept the interpretation has to do with aesthetic richness rather than authorial intention. Where there may be divergences between authorial intentions and textual meanings (that are richer than the putative authorial ones), we go with the latter because maximizing aesthetic satisfaction is our goal. As a matter of aesthetic policy, the best procedure is always to regard authorial intention as irrelevant because it either adds nothing to our aesthetic satisfaction or it may even stand in the way of arriving at the most enjoyable experience of the work.

On Beardsley's view, there is generally a determinate best interpretation. However, the aesthetic argument can also be mobilized by theorists who eschew determinate meanings, preferring the "play of signification of the text." Here, the argument might begin by recalling that a text can be interpreted either as the utterance of an author or as a word sequence.[36] Read as a word sequence, the text may have multiple meanings compatible with the conventions of language. Given this, the question becomes, What is the best way to read the text – authorially or, so to speak, textually?

In defense of reading the text as a word sequence, one can invoke the Kantian notion that aesthetic experience involves the play of understanding and imagination. That is, taking the text as a word sequence allows us to contemplate it for multiple, diverse meanings and their possible connections. It provides the best way for us to maximize our aesthetic experience of the text, permitting us to track the text for its play of meaning and alternative import. Reading for authorial intent, where the author intends a determinate meaning rather than an "open text,"[37] may obstruct the delectation of the various shifts in meaning that would otherwise be available to the reader who takes the text as a word sequence. Thus, for the purpose of maximizing our aesthetic experience – construed here to be a matter of cognitive play with meanings – the best policy is to attend to the work as a word sequence rather than as an authorial utterance.

The conservative version of this aesthetic argument might hold that texts could be read as word sequences or as authorial utterances and that there is no reason why the intentionalist preference for authorial utterance must be given priority over the possibility of reading the text as a word sequence. Both readings are possible, and neither recommendation is binding.[38] So, if a good reason – like the Kantian aesthetic invoked earlier – can be advanced for anti-intentionalist interpretive practices, then the claims of intentionalism can be suspended. This does not preclude intentionalist interpretation, but only denies that interpretation must always be constrained by intentionalist considerations.

A more radical version of the aesthetic argument would advocate that intentionalist considerations are *always* best bracketed because they stand in the way of, or are irrelevant to, maximizing interpretive play.[39] Concern for authorial intent "closes" down the text; it limits the artwork as a source of interpretive enjoyment; it restrains the imagination (of the audience) unduly. This recommendation may be accompanied by the vague and perhaps confusing cliché that artworks are inexhaustible, insofar as word sequences, ex hypothesi, will tend to have more meanings than authorial utterances. But the argument can proceed without claiming that artworks are literally inexhaustible; only to urge that, for the purpose of making literary experience more exciting, we should treat artworks that way, rather as Morris

Zapp in David Lodge's *Changing Places* keeps reinterpreting Jane Austen in the light of every literary theory that comes down the pike. That is, keeping artworks interpretively open – for example, by reading for word sequence meaning rather than authorial meaning – makes for more zestful encounters with art.

The radical version of the aesthetic argument seems to me to underwrite a great deal of contemporary literary criticism. Ironically, where someone like Beardsley supports anti-intentionalism because of his convictions about the autonomy of the artwork and the literary text,[40] contemporary literary critics advocate anti-intentionalism for the sake of the freedom and autonomy of the reader. In Barthes, for example, the "death of the author" corresponds to the birth of the reader.

Admittedly, for Barthes, this is grounded in ontological arguments about the nature of writing. Yet one feels that, with Barthes and his followers, the ontological argument itself is attractive because its conclusion suits their preference for an autonomous reader, one who creatively participates in making the meaning of the text by tracing the multiple and not necessarily converging linguistic trajectories that reading divorced from a concern with authorial utterance allows.[41]

Aesthetic arguments for anti-intentionalism are a subclass of the general view that interpretations are purpose-relative.[42] One could advance anti-intentionalism, then, for purposes other than aesthetic gratification under the banner of purpose-relative interpretation; one could, for example, maintain that anti-intentionalism best realizes some moral or ideological goal, which outweighs whatever aims intentionalism supports.[43] Since I believe that the purpose that critics most often presuppose anti-intentionalism serves best is aesthetic enrichment, however, I focus the discussion on this issue.

With aesthetic arguments, the anti-intentionalist admits, in my reconstruction of the debate, that one could read for authorial intent, but maintains that we have certain aims in pursuing artworks that, so to speak, trump our concerns with authorial meaning. These aims center on the maximization of aesthetic satisfaction. Aesthetic satisfaction is the overriding interest that we have in consuming artworks. So in order to secure said satisfaction, we are best advised to take it that the aesthetically most satisfying interpretation outranks all others, most notably where a competing view is an intentionalist interpretation.

In order to develop this argument fully, the anti-intentionalist needs to say something about aesthetic satisfaction. This may cause difficulties in several registers. The first is the long-standing problem of defining the way in which we are to understand "the aesthetic" in *aesthetic satisfaction*. Moreover, there may be rival views of what constitutes aesthetic satisfaction – Beardsleyan determinate meaning of a certain sort, or the inexhaustible play of meaning in the text. Which of these views must the anti-intentionalist endorse? But even supposing these technical difficulties with characterizing aesthetic satisfaction can be met, I remain unconvinced by aesthetic arguments for anti-intentionalism.

The heart of my disagreement is that it seems unproven that we have overriding interests in maximizing aesthetic satisfaction with respect to artworks. My reason for reservations here have to do with my suspicion that in dealing with art-works we have more interests than aesthetic interests – as "aesthetic interests" are usually construed within the philosophical tradition – and that there is no reason to think that these interests are always trumped by aesthetic ones. Indeed, as I argue, these other-than-aesthetic interests may in fact mandate constraints on the pursuit of aesthetic interest in ways that count against anti-intentionalism and for intentionalism. I would not wish to deny that we have interests in securing aes-thetic satisfaction from artworks. But that interest needs to be reconciled with other, potentially conflictive interests that we also bring to artworks.

What are these other interests or purposes? Broadly speaking, I would call them "conversational." When we read a literary text or contemplate a painting, we enter a relationship with its creator that is roughly analogous to a conversation. Obviously, it is not as interactive as an ordinary conversation, for we are not receiving spontaneous feedback concerning our own responses. But just as an ordinary conversation gives us a stake in understanding our interlocutor, so does interaction with an artwork.

We would not think that we had had a genuine conversation with someone whom we were not satisfied we understood. Conversations, rewarding ones at least, involve a sense of community or communion that itself rests on communi-cation. A fulfilling conversation requires that we have the conviction of having grasped what our interlocutor meant or intended to say. This is evinced by the extent to which we struggle to clarify their meanings. A conversation that left us with only our own clever construals or educated guesses, no matter how aesthet-ically rich, would leave us with the sense that something was missing. That we had neither communed nor communicated.

Not all conversations involve both communion and communication. Probably many firings do not. But what, for want of a better term, we might call serious conversations do have, as a constitutive value, the prospect of community. Like-wise, I want to maintain, this prospect of community supplies a major impetus motivating our interest in engaging literary texts and artworks. We may read to be entertained, to learn, and to be moved, but we also seek out artworks in order to converse or commune with their makers. We want to understand the author, even if that will lead to rejecting his or her point of view.

An important part of why we are interested in art is that it affords not only an opportunity to reap aesthetic satisfaction but is an opportunity to exercise our interpretive abilities in the context of a genuine conversation. Clever con-struals, even if aesthetically dazzling, do not necessarily serve our desire to commune or communicate with another person. Insofar as our pursuit of art is underwritten by, and is an exemplary occasion for, a generic human interest in communicating with others, it is not clear that a concern with aesthetics alone serves our purposes best.

Moreover, in stressing our conversational interest in artworks in terms of understanding the artist, I am not reverting to the notion that we pursue art in order to commune with remarkable personalities. Instead, I am making the more modest claim that art is obviously in part a matter of communication and that we bring to it our ordinary human disposition to understand what another human being is saying to us.

The idea of the maximization of aesthetic satisfaction has a very "consumerist" ring to it. In Buberesque lingo, it reduces our relation to the text to an I/It relationship. What I am trying to defend is the idea that, with artworks, we are also interested in an I/Thou relation to the author of the text. This interest in communicating with others is perhaps so deeply a part of our motive in, for example, reading that we may not have it in the forefront of our attention. But when we pick up Tom Wolfe's *Bonfire of the Vanities,* surely one of our abiding interests is to learn what someone else, namely Tom Wolfe, thinks about contemporary New York. And, the extent to which we have this conversational interest in the text limits the range of aesthetically enhancing interpretations we can countenance. That is, the purpose of aesthetic maximization will have to be brought into line with our conversational interests, which interests are patently concerned with authorial intent.

Furthermore, if I am right about the conversational interests that we have in artworks and literary texts, then our concern with authorial intention will not simply issue from the mutual respect we have for our interlocutor; it will also be based on an interest in protecting our sense of self-respect in the process of conversation. In order to clarify this point, a somewhat extended example may be useful.

In contemporary film criticism, films are often commended because they *transgress* what are called the codes of Hollywood filmmaking, thereby striking this or that blow for emancipation. Within the context of recent film criticism, it is appropriate to regard disturbances of continuity editing, disorienting narrative ellipses, or disruptions of eyeline matches as subversions of a dominant and ideologically suspect form of filmmaking, and given the historical evolution of the language game in which avant-garde filmmaking is practiced, the attribution of such meanings to contemporary films is warranted, especially on intentionalist grounds.

Once interpretations of narrative incoherences in recent films as subversions or transgressions of Hollywood International were in place, however, film critics, such as J. Hoberman of the *Village Voice,* began to attempt to project those readings backward. That is, if a narrative incoherence or an editing discontinuity in a film in 1988 counts as a transgression, why not count a similar disturbance in a film of 1959 as equally transgressive? Thus, a hack film by Edward Wood, *Plan 9 from Outer Space,* is celebrated as transgressive as if it were a postmodernist exercise in collage.[44]

Plan 9 from Outer Space is a cheap, slapdash attempt to make a feature film for very little, and in cutting corners to save money it violates – in outlandish ways – many of the decorums of Hollywood filmmaking that later avant-gardists also seek to affront. So insofar as the work of contemporary avant-gardists is aesthetically valued for its transgressiveness, why not appreciate *Plan 9 from Outer Space* under an analogous interpretation? Call it "unintentional modernism," but it is modernism nonetheless and appreciable as such.[45]

One reason to withhold such an interpretation from *Plan 9,* of course, is that transgression is an intentional concept, and all the evidence indicates that Edward Wood did not have the same intentions to subvert the Hollywood style of film-making that contemporary avant-gardists have. Indeed, given the venue Wood trafficked in, it seems that the best hypothesis about his intentions is that he was attempting to imitate the Hollywood style of filmmaking in the cheapest way possible. Given what we know of Edward Wood and the B-film world in which he practiced his trade, it is implausible to attribute to him the intention of attempting to subvert the Hollywood codes of filmmaking for the kinds of purposes endorsed by contemporary avant-gardists.

An intention is made up of beliefs and desires. It is incredible to attribute to Edward Wood the kinds of beliefs that contemporary avant-garde filmmakers have about the techniques, purposes, and effects of subverting Hollywood cinema. Those beliefs (and avant-garde desires) were not available in the film world Edward Wood inhabited, nor can we surmise that even if Wood could have formulated such beliefs, it would be plausible to attribute to him the intention to implement them. For it is at the least uncharitable to assign to Wood the belief that his audiences could have interpreted his narrative discontinuities and editing howlers as blows struck against a Hollywood aesthetic.[46] That is, it is virtually impossible that Wood could have had the intentions – the beliefs and the desires – that contemporary avant-gardists have about the meanings of disjunctive exposition or the effects of such exposition on audiences.

Historically, it is undoubtedly most accurate to regard Edward Wood's narrative non sequiturs and nonstandard editing as mistakes within the norms of Hollywood filmmaking. One would think that the critic interested in transgression would want to have a way to distinguish between mistakes and transgressions. And the most obvious way to make such a distinction is to require that transgressions be intentional, which requires that the filmmaker in question have the knowledge and the will to violate Hollywood norms of filmmaking as a form of artistic protest. Insofar as it is anachronistic to impute the requisite knowledge (of the discourse of avant-garde theory) or the desire to subvert Hollywood codes to Wood, it is better to regard his violations of certain norms as mistakes. And, in general, it would seem that connoisseurs of artistic transgression would have an interest in being able to distinguish mistakes from subversions – interests that should drive them toward intentionalism.

Nevertheless, it is at this point that an aesthetic argument for anti-intentionalism may be brought to bear. To wit: if a transgression interpretation of *Plan 9 from Outer Space* yields a more aesthetically satisfying encounter with the film, and our primary purpose in interpretation is in promoting maximum aesthetic satisfaction, why not suspend qualms about intention and take *Plan 9 from Outer Space* as a masterpiece of postmodernist disjunction *à la lettre?* Here, the anti-intentionalist might agree that such an interpretation cannot be squared with what it is plausible to say of the film, given the possible intentions of the historical director. But why not sacrifice the distinction between mistakes and transgressions if in the long run it supplies us with more aesthetically satisfying experiences?

That is, the argument against taking *Plan 9* as a transgression rests on the supposition that it is not a reasonable hypothesis of what Wood could have meant in producing the film. But so what? If we drop a commitment to discerning authorial intent, and regard any norm violation as a transgression, would not that make *Plan 9* more aesthetically interesting, and if our premium is on aesthetic interest, would not anti-intentionalist criticism be our best bet?

But I submit that insofar as we have a conversational interest in artworks, we will want to reject this sort of aesthetic argument. For if we take ourselves to be aiming at a genuine conversation, ignoring Wood's palpable intentions, it seems to me, can only undermine our sense of ourselves as authentic participants in the conversation. For, from the point of view of genuine conversation, we are being willfully silly in regarding *Plan 9* as a transgression of Hollywood codes of filmmaking. We are behaving as if we believed that a randomly collected series of phrases, derived from turning the dial of our car radio at one-second intervals, harbored the message of an oracle, while simultaneously we agree that all forms of divination are preposterous.

In his *Concluding Unscientific Postscript,* Kierkegaard notes that a comic moment arises when "a sober man engages in sympathetic and confidential conversation with one whom he does not know is intoxicated, while the observer knows of the condition. The contradiction lies in the mutuality presupposed by the conversation, that it is not there, and that the sober man has not noticed its absence."[47] By analogy, in supposing that Wood is a kind of Godard, we are acting as if a stream of drunken incoherencies constitute an enigmatic code. Indeed, we are placing ourselves in an even more ridiculous position than the butt of Kierkegaard's mishap, for we have voluntarily entered this situation.

In Kosinski's *Being There,* the näif Chance utters all sorts of remarks about his garden, which other characters take to be of great gnomic significance. Since they are unaware that Chance is a simpleton, they are, in effect, applying something like Culler's anti-intentionalist rule of significance[48] to the sayings of a fool. The result, as with Kierkegaard's imagined conversation with the drunk, is comic. Taking something like *Plan 9* to be a radical transgression of Hollywood International seems to me to be a matter of willingly adopting the ludicrous position that those characters suffer inadvertently. It undermines any self-respecting view we could have of ourselves as participants in a conversation. Whatever aesthetic satisfaction we could claim of such an exchange would have to be bought at the conversational cost of making ourselves rather obtuse.

Aesthetic arguments for anti-intentionalism proceed as if aesthetic satisfaction were the only important interest we could have with respect to artworks. Thus, wherever other putative interests impede aesthetic interests, they must give way. But aesthetic satisfaction is not the only major source of value that we have in interacting with artworks; the interaction is also a matter of a conversation between the artist and us – a human encounter – in which we have a desire to know what the artist intends, not only out of respect for the artist, but also because we have a personal interest in being a capable respondent. In endorsing the anti-intentionalist view that aesthetic satisfaction trumps all other interests, we seem to be willing to go for aesthetic pleasure at all costs, including, most notably, any value we might place on having a genuine conversational exchange with another human being. For, as the *Plan 9* example suggests, we are willing to act as if we encountered a profound, reflexive meditation on the dominant cinema, when, in fact, it is readily apparent that we are dealing with a botched and virtually incoherent atrocity.

Aesthetic arguments in favor of anti-intentionalism presume a species of aesthetic hedonism. They presuppose that aesthetic pleasure or satisfaction is our only legitimate interest with regard to artworks. Here it is useful to recall Robert Nozick's very provocative, antihedonistic thought experiment – the experience machine.

> Suppose there were an experience machine that would give you any experience you desired. Super-duper neuropsychologists could stimulate your brain so that you would think and feel you were writing a great novel, or making a friend, or reading an interesting book. All the time you would be floating in a tank, with electrodes attached to your brain. Should you plug into the machine for life, preprogramming your life's experiences?[49]

Nozick thinks that our answer here will be obviously no, and part of the reason is that we wish to be a certain kind of person and do various things and not just have experiences as if we were such a person and as if we were doing those things. In other words, the pleasure of these simulated experiences is not enough; we have a stake in actually having the experiences in question. Applied to the aesthetic case, what I am trying to defend in the name of conversational interests is the claim that we have an investment in really encountering interesting and brilliant authors, not simply in counterfeiting such encounters. Knowing that *Plan 9* is a schlock quickie, but responding to it as if it were superbly transgressive, is akin to knowingly taking the heroics performed in Nozick's experience machine as if they were actual adventures. It is a matter of sacrificing genuine conversational experiences for aesthetic pleasures. And in doing so, one is willing to lower one's self-esteem for the sake of an aesthetic high.[50]

Of course, the problem I have raised with the use and abuse of the concept of transgression by contemporary film critics brings up general problems with aesthetic arguments in favor of anti-intentionalism. For example, the pervasive problems of allusion and irony are strictly analogous to the problems that we have sketched with respect to transgression. One could render both Richard Bach's *Jonathan Livingston Seagull*[51] and Heinrich Anacker's anti-Semitic, pro-Nazi "Exodus of the Parasites"[52] more aesthetically satisfying by regarding them as ironic. Yet I suspect that we resist this kind of interpretive temptation. And this resistance, I think, can be explained by our conversational interests in artworks.

We have every justification for believing that these works are tawdry but sincere, and behaving as though they were ironic – whatever aesthetic satisfaction that might promote – would place us in what we recognize to be an ersatz conversation. We would be, respectively, laughing *with* what we know we should be laughing *at,* and appalled *along* with what we know we should be appalled *at.* Our conversation would not be authentic in either event, and whatever aesthetic satisfaction we secured would be purchased by making ourselves conversationally incompetent. Insofar as one of the abiding values we pursue in encounters with artworks is conversational, we are not willing to turn these particular pig's ears into silver purses.

Stanley Cavell has argued that one of the audience's major preoccupations with modern art is whether it is sincere. Given the dadaist tendencies of contemporary art, the spectator cares whether he or she is being fooled by the artist.[53] The encounter with the artwork is a human situation in which our self-esteem may be felt to be at risk. Likewise, I want to stress that insofar as the artistic context is a kind of conversation, we also may be concerned not only that the artist is given his or her due but that we carry through our end of the conversation. In terms of self-esteem, we have an interest not only in not being gulled by the artist but also in not fooling ourselves. And this interest gives us reason to reject interpretations of artworks that, however aesthetically satisfying they may be, cannot sensibly be connected to the intentions of their authors. The simulacrum of a brilliant conversation cannot be willfully substituted for a brilliant conversation and be a genuinely rewarding experience.

If these thoughts about our conversational interests in works of art are convincing, then they indicate that it is not true that the prospect of aesthetic satisfaction trumps every other desideratum when it comes to interpretation. Aesthetic satisfaction does not obviate our conversational interests in artworks. Moreover, our conversational interest in artworks is best served by intentionalism. Thus, in order to coordinate our aesthetic interests and our conversational interests, the best policy would not appear to be anti-intentionalism but the pursuit of aesthetic satisfaction constrained by our best hypotheses about authorial intent.

These hypotheses, moreover, will often depend on facts available to us about the biography of the artist. That the artist lived in fifteenth-century Italy, for example, will constrain attribution of his supposed intent to explore the themes of Greenbergian modernism in his canvases. Biographical data, in other words, can play a role in hypothesizing the artist's intention, while the recognition of the artist's intention, in turn, constrains the kinds of satisfactions, and, correspondingly, the kinds of interpretations we may advance with respect to artworks.[54] Not only is authorial intention derivable from artworks, *pace* the ontological arguments reviewed in the previous section; authorial intention – and biographical information – are relevant to the realization of the aims, particularly the conversational aims, we bring to artworks. Aesthetic arguments do not show that anti-intentionalism is the best interpretive policy to endorse given our purposes with respect to artworks. For we are interested in art as an occasion for communication with others as well as a source of aesthetic pleasure. And to the extent that communication or communion is among the leading purposes of art, authorial intention must always figure in interpretation, at least as a constraint on whatever other purposes we seek.

Anglo-American Aesthetics and Contemporary Criticism: Intention and the Hermeneutics of Suspicion

I. INTRODUCTION

The fiftieth anniversary of the American Society for Aesthetics comes at a time of ostensible turmoil in academia. Many fields of inquiry – so many, in fact, that it would be cumbersome to enumerate them – claim to be undergoing fundamental identity crises; old paradigms are declared outmoded on every side, and new approaches heralded. In such a context, contemplating the health of Anglo-American-style aesthetics is natural.[1] Indeed, since our colleagues in adjacent fields – including literary theory, film studies, art history, and so on – seem convinced that if aesthetics is not dead, then it should be killed, we might spend some of this anniversary not only celebrating the past, but also worrying about the future.

The charges arrayed against Anglo-American aesthetics at present are legion. One could not hope to identify, let alone to address, them all in such a brief note. Thus, I will focus on just one issue in order to demonstrate that not only is Anglo-American aesthetics not always at loggerheads with contemporary art criticism, but that contemporary criticism may even profit from the insights of aesthetics.

Like the art of the past decade or so, contemporary criticism has become increasingly political in its orientation. One aspect of this is the familiar interpretation of artworks – often indiscriminately called "texts" – for their symptomatic political content, including especially: latent or repressed sexism, racism, classism, imperialism, and so forth.

Moreover, at the same time that contemporary critics have opted for this variety of the hermeneutics of suspicion, a movement reinstating the relevance of the artist's intentions for interpretation has begun to take hold among philosophers of art.[2] That is, after several decades of living with the so-called "intentional fallacy," many – though, of course, hardly all – Anglo-American aestheticians are beginning to perceive fallacies in one of their founding doctrines.

From: *The Journal of Aesthetics and Art Criticism,* 51,2 (Spring 1993), 245–52.

However, an anxiety arises in this context about whether this movement on the part of philosophers of art is not on a collision course with interpretive developments in contemporary criticism. For quite frequently the sexism, racism, and imperialism attributed to artworks by contemporary critics may not accord with what we may reliably hypothesize about the intentions of the artists in question. That is, the intentionalist conception of interpretation favored by many philosophers of art may be at variance with – if not downright incompatible with – the aims of a hermeneutics of suspicion.

Often contemporary critics aspire to attribute properties to artworks where it is difficult to imagine that the creator of said work could have intended said property to be a feature of the work. One reason for this might be that the feature in question – say ablism – is not in the artist's conceptual repertoire. And, in fact, in some cases, contemporary critics may wish to attribute a property – like sexism – to a work when the author may have explicitly intended quite the opposite; one may, for example, find sexism in the creations of George Bernard Shaw, though he was a self-proclaimed proponent of women's rights. So, if interpretations are supposed to track – or, at least, to be constrained by – authorial intentions, contemporary critics may complain that the intentionalist leanings of many contemporary philosophers of art are a logical impediment to their critical practices.

From the viewpoint of contemporary criticism, the hermeneutics of suspicion is a powerful interpretive stance. Furthermore, even old-fashioned humanists can acknowledge that there is some value in many of the moral and political concerns and insights of contemporary criticism. Thus, where a philosophical commitment to intentionalism stands in the way of the robust and often humane practices of contemporary political criticism, the temptation to reject the philosophical theory presents itself.

Surveying the apparent incompatibility of intentionalism and the hermeneutics of suspicion, the contemporary critic is likely to decry it as further evidence of the obsolescence and moribund corruption of philosophical aesthetics. The contemporary critic has available a number of scary accounts here with which to discredit Anglo-American aestheticians. It may be argued that intentionalism shows residues of such horrifying notions as: bourgeois individualism, the metaphysics of presence, the notorious Cartesian ego, and so on. However, in order to simplify matters, let me conjecture that the deepest fear of the suspicious hermeneut is that intentionalism thwarts a lively and productive critical practice.

The nightmare vision is this: the philosopher/legislator posts the sign – "No symptomatic reading allowed." But confronted with this directive, the contemporary critic surmises: "So much the worse for philosophy." Aesthetics is dead; critical results are what count. Perhaps some hardline philosophers are willing to negotiate the apparent incompatibility by abjuring the new political criticism. However, neither response seems to me necessary or advisable. As I will attempt to demonstrate, the claims of intentionalism and the aims of politicized contemporary criticism can be reconciled in this matter in a way

that may suggest a strategy for the fruitful co-existence of critics and philosophers of art in the future.

II. A NOTE ON INTENTIONALISM

Fifty years ago, at the dawn of Anglo-American aesthetics, the philosophy of criticism marched in lockstep with the most significant emerging paradigm in literary
studies in the English speaking world, the New Criticism.[3] One of the earliest,
exemplary exercises in Anglo-American aesthetics was the putative discovery of
the intentional fallacy, a cornerstone of the New Criticism. However, as Anglo-
American aesthetics evolved, that position was predictably subjected to powerful
criticism, to the point where its antithesis began to attract a substantial following.
Where the New Critic and his or her philosophical allies maintained that authorial intention was never relevant to interpretation, arguments began to be
advanced that, in various ways, maintained that authorial intent is not only relevant, but crucial, to interpretation.

Critical practice, of course, has evolved as well. However, oddly enough, for a
variety of reasons, anti-intentionalism, despite minority resistance, continues to
dominate literary studies in particular and humane studies in general.[4] Thus, on
one issue where philosophical aesthetics and criticism once significantly con-
verged, now they tend to part company.

Philosophical arguments for intentionalism and against anti-intentionalism have
been launched from many directions. One very compelling source of the brief
against anti-intentionalism has been a hearty skepticism with respect to essentialist
claims in art theory. For, fundamental to most of the previous philosophical arguments in favor of anti-intentionalism is the view that whereas when it comes to
ordinary words and deeds, understanding is legitimately informed by intentions,
when it comes to literature in particular and art in general, resort to intentions is
inadmissible because literature and the rest of the arts are so essentially different
from ordinary words and deeds – either in terms of their ontology or their aims –
that reference to artistic intentions is either impossible or counterproductive.

For example, some theorists defend anti-intentionalism by contending that literature is either an essentially distinct sort of illocutionary act or a representation
of an illocutionary act, such that it is impossible ontologically to locate authorial
intentions; while others defend anti-intentionalism on the grounds that the point
of art is to maximize interpretive play and that tying interpretation to intention
unduly restricts interpretive invention.[5] That is, either the peculiar nature or aim
of the arts recommends anti-intentionalism.

The anti-intentionalist agrees that, in the interpretation of ordinary words and
deeds, attention to intention is relevant. However, the anti-intentionalist goes on to
claim that the practices of literature and art, and the appreciation thereof, are so different from the comprehension of ordinary behavior, linguistic and otherwise, that
intentionalist understanding is altogether out of place. The burden of proof here, of
course, falls to the anti-intentionalist who must show what it is about literature and

art – in terms of their nature or fundamental aims – that renders intentionalist understanding with respect to them irrelevant, impossible, or counterproductive. And, of course, as candidates for the special status of literature and/or art are advanced by the anti-intentionalist, the skeptical intentionalist has the opportunity to undermine each putative differentia between art and ordinary words and deeds in such a way that our intentionalist inclinations remain unscathed.

That is, if we begin with the presumption that with respect to ordinary behavior (linguistic and otherwise) intentionalist interpretation best suits our explanatory aims, then it falls to the anti-intentionalist to provide reasons why things should stand differently with literature and art. But if no compelling distinction can hive off literature and art from ordinary words and deeds, then the presumption in favor of intentionalist interpretation stands intact.

Artworks, including literary texts, are the products of human action. Typically our understanding of artifacts is enabled by grasping how and why they were made. Understanding how an artifact is made – which involves grasping the maker's intentions – is generally relevant to understanding the artifact. Prima facie, what is appropriate to the understanding of the results of human action in general is appropriate to the understanding of artworks and texts.

The case for intentionalism is often obscured by the tendency of arguments in this arena to be fixated on the interpretation of literary language – that is, the interpretation of literature at the level of the meaning of words and sentences. For at this level of interpretation, one might be readily disposed to agree that meaning can be derived without recourse to intention, but instead through linguistic conventions of the sort easily available in dictionaries, grammars, and, perhaps, tropologies. That is, the meaning of words and sentences are putatively fixed by these conventions in a way that arguably renders speaker intention redundant or misleading.

Of course, it is far from settled that such linguistic conventions banish concern with a speaker's intention. For it can be argued that, in fact, we use linguistic conventions as a means both to communicate and to discern speaker/author intention – or, in other words, that even at the level of words and sentences the object of interpretation is authorial intention. But rather than keep the argument stalled at this level of debate, it is worthwhile to point out that most of our interpretive activity with respect to art in general, but also with regard to literature, is not devoted to linguistic interpretation, and, therefore, not so governed by convention.

When attempting to determine the significance of a character, of a plot structure, of the placement of figures on a picture plane, of a recurring motif, of a stretch of film editing, of a modern dance solo, of the roof of a postmodern medical center, and so on, we are not dealing with articulations whose significance is fixed with anywhere near the determinateness that a dictionary assigns to a word. Thus, even if the appeal to convention alone has some intuitive appeal in discussions of the interpretation of linguistic meaning proper, the attraction vanishes as we proceed to other levels of interpretation. For most artistic activity, including a great deal of literary composition, simply lacks the relatively determinate meaning conventions of words and sentences. Most art cannot be simply "read" in the strictest sense of the word. Rather, we comprehend it as we do any other sort of human action and the products thereof – by tracking it, explaining it, interpreting it in the light of our best hypotheses about intentions.

Even if the interpretation of linguistic meaning could advance considering linguistic conventions alone – an extremely controversial (and, I think, dubious) premise – this kind of interpretation could not be generalized as a model for all literary and artistic interpretation. For although every artwork depends upon conventions, most of these conventions are not of the code-like sort of linguistic conventions that anti-intentionalists rely upon so heavily in order to motivate their case. We approach artworks not as codes to be deciphered, but as actions and the products of action issuing from the intentional activity of rational agents – albeit against a backdrop of artistic traditions and relatively fluid conventions.

Artworks are naturally explained and understood in the way in which it is natural to explain and understand any other kind of intentional activity or the products thereof. We approach artworks as the productions of rational agents, negotiating the logic of a concrete situation. In this light, intentions are relevant to understanding artworks and their invocation is legitimate. *Pace* the anti-intentionalists, there are no special metaphysical or epistemological barriers standing in the way of intentionalist understanding when it comes to artworks. Indeed, despite the claims of the anti-intentionalists about the peculiar aims of art, our abiding aim and interest in understanding human action and its products warrants our references to intention when it comes to explaining artworks.

What the intentionalist wants to establish is that intention has a legitimate role and relevance in understanding and explaining artworks. In this way, that which I am calling "intentionalism" stands at odds with "anti-intentionalism." However, this conception of intentionalism does not entail the stronger claim that in explaining the intention manifested by an artwork, we have, in every case, delivered the final word on the object. Criticism may have more things to say about an artwork than isolating or illuminating authorial intent. Rather, what intentionalism maintains, in the face of anti-intentionalism, is that reference to intention is relevant and legitimate.

However, insofar as intention is at least relevant to our understanding and explanation of artworks, our best hypotheses about the creative intentions manifested in a work do serve to constrain whatever else we wish to say about the work. That is, whatever we want to say about the artwork should be consonant with the ways in which we speak of intentional activity generally. This does not preclude discussion of the unintended consequences of the artist's activity. Nevertheless, talk of unintended consequences needs to take shape against a background understanding of what was intended.

Now, the recognition that intentionalism is compatible with the discussion of unintended consequences, should, I think, reassure the practitioner of the hermeneutics of suspicion that a philosophical commitment to intentionalism is no impediment to his or her critical project. What more does the project require than the preceding, qualified concession of the possibility of the unintended consequences of action? However, there is a certain sort of problem, I suspect, that continues to vex suspicious hermeneuts, despite this abstract resolution – namely, the question of how interpretation is to proceed in cases where the critic wishes to impute to a work some significance that contradicts our best hypotheses about the intended import of a particular work. In order to address this issue, let us look at a specific example.

III. THE CASE OF JULES VERNE

Jules Verne's *Mysterious Island* was published in 1874. It belongs to the genre of the robinsonade that was inaugurated by Daniel Defoe's *Robinson Crusoe* (1719) and continued by Johann Rudolf Wyss' *The Swiss Family Robinson* (1813). The basic saga that such stories rehearse is that of marooned wayfarers who, in the face of natural adversity, transform their deserted islands into outposts of civilization.

In Verne's *Mysterious Island,* a band of Union loyalists escapes from the Confederacy during the throes of the American Civil War by hijacking a hot-air balloon. The all-male company includes an engineer, a journalist, an educated, presumably middle-class adolescent, an ordinary sailor, a former slave, and a dog. Once aloft, their balloon is blown wildly off-course until – during a whirling tempest – it finally sets down on an island somewhere in the Pacific. Most of the story is preoccupied with their exploration of the island, their discovery of the means to survival, and, gradually, their introduction of American techniques of agriculture and, then, industry to their habitat. The text is an exercise in applied science. Eventually, the marooned balloonatics transform their island into a thriving, productive, fantastically efficient, modern hamlet.

However, they do not achieve this singlehandedly. They are surreptitiously provided all sorts of advantages by an invisible benefactor – Captain Nemo, commander of the *Nautilus* whose adventures had been previously recounted in Verne's *Twenty Thousand Leagues Under the Sea*. Captain Nemo's interventions are revealed toward the end of the novel, which concludes with a volcanic eruption, the destruction of the island, and the fortuitous rescue of the island colony.

Mysterious Island has already been subjected to a famous symptomatic reading by Pierre Macheray.[6] According to Macheray, the novel rests on a contradiction. On the one hand, Macheray contends, the novel – as a kind of scientific-industrial celebration – is committed to a faith in the inevitable subjugation of nature to the forces of enlightened progress. But, on the other hand, insofar as the volcano wipes out the accomplishments of not only the Union settlers but those of the super-scientist Nemo as well, it signals a certain pessimism toward the ultimate prospects of technological progress.

Now I am not really convinced by this interpretation. It is far from clear that we should interpret the volcano allegorically as the sign of an irrevocable limit to human progress. Nor is it evident that Verne is aligned to such a delirious confidence in science that the volcanic explosion can serve as a refutation of his (Verne's) putative view. However, there does seems to be another contradiction in *Mysterious Island* – one that is directly relevant to the claims of a hermeneutics of suspicion.

Quite clearly, the narrative of *Mysterious Island* is pro-Union and pro-abolitionist. The novel shows no sympathy for the Confederacy or for slavery. Abraham Lincoln is spoken of in reverential tones; the settlers call their new land "Lincoln Island" in his honor. The Civil War is presented as a struggle to end slavery, and this is never represented as anything less than a holy crusade. The author forthrightly allies himself against racism throughout the text.

Nevertheless, readers of our own day cannot fail to note a great deal of residual racism in the book. The former slave, Neb, continues to call the engineer "Master" throughout the text. Neb is represented as superstitious, naive, docile, and childlike. Neb develops a special affinity for the monkey that the colonists domesticate, and, indeed, the monkey comes to perform as well as assist in many of Neb's kitchen duties. It is hard not to discern an implicit analogy between the monkey and Neb in the text. It is true that the monkey also has a special relationship to Pencroft, the sailor, but Pencroft — as the representative of the working class — is only one notch above Neb in the social order of the island. A character's place in the social hierarchy of the colony can be charted in proportion to his intimacy with the monkey. And the monkey is virtually Neb's double.

Though drawing generalizations from characters to whole classes of people can be problematic in the analysis of literary works, since all the characters in *Mysterious Island* are patently types, the inference from Neb to the idea that Verne is portraying African Americans as docile, childlike, naive, and rather close to the simian origins of the human race seems irresistible.[7] And, of course, in recent years, we have come to see the racism inherent in this variety of paternalism, even if Verne thought that characterizing African Americans as children served as a means for advancing the case for the humane treatment of people of color.

Reading *Mysterious Island,* we take Verne's writing to intentionally portray African Americans as docile, gentle, childlike, and somewhat akin to the intelligent higher primates. We can also glean from the context of the novel that Verne intends this portrayal to bolster his apparent conviction that African Americans deserve humane treatment. The paternalism here is benign in the sense that it is not intended to advance racial oppression. It opposes racist practices like slavery. And yet, at the same time, the portrayal of Neb strikes us as racist. But this appears to yield a contradiction: that *Mysterious Island* is both anti-racist and racist at the same time — anti-racist when read intentionalistically and racist when read from the standpoint of the hermeneutics of suspicion.

Persuaded of the intractability of this apparent contradiction, the contemporary critic, committed to the importance of emphatically identifying the racist tendencies of *Mysterious Island,* may be prompted to discount altogether the relevance of the textual evidence of Verne's intentions by means of a radical gesture: declaring intentionalist interpretation illegitimate *tout court.* That is, such a critic may argue that if intentionalist interpretation is somehow an impediment to attributing racist biases to *Mysterious Island,* then it should be forsaken. However, this line of attack is unnecessary. For not only is intentionalism no impediment to attributing racism to *Mysterious Island,* but, in fact, the attribution of racism in this case — as with similar attributions of racism, sexism, classism, imperialism, and so on — actually requires that *Mysterious Island* be approached intentionalistically.

IV. DEFENDING INTENTIONALISM

Clearly, interpreting *Mysterious Island* intentionalistically is no impediment to finding its treatment of Neb to be racist. Of course, the evidence indicates that Verne did not intend the book to be racist. But the same evidence indicates that he did intend to portray Neb as childlike, naive, and docile; and in doing so, he intentionally performed an act — he intentionally wrote — in such a way that what he produced was racist. He may not have intended to write "racistically," but in intentionally writing in the way he did, he produced something that was racist.

Perhaps Verne in fact wrote intentionally in the way he did — intentionally portraying Neb as docile — in the belief that this would be a beneficial rather than an oppressive way of representing African Americans. But this intentionalist account of Verne's writing of *Mysterious Island* is compatible with noting that — in fact and at the same time — the product of Verne's intentional activity was racist, albeit unintentionally racist.

Intentionalism, as I have advocated it, requires that we acknowledge artistic activity to be intentional activity and that we be constrained to speak about it in the ways we are constrained to speak about intentional activity generally. However, when speaking of intentional activity generally, there is no problem in admitting that in doing something intentionally under one description, one may be also doing something else under another description, even though one is unaware of the applicability of this alternate description.

Consider that someone intentionally lighting a cigarette in 1910 might have also at the same time been incurring lung cancer. Indeed, convinced by cigarette advertisements that proclaimed smoking to be healthful, such a smoker might inhale with the intention of improving his body when in fact he was harming it. Similarly, Verne by intentionally portraying Neb as docile — in a way that an intentionalist interpretation of the text could elucidate — did produce a representation that was racist, even though Verne did not know it to be racist. Verne intended to depict Neb as childlike, though Verne did not realize that this activity is subsumable under the category of racism. Thus, illuminating Verne's intentions does not preclude going on to say that he produced something that is racist, even if he did not know it.

Indeed, Verne may have produced something that was racist even in the process of intending to produce something that was anti-racist. This should come as no surprise. A lot has been learned about the nature of racism since 1874.

Thus, intentionalist criticism does not impede criticism in terms of attributions of racism of the preceding sort. For one can identify the product of intentional activity to be racist even if racism as such is not intended by the activity. Moreover, this, it seems to me, is all that a hermeneutics of suspicion requires. Therefore, it is a mistake to think that intentionalism is incompatible with contemporary symptomatic criticism.

Undoubtedly, the intuition that intentionalism is incompatible with the hermeneutics of suspicion derives from the view that intentionalism mandates that if, for example, a text is said to be racist, then the author should be cognizant of that racism: that he must have intended it; and, perhaps, even that he must be prepared to recognize accusations of racism. However, it is hard to see why intentionalism should be committed to these tests. For they go beyond the view that the work is a product of a rational agent such that, *pace* anti-intentionalism, the artist's intentions are always relevant to understanding and explaining an artwork.

Surely identifying Verne's paternalist intentions is relevant to understanding and explaining Verne's treatment of Neb in *Mysterious Island*. But claiming the relevance of hypothesizing Verne's intentions for understanding *Mysterious Island* does not entail that everything we may want to say about *Mysterious Island* is something that Verne intended to say or to imply by means of *Mysterious Island*. There is no reason to suppose that everything implied by *Mysterious Island* is something that Verne intended to imply, just as there is no reason to think that I know or believe everything that is implied by my actual mathematical beliefs.

The conviction that the intentions of artists are relevant to interpretation is not the view that interpretation is solely a matter of tracking authorial intention. Call the latter view authorism. If anyone holds it, authorism may conflict with the hermeneutics of suspicion. But intentionalism does not.

So far, I have argued that intentionalism is no impediment to the hermeneutics of suspicion. For properly understood, in its claim that authorial intentions are relevant to interpretation, intentionalism is compatible with all that is necessary for hermeneutical suspicion. Of course, this is not much of a finding. It only has what weight it does in a dialectical context in which many too hurriedly surmise that these forms of interpretation are fated for conflict. However, a more ambitious thesis is also worth contemplating here, namely: intentionalism is not only compatible with a hermeneutics of suspicion; the latter requires the former.

Recall the analysis of Neb in *Mysterious Island*. We reason from the paternalistic portrayal of Neb as docile, as childlike, and as naive, and from the implicit comparison of Neb in the chain of being with a monkey, that, at least in terms of its representation of African Americans as a type, *Mysterious Island* is racist (or has racist tendencies).[8] But in making this attribution, we are presuming that Verne's writing is informed by certain intentions. For instance, we infer that in writing about Neb's obedience toward and faith in the white engineer Harding, Verne intends to portray Neb as docile. When in the dialogue Verne has Neb address Harding as "Master," we presuppose that Verne intends us to take Neb's language as sincere rather than sarcastic. Throughout, we assume that Verne means us to take the portrayal of Neb "straight." That is, Verne did not – if our own interpretation of the text as racist is to have any purchase value – intend irony.

An interpretation of *Mysterious Island* as having racist tendencies would be undercut if we believed that Verne's portrayal of Neb was ironic – a satire intended to send up racist stereotypes. The reading of *Mysterious Island* as racist requires that we are satisfied that our best hypothesis about Verne's intentions is that in writing and composing Verne intended the character of Neb to be docile and naive. We proceed under the supposition that Verne was not being ironic – that Verne did not intend us to take his writing to signal that Neb in particular is not and that African Americans by extension are not docile, naive, childlike, and even somewhat simian. For, of course, had Verne intended irony – had he intended that the character be understood to be not docile and so on – then political criticism of *Mysterious Island* of the sort attempted above would be inappropriate.

In a related vein, if we want to criticize Ian Fleming for sexism because he portrays James Bond as heroic – not in spite of, but in part because of his treatment of women as sex objects – then we must take it that it is not the case that Fleming intends us to regard James Bond as a complex character – as a compound of good and bad – whose badness is in large measure a function of his sexual ruthlessness. In order to rebuke Fleming's sexual politics, we rely on the premise that Fleming intends to portray Bond simply as some sort of male paragon. Were we to entertain the notion that Fleming intends the portrayal of Bond to be a mixed one, with his sexism counting as a negative attribute, there would be, all things remaining equal, little point in criticism.

Of course, the text or the artwork itself is a primary source for our hypotheses about what the artist intended in writing or composing. Intentionalism does not entail that we ransack the artist's archives for confessions of temporally remote, psychological episodes. Though biographical and historical information may play a role in isolating the artist's purposes, artworks themselves typically provide the basis for hypothesizing with conviction that, for example, Verne meant Neb to be sincere rather than sarcastic and that Fleming intends Bond to be a male ideal rather than a hero also marked by troubling sexual proclivities. Without such grounds for hypothesizing the relevant intentions and without faith in such hypotheses, political criticism cannot get off the ground.[9]

Therefore, appearances notwithstanding, intentionalism is not at odds with the hermeneutics of suspicion. Rather, it is presupposed by such criticism. Understanding a text or an artwork cannot but be informed and guided by our best construals of the artist's intentions. Intentionalist criticism is logically prior to the application of a hermeneutics of suspicion. If this relation has been overlooked by contemporary critics, the reason may be that intentionalism is in fact so very deeply entrenched in the process of our discovery of significance in artworks that we may forget our reliance upon it.

V. AESTHETICS AND CRITICISM

As we prepare to celebrate the fiftieth anniversary of the American Society for Aesthetics, many of our colleagues in neighboring disciplines think that a funeral might be more in order. For them, aesthetics is dead, and Anglo-American philosophy is seen as an obstacle to explaining art.

The point of this essay has been to argue that – at least on one score – the leading tendencies in the philosophy of art and advanced criticism need not be irreconcilable. Moreover, though this brief exercise has focused narrowly on only one controversy, its result, broadly conceived, may have wider import.

There is no reason for the relation between aesthetics and contemporary criticism to deteriorate into shouting matches across a great divide. The aims of much contemporary criticism are humane and reasonable. The philosophy of art can serve the purposes of such criticism by clarifying its premises, thereby saving contemporary criticism from discarding the baby with the bathwater. Philosophy, that is, can protect otherwise reputable critical innovations from making the sort of extravagant commitments that tend to render them vulnerable to easy refutation and compromise.

One of the earliest projects of Anglo-American aesthetics was meta-criticism. In circumstances like our own in which new critical methodologies are proliferating at a geometric rate of expansion, meta-criticism is one aspect of the philosophy of art whose continued practice is both urgent and useful.

At present and into the foreseeable future, a major challenge to aesthetics is to remain open to what is humane and reasonable in evolving critical discourses. Though our colleagues in other disciplines often fail to see it, Anglo-American philosophy has the resources to facilitate many of their most pressing agendas, including, most significantly, their political agendas. If Anglo-American aesthetics began in a metacritical moment – with the popularization of the so-called "intentional fallacy" – the future of aesthetics still has room for even more metacritical underworkers as our critical horizons flourish in new and exciting directions.

The Intentional Fallacy:
Defending Myself

In "The Intentional Fallacy: Defending Beardsley,"[1] George Dickie and Kent Wilson raise certain objections to my essay "Art, Intention, and Conversation."[2] In my essay, I attempted to defend the intentionalist interpretation of artworks. I offered a number of arguments against anti-intentionalism, a view that I take to hold that reference to artistic intentions and the biography of the artist are never relevant to the interpretation of the meaning of artworks. In a more positive vein, I also argued that interpretations of artworks should be constrained by our knowledge of the biography of the historical artist and our best hypotheses about the artist's actual intentions concerning the artworks in question. Thus, I maintain that authorial intentions and biographies are relevant to the interpretation of artworks.

From: *The Journal of Aesthetics and Art Criticism,* 55,3 (Summer 1997), 305–9.

A number of my arguments, both positive and negative, depend upon a rough analogy with ordinary conversations. I rely on the claim that in such conversations we typically aim at understanding the intentions of our interlocutors. I further argue that I see no principled reasons to suppose that things stand differently with our "conversations" with artworks. Dickie and Wilson challenge this supposition by arguing that I have misconstrued the nature of ordinary conversations. Specifically, in their terminology, they maintain that typically in conversations we are concerned with understanding the meaning of the speaker's utterance and not the speaker's intended meaning. On their view, we are only concerned with the speaker's intended meaning in extraordinary cases where some puzzle arises about the speaker's intended meaning. But, in the main, we are not involved in making conjectures about the speaker's intended meaning. Thus, they conclude that any advantage for intentionalist art interpretation that I hope to derive from a view of our conversational interest in the intended meaning of speakers is flawed from the outset due to my misconception of conversations.

In what follows, I will respond to the charges of Dickie and Wilson in three ways. First, I will compare the scope of their anti-intentionalism with my intentionalism in the hope of showing that even if they are right concerning the narrow linguistic phenomena about which they theorize, their findings are largely irrelevant to the larger issues in the intentionalist/anti-intentionalist debate in aesthetics. Second, I will try to demonstrate that my argument about the intentionalist interpretation of artworks can go through even if we grant them what they say about conversations. And lastly, I will defend my conception of conversations against their denial that in the course of ordinary discourse we are involved in ascertaining the intended meanings of other speakers.

I. A QUESTION OF SCOPE

Dickie and Wilson draw a distinction between different ways in which the intentional fallacy can be construed. The broader interpretation of the intentional fallacy concerns whether an artist's intention is ever relevant to the meaning of the artwork; the narrower interpretation concerns whether the meaning an artist intended is identical with the meaning of the artwork. Their major effort is devoted to refuting the narrower version of the fallacy, which can also be called the "identity thesis." Furthermore, they claim that the debate over the identity thesis has replaced the issues associated with the broader interpretation of the intentional fallacy.

Since my view, as they acknowledge, pertains to the broader interpretation, their objections to the identity thesis do not cut against my account. That is why they raise special considerations against my position. However, before turning to those objections, I would like to question whether Dickie and Wilson are correct in their assertion that nowadays the debate really concerns the identity thesis.

The identity thesis is a conjecture about the meaning of words and word sequences, such as sentences. People like Dickie and Wilson maintain that it is a bad theory of linguistic meaning. But as I understand the intentional fallacy, it is not simply a debate about linguistic meaning, though linguistic meaning is the favorite intuition pump of anti-intentionalists. Rather, the intentional fallacy is a general theory of artistic interpretation, one that precludes the invocation of artistic intention whether the artwork in question is linguistic or nonlinguistic.

Monroe Beardsley, whom Dickie and Wilson are ostensibly defending, would appear to agree with me on this point, since he has noted transgressions of the fallacy in nonlinguistic art forms.[3] Perhaps even Dickie and Wilson might concede this point, since on occasion they also use the language of "the meaning of the artwork."[4]

But if we are talking about the meaning of artworks across the board, then the intentional fallacy does not reduce without remainder to the denial of the identity thesis, since in that case it would only concern one dimension of literary meaning, namely linguistic meaning, whereas the intentional fallacy is generally thought to apply to artistic interpretation of nonlinguistic arts – arts other than literature – and to nonlinguistic features of artworks – such as characterization and plotting – whose meaning, unlike the meaning of a word or a phrase, is not reducible to linguistic meaning.

Dickie and Wilson concede that their conception of the intentional fallacy is narrow. But they are perhaps unaware of how narrow it is, since meaning across the arts is not reducible to linguistic meaning. Thus, even at its very best, their denial of the identity thesis does not get them a comprehensive version of anti-intentionalism with respect to the interpretation of artworks. Even if they were correct about the identity thesis, it would only warrant anti-intentionalism with respect to one kind of artistic interpretation – namely the literary interpretation of words and word sequences.

Against the identity thesis, Dickie and Wilson argue that linguistic conventions rather than speaker intentions determine the meaning of utterances. But even if they are right about this issue in the philosophy of language, this argument cannot be extrapolated very widely across the arts. For many art forms – most art forms? – do not possess anything analogous to linguistic conventions. Therefore, in interpreting them, we cannot be relying on linguistic conventions. For example, in the Bournonville ballet *La Sylphide,* a particular step, the *rond de jambe en l' air,* occurs several times. When the sylph executes it, it is about airiness; when Effie does it, it is about precision. The *rond de jambe en l' air,* a common step in ballet, does not have a conventional meaning. When we reflect about the meaning of the step in its various occurrences, there are no conventional balletic meanings available for us to invoke. Rather, it seems far more likely that as we reflect on the steps in question, we consider what the choreographer and the dancer intend to convey by means of them.

Similarly, in *Man with a Movie Camera,* when the filmmaker Dziga Vertov intercuts shots of the activities of a Soviet cameraman with shots of the activities of all sorts of other Soviet workers, we interpret these juxtapositions as promoting the assertion that the Soviet cameraman is a worker, just like any other. However, this interpretation cannot rely upon the conventional meaning of juxtaposition in the cinema. Juxtaposition has no conventional meaning in film. Instead, in order to understand the shot chain, we ask ourselves what point Vertov intends to impart by means of these juxtapositions. Moreover, examples of this sort, where interpretation cannot fall back upon anything remotely like conventional linguistic meanings, can be endlessly duplicated across the nonlinguistic arts.[5]

Indeed, even in literature, it is implausible to think that all of our interpretive questions revolve around conventional linguistic meaning. In Salman Rushdie's *Satanic Verses,* there are two major characters, both of them Indian, both of them actors – that is, people who take on different roles. And throughout the novel they undergo astounding metaphysical transformations as well. A central question in interpreting *Satanic Verses* is why Rushdie constructed characters such as these – that is, what is their point? One interpretation – one that could be supported by other works by Rushdie, such as *The Moor's Last Sigh* – might be that Rushdie is illustrating the postmodernist conception of personal identity as unstable.

But be that as it may, such an interpretation cannot rely on invoking conventional linguistic meaning, since there are no conventions that correlate such characters with theses about the instability of personal identity. Rather, in interpreting the symbolic significance of these characters, we are asking ourselves about what Rushdie intends to communicate by means of them. Moreover, a great many interpretive questions about literature are of this sort. What is the significance of Dickens's employment of two narrators in *Bleak House?* What does the circular plot structure in the play *La Ronde* portend? These questions cannot be answered by reference to conventions, because there are no conventional meanings in the relevant neighborhoods. Instead, we proceed by conjecturing what the authors intend us to understand by means of these essentially nonlinguistic devices.

Thus, the anti-intentionalism that rests on a denial of the acceptability of the identity thesis for linguistic meaning is not a comprehensive form of aesthetic anti-intentionalism. For a great many questions of artistic interpretation, such as the ones I have adduced, the form of anti-intentionalism Dickie and Wilson defend is, at best, strictly irrelevant. Inasmuch as the debate about intentionalism has been about and continues to pertain to a comprehensive theory of artistic interpretation, Dickie and Wilson have failed to reinstate the intentional fallacy across the arts. Moreover, if anti-intentionalism is understood as the universal, negative proposition that art interpretation must never advert to artistic intentions, then it is a mistake to think that the denial of the identity thesis is a satisfactory defense of anti-intentionalism *tout court*. And, furthermore, if what we seek is a more comprehensive approach to art interpretation, other options, such as my own, may be more attractive than the sort of anti-intentionalism that Dickie and Wilson appear to champion.

II. THE NATURE OF INTERPRETATION

In "Art, Intention, and Conversation," I argued that in everyday conversations our goal is to understand what our fellow speakers intend by their words, and I further argued that there are no pressing philosophical considerations that would lead us to think that things stand otherwise with respect to artistic communication. Dickie and Wilson reject this on the grounds that I have misunderstood what goes on in ordinary conversations. They argue that in the standard case, we are concerned with the meaning of the speaker's utterance, not the speaker's intended meaning. They concede that in certain cases of utterance failures – which may occur, for example, when a speaker misspeaks – and in other unusual circumstances, we may be concerned with the speaker's intended meaning, but they argue that these constitute the exception, rather than the rule. Furthermore, they contend that my case is built on focusing on cases of misspeaking, and that this not only misrepresents that which typically goes on in conversations, but also that it is a rather bizarre basis on which to build a conception of our response to artworks.

Though I do not believe that I have misconstrued the nature of conversation, in this section I will, for the purposes of argument, grant Dickie and Wilson's allegations in order to show that even if I had made the error they suggest about conversations, my overall position about the interpretation of artworks would remain intact, given what they say about conversations.

The first thing to note about Dickie and Wilson's argument is that it does concede that sometimes we do have the conversational goal of understanding the speaker's intended meaning. Thus, they do appear to allow for some measure of intentionalism in conversations, even if they regard it as the exception rather than the rule. Therefore, their anti-intentionalism with respect to conversations is not universal. Consequently, there may be some cases where my analogy between conversations and artworks obtains. The question is, how many cases?

In examining my argument, Dickie and Wilson note that I use cases where authors misspeak themselves in order to advance my case. And they appear to agree that in such cases, our goal might indeed be to discern what the speaker/author intended to mean. They also think we may have such a goal when confronted with ambiguous utterances. What is it about cases like these that prompts us to become concerned with the speaker's intended meaning? Dickie and Wilson indicate that it is because such cases are puzzling – that is, because we are puzzled by what the speaker is saying. But then Dickie and Wilson further suggest that it would be odd to base a theory of the interpretation of artworks on cases like these.

But why? I agree that it would sound odd to base such a theory on conversational mistakes. But it is not odd to base a theory of interpretation on the way in which we respond to that which is puzzling. It is of the nature of artistic interpretation that it takes as its object what is puzzling and nonobvious.[6] It is because artworks are frequently puzzling and that the significance of their various articulations is nonobvious that we engage in the interpretation in the first place. So if, as Dickie and Wilson appear to agree, it is appropriate to be concerned with authorial meaning when puzzles or questions arise, then it would seem to be apposite to adopt intentionalism in response to artistic articulations that warrant interpretation.

The outlandish, enigmatic events, irrational character motivations, unusual metaphors, oxymoronic sentences, and sentence fragments, as well as the gaping narrative ellipses in Kathy Acker's *Pussy, King of the Pirates* strike the reader as puzzling and call for interpretation. They are not mistakes; they are the sort of artistic innovations and defamiliarizations that we expect from avant-garde novelists. They do not rely upon fixed conventions. So we ask ourselves what Acker intends us to understand by them. Admittedly, this is an extreme case. But it illustrates a standard characteristic of artworks – namely, that they often come with features that are unusual, puzzling, initially mysterious or disconcerting, or with features whose portents are far from obvious. These features of artworks are the natural objects of interpretation, and inasmuch as they defy, redefine, or complicate standing conventions, we do not explicate them by applying meaning conventions, but we ask ourselves what the artists in question intend to mean by them.

How often does this happen? Quite often. Indeed, when it comes to the artworks and constituent parts of artworks that we feel are worthy of interpretation, this may be the rule, not the exception.

Dickie and Wilson think that it is strange to motivate an approach to artworks by pointing to conversational failures. Of course, I do not try to motivate my position exclusively by means of such cases. But even if I did, my position would only sound strange when put in terms of mistakes. However, when the relevant feature of mistakes is identified as a response to what is puzzling, then my position does not sound strange, once we recall that what is puzzling is the appropriate object of interpretation. Thus, even if Dickie and Wilson were right in their claim that I misinterpret the nature of typical conversation, given what they say about the way in which we respond to conversational puzzles, I can reinstate my conclusions about our response to artworks by pointing to the nature of interpretation.

III. PLACING THE ARTIST

According to Dickie and Wilson, my conception of ordinary conversations is incorrect. On my view, when we speak with others our goal is to figure out what they intend to say. But for Dickie and Wilson, we standardly only attend to the meaning of the speaker's utterance.

Of course, I would not wish to dismiss the importance of the meaning of the utterance in conversation. Indeed, I think that in large measure utterance meaning is the best guide to speaker meaning. But I still think intentionalist considerations go into the typical comprehension of our fellow conversationalists, not only in cases of obvious misspeaking, but in the normal case as well.

If I am stopped at a street corner in New York City and I am asked for the whereabouts of the Empire State Building, I will try to figure out what I am being asked by tacitly or consciously hypothesizing what my interlocutor wants to know. This will involve presumptions and/or conjectures about who she is and about the purposes behind her question. Is she a traveler, for example, or a pollster? If she is a traveler, with suitcase in hand, I will tell her that the Empire State Building is on 34th Street and Fifth Avenue. If she is a pollster, with clipboard in hand, doing research on the geographical knowledge of middle-aged Americans, it will be enough to tell her that the Empire State Building is in New York City. In order to respond to my interlocutor, in other words, I will either presume or conjecture a certain framework – the traveler framework or the pollster framework – which enables me to place both her and her question. That is, I presume or conjecture a framework that will situate what she intends to learn by means of saying "Where is the Empire State Building?"

When asked by a clergyman about why he robbed banks, Willie Sutton said, "Well, that's where the money is." One thing that this miscommunication reveals is that both the clergyman's question and Sutton's answer depended upon certain assumptions. In this case, the assumptions went in different directions. Generally, however, the assumptions of conversationalists tend to mesh. But even where they mesh, it is nevertheless the case that assumptions underwrite conversations, whether the assumptions in question are presumed or conjectured. Moreover, in making these sorts of assumptions, which obtain in all conversational exchanges, conversationalists are involved in the process of each trying to figure out what the other intends by their words.

In many cases, the relevant assumptions may be default assumptions. If someone with a cigarette in his mouth asks me for a match and all I have is a lighter, I will hand him the lighter, on the assumption that he wants to ignite his cigarette. I will do this rather than doing nothing at all on the assumption that he, say, is a match collector. That he wants a light, in other words, is my default assumption. Moreover, default assumptions are often not brought before the court of consciousness, but are tacit. Nevertheless, default assumptions are still assumptions. They are presumed. And these presumptions constitute part of what is involved in the process of figuring out what my interlocutor has in mind. Of course, sometimes our attempts at placing the interlocutor and his intentions will take the form of explicit conjectures. But whether presumptions or conjectures, tacit or explicit, assumptions of these sorts are, I maintain, a necessary ingredient in all conversational exchanges. And if this is true, then, pace Dickie and Wilson, attempting to figure out what the speaker intends to say is a standard feature of conversations.

Thus, my own account of conversations is not flawed, and my analogy between artworks and conversations cannot be dismissed on the basis of my alleged misconstrual of the nature of conversations. In "Art, Intention, and Conversation." I used the analogy to claim that we have conversational interests in our commerce with artworks. These are not our only interests. But I argue that they are central enough that our knowledge about the biography of the historical artist and our best hypotheses about their actual intentions should constrain our interpretations of artworks. That is, how we place the artist and her purposes is relevant to artistic interpretations. Nothing Dickie and Wilson have said so far demonstrates that this is false.

ℰ⌒

INTERPRETATION AND INTENTION:
THE DEBATE BETWEEN HYPOTHETICAL
AND ACTUAL INTENTIONALISM

Regarded for decades as a fallacy, intentionalist interpretation is beginning to attract a following among philosophers of art.[1] Broadly speaking, intentionalism is the doctrine that the actual intentions of artists are relevant to the interpretation of the artworks they create. For intentionalists, interpretation is a matter of explaining why artworks have the features, including meanings, that they possess. Since artworks possess these features as a result of the actions of artists, it seems natural to explain them, as we explain the results of actions in general, with an eye to the intentions of the pertinent agents, who are, in this case, artists.

Actual intentionalism holds to the conviction that interpretation with respect to artworks is on a continuum with interpretation of intentional action in daily life. Just as in ordinary affairs we interpret with the goal of identifying the actual intentions of the words and deeds of others, so with respect to art the actual intentions of artists are relevant to our interpretations of their productions.

Actual intentionalism, however, comes in different forms. The most extreme form maintains that the meaning of an artwork is fully determined by the actual intentions of the artist (or artists) who created it.[2] It is this extreme form of actual intentionalism that one suspects has encouraged the view that actual intentionalism is a fallacy. For this view leads to the unpalatable conclusion that the meaning of an artwork is whatever the author intends it to mean, irrespective, if we are talking about literary texts, of the word-sequence meaning of the text (the meaning of the text derivable solely by consulting dictionaries, the rules of grammar, and the conventions of literature). This variant of actual intentionalism is clearly unacceptable, since it leads to what has been called "Humpty-Dumpty-ism": the idea that an author could make a work mean anything simply because he wills it so – as Humpty Dumpty tries to do when he says to Alice that "glory" means "there's a knockdown argument."[3] Or, to advert to nonverbal art, this view

From: *Metaphilosophy,* 31, nos. 1/2 (January 2000), 75–90.

would, according to Monroe Beardsley, compel us to regard a blue sculpture as pink simply because the artist says it is.[4]

But extreme actual intentionalism is not the only sort of intentionalism abroad today, nor is it the form of actual intentionalism to be defended here. For convenience, we can call the form of actual intentionalism to be discussed "modest actual intentionalism." In contrast to extreme intentionalism, modest actual intentionalism does not hold that the correct interpretation of an artwork is fully determined by what the artist intended. Rather, modest actual intentionalism only claims that the artist's actual intentions are relevant to interpretation. Specifically, the artist's actual intentions constrain our interpretations of artworks. With reference to literary texts, the modest actual intentionalist argues that the correct interpretation of a text is the meaning of the text that is compatible with the author's actual intention.[5]

Modest actual intentionalism blocks Humpty-Dumpty-ism because even if Humpty Dumpty intends "glory" to mean "knockdown argument," that is not a meaning that the textual unit ("glory") can have. The intentions of authors that the modest actual intentionalist takes seriously are only those intentions of the author that the linguistic/literary unit can support (given the conventions of language and literature). But where the linguistic unit can support more than one possible meaning, the modest actual intentionalist maintains that the correct interpretation is the one that is compatible with the author's actual intention, which itself must be supportable by the language of the text.

For example, if one utters "the fish is on the bank" and intends by that to say that the fish is on the shore, and not that it is on the steps of the Citicorp Building, then the meaning of the utterance, for the modest actual intentionalist, is "the fish is on the shore." Attributions of meaning, according to the modest actual intentionalist, must be constrained not only by what possible senses the text can support (given the conventions of language and literature), but also by our best information about the actual intended meaning of the utterer or author in question. Thus, if a given story could support either the interpretation that ghosts are wreaking havoc or only that the relevant fictional characters in the story believe that ghosts are wreaking havoc *and* it is known that the author intended the story to affirm that ghosts are wreaking havoc, the modest actual intentionalist maintains that the correct interpretation of the text is that the ghosts are wreaking havoc.[6] For the modest actual intentionalist, the author's intention here must square with what he has written, but if it squares with what he has written, then the author's intention is authoritative.

One common complaint about all forms of actual intentionalism is that they divert the audience away from the proper object of its attention. Instead of focusing on the text, intentionalism sends the reader outside the text, searching for the author's intention – perhaps in the archive where her private papers are stored. This criticism, however, is misguided here, since the modest actual intentionalist freely admits that the best evidence for what an utterer, artist, or author intends to say or mean is the utterance or artwork itself. Modest actual intentionalism is not an injunction to root for authorial meaning in hidden places. Generally, we find authorial intention expressed in the artworks in question.

Most of our interpretive endeavors, even if we are actual intentionalists, are aimed at the text. The point of actual intentionalism of the modest variety is the recovery of the intentions, conscious and otherwise, of utterers and artists, but this is consistent with close attention to the text. In fact, for the modest actual intentionalist, close interpretive attention to the text is just the pursuit of the actual intentions of the artist; it is an error to think of close attention to the text and the search for actual intentions as opposed enterprises. Moreover, the modest actual intentionalist also requires that putative authorial intentions be shown to square with what is written. So the worry that modest actual intentionalism is at variance with a textually attentive reading is groundless.

In a related vein, actual intentionalism is also frequently dismissed because it allegedly commits the fallacy of paraphrase. The actual intentionalist, it might be said, behaves as though what we really want from criticism is merely what the author intends to say. But were that so, couldn't we just e-mail her for a succinct statement of her message? Why plow through hundreds of pages of a largish novel, if all we are after is her view that money corrupts? But, of course, we value the experience of navigating our way through the novel, and we would not trade it for a compact restatement of what the novelist intended to communicate by means of it. Thus, if actual intentionalism implies that all we care about is identifying the author's intended message, then it is charged that actual intentionalism woefully mischaracterizes what concerns us in reading literature.

But there is no reason to suppose that the aim of modest actual intentionalism is to substitute a paraphrase of the author's intentions for the reading of the text. Rather, the actual intentionalist is interested in the author's intentions because they will enrich the reading of the text. Grasping the author's intentions puts us in a position to appreciate the author's inventiveness (or lack thereof) in structuring the text. The aim of the modest actual intentionalist is not primarily to return home with a paraphrase of the author's intention as pithy as a Chinese fortune cookie, but to use the author's intended meaning as a resource for engaging the text. Thus, the actual intentionalist need not commit the fallacy of paraphrase. Moreover, since engaging the text is itself importantly a process of identifying the author's actual intentions, once again we see that modest actual intentionalism is consistent with the reader's absorption in the text and need not represent a romp outside it.

So far we have been defending modest actual intentionalism from some of the objections leveled at it by anti-intentionalists (those for whom reference to artistic intentions commits some sort of fallacy). And, in truth, much of the energy of actual intentionalists in the past has been spent in neutralizing the criticisms of anti-intentionalism. But in recent years another threat to actual intentionalism has taken shape. Called hypothetical intentionalism or, sometimes, postulated authorism, this view maintains that the correct interpretation or meaning of an artwork is constrained not by the actual intentions of authors (compatible with what they wrote), but by the best hypotheses available about what they intended.

According to the hypothetical intentionalist, the meaning of a text is what an ideal reader, fully informed about the cultural background of the text, the *oeuvre* of the author, the publicly available information about the text and the author, and the text itself, would hypothesize the intended meaning of the text to be.[7] That is, the hypothetical intentionalist claims that the meaning of the text correlates with the hypothesized intention, not the real intention, of the author, and that interpreters are concerned with postulated authors, not real authors.

Epistemologically, what this comes down to is that the hypothetical intentionalist permits the interpreter to use all the sorts of information publicly available to the intended, appropriate reader of a text, while debarring information not publicly available to said reader, such as interviews with the artist as well as his or her private papers. Since modest actual intentionalism is open to the circumspective use of such information, this is where hypothetical intentionalism and modest actual intentionalism part company most dramatically.

With regard to literary texts, the hypothetical intentionalist argues that the meaning of the text is either the meaning of the word sequences in the text, the speaker's meaning, or the utterance meaning. The meaning cannot be word-sequence meaning for a number of reasons, including the phenomenon of irony. The meaning cannot be speaker's meaning, because this would not allow for the fact that sometimes authors fail to mean by a text what they intend to mean by it; to suppose that the meaning of the text in such cases is speaker's meaning would be tantamount to a reversion to Humpty-Dumpty-ism. That leaves utterance meaning as the meaning of the text – the meaning of the text that an ideally informed reader would attribute to the text given the context of utterance.

Utterance meaning, inasmuch as it is a speech act, requires intentions, but the intention in question is a hypothesized intention. It may not be the author's genuine intention, but only, in context, the most plausibly hypothesized intention thereof. Such intentions require authors, but the author is a postulated or constructed author, that is, the author we infer in order to explain the features of the text – where our inferences (or postulations or constructions) are based not only on the language of the text, but also on information about the genre of the text, the author's past work, and what is publicly available concerning the author's career. Determining the meaning of an utterance on a particular occasion requires more than knowledge about the dictionary meanings of the words used to make the utterance. It requires knowledge of the context of the utterance, including certain knowledge about the speaker.

By modeling literary meaning on utterance meaning, the hypothetical intentionalist acknowledges the relevance of context, bidding the ideal interpreter to heed not only word-sequence meaning, but also all the relevant contextual information, including knowledge about the art-historical context, about the genre in question, about the author's past works, and, in addition, common, publicly available information about the life of the artist (e.g., that he was a freedom fighter or is a Republican). The relevant intention for purposes of interpretation is the one that the fully informed, ideal reader would hypothesize on the basis of such knowledge (while, at the same time, ignoring the author's private pronouncements about his or her intentions).

For example, in the concluding pages of *The Ground beneath Her Feet,* Salman Rushdie writes of the assassination of a *rai* singer who has gone into exile to escape a worldwide plot to "wipe out singing altogether." Since "Rai" is also the name of the fictional narrator of the book and since it is widely known that Rushdie himself had to go into hiding in order to evade the vengeance of fanatics, the hypothetical intentionalist, considering the language of the text and Rushdie's public biography, can plausibly hypothesize that the passage is an allusion to Rushdie's own experience.

Obviously the hypothetical intentionalist and the modest actual intentionalist appeal to much of the same evidence. Since the modest actual intentionalist is committed to discerning the author's actual intentions, he too relies on word-sequence meaning, context, the author's *oeuvre,* the author's public biography, and so on, in order to arrive at an interpretation. Thus, since the hypothetical intentionalist and the modest actual intentionalist depend on much the same evidence, they generally deliver the same interpretations.[8] However, there are imaginable cases when the results of the two methods will diverge.

Suppose I utter "The fish is on the bank" while standing on the steps of the Citicorp Building with a large trout clearly in view behind me. Here, the ideal listener will interpret the utterance as "The fish is on the financial institution." On the other hand, if the actual intentionalist learns from me that what I truly intended by my utterance was "The fish is on the shore," then the actual intentionalist will endorse that as the interpretation of the meaning of my utterance. For that *is* the intended meaning of my utterance, which is, furthermore, compatible with what I said. The hypothetical intentionalist maintains that the meaning of the utterance is the one best warranted given the context of utterance without authorial pronouncements, but the actual intentionalist argues that even the hypothesis best warranted on those grounds can be false.

What putatively recommends hypothetical intentionalism over actual intentionalism? The hypothetical intentionalist raises two considerations. The first reason is one we have already encountered: that approaches like actual intentionalism have no way to accommodate the fact that authors can fail to communicate what they intend, and that modest actual intentionalism has no way of dealing with this fact. The second consideration is more complex. It is that hypothetical intentionalism does a better job of reflecting our actual interpretive practices than does modest actual intentionalism. Jerrold Levinson writes that hypothetical intentionalism

> acknowledges the special interests, and attendant constraints of the practice or activity of *literary* communication, according to which works – provided they are interpreted with maximal attention to relevant author-specific context … – are ultimately more important than, and distinct from, the individuals who author them and those individual's inner lives; works of literature thus retain, in the last analysis, a certain autonomy from the men-

tal processes of their creators during composition at least as far as resultant meaning is concerned. It is this small but crucial dimension of distinctness between agent's meaning and work's meaning ... which is obliterated by actual intentionalism but safe-guarded by the hypothetical variety.[9]

These are significant objections. However, before returning to them, I will begin to sketch the case for modest actual intentionalism against hypothetical intentionalism.

Whereas hypothetical intentionalism claims that literary interpretation and everyday interpretation are distinct, modest actual intentionalism argues that they are importantly continuous practices. Outside the literary and artistic contexts, we generally interpret utterances, gestures, and other forms of symbolic behavior with an eye to retrieving authorial intentions. Modest actual intentionalism takes literary and artistic interpretation to be on a par with ordinary interpretation.

The hypothetical intentionalist maintains that literary and artistic practices are discontinuous with our ordinary practices and says that, in consequence, our interpretations have different aims. In the ordinary course of events, the hypothetical intentionalist concedes, our interpretations aspire to discover actual intentions, but in literary and artistic contexts, hypothesized intentions, as postulated by ideal readers, suffice.

But why suppose that there is a discontinuity between ordinary interpretation and artistic interpretation? Interpretation is part and parcel of human life. We fall back on it in order to conduct our social life with conspecifics and for strategic purposes when confronting predators, prey, and human friends and enemies. Some interpretive powers are probably biologically innate, naturally selected for adaptiveness, while many others are refined and developed through enculturation where they are also ineliminably adaptive. However, these interpretive skills are all aimed at detecting the actual intentions and/or behavioral dispositions of conspecifics, predators, prey, and the like. Interpretive skills, as adaptive endowments, would make little sense otherwise. That is why our interpretive powers were and are keyed to discerning actual intentions.

The arts themselves are, among other things, celebrations of our human powers. Like the dancer, we walk, run, and leap – and sometimes we execute fancy footwork to avoid an oncoming bicycle or to scoot to the head of the line. Dancers interest us because they display these capacities (and more) at particularly high levels of accomplishment. They show us what human grace can be not only so that we can compare what they do with what we do (and, perhaps, garner some tips from them), but also so that we can contemplate the possibilities of common human powers. Since we all communicate and express ourselves through word and gesture, we admire poets, singers, and actors who exhibit human expressive possibilities operating at full throttle.

Moreover, in a similar vein, I would like to suggest that we are interested in literary and artistic interpretations because they too exemplify highly developed skills that we all deploy constantly in our everyday commerce with our conspecifics and with their communicative and expressive behaviour. And those skills, at base, are dedicated to detecting the actual intentions of our conspecifics.

Thus, the modest actual intentionalist sees literary and artistic interpretation on a continuum with ordinary interpretive practices, which are aimed at tracking actual intentions. Certainly, even the hypothetical intentionalist must agree that our practices of literary and artistic interpretation evolved from our practices of everyday interpretation – which practices, needless to say, function to detect actual intentions. Of course, the hypothetical intentionalist may claim that artistic and literary interpretation has become detached from the practices that gave rise to it. But that conjecture itself raises a number of questions.

The first question is: Why did the practices of literary and artistic interpretation become detached from the ordinary practices of interpretation? What new purposes are served that supersede the natural purposes of ordinary interpretation? Hypothetical intentionalists have not been very forthcoming about this matter. It cannot be that pursuing hypothetical intentions is more pleasurable than pursuing actual intentions, since both approaches employ much the same methodology. Sometimes, in this context, it is said that we value the activity of literary and artistic interpretation for its own sake. But that hardly seems to be an explanation; rather, it sounds like an evasion. And, as we shall see later, many literary interpreters would appear ready to resist the claims that they engage in exegesis for its own sake rather than for the sake of recovering authorial intentions.

Second, the hypothetical intentionalist is in an extremely poor position to claim that artistic and literary interpretations aim at different purposes than ordinary interpretation – for the simple reason that the interpretive considerations that the hypothetical intentionalist recommends are roughly the same as those the modest actual intentionalist recommends: attention to the text, to the author's *oeuvre,* to the culture context, to the author's publicly available biography, and so on.

Why are these the desiderata that the modest actual intentionalist emphasizes? Because they are the sorts of things that provide a reliable indication of the author's actual intentions. Attention to these factors is what enables us to track the author's actual intentions. Thus, the very methodology of hypothetical intentionalism seems predicated upon tracking actual authorial intention. Indeed, why else would it select precisely the desiderata it does? Consequently, it does not seem that hypothetical intentionalism is calibrated to satisfy different aims than is actual intentionalism, and, therefore, it does not seem to make much sense to claim that it serves a different purpose than does actual intentionalism – which purpose, of course, is identifying the actual intentions of the author, not merely his or her plausibly hypothesized intentions.

Hypothetical intentionalism identifies the correct interpretation with whatever the ideal reader identifies as the author's hypothetical intention, whereas modest actual intentionalism goes with the author's actual intention (where it is supported by the text), should that diverge from what the ideal reader hypothesizes. However, it is somewhat perplexing that hypothetical intentionalism recom-

mends going with the ideal reader's hypothesis, since the methodology of hypothetical intentionalism is itself designed to track the author's actual intention.

Consider an analogy. We employ scientific method in order to approximate
the truth. Were we to discover that our best scientific hypothesis were false – that
something else were the case – would we stick with a methodologically sound but
false hypothesis, or would we go with what we knew to be true? Clearly, the very
aims of science would recommend that we live with the truth. Similarly, where
actual intentionalism and hypothetical intentionalism diverge in their results,
given the comparable aims of their methodologies, why would we stick with the
results of the hypothetical intentionalist's interpretation when a true account of an
author's actual intention is available?

As already observed, the desiderata the hypothetical intentionalist respects are
all designed to deliver our best approximation of the author's actual intention.
Thus, if we establish the author's intention by means unavailable to the hypothetical intentionalist – perhaps through the discovery of the author's notebook – isn't
that the result that we should care about? Otherwise, we appear to be fetishizing
our method over what the method is designed to secure.

I submit that we respect the interpretive protocols the hypothetical intentionalist cherishes because they are reliable indicators of actual intentions. The
hypothetical intentionalist provides no other reasons for our acceptance of just
the sorts of information he emphasizes. It is true that the hypothetical intentionalist's protocols yield hypotheses about authorial intentions, but they are
plausible hypotheses about actual intentions, not hypotheses about plausible
possible intentions.

The method of hypothetical intentionalism is parasitic on the aims of actual
intentionalism. That is, we attend to the things to which the hypothetical
intentionalist adverts because interpretation, or at least intentionalist interpretation, aims at recovering actual intentions. That is what our interpretive practices are designed to track. If those generally reliable methods are sometimes
supplemented by other creditable resources – such as the author's correspondence – why should those further resources be ignored, if they supply a more
effective means to our ends?

Recall that the modest actual intentionalist is not using this evidence to claim
that a text means something that the written text fails to support. He employs the
author's intention to fix a meaning to the text that the text could have. He simply
goes beyond the evidence permitted by the method of hypothetical intentionalism – a method that is, admittedly, quite warranted. But as in science, even a well-
justified methodology can fail to zero in on the truth.

Here the hypothetical intentionalist may wish to dispute the analogy with science. A realist epistemology makes sense in science, he might say, because there is
a fact of the matter that is independent of the best-warranted theories. But with
respect to literature, it is claimed, there is no difference between our best interpretation of the text and the meaning of the text. But this claim appears to be either
false or question-begging.

It seems false, since it is eminently conceivable that our best interpretation of a text from a remote ancient civilization could diverge from the utterance meaning of the text. But if the hypothetical intentionalist responds that there can be no gap because our best hypothesis, following his protocols of interpretation, *is* the meaning of the text, then all he has done is to reaffirm the claims of hypothetical intentionalism.

In effect, what the hypothetical intentionalist has done is to substitute the notion of warranted assertibility for truth when it comes to literary interpretation. But since we need not accept this relativizing move with respect to other forms of inquiry, it is not evident that we need to make it with respect to literary texts and artworks. We are interested in warranted assertions because they generally track truth. Thus, we are interested in warranted assertions (justifiable hypotheses) about authorial intentions because they are good indications of actual authorial intentions. So, if we come upon the author's actual intention, even if it departs from our best theory of it, then that is what we should prefer. Though Sir Richard Burton's criticisms of John Hanning Speke may have been methodologically sound, nevertheless it is to Speke that we owe the discovery of the headwaters of the Nile.

Hypothetical intentionalists may attempt to advance their approach by arguing that it accurately describes what literary interpreters do. They construct *hypotheses* about authorial intentions, ones that are presumably open to revision with the onset of further information. They don't pretend to be mind readers; they don't have cerebroscopes that enable them to peer into the minds of authors. Their interpretations are hypotheses, conjectures, or constructions. And, of course, the modest actual intentionalist agrees with this, but adds that they are hypotheses about actual intentions. Thus, when literary interpreters explore texts by considering not only their language, but also their historical context, the author's *oeuvre,* the author's public biography, and the like, they are behaving exactly in the way that the modest actual intentionalist predicts. Their behavior in regard to what they typically view as their primary data base does not favor hypothetical intentionalism over modest actual intentionalism.

The book reviewer interpreting a new novel looks in all the places the hypothetical intentionalist advises and comes up with a hypothesis, rather than hiring a private detective to rifle through the author's trash for secret statements of intention. But this is a hypothesis about the author's actual intention, not about some theoretical fiction that might be called a hypothetical or constructed or postulated intention.

Reading in accordance with the protocols of hypothetical intentionalism is simply reading for actual intentions, as the hypothetical intentionalist himself admits. However, the hypothetical intentionalist regards this search for actual authorial intent as a "heuristic."[10] And yet if hypothetical intentionalism is supposed to reflect our actual practices of interpretation, it must be noted that many pedigreed interpreters do not act as though they regard the goal of determining actual authorial intention as merely heuristic. They appear to regard it as their final goal.

Some hypothetical intentionalists speak of postulated authors rather than hypothesized intentions. The aim of interpretation on this view is to construct the most plausible author of the text, according to the interpretive protocols of hypothetical intentionalism, in order to explain why the text has the features it has. This author-construction, the postulated author – a sort of theoretical entity – is the object of criticism, not the actual writer who composed the text. But it is difficult to see how this theoretical construct could really explain the features of a text, since this theoretical construct could not have causally influenced the text in any way.[11]

Of course, if the postulated author is to be understood as some kind of theo-retical entity or construction, then it is important to remember that theoretical entities in science are designed to approximate real processes, not hypothetical processes. That is, they are hypotheses about actual processes, not hypotheses about hypothetical processes – otherwise, they would not possess genuine explanatory power. And, given this, in science we ultimately prefer the truth to postulations that are merely well warranted. Similarly, with respect to interpretation, parity of reasoning would suggest that this is why true characterizations of authorial processes should trump postulated authorial processes.

So far we have been exploring the modest actual intentionalist's reservations about hypothetical intentionalism. But now let us return to the hypothetical intentionalist's objections to modest actual intentionalism. As you may recall, they are two in number. The first charges that modest actual intentionalism has no way to deal with the fact that sometimes authors fail to realize their intentions through their texts. But though this may be an apt criticism of extreme forms of actual intentionalism, it is not a fair criticism of modest actual intentionalism.

For the modest actual intentionalist acknowledges that authors may fail to realize their intentions; this occurs when the authors fail to produce texts that support their intentions. Where the author wrote "green," but intended "black," the modest actual intentionalist will not say the text means black, since for the modest actual intentionalist meaning is not simply a function of what the author intended, but must also be supported by what the text says.

The second objection that the hypothetical intentionalist makes concerning modest actual intentionalism is doubly important, since it not only raises a poten-tial problem for modest actual intentionalism but, in addition, suggests a way of deflecting many of the reservations that we have already expressed about hypo-thetical intentionalism. Many of our criticisms have been based on the observa-tion that the methodology of hypothetical intentionalism seems on a continuum with the methodology of everyday interpretation and, consequently, that the hypothetical intentionalist, like the ordinary interpreter, should prefer the discov-ery of the author's actual intention (where that is consistent with the text) over our best-warranted hypothesis about it (i.e., should the author's intention and the one isolated by the hypothetical intentionalist diverge).

But the hypothetical intentionalist responds that this is not the case, since the aims of literary interpretation are different in crucial ways from the aims of every-day interpretation. Thus, the modest actual intentionalist is wrong when he advances his cause by invoking a continuum between ordinary interpretation, on the one hand, and literary and artistic interpretation, on the other hand; and wrong again when he says an interpreter should prefer statements of genuine authorial intention to the best hypotheses of authorial intent. For given the nature of our literary practices – given their special interests – the hypothetical intentionalist claims that well-warranted hypotheses, derived without the benefit of authorial avowals, are, in fact, what we really care about with respect to literary communication.

For example, Jerrold Levinson writes:

> I agree that when an author proffers a text as literature to a literary audience, just as when he or she speaks to others in the ordinary setting, the author is entering a public language game, a communicative arena, but I suggest that it is one with different aims and understandings from those that apply in normal, one-on-one, or even many-on-many, conversational settings. Although in informative discourse we rightly look for intended meaning first, foremost and hindmost, in literary art we are licensed, if I am right, to consider what meanings the verbal text before us, viewed in context, *could* be being used to convey, and then to form, if we can, in accord with the practice of literary communication to which both author and reader have implicitly subscribed, our best hypothesis of what it is being used to convey, ultimately identifying that with the meaning of the work. What distinguishes our forming that hypothesis in regard to a literary work, as opposed to a piece of conversation, is that we do so for its own sake, the contextually embedded vehicle of meaning in literature being indispensable, not something to be bypassed in favor of more direct access to personal meaning when or if that is available.[12]

That is, literary communication is a different language game than ordinary conversation, and whereas actual authorial intentions are preferred over the best hypotheses thereof in the latter, in the former we are only interested in the most plausible attribution of authorial intention. Why? Well, that's the nature of the game. (One wonders, however, why the debate over intentionalism is so intense if the rules of the game are supposedly so clear-cut).

Here the hypothetical intentionalist seems to me to be making some extremely substantial empirical claims about the nature of our literary practices. And I, at least, am not convinced that the evidence will bear out these claims. Literary reviewers give every appearance that they are concerned with the author's actual intention, not just the best-warranted hypothesis thereof. For instance, when Peter Kurth asserts, "Writing is an act of the will, she [Chu Tien-Wien] says – and, in the end, will is the only trick we have left in our bags," I take him to be claiming that this is what she actually meant, not that this is the best available hypothesis.[13] That at least is what he says. If he is questioned about it, I conjecture that Kurth would predict that Chu Tien-Wien would assent to his interpretation, and that he would be willing to revise it if she said she had something else in mind (so long as the text supported it).

The hypothetical intentionalist cannot say that Kurth prefers hypothesized intentions over actual intentions on the grounds that Kurth has not consulted the author, relying only on text and context for his interpretation, since that is generally the way of identifying actual intentions. Moreover, his writing, like the writing of the vast majority of reviewers, gives no indication that he is making an assertion about the postulated author or the most plausible hypothesis about authorial intention; rather, he appears to be making a clear-cut assertion about actual authorial intent, one that he probably thinks could be verified.

Likewise, when ordinary readers discuss the meaning of novels, they too appear to be making assertions of actual authorial intent. They, like the reviewers, seem to be unaware of the implicit rules of literary communication as alleged to hold sway by the hypothetical intentionalist. But if most are not playing by such "implicit rules," perhaps there are no such rules.

The hypothetical intentionalist may respond that at best I have offered a hypothesis about the behavior of reviewers or ordinary readers. In effect, I have just moved the battle lines back a little – from a debate about authorial intention to a debate about the intentions of literary reviewers and ordinary readers. However, since the rules of ordinary conversation should apply to the pronouncements of literary reviewers and other readers, we should perhaps be willing to poll them about whether they intend to be speaking about hypothesized authors or intentions, or are aiming at and prefer actual intentions.

Of course, among academic critics there are theoretical positions, like New Criticism and poststructuralism, that eschew the pursuit of actual authorial intentions. But the New Critics and poststructuralists should offer no comfort to hypothetical intentionalists, since they are anti–intentionalists, not hypothetical intentionalists. Nor does it seem to me that our best evidence for the nature of our literary practices should be critics with robust theories of the practice. That they practice their own methods consistently does not demonstrate that they serve as models of the practice, especially since their methodologies, outside the circle of the converted, are generally regarded as revisionist.

Furthermore, even within the precincts of academic interpretation it is not clear that the hypothetical intentionalist's implicit social contract reigns. Recent debates about the interpretation of the work of Willa Cather rage over the actual Willa Cather, not some postulated author, and over what she actually, albeit unconsciously, intended. One side claims that she expressed conflicted lesbian desires, solidarity with women, and rebelliousness against the Nebraskan patriarchy.[14] The other side rejects this on biographical grounds.[15] Both sides show every evidence that they are talking about the real Willa Cather, not a theoretical entity. Furthermore, both sides appeal to paraphrases of Cather's private correspondence.[16]

Moreover, as this example reminds us, much criticism today, as well as much criticism from yesteryear, involves a moral and/or a political dimension. Authors are praised and blamed for the ethical import of their work. But surely if this moral criticism is serious, it must be directed at the actual author, not the postulated author, and at what she said, not what she could be taken to have said. And

since much literary and artistic interpretation comes in tandem with moral evaluation, it is hard to believe that our literary practices, as a matter of fact, always
value mere hypotheses about intent over determinations of actual intent, when
actual intent can be confirmed.

It may be true that readers are often satisfied with well-warranted hypotheses
of intention, but that is only because their default assumption is that these interpretations are successful. There is no reason to suppose that they will not revise
their thinking if they learn, perhaps through the discovery of notebooks, that the
best-warranted hypothesis (one that rejects recourse to things like notebooks)
failed to identify the relevant authorial intention correctly.

Suppose, for example, that we learn, through the discovery of heretofore hidden personal correspondence, that Jonathan Swift really despised the Irish and
that, in addition, he had a secret passion for the taste of human flesh. Suppose, as
well, he reports the pleasure he has derived from tricking do-gooders into
applauding his sincere proposal about eating Irish children as irony. Finally, suppose that this evidence is so compelling that it overturns all the other evidence
about Swift's opinions found in his publicly available biography. Would we continue to treat his "A Modest Proposal for Preventing the Children of the Poor
People of Ireland from Being a Burden to their Parents or Country, and for Making Them Beneficial to the Public" as an example of irony?

I suspect not – partly due to the fact that our imputations of irony to the essay
in the first place were primarily based on our beliefs about his *actual* biography
(which we would now understand in a new light) and partly due to the fact that
we would not wish to commend Swift for his opposition to prejudice if it turns
out that he is really, rather, an example of that very prejudice. But if this conjecture
is correct, then that suggests, with respect to our actual practices of literary interpretation, that we do not always value well-warranted hypotheses about authorial
intentions over actually establishable intentions.

Indeed, there may be occasions when audiences expressly desire reports of
authorial intention in order to solve their interpretive quandaries. I remember
that after the film *Stand by Me* was released in 1986, a question arose among film
buffs over the meaning of the last few frames of the film. According to the fiction,
the film was being narrated to us by a writer composing his story of a traumatic
childhood event on a personal computer. After the story was told, he turned off
the machine, but without saving what he had written. This film was made at a
time when knowledge about computers was not widespread among film viewers.
But some film buffs were informed, and this raised an interpretive query.

Did the fictional narrator's failure to save his text mean that, having worked
through his memory, he was now prepared to let it go? That is, was it that, having exorcised the trauma, the writing had served its purpose and could be
aborted? Or did the scene end that way simply because the producers of the
image did not know enough about the operation of personal computers to
realize what they might be fictionally portraying? Here I think that concerned
viewers were not interested in what *could* have been meant by the scene, but by

what *was* meant. After all, they did not wish to applaud the subtlety of the scene that the exorcism interpretation might merit, if in fact the fictional narrator's gesture was just the result of a mistake. That would be as ridiculous as crediting a slip of the tongue as a *bon mot.* Certainly what film buffs wanted, but to my knowledge never got, was a sincere authorial avowal (confession?) of what was intended by the shot.

Dissolving this interpretive ambiguity can, in principle, be solved satisfactorily by the modest actual intentionalist, who is willing to weigh cautiously statements of authorial intention, but not by the hypothetical intentionalist, who brackets such information from the interpreter's purview.

At this point, the hypothetical intentionalist is likely to remind us of a complication in his theory, heretofore unmentioned, that might enable him to deal with the *Stand by Me* case. When the hypothetical intentionalist endorses a hypothesis of authorial intention, he considers not only the epistemically best hypothesis available under his interpretive protocols, but also the aesthetically best hypothesis – that is, the interpretation, where there is room for competing interpretations, that makes the work a better work.[17] Applied to *Stand by Me,* this might dispose the hypothetical intentionalist to say that the exorcism interpretation is the best interpretation, even if we know the author's actual intention was otherwise (say, through personal communication), because it makes the film a better film aesthetically.

Unfortunately, I do not see that the hypothetical intentionalist gives us any grounds for accepting his aesthetic criterion for interpretation. It is not a straightforward extension of interpretive principles of charity. If the aims of the practice of literary communication rule that makers always be given the benefit of the doubt in cases like *Stand by Me,* what exactly are those aims? I confess that they elude me. Rather, it seems to me that the art world is a place where people are praised for their control of their materials. They are not applauded when, unintentionally, their work gets out of control.

I suspect that most viewers would be loath to commend the producers of *Stand by Me* if it turned out that they just didn't know what they were doing. But if we discovered, perhaps by asking them, that they did make the relevant scene with the exorcism interpretation in mind, the modest actual intentionalist would be happy, as I imagine most viewers would be, to appreciate their expressive finesse. Yet if you find the modest actual intentionalist's recommended handling of the *Stand by Me* case intuitively acceptable, that supplies further evidence that our practices of interpretation are not adverse, in principle, to consulting authorial intentions in order to answer hermeneutic questions – even if that entails going beyond the information the hypothetical intentionalist endorses – to the point of consulting artists and authors by means of interviews or through an examination of their journals, correspondence, and the like.

The hypothetical intentionalist conjectures that our practices of literary communication are satisfied by the best-warranted hypotheses of actual authorial intention based on publicly available sources but violated by recourse to authorial confidences derived from interviews, private correspondence, the author's unpublished journals, diaries, and so on. His primary reason for this seems to be that in addressing a public, the artist enters an implicit contract with that public, guaranteeing that they should be able to understand the work without doing research into the author's private life. It is probably good advice to authors who aspire to a general public to behave this way, but it dubiously represents an implicit contract that underwrites all literary communication. Literary communication is more unruly than the stipulated regulations the hypothetical intentionalist imputes to it.

Some authors trade in secret meanings, reserved for a specialized audience – indeed, meanings that are intended to exclude outsiders. This practice lies deep in our hermeneutical tradition. In the New Testament Gospel according to Mark,[18] when discussing the parable of the sower, Jesus tells his apostles that his parables are designed so that outsiders will not understand them; the only ones who are intended to understand them are the apostles, those to whom Jesus goes on in the text to reveal the true meaning of the parable. Thus, here we find an *ur*-practice of literary communication where the correct interpretation is explicitly not the best-warranted hypothesis of Christ's actual intention, but the authorial intention disclosed to a chosen audience by the utterer, in this case Jesus.[19]

The use of secret meanings targeted for specially informed audiences did not stop with Jesus. Rabelais is said to have employed it in *Gargantua*,[20] and modern poets, like Stefan George, have attempted personally to cultivate elite visionary followers for whom their poems carry secret meanings. In the case of occulted meanings, it seems obvious that authorial intention – where it is supportable by the text – should provide the bottom line for interpretation. And since the communication of such secret meanings is part of literary history, the hypothetical intentionalist's protestations about implicit rules of publicity in literary interpretation appear exaggerated.

Perhaps the hypothetical intentionalist will say that in cases like this the reader should not be concerned with the author's intended meaning of the text, but should stick to her guns with the publicly, "democratically" available meaning of the text. But such encouragement is useless; if people are really interested in a text, they will want to know its secret meaning, even if securing it involves violating the hypothetical intentionalist's "implicit contract." And this means that the hypothetical intentionalist's rules do not really reflect the practice of literary communication. The hypothetical intentionalist's characterization of the literary institution, though in ways commonsensical, is poor sociologically.

On the other hand, the hypothetical intentionalist may allege that his position allows the interpreter all the information available to the intended, appropriate audience of the text, where that audience is the one the text requires in order to be understood.[21] So if the intended audience for Christ's parables is the apostles, then the interpreter is entitled to all the information they have. However, this maneuver incurs paradoxical results for the hypothetical intentionalist, since the enabling information the apostles had was just the direct revelation of Christ's intentions.

Apart from the issue of secret meanings, other practices also fly in the face of hypothetical intentionalism's generalized rules of artistic communication. Some artists, like Frida Kahlo, are intensely autobiographical; penetrating their work interpretively may just be impossible, unless we look at their private life and whatever documentation we can find about it. And where people are intrigued by the work, they will be grateful to learn about the work's intended significance from sources otherwise off-limits according to the hypothetical intentionalist.[22]

The hypothetical intentionalist may ask why we should be interested in the meaning of the work for the artist. But if what a work is about is the artist's personal journey *and* we accept, as we often do, that this is a legitimate artistic enterprise, then we should ask in response: Why should we foreclose inquiry into the artist's private, not publicly documented life and abjure examining his personal papers and gingerly interviewing her friends and acquaintances? Some artforms may include in their contract with the audience a willing preparedness to be informed of private authorial intentions.[23] And if that is so, then the hypothetical intentionalist cannot be right in alleging that the best-warranted hypothesis derived from publicly available materials is the one always preferred, over privately divulged intentions, by our interpretive institutions.

Of course, the private/public dichotomy presupposed by the hypothetical intentionalist is also worth questioning. The hypothetical intentionalist permits the interpreter to use published biographical information about an author when unraveling the meaning of a text, but forbids the use of private information, garnered from unpublished papers, interviews, and so on. But it seems that much of what is found in public accounts of artists at one time or another got there because scholars interviewed authors and their associates or found information among private papers and the like. Is the hypothetical intentionalist willing to employ any reliable reports about the author's life and intentions so long as they have been published? But sometimes the published material comes from private material.

On the one hand, it would seem utterly arbitrary for the hypothetical intentionalist to allow interpreters to use biographical facts about authors once they are published, while disallowing reference to the same facts before they are published. On the other hand, it would seem impracticable for the hypothetical intentionalist to rule that the interpreter can use published biographical information about authors only if it is known to be derived from public sources, rather than private ones. And, in any event, this is not how interpreters behave. Once it is published, no matter its provenance, interpreters will use the information.

Much of Stuart Gilbert's famous *James Joyce's Ulysses* is, as Gilbert himself makes clear in his preface, the result of close consultation with Joyce about his intended meanings, structures, and associations.[24] Does hypothetical intentionalism permit interpreters access to *James Joyce's Ulysses,* still surely an important commentary on Joyce's novel? If the hypothetical intentionalist allows the interpreter to use Gilbert's work as historical background information about *Ulysses,* then the hypothetical intentionalist's distinction between public and private appears arbitrary. But if the hypothetical intentionalist objects to the use of *James Joyce's Ulysses,* then he has failed to discover the actual norms of our practices of literary communication, since interpreters resort to Gilbert's discoveries shamelessly.

Perhaps the hypothetical intentionalist has a way of framing the private/public distinction in a way that can avoid criticisms like these. But until he says something more precise about that distinction than he has, we must remain skeptical of the hypothetical intentionalist's claim to have accurately captured the underlying rules of literary communication.

In summary, modest actual intentionalism argues that actual authorial intention is relevant to the meaning of artworks. With respect to literary utterances, the modest actual intentionalist takes meaning to be a function of the author's actual intention, where that intention is supportable by what has been written. In this regard, modest actual intentionalism maintains that artistic and literary interpretation is seamlessly linked with ordinary, everyday forms of interpretation. In both cases, we take utterance tokens to mean what the utterer intends, where that is supportable by what has been said.

Whereas modest actual intentionalism claims that the aim of literary interpretation is to recover actual authorial intentions (that are consistent with the relevant texts), hypothetical intentionalism alleges that the aim of literary interpretation is merely to establish the most plausible hypothesis about authorial intention. The modest actual intentionalist objects that this confuses warranted assertibility for the truth, whereas the shared methodologies of modest actual intentionalism and hypothetical intentionalism both indicate that we should prefer establishing actual authorial intent, when possible, rather than remaining satisfied with only the best-warranted hypothesis about said intent.[25]

In turn, the hypothetical intentionalist concedes that this would be so were literary interpretation on par with ordinary interpretation. But the hypothetical intentionalist argues that this is not the case. Because of its special interests, literary interpretation, the hypothetical intentionalist avers, prizes warranted assertibility over the truth about authorial intentions (where those part company). Lamentably, the hypothetical intentionalist does not tell us much about those special interests or about their grounds. Moreover, as I have tried to show at length, the overarching rules that the hypothetical intentionalist presumes reign over our interpretive institutions and practices are liable to many criticisms – criticisms that, in fact, suggest that modest actual intentionalism provides us with a far better picture of our existing interpretive practices.

PART IV: ART, EMOTION, AND MORALITY

❧

ART, NARRATIVE, AND EMOTION

I. INTRODUCTION

Despite the great interest in the reception of art and media in recent years, little attention has been paid to the way in which narrative fictions, whether high or low, address the emotions of readers, listeners, and viewers. Instead, emphasis is generally placed on hermeneutics. Interpretation of what is loosely called the meaning of the work has preoccupied attention in the humanities. New interpretations, often called symptomatic readings, of what are generically identified as "texts" are still the order of the day in liberal arts journals. And even what some in cultural studies call "recodings," and what some feminists call "readings against the grain," focus on the putative interpretive activities of certain groups of readers, listeners, and viewers. What is not studied in any fine-grained way is how works engage the emotions of the audience. What I wish to deal with in this essay is how we might go about doing just that.

It is not my contention that, in principle, hermeneutics is illegitimate. Rather, I think that our research into the arts should be supplemented by considering their relation to the emotions, especially if we are interested in audience reception. Moreover, the present moment is particularly propitious in this respect, since recent research into the emotions over the last two decades in fields like psychology and philosophy have made the possibility of interrogating the relation of art to the emotions feasible with a heretofore unimagined level of precision.[1]

Perhaps it will be felt that I have already misdescribed the situation. One might argue that I have overstated the degree to which scholars in the humanities have ignored the emotions. For a great deal of recent humanistic research is psychoanalytic, and, at least ostensibly, psychoanalysis is concerned with the emotions. And yet I would respond that psychoanalysis of the sort that is popular among scholars in the humanities today is not really concerned with the garden-variety emotions – that is, the emotions marked in ordinary speech, like fear, awe, pity, admiration, anger, and so on – which garden-variety emotions, in fact, are what keep audiences engaged with artworks.

From: *Emotion and the Arts*, ed. by Mette Hjort and Sue Laver (Oxford: Oxford University Press, 1997), 190–211.

Psychoanalytic critics seem more concerned with certain generic, ill-defined forces like desire and pleasure that they speak of without prepositional modification. For example, they write of Desire with a capital "D," rather than of small *d*-desires *for* this or that. Or they seem preoccupied by certain anxieties, like male castration anxiety or anxieties about the dissolution of the unity of the subject whose purchase on the reading, listening, and viewing activities of audiences are highly suspect and controversial. Indeed, one might speculate that psychoanalytic critics pay scant attention to the operation of the garden-variety emotions of readers, listeners, and viewers exactly because psychoanalytic theory itself has little to say about the nature of such emotions, but often merely assumes the definition of emotions, like fear, that are already in operation in ordinary language.[2]

Nevertheless, it seems to me that if we are really concerned with audience reception, we should pay more attention than we do to the dynamics of the audience's emotional involvement with narrative artworks, both high and low, and especially to the way in which such artworks are designed to elicit garden-variety emotional responses from readers, listeners, and viewers. For in large measure, what commands and shapes the audience's attention to the artwork, what enables the audience to follow and to comprehend the artwork, and what energizes our commitment to seeing the narrative artwork through to its conclusion is the emotional address of the narrative artwork. Speaking metaphorically, we might say that to a large extent, emotions are the cement that keeps audiences connected to the artworks, especially to the narrative fictions, that they consume. Moreover, the emotions in question here are generally garden-variety ones – fear, anger, horror, reverence, suspense, pity, admiration, indignation, awe, repugnance, grief, compassion, infatuation, comic amusement, and the like.

One way to suggest partial substantiation for this assertion might be simply to consider the degree to which popular fictions rely so heavily on the activation of specific, garden-variety emotions. So many melodramas, for example, rely upon the audience's concern for protagonists, whom we not only pity for their misfortunes, but whom we also admire for their character, especially as it is manifested in their self-sacrificing behavior, such as Stella Dallas's self-willed separation from her daughter.[3] Horror fictions, of course, require not only that we be thrown into a state of fear toward and repulsion by the monsters that threaten the human race, but that we feel mounting anxiety as the protagonist ventures into the hidden recesses of the old dark house. But, of course, the evidence for the importance of emotional involvement for the reception of narrative art is not simply that it is a recurring feature of the popular arts. For as Aristotle pointed out long ago, essential to the tragic response to high art is the elicitation of pity and fear in the audience.

With much art, especially narrative art, eliciting the appropriate emotional response from the audience is a condition of our comprehending and following the work. For example, if we do not hate certain characters, then the trajectory of a narrative bent upon punishing them will not only be unsatisfying, but even unintelligible. What, we might ask ourselves, is the author's point in detailing their comeuppance? Why is so much time and elaboration being spent on showing us how this vicious character comes into his just deserts? It will not compute, unless we are attending to the story in the emotionally appropriate way.

But the emotions engaged by the plot are generally not only a condition of the intelligibility of the story. They are often typically what keeps us glued, so to say, to the story. The emotions in life and in art have the function of focusing attention. And with narrative fictions, they keep us focused on the plot on a moment-to-moment basis. They organize our attention in terms of what is going on in a scene *and* they also prime our anticipation about the kinds of things to expect in future scenes. To be more specific: our emotional responses to earlier scenes will generally contribute to organizing the way in which we attend to later scenes. If we are indignant about a character's behavior when we first encounter her, then, when she next appears, we will be on the lookout for more evidence of nastiness in her behavior. Emotions organize perception. Emotions shape the way in which we follow character behavior, just as in everyday life they enable us to track the behavior of others.

Moreover, although most of my examples so far have relied on our emotional involvement with characters, clearly what I have said can also apply to situations and events. The horror that we feel about the initial outbreak of vampirism in a novel like *Salem's Lot* emotionally colors the way in which we attend to subsequent scenes. Our emotional involvement alerts us to the potential dangers in situations that we might otherwise overlook. Indeed, it quite frequently alerts us to dangers in situations that the characters overlook. Small animal bites on the neck may mean little to them, but they loom large in our attention.

Though I think that what I have said so far is fairly obvious, there is one line of misunderstanding that I would like to neutralize before it takes root. I do think that we should pay more attention to the role of the emotions in our commerce with artworks, but I am not advocating a reversion to the sorts of expression theories of art that were advanced by theorists like Leo Tolstoy and Robin Collingwood.[4] Tolstoy and Collingwood were in the business of developing universal theories of art. As such, they maintained, in different ways, that the communication or expression of emotion was an essential or defining feature of art. Their theories were universal characterizations of the nature of all art. In contrast, I am not defending a theory about all art, or even all narrative art.[5] I simply wish to talk, albeit theoretically, about the operation of the emotions in art, especially narrative art, where it occurs. And this is logically consistent with eschewing an expression theory of art in general.

I do not want to deny that there may be some art that does not traffic in emotions, especially in what I have called garden-variety emotions. Some paintings may be about the nature of painting – maybe much of Frank Stella's work is about the conventions of framing; and some films, like *Zorn's Lemma* by Hollis Frampton, may be about the nature of film. These works may be articulated in such a way that they address cognition exclusively. Unlike Tolstoy and Collingwood, I would not argue that these works are not art inasmuch as they are not connected to the emotions. For my claim is not that all art is involved in the elicitation of the emotions, but only that some is – indeed, much is – and, furthermore, I contend that it is useful to develop a theory about the relation of art to the emotions for these works, even if the result is not a universalizable theory that pertains to all art, or even all narrative fiction.

There are also other important issues of detail that distinguish my approach from those of Tolstoy and Collingwood. Tolstoy maintained that the relevant emotions requisite for art status were those that were felt by both the author in making the work and the audience in consuming it. That is, he thought it criterial of art status that the emotion experienced by the audience be the same emotion that had been sincerely undergone by the artist. But I am interested in the emotions elicited by artworks whether or not they parallel the emotions felt by the artist in creating the work. As Denis Diderot so forcefully argued, actors typically evoke emotional responses from audiences that they may not have felt; a performer can communicate Othello's jealousy without being jealous.[6]

For Collingwood, art expresses emotion, by which he maintained that the artwork, properly so-called, was an occasion for the artist to work through or clarify some initially vague feeling. This process of clarification is supposed to stand in contrast to the arousal of emotion, which Collingwood thought of as the aim of pseudo-art. It was pseudo-art according to Collingwood because it relied on the deployment of tried-and-true formulas to arrive at preordained effects. And given Collingwood's somewhat Kantian biases in this regard, anything that smacked of rules or formulas could not count as art properly so-called.

But I, in contrast, take it to be an empirical fact that much of what we correctly call art does traffic in arousing emotions; or, if arousal talk strikes you as too strong, much art is involved in promoting, encouraging, or eliciting preordained emotional responses from readers, listeners, and viewers, often by routine techniques and formulas; and it is my purpose in what follows to look at that art with an eye to developing a theoretical framework for discussing some of the structures artists use to elicit such emotional responses from readers, listeners, and viewers.

II. PLATO VERSUS THE COGNITIVE THEORY OF THE EMOTIONS

Of course, as Collingwood knew, not all philosophers have been opposed to associating art with the arousal of emotion. The Greeks were not, and, as a result, Collingwood called their view the technical theory of art. Plato articulated this view very elaborately in the *Republic,* although, as is well known, he did it in order to banish the arts from the good city. Nevertheless, Plato does provide us with a coherent picture of the relation of the arts to the emotions and, as such, a quick review of his theory and its shortcomings can still afford us an instructive point of entry through which we can dialectically develop a better theoretical framework for the discussion of the relation of art, specifically narrative fiction, and the emotions.

Plato had a battery of arguments against dramatic art and painting, many of which revolved around the way in which works of that kind addressed the emotions of spectators. His central argument hinged on his conviction that the emotions are irrational in the sense that they undermine the rule of reason both in the individual and, in consequence, in society. Certain emotions, like pity and the fear of death, were of particular concern for Plato, since they would undermine the citizen-soldier's capacity to wage war. That is, Plato thought that these emotions were maladaptive. One did not want troops disposed to pity themselves or the enemy, nor troops who feared death. Plato believed that by using dramatic texts as the Greeks did, reading them aloud in the process of education, people would acquire these untoward emotional dispositions by playing certain roles, that is, by identifying with the characters who vented these emotions.

But Plato was not simply concerned that certain unsavory emotions would be disseminated through the influence of and identification with dramatic poetry. He distrusted the emotional address of poetry and painting irrespective of the specific emotions they elicited, because he believed that the promotion of the emotions in general is problematic. For the emotions, on his view, oppose reason, and any threat to reason constitutes a threat to the community at large. Moreover, Plato thought that drama is bound to promote emotion over reason, because artists would have to pander to the emotions of the untutored masses if they were to have audiences at all. That is, Plato argued, the general audience, knowing little, has to be addressed in terms of its emotions rather than reason. That is why, a latter-day Plato might say, shows like *L.A. Law* are preoccupied with the drama of office romance rather than the drama of legal research. The latter requires a background of legal education in order to be comprehended; the former, merely gut reactions. Thus, Plato, in effect, proposed the first economic theory of art, explaining why consumption dictated the unavoidably emotional address of drama.

Of these Platonic arguments, the most general and the deepest is that art essentially addresses the emotions and thereby undermines reason, presenting a clear and present danger to the community. The presupposition here is that reason and the emotions are in some sense at odds. Reason must dominate the emotions. Left to their own, so to speak, the emotions will gravitate toward the irrational. In Plato's conception of human psychology, reason and emotion appear to occupy different regions. There is no expectation from Plato's point of view that they will converge and even more grounds to anticipate that they will pull in opposite directions.

Plato's tendency is to think that the emotions are irrational or opposed to reason. Thus if art or drama addresses the emotions, it will address the irrational in us and thereby undermine reason's control over us. But the obvious question to ask about this argument is whether in fact the distinction between reason and the emotions is as sharp as Plato maintains. Are the emotions necessarily irrational forces in the way Plato supposes?

The tendency in contemporary psychology and in analytic philosophy is to reject Plato's presupposition that the emotions are irrational. Instead, it is more common to maintain that reason and the emotions are not opposed, inasmuch as reason is an ineliminable constituent of the emotions. Thus, in order to undercut Plato's argument and to set the stage for our own positive account of the relation of the emotions to art, specifically to narrative fiction, it is profitable to look at the picture of the emotions – often called the cognitive theory of emotions[7] – that has been developed by contemporary researchers and that challenges the prejudice that the emotions are by their very nature irrational.

In order to determine whether emotions are irrational, we need some conception of what an emotion is. Perhaps the first answer we might naturally turn to in order to answer this question is that an emotion is a feeling. When we're in an emotional state, our body changes. Our heart rate may alter; we may feel our chest expanding or contracting. Physical changes occur as we move into an emotional state – the adrenal glands produce corticosteroids; and there are psychological or phenomenological changes as well. When we are angry, we may feel "hot under the collar." But are these physical and phenomenological changes in the body the whole story? Supporting this view, we might notice that in English we often do refer to emotions as "feelings."

But proponents of cognitive theories of the emotions deny that emotions are simply feelings – neither merely physical alterations, nor phenomenological feelings, nor a combination thereof. Why not? Because it is easy to imagine chemically inducing the sorts of bodily feeling states that are associated with emotions where there is no question of our being in an emotional state. Suppose we chemically induce the feeling states in you that you exhibited the last time that you were angry. Here you are now alone in a room in exactly the same physical state you were in when your colleague said something sarcastic to you in a faculty meeting last month. Are you angry? Not if there is no one or no thing with whom or with which you are angry. Remember that you are in the same physical state you were in last month. But you are not in the same mental state. You are not thinking about your colleague or anyone else. The chemicals only induce certain changes in your body.

Admittedly, you may be in an unpleasant physical state. But you cannot be said to be in an emotional state of anger unless there is someone who or something that you think has done you or yours some wrong. For emotional states are directed – you are afraid of war, or you are in love *with* Mary. Bodily feelings, however, are not directed at anything. They are physical states. They are internal events without external reference.

But what is it that links our internal feeling states to external objects and situations? What's the bridge, so to speak? Cognitive theorists of the emotions say that it is our cognitive states (that's why they are called cognitive theorists). For example, it may be our states of belief that connect our internal feelings to external situations. Suppose that I believe that George took my money and that, in doing so, he has wronged me. This is apt to give rise to anger. That is, taken by this belief – which is directed at George – my sympathetic nervous system is activated, and I begin to feel tension throughout my body. I feel myself tightening up. The reason that I am in this physical state is my belief that George has stolen my money. That's why my blood boils whenever I see him. In short, my belief that George has stolen my money *causes* my blood to boil.

So as an initial approximation, let us say provisionally that an emotion is made up of at least two components: a cognitive component, such as a belief or a thought about some person, place, or thing, real or imagined; and a feeling component (a bodily change and/or a phenomenological experience), where, additionally, the feeling state has been caused by the relevant cognitive state, such as a belief or a belief-like state.[8] Furthermore, a conception of the emotions like this one is bad news for someone like Plato, since it incorporates cognition into the structure of the emotions, thereby denying that reason is totally opposed to the emotions; for if reason/cognition is a constituent of an emotion, emotion cannot be the antithesis of reason/cognition. But in order to make the problem for Plato even more explicit, let's look a bit more closely at the cognitive component of an emotion.

I am angry at George because I believe that he has stolen my money. But theft of my property is only one of many occurrences that might, under suitable circumstances, provide grounds for anger. I could be angry at George for cutting ahead of me in line, or for throttling my little brother. Theft, queue breaking, throttling, and so on are instances of a broader class of things, any of which might warrant anger. What is the relevant broader class of things – that is, what must I believe about someone if I am to be angry with him? I must believe that he has done wrong to me or mine. I think that George has stolen my money, and that falls into this larger class of things. So, in order to be angry with someone, I must believe that the object of my anger has done some wrong to me or mine.

Similarly, other emotions are directed at objects that belong to a specifiable or delimited class of things. In order to be afraid of x, I must think that x is dangerous – that it belongs to the class of harmful things. X might not really be dangerous. But to fear x, I must perceive it to be harmful, even if it is not. In order to pity x, I must think that x has suffered misfortune. I cannot pity someone who I think is on top of the world in every way. In order to envy x, I need to think that x has something that I lack. I cannot envy Quasimodo's good looks, if I believe Quasimodo is grotesque. And so on. In short, what emotional state I am in is determined by my cognitive state – by, for example, beliefs or thoughts about the objects of the emotional state in question.

If I believe that I've been wronged, and this causes a feeling of agitation in me, then, all things being equal, the state I am in is anger; but if I believe that I'm in danger, and this causes my blood to freeze, then the emotional state I am in is fear. That is, as these examples should indicate, emotional states are governed by *criteria*. But what exactly does that mean?

In order to be angry at x, in the standard case, I must believe that certain criteria have been met, for example, I must believe that x has wronged me or mine. To fear x, I must believe that x is harmful; to pity x, I must believe that x has suffered misfortune; to envy x, I must believe that x has something I have not got. To be in these emotional states, I must be in the relevant cognitive states. These cognitive states are constitutive of the identity of the emotional state in which I am. Having the relevant cognitive states is a necessary condition for being in these emotional states.[9] These cognitive appraisals of the situations in question are criterial for being in just these states. Indeed, the relevant cognitive appraisals are the reasons that I am in these states.

If you ask me why I am angry, my reason is that I think that I or mine have been wronged. If you ask me why I'm afraid, my reason is that I've been threatened. Why do I pity Oedipus? Because he's suffered grievous misfortune. Why do I envy Donald Trump? Because he's got lots of money and I don't.

Now if what I've said so far is persuasive, then it looks as though the emotions are necessarily governed by reasons. Indeed, to say that I am in one of these emotional states, sans the requisite cognitive appraisal, would be virtually self-contradictory, the very height of irrationality. To say that I am afraid of potatoes at the same time that I genuinely believe in my heart of hearts that they are not harmful is sheer nonsense, a logical absurdity – what Gilbert Ryle called a category error. Indeed, if I made such a claim, you would probably either attempt to find some hidden, unacknowledged reason why I think that potatoes are dangerous or suspect that I did not understand the meaning of my own words. These explanations might account for the utter irrationality of my assertion. But the very search for these kinds of accounts shows that, in the standard case, we think that the emotions, contra Plato, naturally possess a kind of rationality.

Perhaps some evidence for the view that emotions possess some sort of rationality – that is, that they are governed by reasons – is that our emotions can be modified or changed by changing our beliefs or reasons. Our emotions are educable. If reasons can be given to show that the object of our fear is not harmful, then the emotion of fear typically evaporates. We try to convince the child not to be afraid of the monster underneath the bed by proving to her that there is no such monster. Furthermore, if I can be shown that an action that I thought was cowardly is courageous, then my emotion standardly will shift from contempt to admiration. Why does this happen? Because inasmuch as emotions are determined by cognitive states, like belief, a change in the relevant cognitive state will change the emotional state, either by transforming it into another emotional state altogether or by sublating it entirely. The relation of emotions to cognitive states, like beliefs, is, of course, the basis for the psychoanalytic talking cure, which, in effect, modifies dysfunctional or inappropriate emotional behaviors by disentangling our sedimented, mistaken, or erroneously associated beliefs and patterns of attention. Thus, though certain emotional episodes may be irrational in the sense that they are based on defective beliefs, the emotions as such are rationally tractable.

Moreover, if emotions are susceptible to being changed by reasons and to being modified by cognitive states, such as belief states, then we must conclude, contra Plato, that the emotions respond to knowledge. They respond to knowledge naturally, since knowledge-like cognitive states, such as beliefs, are components of all emotional states. The consequences of these observations for Plato's view should be straightforward. The emotions are not necessarily irrational. They have rational criteria of appropriateness that are open to logical assessment. They are naturally responsive to reason and knowledge. Thus, addressing the emotions in the manner of drama and narrative need not necessarily undermine reason.

Indeed, the emotions may serve reason in general by effectively guiding our attention to important information. Thus, there are no grounds for worrying that the emotions, such as the emotions elicited by art, will necessarily subvert reason, since, among other things, reason or cognition is an ineliminable constituent, indeed a determining force, of the emotions. Therefore, it is not the case that all representations threaten reason; only those that encourage defective cognitive states, like false beliefs, are affronts to reason – and not because they are emotional states, but only because they are epistemically defective. Or, in short, Plato's most general argument about the relation between art and the emotions must be rejected.

In addition to his general argument about art and the emotions, Plato also claims that the specific emotions – like pity and fear – that are engendered by dramatic poetry are maladaptive. Encouraging these emotions would, he believes, contradict certain reasons of state. Perhaps that is another reason that Plato thinks that these emotions are irrational. Of course, whether these emotions do contravene larger purposes raises at least two kinds of questions that are not of direct interest to us: whether, in fact, these emotions really have the consequences that Plato attributes to them, and whether, in the specific cultural circumstances, these emotions are dysfunctional. However, if Plato fears that the emotions are maladaptive in general, he is surely wrong.

For emotions are part of our biological makeup. This is not to deny that they are culturally modified. To be angered, we must believe that we have been wronged, but, of course, what counts as a wrong is in large measure a matter of cultural determination. Yet, along with the influence of culture, the emotions are also rooted in biology. And as biological phenomena, their persistence can be explained according to the principles of natural selection. That is, in opposition to the suspicion that the emotions are maladaptive, we may argue that we have the emotions because they contribute to the fitness of the human organism. In other words, we have the emotions because they enhance our prospects for survival. Undoubtedly this is connected to the fact that they respond to knowledge and reason. But in any case, the emotions are hardly impediments to adaptation; rather, they are devices in the service of adapting to the environment.

Moreover, we need not base this claim on the abstract supposition that any biological component as entrenched as the emotions must provide some adaptive advantage. I think that we can begin to specify with some precision the evolutionary service that the emotions perform for the human organism. Of course, the most obvious service that the emotions perform for the organism is to motivate behavior, since the emotions are typically made up of desires, as well as cognitive states. Emotional states cognitively organize our perceptions of situations in light of our desires and values, and thereby prepare the organism to act in its perceived interests. Anger and fear, for example, prime the organism to fight or to flee, respectively.

The bodily effects that the emotions induce ready the organism to carry out certain activities effectively. But connected to their role in the preparation of the organism for action, the emotions also shape our perception of situations.[10] And this, of course, rather than their action-motivating potentials, is what should be most interesting for aestheticians.

Perception and the emotions are interrelated in a number of ways. First, it is our attention to certain aspects of a situation – say, the harmful ones – that moves us into certain emotional states in the first instance. But the emotions provide feedback to our processes of attention. Once alerted to the harmful aspects of a situation, our fear will impel us to search the situation – to scan the scene – for further evidence of harmfulness. The emotions focus our attention. They make certain features of situations salient, and they cast those features in a special phenomenological light. The emotions "gestalt," we might say, situations. They organize them. They make certain elements of the situation stand out. They are sensitive to certain aspects of various recurring situations, like danger, and they size up and organize certain situations rapidly. And then they hold our attention on the relevant features of the situation, often compelling us to pick out further aspects of the situation under the criteria that define the emotional state we are in. As Jenefer Robinson puts it: "If I respond emotionally … then my body alerts me to my conception of the situation and registers it as personally significant to me."[11] For example, we might first detect the large wave coming at us, and then our fear further apprises us of its lethal velocity.

Clearly, the attention-guiding function of the emotions is connected to the role the emotions play in determining action. The emotions focus attention on those elements of situations that are relevant for action, given our desires. The emotions are evolutionary devices for identifying the significance – generally the significance for effective action – of the situations in which we find ourselves. And they are very economical devices in this respect, especially when contrasted to other, slower mental processes like deliberation. The emotions are good things to have when the organism has to scope out a situation immediately. Thus, in terms of both their action-guiding potential and their service to attention, the emotions are optimal adaptive mechanisms. This is not to say that particular emotional episodes are not frequently out of place or inappropriate, just as certain logical deductions may be unsound. Nevertheless, the emotions as a general feature of human nature are adaptive.

Thus, Plato is wrong in his suspicion that the emotions are maladaptive. Nor do I think that he can make the case that certain emotions – like pity and fear – are always maladaptive. For example, fear of death may be maladaptive for a soldier in battle, but it is not for someone, like a philosopher king, stepping out of the way of an oncoming chariot.

As you will recall, Plato also has a theory of the way in which the emotions are engaged by drama. His theory is probably the first theory of identification in Western civilization. He thought that when people read plays aloud, a practice that was quite common in Athenian culture, they would take on the emotions of the characters whose parts they were reading. And this was problematic, he thought, because in doing so, not only would they risk contamination by unsavory emotions, but also, in giving vent to the emotions through playacting, reason would be sent on a holiday. We have already seen why these worries about irrationality were misplaced. But it also pays to note that Plato's theory of how the emotions are communicated by drama is mistaken.

In the standard case, we do not identify emotionally with characters by, so to say, taking on their emotions. When we are happy at the end of the movie because the lovers have finally gotten together, that is not a function of the fact that we are in love with the characters. Which one of the characters would it be, anyway? Both? But if we are in love with both the characters, then we are in an emotional state that neither of the characters is in, since each of them is only in love with one person. And actually, we are in love with neither of them. We are happy that they have gotten together, but we are happy in the way of onlookers, not participants. Our emotions do not duplicate theirs, although our recognition of what their emotions are and that the lovers' desires have been satisfied are ingredients in our rather different emotional states.

Similarly, when we are angered by the behavior of both Antigone and Creon, our anger is based on our assessment that both of them are unyieldingly stubborn, an emotional assessment that neither of them shares with us. And when Creon's son and wife commit suicide, we pity him, whereas his emotional state is one of self-recrimination. In short, in the standard case, there is an asymmetrical relation between the emotional state that characters undergo and those of the audience, whereas identification requires identity (of emotions), which is a symmetrical relation. Therefore, the notion of identification cannot provide us, contra Plato and his contemporary avatars, with a general theory of our emotional involvement with dramas in particular or with narrative fictions in general.

I have spent a great deal of time elaborating the problems with Plato's conception of our emotional involvement with art for heuristic purposes. For in laying out what is wrong in Plato, I have been able to introduce enough information about the emotions to construct a positive account of the way in which our emotions are engaged by narrative fictions. In my criticisms of Plato, I have rejected the possibility that emotional identification characterizes the general mechanism or structure that elicits the audience's emotional response to narrative fiction. Let me begin my positive account of our emotional involvement with fiction by proposing an alternative structure.

III. AN ALTERNATIVE ACCOUNT OF THE RELATION OF EMOTION AND NARRATIVE

Emotions are intimately related to attention. It is this feature of the emotions that should be important to art theorists, rather than the action-mobilizing feature of the emotions, since artworks, in the standard case, command attention, not action. I have suggested, furthermore, that the emotions are related to our attention-focalizing mechanisms. They direct our attention to certain details, rather than others; they enable us to organize those details into significant wholes or gestalts, so that, for example, our attention selects out or battens on the concatenation of details in the situation that are, for example, relevant to harm or to misfortune. The emotions operate like a searchlight, foregrounding those details in a special phenomenological glow. And, as well, once we are in the midst of an emotional state, we not only hold to those details, often obsessively, but are prompted to search out more details with similar relevance to our emotional assessment of the situation. The emotions manage our attention when we are in their grip. And that management undergoes changes in the sense that it first alerts our attention to certain gestalts and holds our attention on them, and then encourages further elaboration of our attention, inclining us to search for further elements of the relevant gestalt in the stimulus and leading us to form expectations about the kinds of things we should be on the lookout for as the situation evolves.

Now if this picture of the way in which our emotions and attention mesh is accurate, it should provide us with a useful way in which to think about our emotional involvement with narrative fictions. In life, as opposed to fiction, our emotions have to pick up on the relevant details of a situation out of a welter of unstructured details. We are sitting in a room talking distractedly to some friends; we notice a faint smell of something burning. Our emotions alert us to danger; our attention is riveted on the odor. We begin to look and to sniff about for further evidence of fire, readying ourselves to confront it or to flee.

But in fiction, of course, the situation has already been structured for our attention. The author has already done much of the work of focusing our attention through the way in which she has foregrounded what features of the event are salient. After all, the author has not only chosen, indeed invented, the situations we encounter, but she has also decided what features of those events are worthy of direct comment or implication. Thus, again and again in *Uncle Tom's Cabin*, Harriet Beecher Stowe confronts us with scenes of families being separated, and, in case after case, she emphasizes the innocence and decency of the slaves whose family ties are being sundered, and the cruelty and callousness with which it is being done. These perhaps non-too-subtle promptings lead us to perceive the scenes under the category of injustice, which, in turn, elicits the affect of indignation from us. And this indignation, in consequence, bonds us to the details of the text as well as preparing us to anticipate and to be on the lookout for further evidence of injustice, which, of course, Stowe's text delivers in abundance.

Or consider the character Fledgeby in Dickens's novel *Our Mutual Friend*. As Fledgeby taunts his factotum Riah, Dickens keeps in the foreground of our attention Fledgeby's viciousness, underscoring his abusiveness and his unflinching anti-Semitism, which he, Fledgeby, attempts to pass off as humor. Through Dickens's descriptions, Riah is shown to the Fledgeby's moral and human superior in every way. All Fledgeby has is money, which he uses to subordinate everyone else, including Riah. Dickens does not have to come right out and say that Fledgeby is contemptible. Rather, the way in which he has described the situation engenders hatred of and contempt for Fledgeby in us, which primes the way in which we attend to his appearance in other scenes, and encourages us to hope for his downfall.

Or think about how suspense is engendered in fictions and how it keeps us riveted to the action. Suspense is an emotion, one that in fictions generally involves an event where some outcome that we regard to be morally righteous is improbable. For example: in the motion picture *Speed,* it is likely that the bus will explode; in *True Lies,* that the nuclear device will detonate; and in *Outbreak,* that the antidote will be blown away with the rest of the town when the army drops its firebomb. In each of these cases, the outcome that I've mentioned has been depicted as immoral in the relevant fictions, but at the same time, it is the one that is most likely, given the world of the fiction as it has been presented to us. Or, to put it alternatively, the moral outcome is presented as if it were improbable. When confronted with such prospects, we attend to the events onscreen with suspense; the emotion rivets us to the screen and shapes our attention in such a way that our mind is preoccupied with tracking the features of the event that are relevant to the emotional state in which we find ourselves. And with suspense, that means keeping track of the shifting probabilities for the forces of good versus the forces of evil.[12]

I have chosen examples in which the emotions involved are somewhat intense and in which their elicitation has a forceful, one might say, an "in-your-face" character. I have opted for such examples because I think that they show the dynamics of our emotional responses to fiction in bold relief. However, there is no reason to think that the elicitation of emotions by narrative fictions is always as aggressive as it is in these examples. The emotional cues in the text may be more recessive or subtle, they may be initially obscured by irony or ambiguity, and it may take them longer to hit the reader than the examples I have mentioned. This may especially be the case as we ascend from examples of popular culture to so-called high art. And yet, even in these cases, I think that we will discern the same regularities in operation.

Whether verbal or visual, the text will be prefocused. Certain features of situations and characters will be made salient through description or depiction. These features will be such that they will be subsumable under the categories or concepts that, as I argued earlier, govern or determine the identity of the emotional states we are in. Let us refer to this attribute of texts by saying that the texts are criterially prefocused.[13]

For example, horror is an emotion that involves fear and revulsion.[14] The criterion of fear is the harmful; the criterion of revulsion is the impure. Events are horrific when they are subsumable under the categories of the harmful and the impure, that is, when they satisfy the criteria for horror by being harmful and impure. Thus, when authors of horror describe or depict events that they intend to elicit horror from us, they will describe or depict events, situations, and characters that are harmful and impure – for instance, slavering, fetid mounds of cankerous flesh with razor sharp claws and cosmic antipathy toward all things human. That is, the author will describe or depict the putative objects of our emotional state so that the *salient* features of that object are apt, for the normal audience member, to be slotted under the categories of the harmful and the impure. This categorization need not be a conscious operation, no more than my recognition that an oncoming car is potentially harmful need be accompanied by my saying it.

So the first step in the elicitation of an emotional response from the audience is a criterially prefocused text – a text structured in such a way that the description or depiction of the object of our attention is such that it will activate our subsumption of the event under the categories that are criterially relevant to certain emotional states. Once we recognize the object under those categories, the relevant emotion is apt, in certain conditions to be discussed below, to be raised in us. We will undergo some physical changes – with horror fictions our flesh may begin, as they say, to crawl; with suspense, we may feel our muscles tense; with melodrama, we may shed a tear; with comedy, we may laugh – and, in addition, our attention becomes emotively charged: the object of the emotion rivets our attention, while our emotionally governed perception casts its object in a special phenomenological light. The emotion glues our attention to those features of the object of the emotion that are apposite to the emotional state we are in; it encourages us to survey the event for further features that may support or sustain the presiding emotional state in which we find ourselves; and, protentively, our emotively charged state shapes our anticipation of what is to come by priming us to be on the lookout for the emergence or appearance of details subsumable under the categories of the reigning emotion. Or, in short, the criterially prefocused text gives rise, in the right circumstances, to emotive focus in the audience, where by "emotive focus" I am referring to the way in which the emotional state of the reader, viewer, or listener both fixes and shapes her attention.

Plato's story of our emotional involvement with the text posits characters, venting certain emotions, with whom we identify in such a way that their emotions are transferred to the audience. In contrast, I maintain that the structure involves a criterially prefocused text that elicits an emotively focused response. That is, a criterially prefocused text brings our attention to certain details, stimulating an emotional response, which quickens our attentiveness and which binds us to the text so that we are ready to assimilate it in the relevant way. Relevant to what? Relevant to the presiding emotion state, which, in the standard case, is the one that the author designed the text to engender in us.

The emotional states of characters may be pertinent to the emotional state we are in: that we perceive a character to be in anguish may be material to our pity for that character. But it is the way in which the text is criterially prefocused that is crucially determinant to the audience's emotive response, and not some putative process of character identification. Rather than character identification, it is our own preexisting emotional constitution – with its standing dispositions that the text activates – that accounts for our emotional involvement with narrative fictions.

Of course, simply presenting a reader, viewer, or listener with a criterially prefocused text does not guarantee that the reader, viewer, or listener will respond emotionally. For a criterially prefocused text can be read dispassionately. Something more is required to elicit a passionate response. And what that "something more" is amounts to a concern or a pro attitude on the part of the reader, viewer, or listener of the fiction regarding the way in which the situation depicted in the fiction is or is not going. That is, in addition to being criterially prefocused, the narrative must instill certain concerns about the fictional characters and events in the reader, viewer, or listener. These concerns function like the desires in many everyday emotions, and when added to the mental content or conception derived from the criterially prefocused text, the combination, all things being equal, should elicit an emotional response in accordance with the criterial features of the situation that the text has made pertinent for attention.

The structure of our emotional involvement with a narrative comprises at least a criterially prefocused text plus certain concerns or pro attitudes, and together these are apt to elicit broadly predictable responses in standard audiences. The criterially prefocused text embodies a conception of a situation. But a conception of a situation alone is not sufficient to motivate an emotional response, as is evident from the reactions of certain sociopaths. To prompt such a response requires that audiences be invested with concerns – certain pro and con attitudes – about what is going on in a story.[15]

This suggestion makes the assumption that narrative structures can enlist audiences in preferences about the ways in which a story might go. This is not to say that all stories do this – narrative instructions about how to fix a broken water pipe may not. Nevertheless, I think that it is equally noncontroversial to suppose that many narratives do induce readers, listeners, and viewers to form preferences about how the story should evolve. For example, in Grant Allen's *The Woman Who Did* – called "the bestseller that scandalized Victorian Great Britain" – the implied reader is concerned for Herminia Barton (the woman who believed in sexual relations outside of matrimony). Said readers respect her sincerity and prefer that Herminia be spared from harm. Thus, at the end of the story, when Herminia feels compelled to commit suicide, the reader is moved to sadness, not simply because the story has portrayed her plight melodramatically, but because the story has elicited a pro attitude toward Herminia from the reader as well.

Typically, stories develop in such a way that readers, viewers, and listeners have a structured horizon of expectations about what might and what might not happen. And, in addition to having a sense of the possible outcomes of the ongoing courses of events, one also, generally under the guidance of the author, has convictions about what outcomes one would, in a certain sense, prefer to obtain versus those one would prefer not to obtain. In some cases, the preferred course of events correlates with the express goals and plans of the protagonists of the story; what they want to happen – say, averting nuclear disaster – is what the audience wants to happen. However, in a great many other cases, the story may proffer preferred outcomes independently of the express goals and plans of any of the characters. That is, the story may have its own agenda, as in the cases of all those fictional lovers who find themselves amorously involved in ways they never planned and even might have abhorred antecedently.

But however motivated, audiences develop concerns regarding the situations in stories, and when those concerns are threatened, we tend to react with dysphoric (or discomforting) emotions, whereas, when the concern in question is abetted by narrative developments, our emotions tend to be euphoric.[16] Which particular dysphoric or euphoric emotion is engaged, of course, depends upon the way in which the text is criterially prefocused. For example, considering some dysphoric emotions, if I have a pro attitude toward a character and he is morally wronged in a way that the text makes criterially salient, then, all things being equal, I will feel anger, particularly toward those characters who have wronged him; whereas, if presented with the gross misfortune of a group that has elicited my concern in a criterially prefocused way, I am apt to feel pity for them.

Furthermore, euphoric emotions of different sorts also are likely to evolve in accordance with the way in which the text is criterially prefocused (where our concerns or desires about the direction of courses of events are also satisfied). When a character toward whom we bear a pro attitude overcomes obstacles, saliently posed in the text, we are likely to respond with admiration, whereas the manifestation of virtually limitless power by an agency of which we approve – for instance, nature or a god – will tend to evoke reverence.

Authors of narratives are able, fairly reliably, to induce the emotions they set out to evoke – especially basic emotions (like anger, fear, hatred, and so on) – because of the fact that they share a common background (cultural, but biological as well) with their audiences, both in terms of the criteria relevant to the experience of specific emotions as well as in terms of what it standardly takes to elicit concern for given characters and their goals, and for the alternative directions that situations may take. Inasmuch as authors generally share a common background, cultural and otherwise, with their audiences, they may use themselves as detectors to gauge how audiences are likely to respond to their texts. They can use their own reactions to predict the direction of the standard audience member's concern, as well as the specific emotional states the criterial prefocusing will encourage.

Of course, authors are not infallible in this regard. In his book *American Psycho,* Brett Easton Ellis expected audiences to respond with hilarity – because he intended a postmodern parody – whereas they greeted the book with disgust. Nevertheless, with most narrative fiction, such wild mismatches of intended affect with actual affect are the exception rather than the rule. Most narratives are relatively successful in raising the kind of emotion at which they aim, though not always in the degree to which they aspire (frequently eliciting too much or too little of the intended affect).

The reason for what accuracy there is in this matter is that generally, in sharing a background (an ethos, a moral and emotive repertoire, a cognitive stock, and so on) with audiences, authors are able to conjecture what their confrères' reaction should be in terms of which emotional responses are appropriate to situations depicted in certain ways. Within the boundaries of certain cultures, there are certain criteria concerning which emotional responses are normatively correct – that is, which emotions certain situations are supposed to elicit. Authors, as members of that culture, possessed in common with audiences, use their knowledge of what is normatively correct in terms of emotional responses and compose narrative situations accordingly. Thus, authors can broadly predict how readers will respond to the events they construct because they know the way in which members of their culture are supposed to respond emotionally to situations of various sorts. Where most storytellers fail (when they fail), it seems to me, is usually not in evoking the emotions they intend to evoke, but in evoking them at the wrong level of intensity. And this, I speculate, is very frequently a matter of the failure to elicit the appropriate amount or type of concern for the characters and situations depicted.

But, be that as it may, emotional involvement with a narrative depends upon the combination of a criterially prefocused text with pro and/or con attitudes about the ways in which the narrative situation can develop – that is, a combination of a conception of the situation along with some relevant concerns, preferences, and desires. Together, these provide necessary and sufficient conditions for an emotional response to the text to take hold in such a way that the reader, viewer, or listener becomes emotionally focused, that is, in such a way that the abiding emotional state fixes and shapes her attention.

Insofar as audience concern often takes its cue from the goals of characters, it may be tempting to reintroduce the Platonic notion of identification at this point, claiming that audiences take on the goals of characters in fictional narratives by identifying with the characters and deriving their (the audiences') concerns by means of this process. But this brand of identification cannot provide us with a general theory of how concerns are engendered by narratives, since the direction of our concern in many stories runs in different directions from those of the protagonists. So it cannot, across the board, be the case that, in order to form our concerns, we must be identifying with characters and their express goals. Often we form our concerns about how the story should go in a paternalistic rather than an identificatory fashion. Frequently, we do not think that the characters should get what they want. Thus, identification once again fails as a general account of how we are emotionally engaged by narratives.

Contra Plato, the mechanism is not a matter of identification. We do not become the character and acquire her goals. The character's emotion does not transmigrate into us. Rather, our preexisting emotional makeup with its standing recognitional capacities and our preexisting dispositions to certain values and preferences are mobilized by the text's providing an affective cement that fixes our attention on the text and shapes our attention to the evolving story.

Moreover, it will be recalled that Plato tried to explain the function of the emotions in drama purely in terms of economic necessity. The audience understands little, Plato contends, so the only way to engage it is through the emotions, understood as irrational forces. I reject this account, because I think that the emotions are connected to cognition. Indeed, addressing the emotions may, in fact, provide understanding. Thus the elicitation of emotional responses from audiences is not an alternative to cognition and understanding. Rather, the real function of the emotions for narrative fictions is, on my account, the management of the audience's attention. Of course, successful management of the audience's attention may be economically beneficial. But this may be regarded as a secondary effect and not the primary reason that emotions are virtually indispensable to fictions.

IV. RAMIFICATIONS FOR RESEARCH

If my account of the emotional involvement of the audience with regard to narrative fiction is acceptable, it suggests a certain direction of research. In order to analyze how a text elicits an emotional response, it is of central importance to isolate the way in which the text is criterially prefocused. Using herself as a detector, the critic begins with a global sense of the emotions that the text has elicited in her. Then, using the criteria of the emotion in question as a hypothesis, she may review the way in which the text is articulated to isolate the relevant descriptions or depictions in the text that instantiate the concept of the emotion in question. In following this procedure, one can pith the emotive structure of the text.

What "pithing the emotive structure of the text" amounts to here is finding the aspects of the depictions or descriptions of the object of the emotion that satisfy the necessary conditions for being in whatever emotional state the audience is in. This is what explaining the emotional state of the audience generally comes to (along with identifying the concerns or preferences with which the narrative invests the audience).

For example, I cite the descriptions of the putatively rancid odor of the monster in a horror fiction because it contributes the satisfaction of one of the necessary conditions of one's being horrified (viz., that the object of the emotion be perceived as impure) and thus my citation contributes to explaining why the audience is horrified by the novel. Of course, it is impossible to predict exhaustively every way in which authors will satisfy the necessary conditions of the emotional states that concern them. After all, artists can be original. However, there is room for limited generalization in this area where theorists are able to identify recurring formulas – both in terms of constructing emotive salience and enlisting audience preferences – that are routinely used to secure certain affects.

Admittedly, this order of research may not always be practicable. For example, one may not always be able to articulate with precision one's emotional response to a text. In that case, one might be better advised to tackle the descriptions and depictions with an eye to seeing what they make salient and then compare those saliencies with the criteria for the better known emotional states. This may lead to a clarification of the emotional address of the text in question. Needless to say, I would not wish to claim that the emotional address of a text is always unambiguous, nor would I deny that some texts may introduce novel emotional timbres. Nevertheless, in these cases the procedure that I have recommended is still valuable, because it will enable us to identify the general contours of the emotional ambiguities and novel emotional timbres in the text.

Of course, in many cases, especially those in which we as ordinary readers are dealing with texts that are remote from us in time and place, we will not be able to depend on our own emotional responses to the text because we do not have the appropriate cultural background. This is exactly where literary history, film history, art history, dance history, and the like have an indispensable role to play. For historians can supply us with the background necessary to make the emotive address of texts from other cultures and other periods in the history of our own culture emotionally accessible to us.

My emphasis on the emotional address of texts may trouble some readers who worry that it makes textual analysis too much like sociology. It may sound as though I am advocating that we must go out into the field and find out how audiences actually respond to texts. And yet, I am not proposing that sort of empirical sociology. For I am concerned with the normatively correct address of the text – the emotive effect that the text is supposed to have, or is designed to have on the normal audience. Some people may find beheadings humorous; but that is not the emotional response that *A Man for All Seasons* is designed to promote. Throughout this essay, I have been concerned with the normatively correct emotional response to texts and with the structure that encourages that response. This is a matter of textual analysis, albeit against the background of the culture of the emotions in which the text is produced. It is not a matter of sociological polling. This, of course, is not said to deny that the results of sociological polling may be interesting. But in many cases, I suspect that it is redundant, since to a surprising extent, it seems to me, texts tend to elicit actual emotional responses that are normatively appropriate to them.

V. FICTION AND THE EMOTIONS

So far, I have been developing a framework for understanding our emotional engagement with fictional narratives. In doing so, I have presumed that such engagement is logically possible. But there are certain theoretical considerations that suggest that the relations I have attempted to unravel simply can't obtain. So for the brief remainder of this essay, let me address those worries in order to allay them.

I have embraced a cognitive theory of the emotions in order to characterize our involvement with fictional narratives. Cognitive theories of the emotions maintain that a central component of the emotions is a cognitive state, such as a belief. But if the requisite cognitive state that is partly constitutive of an emotion must be a belief, as some cognitive theorists contend, then it is difficult to understand how readers, viewers, and listeners can be emotionally moved by narrative fictions, because such audiences know the narratives in question are fictions, and, therefore, do not believe them. To fear *x,* under one standard analysis, is, among other things, to believe that *x* is harmful. But then how can I be in a state of fear with regard to a vampire novel, since I know that the novel is a fiction, that vampires do not exist, and, consequently, that the vampires mentioned in the novel cannot really be harmful? Similarly, insofar as other emotions involve other sorts of beliefs, which, like fear, putatively cannot be sustained for persons, objects, and events we know, and, therefore, believe do not exist, how is any emotional response to fiction possible at all? Perhaps emotional responses to fiction are just impossible.

My answer to this challenge relies on my rejection of the supposition that emotions require beliefs in all cases.[17] The cognitive theory of emotions requires a cognitive component, but, I would argue, the form that component can take is diverse, including not only beliefs, but thoughts and perhaps even patterns of attention.[18] And, furthermore, the form that is most relevant to understanding our emotional responses to fictional narratives is thought, not belief.

But what do I mean by "thought" in this context? In order to answer that question, let me contrast what I am calling thoughts with beliefs. A belief, for my purposes, can be conceived to be a proposition held in the mind as asserted. To believe that there is a table in front of me is to be committed to the truth of the assertion of the proposition "that there is a table in front of me." A thought, on the other hand, is a matter of entertaining a proposition in the mind unasserted, as one does when I ask you to suppose that "Albania has conquered the United States" or to imagine that "Manhattan Island is made of pizza." To imagine is to remain neutral about whether we know or believe whatever it is that we imagine. It is to entertain a thought-content, to entertain a proposition as unasserted, to understand the meaning of the proposition (to grasp its propositional content), but to refrain from taking it as an assertion, and, therefore, to be neutral about its truth value.

Moreover, it seems to be indisputable that emotions can be engendered in the process of holding propositions before the mind unasserted. While cutting vegetables, imagine putting the very sharp knife in your hand into your eye. One suddenly feels a shudder. You need not believe that you are going to put the knife into your eye. Indeed, you know that you are not going to do this. Yet merely entertaining the thought, or the propositional content of the thought (that I am putting this knife into my eye), can be sufficient for playing a role in causing a tremor of terror. For emotions may rest on thoughts and not merely upon beliefs.

We can evoke bodily changes in ourselves by means of thoughts. We do this all the time when we stimulate ourselves sexually in the process of imagining compliant beauties beckoning us to embrace them. Arachnophobes can send a chill of fear down their spine by imagining that a tarantula is on their back, and most of us can make ourselves gag with disgust, if we suppose that the food in our mouth is really someone else's vomit. Thoughts, that is, can play a role in generating emotional states.

Furthermore, this aspect of the emotions is particularly pertinent to our commerce with fictional narratives. For fictions are stories that authors intend readers, listeners, and viewers to imagine.[19] Fictions comprise sentences, or other sense-bearing vehicles, that communicate propositions to audiences, which propositions the author of the fiction intends the audience to imagine or to entertain in the mind unasserted as a result of audience members' recognition of the author's intention that that is what they are meant to do. In making a fiction, an author is creating an assemblage of propositions for prospective readers, viewers, or listeners, which the author intends to be entertained in thought. The author presenting a fiction in effect says to the audience: "hold these propositions before your mind unasserted" – that is, "suppose p" or "imagine p" or "entertain p unasserted."

Thus, if thoughts, as distinct from beliefs, can also support emotional responses, then we may have emotional responses to fictions concerning situations, persons, objects, and things that do not exist. For we can imagine or suppose that they exist, and entertaining unasserted the propositional content of the relevant thoughts can figure in the etiology of an emotional state. Fictions, construed as propositions to be imagined, supply us with the relevant, unasserted propositional content, and in entertaining that content as the author mandates, we can be emotionally moved by fictions. It is not impossible to be moved by fictions. It is quite natural, as we can see by putting together two theses: (1) the thesis that fictions are propositions that authors proffer to us with the intention that they be imagined or entertained as unasserted and (2) the thesis that thoughts, construed as propositions held in mind unasserted, can play the role of the cognitive constituent in the activation of an emotional state.

On my account of our emotional involvement with fictional narratives, authors present readers, listeners, and viewers with propositions to be imagined that depict or describe situations that have been criterially prefocused and that arouse our concern so that we become emotionally focused on the text – that is, our attention (1) becomes riveted to the objects of our emotional state (said objects are lit, in a manner of speaking, in a special phenomenological glow), (2) our attention is inexorably drawn to those features of the object of the emotion that are apposite to the emotional state we are in, (3) we are encouraged to search the situation for more features of the sort that will support and sustain the prevailing emotional state, and (4) we are prompted to anticipate further details of the evolving story that are subsumable under the categories of the presiding emotion. Emotions are a central device that authors have for managing the attention of readers, listeners, and viewers. Not only do authors use our already existing emotional constitution to direct our attention and to fill in the story in a way that makes it intelligible; our emotions keep us locked on the text on a moment-to-moment basis.

HORROR AND HUMOR

During the last decade or so, the subgenre of the horror-comedy has gained increasing prominence. Movies such as *Beetlejuice,* a triumph of this tendency, are predicated on either getting us to laugh where we might ordinarily scream, or to scream where we might typically laugh, or to alternate between laughing and screaming throughout the duration of the film. One aim of this genre it

From: *The Journal of Aesthetics and Art Criticism,* 57,2 (Spring 1999), 145–60.

would appear, is to shift moods rapidly – to turn from horror to humor, or vice versa, on a dime. *Gremlins* (both versions), *Ghostbusters* (both versions), *Arachnophobia, The Addams Family* (both versions), possibly *Death Becomes Her,* and certainly *Mars Attacks* and *Men in Black* are highly visible, "blockbuster" examples of what I have in mind, but the fusion of horror and comedy also flourishes in the domain of low-budget production, in films like *Dead/Alive* as well as in the outré work of Frank Henenlotter, Stuart Gordon, and Sam Rami.

Nor is the taste for blending horror and humor restricted to film. The recently discontinued daily comic strip by Gary Larson, *The Far Side,* consistently recycled horror for laughs, as do the television programs *Tales from the Crypt* and *Buffy the Vampire Slayer.* And even the usually dour, intentionally deadpan television series *The X-Files* makes room for comedy in episodes like "Humbug."

Likewise, Tom Disch's recent novel *The Businessman* generates humor by sardonically inverting one of the fundamental conventions of the horror genre – representing a ghost who is stricken with disgust by the human she is supposed to haunt, rather than the other way around. And Dean Koontz's best-selling novel – *TickTock* – moves easily between horror and screwball comedy, while James Hynes's *Publish and Perish: Three Tales of Tenure and Terror* restages classic horror motifs and stories for the purpose of academic satire.

Of course, not every recent attempt to fuse horror and humor is effective. Lavish film productions like *The Golden Child* and *Scrooged* earned far less than anticipated. But what is more perplexing from a theoretical point of view is not that some fusions of horror and humor fail, but that any at all succeed. For, at least at first glance, horror and humor seem like opposite mental states. Being horrified seems as though it should preclude amusement. And what causes us to laugh does not appear as though it should also be capable of making us scream. The psychological feelings typically associated with humor include a sense of release and sensations of lightness and expansion;[1] those associated with horror, on the other hand, are feelings of pressure, heaviness, and claustrophobia. Thus, it may appear initially implausible that such broadly opposite affects can attach to the same stimulus.

And yet, the evidence from contemporary films, television shows, comic strips, and novels indicates that they can. Moreover, though my examples so far are all of recent vintage, the phenomenon is long-standing. From earlier movie cycles, one recalls *Abbott and Costello Meet Frankenstein,* and before that there was the naughty humor of James Whale's *Bride of Frankenstein* and *The Invisible Man,* and, even more hilariously, his *Old Dark House.*

Furthermore, in literature, there has been a strong correlation between horror and comedy since the emergence of the horror genre. Perhaps Walpole's *Castle of Otranto* is already a horror-comedy.[2] But, in any case, soon after the publication of Mary Shelley's classic, stage parodies with titles such as *Frank-in-Steam* and *Frankenstitch, the Needle Prometheus* – in which the mad scientist, appropriately enough, is a tailor – appeared.[3] Throughout the nineteenth century, stories by Sheridan LeFanu, M. R. James, and others were laced with mordant humor, while

Saki's "The Open Window" and Oscar Wilde's "The Canterbury Ghost" are side-splitting masterpieces of the collision of laughter and terror.

Given the striking coincidence of horror and humor, it is not surprising that the correlation has been remarked upon. For example, Stuart Gordon, the director of *Re-Animator* and *From the Beyond,* states:

> When Hitchcock referred to *Psycho,* he always referred to it as a comedy. It took seeing it three or four times before I started picking up on it as a comedy. He said that there was a very fine line between getting someone to laugh and getting someone to scream. One thing I've learned is that laughter is the antidote. When you don't think you have to laugh, then you are basically blowing away the intensity. You have to be careful when you do that, you don't want to be laughing at the expense of the fright. It's best if you can alternate between the two, build up the tension and then release it with a laugh. It is a double degree of challenge. You're walking a tightrope, and if something becomes inadvertently funny, the whole thing is over.
>
> The thing I have found is that you'll never find an audience that wants to laugh more than a horror audience.[4]

If Gordon's revealing comments about the nexus of horror and humor are somewhat meandering, Robert Bloch, the dean of American horror writers and the author of the novel *Psycho,* is more precise. He writes:

> Comedy and horror are opposite sides of the same coin. ... Both deal in the grotesque and the unexpected, but in such a fashion as to provoke two entirely different physical reactions. Physical comedy is usually fantasy; it's exaggeration, as when W. C. Fields comes out of a small town pet shop with a live ostrich. There's a willing suspension of disbelief but we don't generally regard it as fantasy because it's designed to promote laughter rather than tension or fear.[5]

Indeed, even Edgar Allan Poe may have had an intimation of a deep connection between horror and humor, for in his discussion of fantasy – a category that would appear to subsume what we call horror – he notes that it is on a continuum with humor. In his *Broadway Journal* of January 18, 1845, Poe observes:

> Fancy is at length found impinging upon the province of Fantasy. The votaries of this latter delight not only in novelty and unexpectedness of combination, but in the avoidance of proportions. The result is therefore abnormal and to a healthy mind affords less of pleasure through its novelty, than pain through incoherence. When, proceeding a step farther, however, Fantasy seeks not merely disproportionate but incongruous or antagonistical elements, the effect is rendered more pleasureable from its greater positiveness – there is an effort of Truth to shake from her that which is no property of hers – and we laugh.[6]

Indeed, there is also a perhaps perverse way in which our theoretical heritage belies the confluence of horror and humor. Namely, we find that sometimes putative theories of comedy look as though they are equally serviceable as theories of horror. Freud, for example, identifies the object of wit with what can be called the jokework, which manifests repressed modes of unconscious thinking. But, at the same time, in his celebrated essay "The 'Uncanny'" – which is as close as Freud comes to a theory of horror – the object of uncanny feelings is also the manifestation of repressed, unconscious modes of thinking, such as the omnipotence of thought.[7] Thus, in Freud's theory, the road to comic laughter and the road to feelings of uncanniness are unaccountably the same.

Likewise, in Jentsch's study of the uncanny, which Freud cites, the ideal object for eliciting feelings of uncanniness is the automaton that closely approximates animate or human life.[8] But, as students of comic theory will immediately recognize, this observation converges on Henri Bergson's candidate for the object of laughter, namely, humanity encrusted in the mechanical.[9]

The kind of evidence that I have already marshaled in favor of some connection between horror and humor can be amplified in many different ways. But the conclusion is unavoidable. There is some intimate relation of affinity between horror and humor. I have spent a great deal of time motivating this conclusion, however, because, though it appears unavoidable, it nevertheless is paradoxical or at least mysterious.

For, as noted previously, it appears that these two mental states – being horrified and being comically amused – could not be more different. Horror, in some sense, oppresses; comedy liberates. Horror turns the screw; comedy releases it. Comedy elates; horror stimulates depression, paranoia, and dread.

Though these feelings, insofar as they are not propositions, are not contradictory in the logician's sense, they are at least so emotionally conflictive that we would not predict that they could be provoked by what to all intents and purposes appear to be the same stimuli. Yet that counterintuitive finding is where the data point us.

Perhaps what is so troubling about the data is that they reveal that what appears to be exactly the same figure – say the monster in *House of Frankenstein* and the monster in *Abbott and Costello Meet Frankenstein* – can look and act in exactly the same way; they can be perceptually indiscernible.[10] Yet, one provokes horror and the other provokes humor. How can the self-same stimulus give rise to such generically different emotional responses? How can the figure in one film be an appropriate object of horror and in another film be an appropriate object of comic amusement? In order to answer these questions, we will have to develop a theory that explains both how horror and humor are alike and how they are different.

Basically, then, we have two questions before us. The first concerns the apparently facile transition, as in *Beetlejuice,* from horror to humor and vice versa. To explain this, we need to show how horror and humor are alike. Indeed, they are so alike that indiscernibly portrayed monsters can give rise to either horror or humor.[11]

But this phenomenon itself raises another question. For though the self-same monster type that we find in *House of Frankenstein* can give rise to laughter – as the case of *Abbott and Costello Meet Frankenstein* shows – typically, with respect to *House of Frankenstein,* he does not. Standardly we do not laugh at our horrific monsters. So there is some differentia between horror and humor – a differentia whose explanation is made philosophically urgent insofar as it appears that horrific figures and humorous ones can, in principle, be perceptually indiscernible.

In order to answer these questions, I will want to say something about the nature of horror and something about the nature of humor. Thus, in what follows, I will proceed in two stages: stage one will sketch a theory of horror; and then stage two will introduce a theoretical discussion of humor for the purpose of isolating its pertinent similarities to and differences from horror.

I. STAGE ONE: HORROR

Our concern with the relation of horror to humor is motivated by an aesthetic problem – the issue of how within popular genres it is possible to move from horror to comedy with such apparent though counterintuitive ease. Here it is important to note that we are concerned with horror and comedy as they manifest themselves in certain well-known genres. We are not concerned with what might be called "real-life" horror – the horror, say, that overcomes us when we read about urban violence. "Horror," for our purposes, pertains to the sort of emotion that attends reading what are commonly called "horror novels" and the like, and viewing horror movies. To be more accurate, we should speak of "art-horror" here – that is, the sort of horror associated with one particular genre of mass art. But for convenience, I will simply refer to the phenomenon as horror (with the unstated proviso that the relevant sense of horror under discussion is art-horror).

But what is the horror genre? What distinguishes the horror genre from other popular genres like the Western or the detective thriller? Perhaps one useful way to begin to answer this question is to take note of the fact that often genres are identified, among other ways, in terms of the characters who inhabit them. Westerns at the very least are fictions that have cowboys in them, while detection thrillers must contain detectives – either professionals (cops or private eyes) or ordinary folk forced into that role (like the character Thornhill, played by Cary Grant, in *North by Northwest*).

So, are there any characters who typically inhabit horror fictions – characters who may serve to mark off horror fictions in the way that cowboys, in part, mark off Westerns? Here it seems that there is an obvious candidate – namely, the monster. Horror fictions have heroes and heroines just like other types of fiction, but they also seem to contain a special character of their own, the monster: Dracula, the werewolf (of London or Paris), the Creature from the Black Lagoon, Freddie Kruger, King Kong, Godzilla, and the Living Dead. Moreover, as these examples indicate, frequently horror fictions take their titles from the monster that haunts them.

However, if this putative insight is to be of any use, something needs to be said about how we are to understand the notion of a monster. For my purposes, the most effective way of characterizing such monsters is to say that they are beings

whose existence science denies. Worms as long as freight trains, vampires, ghosts
and other revenants, bug-eyed creatures from other galaxies, haunted houses, and
wolfmen are all monsters on this construal. Similarly, though science acknowledges that dinosaurs once existed, the dinosaurs in Michael Crichton's *Jurassic Park*
are monsters in my sense, since the idea that such dinosaurs exist today – or that
such creatures could be concocted in the way the novel suggests – offends science.
Similarly, the squid in Peter Benchley's *The Beast,* his most recent rewriting of
Jaws, is a monster because it appears to possess self-consciousness.

Monsters, then, are creatures – fictionally confected out of either supernatural
lore or science fiction fancy – whose existence contemporary science challenges.
And a horror fiction is in part standardly marked by its possession of one such
monster at minimum.

One objection to this initial approximation of the way to begin to demarcate
the horror genre is that it seems liable to one family of obvious counterexamples –
the psycho-killer or slasher, of whom Norman Bates is perhaps the most illustrious
example. The problem is this: many people, including the owners of video stores and
the compilers of television listings, are inclined to count *Psycho* as horror, but on the
view just propounded, it is not, because Norman Bates and his progeny are psychotic – a category that science countenances – and, therefore, he is not a monster.
Consequently, *Psycho* and the like are not horror fictions. However, since the subgenre of the psycho-slasher strikes many as one of the most active arenas of horror
in the late 1970s and 1980s, such a conclusion appears unpalatable.

Now, in point of fact, the correlation of horror fictions with monsters does
not exclude as many psycho-slashers as one might anticipate. For, very frequently,
the psycho-slashers and other assorted berserkers of the recent horror cycle are
literally monsters according to the previous stipulation. Certainly, the most famous
slashers of the last decade or so are of supernatural provenance: Michael Meyers of
the *Halloween* cycle, Jason of the *Friday the 13th* cycle, Freddie from *Nightmare on
Elm Street,* and Chucky from *Child's Play.*

On the other hand, Hannibal Lector is arguably only a psychotic – albeit one
unprecedented in the annals of psychiatry – rather than a monster. So, if you are
disposed to classify *The Silence of the Lambs* as a horror fiction, you may balk at the
correlation between horror and monsters. However, there is an easy way in which
to adjust the correlation so that it accommodates Hannibal Lector and his peers.[12]
It merely requires the recognition that the psycho-killers one encounters in the
relevant popular fictions are not really of the sort countenanced by contemporary
psychology, but are actually creatures of science fiction, though in these cases we
are dealing with science fictions of the mind, not the body.

Horror fictions may contain lizards larger than small towns, and, though science countenances the existence of lizards, lizards larger than, say, Northfield,
Minnesota, are not creatures of science but of science fiction. Likewise, the relevant psycho-slashers are not the kind of psychotics one finds catalogued in the
fourth edition of the *Diagnostic and Statistical Manual of Mental Disorders.* They are
either fanciful, fictional extrapolations thereof, or drawn from wholly mythologi-

cal material. Hannibal Lector, for example, is merely our most recent version of Mephistopheles – erudite, omniscient, satanic – out to seduce Starling's soul with the promise of knowledge. Thus, horrific psycho-slashers are science fictions of the psyche, veritable monsters from the viewpoint of science proper, which serve, in part, to mark off the fictions in which they thrive as horror fictions.[13]

Nevertheless, even if the correlation between horror and the presence of a monster can be defended as a necessary condition for horror fiction, more must be said. For there are many fictions that contain monsters that we do not classify as horror fictions. For example, the space odyssey *Star Wars* contains the creature Chewbacca, who, for all intents and purposes, is a monster, a monster who looks exactly like the sort of thing we would expect to find in a werewolf movie. In fact, there is a 1940s movie called *The Return of the Vampire* where, to my mind, the vampire's assistant is virtually a dead-ringer for Chewbacca. And yet we do not call *Star Wars* a horror film, even though we might call a werewolf film with a creature made-up exactly like Chewbacca a horror film. So, the question is: What is the difference between a horror fiction proper and a nonhorror fiction like *Star Wars* that has a monster in it?

One obvious difference between a horror fiction and a mere monster fiction – that is, a fiction with a monster in it – revolves around our emotional response to the monster in the horror fiction. We are horrified by the monsters in horror fictions, whereas creatures like Chewbacca in *Star Wars* are not horrifying. We regard Chewbacca emotionally as we do any of the other protagonists in the film. So the solution to the problem of distinguishing horror fictions from mere monster fictions depends upon saying exactly what constitutes our emotional reactions to horrifying monsters.

At first, this may appear to be an impossible task. Is not everyone's emotional reaction to horror unique, and, in any case, insofar as it is subjective, how could we ever hope to get at it in a way that could yield precise generalizations? However, the problem is not so daunting once one realizes that horror fictions are generally designed to guide audience response. Specifically, such fictions are generally designed to control and guide our emotional responses in such a way that, ideally, horror audiences are supposed to react emotionally to the monsters featured in horror fictions in the same manner that the characters in horror fictions react emotionally to the monsters they meet there.

That is, with horror fictions, ideally, the emotional responses of the audience to the monster are meant to mimic the emotional responses of the human characters in the fiction to the monsters therein. The makers of horror fictions, in the standard case, want the audience to shudder at the prospect of encountering the monster when the characters in the plot so shudder. Indeed, most frequently, the emotional responses of the fictional protagonists even prime or cue the emotional response of the audience to the relevant monster in such a way that the audience's responses recapitulate the characters' response. Thus, if we can say something by way of general summary about the standard or generic types of emotional responses that fictional characters evince toward monsters, we will be able to hypothesize something about the way in which, normatively speaking, audiences are supposed to respond emotionally to the monsters in horror fictions.

But how do fictional characters respond emotionally to the monsters they encounter in horror stories? Let this paradigmatic example from Stephen King's novel *Needful Things* serve as a basis for discussion.

The character Polly has been set upon by a spider of supernatural origin. It is growing larger by the moment. It is already larger than a cat. King writes:

> She drew in breath to scream and then its front legs dropped onto her shoulders like the arms of some scabrous dime-a-dance Lothario. Its listless ruby eyes stared into her own. Its fanged mouth dropped open and she could smell its breath – a stink of bitter spices and rotting meat.
>
> She opened her mouth to scream. One of its legs pawed into her mouth. Rough, gruesome bristles caressed her teeth and tongue. The spider mewled eagerly.
>
> Polly resisted her first instinct to spit the horrid, pulsing thing out. She released the plunger and grabbed the spider's leg. At the same time she bit down, using all her strength in her jaws. Something crunched like a mouthful of Life Savers, and a cold bitter taste like ancient tea filled her mouth. The spider uttered a cry of pain and tried to draw back....
>
> It tried to lunge away. Spitting out the bitter dark fluid which had filled her mouth, [and] knowing it would be a long, long time before she was entirely rid of that taste, Polly yanked it back again. Some distant part of her was astounded at this exhibition of strength, but there was another part of her which understood it perfectly. She was afraid, she was revolted.[14]

In this passage, whose essential features one finds repeated endlessly in horror fictions, King informs us quite explicitly about the nature of Polly's emotional response to the spider, which, all things being equal, should be our response as well. What is quite clear is that her response – and, by extension, our response – is not simply a matter of fear, though surely both we and Polly regard this unnatural creature as immensely fearsome. But also – and this is key – we, along with Polly, are disgusted by the monster. We find it loathsome and impure. Polly must force herself by an act of will to touch it; we would certainly cringe if something like that spider were to brush against us.

Confronted by such a creature, our response would be to recoil, not only because of our fear that it might harm us, but also because it is an abominable, repugnant, impure thing – a dirty, filthy thing. So, on the basis of this example, which I claim is paradigmatic, let us hypothesize that horror fictions are distinguished not simply in virtue of their possession of monsters, but also in virtue of their possession of monsters of a certain type, namely, monsters that are not only beings whose existence is not countenanced by science, but also beings designed or predicated on raising emotional responses of fear and disgust in both fictional characters and corresponding audiences.

Crucial to distinguishing horror fictions from mere fictions with monsters in them is the peculiar emotional state that the monsters in horror fictions are designed to elicit. Thus, in order to be more precise about that emotional state, it would be useful for me to be explicit about the view of the emotions to which I subscribe.

Emotions involve feelings. These feelings are comprised of a mix of experiences – some of which, like changes in heart rate, are physiological in nature, and others, like an expansive sensation, are more of the order of psychological changes. Broadly speaking, we can call these feeling states agitations or modifications. Any emotional state involves some accompanying feeling state of these sorts. Being horrified, for example, often involves shivering, gagging, paralysis, trembling, tension, an impression of one's "skin crawling," a quickened pulse, or a sense of heightened alertness, as if danger were near to hand. However, no emotion is reducible to such feelings alone. Why not? Because feeling states such as physiological agitations or psychological modifications can be induced by drugs where there is no question of the subject being in an emotional state.

For example, suppose I could be injected with a drug that replicates all the internal sensations that I underwent the last time I was angry. In such a situation, we would, I suggest, nevertheless refrain from saying that I am angry. Why? Because in the present case, there is no one with whom I am angry. I may feel weird; I may feel internal turbulence. But I am not angry, because in order to be in the emotional state of anger, there must be someone or something with whom or with which I am angry; that is, I must believe that there is someone or something that has wronged me or mine – someone who serves as the focus of my mental state.

Emotions are mental states; they are directed. They are intentional states. They must be directed at objects, real or imagined. In order to be in love, I must be in love with someone. In order to be afraid, I must be afraid of something. An emotion is a mental state that takes or is directed at some object. An emotional state is not merely a feeling state, though it involves feeling. An emotional state involves a feeling that is related to some object.

But how does a feeling get related to an object – an object like my own true love? Clearly, thought must be involved; cognition must be involved. Cognition directs our attention to the objects that give rise to our emotional responses. Thus, emotions are not simply a matter of having certain feelings; emotions also essentially involve having certain thoughts. Emotion is not the opposite of cognition; rather, emotions require cognition as an essential constituent. Indeed, the way in which we identify or individuate emotional states is by reference to the cognitive constituents of an emotion.

The feelings of patriotism and love may be exactly alike in terms of their feeling-tones. In order to distinguish these two emotions, we need to look at the objects to which these mental states are directed. Where the object is one's country, the emotion is apt to be patriotism; where the object is one's spouse, the emotion, one hopes, is likely to be love.

Moreover, as this example suggests, what a given emotion takes as its object is not arbitrary: it is governed by formal criteria. Romantic love, for example, must be directed at a person, or what one believes to be a person. Fear must be directed at something that is perceived to be or believed to be harmful. Standardly, one cannot be afraid of something that one does not believe is harmful. I cannot be afraid of a kidney bean, or, if I am afraid of a kidney bean, then that must be due to the fact that I have some rather strange beliefs about kidney beans, for example, that they are mind parasites from an alternative universe. One who claimed to be in a state of fear with respect to *x*, but who genuinely denied that she thought that there was anything harmful about *x*, would be suspected of contradicting herself.

That is, I cannot be in a state of fear unless I cognize the particular object of my mental state as meeting the formal criterion of *harmfulness*. Or, another way to put it is to say that I cannot be said to be afraid of something unless I adjudge the object in question to be subsumable under the category of the harmful. In order to fear *x*, my beliefs, thoughts, judgments, or cognitions with respect to x must accord with certain criteria of appropriateness. It is in this sense that the cognitive constituent of my mental state determines what emotional state I am in; for how I cognize the object of my emotion – what categories I subsume it under – establish what emotional state I am in.

This is not to say that feeling has no role in the emotions. To be in an emotional state one needs to be in *some* feeling state. However, what emotional state one is in hinges on one's thoughts about the object toward which the emotion is directed. The relation between the thought constituents and the feeling constituents in an emotional state is one of causation. That is, when I am in an emotional state, that is a matter of my having certain appropriate thoughts about a particular object, which thoughts, in turn, cause certain physical agitations and psychic modifications – that is, certain feeling states – in me. To be concrete: in order to be afraid I must have certain thoughts – for example, that the hissing snake before me belongs to the category of harmful things – and such thoughts, in turn, cause certain feeling states in me – for example, a psychological state sensation describable, for example, as my blood running cold, and perhaps a physiological agitation caused by a surge of adrenalin in my circulatory system.

Emotions, then, involve feelings and cognitions, cognitions about the categories to which the objects of the overall state belong. Applying this model to the characteristic emotional state that monsters in horror fiction provoke, we can say that we are horrified when the monsters who are the particular objects of our emotional state are thought of as harmful or threatening (i.e., they are fearsome) *and* they are also thought of as impure (i.e., they are revolting or disgusting), where making these categorical assessments *causes* certain feeling states in us – like shuddering, trembling, chilling (as in "spine-chilling"), a sensation of creepiness, of unease, and so on.

To be horrified, that is, involves our subsumption of the monster in a horror fiction under both the categories of the fearsome and the impure where, in turn, these cognitions cause various psycho-physical agitations, such as that of feeling our flesh "crawl." The horrific response is a compound, as King frankly states in the passage quoted, of fear and revulsion, where the harmfulness of the monster is the criterial ground for fear and the monster's impurity is the criterial ground for revulsion.

A horror fiction, then, is a narrative or image in which at least one monster appears, such that the monster in question is designed to elicit an emotional response from us that is a complex compound of fear and disgust in virtue of the potential danger or threat the monster evinces and in virtue of its impurity.[15] Central to the classification of a fiction as art-horror or genre-horror is that it contains a monster designed to arouse the emotions of fear in the audience by virtue of its harmfulness, and that of revulsion in virtue of its impurity.

The insight that horror fictions contain monsters is admittedly pedestrian, and the claim that the relevant monsters are fearsome is perhaps equally obvious, since the monsters in horror fictions customarily occupy themselves with killing and maiming people, as well as eating them and worse. Where my theory may be innovative, however, is in the hypothesis that horror *also* essentially involves the emotional response of abhorrence, disgust, or revulsion in consequence of the monster's impurity.

Nevertheless, though this may represent an innovation in the theory of horror, it may be an innovation that some readers feel is more obfuscatory than informative. For central to this theory of horror is the notion of impurity, a notion that many may think is so vague that it is of no theoretical value whatsoever. So in order to allay such misgivings, let me say something about the nature of impurity.

According to a number of anthropologists, including Mary Douglas and Edmund Leach, reactions of impurity correlate regularly with transgressions or violations or jammings of standing schemes of cultural categorization.[16] In their interpretation of the abominations of Leviticus, for example, they hypothesize that crawling things from the sea, like lobsters, are regarded by Jews as impure because, for the ancient Hebrews, crawling was regarded as a defining characteristic of earthbound creatures, not creatures from the sea. A lobster, in other words, is a kind of category error or categorical contradiction (or *traif*, in high-powered philosophical jargon).

Similarly, according to Leviticus, all winged insects with four legs are to be abominated because, though having four legs is a feature of land animals, these things fly, that is, they inhabit the air. Things that are interstitial – that cross the boundaries of the deep categories of a culture's conceptual scheme – are primary candidates for impurity. Feces, insofar as they figure ambiguously in terms of categorical oppositions such as me/not me, inside/outside, and living/dead, serve as a ready target for abhorrence as impure, as do spittle, blood, tears, sweat, hair clippings, nail clippings, pieces of flesh, and so on.

Where objects problematize standing cultural categories, norms, and concepts, they invite reactions of impurity. Objects can also raise categorical misgivings in virtue of being incomplete representations of their class, such as rotting, disintegrating, and broken things, including amputees. And, finally, stuff that is altogether formless, like dirt, sludge, and garbage, provokes categorical anxiety since it seems completely unclassifiable; it is matter out-of-place.

Following Douglas and Leach, then, we can somewhat specify the notion of impurity. Things are adjudged impure when they present problems for standing categories or conceptual schemes, which things may do in virtue of being categorically interstitial, categorically contradictory, incomplete, or formless. Moreover, the relevance of this characterization of impurity for the theory of horror should be immediately apparent, since the monsters in horror fictions could be said virtually to operationalize the sorts of categorical problematizations that anthropologists have itemized.

So many monsters, like werewolves, are categorically interstitial, straddling the categories of wolf and man as a result of being composite creatures. Other monsters, like Dracula and mummies, are categorically contradictory, they are both living and dead at the same time; likewise zombies, a phenomenon captured in the title of films like *The Night of the Living Dead* and *Dead/Alive*. And the Frankenstein monster is not only, in some sense, living and dead, it is also newborn at the same time that it is aged. Categorical incompleteness is also a frequent feature of many horrific monsters – headless ghosts and noseless zombies come to mind here. And, finally, formless is just about the only way that one can describe such beings as the Blob.

Not only is the concept of impurity not hopelessly imprecise, it also turns out to be particularly apposite in characterizing the monsters we find in horror fiction. Our emotional response to horror fictions involves not simply fear, but revulsion because such monsters are portrayed as impure – where impurity can be understood in terms of the problematization, violation, transgression, subversion, or simple jamming of our standing cultural categories, norms, and conceptual schemes.

Moreover, the recognition that horror is intimately and essentially bound up with the violation, problematization, and transgression of our categories, norms, and concepts puts us in a particularly strategic position from which to explore the relation of horror to humor, because humor – or at least one very pervasive form of humor – is also necessarily linked to the problematization, violation, and transgression of standing categories, norms, and concepts.

II. STAGE TWO: HUMOR

My aim in this section is twofold. First I want to explain how the movement between the putatively opposite mental states of horror and comic amusement is not only unproblematic, but even somewhat natural. This will involve showing what these two states share in common. On the other hand, horror and humor are not exactly the same. For we do not always laugh at monsters. So, we also want to produce an account of the difference between these mental states. In the previous section, I presented a theoretical account of horror. In this section, I will examine a theory of humor, one that will illuminate its essential similarities and differences with horror.

At present, the leading type of comic theory is what is called the incongruity theory. Historically, it seems that this sort of comic theory took its modern shape in the eighteenth century in reaction to the kind of superiority theory of humor that is associated with Thomas Hobbes. As is well known, Hobbes's theory of laughter is nasty, brutish, and short. In *Leviathan,* Hobbes maintains:

> Sudden glory is the passion which makes all those grimaces called laughter; and it is caused either by some sudden act of their own, that pleases them; or by the apprehension of some deformed thing in another by comparison whereof they applaud themselves.[17]

That is, on Hobbes's view, the source of comic laughter, indeed of all laughter, is rooted in feelings of superiority.

But this view is clearly inadequate. Often laughter, especially comic laughter, arises when we find ourselves to be the butt of a friendly joke. So, superiority is not a necessary condition for comic amusement. And, of course, neither laughter nor comic amusement need occur in all situations in which we find ourselves to be superior. As Francis Hutcheson, reacting to Hobbes, pointed out, we rarely laugh at oysters. So, superiority is not a sufficient condition for comic amusement.

But if superiority is not the wellspring of laughter, what is? Hutcheson suggests that

> generally the cause of laughter is the bringing together of images which have contrary additional ideas, as well as some resemblance in the principal idea: this contrast between ideas of grandeur, dignity, sanctity, perfection, and ideas of meanness, baseness, profanity, seems to be the very spirit of burlesque; and the greatest part of our raillery and jest is founded upon it.
>
> We also find ourselves moved to laughter by an overstraining of wit, by bringing resemblances from subjects of a quite different kind from the subject to which they are compared.[18]

That is, for Hutcheson, the basis of comic amusement is *incongruity* – the bringing together of disparate or contrasting ideas or concepts. Comic teams, for example, are often composed of a tall, thin character and a short, fat one. And European clown performances are frequently composed of an immaculately clean, sartorially fastidious white clown – the epitome of orderliness and civilization – and an unruly, disheveled, hairy, and smudged clown – the lord of disorder and mischief. Indeed, even where the white clown is absent, the unruly clown generally finds a foil in the suavely tuxedoed or smartly uniformed ringmaster. Comedy, that is, naturally takes hold in contexts in which incongruous, contrasting, or conflicting properties are brought together for our attention.

In addition to Hutcheson's, incongruity theories of humor have been advanced by James Beattie, William Hazlitt, Søren Kierkegaard, and Arthur Schopenhauer.[19] As we saw in an earlier quotation, Edgar Allan Poe also seems to have subscribed to this opinion, while Henri Bergson's well-known thought that comic laughter is provoked by the apprehension of the mechanical in the human may be regarded as a special instance of the incongruous yoking together of disparate properties – in this case, those of the human and the machine. More recently, Arthur Koestler, D. H. Monro, John Morreall, and Michael Clark[20] have defended variations on incongruity theories.

The basic idea behind the incongruity theory of humor is that an essential ingredient of comic amusement is the juxtaposition of incongruous or contrasting objects, events, categories, propositions, maxims, properties, and so on. Stated this way, the incongruity approach can seem insufferably vague. However, the view can be given immense precision. Schopenhauer, for example, hypothesized that the requisite form of incongruous juxtaposition in humor was the incorrect subsumption of a particular under a concept – that is, a sort of category error. What he had in mind can be illustrated by the following joke.

On a planet in deep space, the inhabitants are cannibals. One butcher shop specializes in academic meat. Teaching assistants go for two dollars a pound, assistant professors cost three dollars a pound, philosophy professors with tenure are only one dollar and fifty cents a pound, but deans – deans are five hundred dollars a pound. When latter-day astronauts ask why deans are so expensive, they are asked, in turn: Have you ever tried to clean a dean?

On Schopenhauer's view, the crux of the humor here is the incorrect subsumption of a particular – the moral regeneration of a dean – under a very different concept of cleanliness, one pertaining to the preparation of animals for cooking. Similarly, when I define comedy as "you falling down and breaking your neck, while tragedy is when I prick my finger,"[21] a major part of the humor resides in the conceptual inappropriateness of counting a pinprick as tragic. The errors here are logical; they involve the misapplication of or the confusion in applying a given concept to a particular case. One might also speak of the relevant incongruity, as Kierkegaard does, as a contradiction.

Thus, on one very rigorous construal of the incongruity theory of humor, the incongruities that underlie comic amusement are contradictions, indeed, contradictions in terms of concepts and categories. This version of the incongruity theory is very elegant and tidy. But it is also rather narrow, too narrow, in fact, to cover the wide gamut of comic data. Juxtaposing a tall, thin clown and a short, fat one may invite comic laughter, but it is hard to see how such laughter can be traced back to a contradiction.

As a result, the ways in which incongruous juxtaposition is to be understood with respect to comedy, while including contradiction, must also be expanded to encompass other forms of contrast. And some extended ways of understanding the notion of incongruous juxtaposition include: simultaneously presenting things that stand at extreme opposite ends of a scale to one another, like placing something very tall next to something very short; or mixing categories, as in the title *Rabid Grannies;* or presenting a borderline case as a paradigmatic case – a diminutive Buster Keaton in an oversized uniform as a representative of the All-American football hero; or breaches of norms of propriety where, for example, an inappropriate, rather than an illogical, behavior is adopted – for example, using a tablecloth as a handkerchief. Or the incongruity may be rooted in mistaking contraries for contradictories, as in the following exchange: "Would you rather go to heaven or to hell?" "I'd rather stay here, thank you."

Though the relevant incongruity in a comic situation may involve transgressions in logic, incongruity may also be secured by means of merely inappropriate transgressions of norms or of commonplace expectations, or through the exploration of the outer limits of our concepts, norms, and commonplace expectations.

The incongruity theory of humor, of course, is especially suggestive in terms of our questions about the relation of horror and humor. For on the expanded version of the incongruity theory of humor, comic amusement is bound up with transgressive play with our categories, concepts, norms, and commonplace expectations. If the incongruity theory of humor is plausible, then for a percipient to be in a mental state of comic amusement, that mental state must be directed at a particular object – a joke, a clown, a caricature – that meets a certain formal criterion, namely, that it be apparently incongruous (i.e., that it appear to the percipient to involve the transgression of some concept or some category or some norm or some commonplace expectation).

Just as the mental state of fear must be directed at a particular object subsumable under the category of perceived harmfulness, the mental state of comic amusement requires being directed at a particular subsumable under the category of apparent incongruity. Moreover, since apparent incongruity is a matter of the transgression of standing concepts, categories, norms, and commonplace expectations, the relation of horror to humor begins to emerge, since in the previous section it was argued that a necessary condition for being horrified is that the emotional state in question be directed at an entity perceived to be impure – where impurity, in turn, is to be understood in terms of violations of our standing categories, concepts, norms, and commonplace expectations. Thus, on the incongruity theory of humor, one explanation of the affinity of horror and humor might be that these two states, despite their differences, share an overlapping necessary condition insofar as an appropriate object of both states involves the transgression of a category, a concept, a norm, or a commonplace expectation.

So far, I have proceeded as if the incongruity theory of humor is unproblematic. But it is not evident that it is a perfectly comprehensive theory of comedy. For the kind of incongruity that the theory identifies as the quiddity of humor requires structure – a structure against which opposites, extremes, contrasts, contradictions, inappropriateness, and so on can take shape.[22] But not all comic amusement would appear to require this sort of structure in order to be effective. Sometimes we laugh at pure nonsense – a funny sound, perhaps, or a dopey expression, like "see you in a while, crocodile" – where no explicit or implicit foil of the sort the incongruity theory presupposes can be specified (no contrasting category or concept or norm or expectation).

However, even if the incongruity theory is not a comprehensive theory of comedy, it may still be useful for our purposes. For it does appear to identify at least one of the major recurring objects of comic amusement with some precision. That is, the incongruity theory of humor may succeed in identifying part of a sufficient condition for some subclass of humor, and this may be all we need to explain why some horrific imagery can be transformed into an object of laughter.

Of course, the domain of even such a modified incongruity theory of comedy is much broader than that of the theory of horror presented earlier. The object of comic amusement of the incongruity variety can include jokes, people, situations, characters, actions, objects, and events, whereas the object of horror according to my theory can only be an entity or being of a certain sort – what I call a monster. However, it should be clear that this sort of being can be accommodated within the incongruity theory of humor because there is something already straightforwardly within the compass of that theory that is generally very like a monster and, on occasion, can be easily transformed into one.

What I have in mind is the figure of the clown. The clown figure is a monster in terms of my previous definition.[23] It is a fantastic being, one possessed of an alternate biology, a biology that can withstand blows to the head by hammers and bricks that would be deadly for any mere human, and the clown can sustain falls that would result in serious injury for the rest of us. Not only are clowns exaggeratedly misshapen and, at times, outright travesties of the human form – contortions played on our paradigms of the human shape – they also possess a physical resiliency conjoined with muscular and cognitive disfunctionalities that mark them off as an imaginary species.

Moreover, clowns are not simply, literally monstrous. Clowns are also frequently theorized in the language of categorical transgression with which we are already familiar from our discussion of horrific monsters. For example, in "The Clown as the Lord of Disorder," Wolfgang Zucker describes the ritual clown in these terms: "Self-contradiction … is the clown's most significant feature. Whatever predicates we use to describe him, the opposite can also be said with equal right."[24]

Noting the origin of the word "clown" in words that meant "clod," "clot" and "lump" – that is, formless masses of stuff, like earth or clay, coagulating or adhering together – the anthropologist Don Handelman claims that "clown-types are out-of-place on either side of the border, and in place in neither. They have an affinity with dirt (Makarius, 1970: 57), primarily through their ability to turn clearcut precepts into ambiguous and problematic ones."[25] Handelman goes on to note:

> These clowns are divided against themselves: they are "clots," or "clods," often "lumpish," that hang together in seemingly ill-fitted and disjunctive ways. The interior of this clown type is composed of sets of contradictory attributes: sacred/profane, wisdom/folly, solemnity/humor, serious/comic, gravity/lightness, and so forth. Given this quality of neither-nor, this type can be said to subsume holistically, albeit lumpishly, all of its contradictory attributes.[26]

Furthermore, as with horrific monsters, these conflicting attributes may be strictly biological. As described by Pnina Werbner, the clown figure at a migrant Pakistani wedding, who is the magical agent of the bride's transition from a presexual being to a sexual one, is a composite – an old man, played by a nubile young woman – whose shape-changing eventually marks ritual transformations.[27]

The anthropological literature on ritual clowns identifies clowns as categorically interstitial and categorically transgressive beings. That aspect of the ritual clown is still apparent in the perhaps more domesticated clowns of our modern circuses. In my previous allusion to European circus performances, I noted that the unruly clown functions as the double or doppelgänger of the more fastidious clown or of the ringmaster or of some other matinee-idol type, such as the lion tamer or the knife thrower or the equestrian. Not only does the clown, like a horrific monster, indulge in morally transgressive behavior – butting people about and taking sexual liberties – but like the dark doppelgängers of horrific fiction, the clown-monster is a double, a categorically interstitial figure that celebrates antitheses or "ab-norms."[28]

Moreover, given the strong analogy between the clown-figure of incongruity humor and the monster-figure of horror, it should come as no shock that the clown can be and has been used as a serviceable monster in horror fictions. One example of this can be found in Stephen King's novel *It,* which has been adapted for television, in which the presiding monster takes the form of Pennywise the Clown through much of the story. But another, rather imaginative example is the film *Killer Klowns from Outer Space,* where the hero correctly surmises of the eponymous man-eating aliens that they are really animals from another planet that just happen to look like clowns. *And* they also store their victims in huge cocoons that just happen to look like cotton candy.

If, typically, clowns function in incongruity comedy in a manner analogous to the way in which monsters function in horror fictions – that is, as the objects of the relevant mental states – then our question can be focused concretely by asking: What does it take to turn a clown into a monster or to turn a monster into a clown? To answer the latter question, it is instructive to recall a short 1965 stand-up comedy monologue by Bill Cosby. He says:

> I remember as a kid I used to love horror pictures. The Frankenstein Monster, Wolfman, The Mummy. The Mummy and Frankenstein were my two favorites. They would scare me to death. But now that I look at them as a grown-up, I say to you anyone they catch deserves to die. They are without a doubt the slowest monsters in the world. Anyone they catch deserves to go.[29]

Here Cosby very efficiently transforms his favorite monsters into comic butts. How does he do it? By effectively erasing one of their essential characteristics. Earlier I offered a theory of what it takes to be a horrific monster. Among the features that were most crucial in that analysis were that the horrific monsters had to be both fearsome and loathsome, where the basis of that loathsomeness was impurity borne of categorical transgressiveness. What Cosby does in this routine is to subtract the fearsomeness from this monstrous equation. By alerting us to how very slow these monsters are, he renders them no longer dangerous or fearsome. Once their fearsomeness is factored out, what remains is their status as category errors, which, of course, makes them apt targets or objects of incongruity humor. Similarly, in a film like *Beetlejuice,* when the ghostly young couple attempt to haunt their former house, they cause laughter despite their horrific appearance because we know that they are ineffectual, insofar as their victims can neither see them nor be harmed by them. Subtract the threatening edge from a monster or deflect our attention from it, and it can be reduced to a clownish, comic butt, still incongruous, but now harmless, and, as a result, an appropriate object of laughter.

Approaching our question from the opposite direction, clowns, of course, are already categorically incongruous beings. Thus, they can be turned into horrific creatures by compounding their conceptually anomalous status with fearsomeness. In Stephen King's *It,* this is achieved by equipping Pennywise with a sharp, cruel, yellow maw, while in *Killer Klowns from Outer Space,* the monsters not only benefit by having rows of incisors that haven't been brushed for centuries, but also through the possession of super-human strength, quasi-magical powers, and intergalactic blood-lust.[30] Moreover, the latently horrific potential of clowns – along with puppets and ventriloquist's dummies – is well known to the parents of small children who are often terrified by such "funny" creatures exactly because they have not yet mastered the conventions of so-called comic distance.

The movement from horror to humor or vice versa that strikes us as so counterintuitive, then, can be explained in terms of what horror and at least one kind of humor – namely, incongruity humor – share. For the categorical interstitiality and transgression that serves as one of the most crucial necessary conditions for the mental state of horror plays a role as part of a sufficient condition for having the mental state of comic amusement, especially of the incongruity variety. Of course, if we allow that there is a subgenre labeled incongruity humor, then incongruity will be a necessary condition of that type of humor as well as part of a sufficient condition. On the map of mental states, horror and incongruity amusement are adjacent and partially overlapping regions. Given this affinity, movement from one to the other should not be unexpected.[31] The impurities of horror can serve as the incongruities of humor, just as, in certain circumstances, mere reference to the feces, mucus, or spittle we were taught to revile was enough to make us the class wit in second grade.

Often a very bad horror film, like *The Attack of the 50 Ft. Woman* (the first version), will provoke particularly thunderous laughter. On my theory, that can be explained by suggesting that the fearsomeness of the monster has not been sufficiently projected, often because of inept or outlandish make-up and special effects. Parodies such as *Attack of the Killer Tomatoes* succeed, on the other hand, because it is nearly impossible to imagine a tomato being dangerous.

In addition, people have told me that when I read selections from horror novels, such as the earlier passage from *Needful Things,* out loud, the effect is often amusing. And I have also been told that some horror fans enjoy reading lurid parts from horror novels to their friends for fun. In these cases, it seems to me that once one excerpts these quotations from their narrative contexts, the danger that has been building up in the story disappears, and primarily only the anomaly remains in a way which, my theory predicts, is apt to cause laughter.

Of course, standardly, horror does not blend into humor, or vice versa. The reason for this is that though horror and incongruity humor share one condition, they diverge in other respects. Horror requires fearsomeness in addition to category jamming. So, where the fearsomeness of the monster is convincingly in place, horror will not drift over into incongruity humor. But where the fearsomeness of the monster is compromised or deflected by either neutralizing it or at least drawing attention away from it, the monster can become an appropriate object for incongruity humor. Likewise, when typically humorous figures like puppets, ventriloquist's dummies, and clowns are lethal, they can become vehicles of horror.

The boundary line between horror and incongruity humor is drawn in terms of fear. Two visually indiscernible creatures – such as the monsters in *The House of Frankenstein* and *Abbott and Costello Meet Frankenstein* – can be alternately horrifying or laughable depending upon whether the narrative context invests them with fearsomeness or not. Invested with fearsomeness, the categorically interstitial figure is horrific; bereft of fearsomeness, it is on its way toward comedy. Horror equals categorical transgression or jamming plus fear; incongruity humor equals, in part, categorical transgression or jamming minus fear. Figures indiscernible in terms of their detectable, categorically anomalous, outward features can inhabit either domain, depending upon whether we view them or are led to attend to them in terms of fear.

Moreover, this conclusion is consistent with experimental data. In a series of papers, psychologist Mary Rothbart has argued that exposure to incongruity can elicit a series of different behavioral responses, including fear, problem-solving, and laughter. The same stimuli can evoke a fear response or a laughter response, depending upon whether or not it is threatening.[32] For example, a child is more likely to respond with laughter to the antics of an adult when the adult is familiar or safe, such as a caregiver.[33] When a situation is not safe or nonthreatening, for example, where the adult is a stranger, the response to incongruity is more likely to be distress.

Of course, Rothbart is not examining the contrast between horror fiction and comedy. However, her findings – that responses to identical incongruous stimuli can take the form of fear or laughter depending on contextual factors – is consonant with my hypotheses about the relation of the horror response to comic amusement. The fictional environment of *Abbott and Costello Meet Frankenstein* is "safe." Given Costello's hijinks, he is marked as a naive clown figure, the sort of being who can take falls and be hit in the head with impunity. He is indestructible. He is exempt from real bodily threat and, therefore, the fictional environment is marked as safe.[34] On the other hand, the human figures in the *House of Frankenstein* are ordinary mortals, fragile creatures of the flesh, and their vulnerability induces fear in us for them. Thus, we respond with horror when harmful and impure monsters stalk them.

Nevertheless, we do not regard potentially horrific figures in comedy as horrific because comedy is a realm in which fear, in principle, is banished in the sense that typically in comedy serious human consideration of injury, affront, pain, and even death are bracketed in important ways. Comedy, as a genre, is stridently amoral in

this regard. Within the comic frame, though injury, pain, and death are often elements in a joke, we are not supposed to dwell on them, especially in terms of their
moral or human weight or consequences. Most frequently, we do not attend to or
even apprehend the mayhem in jokes or slapstick comedies as having serious physical or moral consequences.[35] And, as a result, fear and fearsomeness are not part of
the comic universe from the point of view of the audience.

Freud claimed that humor involves a saving or economy of emotion. Perhaps
I can commandeer his slogan for my own purposes and say that the emotion in
question is fear, which disappears when the comic frame causes the burden of
moral concern for the life and limb of comic characters to evaporate.

In the horror genre, on the other hand, our attention is focused, usually relent-
lessly, on the physical plight of characters harried by monsters. Ordinary moral
concern for human injury is never far from our minds as we follow a horror fiction. Thus, fear is the métier of the horror fiction. In order to transform horror
into laughter, the fearsomeness of the monster – its threat to human life – must be
sublated or hidden from our attention. Then we will laugh where we would otherwise scream.[36]

THE PARADOX OF SUSPENSE

THE PROBLEM

It is an incontrovertible fact that people can consume the same suspense fiction
again and again with no loss of affect. Someone may reread Graham Greene's *This
Gun for Hire* or re-view the movie *The Guns of Navarone* and, nevertheless, on the
second, third, and repeated encounters be caught in the same unrelenting grip of
suspense that snared them on their first encounter. I myself have seen *King Kong* at
least fifty times, and yet there are still certain moments when I feel the irresistible
tug of suspense.

However, although the suspense felt by recidivists like me is an undeniable fact, it
appears to be a paradoxical one. For there seems to be agreement that a key component of the emotion *suspense* is a cognitive state of uncertainty.[1] We feel suspense as
the heroine heads for the buzzsaw, in part, because we are uncertain as to whether or
not she will be cleaved. Uncertainty seems to be a necessary condition for suspense.

However, when we come to cases of recidivism, the relevant readers and viewers know Anne Crowder will stop the onset of world war, that the guns of

From: *Suspense: Conceptualizations, Theoretical Analyses and Empirical Explorations*, ed. by Peter
Vorderer, Hans J. Wulff, and Mike Friedrichsen (Mahwah, N.J.: Lawrence Erlbaum, 1996),
71–91.

Navarone will plunge into the sea, and that King Kong will be blown away. After all, we have already read the novel or seen the film; we know how the fiction ends, because we have read it before.

How then can it be possible for us to feel suspense the second, the third, or the fiftieth time around? Or is it possible only because recidivists with respect to suspense fictions are somehow irrational, perhaps psychically blinded by some process of disavowal or denial, of the sort psychoanalysts claim to investigate?

And yet this variety of recidivism with respect to suspense fictions hardly seems to portend any psychological abnormality or pathology. It is well known that successful suspense films like *Raiders of the Lost Ark, Die Hard,* and *The Fugitive* require repeat audiences in order to be the blockbusters that they are, and it is also a fact that there are classic suspense stories, like "The Most Dangerous Game" by Richard Connell, that are often reread without diminution in their capacity to deliver a thrill. Furthermore, there are lots of classic suspense films (like *North by Northwest*), as well as TV and radio shows, that entice re-viewing and relistening.

So there is, in short, too much recidivism for it to be regarded as so pathologically abnormal that it requires psychoanalysis, unless nearly everyone is to be diagnosed. Yet, nevertheless, the phenomenon is still strange enough – indeed, some researchers even call it *anomalous suspense*[2] – that an account is in order of the way in which it can be rational for a reader or a viewer to feel suspense about events concerning whose outcomes the audience is certain.

To state the paradox involved here at greater length, we may begin with the assumption that, conceptually, suspense entails uncertainty. Uncertainty is a necessary condition for suspense. When uncertainty is removed from a situation, suspense evaporates. Putatively, if we come to know that the heroine will not be sawed in half, or that she will be, then we should no longer feel suspense. Moreover, if a situation lacks uncertainty altogether, no sense of suspense can intelligibly arise. It would be irrational for people to feel suspense in such contexts. And yet, apparently rational people are seized by suspense on re-encountering well-remembered films like Alfred Hitchcock's *The Thirty-Nine Steps* or novels like Tom Clancy's *Patriot Games.* Indeed, such consumers often seek out these fictions in order to experience once more that same thrill of suspense that they savored on their first encounter with the fiction. But surely, then, they must be irrational.

Of course, one might try to explain away the recidivism here by saying that with something like *The Thirty-Nine Steps,* filmgoers do not return for the suspense, but for something else – Hitchcock's cinematic artistry, the undeniable humor, the acting, the ambience, and so on. And undoubtedly, these features of the film, among others, certainly warrant reviewing. However, although we need to acknowledge that such features might reasonably motivate recidivism, it is not plausible to suppose that we can rid ourselves of the paradox of suspense by hypothesizing that every case of recidivism can be fully explained away by reference to good-making features of the fiction that have nothing to do with suspense. For recidivism may recur not only with respect to works of substantial literary merit by people like Greene, Elmore Leonard, and Eric Ambler or works of substantial cinematic achievement by people like Hitchcock, Fritz Lang, and Carol Reed; we may also be swept into the thrall of suspense on the occasion of re-viewing a fairly pedestrian exercise like *Straw Dogs.*

In some cases, our propensity to be recaptivated by an already encountered suspense fiction may be explained by the fact that we have forgotten how it ends. This happens often. However, I do not think this can account for every case; I know it does not apply to my forty-ninth re-viewing of *King Kong.* Instead, I think that we must face the paradox head-on. There are examples – I think quite a lot of examples – where the consumers of fiction find themselves in the enjoyable hold of suspense while responding to stories, read, heard, or seen previously, whose outcomes they remember with perfect clarity; in fact, quite frequently, these audiences have sought out these already familiar fictions with the express expectation that they will re-experience the pleasurable surge of consternation and thrill that they associate with suspense once again.

But how can they rationally expect to re-experience suspense if they know – and know that they know – the outcome of the fictional events that give rise to suspense? For, *ex hypothesi,* suspense requires uncertainty and I certainly know how *The Thirty-Nine Steps, This Gun for Hire,* and *King Kong* end. To put it formulaically, the paradox of suspense – which might be more accurately regarded as an instance of the paradox of recidivism[3] – may be stated in the following way:

1. If a fiction is experienced with suspense by an audience, then the outcome of the events that give rise to the suspense must be uncertain to audiences.
2. It is a fact that audiences experience fictions with suspense in cases where they have already seen, heard, or read the fictions in question.
3. But if audiences have already seen, heard, or read a fiction, then they know (and are certain) of the relevant outcomes.

Although each of the propositions in this triad seems acceptable considered in isolation, when conjoined they issue in a contradiction. In order to solve the paradox of suspense, that contradiction must be confronted. However, before we are in a position to dismantle this contradiction, we need a more fine-grained account of what is involved in suspense.

A THEORY OF THE NATURE OF SUSPENSE

Before proceeding further, it will be useful to be clear about our topic.[4] First, we are talking about suspense as an emotional response to *narrative fictions.* Inasmuch as we are focusing on fictions, we are not talking about suspense with respect to "real-life" experiences, although some comments about the relation between the two will be made. Furthermore, inasmuch as we are speaking about narratives, we are not talking about so-called musical suspense.

Suspense, as I am using the term, is an emotional response to narrative fictions. Moreover, these responses can occur in reaction to two levels of fictional articulation. They can evolve in reaction to whole narratives, or in response to discrete scenes or sequences within a larger narrative whose overall structure may or may not be suspenseful. For example, the attack on Jack Ryan's home is a suspenseful episode or sequence in Tom Clancy's novel *Patriot Games,* which novel, on the whole, is suspenseful, whereas the ride of the Klan to the rescue in D. W. Griffith's film *The Birth of a Nation* is a suspenseful sequence within a work that is probably not best categorized as a suspense film.

Sometimes fictions are categorized as suspense because they contain suspenseful scenes, especially where those scenes come near the end and appear to "wrap up" the fiction. In other cases, the entire structure of a fiction appears suspenseful – not only are there suspenseful scenes, but these suspenseful episodes segue into larger, overarching suspense structures. For example, in *This Gun for Hire,* scenes in which Anne Crowder averts discovery and death are not only locally suspenseful; they also play a role in sustaining our abiding suspense across the whole fiction about whether she can stop the outbreak of war by virtue of what she knows, a prospect about which we are highly uncertain, because she confronts so many dangers, but which uncertainty is kept alive every time she eludes apprehension or, at least, destruction.

Finally, before proceeding, it needs to be emphasized that the emotion of suspense takes as its object the moments leading up to the outcome about which we are uncertain. As the frenzied horses thunder toward the precipice, pulling a wagonload of children toward death, we feel suspense: Will they be saved or not? As long as that question is vital, and the outcome is uncertain, we are in a state of suspense. Once the outcome is fixed, however, the state is no longer suspense. If the wagon hurtles over the edge, we feel sorrow and anguish; if the children are saved, we feel relief and joy.

However, suspense is not a response to the outcome; it pertains to the moments leading up to the outcome, when the outcome is uncertain. Once the outcome is finalized and we are apprised of it, the emotion of suspense gives way to other emotions. Moreover, the emotion we feel in those moments leading up to the outcome is suspense whether the outcome, once known, is the one we favored or not.

Suspense is an emotion that besets us when we are confronted with narrative fictions that focus our attention on courses of events about whose outcomes, in the standard case, we are acutely aware that we are uncertain. However, suspense fictions are not the only narrative fictions that traffic in uncertainty. So, in order to refine our conception of suspense, an instructive first step is to differentiate suspense from other forms of narrative uncertainty, of which, undoubtedly, mystery is the most obvious.

The mystery story, which engenders a sense of mystery in us, is a near relative to suspense fiction. Indeed, it seems to me that the two species are so close that some theorists often confuse them.[5] However, although they belong to the same genus – call it fictions of uncertainty – they are clearly distinct. For in mysteries in the classical detection mode, we are characteristically uncertain about what has happened in the past, whereas with suspense fictions we are uncertain about what will happen.[6]

In mysteries in the classical detective mode, our uncertainty about the past usually revolves around how a crime was committed and by whom. This is why this sort of fiction is most frequently referred to as a *whodunit*. The TV programs *Perry Mason* and *Murder, She Wrote* are perfect examples of the whodunit. To become engaged in a whodunit is to be drawn into speculation about who killed the nasty uncle, along with the related questions of how and why it was done. We conjecture about an event whose cause, although fixed, is unknown to us. Of course, the cause will be revealed in the process of the detective's analysis of the case, but of that outcome we remain uncertain until it is pronounced.

However, our uncertainty here does have a structured horizon of anticipation. The outcome about which we are uncertain has as many possible shapes as we have suspects. If the nasty uncle could have been killed by the maid, the cousin, the butler, or the egyptologist, then our uncertainty is distributed across these four possibilities. A mystery of the classical whodunit variety prompts us to ask a question about whose answer we are uncertain and about which we entertain as many possible answers as there are suspects. But suspense is different.

With suspense, the question we are prompted to ask does not have an indefinite number of possible answers, but only two. Will the heroine be sawed in half or not? Moreover, when looking at the distribution of answers available in a mystery fiction, one realizes that one has no principled guarantee that the competing answers are ultimately exclusive. After all, some or even all of the suspects can be in cahoots or, as occurs in *Murder on the Orient Express,* a knave can be killed by more than one culprit. So, the classical detective story not only encourages uncertainty about an indefinitely variable number of answers to the question of whodunit, but those answers need not bear any special logical relation to each other.

However, in the case of suspense, the course of events in question can have only two outcomes, and those potential outcomes stand in relation to each other as logical contraries – either the heroine will be torn apart by the buzzsaw or she will not. Both mystery fictions and suspense fictions confront us with questions, but the way in which those questions structure our uncertainty differentiates the two kinds of fictions. For with mystery, our uncertainty is distributed over as many possible answers as there are suspects, whereas with suspense, we are "suspended" between no more than two answers, which answers stand in binary opposition. The answers we entertain with respect to mystery fictions are, in principle, indeterminate and logically nonexclusive, whereas the answers pertinent to suspense are binary and logically opposed.

However, even if we have established that suspense proper in fictions of uncertainty takes hold only when the course of events that commands our attention is one whose horizon of expectations is structured in terms of two possible but logically incompatible outcomes, we still have not told the whole story about fictional suspense. For clearly, one can imagine fictions in which characters and readers alike confess that they simply do not know whether it will snow or not tomorrow (in the land of the story), but where, nevertheless, at the same time, there is still no question of suspense.

Of course, the reason for this is obvious, once we think in terms of "real-life" suspense. For in "real life," suspense only takes charge when we care about those future outcomes about which we are uncertain. We are not inclined toward suspense about whether or not the bus will start unless we have some stake or concern in its starting or not starting. Where we are impervious to outcomes, even though the relevant outcomes are uncertain, there is no suspense, because "real-life" suspense requires a certain emotional involvement with the outcome, along with uncertainty about it. Interests, concerns, or at least preferences must come into play. I feel suspense about the results of my blood test not only because I am uncertain about what they will be, but also because I have a vested interest in them.

Similarly, when it comes to fictions, suspense cannot be engendered simply by means of uncertainty; the reader must also be encouraged to form some preferences about the alternative outcomes. As Rodell put it, speaking from the author's point of view, suspense is "the art of making the reader care about what happens next."[7] Moreover, as an empirical conjecture, let me hypothesize that in suspense fiction, the way in which the author typically provokes audience involvement is through morality.

"Real-life" suspense requires not only uncertainty about which outcome will eventuate from a course of events; it also requires that we be concerned about those outcomes. In constructing suspense, authors must find some way of engaging audience concern. Of course, the author has no way of knowing the personal concerns and vested interests of each and every audience member. So in order to enlist our concern, the author must find some very general interest that all or most of the audience is likely to share. One such interest is what is morally right. That is, one way in which the author can invest the audience with concern over a prospective outcome is to assure that one of the logically opposed outcomes in the fiction is morally correct as well as uncertain. In the novel *Airport* by Arthur Hailey, it is morally correct that the jetliner not be destroyed, but whether this outcome will eventuate is uncertain; similarly, in the novel *Seven Days in May* by Fletcher Knebel and Charles Bailey what is presented and perceived to be morally correct – democracy as we know and love it – is at risk.

If the emotion of suspense presupposes not only uncertainty but concern, then presumably a crucial task in constructing a suspense fiction involves finding some way in which to engage the concern of audiences, of whom the author possesses little or no personal knowledge. Nevertheless, the author is typically able to overcome this debit by resorting to morality in order to appeal to the ethical interests of viewers and readers alike. For, all things being equal, the general audience will recognize that sawing the heroine in half is morally wrong, and this will provoke concern about an outcome of the event about which they are uncertain. Likewise, in *This Gun for Hire,* it is presented and perceived that averting war is morally correct, whereas in *The Guns of Navarone* it is given and accepted that the destruction of the Nazi battery is morally right. In suspense fictions, the audience is provided, often aggressively, with a stake in one of the alternatives by having its moral sensibility drawn to prefer one of the uncertain outcomes.

In general in suspense fictions, then, one of the possible outcomes of the relevant course of events is morally correct, but uncertain. In *Patriot Games,* it is righteous that Ryan's family and the Prince and Princess of Wales survive, but when Miller and the terrorists take over Ryan's property, that survival is uncertain. Indeed, it is not merely uncertain; the odds are against it. Moreover, this is the pattern that recurs most frequently in suspense fictions from classic stories like Karl May's *In the Desert* to bestsellers like Robert Ludlum's *The Scorpio Illusion.* There are two competing outcomes to the relevant course of events, and one of those outcomes, although morally correct, is improbable or uncertain or unlikely, whereas the logically alternative outcome is evil but likely or probable or nearly certain. Or, to be even more precise, suspense takes control where the course of events that is the object of the emotional state points to two logically opposed outcomes, one of which is evil or immoral but probable or likely, and the other of which is moral, but improbable or unlikely or only as probable as the evil outcome.

Of course, the defeat of the moral outcome cannot be an absolutely foregone conclusion; there must be some possibility that the good can triumph. That is why there can be no suspense about whether the protagonist in the movie *Philadelphia* can survive AIDS. For suspense requires that, although what is presented and perceived to be morally right be an improbable option, it must be a live option (i.e., not a completely foregone conclusion) nonetheless. And, for related reasons, in stories, where it is given in the fictional world that the hero cannot be defeated, as it is in many of the scenes in the film *Crow,* there is no suspense.

Summarizing then, as a response to fiction, generally suspense is

1. an emotional concomitant to the narration of a course of events
2. which course of events points to two logically opposed outcomes
3. whose opposition is made salient (to the point of preoccupying the audience's attention)[8] and
4. where one of the alternative outcomes is morally correct but improbable (although live) or at least no more probable than its alternative, while
5. the other outcome is morally incorrect or evil, but probable.

Surely this formula works for run-of-the-mill cases of suspense – as the heroine is inexorably pulled toward the buzzsaw, it seems hardly likely that she will live. On the other hand, the alternative outcome, her death, is evil but probable.

Perhaps one way to confirm this formulation would be to accept it provisionally as a hypothesis and to see how well it accords with our pretheoretical sorting of the data; another way might be to use it as a recipe for constructing fictions and to assess how viable it is in inducing audiences to experience suspense.

This analysis of suspense in fiction corresponds nicely with the definition of suspense advanced by the psychologists Ortony, Clore, and Collins, who stated: "We view suspense as involving a Hope emotion and a Fear emotion coupled with the cognitive state of uncertainty."[9] What we hope for is the moral outcome (which is improbable or uncertain), and what we fear is the evil outcome (which is more likely).

The evil that plays such a key role in suspense fictions need not be human evil, but may be natural evil, as it is in the novel *Jaws* or the film *Earthquake*. In these cases, we still regard the destruction of human beings by brute, unthinking nature to be morally offensive. Of course, it is generally the case that suspense fictions involve pitting moral good against human moral evil: the settlers against the rustlers, the Allies against the Nazis, civilization against the barbarians.

Moreover, the reader's or spectator's moral allegiances in response to a suspense fiction do not always precisely correlate with his or her normal repertory of moral responses, and, indeed, the audience's moral responses are frequently shaped by fiction itself. For example, caper films represent persons involved in perpetrating crimes that we do not customarily consider to be upstanding ethically. However, the characters in such fictions are standardly possessed of certain striking virtues such that, in the absence of emphasis of countervailing virtues in their opposite number, or possibly given the emphasis on the outright vice of their opponents, we are encouraged to ally ourselves morally with the caper. The virtues in question here – such as strength, fortitude, ingenuity, bravery, competence, beauty, generosity, and so on – are more often than not Grecian, rather than Christian. And it is because the characters exhibit these virtues – it is because we perceive (and are led to perceive) these characters as virtuous – that we cast our moral allegiance with them.

Quite frequently in mass fictions, characters are designated as morally good in virtue of their treatment of supporting characters, especially ones who are poor, old, weak, lame, oppressed, unprotected women, children, helpless animals, and so on. Good characters typically treat such people with courtesy and respect, whereas your standard snarling villain, if he notices them at all, usually does so in order to abuse them – to harass the woman sexually, to taunt the child, to kick the dog, or worse. With respect to mass fictions, we may generalize this point by saying that the protagonists typically treat their "inferiors" with courtesy and respect, whereas the villains treat such characters with contempt and disdain, if not violence. I suspect that it is fairly obvious that when it comes to mass entertainments, there is a clear-cut rationale for investing the protagonists with democratic or egalitarian virtue, whereas the villains are painted in the colors of elitist vice.

As these conjectures suggest, it is my view that character – especially at the level of virtue – is a critical lever for guiding the audience's moral perception of the action. This is why one may find oneself morally sympathetic to characters who represent moral causes with which one usually does not align oneself – for example, one may find oneself rooting for the colonialists in *Zulu* even if one is, on the whole, anti-imperialist. Here we are drawn into the film's system of moral evaluations by its portrayal – or lack thereof – of characters with respect to virtues. That is, in many suspense fictions – involving imperialism, war, international espionage, and the like – the protagonists are represented as having some virtues, whereas their opposite number are presented either as having no virtues whatsoever or, more pointedly, only negative personal and interpersonal attributes. And in these cases, the balance of virtue is sufficient to fix our moral assessments of the situation.

If the protagonists are represented as possessed of some virtues and their opponents are less virtuous, altogether bereft of virtue, or downright vicious, suspense can take hold because the efforts of the protagonists and their allies will be recognized as morally correct in the ethical system of the film. Of course, it is probably the case that generally the actions of the protagonists are morally correct in accordance with some prevailing ethical norms that are shared by the majority of the audience. However, in cases in which this consensus does not obtain, the protagonist's possession of saliently underlined virtues will project the moral valuations of the fiction and, indeed, incline the audience toward accepting that perspective as its own. Thus, it turns out that sometimes even an antagonist can serve as an object of suspense, as long as he or she is presented as possessed of some virtues.[10]

The emphasis that I have just placed on the relevance of the characters dovetails significantly with some recent psychological research.[11] There appears to be experimental evidence that suspense is generated in cases in which spectators or readers are said to "like" characters. However, when one looks closely at the factors that contribute to this pro-disposition toward characters on the part of spectators or readers, the most important ones seem to be moral. For example, whether the character is an antisocial recluse, a good man, or a fine individual is relevant to the spectators' or readers' registration of suspense.[12]

Some researchers are prone to discussing this relation between the characters and the spectators in terms of identification.[13] But I, like others, think this is ill advised, insofar as most often characters and spectators are cognitively and emotionally too unalike to warrant any presumption of identity – that is, we know more than Oedipus does for a large part of *Oedipus Rex* and, at the conclusion, when Oedipus is racked by guilt, we are not; we feel pity for him.[14] Thus, it makes little sense to talk about identification in cases like this, which are quite frequent, and, if we can do without identification in cases like this one, economy suggests that we can probably do without it in other cases as well.

Of course, I would not say that suspense necessarily requires that we focus on characters who are presented as virtuous. Suspense may take hold when our attention is not riveted on individual characters but on movements that are perceived to be morally correct – as in the case of the socialist mass hero in films like *Potemkin*. Nevertheless, I suspect that we will find empirically that more fictions project the moral assessments relevant for suspense through the virtues of individual characters than through the rightness of social movements perceived as aggregates.

The factors that I have hypothesized that go into appreciating the morality of the outcomes in a suspense framework are broader than what would be considered matters of morality in certain ethical theories, because in my account, what constitutes the morally correct is not simply a matter of ethical purposes and efforts, but virtues, including pagan virtues, and mere opposition to natural evil. Admittedly, this is a wider conception than what many ethical philosophers would include under the rubric of "morality," but I think that it does converge on the way in which people tend to use the terms "good" and "bad" in ordinary language when they are speaking nonpractically and nonprudentially; and, furthermore, I suspect that one should predict that such an expanded, everyday conception of morality would be the one toward which suspense fictions, which aspire to popularity, would gravitate.

Suspense requires not only that consumers rate certain alternative outcomes to be moral and evil; suspense, with respect to fiction, also requires that the moral outcome be perceived to be a live but improbable outcome, or, at least, no more probable than the evil outcome, whereas the evil outcome is generally far more probable than the moral one. That is, readers, listeners, and viewers of fictions not only rate the alternative outcomes in terms of morality, but also in terms of probability. Of course, the sense of probability that I have in mind here is the probability of the outcomes prior to the moment in the fiction at which one of the alternatives is actualized, because after that moment there is no uncertainty.

Moreover, I am talking here about the probability of the event in the fictional world, or, to state it differently, the probability internal to the fiction, or what falls within the scope of the fictional operator (i.e., "It is fictional that..."). It is the audience's access to this internal probability (henceforth usually called just "probability") that is relevant, because from a viewpoint external to the fiction, there is no probability that King Kong will be killed because King Kong does not exist.[15]

Suspense correlates with the course of events prior to, but not including, the relevant outcomes. For after one of the rival alternatives eventuates, there can be no suspense. Morever, the sense of internal improbability that possesses the audience for the duration of its experience of suspense is relative to the information provided within the scope of the fiction operator to the audience by the narrative up to and including the moments when we are gripped by suspense. This is meant to preclude the relevance of such "real-world" knowledge, as that the hero always wins the day, from our estimates of the probabilities of certain fictional events. Instead, we gauge the relevant probabilities relative to the information available in the story preceding and during the interlude of suspense but bracket the information available after and including the moment when one outcome emerges victorious.

The idea of probability that the spectator works with is not technical; it is not a product of deriving probability from a calculus. Rather, when the reader, listener, or spectator entertains the thought that some outcome is either internally probable or improbable, that means that he or she thinks it is likely or unlikely to occur, or that it can reasonably be expected to occur or not, given all the available information provided for the consumer by the relevant parts of the fiction. This hardly requires a consumer deriving specialized probability rankings subvocally; instead, just as I surmise immediately and tacitly that a baseball headed toward a bay window is likely to shatter it, so my estimate that, in a given fiction, it is unlikely that the detailment of the bullet train can be averted, requires no specialized calculations.

It seems to me that much of the suspense sequence in a novel or a film or whatever is preoccupied with establishing and reemphasizing the audience's sense of the relevant probabilities of alternative lines of action. That is, it appears to be the case that with most suspense sequences we are already apprised of the moral status of the rival parties before the various episodes of suspense take hold. So, what primarily comprises those interludes – at least most frequently – is an emphasis on the relative probabilities of the competing outcomes.

In film and TV, suspense scenes are often elaborated with cross-cutting.[16] As Lois Lane and Jimmy Olsen are apprehended by bandits, we cut to Superman who is struggling to resist the effects of kryptonite. This establishes the probability that evil will befall Lois Lane and Jimmy Olsen and the improbability of their rescue by Superman. By the time that the bandits are mere seconds away from executing Lois and Jimmy, there is a cross-cut to Superman finally aloft, but because he is so far away, the shot reemphasizes how unlikely it is that he will be able to save them.

Likewise, toward the end of *The Guns of Navarone,* the director, J. Lee Thompson, cuts between shots of the British rescue armada and shots of the ammunition hoist for the Nazi artillery, stopping just before the demolition charges that the Allies hope will take out the cannons. But each cut, insofar as they carry the information that the charges fail to detonate, makes it more probable in the fiction that the guns will have the opportunity to wreak havoc on the fleet once it is in range. A great deal of the work that goes into a suspense sequence – whether it is visual or verbal – depends on keeping the relative probabilities of the alternative outcomes of the relevant course of events vividly before the audience.

Certain sorts of events – including chases, escapes, and rescues, among others – are staples of popular fiction just because they so naturally accommodate suspense, possessing, by definition, logically exclusive, uncertain outcomes that can be so readily invested with moral significance. Also, suspense scenes often feature such recurring devices as time bombs. In my view, bombs attached to fizzling fuses or ticking timepieces work so well in generating suspense because, as each moment passes, time is running out on the good, and therefore evil is becoming ever more likely, even as the prospects for righteousness become more and more improbable. I would not want to diminish the importance of time bombs and chase scenes for suspense. I only urge that one be wary of reducing suspense to these devices. Rather, the serviceability of the devices themselves needs to be explained by the kind of general theory of suspense fiction that I have advanced in this section.[17]

SOLVING THE PARADOX OF SUSPENSE

Suspense, in general, is an emotional state. It is the emotional response that one has to situations in which an outcome that concerns one is uncertain. Uncertainty and concern are necessary conditions or formal criteria for suspense. Where care and uncertainty unite in a single situation, suspense is an appropriate or fitting emotional response. That is, suspense is an intelligible response to such a situation. If I have no concern whatsoever for the outcome in question, a response in terms of suspense is unintelligible. Indeed, if I claim to be in a state of suspense about something about which I genuinely protest that I have not one jot of concern, then I sound as though I am contradicting myself; but if I believe that an outcome that I care about is uncertain, then suspense is in order.

The care and concern required for suspense are engendered in audiences of fictions by means of morality. That is, the audience is given a stake in the outcome of certain events in the fiction when the relevant outcome is presented as morally righteous, at the same time that the rival outcome is represented as evil. When the righteous outcome appears improbable, relative to the information provided in the story up to that point, suspense is a fitting or intelligible reaction.

Improbability, relative to the information available at the relevant point in the fiction, and moral righteousness are typically the standard conditions or formal criteria for suspense when it comes to fiction. Where a morally righteous outcome is imperiled to the point where it is improbable, our concern for the morally right can be transformed into suspense. For consternation at the prospect that the morally correct is in danger or that the good is at risk is an appropriate or fitting response. That is, just as fear is an appropriate response to the prospect of harm, suspense is an appropriate response to a situation in which the morally good is imperiled or at risk.

Of course, when we say that fear is an appropriate response to the prospect of harm, we do not thereby predict that everyone will feel fear when confronting what is harmful. After all, bungee jumpers, lion tamers, and mountain climbers do exist. Nevertheless, it is always intelligible to feel fear in the presence of the harmful, and it is always intelligible to feel suspense when we perceive the good to be imperiled.

When we feel suspense with regard to our own projects and prospects, it is because we believe that some outcome about which we care – say winning at bingo – is not certain. Here, the cognitive component of our mental state is a belief. We believe that it is uncertain or improbable that we shall win at bingo. But when it comes to fictions, we need to modify our conception of the cognitive component of our emotional states; since my anger at Leontes in *The Winter's Tale* cannot be based on my belief that he is an unjust person, because I do not believe that there is someone, Leontes, such that he is an unjust person. Leontes is a fictional character, and I know it.

However, it is not the case that the only mental state that can do the requisite cognitive work when it comes to emotion is belief. Emotions may be rooted in thoughts as well as beliefs.[18] What is the difference? If we describe believing *p* as a matter of holding a proposition in the mind as asserted, then thinking *p*, in contrast, is a matter of entertaining a proposition in the mind unasserted, as one does when I say "Suppose I am Charles the Bald."

Furthermore, one can engender emotional states by holding propositions before the mind unasserted. Thus, when I stand near the edge of the roof of a high building and I entertain the thought that I am losing my footing, I can make myself feel a surge of vertigo. I need not believe that I am losing my footing; I merely entertain the thought. And the thought, or the propositional content of the thought (that I am losing my footing), can be sufficient for playing a role in causing the chill of fear in my bloodstream. For emotions may rest on thoughts, and not merely on beliefs.

Fictions, moreover, are readily conceived to be stories that authors intend readers, listeners, and viewers to imagine. Indeed, fictions are the sorts of communication in which the author intends the consumer to recognize the authorial intention that the consumer imagine the story. That is, in making fictions, the author is intentionally presenting consumers with situations that they are meant to entertain in thought. The author, in presenting his or her novel as fiction, in effect, says to readers "hold these propositions before your mind unasserted" – that is, "suppose p," or "entertain p unasserted," or "contemplate p as a supposition."[19] Furthermore, insofar as thoughts, as distinct from beliefs, can support emotional responses, we may have emotional responses to fictions concerning situations that we believe do not exist. For we can imagine or suppose that they exist, and entertaining the propositional content of the relevant thoughts can figure in the etiology of an emotional state.

Needless to say, in maintaining that the imagination of the consumer of fiction is engaged here I do not mean to suggest that the activity is free or unbounded. The consumer's imaginative activity is, of course, guided by the object – by the fiction in question. That object – the fiction – has certain properties. Specifically, it presents certain situations as having certain properties (in terms of morality and internal probability), which properties, given the psychology of normal consumers, induces certain emotional responses or, as Hume might have it, sentiments in us.

That is, I maintain that the fictions in question can be identified as suspenseful in terms of features of the fiction (such as the logical exclusivity of outcomes, and their morality and internal probability ratings) that we can specify independently of the responses they induce in a regular fashion in consumers of fiction. These features are naturally suited to raise the affect of suspense in us. The extension of what counts as being suspenseful in fiction is, then, codetermined by the normal (as opposed to the ideal) appreciator's tendency to respond with feelings of suspense and the independently characterizable structural features of suspense fictions adumbrated earlier.[20] In the relevant cases, the appreciator's attention must be focused on those structural features of the fiction, and his or her imagination is guided or controlled by them. In such cases, the thoughts that he or she is prompted to entertain as unasserted by what is in the fiction (as opposed to whatever passing fancies fleetingly strike her) will raise appropriate feelings of suspense.

Nor should it seem bizarre that thinking various thoughts, in addition to having certain beliefs, should figure in the generation of emotional states. For from an evolutionary perspective, it is certainly a distinctive advantage that humans have the capacity to be moved by thinking p as well as by believing p, because this capacity enables humans to be educated about all kinds of dangers that may come to pass in the future, but that do not exist and do not confront us in the here and now. The imagination is surely an asset from the Darwinian point of view; it provides a way in which not only cognition but the emotions, as well, can be prepared for situations that have not yet arisen. Adolescents vicariously learn about love and parental responsibility by imagining these things, and these acts of imagination serve to educate their feelings.

Certain emotions are cognitively impenetrable, and this impenetrability can be explained in terms of the adaptive advantages it bestows on the organism. Adopting the role of armchair evolutionary biologists, perhaps we can speculate that, in the case of many emotions, they can be induced by mere thoughts and thereby are insulated from exclusive causal dependency on particular beliefs, because of the overall adaptive advantage this delivers to humans in terms of educating the emotions in the response to situations and situation types not already at hand.

However, be that as it may, suspense fictions present audiences with situations that we are to imagine. For example, we entertain (unasserted) the thoughts that the train is about to derail with the much-needed medical supplies and that this outcome is all but unavoidable. Because we entertain this thought as unasserted, we do not call the police to alert them. Nevertheless, this thinking does help generate the affect of suspense in us. And this affect, in the case under discussion, is appropriate, fitting, and intelligible. For it is always intelligible that we feel consternation when we entertain the supposition that the good – something that is morally correct – is threatened or is unlikely to come to pass.

What does all this have to do with the paradox of suspense? According to the paradox, if a fiction is experienced by readers, listeners, or viewers as suspense, then the outcome of the events that give rise to suspense must be uncertain to said listeners, readers, and viewers. On the other hand, it seems that it is simply a fact that audiences experience suspense in reaction to fictions they have already seen, heard, or read. But how is that possible, since if they've already seen, heard, or read the fiction, then they know how the fiction ends – that is, they know the relevant outcome – and, therefore, they cannot believe, for example, that the righteous alternative is uncertain? This contradicts the earlier presumption that audiences gripped by suspense must be uncertain of the outcome.

However, if what has been claimed about the emotions in general, and the emotion of suspense in particular, is right, perhaps there is a way out of this conundrum. A presupposition of the paradox is that the response of suspense on the part of audiences requires that they be uncertain of the relevant outcomes. I understand this to mean that the audiences must *believe* that the relevant outcomes are uncertain or uncertain to them. For example, they must believe that the relevant moral outcome is improbable. Yet the audience cannot believe this if they actually know the relevant outcomes already, because they have encountered the fiction in question beforehand.

But notice that the problem here resides in the assumption that suspense would only take hold if the audience believes the outcome is uncertain. But why suppose this? The audience may not believe that the relevant outcome is uncertain or improbable but, nevertheless, the audience may entertain the thought that the relevant outcome is uncertain or improbable. That is, even though we know otherwise, we may entertain (as unasserted) the proposition that a certain morally good outcome is uncertain or improbable. If an emotional response can rest on a thought, then there is no reason to remain mystified about the way in which audiences can be seized by suspense even though they know how everything will turn out.

For they are entertaining the thought that the morally correct outcome is improbable relative to the information within the scope of the fiction operator that is available up to the relevant point in the fiction. That is, the paradox of suspense disappears once we recall that emotions may be generated on the basis of thoughts, rather than only on the basis of beliefs. Indeed, emotions may be generated in the course of entertaining thoughts that are at variance with our beliefs.

Nor is the recidivist reader, listener, or viewer of suspense fictions irrational or perverse in any way. For in contemplating the proposition unasserted – that the heroine in all probability is likely to be killed – the recidivist, despite what he or she knows about the last-minute rescue, recognizes a situation in which the good is unlikely, and it is always appropriate or intelligible to undergo consternation in reaction to even the thought of such a prospect.

In terms of the way in which I set forth the paradox of suspense in the opening section of this chapter, the strategy that I have just employed to dissolve the paradox involves denying its first premise, namely, that if a fiction is experienced with suspense by an audience, then the outcome of the events that give rise to suspense must be uncertain to the audience. This seems to me to be the best way to dispose of the contradiction.[21]

Competing proposals might suggest that we reconsider the second proposition in our inconsistent triad, to wit: It is a fact that audiences experience fictions with suspense in cases where they have already seen, heard, or read the fictions in question. The motivation for this seems to be a theoretical conviction that it is just impossible to undergo suspense when one knows how a fiction will end – impossible, that is, for anyone who holds the first and the last propositions in the paradox. But here it seems to me that theory is recasting reality in its own image; for it appears obvious that people do re-experience suspense with certain fictions with which they are already familiar. As I noted earlier, the existence of blockbuster movies like *The Fugitive* and *Jurassic Park* depends on recidivists for their astronomical success; it is the people who go back to see the films from six to sixteen to sixty times who turn these films into box-office legends.

Perhaps a more popular route in negotiating the paradox of suspense is to deny the last proposition in the triad – if audiences have already seen, heard, or read a fiction, then they know (and are certain) of the relevant outcomes. One way to do this is to postulate that when confronting fictions, audiences are induced into a special sort of psychological state that might be described in terms of self-deception, denial, or disavowal. This way of dealing with the paradox accepts the phenomenon of anomalous or recidivist suspense as contradictory and then postulates disavowal as a psychological mechanism that enables us to live with the contradiction – it is a mechanism that suffers mental states during which one both knows and does not know by repressing the former. Thus, the disavowal account resolves the paradox (or contradiction) of recidivist suspense by portraying the audience as irrational.

Psychoanalytic theorists are particularly prone to this mode of explanation, because they believe that people are extremely susceptible to disavowal anyway.

For example, male fetishists – of whom (if psychoanalytic film theorist Laura Mulvey is correct[22]) there are more than you might expect – are said to be involved pervasively in the disavowal of their knowledge that women lack penises because that knowledge would stir up male anxieties about castration.

Yet if there is some comparable process of disavowal in operation when audiences consume fictions, then this sort of explanation requires, it seems to me, a parallel motivation for our denial or disavowal of our knowledge of the outcomes of fictions. That is, why would we be compelled to disavow our knowledge of the end of a story? It is hard to imagine generalizable answers to that question.

Recently, a nonpsychoanalytic explanation of anomalous suspense, which also appears to undermine the supposition that recidivist audiences in suspense contexts unequivocally know the relevant outcomes, was advanced by Gerrig. He wrote:

> What I wish to suggest, in fact, is that anomalous suspense arises not because of some special strategic activity but rather as a natural consequence of the structure of cognitive processing. Specifically, I propose that readers experience anomalous suspense because an expectation of uniqueness is incorporated within the cognitive processes that guide the expectations of narratives. … My suggestion is that anomalous suspense arises because our experience of narratives incorporates the strong likelihood that we never repeat a game. Note that this expectation of uniqueness need not be conscious. My claim is that our moment-by-moment processes evolve in response to the brute fact of nonrepetition.[23]

For Gerrig, we are possessed of a uniqueness heuristic, which evolved under the pressure to secure fast, optimal strategies rather than massively time-consuming, rational strategies of information processing; the fact that we can undergo the experience of anomalous suspense is simply a surprising consequence or a kind of peripheral fallout from one of the optimizing heuristics that we have evolved. Gerrig sees this heuristic as an expectation of uniqueness that resides in the cognitive architecture linking inputs to outputs.

In some ways, Gerrig's resolution of the problem of anomalous or recidivist suspense is more palatable than what the disavowal model promises. However, it must be noted that Gerrig's approach still does render recidivists irrational, even if in the long run they are victims of a higher rationality (a.k.a. optimality). And this seems to me to be a problem.

Recidivist readers, listeners, and viewers of suspense fictions very frequently reencounter fictions with the express expectation of reexperiencing the thrill they experienced on earlier encounters. They remember the thrill, and they remember the story, too. Gerrig seems to argue that their cognitive processing of the story the second or sixtieth time around is insulated from that knowledge. This seems to me to be highly unlikely.

Think of a relatively simple version of the game show *Concentration* in which there are so few squares that it is very easy to hold all the matching pairs and the image fragments and the saying that solves the rebus in mind after the game is over.

Run the game several more times. Quickly, I predict, it will become boring. But how can it become boring if we have this uniqueness heuristic? On the other hand, one can sit through several showings of a suspense film like *The Terminator* and never become bored before one is thrown out of the theater. But if it is a uniqueness heuristic that explains anomalous suspense, shouldn't it also predict equal staying power in the *Concentration* example? But that seems hardly compelling.

Suspense recidivists are perfectly normal, and not for the reason that they, like everyone else with the same cognitive architecture, diverge from the canons of strict rationality for the sake of optimality. Rather, it is because it is perfectly intelligible that people respond to suspenseful situations in fictions with consternation, because not only beliefs, but also thoughts can give rise to emotions. Indeed, thoughts that are at variance with a person's beliefs can give rise to emotions. Thus, effectively asked to imagine – that is, to entertain the thought – that the good is at risk by the author of a fiction, the reader appropriately and intelligibly feels concern and suspense.

In this case, we focus our attention on the relevant, available information in the story up to and for the duration of the interlude in which suspense dominates. That we may not use our knowledge of earlier encounters with the fiction to drive away our feelings of suspense here is no more irrational than the fact that our knowledge of entertainment conventions or regularities, such as that the hero almost always prevails, does not compromise our feelings of suspense on a first encounter with a fiction, because our attention is riveted, within the scope of the fiction operator, to the unfolding of the story on a moment-to-moment basis. And so focused, our mind fills with the thought that the good is in peril, a prospect always in principle rationally worthy of emotional exercise.[24]

ART, NARRATIVE,
AND MORAL UNDERSTANDING

With much art, we are naturally inclined to speak of it in moral terms. Especially when considering things like novels, short stories, epic poems, plays, and movies, we seem to fall effortlessly into talking about them in terms of ethical significance – in terms of whether or which characters are virtuous or vicious, and about whether the work itself is moral or immoral, and perhaps whether it is sexist or racist. Undoubtedly, poststructuralists will choke on my use of the phrase "naturally inclined," just because they do not believe that humans are naturally inclined toward anything. But that general premise is as needlessly strong a presupposition

From: *Aesthetics and Ethics,* ed. by Jerrold Levinson (New York: Cambridge University Press, 1998), 126–60.

as it is patently false. And, furthermore, I hope to show that my talk of natural inclinations is hardly misplaced here, for we are prone to respond to the types of works in question in the language of moral assessment exactly because of the kinds of things they are.

Moreover, we do not merely make moral assessments of artworks as a whole and characters in particular; it is *also* the case that these moral assessments are *variable*. That is, we find some artworks to be morally good, while some others are not; some are exemplary, while some others are vicious and perhaps even pernicious; and finally other works may not appear to call for either moral approbation or opprobrium. So, though we very frequently do advance moral assessments of artworks, it is important to stress that we have a gamut of possible evaluative judgments at our disposal: from the morally good to the bad to the ugly, to the morally indifferent and the irrelevant. And it is this availability of different judgments that I am referring to as the variability of our moral assessments of artworks.

Very frequently, then, we make variable moral assessments of artworks. I take this comment to be no more than a pedestrian observation about our common practices of talking about art or, at least, certain kinds of art. But even if the observation is pedestrian, it is, oddly enough, hard to square with some of our major traditions in the philosophy of art. For the ideas (1) that we make moral assessments of art and (2) that these moral assessments are variable each offend certain well-known and deeply entrenched viewpoints in the philosophy of art, albeit in different ways.

First, there is the position in the philosophy of art – which may be called *autonomism* – that has exerted a great deal of influence on thinking about art since the eighteenth century and that continues to muddy our intuitions about art even today. Speaking very broadly, according to the autonomist, the artistic and the moral realms are separate. Art has nothing to do with moral goodness, or with badness, for that matter, and moral value neither contributes anything to nor subtracts anything from the overall value of the artwork. From the perspective of the autonomist, the fact, if it is a fact, that we spend so much time talking about morality with regard to so many artworks appears to be virtually unintelligible – perhaps it can be explained only by attributing deep and vast confusions to those who indulge in such talk.

For the autonomist, an essential differentiating feature of art is that it is separate from morality; this is the autonomist's underlying philosophical conviction. Thus, from the autonomist's point of view, that we make moral assessments of certain artworks is a mystery that must signal either our lack of taste or lack of understanding. For the autonomist, the problem is that we make moral assessments of artworks at all, since, philosophically, the autonomist is committed to the view that all artworks are separate from or exempted from considerations of morality.

On the other hand – to make matters more complex – we are also the beneficiaries of other philosophical traditions that, although they, contra autonomism, find no special problem in our making moral assessments of art, nevertheless consider it mysterious that our moral assessments should be variable. For one of these strands in the philosophy of art – call it *utopianism* – leads us to presume that, in virtue of its very nature, art, properly so called, is always morally uplifting, while yet another strand – call it *Platonism* – regards all art as morally suspect, once again due to its essential features. Both tendencies are clearly philosophical in the strong sense, inasmuch as their overall assessments of the morality of art are entailed by or rest on conjectures about the essential nature of art. And, though the utopian and Platonic traditions espouse opposite conclusions in this matter, they do at least appear to agree in precluding the possibility of *variable* moral assessments of artworks, since for the utopian all art is morally good, while for the Platonist all art is morally bad.

Undoubtedly, the Platonic tradition is the oldest and best known of the two.[1] This tradition situates art in ever-expanding circles of guilt. First, Plato himself chides art for proposing characters who are bad moral role models. But then – perhaps due to the recognition that there may be good moral role models in art – Plato argues that the problem is with the way in which art – mimetic art – is engaged and consumed. For that involves *identification,* and, for Plato, identifying with others is immediately morally suspicious. Here, of course, Plato was not simply thinking of designated actors taking on roles; he also believed that ordinary readers of dramas would become involved in a species of identification with others as well, inasmuch as they spoke the lines of characters. That is, in Athenian households, people would read plays aloud; thus, as they read the dialogue, Plato worried that they would somehow "become" someone else (namely, the character whose lines they recited).

This was putatively grounds for moral alarm, not only because the characters in question might be ethically vicious and because it would threaten Plato's ideal of the social division of labor, but also because it would destabilize the personality. Moreover, were one to challenge the generality of Plato's condemnation of art on the grounds that not all art is what Plato calls mimetic and, therefore, not mired in identification, Plato would respond with another argument, claiming that all art is by its nature aimed, in one way or another, at the emotions and, thereby, undermines the righteous reign of reason in the soul.

Nor is the Platonic spirit dead today. It thrives in our humanities departments, where all artworks have become the subject of systematic interrogation either for sins of commission – often in terms of their embodiment of bad role models or stereotypes – or for sins of omission – often in terms of people and viewpoints that have been left out. Furthermore, if none of these strategies succeeds in nailing the artwork, then it is always possible to excoriate it for – as followers of Lacan and Althusser like to say – positioning subjects, that is, for encouraging audiences to take themselves to be free, coherently unified subjects, a self-conception that is always thought to be a piece of ideologically engineered misrecognition and that is instilled by the formal structures of address of the mass communication media.[2] (Ironically enough, whereas Plato thought that the problem with art was that it destabilizes personalities, the contemporary Platonists of the Althusserian–Lacanian dispensation complain that art in fact stabilizes subjects, though for nefarious ideological purposes.)

Perhaps utopianism emerged as a response to Platonism. Once the Platonic prejudice was in the air, it called forth a rival that was its exact opposite number (a kind of situation that frequently occurs in philosophy). To the charge that all art is morally suspect, the utopian responds that in certain very deep respects art is by nature ultimately emancipatory. For Herbert Marcuse, for example, art is always on the side of the angels, because due to the ontology of fiction and representation, core artmaking practices, artworks have the capacity to show that the world can be otherwise, thus entailing the conviction that it is at least possible to change it – an obvious precondition for radical praxis.[3]

In all probability, Marcuse's idea owes something to Schiller's thought that insofar as the aesthetic imagination is free from nature – in fact, on Schiller's account, it gives form to nature through its free play – the aesthetic imagination is said to be a precondition for moral and political autonomy.[4] But, be that as it may, Marxists like Marcuse and Ernest Bloch nevertheless tend to think that art is essentially liberatory by virtue of the ways in which artworks, ontologically, are distinct from mere real things. In virtue of this contrast, art, so to say, is always on the side of freedom, as far as they are concerned. Indeed, Sartre thought that prose fiction writing was so indissolubly linked to freedom that he claimed it would be impossible to imagine a good novel in favor of any form of enslavement.[5]

The autonomist position is also often taken to be a response to Platonism, and there are perhaps even historical grounds for this conjecture. Inasmuch as the autonomist argues that art is essentially independent of morality and politics, the autonomist goes on to contend that aesthetic value is independent of the sort of consequentialist considerations that Plato and his followers raise. Art on the autonomist view is intrinsically valuable; it should not be subservient to ulterior or external or extrinsic purposes, such as producing moral consequences or inducing moral education. For the autonomist, anything devoted to such ulterior purposes could not be art, properly so called.

Autonomists are also able to bolster their case with supporting arguments. For example, they argue that moral assessment cannot be an appropriate measure of artistic value, since not all artworks possess a moral dimension. We can call this the *common-denominator argument,* because it presupposes that if any evaluative scale can be brought to bear on art, then it must be applicable to all art. That is, any measure of artistic merit must be perfectly general across the arts.

Moreover, the autonomist may challenge the specific notion that art is an instrument of moral education. For if moral education delivers knowledge and that knowledge can be distilled into propositional form, then art cannot be a moral educator, on two counts: first, because much art has few propositions to preach, thereby raising the common-denominator question again, while, second, that art that has something to say that can be put in the form of maxims – like the punch lines to Aesopian fables or the entries in Captain Kirk's log at the end of *Star Trek* episodes – usually delivers little more than threadbare truisms. That is, where artworks either blatantly and out-rightly express general moral precepts, or are underwritten by them, those principles or precepts are typically so obvious and thin that it strains credulity to think that we learn them from artworks. Instead, very often, it seems more likely that a thoughtful preteenager will have mastered them already.

Yes, there is an argument against murder in *Crime and Punishment,* but surely it is implausible to think that it requires a novel as elaborate as Dostoyevsky's to teach it, and even if Dostoyevsky designed the novel as a teaching aid, did anyone really learn that murder is wrong from it? Who, by the time he is able to read such a novel with comprehension, needs to be taught such a truism? In fact, it is probably a precondition of actually comprehending *Crime and Punishment* that the readers already grasp the moral precepts that motivate the narrative.

So it seems that art neither teaches nor, for that matter, does it discover any moral truths on a par with scientific propositions. And if an artwork pretends to such a role, such truths as it disseminates – understood as propositions – could unquestionably be acquired just as readily by other means, such as sermons, philosophical tracts, catechisms, parental advice, peer gossip, and so on. Art, in other words, is an unlikely means of moral education, and even where art professes to have some interesting moral maxims to impart, it is hardly a uniquely indispensable vehicle for conveying such messages.

Of course, the autonomist, utopian, and Platonic tendencies each face many problems. For example, there are scarcely any grounds for Plato's anxieties about identification – neither for the case of the actor, nor for the case of the reader or the spectator. For as Diderot pointed out long ago with respect to the actor, no one could become Oedipus and continue the performance.[6] If I became as jealous as Othello, I would surely forget my lines and my blocking, as well as my rehearsed gestures and grimaces.

Nor do audiences standardly identify cognitively or affectively with characters; not only do we know more than Oedipus does through much of the play, but when Oedipus is crushed by feelings of guilt, we do not share these feelings. Instead, we are overtaken by rather distinctively different feelings of pity for Oedipus. We do not share Oedipus's internal experience of self-recrimination, but have concern for him from an external, observer's point of view.

Moreover, Plato's worries that art heightens the rivalry between reason and the emotions are misplaced because there is no cause to conceive of the emotions and reason as locked in ineliminable opposition. Reason – that is, cognition – is a constituent of the emotions rather than an alien competitor. Thus, it is possible to join Aristotle in regarding arts as such and theater in particular as ways of educating emotions such as pity and fear by means of clarifying them – to put a Collingwoodian spin on the notion of *catharsis* – by providing spectators with, or, more accurately, by presenting cognition with, exemplary or maximally fitting objects for certain emotions such that our capacity to recognize the appropriate objects of said emotions and our disposition to undergo these affective states in the right circumstances are enhanced.

And, of course, the problem with the Lacanian Marxists, our contemporary Platonists, is even easier to pinpoint. For insofar as they identify structural features of mass communication – such as film projection[7] – as the source of all evil, they are in the embarrassing position of lumping every attempt at moral and political progressiveness along with *Triumph of the Will*.

Utopianism confronts rather the same problem, but from the other direction. Given certain conceptions of the nature of art, the utopian is driven to put *Triumph of the Will* in the same boat as genuinely progressive art, because of the utopian conviction that, simply by virtue of being art, *Triumph of the Will* has something morally positive about it. Or, to put the matter in more fashionable jargon, all art must have its emancipatory moment. Thus, the utopian approaches the artwork with a research program – namely, find the emancipatory moment. This can lead to some fairly long stretches of interpretive fancy. I once heard a critic of this persuasion locate the emancipatory moment in *The Godfather* as its yearning for community – after all, everyone wants a family.

Utopianism seems highly improbable. It appears entirely too facile and convenient that the ontology of art should be able to guarantee that all art is morally ennobling. Indeed, I find the conclusion that art is necessarily complicit in moral progress, since by its nature it acknowledges that things can be otherwise, to be a deduction that appears to go through simply because its central premise is so vague and amorphous. The notion that art shows that things can be other than the way they are is too indefinite and unspecified a hook, to my mind, upon which to hang art's moral pedigree. Nor, even if we accept this rather obscure, if not equivocating, derivation of art's moral status, can we be satisfied that its conclusion coincides neatly with reality, since pre-theoretically it is rather apparent that there are irredeemably evil artworks.

Finally, I would protest that the utopian position strikes me as unduly sentimental. Basically, the utopian is committed to the view that art is always morally valuable. But the conceit that art should always turn out to be among the forces of light is nothing but a pious, deeply sanctimonious wish-fulfillment fantasy. (Perhaps a less tendentious way of framing this objection is to complain that utopians make art a category of commendation rather than of classification.)

If it were only the Platonic and utopian traditions that stand in the way of the commonsensical observation that the moral assessment of art can be variable, we could easily affirm common sense. However, as already noted, there is the even more comprehensive objection to moral discourse about art, namely the view of the autonomist who claims that there should be no moral assessment of art whatsoever – indeed, that moral discussion of art is of the nature of a category error. This, of course, flies in the face of ordinary critical and discursive practice with respect to most literature, film and theater, and a great deal of fine art. But the autonomist remains unconcerned by this anomaly, convinced that art is categorically separate from morality and politics.

Nevertheless, the acceptability of this conviction is hardly self-evident; and the fact that art, or at least much art – including, for example, art in the service of religion, politics, and social movements – does not appear disjoined from the realm of moral value, *in conjunction with* the fact that autonomists are not very good at coming up with a satisfying, clear-cut principle with which to demarcate the boundary between art and everything else, makes autonomism a far from overwhelmingly persuasive doctrine.[8] For in a great many cases of art, the putative impermeability of art to other sorts of practices, including morality, seems counterintuitive. What credibility can the autonomist position have when one realizes that simply in order to comprehend literary artworks, one must bring to bear one's knowledge of ordinary language and verbal associations, as well as one's knowledge of "real-world" human nature and everyday moral reasoning?[9]

And yet autonomism has some strong intuitions on its side, too – intuitions with which any philosophical attempt to develop an account of a general relation between art and morality must come to *terms*. Those intuitions include the following:

1. Not all artworks have a moral dimension, and it is therefore unintelligible to attempt to assess *all* art from a moral point of view.

2. Art is not an instrument of morality and so should not be assessed in terms of its moral (a.k.a. behavioral) *consequences*. It is not the function of art to produce certain moral consequences, so it is a mistake to evaluate art in light of the behavior to which it gives rise, either actually or probably. Art is not subservient to ulterior purposes, such as morality or politics.

Furthermore, in addition to this putatively conceptual point, it can be added that we still understand virtually *nothing* about the behavioral consequences of consuming art. For example, we have no precise, reliable account of why the incidence of violence is high in Detroit but low in Toronto, where the respective populations are exposed to the same violent entertainment media, nor do we have anything but exceedingly general ideas about why there is less violent crime in Japan than in the United States, despite the fact that Japanese programming is far more violent than ours. At this point, the notion of a *difference in cultures* may be solemnly intoned, but that is not an explanation. It is what needs to be explained if we are to determine the differential behavioral responses to popular art. Thus, given this, it may be argued that since we don't know how to calculate the behavioral consequences of art for morality, we should refrain from evaluating art in light of moral considerations.

3. It is not the function of art to provide moral education. This is not merely a subsidiary of the preceding point. It can also be bolstered by the observation that if art is supposed to afford moral knowledge of a propositional variety, then the maxims that are generally derivable from artworks are rather trivial. They are so commonly endorsed that it makes no sense to suppose that artists discover them, or that readers, listeners, and viewers come to learn them, in any robust sense from artworks.

I would like to develop a philosophical account – by which I mean a general account – of one of the most important and comprehensive relations of art to morality. This account, moreover, is meant to accord with our practice of making variable moral assessments of artworks. I should also like to explain why, with certain types of artworks, it strikes us as natural, rational, and appropriate that we tend to talk about them in terms of morality. But, at the same time, I will try to develop this account in such a way that it confronts or accommodates the objections of the autonomist.

Autonomism is an attractive doctrine for anyone who approaches the question of the nature of art with essentialist biases, that is, with the expectation that everything we call art will share a *uniquely* common characteristic, one that pertains distinctively to all and only art. This is the card that Clive Bell plays when he announces that unless we can identify such a common, uniquely defining feature for art, then when we use the concept, we gibber.

Of course, by declaring art to be utterly separate from every other realm of human praxis, the autonomist secures the quest for essentialism at a stroke, if only by negation, by boldly asserting that art has nothing to do with anything else. It is a unique form of activity with its own purposes and standards of evaluation, generally calibrated in terms of formal achievement. That those standards do not involve moral considerations, moreover, can be supported, the autonomist argues, by noting that moral assessment cannot be an appropriate measure of artistic value, since not all artworks possess a moral dimension. We have already called this the common-denominator argument. It presupposes that any evaluative measure that applies to art should be applicable to all art. But since certain kinds of works – including some string quartets and/or some abstract paintings – may be bereft of moral significance, it makes no sense, so the argument goes, to raise issues of morality when assessing artworks. Moral evaluation is never appropriate to artworks, in short, because it is not universally applicable.

Moreover, that we are willing to call some artworks good despite their moral limitations – despite the fact that their moral insights may be paltry or even flawed – fits as nicely with the autonomist posit that art has nothing to do with morality as does the fact that with certain works of art, questions of morality make no sense whatsoever. The autonomist accounts for these facts by saying that art is valuable for its own sake, not for the sake of morality, and that art has unique grounds for assessment. Art has its own purposes and, therefore, its own criteria of evaluation.

But however well autonomism suits some of our intuitions about art, it also runs afoul of others. Historically, art seems hardly divorced from other social activities. Much art was religious and much art has served explicitly political goals. Are illustrations of the exemplary lives of saints, or biblical episodes, or pictorial biographies of Confucius, or celebrations of the victories of empires and republics to be thought of as utterly disjunct from other realms of social value? Such works are obviously designed in such a way that viewing them from the perspective of "splendid" aesthetic isolationism renders them virtually unintelligible. Such works are made in the thick of social life and demand to be considered in light of what autonomists are wont to call nonaesthetic interests as a condition of their comprehensibility. Thus, though a taste for essentialism may create a predisposition for autonomism, the history of art and its reception makes the thesis that art is categorically separate from other realms of human praxis somewhat suspect.

To understand a literary work, for instance, generally requires not only that one use one's knowledge of ordinary language and verbal associations, drawn from every realm of social activity and valuation, but also, most frequently, that audiences deploy many kinds of everyday reasoning, including moral reasoning, simply to understand the text. How can the negative claims of autonomism – that art is divorced from every other realm of social praxis – be sustained in such a way as to render literary communication intelligible?

Or, to put the matter differently, much art, including literary art in particular and narrative art in general, has propositional content that pertains not only to the worlds of works of art, but to the world as well. In the face of such an indisputable fact, it is hard, save by an excess of ad hocery, to swallow the autonomist conviction that art is always divorced from other dimensions of human practice and their subtending forms of valuation.

If the negative claim of autonomism – that all art is in pertinent respects separate from other social practices – seems problematic, its positive project is desperately embattled. For no one, as yet, has been able to come up with a characterization of what is uniquely artistic that resists scrutiny for very long. Here the notion of disinterestedness plays a large role, one too complicated for me to rehearse here. Suffice it to say that talk of the aesthetic dimension is perennially popular, but after two centuries of discussion still inconclusive. That is, no one can give a persuasive account of what it might be in a sufficiently comprehensive way that would provide a model for art as we know it. Thus, since no autonomist seems to be able to say successfully, in a positive way, what art – its nature, purpose, and schedule of evaluation – is, the hypothesis seems like so much posturing. What persuasiveness it commands appears to rely upon a promissory note, drawn on the conviction that a certain preconception of essentialism is an unavoidable desideratum, though, as I hope to show, the preconception in question may misconstrue the nature of at least certain kinds of art.

Autonomism rides on the unexceptionable observation that art appears to aim, first and foremost, at being absorbing. The so-called aesthetic experience is centripetal. Thus, if the artwork essentially aims at our absorption in it, then it is valuable for its own sake. The thought that art is valuable for its own sake, in turn, is believed to entail that it is not valuable for other reasons, especially cognitive, moral, and political ones. However, this conclusion is a non sequitur. For, in ways to be pursued at length in what follows, some art may be absorbing exactly because of the way in which it engages, among other things, the moral life of its audience. That is, just because we value art for the way it commands our undivided attention does not preclude that some art commands our attention in this way just because it is interesting and engaging cognitively and/or, for our purposes, morally.

The autonomist is certainly correct to point out that it is inappropriate to invoke moral considerations in evaluating *all* art. This premise of the common-denominator argument is right. Some art, at least, is altogether remote from moral considerations. And, in such cases, moral discourse with reference to the artworks in question – say, a painting by Albers – may be not only strained and out of place, but conceptually confused. Nevertheless, the fact that it may be a mistake to engage moral discourse with reference to some pure orchestral music or some abstract paintings has no implications about whether it is appropriate to do so with respect to *The Grapes of Wrath, Peer Gynt, The Scarlet Letter, Anna Karenina, 1984, Potemkin, The Ox-Bow Incident, Antigone, The Bonfire of the Vanities,* and *Beowulf,* since artworks such as these are expressly designed to elicit moral reactions, and it is part of the form of life to which they belong that audiences respond morally to them on the basis of their recognition that that is what they are intended to do, given the relevant social practices. These works have moral agendas as part of their address to the reader to such an extent that one would have to be willfully blinkered to miss them.

The common-denominator argument presupposes that there must be a single scale of evaluation that applies to all artworks. Whether or not there is such a scale – a controversial hypothesis if there ever was one – can be put aside, however, because even if there is, that would fail to imply that its underlying property was the *only* evaluative consideration that could be brought to bear on every artwork. For in addition to, for example, formal considerations, some artworks may be such that given the nature of the works in question, it is also appropriate to discuss them in terms of other dimensions of value.

We may evaluate eighteen-wheelers and sports cars in terms of their capacities to locomote, but that does not preclude further assessments of the former in terms of their capacity to draw heavy loads or of the latter to execute high-speed, hairpin turns. These additional criteria of evaluation, of course, are related to the kinds of things that eighteen-wheelers and sports cars respectively are. Similarly, the conviction that there may be some common standard of evaluation for all artworks, even if plausible, would not entail that for certain kinds of artworks, given what they are, considerations of dimensions of value, beyond the formal, such as moral considerations, are out of bounds.

It is my contention that there are many kinds of art, genres if you will, that naturally elicit moral responses, that prompt us to talk about them in terms of moral considerations, and that even warrant moral evaluation. The common-denominator argument cannot preclude this possibility logically, for even if there is some global standard of artistic value, there may be different local standards for different art genres. Moreover, with some of these art genres, moral considerations are pertinent, even though there may be other genres where bringing them to bear would be tantamount to a category error.

Certain kinds of artworks are designed to engage us morally, and, with those kinds of artworks, it makes sense for us to surround them with ethical discussion and to assess them morally. Thus, in order to deflect the autonomist's common-denominator argument, we need simply adjust the domain of prospective theories about the relation of art to morality to the kinds of artworks in which ethical discourse and moral assessment are intelligible. Consequently, I will restrict the scope of the theoretical framework that I am about to advance to narratives, specifically human narratives (including anthropomorphized ones like *The Wind in the Willows, Charlotte's Web, Animal Farm,* and *Maus*). This is not to suggest that narrative is the only art genre or category where moral assessment is pertinent – portraiture may be another – but only that it is a clear-cut case. That is, narratives like *Lord of the Flies, To Kill a Mockingbird, Vanity Fair, Pilgrim's Progress, Beloved, L'Assomoir, Germinal,* and *Catch-22* are such obvious, virtually incontestable examples of morally significant art that they provide a useful starting point for getting out from under autonomism.

The common-denominator argument cannot be taken to have shown that it is never appropriate to assess artworks morally, but only, at best, that it is not always appropriate to do so. This allows that sometimes it may be intelligible to assess artworks morally and, I submit, that artworks that are narratives of human affairs are generally the kind of thing it makes sense both to talk about in ethical terms and to assess morally. Moreover, there are deep reasons for this.

As is well known, narratives make all sorts of presuppositions, and it is the task of the reader, viewer, or listener to fill these in. It is of the nature of narrative to be essentially incomplete. Every narrative makes an indeterminate number of pre-suppositions that the audience must bring, so to speak, to the text. All authors must rely upon the audience's knowledge of certain things that are not explicitly stated. Authors always write in the expectation that the audience will correctly fill in what has been left unsaid. Shakespeare presumes that the audience will not suppose that Juliet's innards are sawdust and, with respect to *Oleanna,* David Mamet assumes that the audience will suppose that his characters possess the same structure of beliefs, desires, and emotions that they do and that the characters are not alien changelings possessed of unheard-of psychologies. When the author of a novel about the eighteenth century notes that the characters traveled from one country to another, she expects that, unless she wrote otherwise, we will not imagine that the characters were teleported. No artist can say or depict everything there is to say or to depict about the fictional events she is narrating. She depends upon the audience to fill in a great deal and that filling-in is an indispensable part of what it is to follow and to comprehend a narrative.[10]

Moreover, the kinds of details that authors rely on audiences to supply come in all different shapes and sizes, ranging from facts about human biology to facts about geography, history, politics, religion, and so on. In many cases, the author relies upon what we know or believe about human psychology in order for her narratives to be intelligible. For example, in *Eugénie Grandet,* Balzac presumes that the audience has enough understanding of the ways of the human heart to see how it is that Eugenie's betrayal at the hands of her cousin can precipitate an irreparable bitterness that turns her into the very image of her father. Likewise, in the *Symposium,* Plato supposes that the reader knows enough about flirtation to understand the erotic triangle with Agathon at its apex in order to appreciate the sly maneuverings of Socractes and Alcibiades. And in *The Bluest Eye,* Toni Morrison relies on the reader's understanding of human psychology to see how Pecola's plight derives from her aunt's displacement of her maternal concerns from her own family to that of her white employers inasmuch as the white family can provide her with the material conditions that will enable her to take pride in running a functioning household.

But the audience's activity of filling in the narrative does not simply have to do with recognizing what the text suggests or implies or presupposes about the contours of its fictional world and about the nature and psychology of the human characters that inhabit that world. To understand a text properly also involves mobilizing the emotions that are requisite to the text. Properly understanding Trollope's *Dr. Wortle's School* involves feeling distrust toward Robert Lefroy, while anyone who does not find Uriah Heep in *David Copperfield* repugnant would have missed Dickens's point. One does not understand Hemingway's *For Whom the Bell Tolls* unless one admires Robert Jordan's restraint, just as the reader must ultimately find Casaubon despicable in order to "get" *Middlemarch*. Similarly, "getting" *Medea,* it seems to me, requires finding her actions finally appalling, whereas anyone left unmoved by the experiences of the members of the Joy Luck Club would find the point of that novel incomprehensible.

A narrative by its very nature is selective and, therefore, incomplete in certain specifiable senses. It is for this reason that the successful author requires an audience that can bring to the text, among other things, what is not explicit in it. This further dictates that, to a large extent, the author and the audience need to share a common background of beliefs about the world and about human nature, as well as a relatively common emotional life. That is, authors generally not only possess a shared cognitive stock with audiences, but a shared emotional stock as well. The author designs her work with an implicit working hypothesis about the knowledge that her anticipated reader will bring to the text, along with knowledge of how the reader will feel toward the characters. For unless the readers feel toward the characters in certain ways, they will be unlikely to comprehend the narrative.

Of course, the cognitive stock that the audience needs to possess in order to properly understand a narrative fiction includes not only knowledge of geography and human nature, but moral knowledge as well. And the emotions that the audience brings to bear on a narrative are not only shot through with moral concepts, in the way that, say, anger is – insofar as "being wronged" is conceptually criterial for feeling it – but the relevant emotions are themselves very often moral emotions, such as contempt for wanton brutality and the indignation at injustice that pervades almost every page of *Uncle Tom's Cabin.*

One cannot, for example, admire Schindler in the way the film *Schindler's List* encourages if one does not feel that the Nazis are morally loathsome. And even melodramas, like *Back Street,* typically evoke an emotional response that is a mixture of moral admiration for the protagonists – often as a result of recognizing the nobility involved in their self-sacrificing behavior – and sorrow over their adversity.[11] There is no "melodramatic" response, just as according to Aristotle there is no tragic response, when the audience misconstrues the moral standing of the relevant characters. Nor is it likely that there can be a successful narrative of any substance that would not rely on activating the moral powers of the readership.[12] And finally, of course, in the general case, the author can rely on the audience sharing the relevant cognitive and emotive stock because the audience and the author already share a roughly common culture.

In his *Letter to M. D'Alembert on the Theater,* Jean-Jacques Rousseau argues that theater cannot transform a community morally or reform it.[13] Rousseau believes this because he points out that in order to succeed an author has to write within the moral framework of his times. As Rousseau notes, "An author who would brave the general taste would soon write for himself alone."[14] That is, there are "market pressures," so to speak, that incline authors to design their works in such a way that they rely on a fit between their narratives and a roughly common cognitive, emotive, and moral stock that is shared by the readers, viewers, and listeners who make up the expected audience of the work. If there were no such common background, there would be no communication, since there could be no uptake.

A narrative is built so that its anticipated audience can understand it, and in order to understand a narrative properly, an audience will have to mobilize its knowledge and its emotions, moral and otherwise, in the process of filling in a story. This means that in order to understand a narrative properly, we must use many of the same beliefs and emotions, generally rooted in our common culture, that we use to negotiate everyday human events for the purpose of filling in and getting the point of stories. In this sense, it is not the case that the narrative teaches us something brand new, but rather that it activates the knowledge and emotions, moral and otherwise, that we already possess.

That is, the successful narrative becomes the occasion for exercising knowledge, concepts, and emotions that we have already, in one sense, learned. Filling in the narrative is a matter of mobilizing or accessing the cognitive, emotive, and moral repertoire that, for the most part, we already have at our disposal. Narratives, in other words, provide us with opportunities to, among other things, exercise our moral powers, because the very process of understanding a narrative is itself, to a significant degree, generally an exercise of our moral powers.

Because successful narratives are so inextricably bound up with the opportunity they afford for the exercise of our moral powers, it is quite natural for ethical concerns to recur frequently when we discuss stories. Insofar as narratives necessarily depend upon activating our moral beliefs, concepts, and feelings, it comes as no surprise that we should want to discuss, to share, and to compare with other readers our reactions to the characters, situations, and overall texts that authors present to us with the clear intention of eliciting, among other things, moral responses. That is, it is natural for us to think about and to discuss narratives in terms of ethics, because narratives, due to the kinds of things they are, awaken, stir up, and engage our moral powers of recognition and judgment.

If this account is correct, and if we suppose, in addition, that learning is a matter of the acquisition of interesting propositions heretofore unknown or of freshly minted moral emotions, then, as the autonomist argues, in the standard case there is no learning when it comes to the vast majority of narrative artworks, since those artworks antecedently depend, as a condition of their very intelligibility, upon our possession of the relevant knowledge of various moral precepts, and of concepts of vice and virtue, and so on. Nor do narratives invest us with and thereby teach us new emotions; rather they typically exercise the emotions we already possess. So the autonomist's case against the hypothesis that the relation of art to the emotions cannot be one of moral education looks persuasive.

And yet it does seem that the operative sense of learning in the autonomist's argument is too restrictive. For there is another sense of learning – both moral and otherwise – that the autonomist has ignored and that applies to the kinds of activities that narrative artworks abet. It is this: that in mobilizing what we already know and what we can already feel, the narrative artwork can become an occasion for us to deepen our understanding of what we know and what we feel. Notably, for our purposes, a narrative can become an opportunity for us to deepen our grasp of the moral knowledge and emotions we already command.

This conception of the relation of art, especially narrative art, to morality might be called the *transactional view* (because of its emphasis on the transaction between the narrative artwork and the moral understanding), or it might be called, as I prefer to call it, the *clarificationist view*, in honor of the most prized transaction that can transpire between the narrative artwork and the moral understanding. Clarificationism does not claim that, in the standard case, we acquire interesting, new propositional knowledge from artworks, but rather that the artworks in question can deepen our moral understanding by, among other things, encouraging us to apply our moral knowledge and emotions to specific cases. For in being prompted to apply and engage our antecedent moral powers, we may come to augment them.

In the course of engaging a given narrative we may need to reorganize the hierarchical orderings of our moral categories and premises, or to reinterpret those categories and premises in the light of new paradigm instances and hard cases, or to reclassify barely acknowledged phenomena afresh – something we might be provoked to do by a feminist author who is able to show us injustice where before all we saw was culture as usual. Thus, in *Up the Sandbox,* Anne Richardson Roiphe juxtaposes adventure fantasies with the daily chores of a housewife in order to highlight the inequality of the latter's life when compared to her husband's.

A play like *A Raisin in the Sun* addresses white audiences in such a way as to incite vividly their recognition that African Americans are persons like any other and therefore should be accorded the kind of equal treatment for persons that such audiences already endorse as a matter of moral principle. The play does this by showing that the dreams and the family bonds of the major characters are no different from those of other persons, thereby prompting the subsumption of African-Americans under a moral precept concerning equal treatment that the audience already believes. This, in turn, encourages the white audience to form the moral judgment that the way in which the prospective white neighbors of the black family respond to their purchasing a house in their neighborhood is wrong.

In this case, as in many others, it seems accurate to describe what goes on in the white audience as a discovery about something it already knows; that is, audience members put together previously disconnected belief fragments in a new gestalt in a way that changes their moral perception. Here it is not primarily that white audience members acquire a new piece of moral knowledge; rather they are prompted to make connections between the beliefs they already possess.

The characters and the situations presented by the play afford an occasion to reorganize or reshuffle the moral beliefs that the white audience already has at its disposal. Its system of beliefs undergoes clarification. Its grasp and understanding of what it already knows is deepened in a way that counts, I contend, as learning, though it may not primarily be a matter of learning an interesting new proposition, since in some sense, the white audience already knows that African Americans are persons and that persons deserve treatment as equals. They might even be able to recite the relevant syllogism, but it would not strike home. What the play succeeds in doing is to create a situation that encourages the audience to forge a salient connection between heretofore perhaps isolated beliefs. We are given an opportunity to deepen our grasp and our understanding of what we already know in a way that also counts as learning, though not necessarily as a matter of learning interesting, non-trivial, new propositions.[15] Rather, it is more a matter of grasping the significance of the connections between antecedently possessed knowledge.[16]

I intend here to draw a contrast between knowledge and *understanding* such that understanding is meant to mark our capacity to manipulate what we know and to apply it with a sense of intelligibility – not simply to have access to abstract propositions and concepts, but to employ them intelligibly and appropriately. Understanding is a capacity to see and to be responsive to connections between our beliefs. A person with understanding has the ability to find her way around in the mental geography of her own cognitive stock.[17] Understanding is the ability to make connections between what we already know. With understanding, we acquire increasing familiarity with concepts and principles that are at first bewildering. Understanding is the activity of refining what we already know, of recognizing connections between parts of our knowledge stock, of bringing what we already know to clarity through a process of practice and judgment.[18]

We may possess abstract principles, like "All persons should be given their due," and abstract concepts, such as "Virtue is what promotes human flourishing," without being able to connect these abstractions to concrete situations. For that requires not only knowing these abstractions, but understanding them. Moreover, it is this kind of understanding – particularly with respect to moral understanding – to which engaging with narrative artworks may contribute.[19] For narrative, as we have seen, involves the exercise of moral judgment and it is through the exercise of judgment that we come to understand moral abstractions.

Inasmuch as understanding is often a function of correctly classifying things, fictional narratives frequently present us with opportunities to deliberate about how to categorize behaviors and character traits, and thereby they can enhance our capacity for classifying the human environment – by linking abstract concepts to percepts in ways that can make us more sensitive to applying them to real-world cases. As I have already suggested, it seems to me that the work of many feminist novelists has been to get people to reclassify a great many everyday practices under the category of injustice.[20]

Moreover, insofar as the emotions involve a conceptual component – in terms of formal criteria for what can serve as the object of an emotional state – it is coherent to talk about deepening our emotional understanding. This involves treating the narrative as an occasion for clarifying our emotions or, as Aristotle might put it, of learning to apply the right emotion to the appropriate object with suitable intensity.

As is probably apparent, for the clarificationist, engaging with or coming to understand a narrative artwork can itself simultaneously be a process of deepening one's own moral understanding. Recognizing that there is something deeply wrong with Emma's "guidance" of Harriet in Jane Austen's classic is not only a requisite recognition for properly understanding the novel; it also deepens our moral understanding by providing us with a penetrating portrait of interpersonal manipulation, which, though well intentioned, is ultimately self-deceptive as well as wicked. Moreover, the fact that we must resist the allure of Emma's otherwise attractive moral character before we reach this insight about the wrongness of her interference with Harriet's life makes reading the novel *Emma* all the more serviceable as an occasion where we have the opportunity to expand our moral understanding, though not our knowledge (insofar as we already knew the abstract maxim that treating people merely as a means is immoral).[21]

On the clarificationist view, learning from a narrative artwork through the enlargement or expansion of one's moral understanding is not well described as a *consequence* of engaging with the story. Understanding the work, enlarging one's moral understanding, and learning from the narrative are all part and parcel of the same process, which might be called comprehending or following the narrative. When reading a novel or viewing a drama, our moral understanding is engaged already. Reading a novel, for example, is itself generally a moral activity insofar as reading narrative literature typically involves us in a continuous process of moral judgment, which continuous exercise of moral judgment itself can contribute to the expansion of our moral understanding. When reading a novel, we are engaged in a moral activity already insofar as our powers of moral judgment and understanding have been drawn into play, and, as we shall later see, our moral assessment of a narrative artwork may rest on the quality of that moral activity or experience, rather than on speculations about the probable behavioral consequences of reading, hearing, or viewing that fiction.

Moreover, by talking of the expansion or enlargement of our moral powers, I am not speaking metaphorically, since the process of understanding that I have in mind concerns making *more* connections between what we already know or believe, while by the notion of exercising our moral understanding I mean to signal that successful narrative artworks, as a condition of intelligibility, compel us to make moral judgments.

In order to avoid obscurity, it will be useful for me to provide some examples of the way in which narrative artworks can enhance the understanding. As Sir Philip Sidney and Immanuel Kant point out, we are often possessed of general propositions that are very abstract and that we may not be able to connect with particular situations.[22] That is, they are so abstract that they leave us at a loss about how to apply them. But narrative artworks can supply us with vivid examples that enable us to see how to apply abstractions to particulars. For example, *King Lear* gives us an arresting example with which to understand the general proposition that "a house divided shall not stand"; Brecht's *Three Penny Opera* exemplifies the principle that the quality of moral life is coarsened by poverty; *Measure for Measure* shows how power corrupts; the early-twentieth-century film serial *Judex* dramatizes the adage "Judge not, lest ye be judged"; while *Oedipus Rex* supplied the ancient Greeks with a percept to match the admonitory precept "Call no one happy until he is dead."

This recognition of the importance of examples for moral understanding, of course, was also acknowledged by medieval theologians in their recommendation of the use of the *exemplum,* a recommendation that can be traced back to Aristotle's discussion of illustrations in his *Rhetoric.* Much modern moral theory has placed great emphasis on rules in its conception of moral deliberation. However, this overlooks the problem that often our moral rules and concepts are too thin to determine the particular situations that fall under them. That requires moral judgment, and the capacity for moral judgment is exactly what is ideally exercised and refined through our encounters with narrative artworks. Narrative artworks, that is, supply us with content with which to interpret abstract moral propositions. Here, it is not my intention to disparage the role of rules in moral deliberation, but merely to point out that rules must be negotiated by the capacity for judgment, which capacity can be enhanced by trafficking with narrative artworks just because narrative artworks typically require moral judgments to be intelligible.

For example, Mary Shelley's *Frankenstein* exemplifies the point that evil proceeds from nurture, not nature − from the environment and social conditioning, or the lack thereof − and, hence, that blame must be apportioned with respect to this principle. Moreover, as this example should indicate, the way in which moral understanding is enhanced by narrative artworks need not be thought of as a matter of the fiction supplying readers with templates that they then go on to match to real cases. For, obviously, there can be no real case anywhere like the one portrayed in *Frankenstein.* Instead, the moral understanding can be refined and deepened in the process of coming to terms with this story and its characters, especially the monster and his claims to justice. We are not in a position to measure real-life cases on a one-to-one basis against the story of *Frankenstein,* but after reading the novel our moral understanding may be more sophisticated in such a way that we can identify cases of injustice quite unlike that portrayed in *Frankenstein.* Thus, we see why authors need not, and frequently do not, trade in typical cases, but favor extraordinary ones (consider *The Brothers Karamazov*) in order to provoke an expansion of our moral powers.

In addition, just as narrative artworks enable us to clarify our moral comprehension of abstract principles, so too do they enlarge our powers of recognition with respect to abstract virtues and vices. In *Pride and Prejudice,* Jane Austen presents the reader with an array of kinds and degrees of pride in order to coax the reader into recognizing which type of pride, as Gilbert Ryle puts it, goes best with right thinking and right acting,[23] while in *Sense and Sensibility,* she contrasts these traits through the characters of Elinor and Marianne Dashwood in a way that the reader should come to see redounds morally to the former's virtue. Similarly, so many western novels and movies, like *Shane,* are about restraint, about its proper scope and limits, as exemplified in a case study.

Molière's comedy *The Miser* and Erich von Stroheim's film *Greed* are obvious examples of the way in which narratives limn the nature of the very vices their titles name, while in Chekhov's *The Cherry Orchard,* we are offered a striking contrast between worldly prudence and imprudence in the persons of Lopukhin and Madame Ranevskaya – a contrast staged over the cherry orchard whose loss, due to Madame Ranevskaya's obliviousness to real life, deals a shattering blow to her family.

In *Barchester Towers* by Trollope, Mr. Slope exemplifies a paradigm of manipulativeness, whereas in Dickens's *Bleak House,* the reader gradually comes to see Mr. Skimpole's charm and frivolity as a form of callous egoism, thereby receiving a lesson in what, *avant la lettre,* we might call the passive-aggressive personality. That *Bleak House* and *Barchester Towers* were originally released in serial form, of course, encouraged readers to compare their moral judgments of evolving characters and situations with one another between installments, much in the way that contemporary soap operas provide communities of viewers with a common source of gossip, where gossip itself has the salutary function of enabling discussants to clarify their understanding of abstract moral principles and concepts, as well as their application through feelings, by means of conversation and comparison with others.[24]

Narratives involve audiences in processes of moral reasoning and deliberation. As the father in *Meet Me in St. Louis* considers moving to New York, the viewer also weighs the claims of the emotional cost such a move will exact on his family against the abstract claims of the future and progress. And, of course, some narratives present readers with moral problems that appear not to be satisfactorily resolvable, such as Maggie Tulliver's romance in *The Mill on the Floss.* This too seems to enrich moral understanding by stretching its reflective resources as one struggles to imagine a livable course of action.

As Martha Nussbaum argues, not only may narratives serve as models of moral reflection and deliberation, they may offer occasions for moral understanding. Nussbaum, of course, believes there is little legitimate room for moral principles and abstract moral concepts in literary-cum-moral understanding, emphasizing, as she does, perception as the model for moral reflection.[25] However, though I do not want to preclude that there may be cases of the kind of moral perception that Nussbaum valorizes, I do not feel any pressure to deny that there are also cases where the moral understanding comes to appreciate abstractions via concrete narratives. Why not have it both ways – so long as we acknowledge that the process of reflection involved in understanding narrative artworks is at the same time a process of moral understanding, often, at least in the most felicitous cases, involving the reorganization and clarification of our moral beliefs and emotions.

Rousseau, it will be recalled, claimed that theater could not reform its audience, since a public art form, like theater, had, in order to persist, to root itself in the beliefs and moral predispositions that its audiences already embraced, lest the work appear unintelligible to them, only, in consequence, to be rejected out of hand. Now surely Rousseau is right that, in the standard case, living artworks must share a background of belief and feeling with their audience. But Rousseau over-steps himself when he infers from this that art cannot reform its audiences, at least incrementally. For often moral reform is a matter of reorganizing or refocalizing or "re-gestalting" what people already believe and feel.

For example, by calling attention to and emphasizing the fact that gays and lesbians are fully human persons one can often convince heterosexuals that gays and lesbians are thereby fully deserving of the rights that those heterosexuals in ques-tion already believe should be accorded to all persons. And, of course, this type of gestalt switch, which often contributes to the refinement of moral understanding, is easily within the grasp of narrative, as topical novels and films, such as *Gentle-man's Agreement, To Kill a Mockingbird,* and *Philadelphia,* attest.

Undoubtedly, these particular examples are sometimes criticized for traffick-ing in victims who are too pure, too saintly, or too unrealistic and, so, in that sense, are somewhat misleading in the long run. But I think that, in the short run, these choices are certainly tactically justifiable in order to get the job done, where the job in question is to prompt the reconfiguration of thinking about Jews, Blacks, and gays. And to the extent that people can be incrementally enlightened by nar-ratives that operate on the audience's antecedent framework of ethical beliefs and emotions, Rousseau is wrong. For moral reform can be achieved by deepening our moral understanding of that which we already believe and feel.

By focusing on the nature of narrative and by taking note of the way in which narratives require audiences to fill in stories by means of their own beliefs and emotions – including, unavoidably, moral ones – I think that I have shown why it is natural for us to discuss narrative artworks in terms of ethical considerations. For, simply put, much of our readerly activity with respect to narratives engages our moral understanding. It is a failure of neither intelligence nor taste to discuss narrative artworks in virtue of their moral significance, given the kind of artifacts that stories are. For given the nature of narrative, the activity of reading, in large measure, is a matter of exercising our moral understanding. It is appropriate to think and to talk about narrative artworks in light of morality because of the nature of narrative artworks and the responses – such as moral judgment – that they are meant to elicit as a condition of their being intelligible, *given the kinds of things they are.* It would, rather, be a failure of intelligence and taste if one did *not* respond to narratives morally.

Moreover, if what I have argued so far is compelling, then perhaps the clarifi-cationist picture of the relation of morality to (narrative) art can also suggest cer-tain grounds for the moral assessments that we make of characters and of complete narratives as well. Obviously, the moral judgments and understandings achieved in response to a narrative artwork differ in at least one way from those essayed in everyday life, since the moral experience that we have in respect to a narrative artwork is guided by the author of the story. There is a level of moral experience available from the narrative that depends on the guidance with which the author intends to provide us. I contend that our *moral* assessments of the narrative, then, can be grounded in the quality of the moral experiences that the author's guidance is designed to invite and abet.

Some narratives may stretch and deepen our moral understanding a great deal. And these, all things being equal, will raise our moral estimate of the work, which may, in turn, also contribute to our artistic evaluation of the work, insofar as a narrative artwork that engages our moral understanding will be all the more absorbing for that very reason. *Emma,* as I have already suggested, is an example of this sort. On the other hand, narratives that mislead or confuse moral understanding deserve criticism – as does Michael Crichton's morally frivolous novel, *Disclosure,* which pretends to explore the issue of sexual harassment through a case that really has more to do with thriller-type cover-ups than it has to do with sexual politics. Here the problem is that the novel is essentially digressive, and, in that respect, it misfocuses or deflects our moral understanding from the issue of sexual harassment. Likewise, narratives that pervert and confuse moral understanding by connecting moral principles, concepts, and emotions to dubious particulars – as often happens with cases of political propaganda – also fare badly on the clarificationist model, since they obfuscate rather than clarify.

The film *Natural Born Killers,* for example, advertises itself as a meditation on violence, but it neither affords a consistent emotional stance on serial killing, nor delivers its promised insight on the relation of serial killing to the media, if only because it neglects to show how the media might have affected the psychological development of the relevant characters. Indeed, its very title – *Natural Born Killers* – would seem at odds with the hypothesis of media-made murder. The media references in the film seem to divert our attention from the moral issues at hand, and in confusing, or even perverting, our moral grasp of the issues, they are, along with the film as a whole, candidates for moral rebuke.

Throughout this essay, I have emphasized the importance in narratives of enlisting the audience's emotional response to the situations they present. Because of this, narratives can be morally assessed in terms of whether they contribute to emotional understanding, where that pertains to morality, or whether they obfuscate it. For example, in many fictions about psychotic killers, like *Silence of the Lambs,* the murderers are presented as gay. Gayness is part of their monstrosity, and the audience is encouraged to regard these killers with horror. Gayness is thus represented as unnatural. Gayness and monstrosity are superimposed on each other in such a way that gayness is turned into a suitable object of the emotion of horror.

This is to mismatch gayness with a morally inappropriate emotion. It is to confuse homosexuals with the kinds of creatures, like alien beings, that warrant emotional responses of fear and disgust. But to engender this kind of loathing for homosexuals by enlisting a response to them that is emotionally suitable for monsters is morally obnoxious as a result of the way in which it misdirects our feelings. It confuses matters morally by encouraging us to forge an emotive link between gayness and the horrific.

The ways in which the quality of our moral experience of a narrative artwork can vary, either positively or negatively, are quite diverse. Many different things can go right or wrong in terms of how our moral understanding is engaged or frustrated by a narrative artwork. Thus, it is unlikely that there is a single scale along which the qualities of all our moral experiences of narratives can be plotted or ranked. And since we possess no algorithm, we will have to make our moral assessments on a case-by-case basis, aided, at most, by some very crude rules of thumb, like those operative in the preceding examples.

For example, in the movie version of *Schindler's List,* in the scene in which Schindler leaves the factory, director Steven Spielberg manhandles our emotions by trying to force us to accord Schindler a level of moral admiration that the character has already won from us. As Schindler whines about his Nazi lapel pin, we are coerced into virtually subvocalizing, "It's okay Oskar, you're a hero and the pin probably helped you fool the German officers anyway." Here, our moral emotions are engaged, I think, excessively. But, of course, this flaw is rather different and nowhere as problematic as the case of the gay serial killers. In that case, the emotions get attached to morally unsuitable objects for the wrong reasons. At least Schindler appears to be the right kind of object for the emotion in question.

On the clarificationist model, moral assessments of narrative artworks can be grounded in the quality of our moral engagement with and experience of the narrative object. This engagement can be positive, where our moral understanding and/or emotions are deepened and clarified, or it can be negative, where the moral understanding is misled, confused, perverted, and so on. Moreover, there are many ways in which moral understanding and feeling can be facilitated. For example, a novel may subvert complacent views, prompting a reorganization that expands our moral understanding, where such an expansion may count as a good-making feature of the work.[26] And, of course, many narrative artworks, perhaps most, engage our moral understanding and emotions without challenging, stretching, or degrading them. Such narrative artworks probably deserve to be assessed positively from the moral point of view, since they do exercise our moral understanding and emotions, but maybe it is best to think of them as morally *good, but without distinction.*

One advantage of grounding our moral assessments of narrative artworks in the quality of our moral engagement with said artworks in comparison with attempts to base our moral assessments on the probable behavioral consequences of reading, hearing, and viewing such narratives is that we have little or no idea about how to determine with any reliability the consequences of such activities for real-world contexts. And if we can't predict the consequences with precision, there seems to be no acceptable method here. But, on the other hand, using ourselves as detectors, we can make reasonable conjectures about how those who share the same cultural backgrounds as we do are apt to understand and be moved by given characters and situations. That is, it is difficult to imagine participants in Western culture who could mistake Iago for noble or Darth Vader for generous.

The clarificationist, then, can deal with those who are suspicious of moral assessments of art on the grounds that such assessments appear to rest on unwarranted presumptions about the behavioral consequences of consuming artworks.

For the clarificationist contends that the moral assessment here is keyed to the very process itself of consuming the narrative artwork and not to the supposed behavioral consequences of that process. This is not to deny that the way in which narrative artworks might interact with our moral understanding may have repercussions for behavior. Nor would I reject the possibility that certain narrative artworks might be censored, if (but that is a big *if*) it could be proved that they cause harmful behavior on the part of normal readers, listeners, and viewers systematically. Rather, the clarificationist merely maintains that the moral assessment of narrative artworks continues to be possible, as it always has been, in the absence of any well-confirmed theory about the impact of consuming narratives on behavior.

Moreover, the version of the relation of narrative to moral understanding that I am advancing must be distinguished from the closely related view propounded by Frank Palmer.[27] Palmer, following Roger Scruton, maintains that literature, in mobilizing the kind of moral understanding I have been discussing, feeds and strengthens the moral imagination's capacity for knowing what it would be like to be, for example, a Macbeth, and that this exercise of the imagination is thereby linked to practical knowledge. That is, for Palmer, moral understanding, enriched in this way, has a role in determining what to do. Knowing what it would be like – what it would feel like – to be a Macbeth should figure in our deliberations about doing the kind of things Macbeth does. Indeed, in general, knowing what it would feel like to do x is something one should consider before doing x. For instance, if as a result of such an exercise of the imagination one thinks that doing x would bring about insufferable discomfiture, that should count as a reason for not doing x.

But I am skeptical about this link to the behavioral consequences of consuming narrative fictions, because I think that with respect to most narratives, the audience's role is more of the nature of an observer and that the contribution that narratives make to moral understanding has primarily to do with the assessment of third parties rather than with deliberation about action. Palmer's theory seems to me to suggest a reversion to the notion of identification. This is not to say that moral understandings garnered from literature can have no impact on action, but only that the link, where there is one, is less reliable than Palmer seems to believe.[28]

Furthermore, I think that imagining what it would feel like to be a character is not the norm in experiencing fictions. We are more often in the position of onlookers or observers of how the characters feel. Thus, Palmer's theory does not offer a comprehensive picture of the relation of the moral understanding to narrative artworks. At best, it tracks a special case.

Not only can the clarificationist meet the objection that we cannot assess art morally because we lack the wherewithal to gauge the behavioral consequences of art. The clarificationist can also explain how art might have something to *teach,* even though the maxims and concepts it deals in are so often routinely known. For narrative art can educate moral understanding and the emotions by, in general, using what we already believe and feel, mobilizing it, exercising it, sometimes reorienting it, and sometimes enlarging it, rather than primarily by introducing us to interesting, nontrivial, new moral propositions and concepts.[29]

Since I have attempted to ground moral assessments of narrative artworks in what might be broadly construed as a learning model, it may appear that I have walked into the cross hairs of the autonomist's contention that artworks cannot be instruments of moral education, or have it as their function to promote moral education. However, though I think I have shown how moral learning can issue from commerce with narrative artworks, I have not proposed the reduction of narrative art to an instrumentality of moral education. For the learning that may take place here, though it emerges because of the kind of work a narrative artwork is, need not be the aim of the narrative artwork, but rather a concomitant, one of which the author may take no self-conscious notice. If it is the purpose of the narrative artwork to absorb the audience in it, to draw us into the story, to capture our interest, and to stimulate our imagination, then it is also apparent that by engaging moral judgment and moral emotions, the story may thereby discharge its primary aim or purpose by secondarily stimulating and sometimes deepening the moral understanding of the audience.

It is not the function of a narrative artwork to provide moral education. Typically, the purpose of a narrative artwork is to absorb the reader, viewer, or listener. However, frequently the narrative may bequeath moral learning to the audience while in pursuit of its goal of riveting audience attention and making the audience care about what happens next, by means of enlisting our moral understanding and emotions. That is, what the author explicitly seeks is to engage the audience. And engaging the audience's moral understanding may be a means to this end.

The autonomist is correct in denying that narrative art necessarily serves such ulterior purposes as moral education. Nevertheless, that does not preclude there being moral learning with respect to narrative artworks. For in those cases, which I believe are quite common, moral learning issues, in a nonaccidental way, but rather like fallout or a regularly recurring side reaction, as the author seeks to absorb readers in the narrative by addressing, exercising, and sometimes deepening our moral understanding and emotions. This need not be the author's primary intention, but it happens very often in narratives of human affairs where it is our moral interest in the work and our moral activity in response to the work that keep us interested in the object.

In conclusion, I have tried to show why we are naturally inclined to advert to morality when we discuss narrative artworks, and I have also attempted, in the teeth of autonomist objections, to ground the variable moral assessments we make concerning narrative artworks in our experience of the work.[30] Throughout, I have focused on one very important relation between morality and the narrative artwork, specifically on the way in which the narrative artwork unavoidably engages, exercises, and sometimes clarifies and deepens moral understanding and the moral emotions. Indeed, it is my contention that this is the most comprehensive or general relation we can find between art, or at least narrative art, and morality.

Undoubtedly, there may be other relations between art and morality. Some narratives, like the story of the Roman general Regulus, are designed to make virtues, such as honesty, more and more attractive (in a way that might suit Plato's suggestions about the moral education of the young), while other narratives, like "The Pied Piper of Hamelin," are meant to make vices, like dishonesty, seem profoundly ill advised. However, such overt moral didacticism is not the mark of most narratives, but only of a limited segment, often dedicated to children.

Likewise, some narratives are devoted to extending moral sympathies by inducing some of us to see things from foreign or alien points of view. For example, in *Beloved,* Toni Morrison invites us to understand why a slave mother might prefer to kill her child rather than to have the child grow up in bondage. But though this is an undeniable way in which a narrative might address its audience, it is not a phenomenon operative in all or even most narratives of human affairs, since not all narratives typically possess viewpoints that differ in any appreciable degree from those of their audiences.

Thus, I have stressed the way in which narrative artworks generally, given their nature, unavoidably bring moral understanding into contact with narrative artworks as virtually a condition for comprehending them. I have pursued this line of attack because it seems to me to rest on the most pervasive stratum of the relation of morality to narrative art – though, of course, I would be the first to agree that other strata also welcome further excavation.

Throughout this essay, I have tried to indicate why we are so naturally inclined to considerations of morality when we think about, discuss, and evaluate narrative artworks. I have argued that this disposition is connected to the nature of narrative artworks that concern human affairs. In this respect, I wish to urge that it is not a category error to talk about morality with reference to narrative artworks, given the kinds of things they are. Moreover, contra autonomism, since narrative artworks are designed to enlist moral judgment and understanding, morally assessing such works in light of the quality of the moral experience they afford is appropriate. It is not a matter of going outside the work, but rather of focusing right on it.

MODERATE MORALISM

I. INTRODUCTION

For almost three decades, public discourse about art has become increasingly preoccupied with moral issues. Indeed, the discussion of literature in some precincts of the humanities nowadays is nearly always in terms of morals, or, as its proponents might prefer to say, in terms of politics (though here I must hasten to add that the politics in question are generally of the sort that is underwritten by a moral agenda). Moreover, the artworld itself has begun to reflect this preoccupa-

From: *British Journal of Aesthetics,* 36, no. 3 (July 1996), 223–38.

tion to the extent that disgruntled critics have started to wonder aloud when artists are going to become interested in making art again and are going to give up preaching. Remember the fracas over the 1993 Whitney Biennial? Or, look at virtually any issue of the *New Criterion*.

Of course, by remarking that this is a tendency recently come to the fore, I mean to signal that things have not always been this way. Within living memory, or, at least, within my memory, I still recall being admonished as an undergraduate not to allow my attention to wander "outside the text" – where such things as moral questions lurked, as if, so to speak, on "the wrong side of the tracks."

My own initiation into the artworld occurred during the heyday of minimalism, which was understood alternatively as a project of aesthetic research into the essential conditions of painting or as an exercise in the phenomenology of aesthetic perception. In either case, it went without saying that the appropriate focus of one's attention was what was imprecisely called formal problems rather than, say, moral or political ones. In those days, it remained a common article of faith that the artistic realm is autonomous, somehow hermetically sealed off from the rest of our social practices and concerns. To talk about art from a moral point of view belied a failure of taste or intelligence, or, more likely, both.

The changes in criticism and artistic creativity to which I have already broadly alluded are, in part, explicit departures from and rebellions against the belief in the autonomy of art. Though admittedly often excessive, if not sometimes even downright paranoid, these developments, I feel, provide a generally healthy corrective to formalism and its corresponding doctrine of artistic autonomy. Yet of all the disciplines ready to acknowledge the limitations of the presupposition of art's autonomy, contemporary analytic philosophy of art has been the slowest. A brief examination of the philosophical literature that has been produced since the end of World War II easily confirms that the relation of art to morality is a topic that has received and that continues to receive scant attention.

Perhaps one reason for this temporal lag is philosophy's status as a second-order discipline; the owl Minerva needs a functioning runway from which to take off. But, in any event, the recent resurgence of moralistic art and criticism should remind us, as Plato, Aristotle, and even Hume already knew, that there are intimate relations between at least some art and morality that call for philosophical comment. One of the purposes of this essay is to contribute to the discussion of the relation of art to morality.

Moreover, it is my conviction that philosophy has a useful job to perform within the context of renewed interest in the moral dimension of art. For, although a great deal of contemporary criticism presupposes that art can be discussed and even evaluated morally, little effort has been devoted to working out the philosophical foundations of moral criticism beyond loudly and insistently protesting that the doctrines of formalism and artistic autonomy are obviously wrongheaded, repressive and undoubtedly pernicious. But this stance, it seems to me, simply ignores the powerful intuitions that underlie the claims in favour of artistic autonomy. Thus, in this essay, I will review two forms of autonomism –

what I call radical autonomism and moderate autonomism – in order to argue dialectically for an alternative position that I call moderate moralism.[1]

II. RADICAL AUTONOMISM

Radical autonomism is the view that art is a strictly autonomous realm of practice. It is distinct from other social realms that pursue cognitive, political, or moral value. On this account, because art is distinct from other realms of social value, it is inappropriate or even incoherent to assess artworks in terms of their consequences for cognition, morality, and politics. In fact, according to Clive Bell, perhaps the best known radical autonomist, it is virtually unintelligible to talk of art *qua* art in terms of non-aesthetic concerns with cognition, morality, politics, and so on.[2]

Autonomism of any sort provides an attractive antidote to the views of Plato, Tolstoy, and innumerable other puritanical art critics. Opposing them, the autonomist maintains that art is intrinsically valuable, and that it is not and should not be subservient to ulterior or external purposes, such as promoting moral education. In this, autonomism appeals to the intuition, though maybe it is only a modern intuition already informed by autonomism, that artworks can be valuable, perhaps in virtue of the beauty they deliver to disinterested attention, irrespective of their social consequences.

We value artworks for their own sake, it is said – that is, for the way in which they engage us, apart from questions of instrumental value. Autonomism squares with the intuition that what is valuable about our experiences of art is the way in which artworks absorb our attention and command our interest, which, in turn, is part of the reason that artworks associated with obsolete systems of belief, both cognitive and moral, can nonetheless remain compelling. For, the autonomist claims, it is the artwork's design rather than its content that holds our attention.

In addition, autonomism is a satisfying doctrine for anyone who approaches the question of the nature of art with essentialist biases – that is, with the expectation that everything we call art will share a *uniquely* common characteristic that pertains distinctly to all and only art. This is the card that Clive Bell plays when he announces that unless we can identify such a common, uniquely defining feature for art, then when we use the concept, we gibber.

Of course, by declaring art to be utterly separate from every other realm of human practice, the autonomist secures the quest for essentialism at a single stroke, if only by negation, by bolding asserting that art has nothing to do with anything else. It is a unique form of activity with its own purposes and standards of evaluation, generally calibrated in terms of formal achievement.

That those standards do not involve moral considerations, moreover, can be supported, autonomists argue, by noting that moral assessment cannot be an appropriate measure of artistic value, since not all artworks possess a moral dimension. I call this the common denominator argument. It presupposes that any evaluative measure that can be brought to bear on art should be applicable to all art. But since certain works of art – including some string quartets and some abstract visual designs – may be altogether bereft of moral significance, it makes no sense, so the argument goes, to raise issues of morality when assessing artworks. Moral evaluation is never appropriate to artworks, in short, because it is not universally applicable.

Likewise, that we are willing to call some artworks good despite their moral limitations – despite the fact that their moral insights may be paltry or even flawed – fits nicely with the autonomist contention that art has nothing to do with morality, as does the fact that with certain works of art, questions of morality make no sense whatsoever. The autonomist accounts for these putative facts by saying that art is valuable for its own sake and that it has its own unique grounds for assessment; art has its own purposes, and, therefore, its own criteria of evaluation.

Autonomism rides on the unexceptionable observation that art appears to aim, first and foremost, at being absorbing. The so-called aesthetic experience is centripetal. Thus, if the artwork essentially aims at our absorption in it, then it is valuable for its own sake. The thought that art is valuable for its own sake, in turn, is believed to imply that it is not valuable for other reasons, especially cognitive, moral, and political ones. However, this conclusion is a non sequitur. For, in ways to be pursued later, some art may be absorbing exactly because of the way in which it engages, among other things, the moral life of its audiences. That is, just because we value art for the way in which it commands our undivided attention, this does not preclude that some art commands our attention in this way just because it is interesting and engaging cognitively and/or, for our purposes, morally.

The autonomist is certainly correct to point out that it is inappropriate to invoke moral considerations in evaluating *all* art. Some art, at least, is altogether remote from moral considerations. And in such cases, moral discourse with reference to the artworks in question may not only be strained and out of place, but conceptually confused. Nevertheless, the fact that it may be a mistake to mobilize moral discourse with reference to some pure orchestral music or some abstract painting has no implications about whether it is appropriate to do so with respect to *King Lear* or *Potemkin,* since those works of art are expressly designed to elicit moral reactions, and it is part of the form of life to which they belong that audiences respond morally to them on the basis of their recognition that that is what they are intended to do, given the relevant social practices. That is, with cases like these, it is not peculiar, tasteless, or dumb to talk about the artworks in question from a moral point of view, but normatively correct or appropriate, given the nature of the artworks in relation to the language game in which such talk occurs.

The common-denominator argument presupposes that there must be a single scale of evaluation that applies to all artworks. Whether or not there is such a scale – a vexed question if there ever was one – can be put to the side, however, because even if there is such a scale, that would fail to imply that it is the only evaluative consideration that it is appropriate to bring to bear on every artwork. For in addition to, for example, formal considerations, some artworks may be such that, given the nature of the artworks in question, it is also appropriate to discuss them in terms of other dimensions of value.

We may evaluate sledge hammers and jewelery hammers in terms of their capacities to drive nails, but that does not preclude further assessments of the former in terms of their capabilities to deliver great force to a single point in space or the latter to deliver delicate, glancing blows. These additional criteria are, of course, related to the kinds of things that sledge hammers and jewelery hammers respectively are. Similarly, the conviction that there may be some common standard of evaluation for all artworks, even if plausible, would not entail that for certain kinds of artworks, given what they are, considerations of dimensions of value beyond the formal, such as moral considerations, are out of bounds.

It is my contention that there are many kinds of artworks – genres, if you will – that naturally elicit moral responses, that prompt talk about themselves in terms of moral considerations, and even warrant moral evaluation. The common-denominator argument cannot preclude this possibility logically, for even if there is some global standard of artistic value (a very controversial hypothesis), there may be different local standards for different genres. This much is obvious: decibel level has a role to play in heavy metal music that is irrelevant to minuets. Moreover, with some genres, moral considerations are pertinent, even though there may be other genres where they would be tantamount to category errors.

Though no autonomist to date has been able to offer a positive characterization of the essence of art, the autonomist frequently relies on some conception of the nature of art in order to back up the common-denominator argument. That is, art, given its putatively generic nature, supposedly yields generic canons of assessment. However, we can challenge this appeal to the nature of art with appeals to the natures of specific artforms or genres that, given what they are, warrant at least additional criteria of evaluation to supplement whatever the autonomist claims is the common denominator of aesthetic evaluation.

In order to substantiate this abstract claim, let us take a look at the narrative arts (narrative literature, drama, film, painting and so on). It is of the nature of narrative to be incomplete. No author is absolutely explicit about the situations she depicts. Every narrative makes an indeterminate number of presuppositions and it is the task of readers, viewers, and listeners to fill these in. Part of what it is to follow a story is to fill in the presuppositions that the narrator has left unsaid. If the story is about Sherlock Holmes, we presuppose that he is a man and not an android, though Conan Doyle never says so. If the story concerns ancient Rome, we presuppose the message was delivered by hand, not by fax.

No storyteller portrays everything that might be portrayed about the story she is telling; she must depend upon her audience to supply what is missing and a substantial and ineliminable part of what it is to understand a narrative involves filling in what the author has left out. It is of the nature of narrative to be incomplete in this way and for narrative communication to depend for uptake upon audiences supplying what has been left unremarked by the author.

Furthermore, what must be filled in this way comes in all different shapes and sizes, including facts of physics, biology, history, religion, and so on. Notably, much of the information that the author depends on the audience's bringing to the text is folk-psychological. The author need not explain why a character is saddened by her mother's death. The audience brings its understanding of human psychology to bear on the situation.

But it is not only the presupposed, implied, or suggested facts about the fictional world and human psychology that the audience must fill in in order for narratives to be intelligible. Understanding a narrative also requires mobilizing the emotions that are appropriate to the story and its characters. One does not understand *Trilby* unless one finds Svengali repugnant. Moreover, and this is where the connection with morality begins to enter, many of the emotions that the audience brings to bear, as a condition of narrative intelligibility, are moral both in the sense that many emotions, like anger (inasmuch as "being wronged" is conceptually criterial for its application), possess ineliminable moral components, and in the sense that many of the emotions that are pertinent to narratives are frequently moral emotions, such as the indignation that pervades a reading of *Uncle Tom's Cabin.*

Without mobilizing the moral emotions of the audience, narratives cannot succeed. They would appear unintelligible. One does not, I submit, understand the wedding scene in Ken Russell's production of *Madame Butterfly* unless one feels that Pinkerton is unworthy of his bride. Thus, activating moral judgments from audiences is a standard feature of successful narrative artworks. And this is the case, not only where the moral judgments play a role in emotional responses, but also where the audience understands the logic of a plot that deals wrongdoers their just deserts.

Part of what is involved, then, in the process of filling in a narrative is the activation of the moral powers – the moral judgments and the moral emotions – of audiences. Moreover, it is vastly improbable that there could be any substantial narrative of human affairs, especially a narrative artwork, that did not rely upon activating the moral powers of readers, viewers, and listeners. Even modernist novels that appear to eschew "morality" typically do so in order to challenge bourgeois morality and to enlist the reader in sharing their ethical disdain for it.

Earlier I noted that according to the radical autonomist, moral concern with artworks is regarded to be either a failure in taste or intelligence insofar as such concern is inappropriate with respect to art. Talk about morality is, on this account, out of place, if not conceptually incoherent. However, if understanding a narrative artwork is, as I have argued, so inextricably bound up with moral understanding, then at least with narrative artworks, it will be natural for moral concerns to arise in the course of our appreciation of narrative artworks and our discussions of them.

Since narrative artworks necessarily depend upon activating our antecedent moral beliefs, concepts, and feelings, it is no accident that we will be predisposed to discuss, to share, and to compare our moral reactions with other readers, listeners, and viewers concerning the characters, situations, and the texts that portray them, where, indeed, the authors of said texts have presented them to us with the clear intention of mobilizing, among other things, our moral responses. It is natural for us to discuss narrative artworks by means of ethical vocabularies because, due to the kinds of things they are, narrative artworks are designed to awaken, to stir up, and to engage our moral powers of recognition and judgment. The radical autonomist claims that moral discourse is alien to all artworks. But, given the nature of narrative artworks, it is germane to them. We may discuss the formal features of narrative artworks, but it is also apposite, given the nature of the beast, to discuss them from a moral point of view.[3]

The radical autonomist undoubtedly has a case against what might be called the radical moralist or Puritan — someone, perhaps, like Plato — who maintains that art should *only* be discussed from a moral point of view. But radical moralism is not my position, since I freely admit that some works of art may have no moral dimension, due to the kind of works they are, and because I do not claim that moral considerations trump all other considerations, such as formal ones. My position, moderate moralism, only contends that for certain genres, moral comment, along with formal comment, is natural and appropriate.

Moreover, the moderate moralist also contends that moral evaluation may figure in our evaluations of some artworks. For inasmuch as narrative artworks engage our powers of moral understanding, they can be assessed in terms of whether they deepen or pervert the moral understanding. That is, some artworks may be evaluated by virtue of the contribution they make to moral education.

Of course, there is a longstanding argument against the educative powers of artworks, namely, that what we typically are said to learn from artworks are nothing but truisms, which, in fact, everyone already knows and whose common knowledge may in fact be a condition for the intelligibility of the artworks in question. For example, no one *learns* that murder is bad from *Crime and Punishment* and, indeed, knowing that murder is bad may be a presupposition that the reader must bring to *Crime and Punishment* in order to understand it. Artworks, in other words, trade in moral commonplaces, and, therefore, do not really teach morality. They are not a source of moral education, but depend upon and presuppose already morally educated readers, viewers, and listeners.

However, the characterization that I have offered of the relation of moral understanding does not fall foul of this objection. I agree that the moral emotions and judgments that narratives typically call upon audiences to fill in are generally already in place. Most narrative artworks do not teach audiences new moral emotions or new moral tenets. They activate preexisting ones. Nevertheless, it is a mistake to presume that this may not involve moral education. That is, it is an error to presuppose that moral education only occurs when new moral emotions or tenets are communicated.

Moral education is not simply a matter of acquiring new moral precepts. Moral education also involves coming to understand how to apply those precepts to situations. Moral understanding is the capability to manipulate abstract moral precepts — to see connections between them and be able to employ them intelligibly with respect to concrete situations. Understanding is not simply a matter of having access to abstract propositions and concepts; it involves being able to apply them appropriately. This, of course, requires practice, and narrative artworks provide opportunities to develop, to deepen and to enlarge the moral understanding through practice.[4]

We may believe certain abstract principles – like "all persons should be given their due" – and possess abstract concepts – such as "virtue = that which promotes human flourishing" – without being able to connect these abstractions to concrete situations. For that requires not only knowing these abstractions, but understanding them. Moreover, it is this kind of understanding – particularly in terms of moral understanding – to which engaging with narrative artworks may contribute.[5]

Furthermore, since the emotions have a conceptual dimension – by virtue of possessing formal criteria concerning that which can function as the object of an emotion – it makes sense to talk about deepening or enlarging our emotional understanding. Narrative artworks promote such understanding by providing occasions for clarifying our emotions, or, as Aristotle might say, for learning to bring the right emotion to bear upon an appropriate object with suitable intensity.

So, understanding a narrative artwork may involve a simultaneous process of deepening or enlarging one's moral understanding. And this, in turn, is an important element of moral education. Of course, learning from a narrative artwork through the enlargement of one's moral understanding is not well described as a consequence of engaging the story. Understanding the work, enlarging one's moral understanding and learning from the narrative are all part and parcel of the same process, which might be called comprehending or following the narrative. In reading a novel, our moral understanding is engaged already. Indeed, reading a novel is itself generally a moral activity insofar as reading narrative literature typically involves us in a continuous process of making moral judgments. Moreover, this continuous exercise of moral judgment itself contributes to the expansion and education of our moral understanding through practice.

Thus, we may speak of moral education with respect to narrative artworks without supposing that they trade in new moral discoveries or that moral education is an alien imposition on the narrative artwork. Moral education, in terms of the exercise of moral understanding, is a constituent in the appropriate mode of responding to narratives, i.e. following the story. And, if moral education is built in, so to speak, to responding to narratives, there is a straightforward way to evaluate narratives morally. Those narratives that deepen moral understanding, in the manner of, say, James' *Ambassadors,* are, all things being equal, morally commendable, whereas those that muddy moral understanding, as does *Pulp Fiction,* which suggests that homosexual rape is much worse than murder, are morally defective. Moreover, *pace* radical autonomism, such moral evaluations of narrative artworks are not inappropriate. Given the relation of narrative understanding to moral understanding, and the basis of that relationship in the (incomplete) nature of the narrative artwork, such evaluations are quite natural. It is not a category error to find that *Pulp Fiction,* no matter how formally compelling, is also, in certain respects, morally defective. *Pulp Fiction,* because of the kind of artwork it is, engages the moral understanding and can be assessed in terms of the efficacy of that engagement.[6]

III. MODERATE AUTONOMISM

The radical autonomist contends that all art is autonomous and takes this to entail, among other things, that discussing and evaluating art from a moral perspective is conceptually ill-founded, indeed, incoherent. I have argued that for some artworks, notably narrative artworks, this view is mistaken. For, given the nature of the narrative artwork, it is appropriate to discuss it and evaluate it morally. However, confronted by arguments like the preceding one, the autonomist may reconceive his position, conceding that some art may by its very nature engage moral understanding and may be coherently discussed and even evaluated morally. Nevertheless, the autonomist is apt to qualify this concession immediately by arguing that with such works of art, we need to distinguish between various levels of address in the object.

A given artwork may legitimately traffic in aesthetic, moral, cognitive, and political value. But these various levels are independent or autonomous. An artwork may be aesthetically valuable and morally defective, or vice versa. But these different levels of value do not mix, so to speak. An aesthetically defective artwork is not bad because it is morally defective and that provides a large part of the story about why a work can be aesthetically valuable, but evil. Let us call this view moderate autonomism because, though it allows that the moral discussion and evaluation of artworks, or at least some artworks, is coherent and appropriate, it remains committed to the view that the aesthetic dimension of the artwork is autonomous from other dimensions, such as the moral dimension.[7]

The radical autonomist maintains that moral discussion and evaluation are never appropriate with respect to any artwork. The moderate autonomist maintains only that the aesthetic dimension of artworks is autonomous. This grants that artworks (at least some of them) may be evaluated morally as well as aesthetically, but contends that the moral evaluation of the artwork is never relevant to its aesthetic evaluation. The moral dimension of an artwork, when it possesses one, is strictly independent of the aesthetic dimension.

For the moderate autonomist, the narrative artwork can be divided into different dimensions of value, and, although it is permissible to evaluate such an artwork morally, the moral strengths and weaknesses of an artwork, *vis-à-vis* moral understanding, can never provide grounds for a comparable evaluation of the aesthetic worth of an artwork. That is, an artwork will never be aesthetically better in virtue of its moral strengths, and will never be worse because of its moral defects.

On a strict reading of moderate autonomism, one of its decisive claims is that defective moral understanding never counts against the aesthetic merit of a work. An artwork may invite an audience to entertain a defective moral perspective and this will not detract from its aesthetic value. But this central claim of moderate autonomism is false.

Recall Aristotle's discussion of character in the *Poetics*.[8] There he conjectures that, for tragedy to take hold, the major character must be of a certain moral sort, if we are to pity him. He cannot be evil, because then we will regard his destruction as well deserved. The historical Hitler could not be a tragic character; his ignominious death would not prompt us to pity him. Indeed, we might applaud it. Likewise, Aristotle points out the tragic character cannot be flawless. For then when disaster befalls him we will be moved to outrage not pity. Mother Teresa could not be a figure of tragedy, because she had no fatal flaw. The right kind of character, Aristotle hypothesizes, is morally mixed, elevated, but in other respects more like the average viewer.

If certain characters are inserted into the tragic scenario, in other words, tragedy will not secure the effects that are normatively correct for it. That is, tragedy will fail on its own terms – terms internal to the practice of tragedy – when the characters are of the wrong sort. This failure will be aesthetic in the straightforward sense that it is a failure of tragedy *qua* tragedy. And the locus of the failure may be that the author has invited the audience to share a defective moral perspective, asking us, for example, to regard Hitler as an appropriate object of pity.

A recent example of such a failure is Brett Easton Ellis' novel *American Psycho*. The author intended it as a satire of the rapacious eighties in the United States. He presented a serial killer as the symbol of the vaunted securities marketeer of Reaganonomics. However, the serial killings depicted in the novel are so graphically brutal that readers are not able morally to get past the gore in order to savor the parody. Certainly, Ellis made an aesthetic error. He misjudged the effect of the murders on the audience. He failed to anticipate that the readers would not be able to secure uptake of his themes in the face of the unprecedented violence. He invited the audience to view the murders as political satire and that was an invitation they could not morally abide. His moral understanding of the possible significance of murders, such as the ones he depicted, was flawed, and he was condemned for promoting it. But that defect was also an aesthetic defect, inasmuch as it compromised the novel on its own terms. *American Psycho's* failure to achieve uptake as satire is attributable to Ellis' failure to grasp the moral inappropriateness of regarding his serial killer as comic.

Narrative artworks are, as we have argued, incomplete structures. Among other things, they must be filled in by the moral responses of readers, viewers, and listeners. Securing the right moral response of the audience is as much a part of the design of a narrative artwork as structural components like plot complications. Failure to elicit the right moral response, then, is a failure in the design of the work, and, therefore, is an aesthetic failure. The design (the aesthetic structure) of *American Psycho* is flawed on its own terms because it rests on a moral mistake, supposing, as it does, that the sustained, deadpan, clinically meticulous dismemberments it presents to the reader could be taken in a comically detached manner. A great many of the readers of *American Psycho* reacted to the flawed moral understanding of *American Psycho,* and rejected it aesthetically. Thus, this case, along with Aristotle's observations, indicate that sometimes a moral flaw in a work can count against the work aesthetically. Therefore, moderate autonomism seems false.

Many artworks depend for their effect upon the artist's understanding the moral psychology of the audience. Where the artist fails to anticipate the moral understanding of the audience, as Ellis did, the work may fail on its own terms, which is to say in terms of its own aesthetic aims. Of course, the Ellis example is one in which large parts of the audience rejected the aesthetic contract that Ellis extended to them. They were not about to laugh at prostitutes with holes methodically drilled into their heads.

But, one might ask, what about cases in which there is a defective moral perspective in a work, but the audience is not so aware of it – that is, a case where the average reader, viewer, or listener buys into it. Imagine, for example, a propaganda film that treats enemy soldiers as subhuman, worthy of any amount of indignity. Here, let us suppose, most of the audience embraces the flawed moral perspective that the film promotes. Does it make sense to call the work aesthetically defective because it endorses a flawed moral perspective that is also readily adopted by the average viewer?

I suspect that it may. Because as long as the moral understanding promoted by the film is defective, it remains a potential obstacle to the film's securing the response it seeks as a condition of its aesthetic success. Audiences during the heat of war may not detect its moral defect, but after the war such a defect will become more and more evident. Movies that thrilled people may come to disgust them morally. And even if they do not disgust the majority of viewers, the films are still flawed, inasmuch as they remain likely to fail to engender the planned response in morally sensitive viewers.

Moderate autonomists overlook the degree to which moral presuppositions play a structural role in the design of many artworks. Thus, an artist whose work depends upon a certain moral response from the audience, but who has proffered a work that defies moral understanding, makes a structural, or as they say, aesthetic error. This may be one way in which to understand Hume's contention that a moral blemish in an artwork may be legitimate grounds for saying that the work is defective.[9]

Moreover, as Kendall Walton has pointed out, audiences are particularly inflexible about the moral presuppositions they bring to artworks. Whereas we are willing to grant that the physical worlds of fiction may be otherwise – that objects can move faster than the speed of light – we are not willing to make similar concessions about morality – we are not willing to go with the notion, for example, that in the world of some fiction, killing innocent people is good. Thus, artworks that commerce in flawed moral conceptions may fail precisely because the failed moral conceptions they promote make it impossible for readers, viewers, and listeners to mobilize the audience responses to which the artists aspire in terms of their own aesthetic commitments.[10]

But even where given audiences do not detect the moral flaws in question, the artwork may still be aesthetically flawed, since in those cases the moral flaws sit like time-bombs, ready to explode aesthetically once morally sensitive viewers, listeners, and readers encounter them. That is, it need not be the case that viewers or readers actually are deterred from the response that the work invites. The work is flawed if it contains a failure in moral perspective that a morally sensitive audience could detect, such that that discovery would compromise the effect of the work on its own terms. Thus, a moral defect can count as an aesthetic defect even if it does not undermine appreciation by *actual* audiences so long as it has the counterfactual capacity to undermine the intended response of morally sensitive audiences.[11]

That Nazis *circa* 1943 could fail to recognize morally that Hitler was not a tragic figure does not show that a play encouraging us to pity the dictator is not aesthetically ill conceived. This may not be enough to show that a moral flaw is always an aesthetic flaw. But it is enough to show that it may sometimes be an aesthetic flaw, and that is sufficient to show that moderate autonomism is false.

Many artworks, such as narrative artworks, address the moral understanding. When that address is defective, we may say that the work is morally defective. And, furthermore, that moral defect may count as an aesthetic blemish. It will count as an aesthetic defect when it actually deters the response to which the work aspires. And it will also count as a blemish even if it is not detected – so long as it is there to be detected by morally sensitive audiences whose response to the work's agenda will be spoilt by it. A blemish is still a blemish even if it goes unnoticed for the longest time.

In response to my claim that a moral defect – such as representing Hitler as a tragic figure – counts as an aesthetic defect, the sophisticated moderate autonomist may respond that such defects might be categorized in two ways: as aesthetic defects (i.e., they present psychological problems with respect to audience uptake), or as moral problems (i.e., they project an evil viewpoint). Furthermore, the moderate autonomist may contend that all I have really offered are cases of the first type. And this does not imply that a moral problem *qua* moral problem is an aesthetic defect in an artwork. Thus, the moderate autonomist adds, it has not been shown that something is an aesthetic defect because it is evil; rather it is an error concerning the audience's psychology. Call it a tactical error.

But I am not convinced by this argument. I agree that the aesthetic defect concerns the psychology of audience members; they are psychologically incapable of providing the requisite uptake. But I am not persuaded that this failure is unconnected from the evil involved. For the reason that uptake is psychologically impossible may be because what is represented is evil. That is, the reason the work is aesthetically defective – in the sense of failing to secure psychological uptake – and the reason it is morally defective may be the same. Thus, insofar as the moderate autonomist may not be able to separate the aesthetic and moral defects of artworks across the board, moderate autonomism again seems false.

The moderate autonomist also contends that the moral merit of an artwork never redounds to its aesthetic value. Even if an artwork is of the sort where moral evaluation is legitimate, a positive moral evaluation is never relevant to an aesthetic evaluation. The positive moral evaluation is just icing on the aesthetic cake. But this seems too hasty, especially if our previous discussion of narrative art is accurate, since one of the fundamental aesthetic effects of stories – being absorbed in them, being caught up in the story – is intimately bound up with our moral responses, both in terms of our emotions and judgments.

Let us suppose that the bottom line, aesthetically speaking, with respect to narrative artworks is that we are supposed to be absorbed by them. Let us suppose that this is what authors aim at aesthetically. But if it is the purpose of the narrative artwork to absorb the audience, to draw us into the story, to capture our interest, to engage our emotions, and to stimulate our imaginations, then it should be obvious that by engaging moral judgments and emotions, the author may acquit her primary purpose by secondarily activating and sometimes deepening the moral understanding of the audience.

The autonomist is correct to say that it is not the function of the narrative artwork *per se* to provide moral education. Typically the aim of the narrative artwork is to command our attention and interest. But very frequently the narrative artwork achieves its goal of riveting audience attention and making us care about what happens next by means of enlisting our moral understanding and emotions. The author aims at drawing us into the story. But engaging the audience's moral understanding may be, and generally is, a means to this end.

Narrative art does not necessarily serve ulterior purposes like moral education. Nevertheless, this does not preclude that there may be moral learning with respect to narrative artworks. For in many instances the moral learning issues from following the narrative, in a nonaccidental fashion, but rather like a regularly recurring side reaction, as the author seeks to absorb readers of the narrative by addressing, exercising, and sometimes deepening our moral understandings and emotions. This need not be what the author has in the forefront of his intention, but it happens quite frequently in narratives of human affairs where it is our moral interest in the work and our moral activity in response to the work that keeps us attentive to the object.

The aesthetic appreciation of a narrative involves following the story. The more a narrative artwork encourages us to follow the story intensely, the better the narrative is *qua* narrative. I hope that I have shown that following the story involves our moral understanding and emotions. A narrative may be more absorbing exactly because of the way in which it engages our moral understanding and emotions. That is, the deepening of our moral understanding and emotions may contribute dramatically to our intense absorption in a narrative. And in such cases the way in which the narrative addresses and deepens our moral understanding is part and parcel of what makes the narrative successful.

Imagine, if you will, that Jane Austen had a twin. Let us also agree that part of what makes *Emma* absorbing is the opportunity it affords for deepening our moral understanding. The novel is better for the way in which it engages us in assessing the moral rectitude of Emma's interference with Harriet's love life. Now suppose that Jane Austen's sister wrote an alternative version of *Emma* that told the same story in the same elegant prose, but that did not address our moral understanding at all. All things being equal, I suspect that we would not find the alternative version of *Emma* as aesthetically compelling as the real Jane Austen's version. And the reason would be that it is the moral dimension of the original *Emma* that, in large measure, absorbs us, thereby enabling Jane Austen to discharge her primary goal as artist *qua* narrative author.

But if this is right, then moderate autonomism is false yet again. *Sometimes* it is the case that the way in which some artworks, such as narrative artworks, address moral understanding does contribute to the aesthetic value of the work. Works that we commend because of the rich moral experience they afford may sometimes, for the same reason, be commended aesthetically. This is moderate moralism. It contends that some works of art may be evaluated morally (contra radical autonomism) and that sometimes the moral defects and/or merits of a work may figure in the aesthetic evaluation of the work. It does not contend that artworks should always be evaluated morally, nor that every moral defect or merit in an artwork should figure in its aesthetic evaluation. That would amount to radical moralism, and I have no wish to defend such a view.

In conclusion, I have tried to show why with certain artworks, particularly narratives, we are naturally inclined to advert to morality when we think about and discuss them. I have attempted to defend this view by arguing that this disposition is connected to the nature of narrative. In this respect, I wish to urge that it is not a category error nor is it otherwise incoherent to talk about morality with reference to narrative artworks, given the kinds of things they are. Moreover, contra autonomism, since narrative artworks are designed to enlist moral judgment and understanding, assessing such works in light of the moral experiences they afford is appropriate. It is not a matter of going outside the work, but rather of focusing upon it.[12]

SIMULATION, EMOTIONS, AND MORALITY

Recently, a new theory of the way in which narrative fictions engage the emotions and the moral understanding has come to the fore in Anglo-American philosophy. Advanced by Gregory Currie and others, it attempts to exploit a theory developed in the context of the philosophy of mind in order to characterize our emotional and moral encounters with fictions.[1] This view may be called simulation theory. Stated roughly, simulation theory in the philosophy of mind is the hypothesis that we predict, understand, and interpret others by putting ourselves in their place, that is to say, by adopting their point of view.[2] Philosophers of art like Currie suggest that the apparatus of simulation is also what we use when we read, view, or listen to narratives. The grain of truth in what is informally called "identification" is, *ex hypothesi*, the process of simulation. Currie writes: "What is

From: *Emotion in Postmodernism*, ed. by Gerhard Hoffman and Alfred Hornung (Heidelberg: Universitats Verlag C. Winter, 1997), 383–400.

so often called audience identification with a character is best described as mental simulation of the character's situation by the audience who are then better able to imagine the character's experience."[3]

By simulating the mental states of fictional characters, we come to experience what it would be like – that is, for example, what it would feel like – to be in situations such as those in which the characters find themselves. This is relevant to morality, inasmuch as we learn, by acquaintance, what it would feel like to undertake certain courses of action – what it would be like to murder someone, for instance. Furthermore, knowing what it would be like to murder someone or to steal is relevant information when it comes to moral deliberation, since before we undertake a certain line of action, it is important to have a sense of how we will feel about it, once we act.[4] Thus, engaging fictions by simulation is a source of knowledge, for example, about the emotions, which information, in turn, is relevant to moral deliberation and, therefore, to morality. For in deliberating about whether one will commit adultery, it is pertinent to ask oneself what it will feel like once one has done it. Will one feel unbearable pangs of conscience and remorse? One way to find this out is by simulating the experience of fictional adulterers. Or so the story goes.

The notion of simulation has arisen in a context of debate in the philosophy of mind over the best way in which to explain how we predict the behavior of other people in everyday life. One view of how we do this can be called the Theory Theory. On this view, as we mature, we learn a lot about how people behave. We learn that in certain situations, people will react in certain predictable ways. For example, if you aggressively accuse someone of something, they are likely to deny it. Gradually, our knowledge of other people grows. We acquire a great deal of folk-psychological knowledge about human behavior. Moreover, this folk-psychological knowledge of other people's behavior, it is said, has the structure of something like a theory – a very powerful theory, indeed, when you think about how often we are right in our predictions about the behavior of others.

This view is called the Theory Theory because it is the *theory* that we predict and understand the behavior of others on the basis of our possession of an implicit folk-psychological theory of human behavior, a folk-psychological *theory* whose level of accuracy should be the envy of any social scientist. In other words, the Theory Theory is the theory that folk psychology is a theory. According to the Theory Theory, when we observe another person, we apply our implicit folk-psychological theory of human behavior to predict and to understand what they will do. We mobilize, so the account says, the generalizations of our folk psychological theory, much in the manner of a scientist.

There are some obvious questions, however, that the Theory Theory raises. Is it plausible to think that people really possess such a theory subconsciously – a theory whose predictive power is beyond anything available at present to conscious social scientists? Such a theory would be more complex than our most complicated physical theories. Isn't it quite a stretch to think that we are all in possession of such powerful theory subconsciously, especially given how weak our explicit, formal psychological theories are in terms of their predictive power? How is it that we are so smart in constructing our theories subconsciously, but so bad at replicating them consciously? In addition, the computations that the Theory Theory imputes to us are quite complex and would appear to require a great deal of real time to work through. However, our predictions of how others will behave often transpires in an instant.

Simulation theory is proposed as an alternative to the Theory Theory – an alternative that overcomes its shortcomings. It denies that we possess a complex theory of human behavior. Rather, it argues that when we want to predict or understand the behavior of others, we put ourselves in their shoes. We use our own complement of background beliefs, desires, and emotions in order to see how we would respond were we in the situation of the person in question, and then we predict that that person would act as we would. If we want to know how someone else would feel in a certain situation, we put ourselves in their situation, taking on their beliefs about the situation and their values concerning it, and then we observe how we would feel. We use ourselves, in other words, as simulators.

Your belief-desire *system* and mine are pretty much the same. So, if you want to learn about how I am feeling, put yourself in my position – entertain the specific beliefs and desires that are pertinent for me in the situation at hand – and the emotion that I am feeling is apt to arise in you. This is likely to happen because the network of believing, desiring, and emoting that you and I possess are roughly congruent. So input my beliefs and desires into your cognitive/conative system, and the output is likely to be the same.

Similarly, if one wants to predict what someone else will do, input that person's beliefs, desires, and emotions into your own cognitive/conative system and observe what you yourself are disposed to do. This is how Sherlock Holmes proceeds in the "Musgrave Ritual" when he tells Watson: "You know my methods in such cases, Watson. I put myself in the man's place, and, having first gauged his intelligence, I try to imagine how I should myself have proceeded under the same circumstances."[5] Thus, Sherlock Holmes is able to discover Brunton's behavior by simulating it – by asking what he himself would have done in Brunton's place – by running Brunton's program, so to speak, on his own (Sherlock Holmes') system of beliefs, desires, and emotions. Or, as Kant says: "It is obvious that, if I wish to represent to myself a thinking being, I put myself in his place, and thus substitute, as it were, my own subject for the object I am seeking to consider (which does not occur in any other kind of investigation)."[6]

Of course, simulation theory does not suppose that our mental state is exactly the same as that of our target. For when we simulate another, we decouple, so to speak, our mental system from our action system. Or, as simulation theorists, aping computer jargon, like to say: we go off-line. Our cogitations, that is to say, do not issue in actions; they stop short of that. Simulation is a mode of imagination. According to the simulation theorist, this is how we predict the behavior of others in everyday life. Folk psychology is not a theory; folk psychology is simulation. That is, simulation provides, in large measure, the means by which we predict the behavior of others; we use ourselves as detectors of their intentions.

Moreover, we do not just simulate the behavioral intentions of others. When we deliberate about practical decisions, we simulate our own prospective activities. We imagine different lines of action and run them off-line on our own cognitive/conative system in order to gain a sense of how we would react in different circumstances as well as how we would feel emotionally about undertaking different lines of action. Thus, simulation is a crucial ingredient in practical deliberation about our own actions.

In the case of simulating others, we input their relevant beliefs and desires into the black box of our own off-line cognitive/conative system and then consider the output as a predictor of their behavior. With respect to our own prospective actions, we input our own beliefs about some possible future state into our off-line or disengaged cognitive/conative system and contemplate our reactions, including our emotional reactions, to alternative states of affairs. Obviously, from an evolutionary point of view the capacity to run these off-line simulations is an advantage. It is an economical way to figure out what others (including other people and perhaps sometimes animals) will do. But we do not just simulate the behavioral dispositions of others. We simulate our own prospective, future selves. This enables us to test out alternative strategies in thought.

From the viewpoint of evolutionary theory, the explanation for why we have the faculty of imagination/simulation is that it affords the capacity for strategy testing.[7] By entertaining thoughts about future states, we are able to get a handle on how we will feel and act in alternative situations, and, as well, we are able to work up informed hypotheses about how others are likely to respond to us (which is useful in testing out our own prospective strategies). Simulation is a means for constructing cost-free test runs of future actions that can provide us with knowledge about ourselves and others.

Clearly, the theory that folk psychology is simulation rather than a complex psychological theory avoids some of the problems of the Theory Theory. According to the simulation theory, there is no reason to hypothesize our dubious possession of an immensely elaborate, subconscious psychological theory. Moreover, the mobilization of such an elaborate theory with respect to particular cases would seem to require a large amount of computing time, whereas running a simulation is a much faster process – one whose speed is much more in keeping with our actual, real time predictions of the behavior of others.

Moving from the realm of predicting actual behavior to the realm of aesthetics, the application of simulation theory to the consumption of fiction is very straightforward. When we read, view, or listen to a fiction, we are running our cognitive/conative system off-line already; that is, we are imagining the story. Moreover, simulation is a special case of imagining. It is, the simulation theorist argues, one of the primary resources of the imagination that we employ when following texts.

With respect to fictional texts, Gregory Currie distinguishes between two types of imagining. Primary imagining is a matter of what we may describe as entertaining a proposition in the mind as unasserted. It is imagining, under the guidance of the author, that such and such is the case in the world of the fiction.

But there is a another kind of imagining that Currie believes comes into play in response to the fiction. It involves imagining – that is, simulating – the experience of a character.

Currie writes:

> *Secondary* imagining occurs when we imagine various things so as to imagine what is fictional. Sometimes, secondary imaginings are not required for primary imagining to take place: the story has it that a certain character walked down a dark street, and we simply imagine that. Then we have primary imagining without secondary imagining. Primary imagining most notably requires the support of secondary imagining in cases where what we are primarily to imagine is the experience of character. If the dark street hides something threatening, the character who walks may have thoughts, anxieties, visual and auditory experiences and bodily sensations about which it would be important for readers to imagine something. The author may indicate to greater or lesser degree of specificity, what the character's experience is. But it is notoriously difficult, and in some cases perhaps impossible, for us to describe people's mental states precisely. Authors who adopt stream of consciousness and other subjective styles have failed to do it, and so have film makers like Hitchcock who try to recreate the character's visual experiences on screen. Anyway, the attempt at full specificity and precision in this regard would usually be regarded as a stylistic vice, leaving, as we significantly say, "nothing to the imagination." What the author explicitly says and what can be inferred therefrom, will constrain our understanding of the character's mental state. It will set signposts and boundaries. But if these are all we have to go on in a fiction, it will seem dull and lifeless. It is when we are able, in imagination [through simulation], to feel as the character feels that fictions of character take hold of us. It is this process of empathetic re-enactment which I call secondary imagination.[8]

Simulation or secondary imagining, moreover, can be relevant to moral deliberation.

> We imagine ourselves in a certain situation which the fiction describes, imagining ourselves to have the same relevant beliefs, desires and values as the character whose situation it is. If our imagining goes well, it will tell us something about how we would respond to the situation, and what it would be like to experience it: a response and a phenomenology we can then transfer to the character. That way we learn something about the character. More importantly, from the point of view of moral knowledge, we learn something about ourselves and about the things, we regard or might regard as putative values.[9]

Fictions, by way of simulation, then, supply us with the kind of knowledge that would be relevant to making a moral decision about a course of action – knowledge of what it would be like (e.g., what it would feel like emotionally) to be a liar, a cheat, or a philanthropist. If we killed someone, could we live with ourselves? Simulation can provide some information toward answering such questions.

Moreover, this conception of the relation of fiction to morality provides a means for evaluating narratives from an ethical point of view. For example, "fictions that encourage secondary imaginings, while providing signposts for those imaginings which systematically distort their outcomes, may do moral damage by persuading us to value that which is not valuable."[10] And, presumably, fictions that encourage us to value what is morally valuable are *ceteris paribus,* to be assessed positively from the moral point of view.

There is, of course, a debate in the philosophy of mind about whether simulation is the correct conception of folk psychology.[11] This is not a debate about whether there is such a thing as simulation, but whether folk psychology is basically a matter of simulation. But those arguments, interesting as they may be, are not what we need to consider now. Rather, ours is the question of whether the notion of simulation – whether or not it best models folk psychology – is really relevant to aesthetics, specifically: is it relevant to our typical intercourse (especially our emotional intercourse) with fictions and the moral evaluation thereof.

For Currie, simulation is not the whole story of our engagement with fiction. Nor does he claim that simulation is the only relation of narrative fiction to morality. It is *a* relation, though one does have the impression that Currie thinks that it is a rather central and comprehensive one. But is it really?

Simulation or secondary imagining, as Currie describes it, is not the same thing as identification. For unlike identification, simulation does not presuppose that all of our cognitive and/or emotional states are identical to those of the character whom we are simulating. As in everyday life, simulation only requires rough similarity, not mental fusion. There is psychological evidence that audiences do represent the emotional states of characters mentally.[12] One issue is whether that representation takes the form of simulation. At least one psychologist has suggested that something like simulation might play a role in understanding the emotions of fictional characters; but this has not yet been substantiated empirically.[13] However, supposing simulation sometimes comes into play, the question is how often does this happen? How useful is simulation theory as a comprehensive model of our commerce with fictions, especially with reference to the emotions and morality?

Simulation theory suggests that we become engaged emotionally with fictions by simulating the emotional states of characters. Our emotional responses to the fiction are, so to speak, routed through the emotional states of characters. We experience the fiction as if from inside the characters. But an alternative view might suggest that our emotional responses to the fiction are more direct. We do not typically emote with respect to fictions by simulating a character's mental state; rather, we might argue, we respond emotionally to the fiction from the outside. Our point of view is that of an observer of the situation and not, as simulation theory suggests, that of the participant in the situation. When a character is about to be ambushed, we feel fear for her; we do not imagine ourselves to be her and then experience "her" fear.

In order to contemplate the differences between these two approaches, it is useful to recall a distinction made by Richard Wollheim. With reference to the imagination, Wollheim distinguishes between central imagining and acentral imagining.[14] Acentral imagining is a matter of my imagining *that* such and such; central imagining is a matter of my imagining *x*. Acentral imagination is exemplified by the case in which I imagine that Kubla Khan built Xanadu; central imagining is exemplified by the case where I imagine building Xanadu. Acentral imagining is from the outside, so to speak; central imagining is from the inside. Given this rough distinction, Currie's notion of simulation (or secondary imagining) is a case of central imagining, whereas the alternative view stated in the preceding paragraph is involved with acentral imagining. That is, according to the alternative view, we respond to fictional situations as outside observers, *assimilating* our conception of the character's mental state into our overall response as a sort of onlooker with respect to the situation in which the character finds himself. In contrast, for Currie, when we are involved in simulation or secondary imagining, we are centrally imagining that we are the characters. Which, if either, of these approaches is more comprehensive? Which models our response to fictional narratives better?

I think that quite clearly as consumers of fictions we are typically in the position of outside observers, or, as Richard Gerrig and Deborah Prentice call it, side-participants.[15] Of course, the simulationist can respond that outside observers can employ simulation. However, I wonder how often we do. After all, with most narratives, especially mass narratives, omniscient narrators tell us what is going on in the minds of the characters. Simulation theory putatively informs us about how we go about predicting the behavior of others and understanding their affective states. But most narratives, it seems to me, give us ready access to the mental states – the intentions, desires, and emotions – of characters. So what need do we have for simulation? We have the information already in most cases. Furthermore, this often happens in visual narratives as well; with respect to *Casablanca,* we do not have to simulate Rick's feelings about Ilsa; Rick tells us all we need to know in order to feel sorry for him.

Nor does this entail that the "direct access" to character's inner states renders narrative representations affectively lifeless. For we use that information, along with the information about the situation the character is in, in order to generate *our own* emotional reaction to the character and his or her circumstances. There is no need to suppose that our affective state has to be channeled through a simulation of a character's putative state. We can generate our own emotional reaction directly (i.e., without an intervening stage of simulation) by using the information that the narrator supplies us about the character about whom we are concerned – including explicitly given information about her intentions, desires, emotions, plans, and so on.

There are two parts to this objection. The first is that with the typical narrative, there is little role for simulation with respect to fictions – especially written fictions – because the determination of what is going on in the mind of characters is generally supplied by omniscient narrators. Thus, the pressure for philosophers of art to use simulation to explain our grasp of a character's state of mind does not match up with the pressure for simulation theorists in the philosophy of mind to explain our real-life predictions and understandings.

Second, as with the objections often advanced against the notion of identification, simulation theory seems to overestimate the degree to which responding emotionally to a fiction requires centrally imagining the states of characters. Most often, I would contend, the emotionally appropriate object of our attention is the situation in which a character finds herself and not the situation as the character experiences it. The character feels grief, but we feel pity for her, in part, because she is feeling grief. The object of her emotion is, say, her child. The object of our emotion is her situation − a situation in which she is feeling sorrow. We do not simulate her situation; rather, we respond emotionally with our own (different) feeling of pity to a situation in which someone, namely the relevant character, is feeling sorrow.

Putting these two objections together, then, we can argue that typically we do not need to postulate the operation of simulation because our emotional response is finally that of an observer (not a direct participant, as simulation might suggest), and the relevant information needed to form the appropriate emotional response from an observer's point of view is generally supplied by omniscient narrators. Thus, there is no reason to postulate the operation of simulation in the typical case of responding to fiction.

Of course, this argument, if it is persuasive, might be thought to apply primarily to written and perhaps spoken narratives. It might be said that it is less compelling when it comes to visual narratives like movies and TV programs. For with visual narratives, it is far less customary to have the sort of omniscient narration where we are given direct access to the minds of the characters. Running voiceover commentary on the characters' internal states − in either the first person or the third person − is, for example, rare. So, it might be argued that in general when it comes to visual narration, simulation usually has a role to play of a sort that I have denied it plays with standard cases of written narration. In visual narration, we are given the character's overt behavior and have to go on from there. Might it not be the case that we go on by way of simulation?

My inclination is to resist this suggestion. First of all, as the example of *Casablanca* indicates, characters often tell us about their mental states − their intentions and their feelings − outright. But in addition, once again there is what we may call an asymmetry problem in typical cases of narration. Typically our emotional responses to characters are different from their emotional responses. We are paralyzed by fear when the heroine is trapped by pursuers on the edge of a parapet, but she, undaunted and fearless, plunges into the moat several hundred feet below.[16] We feel sorrow for characters wracked with guilt. That is, the emotion we feel is different from the emotion felt by the character. There is no symmetry between our feelings and the character's feeling − which is what simulation theory would predict. Rather, there is asymmetry, at least in a large number of standard cases. And in those cases, simulation just doesn't seem to be the right model for these audience responses.

But how, it might be asked, do we know the characters are wracked with guilt, since without knowing that, we may not respond with pity? Don't we need simulation to explain this? I think not, and not only because characters often verbalize their internal states. Rather, we can recognize the states of others without simulation.[17] This is not a reversion to the Theory Theory. Rather, we need only suppose that people have the power to recognize certain patterns. This does not require having a full-blown theory, but only a repertory of sometimes related, sometimes unrelated schemas or prototypes for assessing situations. For example, in order to interpret the emotions underlying a convicted criminal's effort to shield his face from a TV camera, I need not simulate his mental state in order to recognize that it is connected to his sense of shame. Likewise, tracking the emotional states of characters in films and TV programs rarely requires simulation. It is easy to recognize their states without simulating them.[18]

For example, consider point-of-view editing. It might be suggested that that is a form of visual narration that must involve simulation. The character looks off-screen, and in the succeeding shot we see molten lava streaming toward the camera. Don't we feel fear because we are simulating the character's response? I don't think so. We know that molten lava is dangerous without imagining ourselves to be in the character's position. If we are concerned about the character, the knowledge that molten lava is heading her way is enough to engender fear for the character in us. The added step of imagining that we are in the character's shoes is unnecessary.[19]

Moreover, we can confirm that this is enough to explain our response by noting that our fear for the character may be no different whether we suppose the character knows she is about to be engulfed in lava or not. Presumably, the simulation theory would predict different responses to these alternative situations, since we would be simulating different mental states. But I suspect that we can vary the mental states of the characters without provoking a difference in our emotional response to the alternative stagings.

Similarly, when a fast movement toward the camera in a point of view schema startles us, it startles *us* directly without our simulating the character's being startled. Our cognitive/conative system may be off-line, but we need not be running the character's program in order to be startled. Nor do we need to simulate the character's mental state in order to recognize that he's been startled. And a similar explanation can be given for our response of disgust when a putrid monster lurches from a dark corridor. We have direct access to our own response; we need not imagine ourselves to be the character. For once again, the character might just be unaware of the putrid monster.

Currie says that when we watch a character walking down a dark street, perhaps in a detective thriller, we enliven the situation by simulating the character's mental state. But I think that this is not usually the case. Rather, we are onlookers. We are more likely to subvocalize our concern in terms of thinking almost aloud: "Get out of there," or "Watch out!" We are not necessarily replicating the mental state of the character. For again, remember that this could be a situation in which the character feels no sense of danger. Will it make a difference or not? Perhaps we need some experiments here, though my prediction about their outcome should be evident.

According to the simulationist, we use simulation in order to predict and understand characters. On the other hand, I claim that simulation doesn't play much of a role in the typical case. Is there any way to motivate my claim? Perhaps our response to villains is relevant here. Often villains are the characters whom it is most difficult to understand – in mass media narratives, they are often evil incarnate. Thus, one would predict that they would be especial targets of simulation. But, I suspect that even simulation theorists will admit that we rarely try to put ourselves in the place of villains, though *ex hypothesi,* these characters would seem to be the ones who cry out most for simulation.

Also, I question how useful simulation is for following narratives. Simulation is supposed to be a device for predicting behavior. But very often, the cognitive stock of characters is beyond what the average audience member can simulate. Who could have simulated the incredible catch that Buster Keaton executes when his girlfriend goes over the falls in *Our Hospitality?* Characters often surprise us just because their imagination is beyond simulation by average viewers, listeners, and readers. Had one been simulating Rick's state in *Casablanca,* it would have been more likely to predict that he would fly off with Ilsa. But he surprises us. Perhaps, most often when we consume fictions our posture is that of expecting the characters to surprise us rather than that of simulating them.[20]

But, in any event, I think that we do have reason to believe that our relation to characters is less often a matter of simulation than of what I have called elsewhere assimilation.[21] That is, rather than centrally imagining that we are the character, we adopt the stance of an observer or an onlooker and form an overall emotional response to the situation in which the character finds herself. This may involve an assessment of the character's emotional state. His anger may be relevant to our indignation. But our access to his anger need not, and I claim, most often does not, require simulation in order to be detected; and, in any case, our emotional response is different than his, since our emotional response has as part of its object a man who has been angered.

I am not prepared to claim that simulation never happens. Perhaps sometimes it even happens as a subroutine in the process of assimilating the situation of the character. But I do think that it happens much less frequently than theorists like Currie appear to think it does. They leave the impression that it is very pervasive. But I think that, supposing it does occur, it is very rare. The simulation theorist, in my view, overestimates the importance of central imagining for our response to fiction. Indeed, sometimes the emphasis on central imagining, where simulation is supposed to tell us something about ourselves (i.e., about how we would act or feel), seems to me to be an inappropriate response to fiction, since the author generally does not intend that we *imagine* how we, as readers, feel. That may be to leave off paying attention to the story and instead to go wandering off into some fantasy of our own.

But, in any case, it is my contention that, in the main, central imaginings, such as simulations, have little to do with our typical response to fictions. That is more a matter of acentral imagining where, on the basis of acentrally imagining the situation of the character (i.e., entertaining it in thought) from the perspective of an onlooker, we go on to formulate our own emotional response to it, often assimilating the character's emotional state as part of the object of our more encompassing emotional state.

Thus far I have been focusing on the story the simulation theorist tells about our emotional response to fiction. I have not addressed the link that the simulation theorist alleges to obtain between simulation and moral deliberation. This linkage, of course, is what the simulation theorist regards as one of the most important relations, if not the most important relation, between narrative fiction and morality. Needless to say, if simulation occurs as rarely as I assert, then this relation to morality cannot be very comprehensive. But even if simulation occurs more often than I have argued it occurs, it also pays to ask how significant this putative link between simulating fictions and morality could really be?

According to Currie, fiction serves moral deliberation by providing information about what it would be like to do certain things. Watching *Sunrise* and simulating the mental state of the husband, I learn what it would feel like to intend to kill my wife. This sort of information is relevant to moral reasoning, since knowing what it would feel like to nurture this intention is something one should consider before embracing it. For example, if as a result of such an exercise of the imagination, one thinks that doing x would bring about insufferable discomfiture (in the form of pangs of conscience), that should count as a reason against doing x.

But I am very skeptical about this picture of the relation of morality to fiction, not only because I think that our perspective on characters is, in the vast majority of cases, that of an onlooker rather than that of a simulator, but also because I doubt whether the simulation of characters plays much of a role in moral deliberation, since we know that the situations that fictional characters find themselves in are contrived. I would not deny that simulation may play a role in moral deliberation. However, I think that when it does play a role, we are simulating ourselves undertaking alternative courses of action tailored to our own situations. Since the situations of fictional characters are known by us to be made up, I doubt that moral agents frequently use simulations of the states of fictional characters to assess alternative lines of action for real-life purposes. Thus, if this kind of simulation occurs rarely in moral deliberation, Currie's account of the relation of fiction to morality is not a very comprehensive one.

Simulation theory comes to aesthetics with impressive credentials, since it has been ably defended by philosophers of mind. However, the phenomena that philosophers of mind are dealing with are subtly different from the phenomena aestheticians must consider when thinking about our emotional responses to fiction and their significance for moral deliberation. In this brief essay, I have tried to show why those differences indicate that there is little call for the concept of simulation in dealing with our emotional response to fictions. Thus, despite the growing popularity of simulation theory among English-speaking aestheticians, I argue that it is a bandwagon that we should allow to pass us by.[22]

PART V: ALTERNATIVE TOPICS

❧

ON JOKES

Traditional comic theory has attempted to encompass a wide assortment of phenomena. Often it is presented as a theory of laughter. But even where its ambit is restricted to amusement or comic amusement, it typically attempts to cover quite a large territory, ranging, for instance: from small misfortunes and unintentional pratfalls; to informal badinage, tall stories, and insults; to jokes, both verbal and practical, cartoons, and sight gags; through satires, caricatures, and parodies; and onto something called a cosmic comic perspective. Thus, predictably enough, the extreme variety of the subject matter – reaching from puns to the comedy of character – customarily results in theories that are overly vague.

For example, the most popular contemporary type of comic theory – the incongruity theory[1] – is generally very loose about what constituted its domain (objects, events, categories, concepts, propositions, maxims, characters, etc.) and, as well, it is exceedingly generous about the relations that may obtain between whatever composes the domain (contrast, difference, contrariety, contradiction, inappropriate subsumption, unexpected juxtaposition, transgression, and so on). Consequently, such theories run the danger of becoming vacuous; they seem capable of assimilating anything, including much that is not, pretheoretically, comic.

Moreover, attempts to regiment such theories by making them more precise tend to result in incongruity theories that are too narrow and, therefore, susceptible to easy counterexample. Schopenhauer, perhaps the most rigorous of incongruity theorists, hypothesizes, for instance, that the relevant sense of incongruity always involves the incorrect subsumption of a particular under a concept – an operation he believed could be uniformly diagnosed in terms of a syllogism in the first figure whose conjunction of a major premise with a sophistical minor premise invariably yields a false conclusion.[2] But, as illuminating as this theory is with respect to certain cases, it is hard to mobilize to account for what we find humorous in a funny gesture, like Steve Martin's silly victory dance at the baseball game in the movie *Parenthood*. Again the problem seems to be that the field of inquiry is so large that any relatively precise theory is likely to exclude part of it, while, at the same time, adjusting for counterexamples appears to send us back in the direction of vacuity.

From. *Midwest Studies in Philosophy,* XVI (1991), 280–301.

Starting with the intuition that the objects of comic theory are too unwieldly, I want to propose that the task of comic research might be better served if we proceed in a piecemeal fashion, circumscribing the targets of our investigations in such a way that we will be better able to manage them. This does not imply that we should ignore the rich heritage of comic theory, but only that we exploit it selectively where this or that observation seems best to fit the data at hand.

In the spirit of the preceding proposal, I will restrict my subject to the joke, which, though it may bear family relations to other forms of comedy, such as the sight gag, I will, nevertheless, treat as a distinctive genre. The purpose of this essay is to offer an account of jokes and, then, to go on to consider certain quandaries that my theory may provoke, especially in terms of ethical issues that pertain to such things as ethnic, racist, and sexist jokes. However, before advancing my own view of the nature of jokes, the leading, rival theory in the field, namely, Freud's, deserves some critical attention.

FREUD'S THEORY OF JOKES

Freud's theory of jokes is certainly the most widely known as well as one of the most developed theories of jokes in our culture. Thus, if we want to field an alternative theory, we must show why this illustrious predecessor is inadequate, along with indicating the ways in which our own view avoids similar pitfalls.

Freud's theory of jokes is part – albeit the largest part – of his general theory of what we might call amusement.[3] He divides this genus into three subordinate species: jokes (or wit), the comic, and humor. Membership in the genus seems to be a matter of economizing psychic energy; the subordinate species are differentiated with respect to the *kind* of psychic energy that each saves. Jokes represent a saving of the energy required for mobilizing and sustaining psychic inhibitions. The comic releases the energy that is saved by forgoing some process of thought. And, lastly, humor is defined in terms of the saving of energy that would otherwise be expended in the exercise of the emotions.

Put schematically: jokes are an economy of inhibition; the comic is an economy of thought; and humor is an economy of emotion. Freud's theory is often characterized as a release or relief theory of comedy[4] for the obvious reason that the energy that would have been spent inhibiting, thinking, and emoting in certain contexts is freed or released by the devices of jokes, the comic, and humor, respectively.

A notable feature of Freud's way of carving up this field of inquiry is that he does it by reference to the types of psychic energy conserved rather than by reference to the structural features of distinctive comedic strategies. Thus, we might anticipate that Freud's way of mapping the territory may diverge from our standard ways of, for example, distinguishing jokes from other comedic genres. But more on this in a moment.

Joking for Freud releases the energy saved by forgoing some inhibition. That is, the joke frees the energy that would have gone into mounting and maintaining some form of repression. What is involved here is readily exemplified by what

Freud calls tendentious jokes – jokes involved in manifesting sexual or aggressive tendencies. Such jokes, so to speak, breach our defenses and liberate the psychic energy we might have otherwise deployed against the sexual or aggressive content articulated by the joke.

Though the gist of Freud's theory is initially easy to see when the jokes in question involve transgressive content, it is also the case, as Freud himself freely concedes, that there are what to all intents and purposes appear to be innocent jokes – jests, nonsense, and ostensibly harmless wordplay. These do not seem predicated on articulating transgressive content. But Freud's general hypothesis is that jokes involve a saving in terms of psychic inhibition. So the question then arises as to what relevant inhibitions are lifted when one hears an innocent joke – one that evinces no sexual or aggressive purposes?

The second problem that Freud's theory of jokes needs to address is the question of *how* – even if inhibitions are lifted when we hear sexual and aggressive jokes – this liberation from repression occurs. That is, supposing that we agree with Freud that our inhibitions are put out of gear by tendentious jokes, we will still want to know exactly how this happens.

Freud's answers to these questions are interconnected. First, Freud establishes that jokes employ certain techniques, notably: condensation, absurdity, indirect representation, representation by opposites, and so on.[5] These techniques – call them the jokework – are the very stuff of innocent jokes, while at the same time they parallel the techniques that Freud refers to as the dreamwork in his studies of the symbolism of sleep.[6] With dreaming, these structures, such as condensation, are employed to elude censorship – to protect the dream from repressive criticism. *And,* at the same time, eluding censorship itself is pleasurable.

So, when tendentious jokes employ the techniques of the jokework, they avail themselves of the kind of pleasure that beguiles our psychic censor and that lifts our initial inhibitions in the first instance in such a way that the sexual or aggressive content in the joke is free to deliver even more uninhibited pleasures in the second instance. With tendentious jokes, inhibitions are thrown out of gear by the jokework, which protects the transgressive content in the manner of the dreamwork, while also facilitating the relaxation of censorship by means of its own beguiling pleasurableness.

This account, of course, still leaves our first question unanswered, namely, what fundamental inhibitions are relieved in the case of innocent jokes? Freud tackles this in two stages in his *Jokes and their Relation to the Unconscious.* The first stage (which is developed in chapter 4) might be thought of as a nonspecialized approximation of his considered view, while the second stage (developed in chapter 6) is his specialized (i.e., technical/psychoanalytic) refinement of his first approximation.

The first approximation correlates the jokework – which is also the essence of innocent wit – with childlike wordplay and thought play: the "pleasure in nonsense" of the child learning the language of her culture. Indulging in this childlike pleasure represents a rebellion against the compulsion of logic and a relief from the inhibitions of critical reason. The saving in psychical expenditure of energy that occasions the jokework, then, involves "re-establishing old liberties and getting rid of the burden of intellectual upbringing."[7]

This pleasure in reverting to childlike modes of thought can be further specified psychoanalytically in light of the analogy between the dreamwork and the jokework. Jokes, even innocent jokes, employ infantile (not merely childlike) modes of thought; they manifest the structures of thinking of the unconscious, structures repressed by critical reason. When critical reason is put in abeyance, regressive pleasure is released. "For the infantile source of the unconscious and the unconscious thought-processes are none other than those – the one and only ones – produced in early childhood. The thought which, with the intention of constructing a joke, plunges into the unconscious is merely seeking for the ancient dwelling place of its former play with words. Thought is put back for a moment to the stage of childhood so as once more to gain childhood pleasure."[8]

The inhibitions lifted by innocent jokes (and by the jokework across the board) are those of critical reason against infantile modes of thought and the regressive pleasures they afford. But, as in the case of tendentious jokes, here again we must ask: what makes the lifting of the inhibitions of critical reason possible? That is, what protects the innocent joke in particular and the jokework in general from the censorship of logic and reason? Freud's hypothesis is that for the word and thought play to be protected from criticism, it must have meaning or, at least, the appearance of meaning. The childlike pleasure in alliteration, for example, can elude criticism in expressions like "see you later, alligator," where the saying has some sense, though, admittedly, not of a resounding sort.

Summarizing this theory, then: all jokes involve a saving in inhibition. Tendentious jokes lift inhibitions against sexual and aggressive content. Innocent jokes and the jokework in general oppose the inhibitions of critical reason and allow pleasure in nonsense and the manifestation of infantile and unconscious modes of thought. What protects the tendentious joke from criticism is the jokework, which, like the dreamwork, beguiles the psychic censor. What protects the innocent joke and the jokework, in all its operations, from criticism is the appearance of sense or meaning in the joke.

Clearly, Freud's theory of jokes is intimately connected to his general theory of psychoanalysis. Consequently, it may be challenged wherever it presupposes psychoanalytic premises of dubious merit. For example, if one finds the hydraulic model of psychic energies unpalatable (as I do), then the very foundation of the theory of jokes is questionable. Likewise, if one is methodologically distrustful of homuncular censorship, the theory is apt to appear unpersuasive. However, for the purposes of this essay, I think that Freud's theory of jokes can be rejected without embarking on the awesome task of contesting psychoanalytic theory as a whole. That is, we can eliminate Freud's theory of jokes as a viable rival and, thereby, pave the way for the formulation of an alternative theory without confronting the entire psychoanalytic enterprise.

For there is a genuine question about whether Freud's theory of jokes is coherent, a question that can be framed independently of the relation of the account of jokes to the rest of the psychoanalytic architectonic. To zero in on this potential incoherence, recall: (1) there are innocent jokes (the operation of the jokework pure and simple); what protects them from censorship is their sense; this implies that there is an inhibition against the jokework that needs lifting; (2) there are tendentious jokes; what protects them from censorship is the jokework (the stuff of innocent jokes).

But, given this, we want to know why the tendentious joke does not auto-destruct. For the meaning or sense that the tendentious joke supplies to lift the inhibitions against the jokework involves the articulation of meanings that are prohibited or forbidden. How can prohibited meanings protect the jokework? Why doesn't the specific sense available through the tendentious purpose of the joke cancel the operation of the jokework?

Moreover, if the jokework cannot be protected by tendentious sense, then the jokework cannot, in turn, serve to neutralize inhibitions against the tendentious purposes of the joke. That is, if the jokework itself is a potential target of inhibition and the tendentious sense of the joke is ill suited to deflect censorship, then how can the jokework, in sexual and aggressive jokes, begin to function in the service of lifting any inhibitions?

One might attempt to remove this functional incoherence in the system by saying that the jokework (and, therefore, innocent jokes) do not require protection – that they are not inhibited. But this yields the concession that not all jokes – specifically innocent jokes – involve an economy of inhibition. And, this concession, of course, would spell the defeat of Freud's general characterization of jokes. Admittedly, there may be other ways to attempt to negotiate the aforesaid functional incoherence; but I suspect that they will be somewhat *ad hoc*. So one rather damning point about Freud's theory of jokes is that it is either functionally incoherent with regard to its account of tendentious jokes, or its generalizations about economizing inhibition are false, or it is probably headed toward *ad hocery*.

Furthermore, the theory of jokes is too inclusive. One might anticipate that given Freud's analogy between the jokework and the dreamwork that the problem here would be that dreams, especially dreams with sexual or aggressive purposes, will turn out to be jokes. However, Freud is careful to distinguish dreams and jokes along other dimensions, particularly with reference to the publicity of jokes and the privacy of dreams. But I think that Freud still has problems of overinclusiveness on other fronts.

Given Freud's theory of symbolism and his views about art, he would appear committed to agreeing that artworks deploy the symbolic structures of the dreamwork and that artworks also may traffic in sexual and aggressive meanings. Perhaps the winged lions of ancient Assyria – a condensation with aggressive purposes – would be a case in point. Why wouldn't these count as tendentious jokes on Freud's view?[9] Obviously, they are not jokes in our ordinary sense, for jokes are identified in common speech by means of certain discursive structures (to be explored below). But Freud's theory of jokes is so divorced from structural differentiae – preferring the somewhat dubious idiom of psychic energies and inhibitions, and a theory of lawlike relations between certain types of symbolism and psychic states – that it is not surprising that Freud's theory will violate pretheoretical intuitions that are grounded in ordinary language.[10]

Freud's theory also seems to me to suffer from being too exclusive. And, again, the problem is traceable to the fact that Freud tries to map the field of comedy not with respect to the structural features of comedic genres but by putative differences in psychic energies. Jokes are distinguished from the comic and the humorous as economies of inhibition are distinguished from economies of thought and emotion. But, structurally speaking, much of the material that Freud slots as comic or as humorous could be rearticulated in what we ordinarily take to be jokes.

For example, Freud's category of the comic, in opposition to his category of the joke, involves a saving in thought when we compare the way a naïf or a comic but does something with the more efficient way in which we might do the same thing. Accepting Freud's account, without questioning whether the talk of psychic savings makes real sense with respect to the putative mental processing, it would appear that many "moron" riddles – Why did the moron stay up all night? He was studying for his blood test[11] – would be comic (in Freud's sense), but, pretheoretically, I believe that we think they should count straightforwardly as jokes. For whether or not something is a joke is a matter of its discursive structure, not a matter of the kind of psychic energy it saves (if, indeed, there is any psychic energy, salvageable or otherwise).[12]

AN ALTERNATIVE ACCOUNT OF THE NATURE OF JOKES

Freud's theory of jokes is perhaps the most comprehensive and authoritative in our tradition. However, as we have seen, it is problematic in a number of respects – not only in some of its more controversial psychoanalytic commitments, but also in terms of its potential functional incoherence at crucial junctures and its failure to track what we ordinarily think of as jokes. As indicated previously, the latter failure appears due to its attempted isolation of jokes in terms of inhibition rather than in respect to what is structurally distinctive about jokes as a comedic genre. Thus, one place to initiate an alternative theory of jokes is to try to pinpoint the underlying structural principles that are operative in the composition of jokes.

Jokes are structures of verbal discourse – generally riddles or narratives – ending in punch lines. In contrast to informal verbal humor – such as bantering, riffing, or associative punning – a joke is an integral unit of discourse with a marked beginning and an end. If it is a riddle, it begins with a question and ends with a punch line; if it is a narrative, it has a beginning, which establishes characters and context, and it proceeds to a delimited complication, and then it culminates, again in the form of a punch line. In order to analyze the joke genre, I propose to consider it in the way that Aristotle considered the genre of tragedy – as a structure predicated on bringing about a certain effect in audiences. (And, perhaps needless to say, the effect that I have in mind is not that of lifting psychoanalytically construed inhibitions.)

The feature that distinguishes a joke from other riddles and narratives is a punch line. Where tragedies conclude with that state that modern literary theorists call closure, the last part of a joke is a punch line. Closure in tragedies is secured when all the questions that have been put in motion by the plot have been answered – when, for example, we know whether Hamlet will avenge his father and what will become of our cast of characters. But, ideally, a punch line is not simply a matter of neatly answering the question posed by a riddle nor of drawing all the story lines of a narrative to a summation. Rather, the punch line concludes the joke with an unexpected puzzle whose solution is left to the listener to resolve. That is, the end point of telling a joke – the punch line – leaves the listener with one last question which the listener must answer, instead of concluding by answering all the listener's questions.

Question: "What do you get when you cross a chicken with a hawk?" Answer: "A Quail." At first the answer seems to be mysterious, until one realizes that it should be spelt with a "'y," that it refers to a vice-president, and that the "chicken" and "hawk" in the question are meant to be taken metaphorically. In order to "get the joke," the listener must interpret the punch line. In fact, the point of the punch line is to elicit an interpretation from the listener. Indeed, this joke is designed to elicit pretty much the interpretation that I have offered.

Or, for an example of a narrative joke, consider this story: "A young priest runs into his abbott's office shouting 'Come quickly, Jesus Christ is in the chapel.' The abbott and novice hurry into the church and see Christ kneeling at the altar. The young man asks 'What should we do?,' to which the wise old abbott replies, whispering, 'Look busy.'"[13]

Initially, the abbott's remark seems puzzling and inappropriate; one would expect the two holy men to walk forward and to fall on their knees in adoration of their Lord and Savior. But very quickly one realizes that the abbott does not view Christ as his Savior, but rather as his boss, indeed a boss very much like a stereotypical earthly boss who is always on the lookout for shirkers. Getting the point of the joke, again, depends on interpreting the confounding punch line.

What the listener must do at the end of a joke is to provide an interpretation, that is, make sense of the last line of the text in light of the salient elements of the preceding narrative or riddle. This may involve reconstruing or reconstructing earlier information, which initially seemed irrelevant, as now salient under the pressure of coming up with an interpretation. For example, in the joke about the two priests, the narrative "field" is reorganized in such a way that it becomes very significant that the abbott is "old" and "wise" (cagey) and that he is "whispering" (a signal of furtiveness), given our interpretation that he believes the boss (rather than the Savior) has arrived on the scene for a surprise inspection.[14]

The punch line of a joke requires an interpretation because, in Annette Barnes's sense,[15] its point is not obvious, or not immediately obvious to the listener. The punch line comes as a surprise, or, at least, it is supposed to come as a surprise in the well-made joke. It is perhaps this moment in a joke that Kant had in mind when he wrote that "Laughter is an affection arising from a strained expectation being suddenly reduced to nothing."[16]

However, if this is what Kant had in mind, he has only partially described the interaction, while also misplacing the point where the laughter arises. For after an initial, however brief, interlude of blank puzzlement (Kant's "nothing"), an interpretation dawns on the listener, enabling her to reframe the preceding riddle or narrative in such a way that the punch line can be connected to the rest of the joke. It is at this point that there is laughter – when there is laughter, rather than a smile or a mere feeling of cheerfulness. Nor is our mind blank at this juncture. It has mental content, namely, the relevant interpretation.[17]

Of course, if the listener cannot produce an interpretation, the net result of the joke will be bewilderment. This may transpire either because of some problem with the listener – perhaps he lacks access to the allusions upon which the joke depends (e.g., in our Quayle joke, he might not know that a "hawk" can mean a militarist); or because of some problem with the joke – for example, there really is no compelling interpretation available. Jokes may also fail if they are too obvious, especially if the listener can anticipate the punch line and its attending interpretation. This is one reason that what is called comic timing is important to jokes; if the punch line is likely to be obvious, the teller must get through the joke – often using speed to downplay or obscure salient details – before the listener is likely to guess it.[18] (Moreover, the preceding account of the ways in which jokes can go wrong should provide indirect evidence for the puzzlement/interpretation model that I am advocating.)

Ideally, a joke must be filled-in or completed by an audience. It is intentionally designed to provoke an interpretation – "to be gotten." This, of course, does not happen in a vacuum; jokes are surrounded by conventions. And, once alerted – by formulas like "Did you hear the one about..." or by changes in the speaker's tone of voice – the audience knows that it is about to hear a joke, which means that its aim is to produce an interpretation, or, more colloquially, "to get it." That is, the aims of the teller and the listener are coordinated; both aim at converging on the production of an interpretation. Indeed, the interpretation that the joke is contrived to produce is generally quite determinate, or, at least, falls into a very determinate range of interpretations. For example, the interpretation I offered of the priest joke is *the* interpretation of the joke, give or take a wrinkle.

Of course, even with a well-made joke there is no necessity that the listener enjoy it. Along with the possible failures noted above, the listener may refuse to accept the "social contract" that has been signaled by conventions like changes in voice. That is, the listener may refuse the invitation to interpret and thereby stonewall the joke. This is a technique employed by school teachers – I seem to recall – in order to chasten unruly students.

A joke, on my view, is a two-stage structure, involving a puzzle and its solution.[19] One advantage of the two-stage model is that it can dissolve the apparent debate between what are called surprise theorists (Hobbes, Hartley, Gerard, Kant) – who maintain that laughter is a function of suddenness or unexpectedness – and configurational theorists (Quintilian, Hegel, Maier) – who see humor as a function of things "falling into place."[20] On the two-stage account, each camp has identified an essential ingredient of the joke: sudden puzzlement, on the one hand, versus a reconfiguring interpretation, on the other. The mistake each camp makes is to regard its ingredient as *the* (one and only) essential feature. The two-stage model incorporates both of their insights into a more encompassing theory. Another way to make this point might be to say that the two-stage model appreciates that a joke is a temporal structure, a feature that many previous theories fail to take into account.

So far this approach to jokes may seem very apparent. However, it does already indicate a striking difference between jokes and what many might be tempted to think of as their visual correlates – sight gags. For sight gags, typically, have nothing that corresponds to punch lines and, therefore, they do not call for interpretations to be produced by their audiences. A comic, say Buster Keaton (in the film *The General*) sitting on the connecting rod of the wheel of a locomotive, is so forlorn a rejected lover that he fails to notice that the train has started up. Our laughter rises as we await his moment of recognition and it erupts when we see that he realizes his plight. Similarly, when a comic heads unawares toward the proverbial banana peel, our levity builds as his fall becomes inevitable. Though the characters in gags like these may be puzzled by the dislocation of their expectations, the audience is not puzzled, no matter how amused it may be. We anticipate the pratfall; there is nothing surprising about it for us. The character may be perplexed, but we are not, and so there is no need for us to interpret anything. What has happened is obvious and predicted.[21]

If the punch line/interpretation structure – what we can call the cognitive address of jokes – serves generally to differentiate jokes from sight gags, more perhaps needs to be said about why it differentiates them from noncomic riddles and ordinary narratives, not to mention puzzles of the sort Martin Gardener concocts or difficult mathematical problems. In order to draw these distinctions, it is important to take note of the *kinds* of interpretations that jokes are designed to elicit from audiences.

Broadly speaking, joke discourse falls into the category of fantasy discourse. In telling a joke-narrative or posing a joke-riddle, one is not constrained to abide by the rules of everyday, serious discourse. We need not avoid equivocation, category errors, inconsistency, contradiction, irrelevance, paradox, or any other sort of incoherence with our standing body of knowledge, whether physical or behavioral, moral or prudential, and so on. Likewise, neither the punch line nor the ensuing interpretation need make sense in terms of consistency, noncontradiction, or compossibility with our standing body of knowledge. In fact, it is the mark of a joke interpretation that it will generally require the attribution of an error – often of the sort itemized in various ways by incongruity theorists of humor – either to a character in a joke or to the implied teller of the joke, or it will require the assumption of such an error by the listener, or it will involve some combination thereof – in order for the interpretation to "work."

For instance, consider this narrative joke: "An obese man sits down in a pizza parlor and orders a large pie. The waiter asks: 'Do you want it cut into four pieces or eight?' The diner replies 'Four, I'm on a diet.'" To get this joke, we must infer that the diner has ignored the rule for the conservation of quantity that entails that the pie is the same size whether it is cut into four pieces or eight and that, alternatively and mistakenly, the diner is employing the heuristic rule that increases in number frequently result in increases in quantity.[22]

Or, in the riddle – "What do you get when you cross an elephant with a fish? Swimming trunks" – we attribute to the implied speaker not only the belief that elephants and fish can mate, but that the result – obtained by fancifully associating certain of their identifying characteristics by means of the pun "swimming trunks" – could count as an answer, thereby violating the principle of charity twice, both in terms of the implied speaker's beliefs and his reasoning. However, this nevertheless succeeds in connecting the anomalous punch line with the fantastical question. The answer is a mistake, but a mistake we can interpret by attributing outlandish errors – at variance with our standing principles of interpretive charity – to the implied speaker.

Likewise, many ethnic and racist jokes involve not only errors on the part of Polish or Irish characters, but also call upon an interpretation from listeners that embrace exaggerated stereotypes of ignorance wildly at odds with the interpretive principles of charity that we find plausible to mobilize in interpreting ordinary behavior.

In contrast, then, to nonhumorous riddles, mathematical puzzles, and the like, jokes end in punch lines that may in some sense be mistaken themselves and that call for interpretations that require the attribution to or assumption of some kind of error by the implied speaker, and/or characters, and/or the listener, implied or actual. The solutions to nonhumorous riddles and mathematical puzzles, if they are solutions, are error free.

So, on the one hand, to put it vaguely, the interpretation elicited by a joke is implicated in at least one error. For, in a well-made joke, the interpretation elicited by the punch line works; indeed, it works better than any other interpretation that could pop into one's head at that moment would. What does *working* mean here? That the interpretation connects the punch line to salient details of the narrative or riddle in such a way that the initially puzzling nature of the punch line is resolved. The interpretation fits the punch line and the rest of the joke after the fashion of an hypothesis to the best explanation, *except that* the explanation is not constrained to be coherent with the body of our standing beliefs and knowledge – it need not avoid category errors, contradictions, inconsistency, paradox, equivocation, irrelevance, the gamut of informal logical fallacies, or uncharitable attributions of inappropriate, outlandish, stereotypically exaggerated, normatively unexpected or wildly unlikely behavior, or even full-blown irrationality to human characters or their anthropomorphized stand-ins, and/or to implied authors, and/or to implied listeners.

The interpretations elicited by punch lines are in one sense *optimal*. They get the job done – where the job at hand is interpreting the joke. In this regard, the joke appeals to the optimizer in the human animal – our willingness to mobilize any heuristic, no matter how suspect, to solve a problem, so long as the heuristic delivers an "answer" efficiently. The interpretations we produce in confronting jokes render the punch line intelligible – that is, understandable rather than believable – in a way that, in short order, fits the prominent, though often hitherto apparently unmotivated, elements of the rest of the joke.

It is this feature of jokes that I think that theorists have in mind when they (ill-advisedly) speak of jokes as rendering the incongruous congruous. Moreover, these interpretations are compelling because they do provide a framework, ready-to-hand, to dispel our perplexities. However, it is not quite right to say that the incongruous has been rendered congruous, because there is always something wrong somewhere in the interpretation, no matter how optimal it is in resolving the puzzle of the joke.[23]

Incongruity theorists of humor have supplied us with many of the recurring errors that must be imputed or assumed in order for our joke interpretations to work. As noted earlier, Schopenhauer believed that it was a matter of the fallacious subsumption of a particular under a category by means of a mediating sophistry. On this view, the error embodied in jokes is always a category error. This works nicely with many jokes, such as our earlier example of the moron and the blood *test* (the relevant category error); but the theory is too imprecise – how are we to understand the range of "concept" (in contrast, say, to maxim) and to know when an incident in a joke counts as introducing a concept rather than a particular? Moreover, the theory is just too narrow; jokes mobilize errors above and beyond category mistakes.

Other incongruity theorists have further limned the kinds of errors that can be brought into play in jokes. Hazlitt speaks of a disjunction between what is and what ought to be; Kierkegaard of contradiction.[24] Raskin introduces the notion of opposed scripts.[25] Each of these suggests slightly different sources of error. Arthur Koestler emphasizes the bisociation or mixing of inappropriate frames.[26] Marie Swabey's inventory of incongruities includes: irrelevance, the mistaking of contraries for contradictories, and the straining of concepts to the limit case (in addition to category errors).[27] Monro talks of the linking of dis-parates, the importation of ideas from one realm which belong to another or the collision of different mental spheres, and of attitude mixing.[28] And majority opinion agrees that transgressions of norms of appropriate behavior – moral, prudential, polite, and "what everyone knows" – can serve as the locus of error in the mandated interpretation.

These are very useful suggestions; and further incongruities can be isolated: for example, Bergson's concept of the encrustation of the mechanical in the living,[29] which might be extended somewhat, *pace* Bergson, to include the continuation of routinized or ordinary modes of thought into the fantastical circumstances of the joke.

Given the success of previous incongruity theorists of humor at identifying so many of the errors that we find operative in jokes, it is natural to entertain the possibility that we should build incongruity into the theory of jokes as a necessary constituent – conjecturing that jokes must contain errors that are ultimately traceable to one or another form of incongruity. However, there is no reason, in my view, to suppose that the range of possibilities so far isolated by incongruity theories exhausts the range of error in which a joke-interpretation may be implicated, and, more importantly, there is no reason to believe that all the errors in that range that are yet to be identified will turn out to involve incongruities.

In order to add some substance to these reservations, let me introduce a brief counterexample from Poggio Bracciolini's *Facetiae*, which was first published in 1470.[30] "A very virtuous woman of my acquaintance was asked by a postal runner if she didn't want to give him a letter for her husband, who had been absent for a long time as an ambassador for Florence. She replied: 'How can I write, when my husband has taken his pen away with him, and left my inkwell empty?' A witty and virtuous reply."

On the account of jokes offered so far, this joke has a punch line that is puzzling until we reconceive the wife's apparently nonsensical answer as a set of sexual innuendoes. We need also to attribute an error to the wife; her response is literally a *non sequitur*. Moreover, to my mind, such a non sequitur is not really an example of incongruity.

For incongruity has as its root some form of *contrast* such that a relatively specifiable normative alternative – whether cognitive, or moral, or prudential – stands as the background against which the incongruous behavior, or saying, or whatever, is compared (generally in terms of some form of structured opposition). But with a genuine non sequitur it is difficult to identify the norm that is in play with any specificity. One might say that a *non sequitur* is just nonsense, but stretching the concept of incongruity to encompass nonsense (a rather amorphous catchall, it seems to me) robs the notion of incongruity of definition.

That is, for something to be incongruous requires that we be able to point in the direction of something else to which it stands in some relation of structured contrast or conflict (above and beyond mere difference or lack of connection). But with the wife's answer in the preceding joke, it is hard to identify a foil with which it contrasts in terms of any structurally determinate relation.[31]

So, though incongruity is very often (most often?) an extremely helpful umbrella concept for isolating what is wrong with the interpretation elicited by the punch line of a joke, I prefer to use the even more commodious hypothesis that the listener's interpretation of a joke simply involves an error somewhere, leaving open the possibility that it may issue from incongruity or elsewhere and, thereby, acknowledging the fact that we humans are eternally inventive when it comes to "discovering" new ways to make mistakes.

A joke is designed to produce a transition in the cognitive state of the listener. We are moved from a standing state (M 1) of assimilating stimuli by means of our conventional conceptual/normative schemes – what I think theorists often misleadingly call our "expectations"[32] – into the state (M 2) of producing an interpretation that does not cohere with or, at least, is not constrained by the principles of our standing assumptions nor assimilatable, without remainder, into our body of knowledge.[33] However, if these interpretations oppose rationality in this broad sense, they are nevertheless optimal. For even if they cannot be linked readily and reasonably with our standing body of beliefs, they expeditiously serve the short-term purpose of resolving the puzzle posed by the punch line and of comprehensively reframing the details of the body of the joke.

The joke-situation is one in which the listener is prompted to produce an interpretation which is optimal, while in the broad sense, it is, in some way, not rational. The tension between optimality and rationality is recognized by the listener, and provides the locus of her amusement. This sort of conflict, ordinarily, might be a source of consternation; but within the joke-situation it is advanced for the purpose of enjoyment. The compelling nature or optimality of the interpretation is entertained, despite its implication in absurdity. In the joke-situation, we are allowed to be vulnerable to the attraction of an interpretation that in other contexts would have to be immediately rejected. Speaking only partially metaphorically, in entertaining the interpretation, cum absurdities, while recognizing the rational unacceptability of such an interpretation, we allow ourselves the luxury of being cognitively helpless – appreciating the cognitive force of the interpretation (for example, its comprehensiveness and its simplicity) without feeling the immediate pressure to reject it because of all those liabilities – such as its unassimilability to our body of beliefs – of which we are aware.

Characterizing our cognitive state with respect to joke interpretations as a variety of helplessness is at least suggestive. Laughter, the frequent concomitant of jokes, is also associated with tickling and slight nervousness. If the focus of our mental state with respect to jokes is an interpretation, in which optimality, with an edge, vies openly with rationality, then it seems plausible to speculate that we are in a state that would standardly evoke nervousness. We are vulnerable, but, as with friendly tickling, that vulnerability does not, given the joking frame, constitute clear and present danger. Moreover, if Ted Cohen is right in saying that the joke-situation is one of community,[34] we might amplify his observations by noting that part of that sense of community is constituted by the willingness of the joke-audience to render themselves vulnerable in a public group.

Summarizing our thesis so far: x is a joke if and only if (1) x is integrally structured, verbal discourse, generally of the form of a riddle or a narrative (often a fantastical narrative), (2) concluding with a punch line, whose *abruptly* puzzling nature, (3) elicits, usually quite quickly, a determinate interpretation (or determinate range of interpretations) from listeners, (4) which interpretation solves the puzzle and fits the prominent features of the riddle or narrative, but (5) involves the attribution of at least one gross error, but possibly more, to the characters and/or implied tellers of the riddle or narrative, and/or involves the assumption of at least one such error by the implied or actual listener, (6) which error is supposed to be recognized by the listener as an error.

This is an account of what constitutes the joke. "Getting the joke" involves the listener's production of the interpretation, the recognition of the conflict or con-

flicts staged between what I have called its optimality versus rationality, and, typically, enjoyment of said tension. Often it is maintained that in order to "get a
joke," one must find it funny, which, I suppose, means that one must enjoy it. But
by characterizing enjoyment as only a "typical" feature of "getting a joke," I intend
to leave open the possibility that one can "get a joke" without finding it funny or
without enjoying it. Speaking personally, I believe that I have heard certain racist
jokes which I "got," but which I did not enjoy.

One counterexample to this account that has been proposed is the trick
exam question. And surely graders are familiar with coming across answers to
quiz questions that strike them as very funny, as if, indeed, they were a joke.
However, such examples, even where the question is designed to prompt a
wrong answer, are not jokes, for surely the test takers who advance such questionable answers neither do nor are they supposed to recognize the errors in
which their answers are implicated.

Another problem case is the sort of jest beloved by children that goes like this:
"Why did they bury Washington on a hill? Because he was dead." Chickens cross-
ing roadways and firemen's red suspenders also come to mind here. Such jokes
violate my preceding characterization because they are not implicated in errors.
Chickens presumably do cross roads to get to the other side and firemen, when
they wear red suspenders, indeed do so to hold their pants up.

What I want to say about such examples is that they are meta-jokes. They are
jokes about jokes; specifically, they subvert the basic underlying conventions of
jokes – that jokes will elicit interpretations that negotiate puzzling punch lines –
in such a way that these presuppositions are exposed. These jokes introduce certain questions in the manner of riddles, while their "answers" reveal both that they
were not riddles at all and that what is involved in the listener's conventional
stance in regard to a riddle is the anticipation of a puzzle.

Of course, the immediate aim of these meta-jokes is less exalted; it is to trick
the listener into adopting the role of a problem solver where no solution is necessary. As an empirical conjecture, I hazard that children come to enjoy this kind of
play soon after they acquire initial mastery of the joke form; in a way, such meta-
jokes provide a means of celebrating their recently won command of this mode of
discourse. Moreover, I do not think that postulating meta-jokes compromises my
theory of jokes. For somewhere along the line, every theory will have to come to
terms with meta-jokes, like the shaggy-dog story.

Also, since my analysis of jokes relies so heavily on the notion of the joke
being filled in by interpretive activity, it may tempt one to indulge the long-
standing commonplace that jokes are strong analogs to artworks. I think that
we should resist this temptation. Jokes, like at least a great many artworks, do
encourage interpretation. However, the interpretation relevant to solving a
joke is not only very determinate, but, in general, has been primed by a very
economical structuring of information such that it calls forth the pertinent
interpretation almost immediately, and, therefore, abets very little interpretive
play. The organization of the joke is, in fact, generally so parsimonious that any

attempt to reflect upon the text and its interpretation for any period of time is likely to be very unrewarding. Jokes are not designed for contemplation – one cannot standardly review them in search of subtle nuances that inflect, enrich, or expand our interpretations.

The interpretation of a joke, so to speak, generally exhausts its organization, virtually in one shot, or, alternatively, the organization of the joke calls forth a determinate interpretation that is barely susceptible to the accretion of further nuance. This is not said to deny the fact that we may retell a joke in order to discern the way in which, structurally, its solution was "hidden" from listeners. But, again, even such structural interests are quickly satisfied. Thus, the kind of interpretation elicited by jokes is at odds with at least our ideals concerning the protracted interpretive play that artworks are supposed to educe.

Earlier I rejected the Freudian theory of jokes, but one might wonder whether our successor theory is really so different. Of course, one difference between our theory and Freud's is that we do not support the hypothesis that the structures of jokes reflect the modes of primitive thought that Freud discovered in the dreamwork.[35] However, Freud's less specialized account – that jokes lift the inhibitions of critical reason – may not seem so very different from our claim that the joke-situation allows us to entertain a puzzle-solution that we know is not rational.

Nevertheless, there is a subtle difference between the two views. Freud's theory implies that with the joke rationality is banished, if only momentarily. But on my theory, the crux of amusement is the tension between optimality and rationality. Rationality is not banished; it remains as a countervailing force to the "absurd" solution; the mental state we find ourselves in is one in which we are, so to speak, trapped between the rational and optimal. If jokes have a general moral, it is that we humans are irredeemable optimizers. Perhaps, that is why we say we "fall" for jokes. But part of our appreciation of the joke is that we recognize our "fall," which would be impossible if Freud were right in thinking that jokes send rationality on a holiday.

One outstanding anomaly, however, still plagues our theory. I claim that it is an essential feature of a joke that the listener recognize that the interpretation the joke elicits be in error. But, on the other hand, we are all familiar with racist, ethnic, sexist, and classist jokes that give every appearance of being told to reinforce the darkest convictions of racists, sexists, and so on. It is a fact that such jokes are often told for evil purposes, but my theory makes it difficult to understand how these jokes could serve such purposes. If my theory is correct, then when a racist hears a joke whose interpretation mobilizes a demeaning view of Asian intelligence, if the racist is to respond to it as a joke, it seems that he should realize that the degrading, stereotypically exaggerated view of Asians proffered by the joke is false.

But if the stereotypically degrading view of the racial target of the joke is false, it is hard to see how such jokes could reinforce the racist's view. How can racism be served by racist jokes, if my theory is accurate? And surely we have more faith in our belief that racist jokes can serve racism than we can have in a philosophical theory of the sort advanced so far. In order to deal with this challenge, I must say something about the relation of jokes to ethics.

ETHICS AND JOKES

Initially, it may be thought that one advantage of portraying jokes as devices for eliciting interpretations from listeners is that it explains why people are so deeply troubled about the moral status of jokes – or, at least, some jokes. If what we have said is correct, then jokes involve listeners in producing errors that they may momentarily embrace. The listener fills in the elliptical joke structure, and, in order to complete it, the listener must supply an optimal interpretation that is implicated in error. Now in the case of many jokes – such as ethnic, racist, or sexist jokes, for example – those errors often involve morally disturbing stereotypes of the mental, physical, or behavioral attributes of the comic butt who stands for an entire social group. Thus, the moralist is worried not only about the moral statement the joke implies, but also about the effect of encouraging the listener to produce and embrace the erroneous and morally suspect thoughts that the interpretation of the joke requires. That is, the moralist may be concerned that, among other things, the very form of cognitive address employed in jokes involving ethnic, sexist, and racist material is ethically problematic.

In this regard, Aristotle contended that the most effective rhetorical strategy was the enthymeme; for by means of this device the orator can draw her conclusions from the audience in such a way that we take them to be our own.[36] Having come upon the conclusion on our own, it strikes us as all the more convincing. That is, in this way, the rhetorical structure reinforces the idea. Jokes, it may be thought, work in this way as well; the audience fills in the interpretation on its own, even though the interpretation is predetermined. Thus, the danger is that where the interpretation requires us to operationalize suspect moral thoughts, such as sexist stereotypes, the very process itself may reinforce the viability of those thoughts. So what is troubling about a sexist joke is not just its content, but its form of cognitive address.

However, as noted previously, my theory of jokes obstructs this conclusion. For a joke-interpretation to "work" requires that the listener not only produce the interpretation but also recognize, at the same time, that it is somehow in error. This recognition is the crux of the humored response. Moreover, racist, ethnic, and sexist jokes seem to presuppose the wrongness of certain stereotypes in order to be gotten.

But, in rejecting the moralist's worry, we seem driven to the conclusion that even a bigot recognizes the error or absurdity of the exaggerated stereotypes presumed in the interpretations proponed by an ethnic joke. If he did not, his response to the punch line would not be laughter, but the matter-of-fact acknowledgment that "yes, that's just how Irishmen or Poles or Italians or Jews or African-Americans really are." But this, in turn, seems to make too many racists appear too enlightened.

However, we need not be forced to this conclusion. Consider: "How do you know that an Irishman has been using your personal computer? There's white-out on the screen." Here the mandated interpretation is something like: any Irishman is so dumb that he can't use a computer properly, *and* he even makes corrections in a way that is ultimately self-defeating. In order to appreciate this as a joke, the listener has to realize that this is literally false. However, the punch line can also be construed figuratively.

Much humor rides on figurative language, employing tropes like litotes or meiosis, and irony. In ethnic and racist jokes involving, for example, stereotypes of exaggerated stupidity, the presupposed interpretation may function as hyperbole. This will be the case when the joke is passed for vicious purposes among those committed to the degradation of persons of another race, sex, class, and so on. Within such circles, the presupposed interpretation will be understood as exaggerated – and, therefore, literally trafficking in error – but the exaggeration will be understood as on the side of truth. The racist speaker will be understood by the racist listener as saying something stronger than the literal truth warrants, but also as saying something with the intention that it be corrected so that, though it will not be taken in its strongest formulation, it will still be taken as a strong statement that preserves the same initial polarity (say "major league" stupidity) that the hyperbole did.[37] One might imagine the anti-Irish appreciator of the preceding computer joke saying, after an initial burst of laughter: "Well, the Irish aren't *that* dumb; but they're really pretty dumb nonetheless."

Ethnic, racist, and sexist jokes are very often used as insults, and insults customarily may take the form of hyperbole. Perhaps few mothers wore combat boots, but many could not afford Guccis either. Though they are literally and even intentionally false, hyperboles can figuratively point in the direction of an assertion.[38] And when racist jokes are told with racist intent to racist audiences, tellers and listeners may regard their presuppositions as strictly and literally false – thereby appreciating them as *merely* jokes – while at the same time correcting the tropological figuration so that it accords with their prejudices.

Thus, if it is agreed that a racist can recognize that the implied interpretation of a racist joke is literally false – thereby "getting the joke" – but also take it figuratively as an instance of hyperbole, then the theory of jokes advanced in the preceding section need not be taken to be incompatible with the view that racist jokes can reinforce racist ideology.

It should be noted that I have claimed that racist, ethnic, and sexist jokes are "very often used as insults." Here I am allowing what may seem troublesome to many, namely, that there may be cases where they are not insults. This seems borne out by the fact that there are many groups, including Jews, the Irish, and African Americans, who tell jokes about themselves that employ the same exaggerated stereotypes that outsiders use.[39] It seems reasonable to suppose that even if some of this joking reflects intragroup rivalry and, in some cases, possibly self-hatred, some of it, at the same time, is indulged without the intention of insulting one's own ethnic group. Whether a racist joke is morally charged, then, depends on the intentions of the teller and the context of reception. Pragmatic considerations of particular jokes in context determine whether the joke is an insult – whether its literal absurdity is to be taken as an indication of a morally obnoxious assertion by means, for example, of hyperbole.[40]

In emphasizing the relevance of use and context here, I mean to deny the simple moralistic view, sketched above, that jokes, even ethnic jokes, are evil simply in virtue of being some sort of rhetorical machine whose form of cognitive address automatically reinforces wicked ideas. Whether a joke is evil depends on the intentions of its teller and the uses its listeners make of it.

Quite clearly, ethnic jokes do not instill beliefs in listeners simply by being told. When I originally heard the preceding computer joke, it was told about Newfoundlanders, not about Irishmen. I laughed; I "got the joke." But it neither instilled nor reinforced any beliefs I have about that group, for I have no well-formed beliefs about people from Newfoundland, except, perhaps, that they live in Canada and people tell jokes about them.

Likewise, I have heard the joke told by people as ignorant as I am about the inhabitants of Newfoundland to the equally ignorant with successful results. This prompts me to suspect that it is possible to derive an almost formal pleasure from ethnic jokes and their ilk that is apart from their derisory potential. The focus of this formal appreciation may be the way in which the joke, particularly the punch line, is so perfectly structured to bring about what I earlier referred to as our change in mental state.

However, the conjecture that ethnic jokes and the like may be formally appreciated does not amount to a license to tell or to laugh at them in any context so long as one's intention in telling or laughing is not, in one's own judgment, connected to derisory hyperbole and the like. Since such jokes can be used to encourage racism, sexism, classism, and so on, one should be morally concerned enough to refrain from telling them in contexts in which they might stoke these sentiments; this probably applies to most of the social situations in which we find ourselves. Of course, it is not just the case that we may not know how our audience may respond to or use such jokes. In matters like sexism and racism, we may not know all there is to know about our own hearts as well. Though we may think that our Irish jokes or Polish jokes do not reflect our beliefs about the Poles or the Irish, the tides of racism and sexism probably run deeper. It is very likely that our own intentions and their background conditions are generally obscure in these matters, in part because what is involved in racism, classism, and sexism is not yet completely understood. Thus, our own judgment about our intentions in telling and laughing at racist and sexist jokes may not be reliable. And this supplies us with further moral reasons against indulging in this type of humor.

I have rejected the simple moralist worry that certain types of jokes may be evil as a function of rhetorically bringing listeners to entertain certain immoral ideas in our process of what I call filling-in the joke. This hypothesis conflicts with my view of what it is to "get a joke"; for I maintain that this requires that the listener know that the interpretation one uses to solve the joke puzzle be implicated in error. On the other hand, I do not want to deny that immoral pleasures may be derived from jokes where, despite the recognition of the literal absurdities or errors that the joke mandates, the joke can be used – figuratively, for example – as a serviceable means to insult or to dominate another social group. Jokes, that is, can be immoral in terms of the motives they serve rather than in terms of their particular structure of cognitive address.[41]

e ⁓

THE PARADOX OF JUNK FICTION

Perhaps on your way to some academic conference, if you had no papers to grade, you stopped in the airport gift shop for something to read on the plane. You saw racks of novels authored by the likes of Mary Higgins Clark, Michael Crichton, John Grisham, Danielle Steel, Sidney Sheldon, Stephen King, Sue Grafton, Elmore Leonard, Sara Paretsky, Tom Clancy, and so on. These are the kinds of novels that, when you lend them to friends, you don't care, unless you live in Bowling Green, Ohio, whether you ever get them back. They are mass, popular fictions. In another era, they would have been called pulp fictions. Following Thomas Roberts,[1] I will call them junk fictions, under which rubric I will also include things like Harlequin romances; sci-fi, horror, and mystery magazines; comic books; and broadcast narratives on either the radio or TV, as well as commercial movies.

There are a number of interesting philosophical questions that we may ask about junk fiction. We could, for example, attempt to characterize its essential features. However, for the present, I will assume that the preceding examples are enough to provide you with a rough-and-ready notion of what I am calling junk fiction, and I will attempt to explore another feature of the phenomenon, namely, what I call the paradox of junk fiction.

The junk fictions that I have in mind are all narratives. Indeed, their story dimension is the most important thing about them. Stephen King, for instance, makes this point by saying that he is primarily a storyteller rather than a writer. Junk fictions aspire to be page-turners – the blurb on the cover of *Stillwatch* by Mary Higgins Clark says that it is "designed to be read at breathtaking speed" – and what motivates turning the page so quickly is our interest in what happens next. We do not dawdle over Clark's diction as we might over Updike's nor do we savor the complexity of her sentence structure, as we do with Virginia Woolf's. Rather, we read for story.

Moreover, junk fictions are the sort of narratives that commentators are wont to call formulaic. That is, junk fictions generally belong to well-entrenched genres, which themselves are typified by their possession of an extremely limited repertoire

From: *Philosophy and Literature,* 18 (October 1994), 225–41.

of story-types. For example, as John Cawelti has pointed out, one such recurring Western narrative is that of the recently pacifist gunfighter, like Shane, who is forced by circumstances to take up his pistols again, with altogether devastating effect.[2]

Junk fictions tell these generic stories again and again with minor variations. Sometimes these variations may be quite clever and unexpected. Agatha Christie was the master of this; she was able to use the conventions of the mystery genre in order to "hide" her murderers. In *The Murder of Roger Ackroyd,* she "secrets" the murderer in the personage of the narrator; in *Ten Little Indians,* the murderer is a "dead man"; while in *Murder on the Orient Express,* all the suspects did it. In each of these cases, Christie's brilliance hinges upon her playing (and preying) upon conventional expectations.

Nevertheless, even these surprising variations require a well-established background of narrative forms. That is, in order to appreciate these variations, the reader must in some sense know the standard story already. And with junk fiction, it is generally fair to say that in some sense, the reader – or, at least, the reader who has read around in the genre before – knows in rough outline how the story is likely to go. Readers and/or viewers of *Jurassic Park* surmised, once the dinosaur enclosures were described, that in fairly short order the dinosaurs would trample them down and go on the rampage – after all, we had already seen or read *The Lost World, King Kong,* and their progeny.

So, junk fictions are formulaic. They rehearse certain narrative formats again and again. And, furthermore, in some very general sense, the audience already knows the story in question. But this knowledge on the part of the audience provokes a question, specifically, why if the reader, viewer, or listener *already* knows the story is she or he still interested in investing time in reading, hearing, or seeing it? If you have read one Harlequin romance, it might be argued, you have read them all. You know how it will turn out. It serves no purpose to read any more of them. Or, at least, our persistent reading or viewing in familiar genres invites the question: what sense can we make out of our continued consumption of junk fictions, since it is probably the case that, for most genres of junk fiction, most consumers can be said to know the story antecedently.

There is something paradoxical here. It seems to be undeniably true that people consume junk fictions for their stories – that is, that what interests and absorbs consumers of junk fictions are the stories. But it also appears eminently reasonable to suppose that if people read a certain sort of fiction, such as junk fiction, for their stories, then knowing these stories already should preclude any interest in the stories. And yet, at the same time, we must agree that, in the main, consumers of junk fiction are generally reading fictions whose stories – or story-types – they already know. So, from these three observations, we can derive the conclusion that, though we should not be interested in junk fictions just because we already know the relevant stories, recurring narratives are precisely that which interests us in junk fiction.

Moreover, this somewhat contradictory finding calls for an explanation. How can we be interested in consuming stories that we already know? How is it rational? Or, is it simply irrational?[3]

This is what I call the paradox of junk fiction. This is rather different from the paradox that Thomas Roberts addresses in his book *An Aesthetics of Junk Fiction*. His question is how can consumers of junk fictions speak so disparagingly of them while, at the same time, they evidently derive such great enjoyment and pleasure from them?

And, the paradox of junk fiction should also be distinguished from what I call the paradox of recidivism, which paradox, in turn, is based on the question of how to make sense of the phenomenon that people often read or see mystery and suspense fictions more than once, despite the fact that they have already read or seen them and, therefore, know how they turn out.

The paradox of junk fiction and the paradox of recidivism are clearly related. The paradox of recidivism inquires into the rationality of consuming particular fictions – like the film *Vertigo* – again and again, despite our knowledge of the ending; whereas the paradox of junk fiction is not about particular fictions but about types or genres. Why persist in reading numerically distinct Conan the Barbarian or Tarzan stories, since not only are they always basically the same, but, more important, the reader in some sense knows this? In what follows, I will attempt to dissolve the paradox of junk fiction and to explain why it is not irrational for us to read plots whose generic structures we already know.

Of course, one response to the putative paradox of junk fiction would be to accept the phenomenon as it has been reported so far – to admit that there is a paradox here – and to contend that the existence of that paradox only confirms once again that people are irrational. They do read for story, and the stories are monotonously repetitive. This irrational behavior undoubtedly requires an explanation, but the explanation that does the job will not show the consumer of junk fiction to be embarked upon a rational activity. Rather, his or her paradoxical behavior is irrational and what explains it is psychoanalysis.

A long-standing psychoanalytic proposal concerning junk fiction is the notion that junk fiction functions in a way that is analogous to daydreaming. In his classic essay, "The Relation of the Poet to Day-Dreaming," Freud explicitly pursues his analysis by focusing upon the authors of what I call junk fiction, whom he describes as "the less pretentious writers of romances, novels and stories who are read all the same by the widest circles of men and women."[4] Freud maintains that many of their central, recurring narrative motifs can be characterized in terms of wish-fulfillment.

Heroes in such stories seem to be under special providential protection. Freud writes, "If at the end of one chapter the hero is left unconscious and bleeding from severe wounds, I am sure to find him at the beginning of the next being carefully tended and on the way to recovery; if the first volume ends in the hero being shipwrecked in a storm at sea, I am certain to hear at the beginning of the next of his hairbreadth escape."[5] Likewise Freud points out that in such stories, all the women fall in love with our hero while the distribution of good guys and bad guys is calculated in accordance with whether they are or are not the hero's rivals.

In the case of the providential protection of the hero, the reader is thought to identify with the hero and the writing answers to our infantile fantasies of invulnerability. The hero's strength would supposedly correspond to our infantile fantasies of omnipotence. The irresistible attraction that the hero exerts on the opposite sex bespeaks our sexual wishes; while the shape of the moral landscape reflects our unflinching egotistical desire to be always right. Through identification with the hero in junk fiction, the psychoanalyst argues, the reader or viewer secures vicarious gratification for his/her infantile and egotistical wishes. Junk fiction is analogous to the daydream insofar as it is an avenue for wish-fulfillment.

It is irrational for us to consume the recurring stories of junk fiction. Our behavior is obsessional. Nevertheless, it can be explained in terms of the way in which the recurring stories of junk fiction vicariously satisfy some of our deepest instinctual desires. Those distant, standoffish men in romance novels all finally succumb to true love, thereby responding to the reader's desire, while it is said that the readers and writers of certain slash lit – concerning homosexual erotica, written and primarily consumed by women, about the crew of the Star Ship Enterprise – are in search of idealized relationships.[6] Thus, on the psychoanalytic account, people read stories they already know and this is irrational, but it can be explained in terms of the compelling, wish-fulfilling capacity of these types of stories. We are driven to reread them, even though it makes little sense, because in rereading them infantile, egotistical, and sexual wishes are addressed.

I have several misgivings about the psychoanalytic solution to the paradox of junk fiction. First, I am not convinced that we should be so quick to concede the irrationality of consuming the recurring stories of junk fiction. We should at least canvass some rational explanations of the phenomenon before consigning it to the realm of the irrational. Indeed, I suspect that the behavior in question can be not merely explained, but even justified rationally.

Furthermore, the psychoanalytic account seems inadequate. It maintains that junk fictions function as wish-fulfillments. Though this may be initially plausible for some types of junk fiction, it hardly applies across the board. For in a substantial number of junk fictions the states of affairs realized in the story fail to correspond to what it is reasonable to presume are the wishes of readers. In Ira Levin's novel *Rosemary's Baby* the heroine is subjugated and the Anti-Christ is born. Do average readers wish for the reign of Satan? Of the film *My Girl,* should we really suppose that typical viewers wish for the death of the small boy? And in the movies *Bonnie and Clyde* and *The Wild Bunch* all the characters with whom the audience might be said to identify are blown apart, while the very notion of identification on which the psychoanalytic theory seems to ride is at least questionable.

Of course, the psychoanalyst may try to negotiate these counterexamples by saying that junk fictions not only compel attention through promising wish-fulfillment but also by manifesting anxieties, perhaps even deep anxieties. However, this move involves several problems. For if junk fictions traffic in anxieties, it is not clear how this helps explain why we would be attracted to them. Here the psychoanalyst may claim that these anxieties themselves merely mask deeper wishes.

But, needless to say, supporting this claim will involve the postulation of a great many theoretically suspicious, ad hoc processes in order to account for the transformation of apparent wishes into effective icons of anxiety that are still simultaneously wish-fulfilling.

Perhaps our horror at the triumph of the Anti-Christ masks our deeper desire for a reign of chaos and unbridled sexuality. But this seems somewhat arbitrary. For, then, how are we to speak of our wishes being fulfilled in all those junk fictions where the birth of the Anti-Christ is aborted? Turning all the apparent counterevidence into subterranean wish-fulfillment involves too much theoretical "improvisation." But, at the same time, saying that junk fiction commands attention by virtue of manifesting wishes and/or anxieties robs the theory of its specificity. Hypothesizing that junk fictions are wish-fulfillments is an informative conjecture. Saying that junk fictions either involve wishes or they do not isn't merely unfalsifiable, it is also uninformative.

Thomas J. Roberts has recently advanced an alternative account of reading junk fiction that would explain the way in which consuming generic stories is no affront to rationality. According to Thomas, reading junk fictions is always a matter of reading in a system. He says, "In reading any single story, then, we are reading the system that lies behind it, that realizes itself through the mind of that story's writer. And here lies the fundamental distinction between reading one book after another and reading in a genre, between reading with that story focus and reading with the genre focus. Genre reading is system reading. That is, as we are reading the stories, we are exploring the system that created them."[7]

Thus, for Roberts junk fiction reading is genre reading and genre reading is always intertextual. It is reading with some awareness of a background of norms against which the variations in the story before us are to be appreciated. For example, Roberts maintains that Nora's line in Dashiel Hammett's *Thin Man* – "Tell me something Nick. Tell me the truth: when you were wrestling with Mimi, didn't you have an erection?" – stood out, so to speak, because it was unprecedented in comparable detective stories. Likewise, the murder in *Psycho* takes on further significance because of the way in which it subverts a certain genre norm by killing off the putatively main character in the first act.

Moreover, if I understand Roberts correctly, reading in a system is not primarily subliminal. It is not simply that we possess these genre norms tacitly and that we register their disturbance as we might the grammaticality of a sentence. Rather it seems that for Roberts reading in the system is done with self-awareness that includes comparing and contrasting devices across stories.

Given the notion of reading in a system, the fact that the stories in question are simple and broadly repetitive is not problematic. Indeed, these very design-features facilitate what Roberts calls reading in the system. Furthermore, even if the individual stories appear simplistic and routine, the system is complex. Thus, though in reading junk fiction, we read for the story in some sense, the actual focus of our attention is the system in which we track the place of the story and its elements as variations, subversions, echoes, expansions, and so on. That we know the story-type is no impediment to our interest because what concerns us are convergences, contrasts, and extensions within the story type. The roughly repetitive aspect of these stories makes our fine-grained appreciation of their differences possible.

Perhaps there is an element of reading in a system in much genre consumption. One sword-and-sorcery saga may recall to mind another, just as conversations about a TV program often involve tracing recurring or opposing incidents and episodes in the series before moving on to a discussion of analogous shows. That is, there is no denying that a comparative sense is relevant to the consumption of junk fiction. And, of course, fans elevate that comparative sense into a baroque art. Yet, it seems to me that, though what Roberts calls reading in a system (which I prefer to call comparative reading – and/or viewing) is not infrequent, it is not a necessary component of consuming junk fiction. That is, there is a core phenomenon of reading junk fiction where the consumer knows the story-type and derives justifiable satisfaction from the fiction, but not because he or she is reading in a system.

Admittedly, most fans and connoisseurs read comparatively in a genre, as do both academic and journalistic critics. And where someone reads in this way, we have an answer, for the group in question, to the paradox of junk fiction. But this is a somewhat specialized, though not arcane, mode of consumption. And, of course, many readers and viewers are neither fans nor connoisseurs nor critics. A more basic mode of reading junk fiction, I submit, is to focus on the story, not on the genre of which it is a part. Quite often we become absorbed in a mystery story of the locked-room variety without that experience bringing to mind particular stories of the same sort that we have already encountered (such as Poe's *Murders in the Rue Morgue*), though, at the same time, we recognize that this is a sort of setup we have been confronted with before.

One cannot rule out the possibility of this kind of reading by claiming that all junk fiction reading is, by definition, reading in a system. There is also reading junk fiction noncomparatively, though with a sense of familiarity with the story-type. And for this type of reading, which I suspect is quite pervasive, the paradox of junk fiction still threatens.

The notion that reading junk fiction is reading in a system does not provide a comprehensive solution to the paradox of junk fiction. For though this kind of reading is not uncommon, it is special, and not all, nor perhaps even most, junk fiction reading is of this sort. However, despite its failure in terms of comprehensiveness, the reading-in-a-system approach does suggest a fruitful way in which to solve the paradox of junk fiction. For the reading-in-a-system approach involves the explicit recognition that our interest in a story may not be exhausted by knowledge of how it turns out. We may be interested in a story because of what we can do with it, that is, by virtue of the kind of activities it can support.

The reading-in-a-system hypothesis locates our interest in a particular junk narrative in terms of the way in which junk fiction invites our contemplation of themes and variations within a genre. This phenomenon does not seem comprehensive enough to solve the paradox of junk fiction in general. But it does suggest that we may answer the paradox by identifying some activity or range of activities that junk fiction affords, the pursuit of which motivates our consumption of junk fiction despite our knowledge of the story.

What sorts of activities might these be? Perhaps the easiest way to begin to characterize them is to start with an obvious example, mystery stories. We open the book. We recognize familiar surroundings – say a house in the country. The master of the house is a real bastard – he manages to do something churlish to every other character he meets. We realize that he is not long for this world; for the author is setting things out in such a way that virtually everyone in the fictional world will have a motive to kill him. We have been here before; we know what kind of story we are in; we have met the characters already. And yet we read on. We play the game of whodunit, which, of course, involves our doing something: to wit, performing a range of activities that could be roughly labeled interpreting and inferring.

Clearly the paradox of fiction disappears when we are thinking of what is called classical detective fiction. Whether we are reading stories by Arthur Conan Doyle or more sundry items like *McNally's Luck* by Lawrence Sanders or *Murder at the MLA* by D. J. H. Jones, we have no difficulty in explaining why, even though we know the story-type, we continue reading. The reading enables us to exercise our interpretive and inferential powers. Perhaps it is even the case that the repetitiveness of the story-types aids us in entering the game, since experience with very similar stories may make certain elements in the relevant stories salient for interpretive and inferential processing.

Nevertheless, be that as it may, it is clear that when it comes to mysteries, the fact that we already know the story-type and, in many cases, even the kind of solution eventually used to ascertain whodunit does not preclude our interest in the fiction, nor indeed our interest in the story aspect of the fiction. For the familiar story serves as a vehicle for such readerly activities as interpretation and inference.

Though this sort of readerly activity is very evident with respect to mystery fiction, it should be noted that it is also available in every other sort of junk fiction. Let a few examples from different genres illustrate this point. When reading Isaac Asimov's science fiction novel *Foundation,* the reader infers that the Empire has settled into a kind of medieval stagnation – where the capacity for original research and invention has been lost and, in fact, is repressed in favor of reliance on the authority of the past – before this social malaise is explicitly diagnosed in the book; just as the attentive reader has surmised the identity of the Mule in Asimov's sequel, *Foundation and Empire,* way in advance of its explicit revelation in the text.

Or, for a more localized example, in the concluding pages of *The Rustlers of West Fork,* by Louis L'Amour, the reader knows that Hopalong Cassidy is about to be set upon in the wintery street by Johnny Rebb. Johnny Rebb is hiding out in a house that Hopalong has been told is empty. When Hopalong steps into the street, we learn that he is looking intently at something. L'Amour writes: "No snow on the roof. He smiled." And, then, we infer that Hopalong knows Johnny Rebb is in the house, because the house is obviously heated, and that inference, in turn, is confirmed on the very next page.

Harlequin romances are often held up as the epitome of the formulaic. So many of these novels mobilize the same scenario: girl meets boy; girl misunderstands boy, or vice versa; the misunderstanding is cleared up; girl gets boy. But despite the formulaic structure of these stories, each novel affords the reader the opportunity to exercise her interpretive powers.

In *The Lake Effect* by Leigh Michaels, Alex Jacobi, a high-powered woman lawyer, dressed to the nines for success, has been told to lure Kane Forrestal back to Pence Whitfield, the largest law firm in the Twin Cities. Kane says that he prefers beachcombing to big-time law. Alex assumes that this is a bargaining ploy and that her job is essentially to renegotiate Kane's contract. But the reader gradually hypothesizes that Kane is sincere in his distaste for Pence Whitfield, that he is attracted to Alex, and that she is attracted to him. Alex – one might say *of course* – is the last to know. She consistently misinterprets Kane's avowals and advances as negotiating gambits. Thus, the reader is constantly reinterpreting Alex's interpretations of what is going on.

Or, for a more compact example of the kind of interpretation that I have in mind, consider the Harlequin romance *The Quiet Professor* by Betty Neels. Nurse Megan Rodner is convinced that Doctor Jake van Belfeld is married. The reader realizes that despite his gruffness, he is attracted to Megan, and it also slowly but surely dawns on us that we have no real evidence that van Belfeld is married. In a conversation with Megan, he says his house is too large, but that that can be remedied. She says, "Oh, of course, when your wife and children live here." We know that by this she means van Belfeld's supposed present wife and children. He answers, "As you say, when my wife and children live here," which the reader understands is likely to mean van Belfeld's future wife (whom Megan might become) and their children.

Reading such sentences and situations for their ambiguities is an essential ingredient in appreciating Harlequin romances. Even if one grasps the Harlequin formula, one still derives value – call it transactional value – from reading the story by means of exercising and applying one's interpretive powers. There is no paradox in reading Harlequin romances, even though you already know the story-type inside and out, for each different novel provides you with the opportunity to exercise your interpretive powers on a different set of details and misunderstandings, and, most importantly, on different *kinds* of misunderstandings.

Junk fiction, then, can serve as an occasion for transactional value. This is the value that we derive by, among other things, exercising our powers of inference and interpretation in the course of reading. Here reading is construed as a transaction. The transactional value in consuming junk fiction does not come from simply learning or knowing the details of the story but from the pleasure we derive from the activity of reading or viewing the story. For example, at one point in the movie *Jurassic Park,* the hunter Muldoon explains how packs of velociraptors destroy their prey by outflanking them. Later in the film, when Muldoon is tracking one raptor, we anticipate that flanking maneuver by another raptor, even though, for some reason, Muldoon does not. When the second raptor finally appears, we feel gratified because our conjecture has been borne out and here, just as in the other cases that I have cited, a sense of satisfaction obtains when our inferences and interpretations are correct.

Where junk fictions encourage or invite us to make conjectures about what is going to happen, they keep us riveted to, or at least engaged with, the fiction insofar as we want to see whether our conjectures will be confirmed; and, moreover, when they are confirmed, we derive the kind of pleasure that comes with any successful prediction. In Danielle Steel's *Mixed Blessings,* Barbie's behavior leads the reader to suspect that she's cheating on Charlie Winwood. We read on to ascertain whether or not this is so; we feel excitement as we sense that what we have inferred is about to be revealed; and then once the secret is out of the bag, we feel a flush of self-satisfaction. Junk fiction can sustain interest, in part, because it affords the opportunity for self-rewarding cognitive activity, which, if it is not as arduous as higher mathematics, is not negligible either.

Reading or viewing junk fiction involves the consumer in various activities. At the very least, the reader is involved in following the story, which is not simply a matter of absorbing the narrative but involves a continual process of constructing a sense of where the story is headed. This may include predicting exactly what will happen next. But it need not.

Generally, however, following the story does engage us, at the very least, in envisioning or anticipating the *range* of things – will she get the job or not – that are apt to happen next. In the movie *Sleepless in Seattle,* once the heroine finds the boy's backpack, the viewer tracks the action in terms of the question of whether our heroine and our heroes will meet or pass each other on the elevators. Earlier scenes in popular narratives are most frequently necessary conditions for later scenes. For this reason, earlier scenes implicate a range of options concerning what will happen next, and a crucial aspect of what it is to follow a story is to evolve and to project a reasonable horizon or set of expectations about the direction of the events the story has put in motion. Indeed, it is only within the context of such a horizon of expectations that the reader or viewer can be said to know what is at stake in the action.

Furthermore, following the story also requires filling in the presuppositions and implications of the fictional world of the narrative, an activity that can become challenging with cyberpunk fiction such as William Gibson's *Virtual Reality.* Undoubtedly, the implied background of much popular fiction is not as arcane as one finds in cyberpunk. Nevertheless, there is never any narrative so simple and self-sufficient in terms of information that audiences need make no contribution in order to render the story intelligible. Thus, as of any fiction, junk fictions require active consumers.

So far the readerly activities I have called attention to have been what might be called cognitive. But, of course, the consumers of junk fiction not only derive satisfaction and value from the cognitive judgments they make, they also derive satisfaction from the moral and emotional judgments that are part and parcel of their reading. If in Ben Bova's novel *Mars,* our growing conviction – on the basis of various hints and clues before it is stated – that the expedition is deteriorating physically and psychologically is a cognitive judgment, then our classification of the newscaster Edith as an opportunist is a moral judgment and our hatred for the vice-president is emotional.

Quite often in junk fictions, readers and viewers know more than the characters in the stories about what is going on. For example, in *North by Northwest,* the audience knows that George Kaplan does not exist, but Roger Thornhill, who has been mistaken for George Kaplan, does not. This not only enables us to anticipate what will happen in scenes where Thornhill searches out George Kaplan, but also raises the emotion of suspense in us about whether and when Thornhill will learn the truth. In this case, knowledge, emotion, and morality – since our sense that Thornhill is morally right contributes to the substance of our suspense – lock us into the story.[8] And, in general, our engagement with a junk fiction depends upon the mobilization of our cognitive, moral, and emotive powers, for it is the active exercise of these powers that gives junk fiction a transactional value for its consumers.

The paradox of junk fiction arises from supposing that it is true that people read popular fictions for their stories – that is, that people are interested in junk fictions for their stories; and, that if people read a certain sort of fiction for their stories, then knowing the story precludes any interest in the fiction; and, finally, that people who read junk fiction read stories (story-types) that they already know. This, in turn, implies that people are and are not interested in junk fictions. The psychoanalyst and the proponent of genre reading as reading in a system avert this contradiction by denying that the readers of junk fiction read for stories – rather they read for wish-fulfillments, on the one hand, and for systems, on the other.

Not attracted to either of these approaches, I propose that we dissolve the contradiction by denying the proposition that if people are interested in a certain sort of fiction, then knowing the story precludes any interest in the fiction. Why? Because we can be interested in the story as an occasion to exercise our cognitive powers, our powers of interpretation and inference, our powers of moral judgment and emotive assessment. Junk fictions can support these activities; indeed, they are often designed to encourage them. That we know the story-types already in no way deters our deriving this sort of transactional value from junk fictions. Perhaps in many circumstances knowledge of these story-types may make our active engagement with junk fictions more zestful in the way that playing games with well-defined rules enables us to hone our abilities more keenly.

If I am right and junk fictions afford transactional value to readers and viewers, then there is nothing mysterious or irrational about consuming junk fictions. For within the context of recurring story-types, it is possible to exercise our cognitive, moral, and emotional powers. Baseball games are repetitive, but we play them again and again because they afford the opportunity to activate and sometimes even to expand our powers. There is nothing mysterious or irrational about this when we realize that performing the activity itself is a source of pleasure and satisfaction. Likewise with junk fictions, the activities of following the story, of morally assessing situations and characters as well as of admiring or despising them

occupy our time with varying degrees of satisfaction even if we are already familiar with the generic plot.

Undoubtedly it sounds strange to attempt to justify the rationality of consuming junk fiction on the grounds of the activities that it abets. For one of the
hoariest commonplaces concerning such fiction is that it renders its audiences
passive;[9] that it stupefies them; that it is a kind of narcotic. But this view of junk
fiction is unwarranted. First, if the truth be told, the active/passive distinction is
unpersuasive. After all, it is very difficult to conceive of a completely passive
response to anything, especially to anything like a text. Doesn't the most lack-
adaisical response involve some cognitive processing?[10] Is there such a thing as a
thoroughly passive response?

So, at the very least, the burden of proof lies with the detractors of junk fiction
to define, in some reasonable way, whatever they mean by passivity. For unless they
are able to propose some plausible notion of passivity with respect to junk fiction,
we need not hesitate to think of junk fiction in terms of activity.

Detractors of junk fiction or, as it is sometimes called, kitsch, maintain that the
audience for junk fiction is passive when compared to the audience for high art.
Moreover, they explain this by claiming that junk fiction is "easy" while high art,
or at least high art of the twentieth century, is "difficult." The idea seems to be that
high art demands effort and, hence, activity on the part of its consumers, while
kitsch and junk fiction can be consumed effortlessly and, therefore, passively.

Now it is true that popular art, including junk fiction, is designed for effortless
consumption and that it is rarely difficult. However, it is a logical error to presume
that ease of consumability entails passivity, or that activity only correlates with
what is difficult. Though difficulty may function to goad activity, there can be
activity where there is no difficulty. And this concession is all that we need in
order to dissolve the paradox of junk fiction by reference to the activities of the
reader of junk fiction.

Someone might charge that the activities that I have invoked with respect to
junk fiction are not unique to this sort of narrative. Canonical classics and modernist narratives also support the kinds of activities I have discussed; in fact, they
may even in general stimulate these kinds of activities more than standard examples of junk fiction.

Of course, I freely admit both of these claims. The readerly activities in virtue
of which consuming junk fictions is rational are the same or, at least, are on a continuum with many of the activities elicited by canonical and modernist fictions.
And these latter sorts of fiction may stimulate more readerly activity than junk fiction; and, in that sense, may even be of greater or higher value. However, admitting all this does not undercut my more modest conclusion: that typically junk
fiction does promote certain rewarding, readerly activities that make it rational to
consume junk fictions in cases where we are already familiar with the story. That
these activities can be engaged elsewhere, perhaps even more intensively, does not
compromise the fact that they are also available in junk fictions where they serve
to make reading, viewing, and listening worthwhile.

Here it is important to note that unlike some defenders of junk fiction, I am not claiming that junk fiction has some unique standard of value of its own that is incommensurable with the standards of what might be called ambitious literature. For the activities that make consuming junk fictions worthwhile are on a continuum with those available in ambitious fiction.

This, of course, does not imply that junk fiction is an evolutionary way-station on the trajectory to ambitious fiction; in fact, I doubt that reading junk fiction necessarily puts one on the pathway toward reading more ambitious fiction. But this is compatible with maintaining that the value in junk fiction is on a continuum with the value of ambitious fiction, even if consuming junk fiction does not lead one inexorably to cultivate more of the same value in ambitious fiction.

Just as a taste for beer does not inevitably lead to a taste for champagne, an appreciation of the transactional value of junk fiction does not lead typical readers to a taste for high literary culture. And even persons accustomed to the transactional value of ambitious literature can savor the perhaps lesser virtues of junk fiction in the same way that a connoisseur of champagne can appreciate beer. Indeed, even the wine taster may think beer is what one should have some of the time, though she values champagne, overall, as finer.

Lastly, the kinds of readerly activities that I have been discussing should not be confused with either games of make-believe, on the one hand, or resistant readings, a.k.a. recodings, on the other. For I am not convinced that while watching *The Fugitive* the viewer must make believe that she sees a train hitting a bus, whereas the viewer cannot appreciate the film without at numerous points structuring what she sees in terms of whether or not the hero is about to be captured, that is, without following the plot protentively in light of how the story is likely to unfold.

Moreover, the relevant readerly activities are not of the type that people in cultural studies refer to as recodings or resistant readings. For so-called recodings involve audiences in using junk fictions for creating meanings that serve their own special purposes. Australian aborigines viewing Western movies and cheering when the Indians annihilate the white settlers are said to recode those movies – to derive a significance from the story that was unintended by the makers of the narrative and yet is politically galvanizing for the aboriginal community (and its political struggles).[11] Recodings, in this sense, either reconfigure or add something alien to the narrative, something that corresponds to the political needs of the consumers.

Now I have no reason to doubt that, as a matter of sociological fact, recoding and resistant reading occurs. I am not so convinced that it occurs with the frequency and the invariantly progressive cast claimed for it by certain leading figures in cultural studies. There may be recoding going on, but recoding is not the sort of readerly activity on which I rest my case for the dissolution of the paradox of junk fiction.

For recodings are ultimately arbitrary. Any group, in a certain trivial sense, can make anything mean anything else for its own purposes. However, the readerly activities that I have been talking about are not arbitrary responses to the text. Rather they are normatively correct – they are the responses that the ideal reader of the text should have to the text. Reading the comic novel *Artistic Differences* by

Charlie Hauck, you should come to hate Geneva Holloway. That is what the text or, more precisely, the author expects you to do. The text has been designed to elicit that response. The text requires a reader who fills it in by hating Geneva Holloway, but that hatred is not a readerly invention *ex nihilo*. Nor is it a recoding. For it is not arbitrary, but rather proposed by the text in a structured way.

Perhaps one might attempt to dissolve the paradox of junk fiction by invoking the phenomenon of recoding. My own tendency, however, is to resist this move. For, in the first place, I am not convinced that there is as much recoding going on as is commonly supposed by academic critics and, if I am right about this, then recoding would not yield a comprehensive solution to the paradox. But, as well, I suspect that it is very likely that recoding as it is most frequently described may not usually be a straightforwardly rational response to a text, and that, therefore, the invocation of recoding will not usually rationally justify our consumption of junk fiction.

Instead, I argue that the kinds of rational activities that junk fictions afford – such as interpreting, inferring, following the story, issuing moral judgments and emotive assessments – make sense of our consumption of stories that are admittedly formulaic. That other sorts of fiction might be even more stimulating along these dimensions in no way precludes the possibility that consuming junk fictions can be a self-rewarding activity, albeit one that is limited relative to certain other alternatives. So, inasmuch as it is reasonable to anticipate that junk fiction can be the source of transactional value, choose your reading for the flight to your next professional convention with an easy conscience.

Visual Metaphor

I. INTRODUCING VISUAL METAPHOR

It is the contention of this essay that there are visual metaphors. That is, there are some visual images that function in the same way that verbal metaphors do and whose point is identified by a viewer in roughly the same way that the point of a verbal metaphor is identified by a reader or a listener.

The term "image" here is intended to refer only to human artifacts. It is not, for instance, meant to apply to the outlines of animals or the suggestions of faces discernible in clouds. The visual images that I have in mind in this essay are the products of intentional human activity.

By calling the images in question "visual," I wish to signal that these images are of the sort whose reference is recognized simply by looking, rather than by some process such as decoding or reading. One looks at a motion picture screen and

From: *Aspects of Metaphor,* ed. by Jaakko Hintikka (Kluwer Publishers, 1994), 189–218.

recognizes that a woman is represented; one looks at her hand and recognizes that she is holding a gardenia.

Such images, of course, are symbols. But comprehending such image-symbols does not rely upon codes nor could there be a dictionary according to which one might decipher or read such images. Rather one looks at the screen and recognizes that which the images represent, that is, wherever one is capable of recognizing the referents of the images in what we might call normal perception (perception not mediated by codes).

What in common speech are called "pictures" are prime examples of visual images in the sense that I am using this concept. In the case of a picture, I can recognize what it is a picture of simply by looking in those cases where what it is a picture of is something with which I am already familiar or that I am already capable of recognizing in, so to speak, "nature."

For example, in the case of Gericault's *Portrait of an Officer of the Chasseurs Commanding a Charge* (1812), I recognize it as a depiction of a man on a white horse in military attire as well as recognizing that in his right hand he holds a saber.[1] I understand that this is a saber not by virtue of a correlation of this inscribed shape to a dictionary-like entry, but by looking.

Arguably, we learn to recognize pictures of things in tandem with the development of our capacity to recognize the very things that are pictured.[2] The capacity to recognize x perceptually comes with the capacity to recognize pictures of x perceptually. Pictures belong to the class of symbols I call visual images because they are comprehended perceptually, that is, without recourse to any subtending code.

Of course, pictures are not the only types of visual images. Sculptures can also be visual images, as can typical theatrical scenes when we perceptually recognize that the actors depict people. Visual images, then, are symbols whose overall reference as well as the reference of their elements – such as the officer's saber above – are recognized perceptually.

Visual metaphors are a subclass of visual images – symbols whose elements are recognized perceptually. Moreover, there is a striking structural analogy between what I am calling visual metaphors and verbal metaphors: namely, where verbal metaphors are frequently advanced via grammatical structures that appear to portend identity – such as the "is" of identity or apposition – visual metaphors use pictorial or otherwise visual devices that suggest identity in order to encourage metaphorical insight in viewers. The relevant visual device of this sort that will be emphasized in this essay – which will be elucidated below – is what can be called *homospatiality*.[3]

The possibility of producing visual metaphors is available in every artistic medium that employs visual images. Furthermore, this is a possibility that has been realized. For there are some visual metaphors in every existing artistic medium that traffics in visual images, including: painting, sculpture, photography, film, video, theater, and dance.

The purpose of this essay is to characterize visual metaphors: to suggest how we identify them; to note their recurring features; to indicate how they function;

and to discuss the ways in which they are interpreted. In order to facilitate this project, it is probably useful to begin by providing a list of what I take to be straightforward cases of visual metaphors. Here are six examples.

1. Rene Magritte's 1945 painting *Le Viol* (*The Rape*) is a composite portrait. At the bottom of the painting we immediately recognize a right shoulder and a neck. But as our eyes move up the painting, where we would expect to find a head, we instead see the naked, headless front of a torso of a woman, beginning at the top of her thighs and extending to the upper reaches of her chest, just above her breasts. Atop the headless torso are somewhat unruly, loosely flowing, shoulder-length tresses, parted on the right side. We immediately recognize the constituent elements of the painting – the neck, the torso, the hair. And, furthermore, we easily grasp the metaphorical point of the painting as a whole – that the face is a torso.

That is, we use the image of the torso as an opportunity to see faces in a new light – to see eyes as breasts, noses as navels, and smiles as the triangle formed by the intersection of the torso with the juncture of the legs. Of course, we may also comprehend this image as projecting the metaphor that the body is a face; the image, that is, may invite us to think about the visual appearance of bodies in the light of visual features of faces. This tendency in certain visual metaphors to afford alternative, symmetrical insights with respect to central elements of the image is a feature of visual metaphors to which we will return.

2. Pablo Picasso's 1951 sculpture *Baboon and Young* is surely an example of the sort of thing that Picasso had in mind when he wrote that "My sculptures are visual metaphors."[4] We immediately recognize a depiction of an erect primate with a smaller creature, presumably her offspring, sprawled across her chest and riding on her belly. But as we look at the sculpture, we also notice that the baboon's head is composed of a toy car of a late forties' vintage. The hood of the toy car serves as the snout of the simian, the fender as the mouth, the windshield as the eyes and the roof of the car as the skullcap. One appropriate response to this visual image is to take it as metaphorically suggesting that a baboon's head is a car. But as in the Magritte case, an equally satisfactory, alternative, symmetrical interpretation is also ready at hand, namely, that cars of this period are monkeys' heads.

Also, like *Le Viol, Baboon and Young* launches its metaphor by way of presenting the viewer with a composite construction. The sculpture has been produced by attaching or fusing a toy car to the body of a baboon at exactly the point in space where we would expect the head of a baboon to be. The result of this act of fusion or assemblage is a single, unified, spatiotemporally continuous entity that we readily comprehend as at least a depiction of a baboon.

But the figure is also composite, and we need to notice the discrete elements – such as the toy car – that compose it. Moreover, the discrete elements that compose it coexist in the same space – they are *homospatial* – insofar as they are integral features of a single entity, parts of a unified whole that coexist within the unbroken contour, or perimeter, or boundary of a single unified entity.

3. If so far our examples have been what might be called face metaphors, Man Ray's 1924 *Violon d'Ingres* provides a case where the face plays no role in the

metaphorical insight promoted by the image. In this famous photomontage, the bare back of a model dominates the picture – a bare back noteworthy for the sort of rounded monumentality one recalls from Ingres' well-known paintings of harem odalisques. Undoubtedly, the allusion to Ingres is also enhanced by the kind of turban the model wears. However, this is not merely a photograph of an odalisque. For superimposed on the model's back are images of the kind of f-holes one finds in cellos and violins. The presence of these f-holes encourages us to note that the ways in which Ingres renders his models are cello-like, or, as the title of the photograph would have it, violin-like.

The photomontage plus the title provoke the metaphorical insight that Ingres' odalisques are violins. Also available is the alternative, symmetrical insight: violins are odalisques, or violins are Ingres-esque odalisques. Undeniably, comprehending the visual metaphor in any of the preceding ways probably depends on the viewer having some acquaintance with Ingres' masterpieces. One is prompted to mobilize this knowledge by the title, though, of course, someone really savvy about art history could most likely pick up the allusion to Ingres through the iconography alone, even if the title were withheld from her.

Furthermore, I suspect that even where the viewer is ignorant of Ingres, the viewer is still apt to derive metaphorical insight from the photomontage. These metaphors will not make reference to Ingres, but might be expressed by: "A woman's body is a violin (or a cello)"; or, "A violin (or a cello) is a woman's body." Moreover, a viewer may go on to note other than visual correspondences as a result of the imagery. For, example, a viewer might entertain such thoughts as: a violin (or cello) is to be caressed as one caresses a woman's body; or, a woman's body may be played like a violin or a cello. Whether these metaphorical expansions are offensive or sexist is not of immediate concern for this essay.[5] However, if one were to find *Violon d'Ingres* offensive or sexist, that would probably be best explained in terms of the efficacy of visual metaphors as a means of expression.

4. Though the preceding visual metaphors have all pertained to at least one animate category, it is easy to produce examples of visual images that are not involved in illuminating features of animate beings. For instance, consider Claes Oldenburg's drawing *Typewriter-pie*.[6]

Here, of course, the title of the drawing itself is probably best understood as a metaphor – one secured by parataxis. However, even if the linguistic juxtaposition of the pertinent terms is best glossed as a metaphor, the linguistic metaphor is in no way as perspicuous as the visual metaphor. Indeed, this example is most likely a case in which the visual metaphor clarifies the metaphor in the title of the work rather than vice versa. For the point of this visual metaphor is far more easy to negotiate than is the point of the verbal metaphor.

Looking at Oldenburg's *Typewriter-pie,* we see how the typewriter carriage and paper blend with the raised crust at the back of a piece of pie, while the downward trapezoidal convergence of the keys of a typewriter are captured by the triangular shape of a typical slice of pie. Oldenburg's drawing produces the metaphors that typewriters are slices of pies or that slices of pies are typewriters.

Oldenburg's drawing calls our attention to the visual ways in which, for instance, typewriter carriages are crust-like and pie crusts are typewriter-carriage-like. In fact, in the case of Oldenburg's drawing it may even be accurate to say that Oldenburg has created an unprecedented analogy between typewriters and pieces of pie rather than simply taking note of commonly acknowledged correspondences between the two.

Moreover, in the Oldenburg case, it should be stressed that the metaphorical relation in the drawing should not be misconstrued as an instance of the well-known phenomenon of seeing-as. For in the example of *Typewriter-pie*, it is not the case that one's experience of the visual field shifts in such a way that one first sees a typewriter and then one sees a pie, or vice versa. Rather, one sees a composite figure – a visually stable figure in which the typewriter element and the pie element are constantly discernible at the same time. This contrasts strongly with the infamous duck-rabbit figure where one first sees a duck and *then* a rabbit (or vice versa).

In the case of seeing-as, the duck element and the rabbit element are not simultaneously present for perception. Rather, they become manifest sequentially. However, in the case of *Typewriter-pie*, and in the cases of our previous visual metaphors, the images do not reconfigure themselves. Our examples of visual metaphors are best described as composite images: images in which elements calling to mind different concepts or categories (such as that of the typewriter and that of the slice of pie) are co-present in the visual array and are recognized to be co-present simultaneously in a single, spatially homogeneous entity (this is the feature of visual metaphors that we have already called "homospatiality").

Visual metaphors proffer unified visual arrays in which the terms of the metaphor of both are perceptually co-present at once. Unlike paradigmatic cases of seeing-as, exemplified by ambiguous switch-images, *Typewriter-pie* is an image in which we simultaneously, rather than sequentially, apprehend features of typewriters and pies in such a way that these two categories mutually inform each other.

5. Even if my examples up until now have been static, there is nevertheless no reason to suppose that visual metaphors cannot be evolved or developed over time. One example that immediately springs to mind in this regard is the identification between the machine and Moloch in Fritz Lang's 1926 silent film *Metropolis*.

In the third scene of this film, the son of the ruler of the vast, futuristic city Metropolis ventures to the underground factory precincts. Here, huge engines, manned by stupefied, regimented workers, run the city above. Through the point-of-view of the son, we see a colossal machine. At its foot are two enormous turbines. A giant stairway, flanked by rows of work stations, leads up to an open space in which rotary jacks whirl furiously.

There is an explosion. The screen fills with smoke. As the smoke clears, we not only see dead and wounded workers everywhere; we also see, again through the son's point-of-view, the machine transformed into Moloch, a spurious deity of the Old Testament whose worship involved the sacrificial immolation of children.[7]

Cinematically, the image of Moloch has been superimposed over the machine. The machine becomes a monster. The stairs become Moloch's tongue and the cavern at the top of the stairs becomes Moloch's maw. In one shot, the aforesaid turbines are replaced by Moloch's paws. But in subsequent shots we see the turbines as turbines, figuring in the overall composition perhaps as modernist versions of gigantic votive candles.

We know that the monstrous face that has been superimposed over the machine is Moloch because the son identifies it as such in an intertitle. But even if the son had not specified the face in his vision as Moloch, we would nevertheless be able to recognize the superimposed visage as that of a monster.

The machine, or at least parts of the machine have been transformed into parts of a monster, Moloch. At the same time, however, the machine is still recognizable as a machine. The co-present monster elements and the machine elements interanimate in such a way that we grasp the point of the image: that the machine is Moloch or, more broadly, that such modern machines are man-eating monsters.

Whereas in most of our previous examples, the visual metaphors called attention to visual correspondences between their constituent elements – correspondences between, for example, the *look* of a typewriter and the *look* of a slice of pie – the machine/Moloch example, though motivated by blending features of machines and monsters, is predicated on calling attention to features of machines (and modern industry) over and above the simply visual (just as *Violin d'Ingres* perhaps alerts us to the not simply visual idea of caressing a violin).

The machine/Moloch image invites us to map part of what we know about Moloch onto the machines of modern industry. The concept of Moloch is, so to say, supposed to serve as a template that we lay over the concept or category of modern machines in order to focus on or attend to certain pertinent properties of modern machinery. And, commonplace associations that pertain to Moloch are tested with respect to modern machinery in order to see whether those commonplace associations can be transferred from their source domain (Moloch) in such a way that they pertain to modern machinery (what we may call the target domain of the metaphor).[8]

Of course, the obvious interpretation of the machine/Moloch image is that the machines of modern industry devour workers just like man-eating monsters; or, workers are sacrificed to modern machines as children were sacrificed to cruel gods like Moloch. Through the superimposition of Moloch on the machine, the film director Fritz Lang alerts the viewer to such putative properties of modern machines as that they are consumers of workers, construed as human sacrifices.

This putative property of modern machinery, of course, is not a visual property, strictly speaking, though we are alerted to it by means of the visual fusion of elements of the machine and Moloch. Rather, we might call this putative property a thematic property of the machine. Thus, the machine/Moloch image indicates that visual metaphors need not pertain only to visual correspondences between their respective source domains and target domains. Visual metaphors can also be deployed in such a way that they call attention to non-visual, thematic properties of things.

The machine/Moloch image differs from our previous examples in several noteworthy respects. It is developed over time through superimposition (and narration), whereas our earlier examples were literally static, unchanging images. The machine/Moloch image also calls our attention to more than merely visual properties of modern machines, whereas most of our earlier examples mapped visual aspects of the source domain (such as the curvaceousness of violins) onto the target domain (odalisques).

Furthermore – and this is a point to which we will need to return – the machine/Moloch image does not seem easily susceptible to alternative, symmetrical interpretations. For while it makes sense to comprehend the visual metaphor as assimilating machines to Moloch, it does not seem to the point to take the imagery to be inviting the thought that either Moloch is a machine or that monsters are machines. So, whereas with *Le Viol* it seems unproblematic to regard the face as alternatively the source domain ("the body is the face") and the target domain ("the face is a body"), it appears scarcely intelligible in the context of *Metropolis* to flip the source domain and the target domain – that is, the direction of mapping in the machine/Moloch metaphor is asymmetrical ("the machine is Moloch" works; "Moloch is a machine," in context, does not work).

However, despite these differences between the example from *Metropolis* and earlier examples, the machine/Moloch image still counts as a visual metaphor insofar as it depends upon what has been called homospatiality. The machine/Moloch metaphor proceeds by situating recognizably disparate elements (machine elements and Moloch elements) in the same space – in the same *bounded,* physical entity – in such a way (to be explained later) that these elements call to mind different categories or concepts that we interanimate by mapping part of what we associate with one of the categories onto the other category.

In this case, the precise technical device that is employed by the filmmaker in order to secure homospatiality is superimposition. This is also a technique that is likewise available literally in photography. A comparable technology in video is available through what is called image-processing. Moreover, since image-processing is a particularly easy technique to execute in video, we tend to find a great many visual metaphors in video art. Indeed, some video artists have even maintained that metaphor is the most appropriate – that is, medium-specific – line of aesthetic development in the video medium.[9] But whether such a predilection can be sustained theoretically, it is undeniably the case that due to the ease with which the technology of image-processing facilitates superimposition, visual metaphors occur with pronounced frequency in video. This can be observed readily by attending not only to the video works of gallery artists but also by attending to the special effects in the more popular tapes on MTV that often project visual metaphors. And this tendency toward the use of visual metaphor is likely to increase dramatically as this sort of video becomes even more influential.

6. Although all the preceding examples have been drawn from the art of the twentieth century, there are myriad examples of visual metaphors from earlier periods. Many instances of visual metaphors can be found in the work of the sixteenth-century painter Hieronymus Bosch. In the central panel of *The Temptations of Saint Anthony,* next to the figure with the funnel on its head, there is an image

of a priest, garbed in sacred vestments, reading a missal or bible. His face is that of a pig, although he also wears spectacles, has human ears, and sports a tonsure.

This is a composite image. Clearly it invites us to think of priests in terms of pigs. It insinuates the anticlerical thought that [some] priests are pigs. In the medieval bestiary, pigs could be thought of as animals whose most salient property was that they were devoted solely to the selfish pursuit of their own happiness;[10] so by fusing priest-elements and pig-elements in this painting, Bosch polemically focuses our attention on the piggish properties of the priestly estate.

In this image, the pig-elements function as the source domain and the priest-element function as the target domain. That is, we map part of what we know or associated with pigs onto priests. We use what we know about pig-properties in order to pick out and focus upon putative priest-properties. The homospatiality of the pig-elements and the priest-elements in the same bounded figure invites interaction between the categories or concepts that these elements call to mind in such a way that what we think of pigs, including commonplace associations, serves as the means for organizing our thoughts about priests by selecting putatively corresponding properties of priests for emphasis. That is, we use information that we possess about the category of pigs to focus selectively on certain putative properties of priests.[11]

From my descriptions of the preceding examples, it should be clear why I call them visual *metaphors*. Just as verbal metaphors most frequently intimate some form of identity or at least intersection between the categories they mobilize – "Man *is* a wolf unto man" – the previous cases employ homospatiality, which visually incorporates disparate elements (calling to mind disparate categories) in one, spatially bounded, homogeneous entity. Elements are fused in a composite, but nevertheless self-identifiable construct, thereby visually indicating that these are elements of the self-same entity.

The elements are features of the same thing in virtue of inhabiting the same spatial coordinates – in virtue of inhering in the same body – that is, within the same continuous contour, or perimeter or boundary. The elements fused or superimposed or otherwise attached are recognizable as belonging to the same unified entity.

Homospatiality, in this sense, is a necessary condition for visual metaphor. It serves to link disparate categories in visual metaphors physically in ways that are functionally equivalent to the ways that disparate categories are linked grammatically in verbal metaphor. Where verbal metaphors assert or appear to assert identity between distinct, nonconverging categories, visual metaphors, by means of homospatiality, intimate categorical identity by presenting nonconverging categories as applying to the same entity. Thus, the way in which homospatiality in our examples functions as a visual equivalent to asserted identity in verbal metaphor provides one reason to suspect that certain visual images can be metaphors.

Although in virtue of homospatiality, the visual metaphor is projected via a recognizably unified entity, certain of the elements that comprise the visual metaphor come from discernible disparate categories, categories that are not physically composible. Baboons cannot physically have cars for heads; navels cannot function as noses; priests cannot be pigs, nor machines monsters. And women cannot have f-holes in their backs. Commentators agree that verbal metaphors are generally either false or not literally true.[12] Visual metaphors cannot be false or literally not true since they are not propositional. However, visual metaphors do possess a feature that roughly corresponds to falsity or apparent falsity. Namely, visual metaphors identify or link disparate categories by means of homospatiality that are not physically composible in the sorts of entities they propose. Whereas verbal metaphors are generally false or apparently false, visual metaphors portray homospatial entities that are composed of elements that are not generally physically composible.

Although more needs to be said about this, a further requirement or necessary condition for a visual image to count as a visual metaphor, then, is that, in addition to homospatiality, discernible elements in the unified entity presented by the figure must be physically noncomposible. Moreover, if this is correct, then the fairly obvious analogy between the falsity or apparent falsity of verbal metaphors and the physical noncomposibility of the elements of the kind of visual images we are talking about supply us with a further reason to call these images visual metaphors.

Because the homospatially linked elements in such figures are physically noncomposible, the viewer of such symbols seeks some way to make the image intelligible apart from resorting to the norms of physical possibility. The viewer explores the possibility that the physically noncomposible elements in the array allude to the categories to which they belong and that those disparate categories (or, more precisely, members thereof) have been elided in a way that defies physical possibility not to represent a state of affairs but to interanimate the categories in question. Specifically, the viewer explores the possibility that those categories have been evoked in order to focus on aspects of one of the categories in terms of aspects of the other category.

The physical noncomposibility of the homospatially fused but disparate elements in the visual array invites the viewer to comprehend the image not as a representation of a physically possible state of affairs but as an opportunity to regard one of the categories as providing a source for apprehending something about the other category (the target domain), or as an opportunity for regarding each of the categories as mutually informative (as alternatively the source and the target domain for each other).

Moreover, since the structure of the six visual images previously discussed can so readily be assimilated in terms of the language of source domain and target domain, and insofar as the function of these domains in the pertinent images can be persuasively modeled on a mapping relation from source domain to target domain, we have further reason to call these visual images metaphors.

By now, I hope that I have provided some grounds to support the contention that there are *some* visual metaphors. In what follows, I would like to suggest in more depth the ways in which we go about identifying these visual metaphors. However, before attempting to say more about how we identify visual metaphors, two hypotheses — that are at variance with my own — need to be confronted. I claim that there are *some* visual metaphors. Consequently, I must consider the view that there can be no such thing as a visual metaphor. Moreover, since I believe that some visual images are visual metaphors and that some are not, I must also undermine the suggestion that all visual images are metaphors. Thus, it is to these competing hypotheses which I now turn.

II. COMPETING HYPOTHESES

IIA. THERE ARE NO VISUAL METAPHORS

One consideration that has been advanced against the possibility of visual metaphor has been raised with respect to the film image,[13] though it is easy to imagine it being raised specifically with any sort of visual image. Of the film image, it may be said that it is always concrete; it is always a representation of a particular. Similarly, it might be added, adapting freely from Berkeley, that any picture is also a picture of a particular. But metaphors require abstraction. Metaphors interanimate the relation between classes. Metaphors putatively require that we pull free of the apprehension of concrete particulars in order to imaginatively play with categories. In the metaphor "life is a journey," we are invited to map generic features of journeys onto lives in general. Therefore, insofar as visual images are concrete and particular, they cannot serve as vehicles for metaphors which are abstract.

Of course, the supposition that metaphor is abstract, in the sense in which it is understood in this argument, is false. Many verbal metaphors refer to particulars. In describing an overly ambitious colleague to a newcomer, I might say "That's Napoleon over there." This is a noncontroversial example of a metaphor, but both its source domain and its target domain are particulars. Moreover, such well known metaphors as "Juliet is the sun" and "The moon is a ghostly galleon" also contain reference to particulars.

Furthermore, the second presupposition of this argument is contestable. Though every visual image may be a particular image in some sense (barring the complexities of mechanical and electronic reproducibility), it is not true that every visual image refers to particulars. Some visual images are depictions, that is, some visual images are not intended to refer to particular persons, places, or things, but to refer to classes or sets of persons, places or things. The illustrations in dictionaries are examples of this use of visual images, while the workers pictured in certain Socialist Realist paintings are intended and are understood to refer to the proletariat as a class. Thus, since both of the premises of the preceding argument are false, the argument as stated is not sound.

But perhaps the argument from abstraction should be understood to have a more psychological cast than I have so far conceded. Maybe the idea is that metaphor requires abstract thinking in terms of the interanimation of categories, but the particularity of visual images blocks abstract thinking by keeping the viewer rooted in the perception of the particular. However, I see no reason to accept this psychological hypothesis.

I have, for example, conjectured a rival hypothesis. I have argued that there is a mechanism in certain visual images that prompts the viewer to abandon the attempt to regard the image as the representation of a particular and to attempt to interpret it in terms of the interaction of categories. Specifically, the physical non-compossibility of disparate elements that have been fused homospatially encourages the spectator to find a way to assimilate the image as something other than the representation of a particular. One alternative available to the viewer is to explore the possibility that the visual image provides an opportunity to plumb the metaphorical insights suggested by the linkage of disparate elements and the categories they call to mind.

The scenario that I have just offered is a plausible one. It provides an account of how the structure of visual metaphor can move a viewer from the perception of the visual image as the representation of a particular to abstract thought about the interaction of categories. Thus, unless some flaw can be found in my hypothesis, the burden of proof lies with the skeptic to show that visual imagery perforce thwarts the sort of abstract thinking that they maintain is characteristic of metaphor.

Whereas the preceding line of argument denies that visual images can be *metaphors,* another line of argument might maintain that, although my examples are indeed metaphors, they are not *visual* metaphors. Rather, they are really verbal metaphors in pictorial garb. That is, the presumption here is that if there are such things as *visual* metaphors, then they must be uniquely visual. "The clergy today are pigs" is a thought that one can readily imagine originating in language – only to be illustrated afterwards – and, in any case, it does not rely on any visual correspondences between its source domain and its target domain in order to make its point. Therefore, it is not a uniquely visual metaphor. Moreover, it might be claimed that any example that we might advance will confront the same problems. Indeed, the skeptic with respect to visual metaphors may go so far as to assert that all so-called visual metaphors are nothing but the illustration of commonplace metaphors that already exist antecedently in language. And from this standpoint, the skeptic maintains that there are no *visual* metaphors.

I am suspicious of the idea of uniquely visual metaphors. But even if we grant, for the moment, the notion of uniquely visual metaphors, the previous argument is too strong. For example, if the idea of uniquely visual metaphors depends on the requirement that such metaphors have all and only visual content, then it would seem that some of my previous metaphors, though not all, are uniquely visual. *Le Viol* maps the look of the face onto visual features of the body.

Furthermore, whether a metaphor originates verbally or visually seems too contingent a standard on which to hang a categorical distinction between visual and verbal metaphors. It is just as likely that Phillipon's caricature 1834 *Les Poires* – which engenders the thought that Louis Phillippe is a pear – originated in a context in which visual correspondences rather than verbal associations motivated it. And, of course, it does mobilize recognition of visual correspondences between its source domain and its target.

Of course, the charge that there are no uniquely visual metaphors may rest on another idea, namely, that there are no visual metaphors because they can all be stated in language. But even if this is the relevant standard of uniquely visual metaphors, it is not clear that there are absolutely no visual metaphors. Reconsider the case of Oldenburg's *Typewriter-pie*.[14] As a linguistic metaphor, I submit, it is very obscure, if not completely inert. The visualization, however, is absolutely clear. If anything, it takes the visualization to make sense of the verbal metaphor. And, furthermore, it is not evident that one can really paraphrase all the relevant visual correspondences that the visual metaphor raises in language. This is at least a case where it is very hard to reduce the visual metaphor to a linguistic statement. Indeed, it may be practically impossible. Moreover, this example not only pertains strictly to visual content, but it is also easy to imagine this visual metaphor succeeding independently of language and, in fact, preceding its title. Surely, *Typewriter-pie* counts as a uniquely visual metaphor in terms of all the criteria canvassed so far. Therefore, there are at least some visual metaphors.

The case of *Typewriter-pie* might force the skeptic to concede that there is at least one visual metaphor, but the requirement that such metaphors be uniquely visual may seem to disqualify my other examples as candidates for the status of visual metaphor. But this relies upon the plausibility of the notion of uniquely visual metaphors. I cannot say that I find this to be a compelling category. For, on the most straightforward understanding of its application, it certainly would undermine our ordinary classifications of metaphors.

The presumption that if a metaphor has visual content (refers to visual correspondences), it is a visual, rather than a verbal, metaphor, implies that a spoken metaphor – such as the utterance "The sun is a red rubber ball" – is really a visual metaphor, rather than a linguistic one. But this is a peculiar, counterintuitive result. Moreover, the distinction between where metaphors appear first – in language or in pictures – seems a completely arbitrary way of classifying metaphors, while the notion that uniquely visual metaphors cannot be fully paraphrased in language fails to mark a reliable distinction between visual and verbal metaphors for a reason not stated so far, namely, many linguistic metaphors are said to be such that they cannot be fully paraphrased.

Thus, I reject the idea that whether there are visual metaphors hinges upon whether there are uniquely visual metaphors. Something is a visual metaphor if it encourages the mapping of source domains onto target domains *by visual means* – specifically through the homospatiality of physically noncompossible elements. In this sense, all my previous examples are visual metaphors; so, there are some visual metaphors.

One may want to deny that there are visual metaphors because one holds that metaphors are essentially linguistic.[15] But such a view simply begs the question against the notion of visual metaphors unless some reason can be supplied to support it. One such reason might be that the best the sort of visual images that I have cited can do is to provoke comparisons between the disparate objects co-presented in the homospatial figure. However, as proponents of the "Verbal–opposition theory of metaphor" have pointed out, metaphor involves more than object comparison.

In his discussion of T. S. Eliot's "smoke is briars" metaphor from "East Coker," Monroe Beardsley argues that the metaphor cannot be grasped simply by comparing smoke and briars. One must also recognize that the word "briars" carries certain biblical connotations, recalling to mind Christ's crown of thorns. Thus, an adequate mapping of the source domain – "briars" – onto the target domain – "smoke" – requires access to the history of the word "briars."[16]

Putatively, this is not an adventitious feature of metaphors. No metaphors can be adequately grasped by object comparisons; all require some sense of the historical connotations of the words that are in metaphorical play. So, it might be argued, since so-called visual metaphors can at best motivate object comparisons and since they do not mobilize knowledge of verbal connotations, they are not genuine metaphors. Genuine metaphors are essentially linguistic (insofar as they rely upon the historical connotations of words).

I am not aware of anyone who has made this argument so explicitly. However, were one to attempt to do so, certain objections would appear inevitable. First, it is not the case that visual images only call attention to the objects they portray. Visual images, apart from visual metaphors, can make allusions to other visual images, to the history of certain visual motifs, to ideas related to the history of certain visual motifs, and to concepts. Thus, there is no reason to suppose that visual metaphors would be restricted to guiding the viewer's attention solely at the level of object comparisons. In the "man-eating machine" metaphor from *Metropolis,* we are prompted to think of human sacrifice that also, I submit, makes us think of injustice. The "man-eating machine" metaphor carries the connotation that the machine in question is unjust. Consequently, it is a mistake to suppose that our visual metaphors can only induce object-comparisons and cannot mobilize knowledge of connotations.[17]

Perhaps at this point, it will be claimed that all the connotations that such metaphors mobilize are essentially verbal. But if this means that they all concern the history of words, this is false. Some may involve the history of images and nonverbal features of the typical ways in which things are portrayed (such as the way in which *Typewriter-pie* exploits one of the customary approaches for illustrating slices of pies).

And, in any case, it seems to me to be wrong to believe that even with verbal metaphors the only knowledge we bring to bear is knowledge of words and their history. The knowledge that we bring to bear comes from many sources, including what we know about the world and what we understand about our concepts apart from what is written in our dictionaries. In expanding the insights offered to us by verbal metaphors we depend upon more than linguistic knowledge. And this is also the case with visual metaphors.

Metaphors do not essentially involve the interaction of words, though words are one of the means of securing metaphorical interaction. Rather, metaphors mobilize the interaction of categories and concepts that include all sorts of infor-mation – including beliefs about the world and systems of commonplaces – some of which may be verbal, some of which may be visual, and some of which may not be easily classifiable as either. Any of this information may be brought into play by a metaphor. Moreover, conceptual systems of commonplaces can be acti-vated by visual juxtapositions as well as verbal juxtapositions. Insofar as metaphors are conceptual and categorical, rather than exclusively verbal, there is no reason to suppose that there are necessarily no visual metaphors.

IIB. ALL VISUAL IMAGES ARE METAPHORS

I have maintained that there are some visual metaphors. But this position is triv-ially and uninformatively true if all visual images are metaphors. And though no one has defended this position openly, it would seem to follow from certain recent views of the nature of art. That is, a number of recent philosophers of art have been arguing lately that all artworks are metaphors.[18] Granted, this does not com-mit them to the view that all visual images are metaphors. It only commits them to the view that all visual images that are artworks are metaphors. And, if like me, one counts a metaphor as visual if it is secured by visual means, then such a posi-tion implies that any visual image that is also an artwork is a visual metaphor. Moreover, if you accept that any visual image is an artwork, then, of course, you will be driven to the conclusion that all visual images are metaphors.

Admittedly, unless one views all visual images as art (which is not an altogether inadmissable position for the contemporary art theorists), this will fall short of a commitment to the idea that all visual images are visual metaphors. But since even this view populates the world with far more visual metaphors than I am prone to countenance, I regard it as a rival position to my own.

Perhaps the most obvious problem with the conclusion that all visual images that are artworks – which some may regard as a class to which all visual images belong – are metaphors is that it depends on the premise that all artworks are metaphors. But this strains credulity. It seems to me obvious that there are naturalist paintings such as Thomas Eakins' 1873 *The Biglen Brothers Turning the Stake* that defy metaphorical readings of the paintings as a whole as well as metaphorical readings of any of their constituent elements. Such paintings are art; but there is a daunting burden of proof to be met by anyone who would claim them to be metaphors.[19]

It may be that the temptation to regard artworks as metaphors rests upon the hunch that all artworks invite some sort of exploration from audiences – such as interpretive activity – just as metaphors invite audiences to test the extent to which the source domain can be mapped onto the target domain. But, of course, it is not clear that all artworks invite interpretations in any full-blooded sense; there is, for example, nothing enigmatic or nonobvious – nothing that would call for an interpretation – about the Eakins' painting cited above.

Moreover, *even if* there is some very weak sense in which any artwork invites exploration, that is not enough to establish the putative correlation between artworks and metaphors. For metaphors do not invite just any kind of exploration. They invite exploration of the interaction between the source domain and the target domain and the categories they call to mind. Not every artwork, not even every artwork that invites exploration, invites the kind of exploration that metaphor activates. Therefore, not every visual artwork, including the case where every visual image is counted as a visual artwork, is a metaphor.

However, there may be another way to motivate the notion that all visual images are visual metaphors. There is a view of visual metaphor, different from the one propounded in this essay that would appear to send us in the direction of the conclusion that all visual images are visual metaphors. According to Virgil Aldrich, a visual metaphor can be characterized in terms of three components: the material of the visual image, its subject matter, and its content.[20] The material of a visual image comprises its shaped properties: its texture, color, line, mass, form, and the ways in which these are handled. The subject matter of the visual image is whatever it represents. And the content of the visual image is the result of the interaction of the material and the subject matter. Viewers are said to gain access to this content through a special mode of attention called prehension.

Though Aldrich is somewhat obscure, I think that what he has in mind is that the subject matter of the visual image provides us with the target domain and the organization or the form of the material functions as the source domain. The content of the visual image is metaphorical – the product of the interaction of the form of the material and the subject matter which interaction constitutes an expressive portrayal. Presumably, since all visual images involve shaped material and subject matter, all visual images will involve metaphorical content understood as the expressive portrayal of subject matter.

Putting aside the question of whether the interaction of the material of the visual image and the subject matter always results in an expressive portrayal, the major question one wants to ask is whether the phenomenon Aldrich has in mind is usefully called metaphor. It is undeniably true that quite often what Aldrich calls the material of the image and the subject matter interact in such a way that an expressive portrayal of the subject matter emerges. But is it fruitful to regard this interaction as a matter of metaphor? The phenomenon that Aldrich seems to have in mind is usually called expression, not metaphor.

Gaston Lachaise's 1932 bronze *Standing Woman* expresses a feeling about the monumental strength of his subject, woman. Through his handling of scale and proportion, through his clear articulation of the subject's musculature, and through his emphasis on the clean, impenetrable surface of the figure, Lachaise imbues his subject matter with a quality of elemental power. Through his treatment of the materials with reference to the relevant subject matter, Lachaise makes us aware of a certain quality – say, the elemental power of woman. That is, we can characterize that Lachaise has done within Aldrich's framework. But it is not a metaphor.

There are not two concepts here. The handling of the material imbues the subject matter with a quality of elemental power or expresses a feeling of elemental power with regard to the subject matter. It is difficult to specify a source domain and a target domain in this case. Of course, Aldrich does invoke the possibly contestable distinction between material and subject matter, but these do not seem like units of metaphor if only because it is difficult to think of the handling of materials as typically a concept or a category. If one wants to speak of the material and the subject matter of an image, these distinctions may sometimes be useful for explaining the expressive qualities of images. But it seems wrong to me to reduce expression to metaphor. Thus even if all visual images involved expression (a very controversial claim), one should not go on claim that all visual images involve metaphor.

Aldrich's view of visual metaphor is too broad. It appears to me to conflate expression with metaphor. There are some visual metaphors. But we need a different account than Aldrich's in order to identify them.

III. IDENTIFYING VISUAL METAPHORS

Up to this point, our conception of a visual metaphor has been that a visual metaphor is a visual image in which physically noncompossible elements belong to a homospatially unified figure which, in turn, encourages viewers to explore mappings between the relevant constituent elements and/or the categories or concepts to which they allude.[21] This is a useful starting point for identifying visual metaphors. But more needs to be said.

A visual metaphor is a visual image. This signals that the figure as a whole is recognizable perceptually as well as that the elements that serve in the viewer's mappings be perceptually recognizable.[22] This latter condition amounts to the requirement that the relevant elements be recognizable by looking. Of course, in order to negotiate a visual metaphor, the viewer must not only be able to recognize the relevant elements. Her attention also needs to be drawn to them. So the relevant elements must stand out; they must be visually salient or prominent. There is no way to anticipate all the ways in which image-makers can make visual elements prominent. That is part of the image-maker's art. All we can say by way of theory on this matter is that the elements be salient.

These elements are presented as inhering in homospatially unified figures and they co-habitate within the continuous contour or perimeter of spatially bounded wholes. However, these spatially bounded wholes or homospatially unified figures strike the viewer as anomalous. For certain of the saliently posed elements in the homospatial array are at odds with settled notions of physical possibility. It is not possible, ceteris paribus, for women to have f-holes in their backs; they would lose too much blood.

However, in determining whether the elements in an array are physically noncompossible, we cannot rely simply on a look at the image plus our knowledge of science. We need to consider the context in which the image is presented and the intentions of the image-maker in presenting it.

Why? Because there are homospatial figures with apparently physically noncompossible elements that in virtue of their context and the intentions of their makers are not designed to be taken metaphorically. For example, in horror films there are many images of entities that are physically noncompossible by the lights of science – for example, lizard men and ape women. But given the context of the genre, and the evident intentions of the filmmaker, these entities are not metaphors. In a certain sense, they are being presented as physically compossible in a context ruled by the understandings of the horror genre.

The figures in *Le Viol* and *Baboon and Young* could be set in fictional contexts where they were not being presented as physically noncompossible. One can imagine science fictions in which there are pig-priests, violin-women, and monsters that are part flesh and part machine.[23] In order to interpret such figures metaphorically, we must at least have grounds to believe that the image-maker is presenting them as physically noncompossible entities and not as physically possible entities in some fantastic-fictional world that is ruled by laws different from our own. That is, to explore these entities for metaphorical insight, one must have reason to believe that they are being presented as physically noncompossible rather than as fictionally possible.

Of course, apparently physically noncompossible figures may be presented in order to serve intentions other than fiction-making. The presentation of such figures may be religiously motivated. The gods of ancient Egypt were represented as composite figures. Some Christians continue to represent the devil as part human, part goat, part reptile, and so on. The fundamentalist viewers of such images do not take them to be representations of physically noncompossible entities. For them, pictures of the devil as part man and part goat show how the devil actually looks. Such pictures represent the physical composition of the devil from the perspective of their religion. Operating in a religious context, a fundamentalist image-maker and a fundamentalist viewer do not believe that what is represented is physically noncompossible. In their view, it is the short-sightedness of our scientific outlook that leads the rest of us to think that such images represent physically noncompossible entities.

A visual metaphor rests on the shared recognition on the part of the image-makers and the viewers that the disparate elements fused in the homospatial image are being presented as physically noncompossible. In order to determine whether the homospatial figure presented in the image is to be taken as representing a physically noncompossible state of affairs, certain conditions must be met.

The first is that the image-maker believes that the image represents a physically noncompossible state of affairs and believes that in presenting the image, she is presenting a representation of something that is physically noncompossible (rather than something that is physically possible, religiously actual or fictionally possible and so on). Of course, if the image-maker intends the image to be taken metaphorically, she must also believe that the standard, intended viewer believes that the image represents a physically noncompossible state of affairs (rather than an actual state of affairs, a physically possible state of affairs, a state of affairs in a certain fictional world, and so on).

Furthermore, needless to say, in order for a visual metaphor to succeed, the standard intended viewer will in fact believe that the state of affairs represented by the image is physically noncompossible and that it is meant to be taken as physically noncompossible, rather than as a representation of some supernatural actuality or as a state of affairs that obtains in the context of some fiction that abides by some alternative set of laws. That is, if the viewer is to take the image metaphorically, the viewer must believe that the image-maker believes the state of affairs is physically noncompossible and that the image-maker is presenting the image as physically noncompossible. The viewer believes that the entity in Le Viol is physically noncompossible, that Magritte believes that it is physically noncompossible, and that Magritte presents it with the intention that it be recognized to be physically noncompossible. The viewer does not take the image to represent a monster – neither an existing monster nor a science fiction monster – nor a god.

If the image-maker intends to propose a visual metaphor, then the image-maker believes that her juxtaposition of physically noncompossible elements in a homospatially unified array will serve as an invitation to the viewer to explore the ways in which the noncompossible elements and their corresponding categories illuminate each other when they are interpreted as source domains and target domains that are related by mappings onto each other. That is, the image-maker must believe that the homospatially unified figure and its noncompossible elements have what Ina Loewenberg calls heuristic value.[24]

The image-maker, in other words, intends the viewer of her visual image to take the image as a proposal to consider the referents of the noncompossible elements and their related categories as interacting in an illuminating way. In making the image, the image-maker believes that the juxtaposition of elements will intimate a relation or fact and will encourage the viewer to notice or focus on that fact or relation. The visual metaphor will have heuristic value in the sense that it will facilitate the viewer's apprehension of that fact or relation, for example, that odalisques have violin-like curves. It is in this sense that the image-maker believes that the physically noncompossible, homospatial image has heuristic value.

In making a visual metaphor, the image-maker believes that the image has heuristic value and intends the viewer to consider the image as an invitation to consider its heuristic value. This does not mean that the image-maker antecedently knows all of the discoveries the viewer may make in exploring the image. Viewers may find more connections between the elements in the image than the image-maker was aware of, just as verbal metaphors may contain an indefinite number of resonances that no reader, including the original author, ever fully comprehends.

The image-maker invites the viewer to make discoveries by way of saliently posing physically noncompossible elements. The juxtaposition of physically noncompossible elements prods the viewer to try and make some sense of the image. The image cannot be taken as a realistic representation. However, the viewer will, on the supposition that the image has been proffered in order to make some point,[25] attempt to negotiate it by means of another sort of interpretation. In visual metaphors, the saliently posed juxtaposition of the noncompossible elements as well as the fact that even on an initial viewing they mutually inform each other ideally prompts the viewer to take the image as a proposal to explore the image for metaphorical insight. That is, the viewer takes this as the best explanation of the image-maker's presentation of the physically noncompossible elements in a homospatially unified entity.

Though the image-maker guides the viewer's exploration of the image to a certain extent, the invitation is a somewhat open one. The viewer expands the metaphor through her own imaginative play. The viewer tests to see whether the visual metaphor is open to what I earlier called symmetrical interpretations. The viewer determines whether the metaphor is to be expanded only in terms of the referents of the noncompossible elements or in terms of the categories to which they belong. And, as with verbal metaphor, the audience explores what Lakoff and Turner call the various "slots" of the source domain schema to see if they have bearing on the target domain.[26]

Without taking a stand one way or the other on Davidson's theory of *verbal* metaphor, I think that it is clear that his position is appropriate for *visual* metaphor. It makes little sense to talk about some special kind of meaning with respect to visual metaphors since they are not propositions. They do not carry some special encoded message for there is nothing, strictly speaking, that can count as a code when it comes to visual metaphors. If for no other reason, this follows from the fact that visual metaphors are visual images that are not read in terms of a code, but, rather, are recognized by looking. Nor is there a grammar or syntax of visual metaphor; one would be hard put to set forth the conditions under which such a metaphor would be ill formed. One does not read off the meaning – metaphorical or otherwise – of a visual metaphor. Rather, one interprets visual metaphors, in part in the ways suggested in the previous paragraph.

A visual metaphor is a device for encouraging insights, a tool to think with. This is not to deny that visual metaphors can provide insight, but only that they do so by way of having a meaning. Of verbal metaphors, Davidson writes:

> What I deny is that metaphor does its work by having a special meaning, a specific cognitive content. I do not think … with Black that a metaphor asserts or implies certain complex things by dint of a special meaning and *thus* accomplishes its job of yielding an "insight." A metaphor does its work through intermediaries – to suppose it can be effective only by conveying a coded message is like thinking a joke or a dream makes some statement which a clever interpreter can restate in plain prose. Joke or dream or metaphor can, like a picture or a bump on the head, make us appreciate some fact – but not by standing for, or expressing, the fact.[27]

Whether this is a useful way of thinking of verbal metaphors, it is apt for the case of visual metaphor. Visual metaphors prompt insights rather than stating insights in a language. Visual metaphors "work through intermediaries" – the salient posing of physically noncompossible elements. Visual metaphors are of the nature of what Kant called an aesthetic idea – a representation of the imagination that occasions much thought, without however being reduced to any *definite* thought.[28] That is, with visual metaphors, the image-maker proposes food for thought without stating any determinate proposition. It is the task of the viewer to use the image for insight. This is not to say that the image-maker has not provided some direction for the viewer to follow. And the ingredients in the image obviously constrain the viewer's imaginative flights. Rather, there is no single, fixed propositional meaning, for the visual metaphor is not a proposition.

Some commentators have criticized Davidson's theory of verbal metaphor on the grounds that Davidson presupposes that metaphors are reversible, whereas they argue that they are not.[29] However, as we have seen, visual, as opposed to verbal, metaphors are very often susceptible to symmetrical or reversible interpretations. Magritte's *Le Viol* may introduce either the thought that the face is a body or that the body is a face. Whether a visual metaphor is symmetrical or not depends upon whether the viewer can produce suitably constrained interpretations of the image by reversing the source domain and the target domain. The visual metaphor is an invitation to the viewer to explore it imaginatively. And part of that imaginative exploration involves testing to see whether the terms of the visual metaphor can be reversed.

In presenting a visual metaphor, the image-maker intends the viewer to consider it in terms of its heuristic value, that is, in terms of the ways in which the interaction of the referents and/or categories mobilized by the figure yield insight. Thus, a successful presentation of a visual metaphor requires that the viewer know that the image is being proposed as an invitation to explore it for heuristic value. The viewer is undoubtedly helped in this by the fact that the image fuses physically noncompossible elements. This blocks the viewer's assimilation of the image as a realistic representation. The viewer must find an alternative interpretation of the image. The viewer must suppose that the figure is not a fictional inhabitant of some fantastic world or a supernatural being in some or another theology.

Confronted by a homospatially unified figure that fuses physically noncompossible elements, the viewer, employing the principle of charity, seeks an interpretation that will render the image intelligible. The viewer will have to be prepared to reject religious and science-fiction interpretations. The viewer will have to discount the possibility that the image-maker has outlandish opinions about what there is. And the viewer will also have to determine that the image is not simply a display of cleverness on the part of the artist.

For example, Guiseppe Arcimboldo's 1566 painting *The Librarian* seems to fuse elements in a way that suggests that the referent is part human and mostly books. However, in this case, there does not seem to be a metaphor in the offing – for, among other things, it would be hard to specify it. Rather, the image seems to provide an occasion for appreciating Arcimboldo's visual ingenuity and wit.[30]

However, if the viewer cannot find interpretations of the preceding sorts to account for the point of the anomalous image, then the viewer is apt to take the image as a proposal to explore it as a locus of heuristic value. Moreover, since taking visual images in this way is well-precedented in our visual culture – recall innumerable newspaper caricatures – the viewer easily moves into this interpretive framework. Of course, for the visual metaphor to succeed, the viewer must regard the visual image as an invitation to explore its heuristic potentials; otherwise the image-maker's intended communication lacks uptake. Thus, for the visual metaphor to succeed, the viewer must come to regard it to be the case that the image-maker intends her to take the visual image as an invitation to consider the referents of the physically noncompossible elements and/or their related categories and concepts in terms of mappings onto each other.

Summarizing the preceding remarks: An image-maker successfully presents a visual metaphor if and only if

1. she makes a visual image in which
2. at least two physically noncompossible elements are
3. saliently posed in
4. a homospatially unified figure;
5. the image-maker believes what the figure represents is physically noncompossible and presents it as being physically noncompossible;
6. the image-maker believes the standard, intended viewer will believe that it is physically noncompossible;
7. the standard, intended viewer does believe that it is physically noncompossible;
8. the standard, intended viewer also believes that the image-maker believes that it is physically noncompossible;
9. the image-maker believes that posing the noncompossible elements saliently in a homospatially unified figure has heuristic value in terms of potential mappings of the referents of the elements and/or their related categories onto each other;
10. the image-maker intends the viewer to take the image as an invitation to consider the referents of the physically noncompossible elements and/or their related categories in terms of their heuristic value and the image-maker also intends the viewer to know that she intends this;
11. the viewer believes that the image-maker intends her to take the image as an invitation to consider the referents of the physically noncompossible elements and their related categories in terms of mappings onto each other.

IV. CONCLUSION

I began by announcing my contention that there are visual metaphors. I have defended this view by examining some objections to the very idea of visual metaphors, and by indicating that it is not the case that being a visual metaphor is an unremarkable feature of all visual images or, at least, all visual images that are art. I have tried to show that there are visual metaphors by isolating a certain class of existing visual images and by showing that they can be readily understood within frameworks designed for characterizing metaphor.

If my case is persuasive, then the existence of visual metaphors of the sort that I have identified leds credence to the view that metaphor is primarily a matter of categories and concepts rather than merely a matter of words. On the other hand, I do admit that the range of things that my theory counts as visual metaphors is probably much more narrow than the language of art critics and artists would seem to demand. They call more things "visual metaphors" than I do. Nevertheless, it is my sense that even if further research shows that there are more types of visual metaphor than my theory pinpoints, I have still managed to circumscribe the most central and least controversial core cases of visual metaphor.

On Being Moved by Nature: Between Religion and Natural History

I. INTRODUCTION

For the last two and a half decades – perhaps spurred onward by R. W. Hepburn's seminal, wonderfully sensitive and astute essay "Contemporary Aesthetics and the Neglect of Natural Beauty"[1] – philosophical interest in the aesthetic appreciation of nature has been gaining momentum. One of the most coherent, powerfully argued, thorough, and philosophically compelling theories to emerge from this evolving arena of debate has been developed over a series of articles by Allen Carlson.[2] The sophistication of Carlson's approach – especially in terms of his careful style of argumentation – has raised the level of philosophical discussion concerning the aesthetic appreciation of nature immensely and it has taught us all what is at stake, logically and epistemologically, in advancing a theory of nature appreciation. Carlson has not only presented a bold theory of the aesthetic appreciation of nature; he has also refined a methodological framework and a set of constraints that every researcher in the field must address.

Stated summarily, Carlson's view of the appreciation of nature is that it is a matter of scientific understanding; that is, the correct or appropriate form that the appreciation of nature – properly so called – should take is a species of natural history; appreciating nature is a matter of understanding nature under the suitable scientific categories. In appreciating an expanse of modern farm land, for example, we appreciate it by coming to understand the way in which the shaping of such a landscape is a function of the purposes of large-scale agriculture.[3] Likewise, the appreciation of flora and fauna is said to require an understanding of evolutionary theory.[4]

From: *Landscape, Natural Beauty and the Arts,* ed. by S. Kemal and I. Gaskell (Cambridge: Cambridge University Press, 1993), 244–66.

Carlson calls his framework for nature appreciation the natural environmental model.[5] He believes that the strength of this model is that it regards nature as (a) an environment (rather than, say, a view) and (b) as natural. Moreover, the significance of (b) is that it implies that the appreciation of nature should be in terms of the qualities nature has (and these, in turn, are the qualities natural science identifies). Carlson writes "for significant appreciation of nature, something like the knowledge and experience of the naturalist is essential."[6]

My major worry about Carlson's stance is that it excludes certain very common appreciative responses to nature − responses of a less intellective, more visceral sort, which we might refer to as "being moved by nature." For example, we may find ourselves standing under a thundering waterfall and be excited by its grandeur; or standing barefooted amidst a silent arbor, softly carpeted with layers of decaying leaves, a sense of repose and homeyness may be aroused in us. Such responses to nature are quite frequent and even sought out by those of us who are not naturalists. They are a matter of being emotionally moved by nature. This, of course, does not imply that they are noncognitive, since emotional arousal has a cognitive dimension.[7] However, it is far from clear that all the emotions appropriately aroused in us by nature are rooted in cognitions of the sort derived from natural history.

Appreciating nature for many of us, I submit, often involves being moved or emotionally aroused by nature. We may appreciate nature by opening ourselves to its stimulus, and to being put in a certain emotional state by attending to its aspects. Experiencing nature, in this mode, just is a manner of appreciating it. That is not to say that this is the only way in which we can appreciate nature. The approach of the naturalist that Carlson advocates is another way. Nor do I wish to deny that naturalists can be moved by nature or even to deny that something like our nonscientific arousal by nature might be augmented, in some cases, by the kind of knowledge naturalists possess. It is only to claim that sometimes we can be moved by nature − *sans* guidance by scientific categories − and that such experiences have a genuine claim to be counted among the ways in which nature may be (legitimately) appreciated.

Carlson's approach to the appreciation of nature is reformist. His point is that a number of the best-known frameworks for appreciating nature − which one finds in the literature − are wrongheaded *and* that the model of appreciation informed by naturalism which he endorses is the least problematic and most reasonable picture of what nature appreciation should involve. In contrast, I wish to argue that there is at least one frequently indulged way of appreciating nature that Carlson has not examined adequately and that it need not be abjured on the basis of the kinds of arguments and considerations Carlson has adduced. It is hard to read Carlson's conclusions without surmising that he believes that he has identified the appropriate model of nature appreciation. Instead, I believe that there is one form of nature appreciation − call it being emotionally moved by nature − that (a) is a long-standing practice, (b) remains untouched by Carlson's arguments, and (c) need not be abandoned in the face of Carlson's natural environmental model.

In defending this alternative mode of nature appreciation, I am not offering it in place of Carlson's environmental model. Being moved by nature in certain ways is one way of appreciating nature; Carlson's environmental model is another. I'm for coexistence. I am specifically not arguing that, given certain traditional conceptions of the *aesthetic,* being moved by nature has better claims to the title of *aesthetic* appreciation whereas the environmental model, insofar as it involves the subsumption of particulars under scientific categories and laws, is not an *aesthetic* mode of appreciation at all. Such an objection to Carlson's environmental model might be raised, but it will not be raised by me. I am willing to accept that the natural environmental model provides *an* aesthetic mode of appreciating nature for the reasons Carlson gives.

Though I wish to resist Carlson's environmental model of nature appreciation as an exclusive, comprehensive one, and, thereby, wish to defend a space for the traditional practice of being moved by nature, I also wish to block any reductionist account – of the kind suggested by T. J. Diffey[8] – that regards our being moved by nature as a residue of religious feeling. Diffey says, "In a secular society it is not surprising that there will be a hostility towards any religious veneration of natural beauty and at the same time nature will become a refuge for displaced religious emotions."[9] But I want to stress that the emotions aroused by nature that concern me can be fully secular and have no call to be demystified as displaced religious sentiment. That is, being moved by nature is a mode of nature appreciation that is available between science and religion.

In what follows I will try to show that the kinds of considerations that Carlson raises do not preclude being moved by nature as a respectable form of nature appreciation. In order to do this, I will review Carlson's major arguments – which I call, respectively: science by elimination, the claims of objectivist epistemology, and the order argument. In the course of disputing these arguments, I will also attempt to introduce a positive characterization of what being moved by nature involves in a way that deflects the suspicion that it should be reduced to displaced religious feeling.

II. SCIENCE BY ELIMINATION

Following Paul Ziff, Carlson points out that in the appreciation of works of art, we know what to appreciate – in that we can distinguish an artwork from what it is not – and we know which of its aspects to appreciate – since in knowing the type of art it is, we know how it is to be appreciated.[10] We have this knowledge, as Vico would have agreed, because artworks are our creations. That is, since we have made them to be objects of aesthetic attention, we understand what is involved in appreciating them.[11]

However we explain this feature of artistic appreciation, it seems clear that classifying the kind and style of an artwork is crucial to appreciating it. But with nature – something that in large measure it is often the case that we have not made – the question arises as to how we can appreciate it. By what principles will we isolate the appreciable from what is not, and how will we select the appropriate aspects of the nature so circumscribed to appreciate? In order to answer this question, Carlson explores alternative models for appreciating nature: the object paradigm, the landscape or scenery model, and the environmental paradigm.[12]

The object paradigm of nature appreciation treats an expanse in nature as analogous to an artwork such as a nonrepresentational sculpture; as in the case of such a sculpture, we appreciate its sensuous properties, its salient patterns, and perhaps even its expressive qualities.[13] That is, the object model guides our attention to certain aspects of nature – such as patterned configurations – that are deemed relevant for appreciation. This is clearly a possible way of attending to nature, but Carlson wants to know whether it is an aesthetically appropriate way.[14]

Carlson thinks not; for there are systematically daunting disanalogies between natural expanses and works of fine art. For example, a natural object is said to be an indeterminate form. Where it stops is putatively ambiguous.[15] But with artworks, there are frames or framelike devices (like the ropes and spaces around sculptures) that tell you where the focus of artistic attention ends. Moreover, the formal qualities of such artworks are generally contingent on such framings.[16]

Of course, we can impose frames on nature. We can take a rock from its natural abode and put it on a mantlepiece. Or, we can discipline our glance in such a way as to frame a natural expanse so that we appreciate the visual patterns that emerge from our own exercise in perceptual composition. But in doing this, we work against the organic unity in the natural expanse, sacrificing many of those real aesthetic features that are not made salient by our exercises in visual framing, *especially* the physical forces that make the environment what it is.[17] And in this sense, the object paradigm is too exclusive; it offends through aesthetic omission.

Thus, Carlson confronts the object paradigm with a dilemma. Under its aegis, either we frame – literally or figuratively – a part of nature, thereby removing it from its organic environment (and distracting our attention from its interplay with many real and fascinating ecological forces) OR we leave it where it is, unframed, indeterminate, and bereft of the fixed visual patterns and qualities (that emerge from acts of framing). In the first case, the object model is insensitive; in the second, it is, putatively, inoperable.

A second paradigm for nature appreciation is the landscape or scenery model. This also looks to fine art as a precedent; it invites us to contemplate a landscape as if it were a landscape painting. Perhaps this approach gained appeal historically in the guidebooks of the eighteenth century that recommended this or that natural prospect as affording a view reminiscent of this or that painter (such as Salvator Rosa).[18] In appreciating a landscape as a piece of scenery painting, we attend to features it might share with a landscape painting, such as its coloration and design.

But this, like the object model, also impedes comprehensive attention to the actual landscape. It directs our attention to the visual; but the full appreciation of nature comprises smells, textures and temperatures. And landscape painting typically sets us at a distance from nature. Yet often we appreciate nature for our being amidst it.[19] Paintings are two-dimensional, but nature has three dimensions; it offers a participatory space, not simply a space that we apprehend from outside.

Likewise, the picture frame excludes us whereas characteristically we are included as a self in a setting in the natural expanses we appreciate.[20] Thus, as with the object model of nature appreciation, the problem with the scenery model is that it is too restrictive to accommodate all the aspects of nature that might serve as genuine objects of aesthetic attention.

Lastly, Carlson offers us the natural environment model of appreciation. The key to this model is that it regards nature as nature. It overcomes the limitations of the object model by taking as *essential* the organic relation of natural expanses and items to their larger environmental contexts. The interplay of natural forces like winds are as significant as the sensuous shapes of the rock formations that are subject to them. On this view, appreciating nature involves attending to the organic interaction of natural forces. *Pace* the scenery model, the totality of natural forces, not just those that are salient to vision, are comprehended. Whereas the scenery paradigm *proposes* nature as a static array, the natural environment approach acknowledges the dynamism of nature.

Undoubtedly the inclusiveness of the natural environment model sounds promising. But the question still remains concerning which natural categories and relations are relevant to attending to nature as nature. It is Carlson's view that natural science provides us with the kind of knowledge that guides us to the appropriate *foci of* aesthetic significance and to the pertinent relations within their boundaries.

In order to aesthetically appreciate art, we must have knowledge of the artistic traditions that yield the relevant classificatory schemes for artists and audiences; in order to aesthetically appreciate nature, we need comparable knowledge of different environments and of their relevant systems and elements.[21] This knowledge comes from science and natural history, including that which is embodied in common sense. Where else could it come from? What else could understanding nature as nature amount to? The knowledge we derive from art criticism and art history for the purposes of art appreciation come from ecology and natural history with respect to nature appreciation.

Carlson writes: "What I am suggesting is that the question of *what* to aesthetically appreciate in the natural environment is to be answered in a way analogous to the similar question about art. The difference is that in the case of the natural environment the relevant knowledge is the commonsense/scientific knowledge which we have discovered about the environment in question."[22]

The structure of Carlson's argument is motivated by the pressure to discover some guidance with respect to nature appreciation that is analogous to the guidance that the fixing of artistic categories does with works of art. Three possibilities are explored: the object paradigm, the scenery paradigm, and the natural environment paradigm. The first two are rejected because they fail to comprehensively track all the qualities and relations we would expect a suitable framework for the appreciation of nature to track. On the other hand, the natural environment model is advanced not only because it does not occlude the kind of attentiveness that the alternative models block, but also because it has the advantage of supplying us with classificatory frameworks which play the role that things like genres do with respect to art, while at the same time these categories are natural (derived from natural history).

Stated formally, Carlson's argument is basically a disjunctive syllogism:

1. All aesthetic appreciation requires a way of fixing the appropriate *loci* of appreciative acts.
2. Since nature appreciation is aesthetic appreciation, then nature appreciation must have a means of fixing the appropriate *loci* of appreciative acts.
3. With nature appreciation, the ways of fixing the appropriate *loci* of appreciative acts are the object model, the scenic model and the natural environment model.
4. Neither the object model nor the scenic model suit nature appreciation.
5. Therefore, the natural environment model (using science as its source of knowledge) is the means for fixing the *loci* of appreciative acts with respect to nature appreciation.

Of course, the most obvious line of attack to take with arguments of this sort is to ask whether it has captured the relevant field of alternatives. I want to suggest that Carlson's argument has not. Specifically, I maintain that he has not countenanced our being moved by nature as a mode of appreciating nature and that he has not explored the possibility that the *loci* of such appreciation can be fixed in the process of our being emotionally aroused by nature.

Earlier I conjured up a scene where standing near a towering cascade, our ears reverberating with the roar of falling water, we are overwhelmed and excited by its grandeur. People quite standardly seek out such experiences. They are, pretheoretically, a form of appreciating nature. Moreover, when caught up in such experiences our attention is fixed on certain aspects of the natural expanse rather than others – the palpable force of the cascade, its height, the volume of water, the way it alters the surrounding atmosphere, and so on.

This does not require any special scientific knowledge. Perhaps it only requires being human, equipped with the senses we have, being small and able to intuit the immense force, relative to creatures like us, of the roaring tons of water. Nor need the common sense of our culture come into play. Conceivably humans from other planets bereft of waterfalls could share our sense of grandeur. This is not to say that all emotional responses to nature are culture-free, but only that the pertinent dimensions of some such arousals may be.

That is, we may be aroused emotionally by nature, and our arousal may be a function of our human nature in response to a natural expanse. I may savor a winding footpath because it raises a tolerable sense of mystery in me. Unlike the scenery model of nature appreciation, what we might call the arousal model does not necessarily put us at a distance from the object of our appreciation; it may be the manner in which we are amidst nature that has moved us to the state in which we find ourselves. Nor does the arousal model of nature restrict our response to only the visual aspects of nature. The cascade moves us through its sound, and weight, and temperature, and force. The sense of mystery awakened by the winding path is linked to the process of moving through it.

Perhaps the arousal model seems to raise the problem of framing, mentioned earlier, in a new way. Just as the object model and the scenery model appeared to impose a frame on an otherwise indeterminate nature, similarly the arousal model may appear to involve us in imposing emotional gestalts upon indeterminate natural expanses. Nevertheless, there are features of nature, especially in relation to human organisms, which, though they are admittedly "selected," are difficult to think of as "impositions."

Certain natural expanses have natural frames or what I prefer to call natural closure: caves, copses, grottoes, clearings, arbors, valleys, etc. And other natural expanses, though lacking frames, have features that are naturally salient for human organisms – that is they have features such as moving water, bright illumination, and so on that draw our attention instinctually toward them. And where our emotional arousal is predicated on either natural closure or natural salience, it makes little sense to say that our emotional responses, focused on said features, are impositions.

An emotional response to nature will involve some sort of selective attention to the natural expanse. If I am overwhelmed by the grandeur of a waterfall, then certain things and not others are in the forefront of my attention. Presumably since I am struck emotionally by the grandness of the waterfall, the features that are relevant to my response have to do with those that satisfy interests in scale, notably large scale. But my arousal does not come from nowhere. The human perceptual system is already keyed to noticing salient scale differentials and the fact that I batten on striking examples of the large scale is hardly an imposition from the human point of view.

Suppose, then, that I am exhilarated by the grandeur of the waterfall. That I am exhilarated by grandeur is not an inappropriate response, since the object of my emotional arousal is grand – that is, meets the criteria of scale appropriate to grandeur, where grandeur, in turn, is one of the appropriate sources of exhilaration. In this case, our perceptual makeup initially focuses our attention on certain features of the natural expanse, which attention generates a state of emotional arousal, which state, in turn, issues in reinforcing feedback that consolidates the initial selective gestalt of the emotional arousement experience. The arousal model of nature appreciation has an account of how we isolate certain aspects of nature and why these are appropriate aspects to focus upon; that is, they are *emotionally* appropriate.

Perhaps Carlson's response to this is that emotional responses to nature of the sort that I envision are not responses to nature as nature. This route seems inadvisable since Carlson, like Sparshott, wants us to think of the appreciator of nature as a self in a setting which I understand as, in part, a warning not to divorce human nature from nature.[23] Admittedly, not all of our emotional arousals in the face of nature should be ascribed to our common human nature, rather than to what is sectarian in our cultures, but there is no reason to preclude the possibility that some of our emotional arousals to nature are bred in the bone.

Conceding that we are only talking about *some* of our appreciative responses to nature here may seem to open another line of criticism. Implicit in Carlson's manner of argument seems to be the presupposition that what he is about is identifying the one and only form of nature appreciation. His candidate, of course, is the environmental model, which relies heavily on natural science.

I have already argued that this model is not the only respectable alternative. But another point also bears emphasis here, namely, why presume that there is only one model for appreciating nature and one source of knowledge – such as natural history – relevant to fixing our appreciative categories? Why are we supposing that there is just one model, applying to all cases, for the appropriate appreciation of nature?

That the appreciation of nature sometimes may involve emotional arousal, divorced from scientific or commonsense ecological knowledge, does not disallow that at other times appreciation is generated by the natural environment model. Certainly a similar situation obtains in artistic appreciation. Sometimes we may be emotionally aroused – indeed, appropriately emotionally moved – without knowing the genre or style of the artwork that induces this state. Think of children amused by capers of *Commedia dell'arte* but who know nothing of its tradition or its place among other artistic genres, styles, and categories. Yet the existence of this sort of appreciative response in no way compromises the fact that there is another kind of appreciation – that of the informed connoisseur – that involves situating the features of the artwork with respect to its relevant artistic categories.

I want to say that the same is true of nature appreciation. Appreciation may sometimes follow the arousal model or the natural environment model. Sometimes the two models may overlap – for our emotions may be aroused on the basis of our ecological knowledge. But, equally, there will be clear cases where they do not. Moreover, I see no reason to assume that these are the only models for the appropriate response to nature. In some cases – given the natural closure and salience of arrays in nature – the object model may not be out of place for, given our limited perceptual capacities, structured as they are, nature may not strike us as formally indeterminate.

My basic objection to Carlson is that emotional arousal in response to nature can be an appropriate form of nature appreciation and that the cognitive component of our emotional response does the job of fixing the aspects of nature that are relevant to appreciation. Here, I have been assuming that emotional arousal, though cognitive, need not rely on categories derived from science. But Carlson sometimes describes his preferred source of knowledge as issuing from common sense/science. So perhaps the way out of my objection is to say that with my cases of being moved by nature, the operative cognitions are rooted in commonsense knowledge of nature.

A lot depends here on what is included in commonsense knowledge of nature. I take it that for Carlson this is a matter of knowing in some degree how nature works; it involves, for example, some prescientific, perhaps folk, under-standing of things like ecological systems. That I know, in my waterfall example, that the stuff that is falling down is water is not commonsense knowledge of nature in the way that Carlson seems to intend with phrases like common sense/science. For the knowledge in my case need not involve any systemic knowledge of nature's working of either a folk or scientific origin. And if this is so, then we can say that we are emotionally moved by nature where the operative cognitions that play a constitutive role in our response do not rely on the kind of commonsense systemic knowledge of natural processes that Carlson believes is requisite for the aesthetic appreciation of nature. And, perhaps even more clearly, we can be moved by nature where our cognitions do not mobilize the far more formal and recondite systemic knowledge found in natural history and science.

III. THE CLAIMS OF OBJECTIVIST EPISTEMOLOGY

One reason, as we have just seen, that prompts Carlson to endorse natural history as the appropriate guide to nature appreciation is that it appears to provide us with our only satisfactory alternative. I have disputed this. But Carlson has other compelling motives for the type of nature appreciation he advocates. One of these is epistemo-logical. It has already been suggested; now is the time to bring it centerstage.

Echoing Hume's "Of the Standard of Taste," Carlson's impressive "Nature, Aes-thetic Judgment and Objectivity" begins with the conviction that certain of the aesthetic judgments that we issue with respect to nature – such as "The Grand Tetons are majestic" – are or can be appropriate, correct, or true. That is, certain aesthetic judgments of nature are objective. Were someone to assert that "The Grand Tetons are paltry," without further explanation, our response would con-verge on the consensus that the latter assertion is false.

However, though the conviction that aesthetic judgments of nature can be objective is firm, it is nevertheless difficult to square with the best available mod-els we possess for elucidating the way in which aesthetic judgments of art are objective. Indeed, given our best models of the way that aesthetic judgments of art are objective, we may feel forced to conclude that aesthetic judgments of nature are relativistic or subjective, despite our initial conviction that aesthetic judgments of nature can be objective.

So the question becomes a matter of explaining how our aesthetic judgments of nature can be objective. This is a problem because, as just mentioned, reigning accounts of how aesthetic judgments of art are objective have been taken to imply that aesthetic judgments of nature cannot be objective.

In order to get a handle on this problem, we need, of course, to understand the relevant theory of art appreciation that ostensibly renders nature appreciation sub-jective or relative. The particular theory that Carlson has in mind is Kendall Wal-ton's notion of categories of art. This theory is an example of a broader class of theories – that would include institutional theories of art – that can be usefully thought of as cultural theories. Roughly speaking, cultural theories of art supply the wherewithal to ground aesthetic judgments of art objectively by basing such judgments on the cultural practice and forms – such as artistic genres, styles, and movements – in which and through which artworks are created and disseminated.

On Walton's account, for example, an aesthetic judgment concerning an artwork can be assessed as true or false. The truth value of such judgments is a function of two factors, specifically: the nonaesthetic perceptual properties of the artwork (e.g., dots of paint), and the status of said properties when the artwork is situated in its correct artistic category (e.g., pointillism). Psychologically speaking, all aesthetic judgments of art, whether they are subjective or objective, require that we locate the perceived, nonaesthetic properties of the artwork in *some* category. For example, if an uninformed viewer finds the image in a cubist painting woefully confused, it is likely that viewer regards the work in terms of the (albeit wrong) category of a realistic, perspectival representation.

However, logically speaking, if an aesthetic judgment is true (or appropriate), then that is a function of the perceived, nonaesthetic properties of the artwork being comprehended within the context of the *correct* category of art. In terms of the preceding example, it is a matter of viewing the painting in question under the category of cubism. Consequently, the objectivity of aesthetic judgments of art depends upon identifying the correct category for the artwork in question.

A number of circumstances can count in determining the category of art that is relevant to the aesthetic judgment of an artwork. But some of the most conclusive depend on features relating to the origin of the work: such as which category (genre, style, movement) the artist intended for the artwork, as well as cultural factors, such as whether the category in question is a recognized or well-entrenched one. These are not the only considerations that we use in fixing the relevant category of an artwork; but they are, nevertheless, fairly decisive ones.

However, if these sorts of considerations are crucial in fixing the relevant categories of artworks, it should be clear that they are of little moment when it comes to nature. For nature is not produced by creators whose intentions can be used to isolate the *correct* categories for appreciating a given natural expanse *nor* is nature produced with regard for recognized cultural categories. But if we cannot ascertain the *correct* category upon which to ground our aesthetic judgments of nature, then those judgments cannot be either true or false. Moreover, since the way in which we fix the category of a natural object or expanse appears to be fairly open, our aesthetic judgments of nature appear to gravitate toward subjectivity. That is, they do not seem as though they can be objective judgments, despite our starting intuition that some of them are.

The structure of Carlson's argument revolves around a paradox. We start with the conviction that some aesthetic judgments of nature can be objective, but then the attempt to explain this by the lights of our best model of aesthetic objectivity with respect to the arts, indicates that no aesthetic judgment of nature can be objective (because there are no *correct* categories for nature). Carlson wants to dissolve this paradox by removing the worry that there are no objective, aesthetic judgments of nature. He does this by arguing that we do have the means for identifying the relevant, *correct* categories that are operative in genuine aesthetic judgments of nature. These are the ones *discovered* by natural history and science.

For example, we know that the relevant category for aesthetically appreciating whales is that of the mammal rather than that of fish as a result of scientific research. Moreover, these scientific categories function formally or logically in the same way in nature appreciation that art historical categories function in art appreciation. Thus, the logical form, though not the content, of nature appreciation corresponds to that of art appreciation. *And* insofar as the latter can be objective in virtue of its form, the former can be as well.

Another way to characterize Carlson's argument is to regard it as a transcendental argument. It begins by assuming as given that nature appreciation can be objective and then goes on to ask how this is possible – especially since there does not seem to be anything like correct categories of art to ground objectivity when it comes to nature appreciation. But, then, the possibility of the objectivity of nature appreciation is explained by maintaining that the categories discovered by natural history and science are available to play the role in securing the objectivity of aesthetic judgments of nature in a way that is analogous to the service performed by art historical categories for art.

Thus, for epistemological reasons, we are driven to the view of nature appreciation as a species of natural history. Effectively, it is advanced as the only way to support our initial intuitions that some aesthetic judgments of nature can be objective. Moreover, any competing picture of nature appreciation, if it is to be taken seriously, must have comparable means to those of the natural environment model for solving the problem of the objectivity of nature appreciation.

Of course, I do not wish to advance the "being moved by nature" view as competing with the natural environment approach. Rather, I prefer to think of it as a coexisting model. But even as a coexisting model, it must be able to solve the problem of objectivity. However, the solution to the problem is quite straightforward when it comes to being emotionally moved by nature.

For, being emotionally moved by nature is just a subclass of being emotionally moved. And on the view of the emotions that I, among many others, hold, an emotion can be assessed as either appropriate or inappropriate. In order to be afraid, I must be afraid of *something*, say an oncoming tank. My emotion – fear in this case – is directed; it takes a particular object. Moreover, if my fear in a given case is appropriate, then the particular object of my emotional state must meet certain criteria, or what are called "formal objects" in various philosophical idioms.

For example, the formal object of fear is the dangerous. Or, to put the point in less stilted language: if my fear of the tank (the particular object of my emotion) is appropriate, then it must satisfy the criterion that I believe the tank to be dangerous to me. If, for instance, I say that I am afraid of chicken soup, but also that I do not believe that chicken soup is dangerous, then my fear of chicken soup is inappropriate. C. D. Broad writes: "It is appropriate to cognize what one takes to be a threatening object with some degree of fear. It is inappropriate to cognize what one takes to be a fellow man in undeserved pain or distress with satisfaction or with amusement."[24]

Of course, if emotions can be assessed with respect to appropriateness and inappropriateness, then they are open to cognitive appraisal. Ronald deSousa says, for example, that "appropriateness is the truth of the emotions."[25] We can assess the appropriateness of the emotion of fear for an emoter in terms of whether or not she believes that the particular object of her emotion is dangerous. We can, furthermore, assess whether the appropriateness of her fear ought to be shared by others by asking whether the beliefs, thoughts, or patterns of attention that underpin her emotions are the sorts of beliefs, thoughts, or patterns of attention that it is reasonable for others to share. Thus we can determine whether her fear of the tank is objective in virtue of whether her beliefs about the dangerousness of the tank, in the case at hand, are reasonable beliefs for the rest of us to hold.

Turning from tanks to nature, we may be emotionally moved by a natural expanse – excited, for instance, by the grandeur of a towering waterfall. All things being equal, being excited by the grandeur of something that one believes to be of a large scale is an appropriate emotional response. Moreover, if the belief in the large scale of the cascade is one that is true for others as well, then the emotional response of being excited by the grandeur of the waterfall is an objective one. It is not subjective, distorted, or wayward. If someone denies being moved by the waterfall, but agrees that the waterfall is large scale and says nothing else, we are apt to suspect that his response, as well as any judgments issued on the basis of that response, are inappropriate. If he does not agree that the waterfall is of a large scale, and does not say why, we will suspect him either of not understanding how to use the notion of large scale, or of irrationality. If he disagrees that the waterfall is of a large scale because the galaxy is much much larger, then we will try to convince him that he has the wrong comparison class – urging, perhaps, that he should gauge the scale of the waterfall in relation to human scale.

In introducing the notion of the "wrong comparison class," it may seem that I have opened the door to Carlson's arguments. But I do not think that I have. For it is not clear that in order to establish the relevant comparison class for an emotional response to nature one must resort to scientific categories. For example, we may be excited by the grandeur of a blue whale. I may be moved by its size, its force, the amount of water it displaces, etc., but I may think that it is a fish. Nevertheless, my being moved by the grandeur of the blue whale is not inappropriate. Indeed, we may be moved by the skeleton of a *Tyrannosaurus rex* without knowing whether it is the skeleton of a reptile, a bird, or a mammal. We can be moved by such encounters, without knowing the natural history of the thing encountered, on the basis of its scale, along with other things, relative to ourselves.

Such arousals may or may not be appropriate for us and for others. Moreover, judgments based on such emotional responses – like "that whale excites grandeur" or "The Grand Tetons are majestic" – can be objective. Insofar as being moved by nature is a customary form of appreciating nature, then it can account for the objectivity of some of our aesthetic judgments of nature. Thus, it satisfies the epistemological challenge whose solution Carlson appears to believe favors only his natural environment model for the aesthetic appreciation of nature. Or, to put it another way, being moved by nature remains a way of appreciating nature that may coexist with the natural environment model.

At one point, Carlson concedes that we can simply enjoy nature – "we can, of course, approach nature as we sometimes approach art, that is, we can simply *enjoy* its forms and colors or *enjoy* perceiving it however we may happen to."[26] But this is not a very deep level of appreciation for Carlson, for, on his view, depth would appear to require objectivity. Perhaps what Carlson would say about my defense of being moved by nature is that being emotionally aroused by nature falls into the category of *merely* enjoying nature and, as an instance of that category, it isn't really very deep.

Undoubtedly, being moved by nature may be a way of enjoying nature. However, insofar as being moved by nature is a matter of being moved by appropriate objects, it is not dismissable as enjoying nature in whatever way we please. Furthermore, if the test of whether our appreciation of nature is deep is whether the corresponding judgments are susceptible to objective, cognitive appraisal, I think I have shown that some cases can pass this test. Is there any reason to think that being moved by nature must be any less deep a response than attending to nature with the eyes of the naturalist?

I would be very suspicious of an affirmative answer to this question. Of course, part of the problem is that what makes an appreciative response to nature shallow or deep is obscure. Obviously, a naturalist's appreciation of nature could be deep in the sense that it might go on and on as the naturalist learns more and more about nature, whereas a case of emotional arousal with respect to nature might be more consummatory. Is the former case deeper than the latter? Are the two cases even commensurable? Clearly, time alone cannot be a measure of depth. But how exactly are we to compare appreciative stances with respect to depth?

Maybe there is no way. But if the depth of a response is figured in terms of our intensity of involvement and its "thorough goingness,"[27] then there is no reason to suppose that being moved by nature constitutes a shallower form of appreciation than does appreciating nature scientifically. The Kantian apprehension of sublimity[28] – and its corresponding aesthetic judgment – though it may last for a delimited duration, need not be any less deep than a protracted teleological judgment.

Again, it is not my intention to dispute the kind of appreciation that Carlson defends under the title of the natural environment model. It is only to defend the legitimacy of an already well-entrenched mode of nature appreciation that I call being moved by nature. This mode of nature appreciation can pay the epistemological bill that Carlson presupposes any adequate model of nature appreciation should accommodate. It need not be reducible to scientific appreciation, nor must it be regarded as any less deep than appreciation informed by natural history.

Of course, it may seem odd that we can appreciate nature objectively this way when it seems that a comparable form of appreciation is not available to art. But the oddity here vanishes when we realize that to a certain extent we are able to appreciate art and render objective aesthetic judgments of artworks without reference to precise art historical categories. One may find a fanfare in a piece of music stirring and objectively assert that it is stirring without any knowledge of music history and its categories. Being emotionally aroused by nature in at least certain cases need be no different.

Carlson may be disposed to question whether being emotionally moved by nature is really a matter of responding to nature as nature. Perhaps he takes it to be something like a conceptual truth that, given the culture we inhabit, attending to nature as nature can only involve attending to it scientifically. However, if I am taken with the grace of a group of deer vaulting a stream, I see no reason to suppose that I am not responding to nature as nature. Moreover, any attempt to regiment the notion of responding to nature as nature so that it only strictly applies to scientific understanding appears to me to beg the question.

IV. ORDER APPRECIATION

The most recent argument that Carlson has advanced in favor of the natural environmental model of nature appreciation is what might be called the order argument.[29] In certain respects, it is reminiscent of his earlier arguments, but it does add certain new considerations that are worth our attention. Like his previous arguments, Carlson's order argument proceeds by carefully comparing the form of nature appreciation with that of art appreciation.

One paradigmatic form of art appreciation is design appreciation. Design appreciation presupposes that the artwork has a creator who embodies the design in an object or a performance, and that the design embodied in the artwork indicates how we are to take it. However, this model of appreciation is clearly inappropriate for nature appreciation since nature lacks a designer.

Nevertheless, there is another sort of art appreciation that has been devised in order to negotiate much of the avant-garde art of the twentieth century. Carlson calls this type of appreciation order appreciation. When, for example, we are confronted by something like Duchamp's *Fountain,* the design of the object does not tell us how to take it or appreciate it. Instead, we rely on certain stories about how the object came to be selected by Duchamp in order to make a point. These stories inform us of the ideas and beliefs that lead an avant-garde artist to produce or to select (in the case of a found object) the artwork.

These stories direct us in the appropriate manner of appreciating the object; they guide us in our selection of the relevant features of the work for the purposes of appreciation. They do the work with unconventional, experimental art that design does with more traditional art. For example, our knowledge, given a certain art historical narrative, of Surrealism's commitment to revealing the unconscious, alerts us to the importance of incongruous, dreamlike juxtapositions in paintings by Dali.

For Carlson, design appreciation is obviously ill suited to nature appreciation. On the other hand, something like order appreciation appears to fit the case of nature appreciation. We can appreciate nature in terms of the forces that bring natural configurations about, and we can be guided to the relevant features of nature by stories. But where do these stories come from? At an earlier stage in our culture, they may have come from mythology. But at this late date, they come from the sciences, including astronomy, physics, chemistry, biology, genetics, meteorology, geology and so on. These sciences, and the natural histories they afford, guide our attention to the relevant forces that account for the features of nature worthy of attention.

Basically, Carlson's most recent argument is that art appreciation affords two possible models for nature appreciation: design appreciation and order appreciation. Design appreciation, however, is clearly inadmissable. That leaves us with order appreciation. However, the source of the guiding stories pertinent to the order appreciation of nature differ from those that shape order appreciation with respect to art. The source of the latter is art history while the source of the former is natural history.

But once again Carlson's argument is open to the charge that he has not canvased all the actual alternatives. One's appreciation of art need not fall into either the category of design appreciation or order appreciation. We can sometimes appreciate art appropriately by being moved by it. Moreover, this is true of the avant-garde art that Carlson suggests requires order appreciation as well as of more traditional art.

For example, Man Ray's *The Gift* is an ordinary iron with pointed nails affixed to its smooth bottom. Even if one does not know that it is a specimen of Dada, and even if one lacks the art-historical story that tells one the ideology of Dada, reflecting on *The Gift* one may readily surmise that the object is at odds with itself – you cannot press trousers with it – in a way that is brutally sardonic and that arouses dark amusement. Similarly, one can detect the insult in Duchamp's *Fountain* without knowing the intricate dialectics of art history, just as one may find certain Surrealist paintings haunting without knowing the metaphysical, psychological, and political aims of the Surrealist movement.

As it is sometimes with art, so is it with nature. In both cases, we may be emotionally moved by what we encounter without any really detailed background in art history or natural history. With respect to both art and nature, emotional arousal can be a mode of appreciation, and it is possible, in a large number of cases, to determine whether the emotional arousal is appropriate or inappropriate without reference to any particularly specific stories of either the art-historical or the natural-history varieties.

A parade or a sunset may move us, and this level of response, though traditionally well-known, need not be reduced to either design appreciation or order appreciation, nor must it be guided by art history or by natural history. Insofar as Carlson's approach to both art and nature appears wedded to certain types of "professional" knowledge as requisite for appreciation, he seems to be unduly hasty in closing off certain common forms of aesthetic appreciation. This is not said in order to reject the sort of informed appreciation Carlson advocates, but only to suggest that certain more naive forms of emotive, appreciative responses may be legitimate as well.[30]

I have argued that one form of nature appreciation is a matter of being aroused emotionally by the appropriate natural objects. This talk of the emotions, however, may seem suspicious to some. Does it really seem reasonable to be emotionally moved by nature? If we feel a sense of security when we scan a natural expanse, doesn't that sound just too mystical? Perhaps, our feeling, as Diffey has suggested, is some form of displaced religious sentiment. Maybe being moved by nature is some sort of delusional state worthy of psychoanalysis or demystification.

Of course, many emotional responses to nature – such as being frightened by a tiger – are anything but mystical. But it may seem that others – particularly those that are traditionally exemplary of aesthetic appreciation, like finding a landscape to be serene – are more unfathomable and perhaps shaped by repressed religious associations. However, I think that there is reliable evidence that many of our emotional responses to nature have a straightforwardly secular basis.

For example, in his classic *The Experience of Landscape,*[31] and in subsequent articles,[32] Jay Appleton has defended the view that our responses to landscape are connected to certain broadly evolutionary interests that we take in landscapes. Appleton singles out two significant variables in our attention to landscape – what he calls prospect (a landscape opportunity for keeping open the channels of perception) and refuge (a landscape opportunity for achieving concealment).

That is, given that we are the kind of animal we are, we take a survival interest in certain features of landscapes: open vistas give us a sense of security insofar as we can see there is no threat approaching, while enclosed spaces reassure us that there are places in which to hide. We need not be as theoretically restrictive as Appleton is and maintain that these are the major foci of our attention to landscape. But we can agree that features of landscape like prospect and refuge may cause our humanly emotional responses to natural expanses in terms of the way they address our deep-seated, perhaps tacit, interests in the environment as a potential theatre of survival.

Thus, when we find a natural environment serene, part of the cause of that sense of serenity might be its openness – the fact that nothing can approach us unexpectedly across its terrain. And such a response need not be thought to be mystical nor a matter of displaced religion, if it is connected to information processing molded by our long-term evolution as animals.

Other researchers have tried to isolate further features of landscape – such as mystery and legibility[33] – that shape our responses to natural expanses in terms of a sense, however intuitive and unconscious, of the sorts of experiences we would have – such as ease of locomotion, of orientation, of exploration and so on – in the environment viewed. That is, our perhaps instinctive sense of how it would be to function in a given natural environment may be part of the cause of our emotional arousal with respect to it. A landscape that is very legible – articulated throughout with neat subdivisions – may strike us as hospitable and attractive in part because it imparts such a strong sense of how we might move around and orient ourselves inside of it.

Earlier I sketched a scene in which we found ourselves in an arbor, carpeted by layers of decaying foliage and moss. I imagined that in such a situation we might feel a sense of solace, repose, and homeyness. And such an emotional state might be

caused by our tacit recognition of its refuge potential. On this view, I am not saying
that we consciously realize that the arbor is a suitable refuge and appreciate it as such.
Rather the fact that it is a suitable refuge acts to causally trigger our emotional
response that takes the arbor as its particular object and responds to it with a feeling
of repose and homeyness, focusing on such features as its enclosure and softness,
which features are appropriate to the feeling of solace and homeyness.

Our feeling is not a matter of residual mysticism or religious sentiment, but is
perhaps instinctually grounded. Moreover, if such a scenario is plausible for at least
some of our emotional responses to nature, then it is not the case that being
aroused by nature is always a repressed religious response. Some responses of some
observers may be responses rooted in associations of nature with the handiwork of
the gods. But other emotional responses, appropriate ones, may have perfectly secular, naturalistic explanations that derive from the kinds of insights that Appleton
and others have begun to enumerate.

Admitting that our emotional responses to nature have naturalistic explanations, of course, does not entail a reversion to the natural environmental model of
nature appreciation. For such explanations pertain to how our emotional
responses may be caused. And when I appreciate a natural expanse by being emotionally aroused by it, the object of my emotional state need not be the recognition of my instinctual response to, for example, prospects. Perhaps one could
appreciate nature *à la* Carlson from an evolutionary point-of-view in which the
focus of our attention is the interaction of our emotions with the environment as
that interaction is understood to be shaped by the forces of evolution. But this is
not typically what one has in mind with the notion of being moved by nature.

In conclusion: to be moved by nature is to respond to the features of natural
expanses – such as scale and texture – with the appropriate emotions. This is one
traditional way of appreciating nature. It need not rely upon natural history nor is
it a residual form of mysticism. It is one of our characteristic forms of nature
appreciation – not reducible without remainder to either science nor religion.

EMOTION, APPRECIATION, AND NATURE

I. INTRODUCTION

In a previous essay entitled "On Being Moved by Nature: Between Religion and
Natural History," I defended a view of nature appreciation that I called the arousal
model.[1] According to the arousal model, *one* very customary appreciative response to
nature is a matter of reacting to it with the appropriate emotions – for example, gaz-
ing over a broad expanse of open prairie and becoming possessed by a feeling of
serenity. An afternoon drive in the country is often undertaken in anticipation of

such experiences. And, indeed, people are frequently willing to travel rather far afield to savor emotionally compelling natural vistas like the Grand Canyon.

In characterizing the arousal model of our response to nature, I did not think that I had discovered some heretofore unrecognized form of nature appreciation. Rather, I took myself to be reporting a common form of intercourse with nature. My point in doing so, however, was motivated theoretically. I intended the arousal model to stand in contrast to the formidable account of nature appreciation that has been developed by Allen Carlson.

Carlson's position – which may be called "the natural environmental model" – maintains that the appropriate aesthetic appreciation of nature depends upon knowledge of nature of the sort supplied by natural history and science, or by their commonsense or folk predecessors.[2] Nature appreciation is a matter of understanding the ecological and evolutionary significance of natural phenomena. For example, in order to appreciate the contours of a stretch of farmland, Carlson suggests we should understand the purposes of large-scale agriculture.[3] The ideal nature appreciator for Carlson, it seems to me, is a naturalist – someone who contemplates nature in light of scientific concepts and laws and whose project is to render nature intelligible. The motive for looking toward nature is scientific curiosity and the pleasure to be had from nature on this view, in short, is the pleasure of scientific understanding.

Unlike Stan Godlovitch, I see no reason to deny that the sort of attitude toward nature – that Carlson depicts so masterfully – should be called nature appreciation.[4] However, *pace* Carlson, I would argue that it is not the *only* form that appropriate appreciative responses to nature may take. Being moved by nature, where our emotional response to nature need not depend upon knowledge of scientific concepts and laws, is also a readily available and perfectly respectable form for the appreciative response to nature to assume. Thus, if we are looking for a comprehensive account of nature of appreciation, I argue that Carlson's natural environmental model must be supplemented, at the very least, by the arousal model.

Perhaps predictably, Professor Carlson does not agree. As a result, he has issued a characteristically thoughtful, ingenious, and rigorous response to the claims that I have made in behalf of the arousal model.[5] He has suggested that either the arousal model is not a proper form of nature appreciation at all, or that, if it is, whatever it has to say can, for the most part, be accommodated by the natural environmental model (i.e., the arousal model is not really a *significant* rival to the natural envionmental model).

Needless to say, I am not convinced by these conclusions. However, since addressing them will – I think – contribute to our understanding of the nature of appreciation, I believe that it is worth addressing them in some detail. Thus, in what follows, I will first deal with the question of the relation of emotional arousal to appreciation and then go on to challenge Carlson's attempted dissolution of the difference between the arousal model and the natural environmental model. Finally, I will draw attention to what I think are some mistaken suggestions that

Carlson makes about Kant for the purpose of showing that Carlson not only still has to contend with the arousal model, but with the *Critique of Judgment* as well.

II. EMOTION AND APPRECIATION

Carlson's first line of attack on the arousal model is to wonder whether it is really a form of appreciation at all. For if it is not really a form of appreciation, then it is not an available form of nature appreciation, and, therefore, not really either a rival or a supplement to the natural environmental model. Carlson is careful to note that he is not disputing the claims of the arousal model to characterize an *aesthetic* response to nature – he puts the contested meaning of that thorny concept to one side. Rather, he is arguing that being moved by nature is not any form of *appreciation* – aesthetic (whatever that might be) or otherwise.

This allegation, of course, depends upon one's conception of what is involved in the appreciation of something. Carlson follows Paul Ziff in this matter. On Ziff's view, outlined in his book *Semantic Analysis,* appreciation is essentially a cognitive affair.[6] It involves "sizing up" a situation.

Ziff claims etymological precedence for this view. An appreciation of a chess game, for example, is an account of the moves in a chess game with an eye to strategy. It is a characterization of how certain moves functioned to contribute to the victory of one player and the defeat of the other.

Similarly, in the military, an appreciation of a battle comprises a recounting of the relevant maneuvers, accompanied with explanations of why they failed or succeeded. In order to deliver an appreciation in this sense, one need not bear any affection or antipathy toward either the winners or the losers. One need not be a war lover or a war hater. An appreciation is an assessment of moves and consequences. It can be delivered dispassionately. Mr. Spock could do it.

Whereas we often tend to conflate the notion of appreciation with notions of "liking" or of "gratitude," the core of the concept, according to Ziff, is starkly cognitive, involved in sizing up a situation, a game, an artwork, and so on – that is, in comprehending their internal interrelations and external relations in terms of their significance (in terms of their implications, consequences, presuppositions, and so on).

This is not to deny that appreciation is connected to evaluation. Rather, it is connected to evaluation by way of providing grounds for it. Likewise, appreciation in this sense is related to gratitude ("I appreciate what you've done") and liking ("After a hard day, I appreciate nothing more than listening to music") because an appreciation of how something came about or how it works supplies us with reasons to admire the state of affairs or the object in question.

Ziff, quite rightly in my opinion, has maintained that aestheticians too often overlook the core or fundamental component of appreciation – its involvement with the essentially cognitive activity of sizing things up. Aestheticians frequently think of appreciation merely in terms of affection, which quickly embroils them in debates about whether or not appreciation is anything more than purely subjective. Ziff's conception of appreciation is surely a healthy corrective in this regard.

Summarizing Ziff, Carlson contends that appreciation, properly so called, has two components: a primary component that is involved in the cognitive activity of sizing something up, and a secondary component that is an appropriate affective response, such as gratitude or liking and so on. This secondary response is not a sufficient condition for appreciation. Indeed, it is not weightiest of the two components. In fact, I wonder whether Carlson even thinks that it is a necessary condition for appreciation. But, be that as it may, Carlson certainly thinks that the affective response component is not sufficient for appreciation, and that this is enough for his argument against the arousal model of nature of appreciation.

Basically Carlson argues that an emotional response to nature only involves the secondary component of appreciation, not the primary component. It is an affective response, not sufficiently involved with the cognitive activity of sizing up to count as a full-fledged instance of appreciation. Or, if it does involve sizing up in the relevant sense, it will be involved with scientific concepts of the sort the natural environmental model pinpoints. So there will be no significant difference between the arousal model and the natural environmental model. Let me take on the first horn of this dilemma in this section and look at the second horn in the next section.

The arousal model maintains that emotionally responding to nature can be an appropriate form of nature appreciation. Carlson, resting on the authority of Ziff, maintains that an affective response is not – analytically speaking – enough for appreciation properly so called. One response to this argument would, of course, be to reject Ziff's analysis of appreciation. However, I share Carlson's admiration of Ziff's insights.[7]

Nevertheless, I do think that Carlson has misapplied Ziff's analysis of appreciation to the arousal model. For Ziff and Carlson, the cognitive activity of sizing up is the real essence or crux of appreciation; the so-called affective response is secondary. Thus, according to Carlson, arousal does not add up to appreciation. But I think that this conclusion is wrong for the simple reason that Carlson has misconstrued the nature of the emotional response to nature – indeed, perhaps his idea of an emotional response in general is ill conceived.

Carlson, of course, acknowledges that an emotion may involve a cognitive dimension. My fear of a snake, for example, rides on my belief that the snake is dangerous. Carlson admits this much. However, what he fails to note is that emotions are also intimately involved in sizing up situations. Our emotions guide attention and shape perception. They organize information for us. They are biologically rooted devices that enable us to navigate our way through situations and filter incoming stimuli.

Emotion and attention are interrelated in a number of ways. At first, our attention may be drawn to certain aspects of a situation – say, for example, certain threatening aspects. This moves us into an emotional state of fear, or perhaps it is our emotional state of fear that first alerts us to these aspects. However, once in that state the presiding emotion supplies feedback to our processes of attention.

Once alerted to the harmful aspects of a situation, our fear will impel us to search the situation – to scan the scene – for further evidence of harmfulness.

The emotions focus our attention. They make certain features of the situation salient, and they cast those features in a special phenomenological light. The emotions "gestalt" situations. They organize them. They make certain elements of a situation stand out. The emotions are sensitive to certain aspects of various recurring situations, like danger, and they size up and organize situations rapidly. From an evolutionary point of view, the emotions are very expeditious adaptations in this regard, since they are far faster than other response procedures like deliberation. The emotions hold our attention on the relevant features of a situation, often compelling us to pick out further aspects of the situation under the criteria (such as harmfulness) that define the emotional state in which we find ourselves. For example, we first detect the automobile hurtling at us and then our fear further apprizes us of its lethal velocity and the absence of any accessible escape routes. Our emotions filter the situation and structure it. We do not attend to the color of the car, but to its direction.

Thus, the emotions are not alien to the cognitive activity of sizing up. Indeed, the emotions are biologically fast mechanisms that very frequently serve exactly the purpose of sizing up a situation. Therefore, there is no reason to think that an emotional response must necessarily fall short of appreciation properly so called, for there is no reason to suppose that an emotional response is bereft of the activity Carlson calls sizing up. Perhaps it might even be argued that the sizing up function of emotional response is, from an evolutionary viewpoint, more central to what an emotional state is than are the bodily and phenomenological perturbations that standardly accompany emotional states.

The sizing-up function of emotion is relevant to any discussion of what is called aesthetic appreciation. Recognition of the sizing-up function of emotion reveals why an emotional response to a work of art, for example, can be an appreciative response. But it is also germane to nature appreciation. Struck by the sheer scale of Mt. Cook, I am enthralled. Its grandeur takes my breath away. My emotional state guides my perception and my thinking. I look to the majestic outline it cuts against the sky; I imagine its great weight; I attend to the vast shadow it casts behind me; it prompts me to notice how small great trees seem next to it; and so on. My emotional response unifies my cognitive and perceptual reaction to the scene. I pick out details of the scene (such as size relations) relative to my presiding feeling of grandeur. Not everything in the scene is pertinent to this state – the discarded candy wrapper to my left is not. My attention is selective and organized. If this does not count as sizing up the scene, then the cognitive activity of sizing things up is more mysterious than I took it to be.

Inasmuch as the cognitive component of appreciation can be easily realized by an emotional response, there is no reason to suspect that the arousal model does not characterize an appropriate form of nature *appreciation*. Carlson's error, it seems to me, involves too sharp a cleavage between what he regards as the primary component of appreciation (cognitive sizing up) and the secondary component (an affective response). Perhaps *some* affective responses – like gratitude – can be clearly distinguished from sizing up; I have no considered opinion on that matter now. However, it is also the case that some affective responses – some emotional responses – are full-blooded instances of sizing up, and, therefore, are not, in principle, detachable from Carlson's primary component of appreciation. In such cases, an emotional response to nature just is an occasion of nature appreciation properly so called. Thus, the arousal model does pertain to an authentic form of nature appreciation, despite Carlson's savvy argument to the contrary.

Carlson's argument appears to work only if we take his second component of appreciation to encompass all affective responses. This may rely upon too neat a distinction between cognition and emotion. But this is an antithesis that we have learned to distrust in discussions of the emotions in the philosophy of mind and I see no profit in rejuvenating it in discussions of aesthetics. Cognition and emotion are not always discrete. In standard cases, the processes that we perhaps inadequately attempt to capture by these labels are generally reciprocal and interacting. There is no reason to suppose that typically the sizing-up activity that Carlson emphasizes and the affective response are separate either temporally or analytically. Indeed, in the standard case of emotional involvement, they are very frequently coeval and mutually informing. This is not to deny that there might be cognitive states without emotional involvement, nor that there might be affective states (like the startle response) that are cognitively impenetrable. But, at the same time, there are emotional processes that are inextricably imbricated in the activity of sizing up situations and objects, and scenes, natural and/or dramatic. Some of our appreciations of nature are like this. And that is what the arousal model was designed to acknowledge.

I have tried to dispel the first horn of Carlson's dilemma by arguing that an emotional response to nature has the credentials that he requires for appreciation properly so called. I have also worried that Carlson may be relying on too implausible a dichotomy between cognition and emotion. Carlson, however, may deny this, since he agrees that emotions have cognitive components such as beliefs. Yet what he has failed to notice is that emotions are not only cognitive with respect to their possession of such cognitive components as beliefs, but also in virtue of their performance of cognitive functions like sizing up.

III. DISSOLVING THE DIFFERENCE?

Though Carlson does not appear to agree that emotions size things up, he does agree that emotions have a cognitive dimension. Nowdays it is common to argue that emotions presuppose cognitive elements like belief. To be angry, for example, presupposes a belief on the part of the percipient that he or she has been wronged. Thus, insofar as the arousal model maintains that nature appreciation may involve being moved emotionally, it is committed to the view that the relevant percipients possess certain beliefs, or, at least, belief-like states. But then, Carlson asks, where do these cognitive states come from? And his answer is: from science and natural history, or from their commonsense or folk forebears. Thus, inasmuch as the arousal model is committed to a cognitive theory of the emotions and insofar as the beliefs pertinent to being moved by nature come from science, the arousal model all but collapses into the natural environmental model.[8]

Either the emotional appreciation of nature is cognitive or noncognitive. If it is cognitive, then it depends ultimately on scientific knowledge. *Ex hypothesi,* it is not noncognitive (or not appreciably).[9] Therefore, it depends on scientific knowledge. This is the second horn of Carlson's dilemma.

Of course, I don't want to deny that emotional responses to nature involve cognition. The question is whether the nature of the relevant cognitions amounts to scientific knowledge. The strongest statement of Carlson's view, repeated in "Nature, Aesthetic Appreciation and Knowledge," has been that the beliefs relevant to his version of nature appreciation are represented *paradigmatically* by the knowledge provided by the natural sciences. In response to the arousal model, however, he seems to be willing to weaken that claim to the point where just about any belief state satisfies the natural environmental model. I worry that by diluting the cognitive requirements of the natural environmental model Carlson may be prematurely trading in a very powerful account of one kind of nature appreciation for a rather dubious and merely apparent dialectical advantage.

According to the arousal model, the percipient is in an emotional state that involves a cognitive state – either a belief or a belief-like cognition. Standing beneath Mt. Cook, I believe that it is a mountain, composed of whatever geological stuff mountains are composed of. Does my emotional state rest on scientific knowledge? I don't think so and my reference to "whatever geological stuff mountains are composed of" should bear me out. This certainly wouldn't make the grade on a science exam.

But at this point, Carlson seems to want to extend our conception of scientific knowledge. It might not count as scientific knowledge, but it counts as scientific belief. Well, there are beliefs here, but are they scientific? Perhaps not, Carlson will concede, but they are beliefs of a commonsensical or folk variety that are predecessors to scientific beliefs. But Carlson hasn't really told us how to tell whether a belief is a predecessor to a scientific belief. Is any belief such a predecessor?

But can any folk or commonsense belief about nature really be a predecessor to scientific beliefs? Clearly, whether a belief is false does not preclude its being a predecessor to a scientific belief. But among those false beliefs are many mythological ones. Are they all predecessors to scientific beliefs?

Suppose that I believe that water is the blood of the earth god. Thus, when I perceive a geyser, I believe that I am seeing the blood of the earth god gushing forth. The force of the explosion moves me; I am absorbed by the heat and force and smell of it. I am emotionally moved by nature. But my beliefs are about the blood of the earth god. Does Carlson really want to assimilate my response to the naturalist's? Does he actually want to say that my belief belongs to a class of beliefs paradigmatically represented by scientific knowledge?

Whereas Carlson makes the case for the natural environmental model primarily on the basis of scientific knowledge, he seems willing to water down the model to the extent where any sort of belief will do the job. This means that by its own lights the natural environmental model countenances all manner of pseudo-scientific junk as a constituent in a legitimate response to nature as long as it is part of some folklore.

Moreover, what Carlson is willing to consider as proto-scientific common sense and folk wisdom too is quite expansive. If I believed that the geyser was spouting water, that would also count as a proto-scientific belief. I won't quibble that it is a belief. But why is the belief that water is water scientific or even proto-scientific? Why is it a predecessor to scientific knowledge? Scientific knowledge is self-consciously systematic and explanatory. But my belief that a geyser is water is neither. At the very least, Carlson owes us a persuasive criterion to tell which beliefs count as proto-scientific and which do not. Without such a criterion we may suspect that he has merely stipulated the comprehensiveness of the natural environmental model. It does not seem plausible to me to regard any old belief derived from one's culture – such as this is water and that is a flower – as a nascent scientific belief, let alone scientific knowledge.

However, even if Carlson retools the natural environmental model so that it claims the existence of every sort of belief as evidence in its behalf, I still wonder whether Carlson has succeeded in showing that it can logically swallow the arousal model without remainder. For emotional responses need not require beliefs, even if they require belief-like components. I may not believe that I am about to fall off a precipice, but I may still undergo a surge of fear if I imagine myself losing my footing. That is, not only beliefs (propositions held before the mind as asserted), but thoughts (propositions entertained or held before the mind as unasserted) can generate emotional responses.[10]

Thus, I may view a cloud formation – entertaining the metaphor that it is a mountain range – and that belief-like state (that imagining) may engender emotions of awe in me, calling my attention to the massive, powerful shapes in the sky. Nor need this imagining on my part be idiosyncratically subjective. Everyone else can see why I see it as a mountain range and can agree that my metaphor is apposite. Since my metaphor directs my attention to natural features of the cloud formation, including its color and contour, I see no reason to deny that my response constitutes an appreciation of some features of nature. But I do not believe that the cloud is a mountain. I merely entertain the thought in a way that raises an emotional response in me, which, in turn, enables me to organize my perception of (i.e., to size up) some of its features.

This, I submit, is an emotional response to nature – a case of nature appreciation – but it does not require a belief state to, so to speak, get off the ground. Thus, even if Carlson tries (ill advisedly, I think) to appropriate every sort of belief state for the natural appreciation model, there will still be a logical difference between the arousal model and his approach, since the arousal model will endorse nature appreciations rooted in imaginings (at least, imaginings of a constrained, intersubjectively apt variety), whereas Carlson has not yet extended the natural environmental model that far. Consequently, the arousal model does not collapse without residue into the natural environmental model.

Carlson wishes to deconstruct the distinction between his natural environmental model and the arousal model by claiming that the beliefs required by the
arousal model will all turn out to be either scientific or proto-scientific. This
seems to me mistaken on two counts. First, it is not plausible to presume that
every belief relevant to being moved emotionally by nature is either scientific or
proto-scientific; Carlson at least owes us both a definition and a demonstration to
support this claim. And second, not every belief-like state that may be relevant to
being moved by nature need be a belief, scientific or otherwise. So even if nearly
every belief turns out to be either scientific or proto-scientific, there may still be
emotional appreciations of nature that cannot be incorporated into the natural
environmental model. There is still logical space for the arousal model to inhabit.

Of course, the arousal model and the natural environmental model are not
inimicable. Scientific knowledge, for example, may enhance my emotional
response to nature. Standing between the two tors that flank the Pali Lookout on
Oahu, I felt dwarfed by their power. Learning that these mountains serve as natural vents, channeling the winds that blow across Kaneohe Bay, made that sense of
power even more acute. I suddenly saw the sailboats below driven under their
aegis. Here, scientific knowledge accentuated an emotional response. I suspect that
this happens quite often. In some cases, then, scientific knowledge complements
emotional arousal. And yet at the same time, arousal may flourish independently of
scientific knowledge. I found the tors moving before I learnt that they were natural vents. In such cases, the natural environmental model needs to be supplemented by the arousal model if we wish to develop a comprehensive account of
nature appreciation.

IV. CARLSON AND KANT

In the opening of "Nature, Aesthetic Appreciation and Knowledge," Carlson cites
Kant on the appreciation of nature. My impression is that Carlson does this in
order to align my view with Kant's. Moreover, I also suspect that Carlson believes
that in putatively disposing of the arousal model, he has also made his peace with
Kant. But if this is what Carlson intends by his reference to Kant, I must disagree
with him on both points.

As I understand Kant, aesthetic judgments – the genus of which I take it
appreciations of nature are uncontroversially a species – are singular. By this Kant
means that they proceed without subsuming particulars under a concept. The
judgment that this horse is beautiful does not subsume this particular horse under
the concept horse and its subtending canons of excellence. I do not reason that
this horse is beautiful because it is a good example of the category horse. Rather,
I look at this entity, which happens to be a horse, and I surmise that it is beautiful
without reference to the category it belongs to (and without reference to the purposes it might serve). The stimulus of the horse gives rise to the free play of my
faculties of undertanding and imagination, and the harmony of those faculties,
engaged in free play, give rise to the feeling of beauty.

This experience does not preclude that I know that the horse in question is a horse. What it precludes is that my judgment that it is beautiful is the result of subsuming it under a concept. The imagination and the understanding peruse the horse freely (without reference to a concept). Nor would I defend my assertion that this horse is beautiful by deducing that judgment from concepts in conjunction with this particular case. Rather I would command the assent of all to my aesthetic judgment of the horse on the basis of my experience of this particular horse – on the basis of the free play of my understanding and imagination in response to this horse. What goes on during the free play of the understanding and the imagination is something that we can talk about at great length. However, Kant is clear that one thing that he believes does not go on is the subsumption of the particular under a concept.

Whether or not one buys Kant's analysis is an open question. However, it seems to me that Kant's account of aesthetic appreciation is not equivalent to the arousal model. One reason for this is that on the arousal model, the percipient does subsume the particular under categories, namely, the categories or criteria relevant for the pertinent emotional states. In order to be afraid, one must subsume the object of the emotional state under the category of the harmful. In order to be enraptured by the grandeur of a mountain peak, one must subsume it at least under the category of the large. It would be inappropriate to regard a molehill as grand, since a molehill is too small to be subsumed under the category of the large. Thus, emotional states, including emotional appreciations of nature, do not fit the Kantian model because they typically involve the subsumption of the objects of the relevant emotions under categories. Therefore, even if Carlson had managed to dispose of the arousal model – something that I have denied – he would not at the same time have dealt with the perhaps more radical Kantian model. For the two models part company on the issue of categories.

Furthermore (and of far greater importance), it does not seem to me that the natural environmental model can accommodate Kantian appreciation under its rubric. The natural environmental model thrives on scientific (or proto-scientific) concepts and laws. Nature appreciation is a matter of seeing how particular natural phenomena fall under scientific concepts and laws (or folk concepts and folk laws). But this is exactly what the Kantian aesthetic judgment eschews. Kant felt that he needed to adduce a critique of aesthetic judgment exactly because it differed radically from judgments of pure reason and practical judgments. Whereas those forms of judgment involved the subsumption of particulars under concepts, aesthetic judgment is putatively singular. Explaining how such judgments are possible is the primary burden of proof that motivates the analysis of free beauty in Kant's *Critique of Judgment*.

But this architectonic ambition would be, in large measure, beside the point if Kant thought that the aesthetic appreciation of nature were characterizable by means of the natural environmental model. For in that case, nature appreciation would be a subclass of judgments of pure reason.

I do not suppose that Carlson, or anyone else, has to accept Kant's account. However, at the same time, I do not believe that Carlson can imagine that the natural environmental model can easily take Kant's view on board. For Kant requires that knowledge of categories and laws be irrelevant for genuine aesthetic responses to both nature and art, whereas the natural environmental model makes little or no sense without access to laws and categories. Thus, even if the natural environmental model could absorb the arousal model, Kant's view of the aesthetic appreciation of nature should remain indigestible to Carlson.

I mention this problem with Kant's theory not in order to endorse that theory, but rather to point out that it remains a competitor to Carlson's natural environmental model. Thus, Carlson's model confronts not only one rival (or supplement) in the form of the arousal model, but at least one other in the form of Kant's theory of aesthetic judgment.

NOTES

INTRODUCTION

1. George Dickie, "The Myth of the Aesthetic Attitude," *American Philosophical Quarterly* (January 1964), pp. 56–64.

2. George Dickie, *Art and the Aesthetic: An Institutional Analysis* (Ithaca: Cornell University Press, 1974).

3. Further arguments against the traditional account can also be found in my "Art and the Domain of the Aesthetic," *British Journal of Aesthetics*, (vol. 40, no. 2 (April 2000), pp. 191–208.

4. My reliance on history in this regard surely shows the influence of the spirit, though not the word, of Arthur Danto's early essay "The Artworld," *Journal of Philosophy*, (October 15, 1964), pp. 571–84.

5. One anti-intentionalist, Kent Wilson, has suggested that where there are no determinate meaning-conventions of the sort found in language, we should not speak of interpreting the meaning of artworks at all. But this seems to be a very ad hoc way of settling the debate over intentionalism, since that debate has always been thought to be relevant to the interpretation of artworks in general. Standardly, nonlinguistic artworks are thought to possess meaning (e.g., montage in film and television). From the perspective of the philosophy of art, to restrict stipulatively the notion of meaning to linguistic matters not only seems arbitrary, but, as well, fails to take seriously our interpretive practices. One does not explain the phenomenon by denying its existence. This is to give up the philosophical project of discovering the presiding conditions of possibility of our interpretive practices. Thus, Wilson's suggestion not only involves exiting the debate, but he also seems to shirk the philosophical responsibility of reconstructing our actual interpretive practices by effectively attempting to regiment them unrealistically. To declare, by fiat, that all nonlinguistic artworks lack meaning because they are not linguistic appears at root to beg the question. See: W. Kent Wilson, "Confession of a Weak Anti-Intentionalist: Exposing Myself," *Journal of Aesthetics and Art Criticism,* (Summer, 1997), pp. 309–11.

6. I also address the debate with hypothetical intentionalism in my "Andy Kaufman and the Philosophy of Interpretation," in *Interpretation: Multiple or Singular?* edited by Michael Krausz (University Park: Penn State University Press, forthcoming).

7. This article has been criticized by: James Anderson and Jeff Dean in "Moderate Autonomism," *British Journal of Aesthetics* (April, 1998), pp. 150–66; and Daniel Jacobson, "In Praise of Immoral Art," *Philosophical Topics* (Spring, 1997), pp. 155–99. I have replied to these objections respectively in: Noël Carroll, "Moderate Moralism versus Moderate Autonomism," *British Journal of Aesthetics* (October, 1998), pp. 419–24 and Noël Carroll, "Art and Ethical Criticism," *Ethics,* vol. 110, No. 2 (January 2000), pp. 350–387.

ART AND INTERACTION

1. Though throughout this essay I maintain that there is a strong tendency among philosophers of art to deploy notions of the aesthetic as definitive of our interactions with art, not all philosophers find the aesthetic to be a congenial idea. George Dickie, for example, challenges its use in his classic "The Myth of Aesthetic Attitude," in *American Philosophical Quarterly* I no. 1 (Jan., 1964). Dickie challenges proponents of the aesthetic to find a plausible

differentia between this concept as a prefix for experiences of art versus ordinary experiences. I am sympathetic with Dickie's reservations as well as with objections that worry about whether the usage of such notions as disinterest and freedom in characterizations of the aesthetic is ultimately coherent. However, for the purposes of this paper. I have not dwelt on these problems with aesthetic theories of art but rather, in a manner of speaking, have attempted to give the devil his due by generally proceeding as if such notions as disinterest could be rendered intelligibly while also wondering whether even with this concession aesthetic theories of art are acceptable. I am prone, especially in regard to what I later call "affect-oriented" characterizations, to think that the notion of the aesthetic is mythic. On the other hand, where the notion of aesthetic experiences is what I label above as "content-oriented," I think there is no problem in speaking of aesthetic experience, that is, of the experience of aesthetic and/or expressive qualities.

2. For an example of the anti-definitionalist stance, see Morris Weitz, "The Role of Theory in Aesthetics," *The Journal of Aesthetics and Art Criticism* 15 no. 1 (Fall, 1956). For an example of an Institutional Theory, see George Dickie, *Art and the Aesthetic: an Institutional Analysis* (Cornell University Press, 1974).

3. Monroe Beardsley, "An Aesthetic Definition of Art," in *What Is Art?,* ed. Hugh Curtler (New York, 1983); W. Tolhurst, "Toward An Aesthetic Account of the Nature of Art," *The Journal of Aesthetics and Art Criticism* 42 no. 3 (Spring, 1984). Also, Harold Osborne's "What Is a Work of Art?" *British Journal of Aesthetics* 21 (1981) represents another attempt at defining art in terms of aesthetic experience.

4. Beardsley, 21.

5. Tolhurst, 265.

6. Monroe Beardsley. "The Discrimination of Aesthetic Enjoyment," in *The Aesthetic Point of View,* ed. Michael Wreen and Donald Callen (Cornell University Press, 1982), p. 42.

7. J. O. Urmson, "What Makes a Situation Aesthetic," *Art and Philosophy,* ed. W. E. Kennick (New York, 1979), pp. 395–97.

8. Monroe Beardsley, "Aesthetic Experience." *The Aesthetic Point of View,* pp. 288–89.

9. The practice of planting oblique meanings and themes in artworks that the audience is meant to discover occurs in varying degrees in different artforms, perhaps most frequently in literature and least frequently in orchestral music. But it has examples in every artform.

10. Peter Hutchinson, *Games Authors Play* (London, 1983), p. 80.

11. For a reproduction of *Black Quadrilateral* see *The Russian Avant-Garde: The George Costakis Collection,* ed. Angelica Zander Rudenstine (New York, 1981), p. 256.

12. David Hume, "Of the Standard of Taste," *Art and Philosophy,* p. 495. This view of Hume in regard to intellection is discussed in my "Hume's Standard of Taste," *The Journal of Aesthetics and Art Criticism* 43 no. 2 (Winter, 1984).

13. Alasdair MacIntyre, *After Virtue* (University of Notre Dame Press, 1981), p. 175.

14. Jerome Stolnitz, "The Aesthetic Attitude." *Introductory Readings in Aesthetics,* ed. John Hospers (New York, 1969), pp. 17–27.

15. MacIntyre, p. 181.

BEAUTY AND THE GENEALOGY OF ART THEORY

1. For example, Monroe Beardsley, "An Aesthetic Definition of Art," in Hugh Curtler (eds.), *What Is Art?* (New York: Haven, 1983); W. Tolhurst, "Toward an Aesthetic Account of the Nature of Art," *Journal of Aesthetics and Art Criticism,* vol. 42, no. 3, Spring 1984; Harold Osborne, "What Is a Work of Art?" *British Journal of Aesthetics,* vol. 21, no. 3, 1981; G. Schlesinger, "Aesthetic Experience and the Definition of Art," *British Journal of Aesthetics,* vol. 19, no. 2, Spring 1979. Extensive reference to the currency of aesthetic definitions of art can be found in Bohdan Dziemidok, "Controversy about the Aesthetic Nature of Art," *British Journal of Aesthetics,* vol. 28, no. 1, winter 1988.

2. George Dickie, "The Myth of the Aesthetic Attitude," *American Philosophical Quarterly*, vol. 1, no. 1, Jan. 1964; George Dickie, "Beardsley's Phantom Aesthetic Experience," *Journal of Philosophy*, vol. 62, 1965.

3. George Dickie, *Art and the Aesthetic* (Ithaca, N.Y.: Cornell University Press, 1974); and George Dickie, *The Art Circle* (New York: Haven, 1984).

4. Morris Weitz, "The Role of Theory in Aesthetics," *Journal of Aesthetics and Art Criticism*, vol. 15, no. 1, Fall 1956; Paul Ziff, "The Task of Defining a Work of Art," *Philosophical Review*, vol. 62, 1953.

5. Maurice Mandelbaum, "Family Resemblances and Generalizations Concerning the Arts," *American Philosophical Quarterly*, vol. 2, 1965.

6. Wladyslaw Tatarkiewicz, *A History of Six Ideas: An Essay in Aesthetics* (Hague, Netherlands: Martinus Nijhoff, 1980), p. 122.

7. Tatarkiewicz, *History of Six Ideas*, p. 122.

8. Francis Hutcheson, *Inquiry Concerning Beauty, Order, Harmony, Design*, edited by Peter Kivy (Hague. Netherlands: Martinus Nijhoff, 1973), p. 40.

9. Hutcheson, *Inquiry*, pp. 31–32.

10. Hutcheson, *Inquiry*, p. 36.

11. In Hutcheson, the relationship of knowledge and interest is complicated. Some knowledge is distinct from interest; however, knowledge also may be connected with interest when it is knowledge of the uses to which an object may be put. Thus, the contrasts between the sense of beauty, and knowledge *and* interest drawn above is not so neat, since knowledge that serves interests cuts across both the contrasts.

12. Hutcheson. *Inquiry*, pp. 36–37.

13. It should also be noted that in contrast to later aesthetic theories of art, due to some of his strange applications of the notion of uniformity in his analysis of what he calls relative beauty, Hutcheson does not appear to be as draconian as later theorists of the aesthetic in terms of separating the aesthetic response from cognition. He does not apparently bracket certain types of knowledge with respect to beauty and art that will be bracketed by theorists influenced by him. Since he regards the relation of similitude of a representation to its referent and of an author's intention and the artwork as "uniformities," he *must* countenance knowledge of reference and of authorial intent as relevant ingredients in the experience of beauty and of beautiful artworks. Needless to say, his use of the notion of uniformities here seems strained beyond the breaking point, which perhaps accounts for the abandonment of these commitments by the tradition. Clive Bell would reject the referent of a painting as part of its significant form. He thus maintains that the similitude of the painting to its referent is aesthetically irrelevant, while Monroe Beardsley attempts to separate the art object from the artist's intention, thereby denying that it is part of the proper focus of aesthetic attention. Obviously, on these matters, Bell and Beardsley diverge with Hutcheson on the appropriate parameters of the object of contemplation in question. Perhaps on these points, it could be argued that they are more consistent with Hutcheson's own suggestion that the knowledge of the genesis of the object is irrelevant to its aesthetic (not Hutcheson's term) appreciation than he is. Hutcheson, they might say, spoils his own theoretical insight when it comes to applying his uniformity amidst variety formula.

14. See J. O. Urmson, "What Makes a Situation Aesthetic," in W. E. Kennick (ed.). *Art and Philosophy* (New York: Saint Martin's Press, 1979), pp. 398–410.

15. That is, grounded in an actual inner sensation of pleasure on the part of the percipient.

16. Since these judgments are disinterested, we are assured that our sensation of pleasure would be shared by all insofar as the differences between us – our interests – have been factored out. Also, this pleasure is rooted in the play of the cognitive and imaginative faculties. These are part of our common humanity. Consequently, the pleasure derived from the engagement of these faculties – where interests have been factored out – should be available to everyone. It is in virtue of this common humanity that Kant defends the objectivity of

judgments of taste, and answers Hume's paradox concerning how judgments based on individual experiences can nevertheless be objective, that is, have intersubjective reach.

17. That is, our judgments of taste, if they are disinterested, and result from the play of common human faculties, can command the assent of everyone, since they are grounded solely on what we share with others. Since our judgments are based on those universal human features that we share with everyone else (see prior note), our pronouncements should necessarily be shared by others in virtue of our common humanity. This answers Hume's quandary about how we can claim that Milton is better than Ogilby while simultaneously admitting that the perception of beauty is in the subject. It is in the subject, but at a level of response common to the constitution of all human subjects.

18. This is the claim that the aesthetic judgment does not rest on the application of rules or of a concept. I would suggest that Frank Sibley's thesis – that the application of aesthetic concepts is not condition-governed – is related to this idea.

19. That is, what engages us in the object of beauty is the sense of purposiveness it conveys – the sense of being designed – independently of any knowledge of the purpose for which it was designed. Just as such objects cannot be subsumed under a rule or concept (condition 5), so they cannot be assimilated in terms of a purpose. The plumage of a bird may serve a purpose in the mating rituals of its species; however, when we find the plumage beautiful, we are not responding positively in virtue of our knowledge that it has this purpose. Rather, the plumage strikes us as configurationally fit or as intentionally patterned without our knowing what principle or purpose motivated its formal articulation. It conveys a sense of purposiveness without a purpose.

20 Immanuel Kant, *The Critique of Judgement,* tr. James Creed Meredith (Oxford: Clarendon Press, 1982), pp. 42–43.

21. Throughout this essay I am leaving open the possibility that the theory of beauty, narrowly construed, that emerges from people such as Hutcheson, Hume, and Kant may be false. I am not really concerned with whether it is true or false. Perhaps another theory of beauty, as narrowly construed, is superior – for example, the one developed by Guy Sircello in his *New Theory of Beauty* (Princeton, N.J.: Princeton University Press, 1975). My major contention is that the theory that invokes things like disinterested pleasure is a reasonable or plausible attempt at a theory of beauty, *whereas* the attempt to extend its basic ingredients into a theory of art is highly dubious.

22. See, for example, Monroe Beardsley, *Aesthetics* (New York: Harcourt, Brace & World, 1958), Chapter 1. This way of speaking, moreover, continues in Beardsley's later writings as well.

23. Indeed, that Bell locates the pertinent aesthetic datum as an inner feeling state in the spectator is also a mark of his implicit, unstated, rather classical empiricism.

24. Clive Bell, *Art* (New York: Capricorn Books, 1958), p. 27.

25. See, for example, Bell, *Art,* p. 55.

26. Bell, *Art,* p. 24.

27. That is, Hutcheson appears to think that with representation the variety component is a matter of there being at least two objects – the referent and the representation – while the resemblance thereof is a matter of unity. One wonders whether there isn't undue strain being put on the notion of variety here and one wants to ask about representations that have no actual referent. Furthermore, knowledge of the nature of the referent would appear to be relevant to ascertaining whether the representation suited it.

28. Bell, *Art,* p. 73.

29. Bell, *Art,* p. 73.

30. That is, Bell seems to have transformed Kant's notion of the *free* play of the faculties into the *freeing* or liberation of the faculties.

31. See Arthur Danto, *The Transfiguration of the Commonplace* (Cambridge, Mass.: Harvard University Press, 1981).

32. See Noël Carroll. "Clive Bell's Aesthetic Hypothesis," in G. Dickie, R. Sclafani, and R. Roblin (eds.), *Aesthetics* (New York: Saint Martin's Press, 1989).

33. Save, perhaps, to certain aspects of art that are beautiful in the narrow sense of the term.

34. Beardsley, *Aesthetics,* Chapters II–V.

35. Beardsley, *Aesthetics,* pp. 527–29.

36. Beardsley, *Aesthetics,* p. 529.

37. This characteristic is perhaps related to Kant's notion of cognitive and perceptual play. About this characteristic, Beardsley notes that until the work of Gombrich and Goodman, he had not realized that he had always regarded the apprehension of an artkind to be a cognitive act ("Aesthetic Experience." p. 292). This is a strange remark. Throughout most of his career, he seemed to be arguing that the aesthetic was distinct from the cognitive, especially against people like Goodman (see their debate about exemplification). And even in the formulation above, the emphasis is affective rather than cognitive since what is underscored is a sense of intelligibility and a corresponding feeling of elation. Thus, despite this remark, I tend to continue to regard Beardsley's approach to aesthetic experience as noncognitivist. Indeed, Beardsley's aesthetic definition of art essentially contrasts the aesthetic/artistic realm from the cognitive.

38. Monroe Beardsley, *The Aesthetic Point of View* (Ithaca, N.Y.: Cornell University Press, 1982), pp. 288–89.

39. Beardsley, "Aesthetic Definition of Art," p. 21. See also. Beardsley, "Redefining Art," in *The Aesthetic Point of View,* p. 299; and Beardsley, "The Philosophy of Literature," in G. Dickie and R. Sclafani (eds.), *Aesthetics: A Critical Anthology* (New York: Saint Martin's Press, 1977), p. 328. It seems to me that due to the prevailing antidefinitional mood in art theory during the period of publication of Beardsley's *Aesthetics,* he did not think that a definition of art was necessary. But toward the end of his career, when the prospect of such a definition again seemed important, he conjectured about the aesthetic definition of art found in these articles to varying degrees.

40. For an elaboration of this argument, see George Dickie, *Evaluating Art* (Philadelphia: Temple University Press. 1988), Chapter IV.

41. See Chapter I of Beardsley's *Aesthetics.*

42. Surely one way to read Beardsley's project is to see him as providing a philosophical foundation – indeed, the most rigorous and systematic one ever devised – for the New Criticism.

43. See Monroe Beardsley, "The Relevance of Art History to Criticism," in *The Aesthetic Point of View,* pp. 219–35.

44. Beardsley's position against Goodman can be found, among other places, in his "Semiotic Aesthetics and Aesthetic Education," *Philosophical Exchange,* vol. 1, 1973, pp. 155–71; and in his "*Languages of Art* and Art Criticism." *Erkenntnis,* vol. 12 (1978), pp. 95–118.

45. Beardsley, *Aesthetics,* p. 507.

46. Beardsley, *Aesthetics,* pp. 556–83.

47. Beardsley, *Aesthetics,* p. 506.

48. Beardsley. "*Aesthetic Definition of Art,"* p. 25.

49. Harold Osborne, "Aesthetic Implications of Conceptual Art, Happenings, Etc.," in *British Journal of Aesthetics,* vol. 20, no. 1, Winter 1980, pp. 6–21. Another author who has used the aesthetic theory of art to challenge the claims of avant-garde art is P. N. Humble. See his "Duchamp's Readymades: Art and Anti-Art," *British Journal of Aesthetics,* vol. 22, no. 1. Winter 1982, and "The Philosophical Challenge of Avant-garde Art," *British Journal of Aesthetics,* vol. 24, no. 21, Spring 1984.

50. Benjamin Tilghman, *But Is It Art?* (New York: Blackwell, 1984), p. 120.

51. One way to attempt to save the aesthetic approach is to effectively redefine what is meant by "aesthetic" in such a way that anything that is an appropriate response to art is redesignated as an *aesthetic* response. So if it is appropriate to read novels with a concern for their moral content, where there is some, then moral engagement with the artwork is reclassified as aesthetic. My own inclination is to categorize such responses as art responses rather than as aesthetic responses. For the standard use of the term *aesthetic* is connected with either attention delimited to form and appearance, generally with notions of disinterest and detachment in the background. To reclassify art responses as aesthetic responses is, in this

context, at best an exercise in stipulative redefinition, if not a downright misuse of language. Moreover, and more important, to redefine "aesthetic" this way is tantamount to giving up the core of aesthetic theories of art, viz., the reliance on a unique aesthetic experience, different in kind from those of other realms of human activity, and, therefore, suited to separating art from morality, utility, knowledge, and so on.

52. Though reliance on aesthetic experience does facilitate an essentialist separation of art from *almost* everything else, as the hedge "*almost*" indicates, it does have some residual problems even from an essentialist point of view. The most notable one, and the one that frequently recurs in the literature has to do with the putative possibility of responding disinterestedly to the forms of mathematical theorems. Needless to say, from our perspective this recurring problem is a predictable one since Hutcheson's theory of beauty, from which aesthetic theories are derived, was in part devised in order to account for the pleasure we take in pure mathematics and geometry.

53. Of course, I do not mean to suggest that all analytic philosophers of art are entrapped in this obsession. Arthur Danto has argued for the importance of art history to philosophy, while Nelson Goodman has championed a cognitive approach to art in direct rivalry with the noncognitivist claims of the aesthetic approach. However, the theories of these philosophers and others, such as Marx Wartofsky, are revolutionary exactly because they go against the dominant tendency. Moreover, as should be clear, Hegel is a philosopher of art who is not being counted as part of the lineage of analytic aesthetics.

54. Including, whatever, if there are any, innate, human perceptual responses to form.

FOUR CONCEPTS OF AESTHETIC EXPERIENCE

1. It must be emphasized that throughout this essay I am concerned with the aesthetic experience of art, not the aesthetic experience of nature or of everyday artifacts. When the term "aesthetic experience" is used here, it should generally be understood as an abbreviation for the "aesthetic experience of artworks." This is not to deny that some of the things said about the aesthetic experience of artworks may also pertain to other things, but only that the domain of discourse in what follows is primarily the aesthetic experience of artworks.

2. For example, recently it has been hypothesized that the brain may generate new cells under the influence of stimulation. This may suggest an evolutionary explanation for our pursuit of aesthetic experiences. Art that engenders aesthetic experiences may be an invention, unbeknownst to our conscious awareness, that contributes in a particularly effective way to abetting the turnover of new brain cells involved in memory and learning. That is, it may be the case that we seek aesthetic experiences, albeit not consciously, in order to replenish brain cells. See: Nicholas Wade, "Brain Cells Grow New Cells Daily," *New York Times*, October 15, 1999, p. 1.

3. John Dewey, "Having an Experience," in *A Modern Book of Aesthetics*, edited by Melvin Rader (New York: Holt Rhinehart and Winston, 1966), p. 172.

4. Ibid.

5. Ibid.

6. Dewey, pp. 172–73.

7. Dewey, p. 173.

8. Herbert Marcuse, *The Aesthetic Dimension: Toward A Critique of Marxist Aesthetics* (Boston: Beacon, 1977), p. 72.

9. Marcuse, *Aesthetic Dimension*, 19.

10. Marcuse, *Aesthetic Dimension*, p. 44.

11. Marcuse, *Aesthetic Dimension*, p. 36.

12. When advocates of the allegorical account speak of "genuine art," they seem to have in mind art that supports disinterested experiences valued for their own sake. Such art is autonomous derivatively in the sense that the experiences it affords are valued intrinsically – that is, genuine

art is such that it encourages aesthetic experience. But if this interpretation is correct, then the allegorical account identifies genuine art, as do aesthetic theories of art, in terms of its capacity to afford aesthetic experience, thereby rendering the allegorical account of art vulnerable to the same kinds of criticisms that are leveled at aesthetic theories of art.

13. T. W. Adorno, *Aesthetic Theory,* translated by C. Lenhardt (New York: Routledge and Kegan Paul, 1984), p. 322.

14. It should be noted that the notion of disinterestedness is a particularly nettlesome one. When it was first introduced in the eighteenth century, it seemed to mean impartiality. That is, if I judge something to be beautiful, then if my judgment is authentic, it should be impartial – the judgment must not be to the judge's direct personal benefit, as it would be if my judgment of the beauty of my house was made in order to enhance its property value. That is, a disinterested judgment is one in which the judge is indifferent to the consequences of his judgment for his own personal benefit.

     This, of course, makes sense. Judgments of artworks should be impartial. But, of course, so should judgments of all sorts of other things. When I evaluate an artwork, I should be impartial. But, then again, if I am a judge of champion pigs at the state fair, or a juror at a murder trial, I should also be impartial. Impartiality does not mark off aesthetic judgments or experiences. It is a property of all sorts of judgments and experiences, including not only aesthetic ones, but moral ones as well. Thus, disinterestedness, construed as impartiality, is not a sufficient condition for aesthetic experience.

     Where pleasure is added to disinterestedness – as it is in Hutcheson and Kant – it may be argued that disinterestedness, if not a sufficient condition, is a necessary condition, which when joined with pleasure yields an essential definition of aesthetic experience. But if we subtract pleasure from the formulation – for the good reason that it does not appear to be the case that all aesthetic experiences need be pleasureable – and we are left only with disinterestedness to define aesthetic experience, then the failure of distinterestedness, understood as impartiality, to supply a sufficient condition for aesthetic experience becomes a major problem.

     Furthermore, it should be obvious that from disinterestedness, construed in the unobjectionable sense of impartiality, it does not follow that moral, political, practical, instrumental, or cognitive concerns must be bracketed from aesthetic experiences properly so-called. For these judgments can all be made, and generally should be made, from a disinterested (impartial) point of view. It is a mistake that lies deep in the tradition to think that the reasonable expectation of impartiality in aesthetic judgments entails that this requires or excludes moral, political, cognitive, and other concerns from aesthetic experience. These are not alien to the state of being indifferent to the direct personal benefits that an experience might afford to the judge in question. Moreover, it should be evident that valuing an experience for its own sake does not follow from the notion, which most might assent to, that aesthetic judgments should be impartial concerning the personal benefit of the relevant judges.

     Impartiality is, in some ways, an empty notion. You can be impartial about anything. So talking about the disinterestedness (the impartiality) of an aesthetic experience as a defining description of said experience has next to nothing to say about the content of the experience; it is flagrantly uninformative.

     Nor does it help to stipulate that aesthetic experience is just the sort of experience that has nothing whatsoever to do with any other kind of experience, not only because this seems palpably false, but also because a thoroughly negative characterization of aesthetic experience like this is completely impoverished.

15. The temptation to use the label "aesthetic experience" for all appropriate experiences of art can, I believe, be traced back to aesthetic theories of art, insofar as such theories identify the intended elicitation of aesthetic experiences as the quiddity of all art. On such theories, it is natural to suppose that all appropriate art responses are aesthetic experiences, since those experiences are what is thought to define art. However, once we abandon the aesthetic theory of art, we may also abandon the subsidiary notion that all appropriate, because definitory, experiences of art are aesthetic. The tendency to continue to correlate all appropriate

art experiences with aesthetic experience is, in my view, merely the confused residue of aesthetic theories of art.

ART, PRACTICE, AND NARRATIVE

1. See William Kennick, "Does Traditional Aesthetics Rest on a Mistake?" in *Mind* 67 (1958): 27.
2. See Morris Weitz, "The Role of Theory in Aesthetics," *Journal of Aesthetics and Art Criticism,* 15 (1956), and Weitz, "Wittgenstein's Aesthetics," in *Language and Aesthetics,* ed. Benjamin Tilghman (Lawrence: University of Kansas Press, 1973).
3. These responses to the open concept approach are derived from Maurice Mandelbaum, "Family Resemblances and Generalizations Concerning the Arts," in *Aesthetics,* ed. by George Dickie and Richard Sclafani (New York: St. Martin's Press, 1977).
4. The classic formulation of the Institutional Theory of Art is to be found in George Dickie's *Art and the Aesthetic* (Ithaca: Cornell University Press, 1974). Dickie has attempted to meet many of the objections to this theory by elaborating its central insights in *The Art Circle* (New York: Haven Publications, 1984), especially chs. IV and V. This reformulation may evade some of the above objections that are directed at the classic statement of the theory. However, I have chosen to focus discussion on the classic statement for heuristic and expositional purposes. Furthermore, I should add that, although I think that Dickie's reformulation of his view is an improvement, it still shares a crucial liability with the classic statement of the theory, namely, a lack of an explicit enough emphasis on the role of art history in the characterization of the internal structure of the artworld. That is, the thrust of Dickie's newer theory remains essentially sociological rather than historical. Dickie's newer theory may, in fact, be strictly compatible with the view propounded in this essay. Nevertheless, Dickie still does not underscore the importance of history in the discussion of the artworld, which topic is the central purpose of this essay.
5. The categories of repetition, amplification, and repudiation are also discussed in my "Film History and Film Theory," in *Film Reader,* no. 4, 1979. At that time, I was committed to an Institutional Theory of Art, a position that I have since attempted to modify in terms of the notion of a cultural practice.
6. For a discussion of the idea of associated values see my "Post-Modern Dance and Expression," in *Philosophical Essays on Dance,* ed. Gordon Fancher and Gerald Myers (New York: Dance Horizons, 1981).
7. By invoking the category of repudiation, one may establish that an object is an artwork. But this, of course, is to establish very little. Whether a repudiation will catch on, whether it is interesting or important to the life of the culture requires further argumentation. Often, repudiating art will be advocated by linking it to political and moral concerns and to other cultural projects. For example, Cunningham's choreography, which repudiates certain forms of Modern Dance, is promoted on the grounds that it is democratic. That is, the successful endorsement and acceptance of repudiating art – as well as other forms of art – involves more than identifying it as art. The admission that "more" can involve reference to broader cultural contexts is meant to allay worries that the view in this paper is exclusively formalist.
8. Other categories for dealing with innovative art readily come to mind. One is synthesis; an artist attempts to fuse existing, even opposed, styles. An example here might be Godard, who in the sixties was involved in developing a style that combined elements of Soviet editing and Italian Neo-Realism. Another category could be called radical reinterpretation; artists take an animating concept of an earlier stage of art and reread it in such a way that radically changes its reference. For instance, in the fine arts modern painters reconstrued the idea of realism in such a way that paintings were reconceived as mere real things (in Danto's sense) rather than as representations of real things.
9. The perspective that art might be identified historically is not original to this paper. It is discussed in Richard Wollheim, *Art and Its Objects* (Cambridge: Cambridge University

Press, 1980 [second ed.], esp. sections 40 and 60–63); and in Jerrold Levinson, "Defining Art Historically," *British Journal of Aesthetics,* vol. 19, no. 3, Summer, 1979. Levinson states his theory explicitly: "X is an art work at t = df X is an object of which it is true at t that some person or persons, having the appropriate proprietary right over X, non-passingly intends (or intended) X for regard-as-a-work-of-art, i.e., regard in any way (or ways) in which objects in the extension of 'art work' prior to t are or were correctly (or standardly) regarded." If I understand this formula correctly, the view propounded in our essay and Levinson's may be at least compatible and perhaps mutually informing. One could take our discussion of repetition, amplification, and repudiation as a detailed exposition of *some* of the precedented ways of correctly regarding artworks. On the other hand, I do disagree with Levinson's suggestion that the artist must have a proprietary right over the object in question; had Picasso stolen into a subway yard at night and, after the fashion of graffiti artists, painted *Guernica* on the side of a train, it would be art no matter what Mayor Koch says.

10. Both Wollheim and Levinson discuss the possibility of recursively identifying art.

11. In his review of Dickie's *Art and the Aesthetic* (*Philosophical Review,* January, 1977), Kendall Walton writes "Perhaps the systems of the artworld are connected by causal/historical ties; perhaps the artworld consists of a limited number of protosystems, plus any other systems which developed historically from these in a certain manner." (p. 98) This paragraph is a speculative sketch of such a protosystem from which other systems could be generated by processes such as repetition, amplification, repudiation, synthesis, radical reinterpretation, and so on.

12. Tribal art, remote from our influences, represents another point at which we begin to reach the boundaries of our tradition and where the identification of objects as art gravitates toward considerations of function (though not necessarily the same type of considerations previously discussed). Here narrative accounts may be replaced by reference to functional analogies between the relevant tribal symbolic practices and the art in our tradition, especially at the level of the protosystem (see previous note). The reason for this is obvious; much tribal art is not part of our tradition, though it may represent a significantly parallel practice. The upshot of this admission for this essay is that historical narration is not the only means of identifying artworks due to the necessity of recourse to certain issues of function in various cases; however, this is consistent with the claim that historical narration is our primary means of identifying objects as art.

13. The preparation of this essay has benefitted from discussion with numerous colleagues including Peter Kivy, Dale Jamieson, Anita Silvers, Joseph Rouse, Joseph Margolis, Richard Eldridge, and the philosophy department of Swarthmore College.

IDENTIFYING ART

1. For a statement of this approach, see my "Art, Practice and Narrative," *The Monist* 71 (1986): 140–56.

2. Nelson Goodman, "When Is Art?" in his *Ways of Worldmaking* (Indianapolis: Hackett Publishing Co., 1978).

3. Kendall Walton, review of George Dickie's *Art and the Aesthetic, Philosophical Review* 86 (1977): 97–101.

4. Monroe Beardsley, *Aesthetics: Problems in the Theory of Criticism* (New York: Harcourt, Brace & World, 1958).

5. The realization that the question "What is art?" may represent different requests for information has been noted by T. J. Diffey in his "The Republic of Art," *British Journal of Aesthetics* 9 (1969): 45–56. My thinking has been influenced by this article and by discussions with Dale Jamieson.

6. Stanley Cavell, "Music Discomposed," in his *Must We Mean What We Say?* (Cambridge: Cambridge University Press, 1969).

7. T. J. Diffey, "Essentialism and the Definition of Art," *British Journal of Aesthetics* 13 (1973): 103–20.

8. George Dickie, *The Art Circle* (New York: Haven Publications, 1984), p. 80.

9. The debate here would center on the issue of whether there is a purely classificatory, nonevaluative sense of "art." Here I agree with Dickie in thinking that there is.

10. Monroe Beardsley, "Is Art Essentially Institutional," in *Culture and Art,* ed. Lars Aagaard-Mogensen (Atlantic Highlands, N.J.: Humanities Press, 1976), p. 106.

11. See Morris Weitz, "The Role of Theory in Aesthetics," *The Journal of Aesthetics and Art Criticism* 15 (1956): 27–35; Morris Weitz, "Wittgenstein's Aesthetics," in *Language and Aesthetics,* ed. Benjamin Tilghman (Lawrence: University Press of Kansas, 1973); William Kennick, "Does Traditional Aesthetics Rest on a Mistake?" *Mind* 67 (1958): 317–34; William Kennick, "Definition and Theory in Aesthetics," in *Art and Philosophy,* ed. William Kennick (New York: St. Martin's Press, 1964); and Paul Ziff, "The Task of Defining a Work of Art," *Philosophical Review* 62 (1953): 58–78.

12. Weitz, "The Role of Theory in Aesthetics."

13. Kennick, "Does Traditional Aesthetics Rest on a Mistake?"

14. Arthur Danto, "Thoughts on the Institutional Theory of Art," a paper delivered at the San Francisco Art Institute, July 10, 1991.

15. Arthur Danto, *The Transfiguration of the Commonplace* (Cambridge: Harvard University Press, 1981). It is interesting to note that Danto's point – that art is something the eye cannot descry – counts against the family resemblance approach to identifying artworks as well as against certain well-known aesthetic theories of art (such as Clive Bell's).

16. See Maurice Mandelbaum, "Family Resemblances and Generalizations Concerning the Arts," *American Philosophical Quarterly* 2 (1965): 219–28; and Anthony Manser, "Games and Family Resemblances," *Philosophy* 42 (1967): 210–25.

17. It is instructive to note that even though George Dickie exploited the criticisms of people like Maurice Mandelbaum in terms of the latter's suggestion that the properties that the family resemblance theorists overlooked were nonmanifest relational ones, he did not also take Mandelbaum's suggestion that the relevant properties might be functional. Perhaps the reason for this is that the most obvious candidate for the pertinent functional properties in this area involved the putative capacity of artworks to engender aesthetic experiences. And, of course, Dickie was already opposed to the invocation of anything aesthetic.

18. Dickie, *The Art Circle,* p. 80.

19. Ibid., pp. 80–82.

20. Dickie's theory of the art circle is also criticized by Robert Stecker in his "The End of an Institutional Definition of Art," *British Journal of Aesthetics* 26 (1986): 124–32. Dickie has answered Stecker in his "Reply to Stecker," in *Aesthetics: A Critical Anthology,* 2nd ed., ed. George Dickie, Richard Sclafani, and Ronald Roblin (New York: St. Martin's Press, 1989). See also Jerrold Levinson, review of Dickie's *The Art Circle, Philosophical Review* 96 (1987): 141–46.

21. Throughout this essay, when it is claimed that identifying narratives are distinct from real definitions, I mean that they are distinct from definitions in terms of necessary conditions that are jointly sufficient. I take this to be the relevant sense of "definition" for a discussion such as the present one because that is the kind of definition which has been at the center of our controversies since the 1950s.

22. This method identifies works as art where the works were art at the moment of their inception. Identifying narratives do not constitute works as art; thus, they are not susceptible to the kinds of objections that were leveled at Dickie's notion of the conferral of status. Identifying narratives are typically mobilized in contexts where questions about whether some work is an artwork are likely to arise. In such contexts, identifying narratives establish the credentials of something that is already art. Identifying narratives do not, so to say, turn nonartworks (or not-yet-artworks) into artworks.

Furthermore, this procedure is classificatory insofar as it in no way implies that the work in question is good. For even if an unproblematic application of the procedure implies that an artist succeeded in making art, that success is logically independent from the question of whether the art is good.

23. Clive Bell, *Art* (New York: Capricorn Press, 1958). For an analysis of Bell's theory in relation to the avant-garde art of his contemporaries, see Noël Carroll, "Clive Bell's Aesthetic Hypothesis," in *Aesthetics: A Critical Anthology*.

24. R. G. Collingwood, *Principles of Art* (Oxford: Clarendon Press, 1935).

25. Susanne K. Langer, *Feeling and Form* (New York: Scribner's, 1953).

26. Arthur Danto, "The Last Work of Art: Artworks and Real Things," *Theoria* 39 (1973): 1–17.

27. Arthur Danto, *The Philosophical Disenfranchisement of Art* (New York: Columbia University Press, 1986).

28. See *Russian Formalist Criticism: Four Essays,* ed. Lee T. Lemon and Marion J. Ries (Lincoln: University of Nebraska Press, 1965); and Victor Erhlich, *Russian Formalism* (New Haven: Yale University Press, 1981).

29. See Roland Barthes, "The Death of the Author," in his *Image-Music-Text* (New York: Hill & Wang, 1977); Michel Foucault, "What Is an Author," in *Twentieth-Century Literary Theory,* ed. Vassilis Lambropoulos and David Neal Miller (New York: State University of New York Press, 1987).

30. Benjamin R. Tilghman, "Reflections on Aesthetic Theory," in *Aesthetics: A Critical Anthology,* p. 161.

31. R. A. Sharpe, "A Transformation of a Structuralist Theme," *British Journal of Aesthetics* 18 (1978): 160.

32. This view of criticism may seem to be at odds with the influential view of Arnold Isenberg, who holds that what critics do, essentially, is to point at specific features of artworks in order to get audiences to see their properties. The view of criticism sketched above, however, does not preclude this sort of critical activity. Rather, it sees this sort of "pointing" as proceeding within a larger framework of contextualization. The critic contextualizes in order to orient and to give sense to her pointings. For Isenberg's view of criticism, see Arnold Isenberg, "Critical Communication," in his *Aesthetics and the Theory of Criticism* (Chicago: University of Chicago Press, 1973).

33. Sharpe, "A Transformation of a Structuralist Theme," p. 170.

34. W. B. Gallie, "Art and Politics," in *The Aristotelian Society* 46 supp. (1972): 111. See also Gallie's "The Function of Philosophical Aesthetics," *Mind* 57 (1948): 302–21; his "Essentially Contested Concepts," *Proceedings of the Aristotelian Society* 56 (1956): 169–98; and his "Art as an Essentially Contested Concept," *The Philosophical Quarterly* 6 (1956): 97–114.

35. For one, perhaps not pellucid, account of these anxieties, see Harold Bloom, *The Anxiety of Influence* (New York: Oxford University Press, 1973).

36. For a discussion of the distinction between chronicle and narrative, see Arthur Danto, *Narration and Knowledge* (New York: Columbia University Press, 1985), pp. 112–43.

37. This picture of historical narration differs from the one proposed by Danto in *Narration and Knowledge*. There Danto maintains that historical narration shows the significance of earlier events in the series by connecting them to their consequences. The point of historical narration, on his construal, is to elucidate the significance of the earlier events in the series. However, the kinds of historical narratives we are talking about – identifying narratives – aim at illuminating the final event in the series; therefore, identifying narratives represent a counterexample to Danto's general view of historical narration.

38. For the view that historical narratives need not have unified subjects, see L. B. Cebik, *Concepts, Events and History* (Washington, D.C.: University Press of America, 1978).

39. Quoted by Bronislava Nijinska, *Early Memoirs* (New York: Holt, Rinehart & Winston, 1981), p. 224.

40. In my "Art, Practice and Narrative," I call this option "repetition."

41. These options are called, respectively, "amplification" and "repudiation" in my "Art, Practice and Narrative."

42. Information on Duncan's career is available in Deborah Jowitt, *Time and the Dancing Image* (New York: William Morrow & Co., 1988), chap. 2, and in Sally Banes, "Twentieth Century Dance," in *The Great Ideas Today: 1991* (Chicago: Encyclopaedia Britannica, 1991), pp. 65–68.

43. Narratives of this sort would seem to be the most straightforward way of representing the "heuristic pathways" that are so crucial in Gregory Currie's *An Ontology of Art* (New York: St. Martin's Press, 1989); see esp. chap. 3.

44. For further discussion of the idea of associated values, see Noël Carroll, "Post-modern Dance and Expression," in *Philosophical Essays on Dance,* ed. Gordon Fancher and Gerald Myers (Brooklyn: Dance Horizons Press, 1981).

45. It has been asserted above that the assessments in question be intelligible. This allows that the assessments might be wrong, especially in the hindsight of historical research. For example, Isadora Duncan supposed that the art of the Greeks was natural. Her assessment might not stand up to the scrutiny of classical scholars today. Nevertheless, her view was intelligible for someone in her situation. That is, we can see how a reasonable person in her situation could, in a perfectly reasonable way, come to develop her view of Greek art even if, when all the research is in, it turns out that her view was incorrect. In terms of our historical narratives, we require that the artists make the assessments we claim they make, but those assessments need only be intelligible – reasonable conclusions reached in a reasonable way – and need not be art-historically correct according to retrospective historical research. This notion of intelligibility is analogous to the way in which Amelie Rorty thinks that the principle of charity should be employed in explaining certain emotions. See Amelie Oksenberg Rorty, "Explaining Emotions," *The Journal of Philosophy* 75 (1978): 139–61.

46. "Generally" has been added here to allow for the possibility that an identifying narrative might be told with reference to a work that is not disputed – for example, a "repetition," to use the language of my essay "Art, Practice and Narrative."

47. "Or reenact" has been added in order to allow for resolutions that do not involve changing the artworld. This adjustment is meant to accommodate the option of repetition (see note 46).

48. Compare my account of the complication with accounts of the logic of the situation in Alan Donagan, "The Popper-Hempel Theory Reconsidered," in *Philosophical Analysis and History,* ed. William Dray (New York: Harper & Row, 1966); and Michael Martin, "Situational Logic and Covering Law Explanations in History," *Inquiry* 11 (1968): 394.

49. For more information on embedding and enchainment, see Shlomith Rimmon-Kenan, *Narrative Fiction* (New York: Methuen, 1983); Claude Bremond, "La logique des possibles narratifs," *Communications* 8 (1966): 60–76; and Claude Bremond, *Logique du récit* (Paris: Seuil, 1973).

50. By including the constraint that identifying narratives track activities localized in art-presentational systems, I think I can provide the kind of framework whose absence from my "Art, Practice and Narrative" Stephen Davies criticizes in his recent *Definitions of Art.* Also, Davies seems too quick to assimilate my notion of repetition with the family resemblance approach's notion of similarity. For, on my account, the similarities in question must be the result of *real* historical processes: that is to say, similarities which are not rooted in real historical relations are not enough. For a statement of Davies's criticisms of the narrative approach, see his *Definitions of Art* (Ithaca: Cornell University Press, 1991), pp. 167–69.

51. See Jerrold Levinson, "Defining Art Historically" and "Refining Art Historically," in his *Music, Art & Metaphysics* (Ithaca: Cornell University Press, 1990).

52. Ibid., p. 15.

53. In his "The Boundaries of Art," Robert Stecker suggests that my narrational approach may be open to the same objections to which Levinson's approach is open. This conjecture is undoubtedly owing to my remark, in "Art, Practice and Narrative," that in certain ways the narrative approach is compatible with Levinson's view. What I had in mind there, but did not fully explicate, was that my notions of repetition, amplification, and repudiation could serve as the basis of some of the art regards that might be relevant to Levinson's theory. That is, artists might create

works with the intention that they be regarded as repetitions, amplifications, and repudiations. Still, I do not think the narrational approach falls with Levinson's in the face of the kinds of objections that Stecker advances, if only because the narrative approach *does not propose a definition of art.* See Stecker, "The Boundaries of Art," *British Journal of Aesthetics* 30 (1990).

54. I have derived this interpretation of Danto's theory from his book *The Transfiguration of the Commonplace.* I have also presented a less restrictive interpretation of Danto's theory in my review of his art theory in the journal *History and Theory.* The less restrictive definition was produced in order to avoid certain of the difficulties with Danto's view that I rehearse above. Nevertheless, though a more charitable version of Danto's theory can be produced, I think that the version of Danto's theory that I attack here is his official theory. See my review in *History and Theory* 29 (1990): 113.

55. See Annette Barnes, *On Interpretation* (New York: Basil Blackwell, 1988).

HISTORICAL NARRATIVES AND THE PHILOSOPHY OF ART

1. See, for example, the section entitled "I. The Nature of Art" in *Art and Philosophy,* ed. William Kennick (New York: St. Martin's Press, 1979, 2nd edition).

   Throughout this essay, I should emphasize that I am using the phrase "philosophy of art" somewhat stipulatively to refer to the philosophical concern with the question "What is art?"

   This essay, furthermore, is a substantial variation on a longer piece of mine, "Identifying Art," in *Institutions of Art: Reconsiderations of George Dickie's Philosophy,* ed. Robert Yanal (Penn State University Press, 1993).

2. See Stephen Davies, *Definitions of Art* (Cornell University Press, 1991), Ch. 2.

3. Ibid., p. 218.

4. See, for example, Benjamin Tilghman's arguments in "Reflections on Aesthetic Theory," in *Aesthetics: A Critical Anthology,* eds. George Dickie, Richard Sclafani, and Richard Roblin (New York: St. Martin's Press, 1989), most notably p. 161.

5. The qualification "most" in the sentence above is introduced in order to admit that some philosophers of art – often proponents of aesthetic theories of art – are sometimes engaged in the somewhat rear-guard action of attempting to impugn the artistic credentials of the avant-garde. However, given the course of art history and the inexpugnable influence of the avant-garde, such maneuvers at this late date strike me as almost quaint.

6. I have previously defended a version of the narrative approach in my "Art, Practice and Narrative," *The Monist* 71 (1988): 57–68. The view of art as a practice is also advanced by Nicholas Wolterstorff in his "Philosophy of Art after Analysis and Romanticism," in *Analytic Aesthetics,* ed. Richard Shusterman (Oxford: Blackwell, 1989).

7. In his "Style Theory of Art," *Pacific Philosophical Quarterly,* No. 72 (1991), pp. 277–89, James Carney attempts to develop certain of the insights in my "Art, Practice and Narrative" into a definitional approach, whereas I am prone to extend those earlier views in a way that is alternative to the definitional approach.

8. See, for example, Morris Weitz, "The Role of Theory in Aesthetics," in *The Journal of Aesthetics and Art Criticism* 15 (1956): 27–35.

9. See: Maurice Mandelbaum, "Family Resemblances and Generalizations Concerning the Art," *American Philosophical Quarterly* 2 (1965): 219–28; Anthony Manser, "Games and Family Resemblance," *Philosophy* 42 (1967): 210–25; George Dickie, *Aesthetics: An Introduction* (Indianapolis, Indiana: Pegasus, 1971), pp. 95–98; Arthur Danto, *The Transfiguration of the Commonplace* (Harvard University Press, 1981), pp. 57–66; George Dickie, *The Art Circle* (New York: Haven Publications, 1984), Ch. III; and Stephen Davies, *Definitions of Art,* Ch. I.

10. In terms of what are called exhibited properties.

11. For older accounts of the evolutionary nature of art, see: Henri Focillon, *The Life of Forms in Art,* tr. Charles Beecher Hogan and George Kubler (New York: Zone, 1989); and George Kubler, *The Shape of Time: Remarks on the History of Things* (Yale University Press, 1962).

12. Quoted in Claude Schumacher, *Alfred Jarry and Guillaume Apollinaire* (New York: Grove Press, 1985), p. 75.

13. R. A. Sharpe, *Contemporary Aesthetics: A Philosophical Analysis* (New York: St. Martin's Press, 1983), p. 171.

14. See Kwame Anthony Appiah, "The Postcolonial and the Postmodern," in his *In My Father's House* (Oxford University Press, 1992), Ch. 7, notably pp. 150–55.

15. Roman Jakobson, "The Dominant," in *Readings in Russian Poetics: Formalist and Structuralist Views,* eds. Ladislav Matejka and Krystyna Pomorska (University of Michigan Press, 1978), p. 83. In the same volume, see also: Boris Ejxenbaum, "Literary Environment;" Jurij Tynjanov, "On Literary Evolution;" and Jurij Tynjanov and Roman Jakobson, "Problems in the Study of Literature and Language." For an overview of the work of the Prague Structuralists concerning literary evolution, see: *Historical Structures: The Prague School Project, 1928–1946,* by F. W. Galan (University of Texas Press, 1984). For contemporary theorizing in this vein see: David Bordwell, "Historical Poetics of Cinema," in *The Cinematic Text: Methods and Approaches,* ed. R. Barton Palmer (New York: AMS Press, 1989).

16. Jeffrey Wieand, "Putting Forward a Work of Art," in *The Journal of Aesthetics and Art Criticism* 41 (1983): 618.

17. Ibid.

18. Insofar as identifying narratives emphasize real genetic linkages between past art and contested works, the narrative approach, *pace* critics like Davies and Carney, cannot be dismissed in the manner of the family resemblance approach.

19. This is not to deny that such narratives may also involve, so to speak, a coda in which the consequences of the work in question are also cited.

20. Aristotle, *Poetics,* in *Classical Literary Criticism,* tr. T. S. Dorsch (New York: Viking Penguin, 1984), p. 41.

21. Though typically the relevant context for initiating an identifying narrative is an artworld state of affairs immediately prior to the introduction of the avant-garde work in question, this, of course, is not always the case. Sometimes the narrative will begin further back in history. However, whenever the narrative begins, it must start with a context of practices about which there is consensus concerning its artistic legitimacy.

22. Schumacher, *Alfred Jarry and Guillaume Apollinaire,* p. 98.

23. Alfred Jarry in *Ubu,* ed. Noel Arnaud (Paris: Gallimard, 1978), pp. 412–13. The above translation comes from Schumacher, p. 105.

24. See Jerrold Levinson, "Defining Art Historically," *The British Journal of Aesthetics* 19 (1979): 232–350; Levinson, "Refining Art Historically," *The Journal of Aesthetics and Art Criticism* 47 (1988): 21–33; and Levinson, "A Refiner's Fire: Reply to Sartwell and Kolak," *The Journal of Aesthetics and Art Criticism* 48 (1990): 231–35. For further criticism of Levinson's position, see my "Identifying Art."

25. Davies, *Definitions of Art,* p. 221.

26. Ibid.

27. For a suggestive discussion of the relation of narration and practical reasoning, see Paul Ricoeur, *Time and Narrative,* tr. Kathleen McLaughlin and David Pellauer (University of Chicago Press, 1984), vol. 1.

28. Davies, *Definitions of Art,* p. 221.

29. This argument is developed at greater length in my "Art, Intention and Conversation," in *Intention and Interpretation,* ed. Gary Iseminger (Temple University Press, 1992).

30. Quoted in Beaumont Newhall's *The History of Photography* (New York: The Museum of Modern Art, 1964), p. 106.

31. For a more developed account of the introduction of an artworld presentational system, see my "Performance," *Formations* 1 (1986): 63–82.

32. See Carroll, "Performance."

33. An identifying narrative is not a necessary condition for art status because there may be artworks for which no identifying narrative can be produced. Certain fossil finds may be rel-

evant to consider here. Such cases, however, do not compromise the efficacy of the narrative approach as a reliable method for identifying art – particularly innovative art – in our own tradition. Moreover, I suspect that Carney's style theory of art may falter as a real definition because there is no reason to believe that every genuine work of art – such as certain exotic finds – can be connected to the kind of historical styles his view requires.

34. This is one of the worries that Richard Shusterman raises in his *Pragmatist Aesthetics* (Oxford: Blackwell, 1992), especially p. 44.

ON THE NARRATIVE CONNECTION

1. Morton White, *Foundations of Historical Knowledge* (New York: Harper and Row, 1965).
2. A number of theorists, including Benedetto Croce, Arthur Danto, and William Dray, have used this term. I am using it in the way Morton White does in *Foundations of Historical Knowledge,* p. 222.
3. See Gerald Prince, *Narratology: The Form and Functioning of Narrative* (Amsterdam: Mouton Publishers, 1982), 145.
4. Dray extrapolates the notion of a causal input from *Narration and Knowledge* by Arthur Danto (New York: Columbia University Press, 1985), Chapter 11. Dray discusses the causal input in the second edition of his book *Philosophy of History* (Englewood Cliffs, N. J.: Prentice-Hall, Inc., 1993), pp. 93–94.
5. This example comes from Danto and Dray, although it has been modified for my own purposes. For references, see the preceding footnote.
6. W. B. Gallie first proposed that the earlier events in narratives might be construed as necessary conditions for later events, though his comments are very laconic and undeveloped. I have refined his approach by talking about *causally* necessary conditions as well as by attempting to support the hypothesis argumentatively and developing it in greater detail. I have also profited greatly from Gallie's discussion of following a narrative, though I hope that I have extended it and clarified it somewhat. For Gallie's views, see: W. B. Gallie, *Philosophy and the Historical Understanding* (London: Chatto & Windus, 1964), Chapter 2.
7. An INUS condition is an *insufficient* but *necessary* part of a condition that itself is *unnecessary* but *sufficient* for an effect event. Throughout this essay, when I refer to the causally necessary conditions in the narrative connection, I have INUS conditions in mind inasmuch as they are necessary ingredients in the relevant causal networks under discussion.

   For J. L. Mackie's discussion of INUS conditions, see his "Causes and Conditions" in *The Nature of Causation,* edited by Myles Brand (Urbana: University of Illinois Press, 1976) and his *The Cement of the Universe* (Oxford: The Clarendon Press, 1980).
8. Mackie, "Causes and Conditions" and *The Cement of the Universe.*
9. Of course, you may not be persuaded by this, in which case you may prefer to conjecture that the earlier event in the narrative connection is only a necessary condition of the later events rather than that it is a causally necessary condition, However, I predictably feel that this formulation is too loose.
10. For discussions of the *syuzhet/fabula* distinction see: Seymour Chatman, *Coming to Terms: The Rhetoric of Narrative in Fiction and Film* (Ithaca, N. Y.: Cornell University Press, 1990), and David Bordwell, *Narration in the Fiction Film* (Madison: University of Wisconsin Press, 1985).
11. I owe my recognition of the need to acknowledge the forward-looking aspect of narration to comments made by audience participants at the University of Leeds.
12. Danto would appear to hold to such a view in his *Narration and Knowledge.*
13. I owe this objection to Gregory Currie.
14. I would like to thank Gregory Currie, Elliot Sober, Berent Enc, Ellery Eels, James Phelan, David Bordwell, Susan Friedman, Sally Banes, Graham McFee, Matthew Kieran, and my audiences at the University of Leeds and the University of Sussex for their helpful comments and criticisms.

INTERPRETATION, HISTORY, AND NARRATIVE

1. See Friedrich Nietzsche, *On the Advantage and Disadvantage of History for Life,* translated by Peter Preuss (Indianapolis, IN: Hackett Publishing Company, 1980). Speaking of "monumental history," for example, Nietzsche claims that this venture risks distorting the past by reinterpreting it according to aesthetic criteria and, thereby, brings it closer to fiction (p. 17). Nietzsche's specific reason for this belief is that insofar as monumental history functions to provide models for emulation, it will occlude attention to sufficient causes in order to produce representations available for imitation.

2. Roland Barthes, "The Discourse of History," in *Comparative Criticism: A Yearbook,* edited by E. S. Shaffer; translated by Stephen Bann (Cambridge: Cambridge University Press, 1981), pp. 7–20.

3. Louis Mink, "Narrative Form as a Cognitive Instrument," in his *Historical Understanding,* edited by Brian Fay, Eugene Golob and Richard Vann (Ithaca, NY: Cornell University Press, 1987), pp. 183–203.

4. See Hayden White, *Metahistory: The Historical Imagination in Nineteenth-Century Europe* (Baltimore, MD: The Johns Hopkins University Press, 1973); White, *Tropics of Discourse: Essays in Cultural Criticism* (Baltimore, MD: The Johns Hopkins University Press, 1978); White, *The Content of Form* (Baltimore, MD: The Johns Hopkins University Press, 1987); White, in "Figuring the Nature of Times Deceased," *Future Literary Theory,* edited by Ralph Cohen (New York: Routledge, 1989), pp. 19–43.

5. For its impact on literary critics and historians see the essays by K. Egan, L. Gossman and R. Reinitz in *The Writing of History: Literary Form and Historical Understanding,* edited by Robert H. Canary and Henry Kozicki (Madison, WI: University of Wisconsin Press, 1978). For an example of a philosopher of history influenced by this view, see F. R. Ankersmit, "The Dilemma of Contemporary Anglo-Saxon Philosophy of History," in the journal *History and Theory,* Beiheft 25 (1986), 1–27. The view is also endorsed in Stephen Bann, "Toward a Critical Historiography: Recent Work in Philosophy of History," *Philosophy,* 56 (1981), 365–85.

6. See White, "Interpretation in History," in *Tropics,* pp. 51–80. The interrelation between these different interpretive registers is also discussed in the "Introduction" to *Metahistory* (pp. 1–42), among other places. That White continues to regard historical narrative as interpretive is evident in his recent "'Figuring the Nature of Times Deceased'; Literary Theory and Historical Writing;" see, for example, p. 21.

7. Here it is important to note that our reservations about White have less to do with his view that historical narratives are interpretative and more to do with his claims that such interpretive narratives are, in decisive respects, fictional.

8. See White, "Historicism, History and the Figurative Imagination," in *Tropics,* for example, pp. 111–12.

9. Claude Lévi-Strauss, *The Savage Mind* (Chicago: University of Chicago Press, 1966).

10. See, for example, Fernand Braudel, "The Situation of History in 1950," in his *On History* (Chicago: University of Chicago Press, 1980), and François Furet, "From Narrative History to History as a Problem," *Diogenes,* Spring 1975. W. H. Dray criticizes the latter article in his "Narrative Versus Analysis in History," in *Rationality, Relativism and the Human Sciences,* edited by Joseph Margolis, Michael Krausz and R. M. Burian (Dordrecht, Netherlands: Martinus Nijhoff, 1986).

11. White, "'Figuring the Nature of Times Deceased,'" p. 27. I take the gnomic, rhetorical question at the end of this quotation to signify that narratives as metaphors (in virtue of their generic plot structures) are true in the way analogies are true—do they provide an insightful fit; are they true *enough?*

12. Paul Ricoeur, *The Reality of the Historical Past* (Milwaukee, WI: Marquette University Press, 1984), pp. 33–34.

13. Joseph Margolis, *Art and Philosophy* (Atlantic Highlands, NJ: Humanities Press, 1980), p. 158.

14. White, "'Figuring the Nature of the Times Deceased,'" p. 18.

15. White, "'Figuring the Nature of the Times Deceased,'" p. 21.

16. For a discussion of the failure of both the narrative and the covering-law models to pith the essence of history, see Gordon Graham, *Historical Explanation Reconsidered* (Aberdeen: Aberdeen University Press, 1983).

17. This is the case even if we accept Maurice Mandelbaum's distinction between inquiry and narrative for it would remain a question as to what kind of knowledge (if any) readers could derive from historical narratives. See Maurice Mandelbaum, "A Note on History as Narrative," in *History and Theory*, VI, 1967; and Mandelbaum, *The Anatomy of Historical Knowledge* (Baltimore, MD: Johns Hopkins Press, 1977).

18. White, "The Question of Narrative in Contemporary Historical Theory," in *Content*, p. 46. White derives this argument from Louis Mink, "Narrative Form as a Cognitive Instrument," pp. 197–98.

19. See, for example: White, "The Historical Text as Literary Artifact," in *Tropics*, p. 90; "Historicism, History and The Figurative Imagination," in *Tropics*, p. 111; "Preface," in *Content*, pp. ix–x; "'Figuring the Nature of the Times Deceased,'" p. 27; among others.

20. See Louis Mink, "History and Fiction as Modes of Comprehension," and "Narrative Form as a Cognitive Instrument" in his *Historical Understanding*.

21. White, "The Historical Text as Literary Artifact," in *Tropics*, p. 4.

22. For example, White, "The Historical Text as Literary Artifact," in *Tropics*, p. 82. Here, *invention* seems to follow from the verbal nature of the historical text.

23. For example, White, "The Burden of History," in *Tropics*, pp. 28–29.

24. For example, White, "The Question of Narrative in Contemporary Historical Theory," in *Content*, p. 42.

25. For example, White, "The Burden of History," in *Tropics*, p. 47.

26. For example, in "Interpretation in History," White uses the metaphor of the mirror of a whole for what narrative *passes* as (*Tropics*, p. 51). Also note the analogies to replicas like model airplanes in "The Historical Text as Literary Artifact" in *Tropics*, p. 88.

27. See White, "Historicism, History and the Figurative Imagination," in *Tropics*, pp. 111–12.

28. See, for example, White, "The Question of Narrative in Contemporary Historical Theory," in *Content*, p. 42.

29. That is, for White, narrative forms are the culture's patterns of story-telling and a given event can be plotted in accordance with more than one such structure (which White sometimes refers to as *codes* [*Content*, p. 43]). And in his "The Value of Narrativity in the Representation of Reality," White says that the relation between historiography and narrative is conventional (*Content*, p. 6).

30. For an account of the argumentative function of intuition pumps, see Daniel Dennett, *Elbow Room* (Cambridge, MA: MIT Press, 1984).

31. See especially, White, "The Value of Narrativity in the Representation of Reality," in *Content*, pp. 1–25.

32. Gerard Genette as quoted by White in *Content*, p. 3.

33. Though White flirts with the notion of the *imaginary* as that figures in Lacanian literary theory, he does not accept it whole cloth. He does apparently agree that narrative seduces us through our desire for the kind of coherence and completeness that it counterfeits. However, narratives are also imaginary for him in the sense of being products of the imagination. And, as we have already noted, White does not regard the imagination as discredited epistemically; it has its own realms of veracity, such as the metaphorical. Thus, unlike many contemporary literary theorists, White is not committed to the view that the imaginary structures of narrative necessarily coerce us into misrecognizing reality. They can, rather, reveal reality if they are construed metaphorically.

34. White, "The Value of Narrativity in the Representation of Reality," in *Content*, p. 24.

35. White, "The Value of Narrativity in the Representation of Reality," p. 3.

36. Northrop Frye, *Anatomy of Criticism* (Princeton, NJ: Princeton University Press, 1957).

37. White, "Historicism, History and the Figurative Imagination," in *Tropics*.

38. Though White thinks that the epic may correspond more closely to the chronicle than to narrative proper.

39. White, "Figuring the nature of the times deceased," p. 29.

40. See Roger Schank and R. P. Abelson, *Scripts, Plans, Goals and Understanding* (Hillsdale, NJ: Lawrence Erlbaum Associates, 1977).

41. I've derived this term from John Passmore, "Narratives and Events," in *History and Theory*, Beiheft 26 (1987), 73.

42. For an expansion of these points, see Frederick A. Olafson, *The Dialectic of Action: A Philosophical Interpretation of History and the Humanities* (Chicago: University of Chicago Press, 1979). In his *Time, Narrative, and History* (Bloomington, IN: Indiana University Press, 1986), David Carr attempts to defend the notion of "real stories" with reference to corporate entities like nations in terms of the shared myths that serve in practical deliberations. For my objections to this way of confronting historical constructivism, see my article-review of Carr's book in *History and Theory*, vol. XXVII, no. 3, 1988.

43. The idea of significance here is derived from Arthur Danto, *Knowledge and Narration* (New York: Columbia University Press, 1985).

44. Of course, if the meaning of events is to be conceptualized at the level of comedy or tragedy, then the issue of fiction cannot be dealt with in the above fashion. But remobilizing the argument in this way depends on the viability of White's theory of generic emplotment, which we will take up shortly.

45. In his reliance on the "copy" standard of truth, one suspects that White is endorsing the myth of the Ideal Chronicler which Danto attacked so persuasively in *Narration and Knowledge*, pp. 142–82.

46. White's analogies to science, as comprehended by the constructivist dispensation, sit uncomfortably with his claims to be concerned with the specificity of history.

47. See, for example, Richard N. Boyd, "The Current Status of Scientific Realism," in *Scientific Realism*, edited by Jarrett Leplin (Berkeley, CA: University of California Press, 1984), pp. 41–82.

48. This may be a big *if* since the "unobservables" the historian deals with are categorically disanalogous to the "unobservables" of scientific theories.

49. For further criticism of the notion of transparency as it is used in contemporary literary theory see Noël Carroll, "Conspiracy Theories of Representation," *Philosophy of the Social Sciences*, vol. 17, 1987.

50. Moreover, the fact that in one story, told for one reason, a causal relation between events A and B is cited while in another story, undertaken for other purposes, that causal relation is not cited does not imply that the causal/narrative linkage in the first story is an "imposition."

51. A related point is made against Louis Mink by William Dray in his review of *Historical Understanding* in *Clio*, vol. 17, no. 4 (Summer, 1988), 397.

52. Michael Harrington, *Socialism: Past and Future* (New York: Arcade Publishing, 1989), p. 21.

53. A related objection can be found in J. L. Gorman's review of *The Writing of History*, *The British Journal of Aesthetics* 20 (1980), 189.

54. See Robert Fogelin, *Figuratively Speaking* (New Haven, CT: Yale University Press, 1988).

55. White, *Metahistory*, p. 190.

56. White, *Metahistory*, p. 34.

57. Leon Goldstein attacks the atomic sentences model for other reasons in his "Impediments to Epistemology in the Philosophy of History," in *History and Theory*, Beiheft 25 (1986), 82–100.

58. See J. L. Gorman, *The Expression of Historical Knowledge* (Edinburgh: Edinburgh University Press, 1982), ch. 3. See also, J. L. Gorman, "Objectivity and Truth in History," in *Inquiry*, 17 (1974), 373–97.

59. See C. Behan McCullagh, "The Truth of Historical Narratives," *History and Theory*, Beiheft 26 (1987), 33–40.

60. It seems to me that Paul Ricoeur makes a similar error in his *Time and Narrative* (Chicago: University of Chicago Press, 1984), vol. I. Pressed to account for historical narrative, he opts for a correspondence theory of truth and maintains that narrative corresponds to temporality. White justifiably rejects this view for its obscurity, but stays with the commitment to truth, modifying it in terms of metaphorical truth. Both White and Ricoeur on my view would do better to recognize that truth is not the only relevant epistemic standard for evaluating narratives. Granting that, they could avoid commitments to strange correspondents (temporality) and special standards of truth.

ART, INTENTION, AND CONVERSATION

1. H. P. Grice, "Meaning," *Philosophical Review* 66 (1957). See also Grice's *Studies in the Way of Words* (Cambridge, Mass.: Harvard University Press, 1989).
2. The idea of interpretations as *hypotheses* about authorial intentions is derived from William Tolhurst, "On What a Text Is and How It Means," *British Journal of Aesthetics* 19 (1979).
3. See W. K. Wimsatt, Jr., and Monroe C. Beardsley, "The Intentional Fallacy," *Swanee Review* 54 (1946). This is an expansion of their "Intention," in *Dictionary of World Literature*, ed. J. T. Shipley (New York: Philosophical Library, 1943).
4. See, for example, E. M. W. Tillyard and C. S. Lewis, *The Personal Heresy: A Controversy* (London: Oxford University Press, 1939). Stein Haugom Olsen makes the very interesting claim that the intentional fallacy evolved from the personal heresy but that the shift to intention talk also changed the debate in fateful ways. See Stein Haugom Olsen, *The End of Literary Theory* (Cambridge: Cambridge University Press, 1987), pp. 27–28.
5. Anti-intentionalists have not always been careful to keep the issues of authorial intention, reports of authorial intention, and biography apart. But one should. For example, one may believe that authorial intent is relevant to interpretation and at the same time maintain strong reservations about the authority of authorial pronouncements about the meaning of their artworks. On the distinction between intention and biography, see Colin Lyas, "Personal Qualities and the Intentional Fallacy," *Philosophy and the Arts: Royal Institute of Philosophy Lectures,* vol. 6 (New York: St. Martin's Press, 1973).
6. Monroe C. Beardsley, *Aesthetics* (New York: Harcourt, Brace and World, 1958), p. 20.
7. For a discussion of the notion of "intuition-pumps," see Daniel Dennett, *Elbow Room* (Cambridge, Mass.: MIT Press, 1984).
8. Monroe C. Beardsley, "An Aesthetic Definition of Art" in *What Is Art?* ed. Hugh Curtler (New York: Haven, 1984); and Monroe C. Beardsley, "Intending," in *Values and Morals,* ed. Alvin I. Goldman and Jaegwon Kim (Dordrecht: Reidel, 1978).
9. Beardsley, "Intending."
10. For related arguments dealing with the problem of arbitrary authorial pronouncements, see P. D. Juhl, *Interpretation: An Essay in the Philosophy of Literary Criticism* (Princeton: Princeton University Press, 1980), esp. chap. 7, sec. 4.
11. Beardsley, *Aesthetics,* p. 458.
12. Thomas Kuhn, *The Structure of Scientific Revolutions* (Chicago: University of Chicago Press, 1970), p. 9.
13. If Kuhn had really meant "weaned" here, he should have written "weaned from," not "weaned on."
14. The *locus classicus* of this view of intention is G.E.M. Anscombe's *Intention* (Oxford: Blackwell, 1959). Mary Mothersill provides a brief but useful sketch of the history of these countervailing views of intention in her *Beauty Restored* (Oxford: Oxford University Press, 1984), pp. 15–21.
15. See, for example, Stanley Cavell, "Music Discomposed," in his *Must We Mean What We Say?* (Cambridge: Cambridge University Press, 1976), p. 181. Also see "A Matter of Meaning It" in the same volume. These originally appeared in *Art, Mind and Religion,* ed. W.H. Capitan

and D.D. Merrill (Pittsburgh: University of Pittsburgh Press, 1967). Also relevant is Richard Kuhns, "Criticism and the Problem of Intention," *Journal of Philosophy* 57 (1960). Other arguments in the neo-Wittgensteinian vein include Frank Cioffi "Intention and Interpretation in Criticism," *Proceedings of the Aristotelian Society* 64 (1963–64); and A.J. Close, "Don Quixiote and the 'Intentionalist Fallacy,'" in *On Literary Intention: Critical Essays,* ed. David Newton-de Molina (Edinburgh: Edinburgh University Press, 1976).

16. Monroe Beardsley himself seems to have agreed that the earlier view of intention upon which his arguments were based are inadequate – which is one reason why he developed what I call the ontological argument for anti-intentionalism that is examined later in this essay. See Monroe C. Beardsley, "Intentions and Interpretations: A Fallacy Revived," in *The Aesthetic Point of View,* ed. Michael J. Wreen and Donald M. Callen (Ithaca, N.Y.: Cornell University Press, 1982), p. 189.

17. Roland Barthes, "The Death of the Author," in his *Image-Music-Text* (New York: Hill and Wang, 1977). See also Roland Barthes, "From Work to Text," in *Textual Strategies: Perspectives in Post-Structuralist Criticism,* ed. Josue V. Harari (Ithaca, N.Y.: Cornell University Press, 1979).

18. In his *American Formalism and the Problem of Interpretation* (Houston: Rice University Press, 1986), J. Timothy Bagwell argues that the notion of a difference between literary and ordinary language underlies the early anti-intentionalism of Wimsatt and Beardsley. In this essay, I want to extend that insight to Beardsley's later arguments in his "Intentions and Interpretations."

19. Barthes, "Death of the Author," p. 143.

20. There may be an interesting parallel with the New Criticism and even Beardsley's defense of it here. Not only may Barthes's infatuation with polysemy correlate to the New Critical valorization of ambiguity, but also the New Criticism, it can be argued, arose as a critical practice allied with modernism – namely, that of Eliot. Indeed, even Beardsley's treatment of allusion fits nicely with Eliot's willingness to ascribe interpretations retrospectively. Moreover, both the New Criticism and Barthes may be involved in generalizing the critical position appropriate to the works of art they champion to all works of art.

    Of course, the analogy I wish to draw is limited. There are also immense differences between Barthes and Beardsley. Barthes moves from the irrelevance of the author to fairly wide-ranging intertextuality, whereas Beardsley, given a commitment to the autonomy of the art work, advances a constrained form of objective interpretation. That is, Barthes's position elicits a great deal of free play on the part of the reader, whereas Beardsley remains committed to the possibility of true interpretations.

    On Eliot's retrospective anti-intentionalist interpretations, see T.S. Eliot, "Tradition and the Individual Talent," in *Twentieth-Century Literary Theory,* ed. Vassilis Lambropoulos and David Neal Miller (Albany: State University of New York Press, 1987).

21. Beardsley, "Intentions and Interpretations," p. 190.

22. Characters, implied or otherwise, do not exist *de re.*

23. This view is also advanced by Graham Hough, who traces it to Austin. See Graham Hough, "An Eighth Type of Ambiguity," in Newton-de Molina, *On Literary Intention.*

24. See Richard Ohmann, "Speech Acts and the Definition of Literature," *Philosophy and Rhetoric* 4 (1971); Richard Ohmann, "Speech, Action and Style," in *Literary Style: A Symposium,* ed. Seymour Chatman (London: Oxford University Press, 1971); Barbara Herrnstein Smith, "Poetry as Fiction," in *New Directions in Literary History,* ed. Ralph Cohen (Baltimore: Johns Hopkins University Press, 1974); see also chap. 2 of Barbara Herrnstein Smith, *On the Margins of Discourse: The Relation of Literature to Language* (Chicago: University of Chicago Press, 1978). Indeed, Smith suggests an argument that somewhat parallels Beardsley's in her "The Ethics of Interpretation," in *On the Margins of Discourse.* For Beardsley's defense of the notion that lyric poems are representations, see his "Fiction as Representation," *Synthese* 46 (1981).

25. To be fair to Beardsley, it is important to note that in his "Philosophy of Literature," he appears to admit that there are literary works that are not fictional; this leads him to develop

an aesthetic definition of literature – that is, one based on aesthetic intentions rather than on fiction. But it is hard to see that that admission will not undercut the argument in "Intentions and Interpretations." See Monroe C. Beardsley, "The Philosophy of Literature," in *Aesthetics: A Critical Anthology*, ed. George Dickie and Richard J. Sclafani (New York: St. Martin's Press, 1977), p. 325.

26. See John R. Searle, "The Logical Status of Fictional Discourse," *New Literary History* 6 (1974).

27. I suspect that one reason for adopting the notion of an implied author as a general hypothesis applying to all literary works by critical theorists may be an attempt – parallel to phenomenalism – to fend off skeptical, epistemological anxieties. That is, lacking a general principle for telling when one is confronted by the views of an actual author versus an implied author, one opts for a kind of reductionism – there are only, always implied authors. But this sort of reductionism hardly explains the behavior of our literary practices in general – we argue not only about but with Mailer's views on sex, death, and manliness.

In regard to my last point, one might respond in the spirit of Boris Tomasevkij, the Russian Formalist critic. He thinks of the public character of an author as a fictional creation – a fabrication existing in newspapers, published journals, and correspondence. Extrapolating from his position, one might try to say that we are arguing, not really with Mailer, but with the character of Mailer as he exists in our literary culture. But, as intriguing as this idea might be, I think we are often arguing with the real Norman Mailer, not a publicity fabrication or an implied author. See Boris Tomasevskij, "Literature and Biography," in Lambropoulos and Miller, *Twentieth-Century Literary Theory*.

Perhaps another motive for commitment to the generalized application of the notion of the implied author is that it is a means of adjusting to and accepting the intentional fallacy. But in this case, the claim that all literary expression is mediated by implied speakers cannot be used in an argument with intentionalism without begging the question.

28. Beardsley, *Aesthetics,* pp. 409–11.

29. This interpretation is derived from Christopher Butler, "Saving the Reader," in *Future Literary Theory,* ed. Ralph Cohen (New York: Routledge, 1989).

30. Jonathan Culler, a literary theorist in the Barthesian tradition, seems to take it that the literary work is divorced from reality because it is fictional, and therefore not a speech act. It functions differently, as a result, than ordinary language. This view sits strangely with his view that in reading literary texts with their consequent, wide-ranging semiosis we learn about the processes of the production of meaning in general. That is, how can the literary texts be essentially different than ordinary discourse, yet shed light on the processes of ordinary discourse? See Jonathan Culler, *Structuralist Poetics* (Ithaca, N.Y.: Cornell University Press, 1975), pp. 139 and 264–65.

31. Furthermore, if the mark of whether language is acting on reality is the presence of the speaker to the listener, then this would seem to make theatrical utterances a case of acting directly on reality, which is a consequence that I infer Barthes would reject.

32. One wonders, of course, whether Beardsley could extend the distinction between performances of illocutionary acts and representations of illocutionary acts across all the arts, since it is not clear that speech-act theory can be made to fit the cases of pictures, statues, and so on.

33. For a more extended account of this, see Noël Carroll, "Trois propositions pour une critique de la danse contemporaine," in *La Danse au défi,* ed. Michele Febvre (Montreal: Editions Parachute, 1987).

34. As well, a great deal of literature will have to be understood in terms of choices and doings rather than solely in terms of manipulations of linguistic conventions. The way in which an author modulates a suspense structure, for example, will have to be explained in terms of what he is trying to do; there are no fixed conventions to fall back on. Instead, the author will adopt a certain strategy that we will have to interpret intentionalistically. Similarly, the remarks about Barthleme's "Alice" indicate that with what I call strategies, the intentionalistic idiom of action is best suited for much of what we think of as the object of literary interpretation.

35. Monroe C. Beardsley, *The Possibility of Criticism* (Detroit: Wayne State University Press, 1970), p. 34. See Chapter 2, p. 34.

36. For elaborations of this distinction, see Tolhurst, "On What a Text Is," and Jack W. Meiland, "The Meanings of a Text," *British Journal of Aesthetics* 21 (1981).

37. This notion is elaborated on by Umberto Eco in his *The Open Work* (Cambridge, Mass.: Harvard University Press, 1989).

38. I take this to be the point of Jack Meiland's "The Meanings of a Text."

39. It stands in the way of maximizing interpretive play if the authorial intent is determinate; it is irrelevant because if we adopt anti-intentionalist interpretive practices, then whether or not the author intended an "open text," we will read it in that like anyway.

40. For a diagnosis of this, see Mary Sirridge, "Artistic Intention and Critical Prerogative," *British Journal of Aesthetics* 18 (1978).

41. See, for example, the high premium Barthes assigns to "writerly reading" in his *The Pleasure of the Text* (New York: Hill and Wang, 1975).

42. This position has been defended by Laurent Stern in his "On Interpreting," *Journal of Aesthetics and Art Criticism* 39 (1980); and Laurent Stern's "Facts and Interpretations," address to the Pacific Division meetings of the American Philosophical Association, Spring 1988.

43. A moral purpose that anti-intentionalism might be thought to advance is the emancipation of the spectator, a view with respect to interpretation that parallels the aspiration of many modern artists. But one wonders here whether the freedom of the reader here is genuinely moral or whether it is merely a strained moralization of the *free* play of cognition enjoined by Kantian aestheticism.

    Or it might be felt that opening the artwork to interpretative play affords some kind of consciousness-raising heuristic; Jonathan Culler seems to have this view at the end of *Structuralist Poetics* where engaging the nonauthorially constrained play of textual signs teaches the reader something about the process of semiosis in general (p. 264). This claim would depend on a very controversial view of how language, in general, functions.

    One could also imagine a literary theorist defending anti-intentionalism as securing an institutional purpose. That is, since the literary-critical institution is predicated on the production of interpretations, anti-intentionalism is facilitating because it keeps more interpretive options open. Nevertheless, the job security of literary critics hardly seems like the kind of overriding purpose that would move the rest of us.

    Interestingly, intentionalism has also been defended for what might be thought of as institutional purposes. E. D. Hirsch, for example, wants to defend literary criticism as a cognitive discipline, and he believes that this requires determinate meaning, a commitment best served, on his account, by authorial intention. In this respect, Hirsch, unlike P. D. Juhl, is advancing intentionalism as a means to secure an end of the literary institution rather than as a thesis about the nature of meaning. See E.D. Hirsch, Jr., *Validity in Interpretation* (New Haven: Yale University Press, 1967); and E. D. Hirsch, Jr., *The Aims of Interpretation* (Chicago: University of Chicago Press, 1976). See Chapter I.

44. This is not an invented example. See J. Hoberman, "Bad Movies," *Film Comment,* July–August 1980. Similar arguments appear in Hoberman's "Vulgar Modernism," *Artforum,* February 1982.

    Moreover, I should stress that the issue raised by Hoberman's critical practice is not isolated. For it is often the case that the developments of avant-garde art are projected or read backward with respect to earlier works in the tradition. Thus, previously we saw Barthes's tendency to regard Mallarmé's modernist aspiration to efface authorship as a feature of all antecedent writing.

45. Hoberman. "Bad Movies."

46. Intentionalist criticism is guided by what a given text or artwork could have meant to the work's contemporary informed audience. Reference to what the audience could have

understood is not to be taken as an alternative to intentionalist criticism, however, but as a means of identifying authorial intent. For, *ex hypothesi,* we begin by attributing to the author the intention of communicating – of getting her audience to recognize her intention. Thus, what we conjecture as the intention of the author charitably, is something that the author could reasonably believe the audience – that is, the informed audience – could recognize. It should also be noted that included under the rubric of intentionalist criticism is the elucidation of the author's presuppositions, especially the elucidation of the stylistic choice structure through which the author's intentional activity takes place. And again, what an informed audience could perceive as a stylistic option guides our hypotheses about the author's intentions for the reasons already given.

47. Søren Kierkegaard, *Concluding Unscientific Postscript* (Princeton: Princeton University Press, 1941), p. 466.
48. Culler, *Structuralist Poetics,* p. 115.
49. Robert Nozick, *Anarchy, State, and Utopia* (New York: Basic Books, 1974), p. 42.
50. Why, it might be asked, if this analysis is correct, do so many critics seem willing to indulge anti-intentionalist criticism? One hypothesis is that by means of theoretical devices like unconscious or ideological motivation, they believe that they are getting at the author's actual intentions.
51. This example comes from Denis Dutton, "Why Intentionalism Won't Go Away," in *Literature and the Question of Philosophy,* ed. Anthony Cascardi (Baltimore: Johns Hopkins University Press, 1987).
52. Juhl, *Interpretation,* pp. 121–24.
53. Cavell, "Music Discomposed."
54. Daniel Nathan has argued that intentionalist arguments often depend on having access to contextual information about the text – rather than biographical evidence – and that the anti-intentionalist also may, in principle, have access to contextual information. I think, however, that an example like Edward Wood indicates that biographical information may also be required. For Wood was a contemporary of the Surrealist filmmaker Buñuel, someone who had the intellectual resources and the will to make a transgressive film. Thus, knowing that the filmmaker was Wood, and knowing something about Wood, and that the film-maker was not Buñuel, is crucial to our dismissal of *Plan 9* as a mistake. See Daniel O. Nathan, "Irony and the Artist's Intentions," *British Journal of Aesthetics* 23 (1982).

ANGLO-AMERICAN AESTHETICS AND CONTEMPORARY CRITICISM: INTENTION AND THE HERMENEUTICS OF SUSPICION

1. Throughout, I will use the terms "aesthetics" and "philosophy of art" interchangeably. I prefer the term "philosophy of art," but since our society carries the label "aesthetics," I will use it in its broadest signification.
2. For an especially notable example, see Richard Wollheim, *Painting as Art* (Princeton University Press, 1987).
3. Here I am taking the argument for the existence of the intentional fallacy to be one of the major founding moments of contemporary Anglo-American aesthetics. That argument was first broached by Monroe Beardsley and W. K. Wimsatt in their article "Intention" in *Dictionary of World Literature,* ed. J. T. Shipley (New York: Philosophical Library, 1943); later their position received its canonical statement in Beardsley and Wimsatt, "The Intentional Fallacy," *The Swanee Review* 54 (1946).
4. For one example of this resistance see: Michael Baxandall, *Patterns of Intention* (Yale University Press. 1985).
5. This diagnosis of anti-intentionalism is developed more elaborately in my "Art, Intention and Conversation," in *Intention and Interpretation,* ed. Gary Iseminger (Temple University Press, 1992).

6. Pierre Macheray, *A Theory of Literary Production* (London: Routledge and Kegan Paul, 1978).
7. See especially the arguments in Richard Levin, *New Readings vs. Old Plays* (University of Chicago Press, 1979).
8. The qualification "at least" is meant to restrict Verne's paternalism to African Americans (in contrast to other persons of color), because Capt. Nemo, Verne's superman, is of Indian extraction.
9. My point above pertains to the conceptual relation between intentionalist findings and political criticism. If Verne's portrayal of Neb is intended as irony – that is, as implying that African-Americans are not docile – then criticizing the characterization of Neb as racist makes no sense. There are, of course, further questions about how one goes about establishing that a characterization is ironic. That is an important issue, but one that I shall reserve for another essay.

The Intentional Fallacy: Defending Myself

1. George Dickie and Kent Wilson. "The Intentional Fallacy: Defending Beardsley," *The Journal of Aesthetics and Art Criticism* 53 (1995): 233–50.
2. Noël Carroll, "Art, Intention, and Conversation," in *Intention and Interpretation,* ed. Gary Iseminger (Temple University Press, 1992), pp. 97–131.
3. See Monroe Beardsley, *Aesthetics* (New York: Harcourt, Brace and World, 1958), p. 20.
4. E.g., Dickie and Wilson, p. 234.
5. I have employed arguments like these against anti-intentionalism in my "Art, Intention, and Conversation," p. 112. See also, Noël Carroll, "Anglo-American Aesthetics and Contemporary Criticism: Intention and the Hermeneutics of Suspicion," *The Journal of Aesthetics and Art Criticism* 51 (1993): 247.
6. For a defense of this view of interpretation, see Annette Barnes, *On Interpretation* (Oxford: Basil Blackwell, 1988).

Interpretation and Intention: The Debate between Hypothetical and Actual Intentionalism

1. Noël Carroll, "Art, Intention, and Conversation," in *Intention and Interpretation,* edited by Gary Iseminger (Philadelphia: Temple University Press, 1992); Noël Carroll, "Anglo-American Aesthetics and Contemporary Criticism: Intention and the Hermeneutics of Suspicion," *Journal of Aesthetics and Art Criticism,* 51 (1993), pp. 245–52; Noël Carroll, "The Intentional Fallacy: Defending Myself," *Journal of Aesthetics and Art Criticism,* 55 (1997), pp. 305–9; Gary Iseminger, "An International Demonstration?" in *Intention and Interpretation,* edited by Gary Iseminger (Philadelphia: Temple University Press, 1992); Gary Iseminger, "Actual Intentionalism vs. Hypothetical Intentionalism," *Journal of Aesthetics and Art Criticism,* 54 (1996), pp. 319–26; Gary Iseminger, "Interpretive Relevance, Contradiction and Compatibility with the Text," *Journal of Aesthetics and Art Criticism,* 56 (1998), pp. 58–61; Paisley Livingston, "Intentionalism in Aesthetics," *New Literary History,* 29 (1998), pp. 831–46.
2. Stevens Knapp and Walter Benn Michaels, "Against Theory," *Critical Inquiry,* 8 (1982), pp. 723–42. This view is criticized in George Wilson, "Again, Theory: On Speaker's Meaning, Linguistic Meaning and the Meaning of the Text," *Critical Inquiry,* 19 (1992), pp. 164–85.
3. Gary Iseminger, "Actual Intentionalism vs. Hypothetical Intentionalism."
4. Monroe Beardsley, *Aesthetics* (Indianapolis: Hackett, 1981), p. 20.
5. Gary Iseminger, "Actual Intentionalism vs. Hypothetical Intentionalism."
6. This example is adapted from Paisley Livingston, "Intentionalism in Aesthetics," pp. 841–44.
7. William Tolhurst, "On What a Text Is and How It Means," *British Journal of Aesthetics,* 19 (1979), pp. 3–14; Alexander Nehamas, "The Postulated Author: Critical Monism as a Regulative Ideal," *Critical Inquiry,* 8 (1981), pp. 133–49; Alexander Nehamas, "Writer, Text,

Work, Author," in *Literature and the Question of Philosophy,* edited by Anthony Cascardi (Baltimore: Johns Hopkins University Press, 1987); Jerrold Levinson, "Intention and Interpretation in Literature," in *The Pleasures of Aesthetics* (Ithaca: Cornell University Press, 1996).

8. There is, however, this difference between the evidence countenanced by the hypothetical intentionalist and that to which the modest actual intentionalist is open: the hypothetical intentionalist will not use nonpublic authorial statements of intent (as found in diaries, journals, correspondence, and the like) as grounds for his hypotheses, whereas the modest actual intentionalist will permit the cautious use of such information. Ultimately, it seems, the hypothetical intentionalist defends this limitation on the evidence on the grounds that it does not reflect our interpretive practices. In response, I will argue later that as an empirical conjecture about our practices, this is false.

9. Jerrold Levinson, "Intention and Interpretation in Literature," p. 194.

10. Ibid., p. 200.

11. See Robert Stecker, "Apparent, Implied and Postulated Authors," *Philosophy and Literature,* 11 (1987), p. 266.

12. Jerrold Levinson, "Intention and Interpretation in Literature," p. 198.

13. Peter Kurth, "This Man Is an Island," *New York Times Book Review,* Aug. 22 (1999), p. 13.

14. Sharon O'Brien, *Willa Cather: The Emerging Voice* (New York: Oxford University Press, 1987); Eve Kosofsky Sedgwick, "Across Gender, Across Sexuality: Willa Cather and Others," *South Atlantic Quarterly,* 88 (1989), pp. 53–72.

15. Joan Acocella, "Cather and the Academy," *New Yorker* 71, Nov. 27 (1995), pp. 56–66; Joan Acocella, *Cather and the Politics of Criticism* (Lincoln: University of Nebraska Press, 2000).

16. Neither side quotes directly from Cather's letters, since the Cather estate forbids it. Presumably, they would be willing to cite Cather's correspondence, were it legally permissible to do so.

17. Jerrold Levinson, "Intention and Interpretation in Literature," p. 179.

18. The New Testament Gospel according to Mark 4.12.

19. This view of the passage from Mark has been endorsed by Pascal and Calvin and, to a certain extent, by Frank Kermode, though Kermode uses it to advance a theory of interpretation different from modest actual intentionalism. See D. P. Walker, "Esoteric Symbolism," in *Poetry and Poetics from Ancient Greece to the Renaissance,* edited by G. M. Kirkwood (Ithaca: Cornell University Press, 1975), pp. 218–32; and Frank Kermode, *The Genesis of Secrecy: On the Interpretation of Narrative* (Cambridge: Harvard University Press, 1979).

20. D. P. Walker, "Esoteric Symbolism," pp. 221–22.

21. Jerrold Levinson, "Intention and Interpretation in Literature," pp. 181–84.

22. The hypothetical intentionalist presupposes that all artworks should be "freestanding" in the sense that all one needs to interpret them is what is available publicly. However, the problem with this is that not all artworks are designed to be "freestanding" in this way, as the example of intensely autobiographical art indicates.

23. For example, the filmmaker Stan Brakhage often makes highly autobiographical films. When he attends screenings of his own films, he often answers questions about the meaning of the films from spectators by reference to the autobiographical significance of the work. This seems an integral part of the author/audience relation with respect to these films. If the hypothetical intentionalist objects that this violates some imaginable author/audience contract, the appropriate response would appear to be that Brakhage's "confessions" represent a fulfillment of the real, as opposed to the stipulated, contract that is pertinent to Brakhage's work.

    Moreover, if the hypothetical intentionalist argues that since Brakhage makes these pronouncements in public, they do not violate the strictures of hypothetical intentionalism, this would seem to open the hypothetical intentionalist to charges of arbitrariness – why are the self-same Brakhagean remarks interpretively available if he utters them during a screening at Millennium Film Workshop, but not if they are filed away among his personal correspondence in the library of Anthology Film Archives?

24. See Stuart Gilbert, *James Joyce's Ulysses* (New York: Vintage Books, 1962), pp. v–ix.
25. That is, where the actual authorial intention and the best-warranted hypothesis about it come apart.

ART, NARRATIVE, AND EMOTION

1. A useful survey of this material in the philosophical literature is John Deigh's "Cognitivism in the Theory of Emotions," in *Ethics,* 104 (July 1994). For a discussion of a wide range of research in psychology, see Keith Oatley, *Best Laid Schemes: The Psychology of the Emotions* (Cambridge: Cambridge University Press, 1992).
2. Oatley remarks, for example, that Freud had no theory of the emotions as such in *Best Laid Schemes,* p. 143.
3. Flo Leibowitz, "Apt Feelings, or Why 'Women's Films' Aren't Trivial," in *Post-Theory: Reconstructing Film Studies,* edited by David Bordwell and Noel Carroll (Madison: University of Wisconsin Press, 1996), pp. 219–29.
4. Leo Tolstoy, *What Is Art?* translated by Aylmer Maude (Indianapolis: Hackett Publishing Company, 1960), and R. G. Collingwood, *Principles of Art* (Oxford: Clarendon Press, 1938).
5. Some modernist narratives may intentionally suppress emotive address entirely.
6. Denis Diderot, *The Paradox of Acting* (New York: Hill and Wang, 1957).
7. For different versions of this view, see, for example: William Lyons, *Emotion* (Cambridge: Cambridge University Press, 1980); George Rey "Functionalism and the Emotions," in *Explaining Emotions,* edited by Amelie Oksenberg Rorty (Berkeley: University of California Press, 1980), pp. 163–96; Robert C. Solomon, *The Passions* (Garden City, N.Y.: Anchor/Doubleday, 1976); Irving Thalberg, "Emotion and Thought," *American Philosophical Quarterly,* no. 1 (1964), pp. 45–55; and Thalberg, "Avoiding the Emotion-Thought Conundrum," *Philosophy,* no. 55 (1980), pp. 396–402.

    Of course not everyone accepts the cognitive theory of the emotions as a universal theory of the emotions. However, even if it is not a universal theory of the emotions, I still think its usefulness in discussing the emotions elicited by narratives is defensible, since most of those emotions appear to fall noncontroversially into the class of cognitive emotions.
8. The caveat "at least" here is meant to acknowledge that desires may also be constituents of many everyday emotions. Some theorists argue that desires are constituents of all emotions. See, for example, Jenefer Robinson, "Emotion, Judgment and Desire," in *Journal of Philosophy,* vol. LXXX, no. 11 (November 1983), pp. 731–41; and O. H. Green, *The Emotions: A Philosophical Theory* (Dordrecht, The Netherlands: Kluwer Academic Publishers, 1992).
9. This is not to say that we always recognize the emotional state that we are in by reference to the necessary criteria for being in that state, nor that everyone can explicitly articulate the necessary criteria for being in a given emotional state. Often, we identify the state we are in by means of what Ronald de Sousa has called "paradigm scenarios" – narrative prototypes that we use to match emotions to certain types of situations. For a discussion of paradigm scenarios, see Ronald de Sousa, *The Rationality of Emotion* (Cambridge, Mass.: The MIT Press, 1987). For an initial attempt to suggest the relevance of paradigm scenarios for aesthetic research, see Noël Carroll, "The Image of Women in Film: A Defense of a Paradigm," *Journal of Aesthetics and Art Criticism,* 48: 4, Fall 1990, pp. 349–60.
10. S. Tomkins, "Script Theory: Differential Magnification of Affects," in *Nebraska Symposium on Motivation,* 26, (1979), pp. 201–36; Kent Bach, "Emotional Disorder and Attention," in *Philosophical Pathology,* edited by George Graham and G. Lynn Stephens (Cambridge, Mass.: The MIT Press, 1994), pp. 51–72; and, Jenefer Robinson, "Startle," *Journal of Philosophy,* vol. XCII, no. 2 (February 1995), pp. 53–74.
11. Robinson, "Startle," p. 65.
12. This theory of suspense is defended in Noël Carroll, "The Paradox of Suspense," in *Suspense: Conceptualizations, Theoretical Analyses and Empirical Explorations,* edited by Peter Vorderer, Hans Wulf and Mike Friedrichsen (Hillsdale, N.J.: Lawrence Erlbaum, 1996), pp. 71–91.

13. I think that it is the fact of criterial prefocusing that Jenefer Robinson leaves out in her essay on the emotions in fiction in her article "Experiencing Art," in the *Proceedings of the 11th International Congress of Aesthetics*, pp. 156–60.

14. This account of horror is defended in Noël Carroll, *The Philosophy of Horror* (New York: Routledge, 1990).

15. As I understand these pro attitudes, they are not themselves emotions; rather, they are like the desires that comprise many everyday emotions.

16. Here, I am extrapolating from what is sometimes called the conflict theory of emotions. Representatives include F. Paulhan, *The Laws of Feeling,* translated by C. K. Ogden (New York: Harcourt, Brace and Company, 1930); G. Mandler, *Mind and Body: Psychology of Emotions and Stress* (New York: Norton, 1984); and Keith Oatley, *Best Laid Schemes,* especially pp. 107–9 and pp. 174–77.

17. This view is defended at greater length in Noël Carroll, *The Philosophy of Horror,* especially Chapter 2.

18. See Amelie Rorty, "Explaining Emotions," in *Explaining Emotions,* pp. 103–26.

19. This view of fiction is advanced in Gregory Currie, *The Nature of Fiction* (Cambridge: Cambridge University Press, 1990); and in Peter Lamarque and Stein Haugom Olsen, *Truth, Fiction and Literature: A Philosophical Perspective* (Oxford: Clarendon Press, 1994).

HORROR AND HUMOR

1. Helmuth Plessner, *Laughing and Crying: A Study of the Limits of Human Behavior,* trans. James Spencer Churchill and Marjorie Grene (Northwestern University Press, 1970), pp. 72–73.

2. Walpole himself described the work as a mixture of "buffoonery and solemnity" in the "Preface to the Second Edition" of *The Castle of Otranto* (London: Collier-Macmillan, 1963), p. 21. For an analysis of *The Castle of Otranto,* see Paul Lewis, *Comic Effects: Interdisciplinary Approaches to Humor in Literature* (SUNY Press, 1989), pp. 116–19.

3. Donald F. Glut, *The Frankenstein Legend* (Metuchen, NJ: Scarecrow Press, 1973), p. 33.

4. Stuart Gordon, as interviewed in *Dark Visions,* ed. Stanley Wiator (New York: Avon, 1992), p. 84.

5. Robert Bloch, as interviewed in *Faces of Fear,* ed. Douglas Winter (New York: Berkeley Books, 1985), p. 22.

6. Edgar Allan Poe, "American Prose Writers, No. 2: N. P. Willis," *Broadway Journal* no. 3, January 18, 1845.

7. Sigmund Freud, "The 'Uncanny,'" in *Studies in Parapsychology* (New York: Collier, 1963), pp. 19–62.

8. E. Jentsch, "Zur Psychologie des Unheimlichen," in *Psychiatrischneurologische Wochenschrift,* numbers 22 and 23, 1906.

9. Henri Bergson, *Laughter: An Essay on the Meaning of the Comic,* trans. Cloudesley Brereton and Fred Rothwell (New York: Macmillan, 1911).

10. I have chosen these two films because in both, the Frankenstein monster is played by the same actor (Glenn Strange, who also played the bartender in the television series *Gunsmoke*).

11. The notion that problems of perceptual indiscernibility are the hallmark of philosophical inquiry is advanced by Arthur Danto in his *Transfiguration of the Commonplace* (Harvard University Press, 1981).

12. I am not fully convinced that we should construct a theory of horror that includes these psychotics. Thus, what follows is a conditional extension of the theory that I presented in *The Philosophy of Horror* under the presumption that the theory should be expanded to accommodate certain psychotics. So, if one wishes to count *The Silence of the Lambs* as a horror fiction, the previous account suggests how that might be done in a way that is maximally consistent with my *Philosophy of Horror.* A similar approach can be found in Peter Penzoldt, *The Supernatural in Fiction* (London: Peter Neville, 1952), p. 12, and S. T. Joshi, *The*

Weird Tale (University of Texas Press, 1990), p. 80. My theory of horror is elaborated in *The Philosophy of Horror, or, Paradoxes of the Heart* (New York: Routledge, 1990).

13. This paragraph repeats an argument that I made in Noël Carroll, "Enjoying Horror Fictions: A Reply to Gaut," *The British Journal of Aesthetics* 35 (1995): 67–72.

14. This scene did not appear in the movie adaptation of *Needful Things*. Perhaps the expenses involved in producing such a scene were prohibitive.

15. I have characterized the relation of fear and disgust as a *complex* compound because horror does not merely involve the *simple* addition of these two components. Horror is not simply the result of adding danger to impurity. For when elements that are independently harmful and impure are yoked together by horrific iconography, the impurity component undergoes a change. It becomes fearsome in its own right. That is, the impurity element comes to be fearsome in itself. It is as if the impurity comes to be, so to speak, toxic. The fearsomeness component in horrific imagery works like a chemical agent in activating or releasing a dormant property of the impurity. It catalyzes the impurity component. The impurity of the monster becomes, in addition to being merely disgusting, one of the fearsome properties of the monster. In *Alien,* when the creature bursts out of the egg, it is fearsome because of its evident power and speed. But the fearsomeness of the creature in light of its power and speed also encourages us to regard its squishy carapace as dangerous in its own terms. You wouldn't want to touch it for fear that it might contaminate you. Horror, then, is not simply a function of fear in response to the overt lethal capacity of the monster to maim plus disgust in response to the monster's impurity. For when fear and disgust are mixed in horror-provoking imagery, what is disgusting becomes additionally fearsome in its own way. Call this process *toxification*.

This process of toxification, moreover, is important theoretically. For one of the things that happens, as we will see in the next section of this essay, is that when fear is subtracted from potentially horrific imagery – as happens in much comedy – the imagery becomes detoxified. This is why what I call category jamming is not a sufficient condition for a horrific response. Impure, incongruous entities can be presented detoxified, so to say, as is the case in much humor.

Lastly, the phenomenon of toxification is important because it suggests a way in which I might be able to answer a recent criticism of my *Philosophy of Horror.*

In the process of answering what I call the paradox of horror, I maintained that being horrified is unpleasant and that the pleasure we derive from horror fictions comes from elsewhere (notably from our fascination with the design of the monstrosity along with certain recurrent forms of plotting). Berys Gaut, in contrast, argues that the pleasure derived from horror fictions comes from being horrified. One of the ways that Gaut defends this view is by pointing out that even if being horrified is *necessarily typically* unpleasant, this is consistent with some people sometimes taking pleasure from being horrified. These will be atypical people in atypical situations. And horror audiences, by hypothesis, are of this sort.

Responding to this proposal, I argue that it is strange to regard either the responses of horror audiences or the situation of being art-horrified by horror fictions to be atypical. Indeed, I contend that the situation of being art-horrified by horror fictions is the norm, since we are rarely, if ever, horrified, in the sense of art-horror, anywhere else but in response to horror fictions. In ordinary experience there are no monsters. So we have little recourse in real life to be horrified in the sense that I use that term.

But Gaut questions my claim that we rarely, if ever, experience the relevant sort of horror in real life. He maintains that we often experience fear and disgust separately. So, if horror is the result of merely conjoining fear and disgust, then there is no reason to suppose that they might not be experienced together with respect to some object in real life. However, in response to Gaut, I would like to argue that what I call horror involves the toxification process discussed in the first paragraph of this note. Thus, art-horror involves fear (divorced from impurity), disgust, and, as a consequence of the mixture of these two elements, a third element, namely, fear-of-toxification. This emotion, particularly with regard to the impression of toxification, is not typical in ordinary life. It is primarily an artifact of the horror genre. So, it does not seem right to characterize the horror audience as atypical with respect to art-horror. Rather, they are definitive of it. Therefore, Gaut cannot exploit the typicality operator, in the way that he suggests, in order to dissolve the paradox of horror.

See: Berys Gaut, "The Paradox of Horror," *The British Journal of Aesthetics* 33 (1993): 333–45; Berys Gaut, "The Enjoyment Theory of Horror: A Response to Carroll," *The British Journal of Aesthetics* 36 (1995): 284–89; and Carroll, "Enjoying Horror Fictions: A Reply to Gaut" (see note 13).

16. Mary Douglas, *Purity and Danger* (London: Routledge and Kegan Paul, 1966); and Edmund Leach, "Anthropological Aspects of Language: Animal Categories and Verbal Abuse," in *New Directions in the Study of Language,* ed. Eric H. Lenneberg (MIT Press, 1964), pp. 23–63.

17. Thomas Hobbes, *Leviathan,* part I, chap. 6.

18. Francis Hutcheson, *Reflections on Laughter* (Glasgow, 1750), reprinted in John Morreall, ed., *The Philosophy of Laughter and Humor* (SUNY Press, 1987), p. 32.

19. James Beattie, "On Laughter and Ludicrous Composition," in his *Essays* (Edinburgh: Creech, 1776); William Hazlitt, *Lectures on the English Comic Writers* (London: George Bell, 1850); Søren Kierkegaard, *Concluding Unscientific Postscript,* trans. David F. Swenson (Princeton University Press, 1941); Arthur Schopenhauer, *The World as Will and Idea,* trans. R. B. Haldane and John Kemp, 6th ed. (London: Routledge and Kegan Paul, 1907), book I, section 13.

20. Arthur Koestler, *The Act of Creation* (London: Hutchinson, 1964); D. H. Monro, *Argument of Laughter* (Melbourne University Press, 1951); John Morreall, *Taking Laughter Seriously* (SUNY Press, 1983); Michael Clark, "Humor and Incongruity," *Philosophy* 45 (1970): 20–32.

21. Adapted from Mel Brooks. See Joshua Halberstam, *Everyday Ethics* (Harmondsworth: Penguin, 1993), p. 83.

22. Noël Carroll, "On Jokes," *Midwest Studies in Philosophy* 16 (1991): 280–301.

23. Interestingly, Beetlejuice, in the film of the same name, resembles a clown. But certainly he is a clown-monster, if there ever was one.

24. Wolfgang Zucker, "The Clown as the Lord of Disorder," in *Holy Laughter,* ed. M. C. Hyers (New York: Seabury, 1960).

25. Don Handelman, *Models and Mirrors: Toward an Anthropology of Public Events* (Cambridge: Cambridge University Press, 1990), p. 247.

26. Ibid., p. 242.

27. Pnina Werbner, "The Virgin and the Clown," *Man,* n.s. (1986): 21.

28. Paul Bouissac, *Circus and Culture: A Semiotic Approach* (Indiana University Press, 1976), p. 165.

29. This routine can be seen on *Great Comedians: TV – The Early Years,* which is distributed by Goodtimes Home Video Corp., 401 5th Avenue, New York, New York (Goodtimes Home Video Corp., 1987; Movietime Inc. Archives, 1986).

30. Similar strategies with respect to the clown-figure are in evidence in the film *Spawn* by A. Z. Dippé, and in the comic book series by Todd McFarlane on which it is based.

31. Of course, I do not mean to suggest that horror and humor are the only mental states in this neighborhood. Certain types of religious awe are also located in the vicinity of incongruity. Recall that the leading mystery in Christianity – Christ as simultaneously both god and man – revolves around an apparent contradiction.

32. Mary K. Rothbart, "Incongruity, Problem-Solving and Laughter," in *Humour and Laughter: Theory, Research and Applications,* eds. Antony J. Chapman and Hugh C. Foot (London: John Wiley and Sons, 1976), pp. 37–54. See also Mary K. Rothbart and Diana Pien, "Elephants and Marshmallows: A Theoretical Synthesis of Incongruity-Resolution and Arousal Theories of Humour," and "Psychological Approaches to the Study of Humour," in *It's A Funny Thing, Humour,* eds. Antony J. Chapman and Hugh C. Foot (New York: Pergamon Press, 1977), pp. 37–40 and 87–94, respectively. Rothbart's work is also discussed by Paul Lewis in

his book *Comic Effects: Interdisciplinary Approaches to Humor in Literature* (SUNY Press, 1989), chaps. 1 and 4.

33. Mary Rothbart, "Laughter in Young Children," *Psychological Bulletin* 80 (1973): 247–56.

34. Moreover, where a fictional environment is "safe," the impurity of incongruity features of the relevant monsters are detoxified. See note 15.

35. There may be certain forms of "black humor" in which this generalization does not appear to obtain. In Roman Polanski's *Cul de Sac,* for example, we are invited to laugh at the bloody death of a self-satisfied bourgeois character. But in cases like these, I wonder whether the laughter is merely comic, rather than a Hobbesian celebration of superiority.

36. Versions of this essay have been read at a number of universities and conferences. The author wishes to thank these audiences for their generous comments, criticisms, and suggestions. Special thanks go to Ted Cohen, John Morreall, Elliott Sober, Robert Stecker, Michael Krausz, Jerrold Levinson, Stephen Davies, Alex Neill, Annette Michelson, David Bordwell, Tom Gunning, Lucy Fischer, and Sally Banes. Of course, no one but the author is responsible for the errors in this essay.

THE PARADOX OF SUSPENSE

1. Examples of theorists who take uncertainty to be a key element of suspense include: Seymour Chatman, *Story and Discourse: Narrative Structure in Fiction and Film* (Ithaca and London: Cornell University Press, 1978), p. 170; Eugene Vale, *The Technique of Screen and Television Writing* (New York: Simon and Schuster, 1982), pp. 178–79; Andrew Ortony, Gerald L. Clore, and Allan Collins, *The Cognitive Structure of the Emotions* (Cambridge: Cambridge University Press, 1988), p. 131; Kendall Walton, *Mimesis as Make-Believe* (Cambridge, Mass.: Harvard University Press, 1990), pp. 259–61; Richard J. Gerrig, *Experiencing Narrative Worlds: On the Psychological Activities of Reading* (New Haven: Yale University Press, 1993), p. 77; Richard Michaels, *Structures of Fantasy,* (Washington, D.C.: MES Press, 1992), p. 266.

2. Richard J. Gerrig, "Reexperiencing Fiction and Non-fiction," in the *Journal of Aesthetics and Art Criticism,* 47 (1989), pp. 277–80; Richard J. Gerrig, "Suspense in the Absence of Uncertainty," *Journal of Memory and Language,* 28 (1989), pp. 633–48; Richard J. Gerrig, *Experiencing Narrative Worlds,* pp. 79–80, 238–39.

3. What I am calling the paradox of suspense may be regarded as a subparadox in the family of paradoxes that might be titled *paradoxes of recidivism* – that is, paradoxes that involve audiences returning to fictions whose outcomes they already know – such as mystery stories and jokes as well as suspense tales – but which they enjoy nonetheless for their being twice- (or more) told tales.

4. This section represents a refinement and attempted updating of earlier essays by me that advance a theory of suspense, including: Noël Carroll, "Toward a Theory of Film Suspense," in *Persistence of Vision,* 1 (1984), pp. 65–89; and Noël Carroll, *The Philosophy of Horror* (New York: Routledge, 1990), pp. 137–44.

5. For example, I would argue that George N. Dove mistook suspense for mystery throughout his book *Suspense in the Formula Story,* which might have been better titled *Mystery in the Formula Story.* See George N. Dove, *Suspense in the Formula Story* (Bowling Green, Ohio: Bowling Green State University Popular Press, 1989).

6. I do not mean to preclude the possibility of fictions that mix elements of suspense and mystery hierarchically. *This Gun for Hire* is probably an example of such a mixed genre case – because, up to a certain point, there are whodunit questions about who is ultimately behind the assassination – however, in the main it seems to be a suspense novel.

7. Marie Rodell, *Mystery Fiction: Theory and Technique* (New York: Hermitage House, 1952), p. 71.

8. Some fictions may contain courses of events that may have rival outcomes that are uncertain but the text may make nothing of them. Thus, they do not generate suspense. The preceding condition acknowledges this possibility and, in consequence, requires that the course of events in question must be one that is made salient, that is, one in which the audience is alerted to the importance of the rivalry between alternative outcomes.

9. Ortony, Clore and Collins, *The Cognitive Structure of Emotions*, p. 131.

10. This happens with the character Raven at points in *This Gun for Hire*.

11. See, for example, D. Zillman and J. R. Cantor, "Affective Responses to the Emotions of a Protagonist," in *Journal of Experimental and Social Psychology*, 8 (1977), pp. 155–65; D. Zillman, T. A. Hay, and J. Bryant, "The Effect of Suspense and Its Resolution in the Appreciation of Dramatic Presentation," in *Journal of Research in Personality*, 9 (1975), pp. 307–23; D. Zillman, "Anatomy of Suspense," in *The Entertainment Functions of Television*, edited by P. H. Tannenbaum (Hillsdale, N.J.: Erlbaum, 1980), pp. 133–63; and P. Comisky and J. Bryant, "Factors Involved in Generating Suspense," *Human Communication Research*, 9, no. 1 (1982), pp. 48–58.

12. See Comisky and Bryant for experimental testing along these lines. These experiments were suggested by earlier findings by Zillman and Cantor that indicated that subjects responded positively to the euphoria of a boy character when that was subsequent to benevolent or neutral behavior on his part, whereas they responded negatively when the euphoria was subsequent to malevolent behavior by the boy.

13. For example, see W. F. Brewer and P. E. Jose, "Development of Story Liking: Character, Identification, Suspense and Outcome Resolution," in *Developmental Psychology*, 20, no. 5 (1984), pp. 911–24.

14. For opposition to the identification model, see D. Zillman, "Anatomy of Suspense"; Noël Carroll, "Character-Identification?" in *The Philosophy of Horror*; D. W. Harding, "Psychological Processes in the Reading of Fiction," in *Aesthetics in the Modern World*, edited by Harold Osborne (New York: Weybright and Talley, 1968), pp. 300–17. Harding's article is a development of an earlier article entitled: "The Role of the Onlooker," in *Scrutiny*, VI, no. 3 (December 1937).

15. This notion of internal probability is crucial to specifying the content of what the audience is to imagine in the course of consuming a suspense fiction. For from a point of view external to the fiction, we do not believe that the events in question have any probability. Likewise by focusing our attention on what is internal to the fiction, we do not imagine that the fiction was, for example, written by Karl May. From the external point of view, we know that *In the Desert* is by Karl May, but we do not imagine that as part of what it is to follow the story. It is not part of the story, nor should it be part of our imaginative response to the story. This is also why our knowledge that heroes almost always triumph in stories does not disturb our internal probability ratings. For it is not information that is inside the fiction operator. It is not part of the story, and, hence, not something we are supposed to imagine.

16. Of course there are comparable narrative structures in literature as well.

17. Because establishing and reemphasizing the relative probabilities of the competing outcomes to courses of events will undoubtedly take time, the expositional duration of the event will reflect this. Thus, I would not deny that the passage of time figures in the articulation of suspense. However, I have not included it as a central ingredient, in its own right, of suspense. In this I perhaps reveal my suspicions with regard to theorists of suspense who claim that it arises as a consequence of time being "distended" or outcomes being "delayed" in the exposition of suspense scenes.

My problem here is that notions like that of temporal distension entail a contrast with something else – presumably the event represented is supposed to contrast to the duration of the event "in nature." However, with fiction, there seems to be nothing "in nature" to which we can compare the represented event.

Recently, however, there has been some psychological research that maintains that – at least in film – there is an available contrast to the representation of the event, which contrast makes talk about temporal distensions and delayed outcomes intelligible. And that contrast is the time that the audience expects the event to take in order to resolve itself. So, for example, suspense will be accentuated where the outcome of an event occurs after that point in time when the audience expected it. Researchers have not claimed that such a temporal prolongation can carry suspense by itself. Rather, they have only claimed a role for time structures in exacerbating or undercutting suspense.

This research is certainly intriguing. However, I still have some reservations. Because so many representations of events in film differ in duration from the same kind of events "in real life" (e.g., wars and the decisive battles of world history are always shorter in the movies than they are in "real life"), one wonders how audiences form expectations about how long cinematic representations of events should take. Here, it has been suggested that we form our expectations insofar as we develop norms about event lengths on the basis of the other representations in the film. But how, then, do we undergo suspense with respect to the opening scenes in a film?

I would feel more comfortable with this conjecture in general if more could be said about the computational mechanism that putatively enables us to estimate what we feel is the right amount of time, for example, for a suspenseful battle to take in a film about inter-galactic revolution. Without a convincing specification of such a mechanism, I am not sure I can make much sense of what people say about their expectations concerning when fic-tional representations of events should (as a matter of prediction) end.

Also, we experience suspense not only while watching films, but in reading literature. It seems to me that the experience of suspense, whether seen or read, is pretty much the same. However, it is virtually unfathomable to me how people could form expectations about on what page a scene should end. Indeed, on the basis of introspection, I find it dif-ficult to observe such expectations in me. Consequently, if the analysis of suspense in liter-ature and the visual arts should be roughly the same, and if it seems unlikely that readers predict what they take to be the appropriate length of the exposition of events in literature, then why should we suppose that a prediction of the length of the exposition of the event is an essential ingredient in film suspense?

On the other hand, if these sorts of worries can be allayed, perhaps I shall have to grant that time plays a more integral role in the generation of suspense than I have acknowledged heretofore.

For interesting research on this topic that favors the conclusion that time is an integral element of suspense, see Minet de Wied, *The Role of Time Structures in the Experience of Film Suspense and Duration: A study of the effects of anticipation time upon suspense and temporal varia-tions on duration experience and suspense* (doctoral dissertation for the Department of Theater Studies of the University of Amsterdam, 1991).

18. For further arguments on behalf of this contention, see Patricia S. Greenspan, *Emotions and Reasons: An Inquiry into Emotional Justification* (New York: Routledge, 1988), Chapter 2, especially pp. 17–20.

19. See Roger Scruton, *Art and Imagination: A Study in the Philosophy of Mind* (London: Rout-ledge and Kegan Paul, 1972), pp. 84–106.

20. I am indebted to Dong-Ryul Choo for pointing out some of the realistic commitments of my theory of suspense. He develops his insights in his *How to be an Aesthetic Realist* (doctoral disser-tation for the Department of Philosophy of the University of Wisconsin-Madison, 1994).

21. As I understand him, Kendall Walton makes a similar move in dissolving the paradox of sus-pense. He draws a distinction between what one knows to be fictional and what is fictional that one knows. Thus, if I have already seen the *Guns of Navarone,* then I know it to be fic-tional that the artillery is destroyed; but as I watch the film a second time and play my game of make-believe, I make-believe that I am uncertain about whether the guns will be destroyed, or, to put it differently, it is fictional that I am uncertain about whether the guns will be destroyed (in my occurrent game of make-believe).

However, I think that my characterization of the mental state in terms of imagination is superior to Walton's discussion in terms of make-believe, because Walton's games of make-believe seem to require so much more activity than mere imagination. For in some games of make-believe, Lauren is paralyzed by her fear for Jack in the Beanstalk, whereas in others, it is fictional that she is hit by the gravity of the situation of Jack's theft of the goose that lays the golden egg, or, yet again, fictionally she is emotionally exhausted when Jack defeats the giant. Playing games of make-believe in Walton's examples seems to involve readers in playing roles or acting. Playing games of make-believe involves more than merely imagining p – merely entertaining the proposition p unasserted. Thus, solving the paradox of suspense in terms of imagination seems more economical than talking about make-believe.

Although Walton sometimes speaks of make-believe as imagination, when he gives examples of what he has in mind, it seems far more structurally complex than mere imagining. Consequently, I maintain that my solution to the paradox of suspense is more economical than Walton's, because all I require is a notion of the imagination that we are already willing to endorse outside the context of fiction, whereas Walton employs the more complicated machinery of make-believe or fictional games, which even if called the imagination is really an elaborate version thereof. For a discussion of the relevant examples, see *Mimesis as Make-Believe,* especially p. 261.

Moreover, Walton's overall argument for the efficacy of his concept of make-believe is indirect. He advances his case by showing that his own approach solves more puzzles – such as the paradox of suspense – than do contending approaches. Thus, if the solution offered here by me is superior to Walton's, then one of the major struts supporting Walton's theory is undermined. For pressure on some of the other struts, see Noël Carroll, *The Philosophy of Horror,* especially Chapter 2.

22. See Laura Mulvey, "Visual Pleasure and Narrative Cinema," in her book *Visual and Other Pleasures* (Bloomington: Indiana University Press, 1989), pp. 14–28.
23. Richard Gerrig, *Experiencing Narrative Worlds,* pp. 170–71. See also his articles: "Reexperiencing Fiction and Non-fiction," and "Suspense in the Absence of Uncertainty."
24. I would like to thank Elliott Sober, David Bordwell, Berent Enç, Gregory Currie, and Sally Banes for their assistance in the preparation of this essay.

ART, NARRATIVE, AND MORAL UNDERSTANDING

I would like to thank Jerrold Levinson, Alex Neill, Berys Gaut, Sally Banes, Kendall Walton, Stephen Davies, Denis Dutton, Ismay Barwell, William Tolhurst, David Novitz, Ivan Soll, John Brown, John Deigh, David Michael Levin, Peter Lamarque, Gregory Currie, Jim Anderson, Jeff Dean, Richard Kraut, Michael Williams, Meredith Williams, Robert Stecker, and David Bordwell for their comments on earlier versions of this essay. They, of course, are not responsible for the flaws in my argument; I am.

1. See Plato's *Republic,* Books 2, 3, and 10.
2. The founding essay in this line of thought is "Ideology and Ideological State Apparatuses (Notes Towards an Investigation)," by Louis Althusser in his book *Lenin and Philosophy* (London: New Left Books, 1971). This approach has been extremely influential in the humanities and notably still is in film studies. For a critical overview, see Noël Carroll, *Mystifying Movies* (New York: Columbia University Press, 1988).
3. See Herbert Marcuse, *The Aesthetic Dimension: Toward a Critique of Marxist Aesthetics* (Boston: Beacon Press, 1977).
4. See Friedrich Schiller, *On the Aesthetic Education of Man (in a Series of Letters)* (Oxford: Oxford University Press, 1967).
5. See Jean-Paul Sartre, *What Is Literature?* (London: Methuen, 1983).

Sometimes Martha Nussbaum sounds as though she may be a member of the utopian school, at least with respect to novels. For example, she contends that "the genre itself [the genre of the novel], on account of some general features of its structure, generally constructs empathy and compassion in ways highly relevant to citizenship." At points, Nussbaum qualifies this in various ways – by claiming that she is speaking only of the *realist* novel or by acknowledging that not all novels are *equally* valuable for citizenship. But, at the same time, she is prone to speak of the novel in general, or at least the realist novel, as a form generically conducive to positive moral perception. But clearly to speak this way would require gerrymandering the extension of the class of things to which the concept of the novel (or even realist novel) applies. The novel, at least in the classificatory sense, is not always morally beneficent. There are evil novels. When Nussbaum refers to the genre of the novel, she must be using that notion honorifically, even if she writes as though she is using it descriptively. See Martha Nussbaum, *Poetic Justice: The Literary Imagination and Public Life* (Boston: Beacon Press, 1995), 10.

6. Denis Diderot, in *The Paradox of Acting, and Masks or Faces?* (New York: Hill & Wang, 1957).

7. For a sympathetic account of this approach, see James Spellerberg, "Technology and Ideology in the Cinema," reprinted in *Film Theory and Criticism,* ed. Gerald Mast and Marshall Cohen (New York: Oxford University Press, 1985), 761–75.

8. For an account of why autonomism maintains its grip on the philosophical imagination, see Noël Carroll, "Beauty and the Genealogy of Art Theory," *Philosophical Forum,* 22, no. 4 (1991): 307–34.

9. This sort of criticism is developed by R. W. Beardsmore in *Art and Morality* (London: Macmillan Press, 1971).

10. Much of the filling-in that audiences do with respect to narratives involves mobilizing the schemas they use in order to navigate everyday life. For example, when encountering a fictional character, we use what some theorists call the *person schema* in order to fill out our understanding of a character. Thus, Arthur Conan Doyle need not inform us that Sherlock Holmes has only one liver rather than three because, unless informed otherwise, we will use our standing person schema to form our conception of Sherlock Holmes. Our person schema is a default assumption, and authors presume that we will use it to fill in their characters, unless notified otherwise by the text. Moreover, insofar as we constantly deploy everyday schemas, like the person schema, to understand narratives and fictional characters, the doctrine of autonomists – like the Russian Formalist Boris Tomashevsky – that art, including literature, and life are separate must be false. Most narratives are unintelligible unless the audience accesses everyday person schemas, as well as other sorts of schemas, in order to follow and comprehend narratives of human affairs. The penetration of life into art is, therefore, a necessary condition of narrative literature. It is not a category error.

On person schemas, see Murray Smith, *Engaging Characters: Fiction, Emotion and Cinema* (Oxford: Clarendon Press, 1995), esp. chap. 1.

11. This characterization of melodrama is defended by Flo Leibowitz in "Apt Feelings, or Why 'Women's Films' Aren't Trivial," in *Post-Theory: Reconstructing Film Studies,* ed. David Bordwell and Noël Carroll (Madison: University of Wisconsin Press, 1996), 219–29.

12. One can imagine an avant-garde novel designed to stifle or to derail the reader's propensity to respond to human events morally. However, experiments of this sort are likely to have as part of their purpose reflexively calling attention to our typical expectations and, in that respect, would involve drawing attention to our standard, moral response by forcefully deactivating our moral powers and intuitions. But even this subversion of expectations would have our typical moral response as a background, and, in fact, such experiments might be undertaken, as they frequently are, for moral reasons – such as disparaging and/or dislodging the reader's "sentimental bourgeois" tendency to read moralistically.

13. Jean-Jacques Rousseau, *Letter to M. D'Alembert on the Theater,* in *Politics and the Arts,* ed. Allan Bloom (Ithaca, N.Y.: Cornell University Press, 1973).

14. Ibid. 19.

15. This view is defended at greater length in Noël Carroll, *A Philosophy of Mass Art* (New York: Oxford University Press, 1998), chap. 5.

16. I would not wish to deny that there is a sense in which one might describe what the audience has learned by means of a general proposition. Perhaps, one might describe the reaction to *A Raisin in the Sun* in terms of the audience's possession of a new proposition – that African Americans deserve equal treatment. But I don't think that the audience has simply deduced this from other general propositions that it holds antecedently. That is something it could have done by rote. Rather, audience members come to see that this perhaps already known moral fact is deeply embedded in their structure of moral beliefs. That is, they come to appreciate it in the sense that one appreciates a chess move. They not only acknowledge that it follows from their beliefs in a formal sense, but apprehend its interrelation to other beliefs in a way that also makes those other beliefs more vivid and compelling inasmuch as their relevance is brought home powerfully with reference to a particular case. What goes on might be better described as "re-gestalting."

    Phenomenologically, it is not like simply acquiring a new proposition such as "The sum of 47,832 + 91,247 = 139,079." Rather, it is a matter of an abstract proposition falling into place, resonating in a larger system of beliefs. Merely describing what happens as the acquisition of a new proposition, even if in some sense this is formally accurate, misses this dimension of the transaction.

    Of course, I would not want to deny that *some* narrative artworks convey general moral propositions to audiences of which they were hitherto unaware. Perhaps from *Native Son* readers learned that racism literally brings its own worst nightmares into existence. However, it is my contention that this is not the standard case. In the standard case, the narrative artwork functions more as a vehicle for promoting (or, as we shall see, degrading) moral understanding by activating moral propositions already in our ken.

17. See Neil Cooper, "Understanding," *Aristotelian Society,* suppl. vol. 68 (1984): 1–26.

18. On one view of the morally educative powers of narrative, it is supposed that audiences derive interesting, novel moral propositions from texts and then apply these propositions to the world. I agree that this is not an accurate, comprehensive account, because most of the propositions derivable from narratives are truisms. But this is not the picture of the educative powers of narrative that I advance. I agree that narratives generally play off the moral beliefs and emotions that we already possess and that we already employ in our intercourse with the world. However, in *exercising* these preexisting moral powers in response to texts, the texts may provide opportunities for enhancing our existing moral understanding. Thus, the direction of moral education with respect to narratives is not from the text to the world by way of newly acquired moral propositions. Rather, antecedent moral beliefs about the world may be expanded by commerce with texts that engage our moral understanding. In stressing the world-to-text relation between moral understanding and narratives rather than the text-to-world relation, my position converges on one defended by Peter Lamarque and Stein Haugom Olsen in their *Truth, Fiction and Literature* (Oxford: Clarendon Press, 1994).

19. Charles Larmore, *Patterns of Moral Complexity* (Cambridge University Press, 1987), 21.

20. This view is close to one expounded by Alex Neill. However, in emphasizing fictional narratives as paradigm cases of the grammatical investigation of concepts, I think that Neill makes the consumption of narratives too philosophical. Readers and viewers may recognize the appropriateness of certain concepts to fictional behaviors and character traits, but that sort of recognition can occur without insight into the formal criteria or grammar of the concepts. Neill's immensely stimulating paper, "Fiction and the Education of Emotion," was read at the 1987 meetings of the American Society of Aesthetics in Kansas City.

21. See Gilbert Ryle, "Jane Austen and the Moralists," *Oxford Review,* no. 1 (1966): 8.

22. Sir Philip Sidney, "An Apology for Poetry," in *Criticism: The Major Texts,* ed. Walter Jackson Bate (New York: Harcourt, Brace, Jovanovich, 1970), 82–106. Immanuel Kant, "Methodol-

ogy of Pure Practical Reason," in *Critique of Practical Reason* (Indianapolis: Bobbs-Merrill, 1956), 82–106. See also what Kant says about judgment in "On the Common Saying:'This May Be True in Theory, but It Does Not Apply in Practice,'" in Immanuel Kant, *Political Writings,* ed. Hans Reiss (Cambridge University Press, 1995), 61.

23. Ryle,"Jane Austen and the Moralists," 8.

24. On this view of soap operas, see Noël Carroll,"As the Dial Turns," in *Theorizing the Moving Image* (Cambridge University Press, 1996), 118–24.

25. See, for example, Martha Nussbaum,"Perceptive Equilibrium: Literary Theory and Ethical Theory," in *Love's Knowledge: Essays on Philosophy and Literature* (New York: Oxford University Press, 1990), 168–94.

26. This sort of value is stressed by numerous authors. It is a view that is important to acknowledge. However, it can be overdone when theorists isolate the subversive power of narrative as *the* morally significant power of art in general or of literature in particular. It is one moral contribution that novels, plays, films, and so on can make to moral understanding. But it is not the only one, since nonmorally subversive narratives can also make a contribution to moral understanding. Overemphasizing the subversive power of certain narratives can suggest a distinction between "literature" and other sorts of narratives, which distinction poses as classificatory but which is ultimately honorific. In this light, such a view may be a subspecies of utopianism. Some theorists who emphasize the morally subversive value of literature include Bernard Harrison, *Inconvenient Fictions: Literature and the Limits of Theory* (New Haven, Conn.: Yale University Press, 1991); R. W. Beardsmore, "Literary Examples and Philosophical Confusion," in *Philosophy and Literature,* ed. A. Phillips Griffiths (Cambridge University Press, 1984), 59–74; John Passmore, *Serious Art* (LaSalle, Ill.: Open Court, 1991); Richard Eldridge, "How Is the Kantian Moral Criticism of Literature Possible?" in *Literature and Ethics,* ed. Bjorn Tysdahl et al. (Oslo: Norweign Academy of Science and Letters, 1992), 85–98.

27. Frank Palmer, *Literature and Moral Understanding: A Philosophical Essay on Ethics, Aesthetics, Education and Culture* (Oxford: Oxford University Press, 1992).

28. The reservations I have raised concerning Palmer's view may also be relevant to Gregory Currie's account of the moral psychology of fiction, given the emphasis that Currie places on our putative simulation of the situations of characters. I worry about whether simulation isn't identification all over again. Rather than simulating or identifying with characters, I think that our relation to characters is typically that of onlookers or outside observers. Undoubtedly, how the character feels from the inside is relevant to our responses to her, but when she feels sorrow over her misfortune, we typically pity her for the sorrows she palpably feels, and this is not something that *she* does. The object of our emotion is different from the object of her emotion. Moreover, I am also not convinced that simulations à la Currie play much of a role in our moral deliberations, since we are aware that the pertinent scenarios are made up. For exposition of the simulation theory, see Gregory Currie, "The Moral Psychology of Fiction," *Australasian Journal of Philosophy, 73,* no. 2 (1995): 250–59. A simulation theory is also advanced by Susan Feagin in *Reading with Feeling: The Aesthetics of Appreciation* (Ithaca, N.Y.: Cornell University Press, 1996). For further criticism of the simulation view, see Carroll, *A Philosophy of Mass Art,* chap. 5.

29. The caveat "primarily" is meant to allow for the possibility that, in exceptional cases, the kind of reorienting, reorganizing, and re-gestalting that I have been talking about may yield some new nontrivial proposition or concept. This is not, I contend, the general course of events, but I would not wish to argue that it could never happen. However, it is rare enough that it cannot provide the basis for a general theory of fictional narratives and moral understanding. Moreover, it should be stressed that even where there is the acquisition of a new proposition or concept, the fictional narrative itself provides no probative force for the acquired "knowledge," since the fiction is made up. If the proposition is to be justified, it must find warrant in the real world. (The concession that new propositions may be acquired in the process of deepening our

moral understanding of fictional narratives is a response to a comment by Jerrold Levinson. But I remain skeptical about his suggestion that the fictional narrative can serve as part of the data base for newly acquired principles and concepts.)

30. In response to my suggestions about the moral assessment of artworks, some autonomists might say that though I have shown how some artworks might be evaluated *morally*, nevertheless this sort of moral assessment is never relevant to the *aesthetic* assessment of artworks. I have tried to deal with this objection in "Moderate Moralism," *British Journal of Aesthetics* 36, no. 3 (1996): 223–37. See also Berys Gaut, "Ethical Criticism," in *Aesthetics and Ethics,* ed. by Jerrold Levinson (New York: Cambridge University Press, 1998).

MODERATE MORALISM

1. Moderate moralism represents a departure from an earlier position of mine that I called soft-formalism. See Noël, Carroll "Formalism and Critical Evaluation," in Peter J. McCormick (ed.), *The Reasons of Art* (Ottawa: University of Ottawa Press, 1985).

2. See Clive Bell, *Art* (London: Chatto and Windus, 1924).

3. Though I have only discussed narrative artworks as a counterexample to radical autonomism, the case could be made with reference to other artforms or genres, such as portraiture.

4. On one view of the morally educative powers of narrative, it is supposed that audiences derive novel, general, moral propositions from texts and then they apply those propositions to the world. I agree that this is not an accurate, comprehensive account because most of the propositions derived from narratives are truisms. But this is not the picture of the educative powers of narrative that I advance. I agree that narratives generally play off the moral beliefs and emotions that we already possess and that we already employ in our intercourse with the world. However, in *exercising* these preexisting moral powers in response to texts, the texts may become opportunities for enhancing our already existing moral understanding. Thus, the direction of moral education with respect to narratives is not from the text to the world by way of newly acquired moral propositions. Rather, antecedent moral beliefs about the world may be expanded by commerce with texts that enlarge our moral understanding. In stressing the world-to-text relation between moral understanding and narratives, rather than the text-to-world relation, my position converges on the one defended by Peter Lamarque and Stein Haugom Olsen in their *Truth, Fiction and Literature: A Philosophical Perspective* (Oxford: Clarendon Press, 1994).

5. This view of moral understanding is defended at greater length in Noël Carroll, "Art, Narrative and Morality," in Jerrold Levinson (ed.), *Aesthetics and Ethics* (Cambridge University Press 1998).

6. See "Art, Narrative and Morality" for further argumentation along these lines.

7. I am not sure that moderate autonomism is explicitly represented in the literature. I have come to construct it as a logically possible position because something like it was a common manoeuvre with which critics confronted me upon hearing the previous arguments in this essay.

8. Aristotle, *Poetics,* in Jonathan Barnes (ed.), *The Complete Works of Aristotle* (Princeton: Princeton U.P., 1984), vol. II, p. 2325.

9. David Hume, "Of the Standard of Taste," in John W. Lenz (ed.), *Of the Standard of Taste and Other Essays* (Indianapolis: The Bobbs-Merrill Company, 1965), pp. 23–24.

10. See Kendall Walton, "Morals in Fictions and Fictional Morality," in *The Aristotelian Society,* Supplementary Volume LXVIII, pp. 27–50.

11. For a more powerful as well as a more elegant argument along these lines, see Berys Gaut, "The Ethical Criticism of Art," in Jerrold Levinson (ed.), *Aesthetics and Ethics.* Gaut delivered this article as a talk at the 1994 national meeting of the American Society for Aesthetics.

12. Earlier versions of this essay were delivered as lectures at Columbia University, Northern Illinois University, and the University of Wisconsin at Madison. I would like to thank those

audiences for their attentive criticisms. Alex Neill, Kendall Walton, Sally Banes, and Berys Gaut have also discussed these issues with me. I have profited from the comments of all these critics. Whatever inadequacies remain in my position are my own fault, not theirs.

SIMULATION, EMOTIONS, AND MORALITY

1. See Gregory Currie, "The Moral Psychology of Fiction," *Australasian Journal of Philosophy* 73.2 (June 1995): 250–59; and Gregory Currie, "Imagination and Simulation: Aesthetics Meets Cognitive Science," *Mental Simulations,* ed. Martin Davies and Tony Stone (Oxford: Blackwell, 1995) 151–69. Susan Feagin also endorses the notion of simulation in her book *Reading With Feeling* (Ithaca, NY: Cornell University Press, 1996), as does Murray Smith in *Engaging Characters* (Oxford: Oxford University Press, 1995).

2. See especially Robert Gordon, "Folk Psychology as Simulation," *Folk Psychology,* ed. Martin Davies and Tony Stone (Oxford: Blackwell, 1995) 60–73; Robert Gordon, "Simulation Without Introspection or Inference from Me to You," *Mental Simulations* 53–67; Alvin Goldman, "Empathy, Mind and Morals," *Mental Simulations* 185–208. These books contain a wealth of information about simulation theory, including arguments for and against. Robert Gordon also discusses simulation in his book *The Structure of Emotions: Investigations in Cognitive Psychology* (Cambridge: Cambridge University Press, 1987) 149–55.

3. Currie, "The Moral Psychology of Fiction" 257.

4. Such a theory of the relevance of literature to moral learning, sans the apparatus of simulation, can also be found in Dorothy Walsh, *Literature and Knowledge* (Middletown, CT: Wesleyan University Press, 1969); Catherine Wilson, "Literature and Knowledge," *Philosophy* 58.226 (Oct., 1983); Frank Palmer, *Literature and Moral Understanding: A Philosophical Essay on Ethics, Aesthetics, Education and Culture* (Oxford: Clarendon Press, 1992); and Roger Scruton, *Art and Imagination: A Study in the Philosophy of Mind* (London: Routledge, 1974). In contrast to propositionalism – which emphasizes *knowing-that* – these authors stress a form of knowledge by acquaintance – that is, *knowing-what-it-would-be-like.* What contemporary simulation theorists do – it seems to me – is to supply the psychological mechanism that makes this possible.

5. Arthur Conan Doyle, "Musgrave Ritual," *The Complete Sherlock Holmes Short Stories* (London: John Murray, 1928) 396–417; 413.

6. Immanuel Kant, *Critique of Pure Reason,* trans. Norman Kemp Smith (London: Macmillan, 1953) 336.

7. Ruth Millikan, *Language, Thought and Other Biological Categories* (Cambridge, MA: MIT Press, 1984).

8. Currie, "The Moral Psychology of Fiction" 256.

9. Currie, "The Moral Psychology of Fiction" 257.

10. Currie, "The Moral Psychology of Fiction" 258.

11. See, for example, Stephen Stich and Shaun Nichols, "Folk Psychology: Simulation or Tacit Theory," *Folk Psychology* 123–58; and Stephen Stich and Shaun Nichols, "Second Thoughts on Simulation," *Mental Simulation* 87–108. Both these volumes also contain answers to Stich and Nichols, as well as further rebuttals and defenses of simulation theory.

12. Morton Ann Gernsbacher, H. Hill Goldsmith, and Rachel R. W. Robertson, "Do Readers Mentally Represent Characters' Emotional States?" *Cognition and Emotion* 6.2 (1992): 89–111.

13. D.S. Miall, "Beyond the Schema Given: Affective Comprehension of Literary Narratives," *Cognition and Emotion* 3 (1989): 55–78. Miall is discussed in Gernsbacher et al. 109.

14. Richard Wollheim, *On Art and the Mind* (Cambridge, MA: Harvard University Press, 1974) 59.

15. Richard Gerrig and Deborah Prentice, "Notes on Audience Response," *Post-Theory: Reconstructing Film Studies,* ed. David Bordwell and Noël Carroll (Madison: University of Wisconsin Press, 1996) 388–403.

16. Moreover, in such a case, is it likely that if we used ourselves as simulators, we would predict that she would take the plunge. Wouldn't we predict that she would surrender? Wouldn't we?

17. In Noël Carroll, "Toward a Theory of Point-of-View Editing," in my *Theorizing the Moving Image* (New York: Cambridge University Press, 1996), I have argued that there is compelling psychological evidence to the effect that the recognition of certain basic emotions on the basis of facial expressions may be an innate capacity. It is not at all clear that when I recognize a picture of a face etched in the characteristic contours of fear that I am simulating. For if I am just shown the picture of a face, I really don't have enough of the character's situation at my disposal to know which of his beliefs, desires, and so on to run off-line. And yet I am able to identify his mental state accurately.

18. Here it might be suggested that recognition just is simulation. But I suspect that this begs the question. Moreover, I think that we need to postulate some capacity of recognition that is independent of simulation. It can't be simulation all the way down. For simulation would appear to require powers of recognition in order to get off the ground. For example, suppose I wanted to simulate the state of someone who is embarrassed by being in the presence of someone else who is suffering an intense state of humiliation. Wouldn't I have to take on board the first person's recognition that the second person is humiliated? Simulators require the beliefs of the simulatee, and some of those beliefs must often be of the nature of recognitions. The possibility that everything is a matter of simulations nested in simulations is too baroque for my sensibilities, unless some compelling reason can be found to force us to postulate it.

19. That we are able to recognize emotions on the basis of facial displays indicates that it cannot be the case that it is always simulation all the way down. For the photos that psychologists like Ekman have used to elicit these responses are simply photos of faces. They are not photos of bodies nor of the situations in which characters find themselves. Thus the percipient does not have enough information to simulate what the person in the photo is believing and feeling. The percipient's response, then, is based on recognition without simulation. Thus, with facial expression, it cannot be simulation all the way down. There is a bedrock of recognition. Simulation then is not a fully comprehensive account of folk psychology. Nor does it appear to handle every case of emotional detection in mass art. It does not fully account for the phenomena of point-of-view editing. Of course, there is still a question of how pervasive simulation really is with respect to fiction in general and mass fiction in particular. My suggestion is that it is at best very rare. For further discussion of Ekman's evidence and for my argument regarding point-of-view editing, see Noël Carroll, "Toward a Theory of Point-of-View Editing," in my *Theorizing the Moving Image.*

20. Also there is a question about how much prediction actually goes on in following a narrative. When a character is surrounded by the villains, are we predicting what he will do, or waiting to see what he will do? Also, it seems to me that when we follow a narrative, we more often than not are keeping track of possible future lines of action – for example, will she be captured or not – rather than making exact predictions about the outcomes of earlier events, since the later events in the narrative are generally so underdetermined by the previous events in the story that precise predictions are out of place. And, of course, sometimes we know what will happen next, because either the narrator or the characters tell us, thereby obviating the need for our own predictions. Prediction, that is, may not be a general model of what we usually do when following narratives. Thus, if prediction is what makes simulation theory attractive to philosophers of mind, it may be of little applicability in aesthetics, since following narratives to a large extent does not call for prediction. For further argumentation about the unimportance of prediction for narratives, see Noël Carroll, "On the Narrative Connection," *New Perspectives on Narrative Perspective,* ed. by Will van Peer and Seymour Chatman (Albany: State University of New York Press, forthcoming).

21. Noël Carroll, *The Philosophy of Horror* (New York: Routledge, 1991) 95–96.

22. For further argumentation against simulation theory and for an alternative account of our emotional and moral engagement with fiction, see Noël Carroll, *A Philosophy of Mass Art* (Oxford: Oxford University Press, 1998) chapters 4 and 5.

ON JOKES

1. For examples of incongruity theories, see: D. H. Monro, *Argument of Laughter* (Melbourne, 1951); Marie Collins Swabey, *Comic Laughter: A Philosophical Essay* (New Haven, Conn., 1961); John Morreall, *Taking Laughter Seriously* (Albany, N.Y., 1983); John Morreall, "Funny Ha-Ha, Funny Strange and Other Reactions to Incongruity," in *The Philosophy of Laughter and Humor*, edited by John Morreall (Albany, N.Y., 1987); Michael Clark, "Humour and Incongruity," in *Philosophy* 45 (1970); Mike Martin, "Humour and the Aesthetic Enjoyment of Incongruities," in *British Journal of Aesthetics* 23, no. 1 (Winter 1983); Michael Clark, "Humour, Laughter and the Structure of Thought," in *British Journal of Aesthetics* 27, no. 3 (Summer 1987). Early modern examples of incongruity theories can be found in Francis Hutcheson's *Reflections Upon Laughter, and Remarks Upon "The Fable of the Bees"* (Glasgow, 1750) and James Beattie's "An Essay on Laughter and Ludicrous Composition," in his *Essays on Poetry and Music* (Edinburgh, 1778). William Hazlitt's *Lectures on the English Comic Writers* (London: 1885) and Søren Kierkegaard's *Concluding Unscientific Postscript*, translated by David F. Swenson and Walter Lowire (Princeton, N.J.: 1941) also advance incongruity theories. John Morreall maintains as well that the rudiments of an incongruity theory are suggested by Aristotle in his *Rhetoric* (3,2); see Morreall's *The Philosophy of Laughter and Humor*, p. 14.
2. Arthur Schopenhauer, *The World as Will and Idea*, translated by R. B. Haldane and John Kemp (London, 1907), supplement to Book I: chap. 8, "On the Theory of the Ludicrous."
3. My discussion in this section focuses on Sigmund Freud's *Jokes and their Relation to the Unconscious*, translated and edited by John Strachey (New York, 1960). In his essay "Humor," Freud further discusses the differences between jokes and humor, attributing to the former the aim of sheer gratification and to the latter the aim of evading suffering. I will not be dealing with these distinctions in my discussion here. Freud's essay "Humor" originally appeared in the *International Journal of Psycho-Analysis* 9 (1928).
4. Other examples of release/relief theories include: Herbert Spencer, "The physiology of laughter," *Macmillan's Magazine* I (1860); Theodore Lipps, *Komic und Humor* (Hamburg, 1898); J. C. Gregory, *The Nature of Laughter* (London, 1924).
5. Freud, *Jokes and their Relation to the Unconscious*, 88.
6. Though unacknowledged by Freud, Bergson also hypothesized a connection between dreams and comedy. See Henri Bergson, *Laughter in Comedy*, edited by Wylie Sypher (Baltimore, Md., 1984), 177–87.
7. Freud, *Jokes*, 127.
8. Ibid., 170.
9. If this counterexample is rejected, an alternative approach would be to consider the overlap between Freud's formulas for jokes and his characterization of the uncanny. When the criteria for the uncanny is spelt out, uncanny phenomena bear an unnerving structural affinity to jokes (in the Freudian dispensation). See Sigmund Freud, "The Uncanny," in *Studies in Parapsychology*, edited by Philip Rieff (New York, 1966).
10. It may seem strange to say that Freud's theory of jokes is not sensitive to discursive structure since chapter 2 ("The Technique of Jokes") is a rather compendious inventory of structure. However, these structures are not unique or even semi-unique to jokes. The kind of discursive structure that I have in mind above will be explicated in the next section of this essay.
11. Derived from Victor Raskin, *Semantic Mechanisms of Humor* (Dordrecht, 1985), p. 252.
12. The argument in the preceding paragraph rides on showing that the kind of material that Freud counts as comic, in contradistinction to what he counts as a joke, can be formatted as

what we regard as a joke in everyday speech quite easily. Similarly, I think that the kind of anecdote that dissipates emotion, which Freud takes as the hallmark of the humorous, can also be rewritten in a joke structure with no loss of effect.

I should also note that Freud also distinguishes jokes, the comic, and the humorous in terms of the size of the respective audiences required to appreciate them. Defenders of Freud might want to block my counterexamples by excluding them through reference to this dimension of differentiation. I have not developed a defense against this line of counterattack since I think it would take us too far afield in an essay of this scope. However, for the record, I should say that I find Freud's speculations about the size of audiences (e.g., *Jokes,* 143: "no one can be content with having made a joke for himself alone") thoroughly unsubstantiated and unpersuasive.

13. Derived from Harvey Mindess, *Laughter and Liberation* (Los Angeles, 1971), 133.

14. The restructuring aspect of joke interpretation is emphasized by Gestalt theorists of humor. And, though I do not agree with all their claims about the ways in which this should be incorporated in a theory of jokes, I do think that the reconstructing process that they point to provides some support for calling what the listener does in response to a joke "an interpretation." For Gestalt theories of humor, see: Norman Maier, "A Gestalt Theory of Humor," *British Journal of Psychology* no. 23 (1932); Gregory Bateson, "The role of humor in human communication," in *Cybernetics,* edited by H. von Foerster (New York, 1953); and P. A. Schiller, "A configurational theory of puzzles and jokes," *Journal of Genetic Psychology* 18 (1938).

15. Annette Barnes, *On Interpretation* (New York, 1988), chaps. 2 and 3. Though I am not sure that Barnes's claims about nonobviousness are perfectly accurate for the case of literary interpretation, I do think that they pertain to joke interpretation.

16. Immanuel Kant, *The Critique of Judgment,* translated by James Creed Meredith (Oxford, 1982), section 54, p. 199.

17. Daniel Dennett appears to allow that the interpretation here might be some sort of mental, visual representation. See Daniel Dennett, *The Intentional Stance* (Cambridge, Mass., 1987), 76–77.

18. Comic timing can also be important as a means of highlighting the puzzling aspect of the punch line. That is, the pause before delivering the punch line is a way of dramatizing it.

19. For other examples of the two-stage view, see: Jerry M. Suls, "A Two-Stage Model for the Appreciation of Jokes and Cartoons, An Information-Processing Analysis," in *The Psychology of Humor,* edited by Jeffrey Goldstein and Paul McGhee (New York, 1972); Michael Mulkay, *On Humor* (New York, 1988); J. M. Willman, "An Analysis of Humor and Laughter," *American Journal of Psychology* 53 (1940). Also, the Gestalt psychologists cited previously may be thought of as contributing to the development of the two-stage model.

20. For information on surprise and configurational theories, see Patricia Keith-Spiegel, "Early Conceptions of Humor: Varieties and Issues," in *The Psychology of Humor.*

21. The joke and the most general sort of sight gag seem typically distinguishable in this way; but there is a sort of quasi-visual humor that is more akin to the joke, namely, cartoons with captions. The latter, I think, is the closest relation to the joke among comic genres, though, of course, it is not exclusively a matter of verbal discourse.

22. Suls, "Two-Stage Model for the Appreciation of Jokes," 83.

23. Loose talk of "incongruity" and "congruity" in comic theory can generate a great deal of confusion. For example, Roger Scruton attacks Michael Clark's incongruity theory of humor (cited previously) on the grounds that caricatures involve "congruity" rather than "incongruity." But, of course, even if caricatures are apt or fitting, they also involve some distortion, which I suppose that someone like Clark would want to call an "incongruity." In another vein, Scruton's claim that humor cannot be an emotion because it involves an attentive stance of demolition rather than a formal object would appear to run afoul of theories of the emotions like Amelie Rorty's which take fixed patterns of attention as marks of

emotions. See Roger Scruton, "Laughter," *Proceedings of the Aristotelian Society* 56 (1982), and Amelie Rorty, "Explaining Emotions," *Journal of Philosophy* 75 (1978).

24. See note 1.
25. Raskin, *Semantic Mechanisms of Humor.*
26. A. Koestler, *The Act of Creation* (New York, 1964).
27. Swabey, *Comic Laughter,* 103–26.
28. Monro, *Argument of Laughter.*
29. Henri Bergson, *Laughter* in *Comedy,* edited by Wylie Sypher (Baltimore, Md., 1984).
30. From Barbara C. Bowen, editor, *One Hundred Renaissance Jokes: An Anthology* (Birmingham, Ala., 1988), 9. This joke was first brought to my attention by John Morreall as a counterexample to my theory. The discussion above should indicate why I do not regard it as such.
31. Some incongruity theorists claim the *non sequitur* as part of their domain. See, for example, Swabey, *Comic Laughter,* 120–21. As indicated, I believe that this makes the often otherwise useful concept of incongruity vacuous.
32. The notion that the punch line of a joke subverts our expectations may be misleading since it suggests that we already have some positive view of how the joke will conclude – that is, a determinate, rival hypothesis to the conclusion that actually eventuates. But often – most of the time? – I think that we have no definite idea of how the joke will end. Thus, if we wish to persevere in speaking of our expectations being subverted, I think that it is best to think of our expectations here as the continuation of our normal modes of thought – though this needs a bit of qualification since we may also bring to a given joke certain "joke expectations" due to the internal structure of the joke (e.g., the expectation of continued regularities in jokes told in "threes"), or "joke expectations" due to the recognition of the genre to which the joke belongs (e.g., light-bulb jokes).
33. The notion of cognitive state transitions derives from Alvin Goldman, *Epistemology and Cognition* (Cambridge, Mass., 1986), 74–80 and chap. 5. An interesting project for future research would be to try to fill out Goldman's format with some example of typical joke-interpretations.
34. Ted Cohen, "Jokes," in *Pleasure, Preference and Value,* edited by Eva Schaper (Cambridge, 1983), 124–26.
35. Although we can incorporate Freud's findings into our theory by noting that sometimes the errors in joke-interpretations, along with the attractiveness of said interpretations, may be a result of the operation of infantile thinking.
36. Aristotle, *Rhetoric* (2, 22–25).
37. See Robert Fogelin, *Speaking Figuratively* (New Haven, Conn., 1988), 13–18.
38. Though I do not want to endorse Davidson's theory of metaphor, something like it may apply to hyperbole, though, of course, an hyperbole does contain certain instructions about the way in which to move from it to its literal counterpart. See Donald Davidson, "What Metaphors Mean," *Critical Inquiry* 1 (1978).
39. Christopher P. Wilson, *Jokes: Form, Content, Use and Function* (London, 1979), 217–18; R. Middleton and J. Moland, "Humor in Negro and White Subcultures," *American Sociological Review* 24 (1959); A.M. O'Donnell, "The mouth that bites itself; Irish humour," address to the Institute of Education, University of London, 1975 (cited in Wilson).
40. Forms of figuration other than hyperbole can be in play in such jokes.
41. I have the impression that the view here conflicts with that of Ronald DeSousa in his *The Rationality of Emotion* (Cambridge, Mass., 1987), 289–93. He appears to believe that when a certain kind of wit – which, following Plato, he calls *phthonic* – induces laughter, this implicates us in wickedness, such as sexism, because it shows that we possess an evil attitude. Such attitudes, he maintains, cannot be adopted hypothetically for the purposes of "getting a joke" in the way we entertain the idea that Scots are cheap in order to appreciate certain jokes about them. I am not sure that I follow all of DeSousa's arguments here; indeed, I would want to challenge the thought-experiments that he offers in defense of his thesis. Also, he does not seem to take into account the view that the interpretations that we supply to jokes are recognized to be

involved in error. However, DeSousa's position really deserves to be addressed in a separate article rather than to be hastily engaged in a brief rebuttal here. Nevertheless, one reservation about his position that can be stated briefly now is that his claims that certain presuppositions of jokes cannot be entertained hypothetically does not seem obviously consistent with his admission that anthropologists can entertain attitudes that are alien to them in order to appreciate the jokes of other cultures (DeSousa, 293).

In retrospect, I should also note that the type of "why-did-the-chicken-cross-the-road" joke that I analyzed as a meta-joke in my section entitled "An Alternative Account of the Nature of Jokes" could be analyzed in a way that is more in keeping with my overall approach. We could, for example, analyze it as eliciting a mistaken framework. See, for instance, Alan Garfinkel's account of the Willy Sutton joke in Chapter 1 of his *Forms of Explanation* (New Haven, Conn., 1981). However, even if this is the right way to go with such jokes, I still think that we need the category of meta-jokes in order to accommodate shaggy-dog stories.

THE PARADOX OF JUNK FICTION

1. In Thomas J. Roberts, *An Aesthetics of Junk Fiction* (Athens: University of Georgia Press, 1990).
2. John Cawelti, *The Six-Gun Mystique* (Bowling Green: Bowling Green University Popular Press, 1971).
3. Here it is important to note that the paradox of junk fiction is not a creature of idle invention on my part. The quandary can frequently be heard with reference to this or that particular junk fiction genre at cocktail parties. Often, for example, people tell me that they see no sense in reading horror novels because the stories are always the same. Similarly, defenders of high culture often deride junk fiction by stigmatizing its formulaic nature. Thus, in framing the paradox of junk fiction, I have not discovered a new problem, but rather merely have sharpened up logically some criticisms of junk fiction that have been voiced for a long time now both in common speech and by modernists.
4. Sigmund Freud, "The Relation of the Poet to Day-Dreaming," in *Character and Culture,* ed. Philip Rieff (New York: Collier Books, 1963), pp. 39–40.
5. Ibid.
6. On slash lit, see Constance Penley, "Feminism, Psychoanalysis and the Study of Popular Culture," in *Cultural Studies,* ed. Lawrence Grossberg, Cary Nelson, and Paula Treichler (New York: Routledge, 1992).
7. Roberts, pp. 150–151.
8. For an analysis of *North by Northwest* in terms of the differential knowledge of characters and audiences, see David Bordwell and Kristin Thompson, *Film Art: An Introduction* (New York: MacGraw Hill, 1993), pp. 75–79 and 370–75.
9. For an influential statement of this view, see Clement Greenberg, "Avant-garde and Kitsch," in *Clement Greenberg: The Collected Essays and Criticism, Volume I: Perceptions and Judgments, 1934–1944,* ed. John O'Brian (Chicago: University of Chicago, 1986).
10. For a theory of some of these processes with respect to film, see David Bordwell, *Narration and the Fiction Film* (Madison: University of Wisconsin Press, 1985).
11. John Fiske, *Understanding Popular Culture* (London: Unwin Hyman, 1989), p. 25. For further objections to Fiske's approach, see Noël Carroll, "The Nature of Mass Art," In *Philosophic Exchange* 23 (1992).

VISUAL METAPHOR

1. The notion of depiction here derives from Monroe C. Beardsley, *Aesthetics: Problems in the Philosophy of Criticism* (New York: Harcourt, Brace, and World, 1958), Chapter 6, section 16. See also: Goran Hemeren, *Representation and Meaning in the Visual Arts* (Lund: Scandinavian Books, 1969), especially Chapter 2.

2. See Arthur Danto, "Description and the Phenomenology of Perception," in Norman Bryson, Michael AnnHolly and Keith Moxey (eds.), *Visual Theory: Painting and Interpretation* (New York: Harper Collins, 1988), pp. 201–15.

3. This name for the phenomenon in question was suggested to me by Albert Rothenberg's notion of homospatial thinking. However, I use the idea of homospatiality far more narrowly than does Rothenberg as will become apparent in this article. He applies the term to music, literature, and all sorts of visual art, whereas I use the term to refer only to certain forms of visual imagery. For Rothenberg's wider conception, see Albert Rothenberg, *The Emerging Goddess: The Creative Process in Art, Science and Other Fields* (Chicago: University of Chicago Press, 1979), pp. 268–328.

4. In Francoise Gilet and Carlton Lake, *Life with Picasso* (New York: Signet Books/ McGraw Hill, 1964), pp. 296–97.

5. Though I agree that this issue would be an appropriate topic of discussion in another sort of essay.

6. This illustration can be found in Claes Oldenburg, *Notes in Hand* (London: Petersburg Press, 1972).

7. See II *Kings* 23:10 and *Jeremiah* 32:35.

8. The distinction between source domains and target domains derives from George Lakoff and Mark Turner. See: George Lakoff and Mark Turner, *More than Cool Reason* (Chicago: University of Chicago Press, 1989), p. 38.

9. See, for example, Hollis Frampton, *Circles of Confusion* (Rochester, N.Y.: Visual Studies Workshop, 1983), pp. 166–67.

10. See the interpretation of this figure in Carl Linfert, *Hieronymus Bosch* (New York: Harry N. Abrams, Inc., 1989), p. 74.

11. Obviously, the language here is adapted from Max Black's classic article 'Metaphor,' from *Proceedings of the Aristotelian Society,* N.S. 55 (1954–55), pp. 273–94.

12. I have added the qualification "generally" since some commentators have claimed that some metaphors are true. One example that has been proposed is "Business is business." Similarly, there may be borderline cases of visual metaphors in which the disparate elements in question are not strictly physically incompossible. For instance, in Horatio Greenough's famous, patriotic statue *George Washington,* our first president is dressed in the garb of an Olympian god. The statue invites the thought "George Washington is Zeus." However, strictly speaking, it is not impossible that Washington wears drapery, though it is impossible, given the facts of his life, that Washington be an ancient anything. Physical noncompossibility, it seems to me, tracks the core cases of visual metaphor, though in certain compelling borderline cases, it may be that the incongruity involved falls short of physical noncompossibility and depends on historical or social impossibility or even unlikelihood.

13. Such an attitude toward film images is often attributed to Siegfried Kracauer. See his *Theory of Film: The Redemption of Physical Reality* (Oxford: Oxford University Press, 1960). For discussions of this position see: Calvin B. Pryluck, "The Film Metaphor Metaphor: The Use of Language-Based Models in Film Study," in *Literature/Film Quarterly* 3, no. 2 (Spring 1975); Pryluck, *Sources of Meaning in Motion Pictures and Television* (New York: Arno Press, 1976); Louis Giannetti, "Cinematic Metaphors," in *Journal of Aesthetic Education* 6, no. 4 (October, 1972); Trevor Whittock, *Metaphor and Film* (Cambridge: Cambridge University Press, 1990), Chapter I.

14. Clearly the case of *Typewriter-pie* also blocks the suspicion that all visual metaphors merely illustrate commonplace, preexisting linguistic metaphors. For to my knowledge there is no preexisting, commonplace verbal metaphor to the effect that "typewriters are pies." That is, whereas in certain anti-clerical circles "priests are pigs" may be a commonplace metaphor, 'typewriters are pies' is not a commonplace linguistic metaphor among any group of English speakers. Moreover, the advent of Oldenburg's sketch did not make it a commonplace among any group of English speakers. Also, it is the case that many of what I am calling visual metaphors do trade in commonplace metaphors. In this respect *some* visual metaphors fall into the class that I have elsewhere called ver-

bal images – images that are predicted not only on commonplace metaphors, but also on commonplace idioms, phrases, sayings and so on. The visual metaphors that rely on homospatiality and that illustrate commonplace metaphors fall into the class of verbal images. On the other hand, verbal images that illustrate commonplace metaphors but which do not do it by means of homospatiality count only as verbal images and not as visual metaphors. For an account of verbal images, see: Noel Carroll, 'Language and Cinema: Preliminary Notes for a Theory of Verbal Images', in *Millennium Film Journal*, nos. 7/8/9 (Fall/Winter, 1980–1981).

15. W. Bedell Stanford. *Greek Metaphor* (Oxford: Basil, Blackwell, 1936), p. 95.

16. See Monroe C. Beardsley, "The Metaphorical Twist," *Philosophy and Phenomenological Research* 22, no. 3 (1962).

17. Moreover, I would want to reject the view that if an image – verbal or visual – only mobilizes object comparisons, then it is not a genuine metaphor. Some metaphors may involve more than object comparisons, but that does not compel us to consign those that only evoke object comparisons to the status of the non-metaphorical.

18. See Arthur Danto, *The Transfiguration of the Commonplace* (Cambridge, Mass.: Harvard University Press, 1981); and A. L. Cothey, *The Nature of Art* (New York: Routledge, 1990). See also Carl R. Huasman, *Metaphor and Art* (Cambridge: Cambridge University Press, 1989). In a somewhat different vein, Michael Baxandall maintains that art criticism is fundamentally metaphorical. See his "The Language of Art Criticism," in *The Language of Art History* (Cambridge: Cambridge University Press, 1991).

19. This objection, first and foremost, is aimed at Danto's view of art as metaphor in his *Transfiguration of the Commonplace*.

20. This position is advanced in: Virgil Aldrich, "Visual Metaphor," *Journal of Aesthetic Education* 2 (1968); and Virgil Aldrich, "Form in the Visual Arts," *British Journal of Aesthetics* 11 (1971). Aldrich's position is somewhat difficult to follow. It has been usefully recounted by Carl Hausman in his *Metaphor and Art,* pp. 149–50. I have benefited a great deal from Hausman's helpful synopsis.

21. The requirement here is that the physically noncompossible elements be literally co-present in the same object. This precludes certain cases that people may be prone to call visual metaphors. For example, in the film *The Gold Rush,* Charlie Chaplin as The Tramp treats the nail of a boot as if it were a turkey-bone (specifically as if it were a wishbone). Due to Chaplin's miming, on seeing Chaplin's performance, one is inclined to entertain the thought that the nail is a wishbone. However, since the nail elements and the wishbone elements are not literally co-present in a single object, the image does not count as a visual metaphor. That is, the wishbone is only a suggestion, conjured up by Chaplin's gestures. No wishbone elements are literally fused with nail elements. Nevertheless, there is a relation between Chaplin's miming and what I call visual metaphors. In both cases, two or more objects are "superimposed;" but in visual metaphor, the fusion is literal, whereas in the Chaplin case it is not. Rather, Chaplin's miming induces the audience to use their imaginations in order to grasp the superimposition. The audience imagines the coincidence of the nail and the wishbone rather than seeing elements that are literally co-present in the object. Due to this difference, I am disposed to categorize the Chaplin case, as well as comparable exercises in pantomime, as an instance of *mimed* metaphor, rather than visual metaphor. For a discussion of mimed metaphor, see Noel Carroll, "Notes on the Sight Gag," in Andrew S. Horton (ed.), *comedy/cinema/ theory* (Berkeley: University of California Press, 1991).

22. It should be noted that this condition entails that nonobjective art is not metaphorical. For insofar as the art in question is nonobjective, it is not perceptually recognizable. This may seem problematic to some since often critics let on that this or that piece of nonobjective are is a metaphor for something or other. But I think that there is a problem here. If a painting is truly nonobjective, then it would appear to me that we have no way of divining the relevant categories whose interplay yields metaphorical insight. Nonobjective paintings can certainly be expressive, they can be moving, they can sym-

bolize things in a noniconic way. But if they are not perceptually recognizable wholes and if they have no perceptually recognizable parts, it is difficult to see how they can enlist metaphorical thinking.

23. The creature in the movie *Alien* would appear to be an example of this sort.

24. Ina Loewenberg, "Identifying Metaphors," in Mark Johnson (ed.), *Philosophical Perspectives on Metaphor* (Minneapolis: University of Minnesota Press, 1981), pp. 175–76. This entire section of this paper has been heavily influenced by Loewenberg's article.

25. This, of course, is a general principle of communication. See, for example, Edward H. Bendix, "The Data of Semantic Description," in D. Steinberg and L. Jokobovits (eds.), *Semantics: An Interdisciplinary Reader* (Cambridge: Cambridge University Press, 1971).

26. Lakoff and Turner, *More Than Cool Reason,* p. 63.

27. Donald Davidson, "What Metaphors Mean," in *Philosophical Perspectives on Metaphor,* p. 217.

28. Immanuel Kant, *Critique of Judgment,* translated by J. H. Bernard (New York: Hafner Publishing Company, 1972), p. 158.

29. Robert Fogelin, *Figuratively Speaking* (New Haven: Yale University Press, 1988), pp. 52–67.

30. It may be the case that some of Arcimboldo's fantastic images are to be deciphered as allegories. However, in the case of *The Librarian,* it seems more accurate to regard it as a representation of a librarian cleverly composed out of books rather than as a visual metaphor. Similarly, though perhaps controversially, I am inclined to regard Picasso's *Bull's Head* as a representation of a bull's head, cleverly composed out of a bicycle, rather than as a metaphor.

On Being Moved by Nature: Between Religion and Natural History

1. R. W. Hepburn, "Contemporary Aesthetics and the Neglect of Natural Beauty," in his *Wonder and Other Essays* (Edinburgh University Press, 1984). This essay appeared earlier in *British Analytical Philosophy,* eds. B. Williams and A. Montefiore (London: Routledge and Kegan Paul, 1966).

2. See especially: Allen Carlson, "Appreciation and the Natural Environment," in the *Journal of Aesthetics and Art Criticism* 37 (spring, 1979); "Formal Qualities in the Natural Environment," *Journal of Aesthetic Education* 13 (July, 1979); "Nature, Aesthetic Judgment and Objectivity," *Journal of Aesthetics and Art Criticism* 40 (autumn, 1981); "Saito on the Correct Aesthetic Appreciation of Nature," *Journal of Aesthetic Education* 20 (summer, 1986); "On Appreciating Agricultural Landscapes," *Journal of Aesthetics and Art Criticism* (spring, 1985); "Appreciating Art and Appreciating Nature," in this volume; Barry Sadler and Allen Carlson, "Environmental Aesthetics in Interdisciplinary Perspective," in *Environmental Aesthetics: Essays in Interpretation,* eds. Barry Sadler and Allen Carlson (Victoria, British Columbia: University of Victoria, 1982); and Allen Carlson and Barry Sadler, "Towards Models of Environmental Appreciation," in *Environmental Aesthetics.*

3. See Carlson, "Appreciating Agricultural Landscapes."

4. Carlson, "Appreciating Art," *Landscape, natural beauty and the arts* (Cambridge University Press, 1993).

5. Carlson, "Appreciation and the Natural Environment," p. 274.

6. Carlson, "Nature, Aesthetic Judgment," p. 25.

7. See, for example, William Lyons, *Emotion* (Cambridge University Press, 1980), especially ch. 4.

8. T. J. Diffey, "Natural Beauty without Metaphysics," in *Landscape, natural beauty and the arts* (Cambridge University Press, 1993).

9. Ibid.

10. Carlson, "Appreciation and the Natural Environment," p. 276.

11. Ibid.

12. This is the way that the argument is set up in "Appreciation and the Natural Environment." In "Formal Qualities in the Natural Environment," the object paradigm and the scenery model, it seems to me, both get assimilated under what might be called the formal-qualities model.

13. Carlson, "Appreciation and the Natural Environment," p. 268.

14. *Ibid.*

15. *Ibid.*

16. Carlson, "Formal Qualities," pp. 108–9.

17. Carlson, "Appreciation and the Natural Environment," p. 269.

18. See for example, Peter Bicknell, *Beauty, Horror and Immensity: Picturesque Landscape in Britain 1750–1850* (Cambridge University Press, 1981).

19. Carlson, "Appreciation and the Natural Environment," p. 271.

20. Carlson, "Formal Qualities," p. 110.

21. Carlson, "Appreciation and the Natural Environment," p. 273.

22. Ibid.

23. Francis Sparshott, "Figuring the Ground: Notes on Some Theoretical Problems of the Aesthetic Environment," *Journal of Aesthetic Education,* 6.3 (July 1972).

24. C. D. Broad, "Emotion and Sentiment," in his *Critical Essays in Moral Philosophy* (London: Allen and Unwin, 1971), p. 293.

25. Ronald deSousa, "Self-Deceptive Emotions," in *Explaining Emotions* ed. Amelie Okesenberg Rorty (Berkeley: University of California Press, 1980), p. 285.

26. Carlson, "Nature, Aesthetic Judgment," p. 25.

27. A test suggested by Robert Solomon in his "On Kitsch and Sentimentality," *The Journal of Aesthetics and Art Criticism,* 49.1 (winter 1981): 9.

28. See Immanuel Kant, *The Critique of Judgment,* trans. James Creed Meredith (Oxford: Clarendon Press, 1952), especially the "Analytic of the Sublime."

29. See Carlson, "Appreciating Art," in this volume.

30. Toward the end of "Appreciating Art," Carlson does refer to certain responses to nature, such as awe and wonder, which sound like the type of emotional responses I have been discussing. He thinks that even armed with the natural environment model, we may become aware that nature is still mysterious to us and *other.* And, in consequence, we feel awe and wonder. I do not want to deny that we may come to feel awe and wonder at nature through the process Carlson describes. However, I do not think that this is the only way that we can be overwhelmed with awe in the face of nature. We may, for example, be struck by the scale of nature, without any reference to scientific categories, and be overwhelmed by awe. Thus, though there may be a route to awe through the natural environment model, it is not the only route. There are still other ways in which we may be moved to awe by nature *sans* natural history. Consequently, the account of awe that Carlson offers does not eliminate the more naive model of emotional arousal that I have been defending.

31. Jay Appleton, *The Experience of Landscape* (New York: Wiley, 1975).

32. Jay Appleton, "Prospects and Refuges Revisited," in *Environmental Aesthetics: Theory, Research & Applications,* ed. Jack L. Nasar (Cambridge University Press, 1988); and Jay Appleton, "Pleasure and the Perception of Habitat: A Conceptual Framework," in *Environmental Aesthetics: Essays in Interpretation.*

33. Stephen Kaplan, "Perception and landscape: conceptions and misconceptions," in *Environmental Aesthetics: Theory,* pp. 49–51. See also Kaplan's "Where Cognition and Affect Meet: A Theoretical Analysis of Preference," in the same volume.

EMOTION, APPRECIATION, AND NATURE

1. Noël Carroll, "On Being Moved by Nature: Between Religion and Natural History," in *Landscape, Natural Beauty and the Arts,* edited by Ivan Gaskell and Salim Kemal (Cambridge: Cambridge University Press, 1993). That essay is included in this volume.

2. Allen Carlson, "Appreciating Art and Appreciating Nature," in *Landscape, Natural Beauty and the Arts.*

3. Allen Carlson, "On Appreciating Agricultural Landscapes," in *Journal of Aesthetics and Art Criticism* (spring, 1985), p. 134.

4. Stand Godlovitch, "Icebreakers: Environmentalism and Natural Aesthetics," in *Journal of Applied Philosophy*, 11 (1994).

5. Allen Carlson, "Nature, Aesthetic Appreciation and Knowledge," in *Journal of Aesthetics and Art Criticism*, vol. 53, no. 4 (Fall, 1995).

6. Paul Ziff, *Semantic Analysis* (Ithaca, New York: Cornell University Press, 1960), pp. 242–43.

7. That is, I think that Ziff is exactly right when it comes to the appreciation of art. To appreciate art *qua* art, as Gregory Currie puts it, is to appreciate the heuristic pathway of a work. In Popperian language, appreciating an artwork as a work of art involves assessing the logic of the situation from which the artwork emerges, since the relevant situation is an *art-historical* situation. Ziff's view of appreciation segues nicely with historical characterizations of art such as Danto's and my own view, which I have called narrativism. Thus, rather than denying Ziff's account of artistic appreciation, I should like, with modification, to embrace it. Consequently, I would not wish to block Carlson's claims about its relevance for nature appreciation.

8. I say "all but" here because Carlson admits that there might be a few cases of the emotional appreciation of nature, though he says that they are minimal (adding, skeptically, "if not nonexistent"). Carlson, "Nature, Aesthetic Appreciation and Knowledge."

9. See the preceding note for an explanation of the caveat "not appreciably."

10. For further defense of this, see Noël Carroll, "The Paradox of Suspense," in *Suspense: Conceptualizations, Theoretical Analyses and Emprical Explorations,* edited by Peter Vorderer, Hans J. Wulff and Mike Friedrichsen (Mahwah, N.J.: Lawrence Erlbaum Associates, Publishers, 1996). That essay is also included in this volume.

INDEX